Roma Britannica

Published with the aid of grants from

The Marc Fitch Fund
The Paul Mellon Centre for the Study of British Art

Roma Britannica

ART PATRONAGE AND CULTURAL EXCHANGE
IN EIGHTEENTH-CENTURY ROME

Edited by
David R. Marshall, Susan Russell and Karin Wolfe

The British School at Rome, London
2011

www.bsr.ac.uk

Registered Charity No. 314176

ISBN 978-0-904152-55-5

Front cover illustration

Pompeo Batoni (1708–87), *Thomas Dundas, Later 1st Baron Dundas*, 1763–4. Oil on canvas. Collection of the Marquess of Zetland, Aske Hall, North Yorkshire. *(Photo: Jerry Hardman-Jones. Reproduced courtesy of the Earl of Ronaldshay.)*

Back cover illustration

Giovanni Battista Piranesi (1720–78), *Ichnographia* (detail showing fictive coin with portraits of Robert Adam and Piranesi), from *Il Campo Marzio dell'antica Roma*, 1762. British School at Rome Library. *(Photo: David R. Marshall.)*

Typeset by Academic + Technical Typesetting, Bristol, Great Britain
Printed by Information Press, Eynsham, Oxford, Great Britain

CONTENTS

List of Figures

CHAPTER 4

CHAPTER 5

CHAPTER 6

List of Plates

Preface

For over 100 years the British School at Rome has had the mission of bringing Italy and the United Kingdom and Commonwealth together in its premises in Rome. We are not the first to have done so. The relationship between Britain and Italy is intense and deep, resting as it does on complex and difficult intellectual games, personal engagement with Italy through the Grand Tour, the exchange of cultural goods, sometimes in a manner we would find unacceptable now, and sometimes, as now, in the free passage of ideas and artists, and in the influence of patronage on the creation of art.

Much of the image we sometimes have of this is of the British traveller in Italy, sometimes indifferent but often enamoured. The British School at Rome has contributed to our understanding of this phenomenon through the publication of James Hakewill's drawings (*Twilight of the Grand Tour*, 1992) and Clare Hornsby's important collection of essays (*The Impact of Italy: the Grand Tour and Beyond*, 2000); and antiquarianism, the passionate intellectual drive to understand and often to appropriate the past is a core theme of recurrent research within the School. Moreover, *Roma Britannica* invites us to reflect on the lasting intellectual importance of the engagement of artists and architects with the historical and contemporary eighteenth-century realities of Rome. The British School at Rome continues to foster and support 21st-century architects and artists in this same engagement, and we are encouraged by this volume to see the potential of these exchanges for our future.

This tradition of scholarship is continued with *Roma Britannica*, and reminds us that there is more at stake in this relationship than the development of impressionable young men on their adventures abroad. The British obsession with the Roman past is of extraordinary significance for understanding our politics then, and, one might argue, now, for our constitution and the historical roots of our social and moral codes lie embedded in arguments within the enlightenment and romanticism that drew upon and reacted against Rome in its ancient, Renaissance and Baroque or Counter-reformation manifestations.

Roma Britannica makes a significant contribution to this exciting and deeply important historical relationship, and itself embodies the values of the British School at Rome, through its interdisciplinarity, internationalism and intellectual seriousness, and it is my pleasure to thank the organizers and editors for this elegant and substantial addition to our publications.

Christopher J. Smith
Director, The British School at Rome

Acknowledgements

In April 1743, Horace Walpole remarked that nominal qualification for membership of the Society of Dilettanti was having been in Italy, and the real one having been drunk in Rome! If this were still the case, the organizers of the conference 'Roma Britannica' would undoubtedly qualify, for it was over a night-cap at the British School in the winter of 2005 that the idea was born. The prime movers in the undertaking were Karin Wolfe and David Marshall, whose energy and intellectual acumen attracted speakers and session chairs at the top of their fields. It was my privilege to be able to facilitate such a conference with the British School's many resources, including the Sainsbury Lecture Theatre, and an exceptional staff who, often stretched to the limit, manage to do a consistently excellent job.

The British School is a place where ideas are naturally stimulated because of the extraordinary variety of scholars and artists who either reside in it for whole or part of the academic year or who pass through its portals as temporary residents, guests or associates. While times have changed, and those living at the British School undoubtedly would object to the label 'dilettanti', the School maintains a spirit of conviviality of which Walpole would certainly have approved amongst those who, though of different disciplines, are members of a universal community of scholars and artists, who still come to Rome to learn from its glorious traditions. Guest speakers at our regular Wednesday evening lectures are invited to a reception and a special dinner afterwards, in the winter distinguished by candlelight and an open fire in Edwin Lutyens's dining-room and in the summer by an alfresco meal in a courtyard embellished with roses and archaeological finds. Such occasions are a reward for long days spent working away, if not at a British School desk, then elsewhere in Rome's libraries, archives, museums, galleries and archaeological sites.

The British School's dedication to research continually fosters new projects in many fields and promotes intellectual and cultural exchange of the kind that results in numerous activities, including such memorable conferences as '*Roma Britannica*: Art Patronage and Cultural Exchange in Eighteenth-Century Rome'. The conference, accompanied by a small exhibition of prints and rare books from the British School Library, was a great success, both in terms of the depth and breadth of the papers presented, and by the attendance of a general public, British School award-holders and residents, and experts and students of the field, several of whom travelled specially from the UK to attend.

The conference was an international affair, with participants from: Australia — David Marshall, Katrina Grant and myself; Great Britain — Brian Allen, Edward Chaney, Edward Corp (transposed to France), James Holloway, Clare Hornsby, Alastair Laing, Carol Richardson, Francis Russell, Desmond Shawe-Taylor, Andrew Wallace-Hadrill and John Wilton-Ely; Germany — Peter Björn Kerber and Elisabeth Kieven; Italy — Tommaso Manfredi and Letizia Tedeschi; Spain — José María Luzón; and the USA — Malcolm Baker (transposed from the UK), Edgar Peters Bowron, Joseph Connors (transposed to Florence), Christopher Johns, Wendy Wassyng Roworth, Kevin Salatino and Karin Wolfe (transposed to Rome). Although they could not be included here, the papers presented by Clare Hornsby, José María Luzón and Elisabeth Kieven were an important addition to the proceedings, and will surely appear elsewhere in due course.

It was my great pleasure not only to make valuable new contacts with academics and museum professionals from around the world, but also to welcome back those with previous and continuing ties to the School: Edward Chaney (Paul Mellon Centre Research Support Grant, tenable at the BSR 2004–5), Edward Corp (Paul Mellon Centre Rome Fellow 2004–5), Katrina Grant (Melbourne Rome Scholar 2007–8), Clare Hornsby (Assistant Director—Art History 1996–8; Paul Mellon Centre Special Projects Fellow 2005–8), David R. Marshall (Trendall Fellow 2006; BSR Honorary Fellow), Carol Richardson (Rome Awardee 1997; Paul Mellon Centre Rome Fellow 2006–7), John Wilton-Ely (in residence during the conference as Paul Mellon Centre Rome Fellow 2005–6) and Karin Wolfe (BSR Research Fellow).

We wish particularly to thank Christopher Johns and Alastair Laing for their good council in recommending scholars currently engaged in research on the subject.

On behalf of the British School and the conference participants, I would like to thank Anna Lo Bianco, who, with Angela Negro, curated the exhibition *Il Settecento a Roma*, which, fortuitously, was showing at the Palazzo Venezia during the conference. She generously gave up a Saturday afternoon to escort a group around the exhibition, providing an unparalleled opportunity to view at first hand several key works discussed in the preceding days, as well as sharing her own invaluable insights. Thanks also to Francesco Colalucci, Maria Giuseppina Lauro and Alessandra Ghidoli, at the Ufficio Conservazione Patrimonio Artistico del Quirinale, for an outstanding visit to the Quirinal Palace, its excavations, Coffee House and Organ Fountain.

Since the volume was submitted for publication, the British School at Rome has had a change of Directors. Andrew Wallace-Hadrill, after fourteen years of overseeing numerous important changes and improvements to the School, left to become Master of Sidney Sussex College, Cambridge. He was actively involved in *Roma Britannica*, as both host and speaker, and supported its transformation from conference to publication. It was a mark of the conference's inclusive nature that he was able to make a significant contribution in a paper directly linking ancient Rome to 'modern' Britain. Christopher Smith is the new Director and, admidst the pressing demands of his new post, kindly agreed to write a brief preface to this volume.

For their generous support, the British School's gratitude and thanks go to the Samuel H. Kress Foundation, the Paul Mellon Centre for Studies in British Art and the Marc Fitch Fund. Thanks also go to Valerie Scott and her colleagues in the British School Library and Archive for the care and exhibition of the rare books and prints that were displayed during the conference. These included several images that have roles to play in succeeding chapters: Lord Castelmaine's dinner at the Palazzo Pamphilj (Marshall and Wolfe), Camillo Buti prints of the Villa Negroni frescoes (Wallace-Hadrill) and Piranesi's map of the Campus Martius (Wilton-Ely). I would like to express my personal thanks to all the participants, who not only made the occasion an extremely enjoyable one, but who also gave me, a scholar of Roman Seicento art, an unforgettable crash course in the art of the Settecento, conducted at the highest level of academic excellence. I particularly want to thank my fellow editors and Gill Clark, whose combined efforts saw the volume to completion, thus providing the opportunity for a much larger audience to share this experience.

Susan Russell
Assistant Director, The British School at Rome

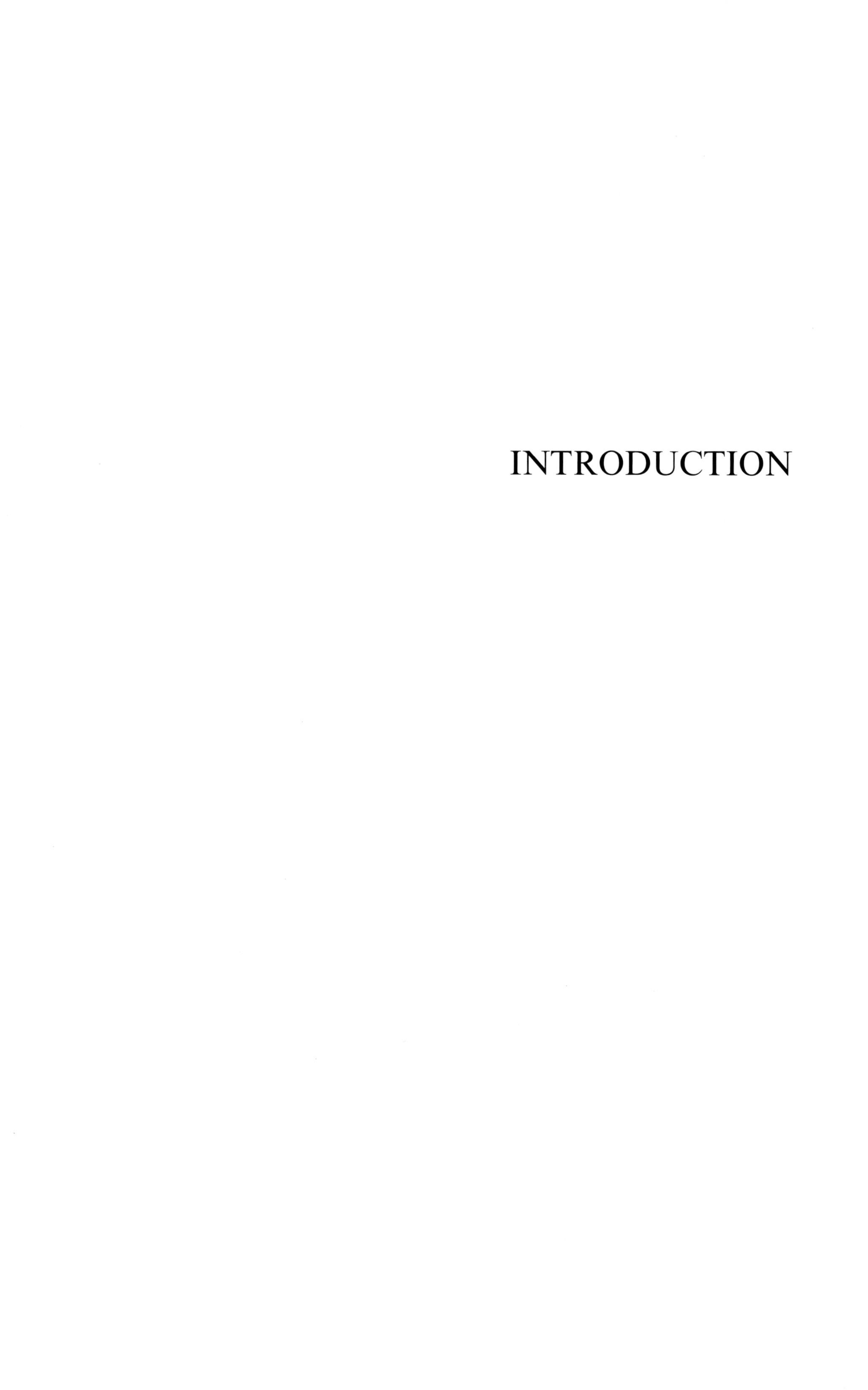

INTRODUCTION

Roma Britannica

David R. Marshall and Karin Wolfe

The Grand Tour — the institution of young British visitors who came to Rome as an integral part of their education — has come to be seen as synonymous with the cultural production of Britain in respect of Rome in the eighteenth century. Its importance cannot be denied: the Grand Tour served to reinforce the principal foundation myth of early modern Europeans that they were the descendants of antiquity, as Julius Caesar had once claimed to be the descendant of Venus. This myth still has the power of living religion today, and indeed the British School at Rome is evidence of it, its existence being predicated on the importance of classical antiquity for contemporary British culture. It was inculcated in the British aristocracy from the beginning of their education, which consisted largely of the study of Latin literature. The values of British culture were, in the eighteenth century, wholly identified with those of Republican Rome. All parties in Parliament identified themselves with the Roman Senate, and that meant that core values of the Roman Republic, such as gravity, virtue and frugality, were considered to be both British and Roman. Hence the importance of the Grand Tour: a trip to Rome served to cause an electrical short across the terminals marked 'Rome' and 'today', thus bypassing the millennium and a half of history that separated the two cultures. This was recognized as early as 1670, when the English Roman Catholic priest Richard Lassels (*c.* 1603–68) first suggested that it was impossible to understand Livy or Caesar if one had not done the 'Grand Tour of France and Giro of Italy'.[1] In a similar vein the Scots traveller and collector Sir John Clerk of Penicuik (1676–1755) wrote evocatively about his youthful passion to visit Italy in his *Memoirs*:

> the vast desire I had to see a country so famous for exploits about which all my time had been hitherto spent in reading the classics, likeways a country so replenished with Antiquities of all kinds and so much excelling all other countries in painting and music, I say these things created such a vast desire in me to see it that I am sure nothing in life had ever made me happy if I had denied myself this great pleasure and satisfaction.[2]

The premise of the *Roma Britannica* conference, however, was that there was more to the cultural relationship between Britain and Rome in the eighteenth century than the Grand Tour, important as that was. This cultural relationship needs to be seen not only from the perspective of a British visitor, but also from the perspective of the Italians, who were beginning to recognize the emerging economic and cultural power of the largely Protestant island that lay beyond their traditional object of attention, France. It also needs to be seen from the perspective of other Europeans: Rome in the eighteenth century stood for cosmopolitanism rather than national rivalry, and had moved beyond being the centre for the renaissance of antiquity to being the place where the cross-pollination of the modern with the ancient allowed the culture of Europe to flower in new and unexpected ways. However, in order to see this larger picture, it is necessary to look not only at the period when the Grand Tour peaked (from 1760 to 1799), but also at a long eighteenth century that began in 1688 and ended in 1799. The first date is the year of the Glorious Revolution, which saw the expulsion of the Stuarts from Britain and their establishment in France and, eventually, in Rome, and the second is the year of the death of Pius VI in exile; a period that extended from the deposing of one Catholic presence to that of another.

By starting with the Glorious Revolution, we start at the moment when the relationship between Britain and papal Rome became problematic. In 1687 the Earl of Castlemaine (1634–1705) had served a banquet in the gallery of one of the great palaces of a papal family, the Palazzo Pamphilj, an event organized by a British painter, John Michael Wright (1617–94), and recorded in a magnificent print produced in Rome by a Dutch printmaker, Arnold van Westerhout (1651–after 1725) after drawings by an Italian, Giovanni Battista Lenardi (1656–1704) (Fig. 1.1).[3] As James II's ambassador in Rome, Castlemaine was no different from French or Spanish ambassadors who regularly put on showy functions to glorify the regimes they represented. The engraving of his banquet, which shows Berninesque sugar *trionfi* designed by a team of artists led by Ciro Ferri, frequently appears in books devoted to the art history of papal Rome. Lovers of Pietro da Cortona (1596–1669), Francesco Borromini (1599–1667) or Gianlorenzo Bernini (1509–1680) sooner or later come across it and recognize it as being germane to their interests. The Earl of Castlemaine's banquet may stand, therefore, as emblematic of the integration of the visual culture of the British in Rome with the culture of papal Rome, an integration that ended with the deposing of the Stuarts and the exclusion of Catholics from the succession. The year after the Glorious Revolution Lord Melfort (1650–1714) arrived in Rome, hoping to procure papal funding for the exiled James II (1633–1701) and to form his own collection, and so inaugurated the season of Jacobite patronage.[4]

A century later, in 1787, when David Allan (1744–96) made a drawing of British Grand Tourists arriving in the Piazza di Spagna, things had changed greatly (Plate 1.1). An end to Stuart hopes of restoration had come with the failure of Bonnie Prince Charlie's uprising of 1745. In 1747 his younger brother, Henry Benedict (1725–1807), was made Cardinal York, thus renouncing any aspirations to the throne. In 1763 his part-namesake, the Protestant Whig Edward Augustus, Duke of York (1739–67), visited Rome, an event that constituted 'a death-blow for the Catholic Stuarts', as Ilaria Bignamini put it.[5] By then, the British in Rome had a cultural identity that was distinctly their own. Rome was, on the one hand, the city of the papacy — the whore of Babylon to a Protestant — and, on the other, the city of antique remains. But it was also a city filled with living people, people who constituted a touristic other, who were both similar to and different from those they knew at home. The Whig landed gentry had grown in power, wealth and influence, and the British presence was manifested in Rome, not as an ambassadorial spectacle, but as a succession of 'milordi', arriving with their bearleaders, hiring *ciceroni*, renting accommodation near the Piazza di Spagna, getting introductions to Italian aristocrats and relieving them of their collections, and taking back with them as many antiquities as they could get away with, not to mention *vedute* and portraits.

THE VIEW FROM ENGLAND AND THE VIEW FROM ROME

Overlaid on these chronological limits are differences of perception: the view from England versus the view from Rome. These differences of perception are exemplified by the situation of the Stuart court. In *A Letter From an English Traveller at Rome to His Father, of the 6th of May 1721*, supposedly a Grand Tour letter written by the Marquis of Blandford, but actually 'a work of fantasy',[6] a young English traveller arrives in Rome in 1721 and meets a Church of England clergyman, who turns out to to be a chaplain at the Stuart residence. They meet the King, James III, and the Queen, Maria Clementina Sobieska (Plate 7.2), and stay to a meal, where fine French and English dishes are offered. The King, however, eats only the English dishes, 'and showed a particular fondness for roast

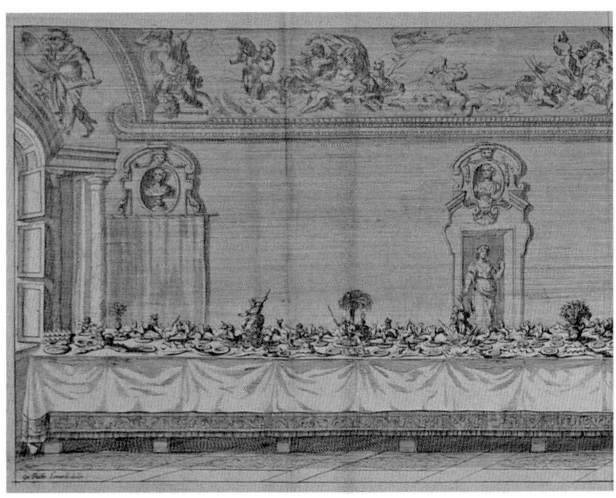

FIG. 1.1. Arnold van Westerhout (1651–after 1725) after Giovanni Battista Lenardi (1656–1704), *Table Setting for the Earl of Castlemaine's Banquet in the Gallery of Palazzo Pamphilj*, 1688. Engraving, 35.3 × 114 cm. *(From J.M. Wright, An Account of His Excellence Roger Earl of Castlemaine's Embassy From His Sacred Majesty James the IId. King of England, Scotland, France, and Ireland &c To His Holiness Innocent XI . . . , London, 1688. Rome, British School at Rome Library. Photo: David R. Marshall.)*

beef and Devonshire pie washed down with English March ale specially imported from Leghorn'.[7] This fictional visitor from England sees the cultural life of English royalty in Rome through English eyes: he sees roast beef and imported English ale, where others at the same banquet may have seen French food, baroque *trionfi* or German porcelain. This is how the Stuarts needed to present themselves to their countrymen, and how their countrymen wanted to perceive the Stuarts.

The view from Rome was rather different. From the perspective of the Roman nobility, the Stuarts were part of their day-to-day life. They paid social calls to the houses of the Roman aristocracy, who would, when they arrived, so to speak, sweep the crumbs under the table to avoid making *brutta figura*.[8] They were special, not because, like the French ambassador, they embodied the power and authority of a superpower, but simply because they were royal: as royals without royal authority, they were a social catch. The opera revolved around them — we see this in works such as Panini's *Musical Performance Given by the Cardinal de la Rochefoucauld in the Teatro Argentina in Rome on 15 July 1747 for the Marriage of the Dauphin of France* (Plate 1.2)[9] — and descriptions of events in Chracas's *Diario ordinario* are always careful to name them at the head (after the pope) of the social hierarchy.[10] In addition they commissioned paintings from the same artists as the local nobility, and contributed to the development of Grand Tour portraiture.[11]

THE PRESENTNESS OF ROME: THE TRUE DEMOCRACY OF ART

For the British, Rome was the present as well as the past, the slippage between them being continuous. A tourist in Rome today is likely to be coming with the past in mind, but may have the present — in the form of traffic and other tourists — filling his or her field of vision. Occasionally, even today, he or she might discover something that is the past alive in the present, a 'living fossil': a gypsy like one in a painting by Caravaggio, or a man with a team of donkeys in the Campagna straight out of a seventeenth- or eighteenth-century *bambocciata*. The British visitor in the eighteenth century confronted with a comparable experience may have imagined he was back in the world of Horace or Virgil. The touristic gaze becomes energized when the past is seen to be alive in the present.

Yet the British visitor in the eighteenth century would have been just as interested in the presentness of Rome as in its past. An art student today goes to New York not to seek out on a construction site some echo of a 1920s workman perched with his lunch-box on a girder of the half-built Chrysler building — an echo of the city's heroic past —, but to discover the action at the galleries of contemporary art dealers, hoping to be part of the scene. The British artist in Rome in the eighteenth century was no different, since his career was as dependent on making it in Rome as the careers of his successors today are dependent on making it in New York or London.

What the Rome of the present had to offer was, above all, internationalism. Rome was a place where foreigners could study art on an equal footing with the Italians, and where artists who wanted to work for a European, rather than a regional, market could come to live. Rome did not belong just to the Romans, but was a place where artists of any nationality could come to drink at the water of the fount of all art, and, having undergone this initiation, were free to return to their native countries, or to spread

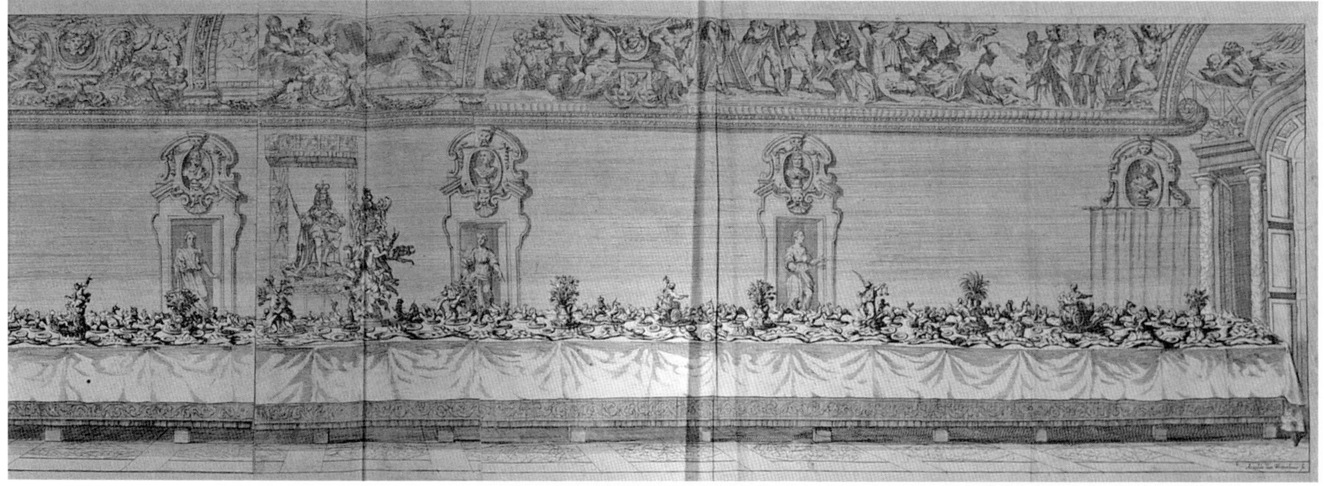

out among the courts of Europe in search of employment. It was the primary centre of cultural exchange. British artists were woven into the everyday Roman scene: William Kent (1685–1748) painting the ceiling of the Belgian national church, San Giuliano dei Fiamminghi; the Irish painter Henry Trench (*c.* 1685–1726) taking part in the annual competitions at the Accademia di San Luca; Gavin Hamilton (1723–98) painting Homeric history paintings to be shipped to British country houses; Christopher Hewetson (*c.* 1736/9–*c.* 1798/9) producing a bust of Pope Clement XIV (1705–74); and James Gibbs (1682–1754), Robert Mylne (*c.* 1734–1811), James Adam (1732–94) and John Soane (1753–1837) everywhere studying, drawing and designing. As Christopher Johns has reminded us, 'because of the remarkable degree of cosmopolitanism during the eighteenth century, Rome was of crucial significance not only as a cultural site but as a promoter of a vigorous school for artists of widely different nationalities; being from Venice or Paris [or London] makes an artist no less Roman in consequence'.[12] British artists, therefore, could also be Roman.

These, then, are the issues running through the contributions to this volume: the necessity of Rome to being British; the relationship between a British court embedded in Roman society and the visitor from Britain; the tension between the nostalgia for an idealized ancient Rome and the excitement of the presentness of modern Rome; international art patronage, cultural exchange and the Romanness of British artists.

*****

The papers in this volume are grouped under five general headings. After this introduction, CHRISTOPHER JOHNS focuses on cosmopolitanism and national identity in eighteenth-century Rome, in an essay that sets out many of the premises of the conference. Johns argues that the city of Rome and the role of Rome in the European imaginary were essential components of Britain's negotiation of the destruction of the *ancien régime*'s institutions and the rise of the modern nationalist tradition from their ashes. Rome played an important part in the definition of what it meant to be British in the modern world, because Britain had successfully appropriated the mantle of world empire inherited from ancient Rome, a legacy that the papacy and the Holy Roman Empire had long contested and that would be claimed ephemerally by Napoleonic France. Britain used the materials of the international neoclassicism whose capital was Rome for the purpose of national self-identification. From this imperial point of view, the British found contemporary Roman artists, and their Renaissance and Baroque predecessors, to be unworthy of the inheritance of ancient Rome. Hence James Barry (1741–1806) referred to the 'vitiated, sickly and dying state' of contemporary Roman art, while Sir Joshua Reynolds (1723–92) made disparaging remarks about the leading lights of the eighteenth-century Roman school, epecially Pompeo Batoni (1708–87). Yet, as Johns argues, this did not mean that British artists profited from the mantle of empire: Barry's remarks were prompted by anger at an important British commission going to the Rome-based Anton Raphael Mengs (1728–79), rather than to a British artist. The imperial attitude meant that British élites viewed art largely as an expensive and high-quality form of colonial import, rather than as a reason to create Rome on the Thames.

The second section deals with Catholic Britain and the Jacobites in Rome. CAROL M. RICHARDSON's paper explores the exposure of British patrons and collectors to an important part of the Roman art world — institutional architecture and large-scale frescoes — through the Venerable English College, founded in 1579. This institution, although ostensibly a place for training priests to be sent back to England to face possible martyrdom, had begun as a pilgrim hospice in 1362, and continued to welcome both Catholic and Protestant English pilgrims until well into the eighteenth century. Catholic visitors could enjoy the triumphalism of English Catholicism celebrated at the College, unavailable to them in Britain. Since the College was administered by the Jesuits, around 1700 the Jesuit painter and architect Andrea Pozzo (1642–1709) was involved in the design of its new church and the frescoes in the oratory, refectory and garden. English visitors were thus exposed to the Jesuit art of Pozzo in an English context. Moreover, Pozzo's designs, including that used for the garden fresco, published in his *Prospettiva de' pittori e architetti*, would be studied eagerly by Protestant English architects, such as Sir Christopher Wren (1632–1723), Nicholas Hawksmoor (1661–1736) and John Vanbrugh (1664–1726), through the English edition published in 1707.

EDWARD CORP focuses on the very heart of the English Catholic dilemma — the presence of the Stuart court established in papal Rome in 1719. In documenting the 'cultural forum' of the court in Rome, Corp illuminates both the practical and formal functions that made up the everyday life of the Stuarts and thereby governed their relations with British visitors and locals alike. Like Richardson, he observes that the ties of language and nationality could override differences of religion, so that the Stuart court took on the role of a surrogate British embassy. The court's political influence may have been limited, but, as Corp establishes, the official role it assumed in the papal city permeated the British presence in Rome. Focusing on the patronage of portrait-painters by members of the Stuart court, Corp shows, for example, that Pompeo Batoni's career as a painter of portraits of British and Irish tourists was launched by the Stuart court, even though his patrons were mainly Whigs and all were loyal Hanoverians.

DAVID R. MARSHALL continues the exploration of the urban stage the Stuart dynasty set for itself when it ventured into the heart of Rome's rich culture of ephemeral celebrations by examining a painting depicting the temporary façade erected on the occasion of the creation of Henry Benedict Stuart as Cardinal York in July 1747, now in the Scottish National Portrait Gallery. The location of this façade hitherto has been uncertain, but Marshall, employing a close topographical analysis, establishes that it could have been erected only on the rear façade of the Palazzo Balestra (the 'Palazzo del Re' of the Stuarts), facing the side branch of the Piazza della Pilotta. Such an apparently undistinguished site may appear to be a surprising choice of location, but Marshall shows it to have been normal for such façades to be so located. He also proposes that James II and his court drew on the earlier experience of their exile in France at the court of Saint Germain, and therefore imported French royal ideas of architectural and ephemeral taste to Rome.

PETER BJÖRN KERBER takes up the issue of recusant patronage from England. He examines the case of a Catholic collector of the second half of the eighteenth century, Henry, 8th Baron Arundell (1740–1808), a devout young man who visited Rome accompanied by a Jesuit governor in 1760. Kerber traces the lengthy and complex negotiations to secure a commission from Batoni, at the time the most fashionable painter in Rome for all European visitors and courts. Arundell had met Batoni in Rome during his Grand Tour in 1760, and commissioned several paintings from him for a collection of over 200 works amassed during the 1760s and 1770s for Wardour Castle in Wiltshire, begun in 1768. At first unwisely attempting to obtain copies from Batoni — including Van Dyck's *The Three Eldest Children of King Charles I*, then in the collection of Charles Edward Stuart in the Palazzo Muti —, followed more predictably, but no more successfully, by attempts to commission family portraits, Arundell began to acquire Batoni's religious works on the secondary market through his agent, and former tutor, the Jesuit priest Father John Thorpe (1726–92). While earlier Catholic visitors to Rome regularly had purchased and commissioned devotional images, such patronage had been on the wane since 1745, and Arundell was unusual in commissioning from Batoni a devotional subject, *The Appearance of the Angel to Hagar in the Desert* (1774–6). Considering the patron, his agent, the artist and the political and religious climate, Kerber posits that this unusual masterpiece coincided perfectly with the suppression of the Jesuit Order in 1773, which bitterly believed itself to have been, like Hagar and Ishmael, 'banished to the wilderness at the instigation of jealous enemies'.

The third section develops the theme of patrons, collectors, agents and the Roman art market. KARIN WOLFE foregrounds the interest of British travellers in Francesco Trevisani (1656–1746), an artist who regularly received British clients at his studio to paint their portraits from as early as 1691. Using new documentation, including the painter's rediscovered inventories, Wolfe demonstrates that the British — and international visitors generally — also became eager buyers of the artist's cabinet-sized devotional pictures, which Trevisani's assistants prepared for this tourist trade, and to which he applied the final touches and glazes. Visitors also acquired the sketches and small-scale *ricordi* (replicas and variants) the artist made after his public commissions. Many of these artistic souvenirs survive today in Britain in the collections of Trevisani's original patrons. A case in point is Lord Burghley (1648–1700), 5th Earl of Exeter, a passionate art collector who travelled to Italy on at least four occasions and who acquired six works by Trevisani. The most striking of these paintings is a *Noli Me Tangere*, a subject that may well have been suggested by Burghley's wife, Anne Cavendish (1643–1703), an heiress in her own right and a devotee of penitential themes, with which she decorated her apartments. In the field of portraiture, Wolfe shows Trevisani to have been an innovator in the creation of the new genre of a specifically British Grand Tour portrait style that would culminate two generations later with Pompeo Batoni.

Trevisani's other important British patron, John Urquhart of Cromarty and Craigston (1696–1756), was an openly avowed Jacobite. Urquhart fought as a Catholic convert at Sherrifmuir as a young man, served as a captain in the Spanish navy and was wounded by the English at Gibraltar, an event depicted in his portrait by Trevisani. He enriched himself through privateering and, as JAMES HOLLOWAY observes in his essay, his life might form the basis for a novel. Drawing on the correspondence of Urquhart with his agent in Rome, the Scottish artist William Mosman (*c.* 1700–71), Holloway shows how Urquhart commissioned from Antonio David the important pair of portraits of Bonnie Prince Charlie and his brother, Prince Henry, now in the Scottish National Portrait Gallery, as well as original works by other Roman artists, including Francesco Fernandi (1679–1740), called Imperiali, Pietro Bianchi (1694–1740), Giuseppe Chiari (1654–1727) and Paolo Monaldi (1720–99), and copies of famous Baroque paintings by Pompeo Batoni (1708–87), Camillo Paderni (1720–70) and Stefano Pozzi (1699–1768). Holloway shows that Urquhart's eagerness to obtain works by Trevisani — he acquired seven works, and would have acquired more if it were not for Trevisani's advanced age and other commitments — was a consequence of his links with the Jacobite court.

An artist more generally supposed to have been much patronized by the British was the painter of *capricci* and *vedute*, Giovanni Paolo Panini (1691–1765), whose works were once common in British collections. However, as ALASTAIR LAING shows, relatively few can be traced back to the artist's lifetime. Like Trevisani, and unlike Canaletto (1697–1768), Panini was not a painter who was exclusively the preserve of the British. He seems not to have had a regular middleman in the way that Canaletto had Owen MacSwiny (1684–1754) and Consul Smith (1682–1770) to promote his interests with English patrons, nor did he develop his own links with them back in England. Nevertheless, he painted a number of important works or sets of works for English patrons. Examining the earliest of these, Laing establishes that it was not until 1734 that his English patronage really took off. He explains this development by referring to changes in the design of interiors in Britain that accompanied the triumph of Palladianism. Italian stuccadors working in England had devised a way of giving Roman gravitas to their interiors by employing rectangular plaster panels and rectangular overdoors and overmantels that were intended either to be filled with classicizing marble or plaster reliefs or with paintings that were often evocative of that same antique past. For such fields, Panini's representations of Roman ruins and buildings were ideal.

Although Trevisani obtained commissions directly from visitors to his studio, and Panini had no apparent middleman, middlemen were none the less of great importance for many patrons. FRANCIS RUSSELL explores one such case: the acquiring of works of art in Italy by the Scottish nobleman, John Stuart, 3rd Earl of Bute (1713–92), with the help of his agent, James Byres of Tonley (1734–1817). Adding to his 2004 monograph on Bute, Russell examines sixteen newly-discovered letters from Byres to Bute written between 1769 and 1771, in conjunction with Byres's itemized accounts for the period. This new information clarifies the range of commissions Byres undertook for Bute, which involved not only pictures and architectural drawings, but also statues, chimney-pieces and a tapestry. Byres's detailed replies to lost letters from Bute show how uniquely qualified he was to act for one of the most determined collectors of the eighteenth century, and how central a position he came to hold in the life of the Grand Tour community at Rome.

The fourth section, 'Confrontations with the antique: the British reception of Egypt and Rome', examines a range of issues involving artists and patrons looking at antiquities, both Egyptian and Roman. EDWARD CHANEY examines the interest in ancient Egyptian obelisks of another Catholic collector, Thomas Howard, 14th Earl of Arundel (1585–1646). Chaney tells the story of the little-known phenomenon of English attempts to acquire and install Egyptian obelisks, first realized in 1821 by Henry Bankes (1757–1834) at Kingston Lacy. Arundel, two centuries before Bankes, had in 1614 seen the obelisks re-erected in Rome by Sixtus V (1521–90) in 1585–90, and, inspired by them, attempted to acquire for his riverside garden in London the obelisk of Domitian that lay broken in the so-called Circus of Caracalla (actually the Circus of Maxentius). (The obelisk in due course would be erected in Piazza Navona as part of Bernini's *Four Rivers* fountain.) Unsuccessful in this endeavour, Arundel, with Inigo Jones (1573–1652), succeeded in persuading Queen Henrietta Maria (1609–69) to erect two massive modern obelisks to flank her watergate at Somerset House. Chaney argues that Arundel's devotion to such antiquities and to the 'ancient religion' of Roman Catholicism were inseparable from his pride in his ancient family, members of which had died as Catholic martyrs in the previous century and were to do so again during the 'Popish Plot' in 1678–81. While English Catholics followed Roman precedent in ascribing a broader spiritual significance to the obelisk, their Protestant compatriots adopted them almost exclusively as funeral monuments.

Continuing this Egyptian theme in the following century, ELIZABETH BARTMAN looks at the British interest in ancient Egypt as it was mediated through Rome. She shows how, inspired by the eclecticism of the great sculpture collections of Rome, many Grand Tourists purchased Egyptian antiquities while in Rome and Italy to display alongside their 'classical' statues. That these Egyptian works have been ignored in studies of Grand Tour collecting underscores the degree to which later attitudes have differed from those of the eighteenth century. Many of the Egyptian works that made their way into British collections were grossly misunderstood; a misinterpretation that is hardly surprising given that they typically represented stray finds — some known as early as the Renaissance — without archaeological context, and given that many were actually Roman works created in an Egyptian idiom. Bartman shows how their interpretation and misinterpretation provide evidence both for the reception of the antique and for the construction of history in eighteenth-century Britain.

Pompeo Batoni's practice of including careful and accurate representations of Roman antiquities in his portraits of Irish, English and Scottish visitors to Rome is well known. But, as EDGAR PETERS BOWRON explains, his youthful practice of making careful drawn copies of antiquities did not at first carry over into his portraits, and well into the 1750s they underplayed the identity of their sitters as visitors to Italy. He was slow to adopt the most characteristic features of the Grand Tour portrait, such as the presence of antique architecture or sculpture, which had been established by earlier Roman painters such as Carlo Maratti (1625–1713) and Trevisani. Bowron argues that, while the repeated presence of certain antiquities in his portraits from the 1750s was undoubtedly a response to the fact that his sitters, exposed to the continued repetition of a relatively small number of ancient works in guidebooks and travel diaries, were favourably inclined towards a canonical group of antiquities, the belief that Batoni employed antique references as mere 'studio props' is unwarranted. He argues that Batoni was thoughtful and deliberate in his use of archaeological allusions, as is confirmed by the number of antiquities that appear in only a single portrait. Unfortunately, the reasons for the choice of antiquity are normally undocumented, but Bowron examines a numbers of instances where it is possible to explore its possible significance for the sitter.

ANDREW WALLACE-HADRILL reminds us that it was not only antique sculpture, but also Roman painting and stucco-work, that could inspire English artists and decorators, as well as their patrons, for whom there was an equivalence between the 'magnificence of ancient [and] the elegance of modern Rome'. These are the words of Frederick Hervey, 4th Earl of Bristol and Bishop of Derry (1730–1803), in connection with the Roman painted stuccoes he had just acquired from a Roman house discovered in 1777 in the Villa Negroni, and which is depicted in the course of excavation in a painting by the Welsh artist Thomas Jones (1742–1803). The site was quickly destroyed and the paintings are now lost, but a project to record them was set in train in 1777, which employed the artists Mengs and Anton von Maron (1733–1808), and which was published in a set of plates produced by Camillo Buti (1747–1808) completed in 1802. (A copy is in the Library of the British School at Rome.) These provided the model for a room decorated by the artist John Grace at Hervey's country seat of Ickworth for the 3rd Marquis of Bristol in 1879. By then the Romanness of the paintings had been forgotten, and the room was known as the 'Pompeian Room'. Moreover, as Wallace-Hadrill establishes, such a designation was not entirely unjustified. The Villa Negroni house probably dated from the second century AD, yet Buti's plates show designs that are unusual for that period, and have elements that are suspiciously close to those recorded in publications of Pompeian frescoes. Wallace-Hadrill therefore proposes that Buti's plates are 'a complex product of accurate observation and reconstruction based on educated guesswork, the guesswork informed by a knowledge of Vesuvian paintings that pre-dated Mau's identification of the four styles by a century, and therefore allowed eclectic use of elements from paintings of very different styles' (p. 199).

The following section deals with the British and the Roman practice of architecture. TOMMASO MANFREDI's contribution focuses on the relationship of the architecture of Filippo Juvarra (1678–1736) and the British architects and patrons with whom he was acquainted. Manfredi discusses the arrival of Juvarra in London, following a trip by the architect to Portugal, in the first half of 1719. Rudolph Wittkower was the first to postulate a link between the motif of the stepped pyramidal spire found in Hawksmoor's Saint George's, Bloomsbury, and one of Juvarra's drawings dedicated to Lord Burlington (1694–1753) made a decade later. Manfredi points out that this motif was present in both architects' work earlier, but that its presence in a drawing by Juvarra datable to 1719, where it appears in conjunction with a monumental double bridge based on Palladio's design for the Rialto bridge, implies a significant confluence of interest between Juvarra and English neo-Palladianism. Through a careful exploration of the intricacies of the movements of Juvarra and the British artists and patrons with whom he was in contact — including Gibbs, Kent, Lord Burlington, the Earl of Harrold (1696–1723) and Thomas Coke (1697–1759) — Manfredi concludes that Juvarra was more responsive to sober, classicizing tendencies in architecture than has been supposed hitherto.

KATRINA GRANT pursues a related theme, the relationship between William Kent's experience of theatre in Italy from 1709 to 1719, during which time he often wrote of his intention to introduce 'ye Italian gusto' to the arts of England and to his practice as a garden designer in Britain immediately afterwards. After tracing the connections between Kent and Juvarra in Rome and London, and exploring echoes of Juvarra's presence in London in theatrical activity there, she argues that the garden style Kent initiated in England in the 1720s and 1730s was influenced by the set designs of Italian opera, particularly Juvarra's. Comparing set designs by Juvarra to such gardens as Stourhead, she sets aside the traditional association of such gardens with the paintings of Claude Lorrain (*c.* 1602–82), and by extension the Picturesque, in favour of theatre sets and the practice of the 'Theateresque'.

JOHN WILTON-ELY's essay deals with cultural exchange in the applied arts in the second half of the eighteenth century. He argues that Robert Adam (1728–92) and James Adam (1732–94) were fully aware that they were launching a major revolution within the visual arts, and were setting out consciously to fashion an attractive and flexible style spread across the full spectrum of the fine and decorative arts from architecture, landscape and urban design to decorative painting, furniture, plasterwork, metalwork, ceramics and textiles. Fundamental to the creation of this style were the Grand Tours in Italy by Robert and James, made in 1755–7 and 1760–3 respectively, during which their residence in Rome — unusually well documented by correspondence and a wide range of drawings — was to prove of major consequence. Not only did Robert's studies in Rome allow him to absorb a prodigious amount of material, extending from classical antiquity to the contemporary world, but both were to make a series of critical contacts with their Italian, British and French contemporaries in terms of professional practice and patronage. Wilton-Ely explores the complexity of Robert Adam's artistic development under the influence of Charles-Louis Clérisseau (1721–1820) and, above all, Giovanni Battista Piranesi (1720–78) and his circle, as well as the theoretical climate of neoclassicism.

LETIZIA TEDESCHI's contribution looks at the patronage of the architect Vincenzo Brenna (1745–), born in Rome to a family from Ticino Canton in Switzerland, by the English collector and scholar-connoisseur Charles Townley (1737–1805). Focusing on the polemic concerning whether Greek or Roman models constituted the more perfect style for modern architects and designers to emulate, Tedeschi carefully examines letters and drawings relating to a trip made by Brenna and Townley to the Doric temples at Paestum in order to demonstrate the extent to which the English ambience in which Townley operated stimulated Brenna in his archaeological and architectural researches. She also considers the architectural models, no longer identifiable, that Brenna fashioned to scale in cork 'for his own pleasure', which were based on the measurements of antique buildings he had taken on site at Paestum and Tivoli, and which were later sent to Townley in England.

The final section is entitled 'Universal neoclassicism: old Rome and new Britain'. The British acquired not only antiquities, but contemporary sculpture in the antique manner. MALCOLM BAKER explores contemporary perceptions of portrait busts, both ancient and modern, in Rome. Although sculptors such as Michael Rysbrack (1694–1770) and Louis-François Roubiliac (1702–62), who were working in Britain, employed models that were as much French or Flemish as antique, for many patrons familiar with Italy the notion of the portrait bust had more to do with the works to be seen in the Farnese collection or busts being produced in Rome by contemporary sculptors, both Italian and French. Sir Thomas Robinson (1703–77), for example, saw commemoration through sculpture as the practice of Italian noblemen. As Baker's review of sculptural portraiture reveals, it was the impetus of British patrons who desired to leave, in Robinson's words, 'themselves to posterity in a more durable and grave manner than by our method by pictures, that is by sculptures in either statues or busts' (p. 274), who initiated a new trend in Roman portrait sculpture. Not only did British visitors set a new taste for antique-style portrait busts, but they redirected this vogue back to England, where Roubiliac and Rysbrack would be influenced by this new aesthetic.

The issue of the contemptuous attitude of the British towards modern Italian artists as unworthy of the inheritance of ancient Rome is explored by DESMOND SHAWE-TAYLOR. Observing that a prime purpose of Reynolds's *Discourses* (1769–73) was to warn students at the Royal Academy against the pernicious influence of Batoni and other living Italian artists, Shawe-Taylor argues that Reynolds's feelings about Batoni derive from his understanding of the concept of ideal beauty. He explores the professional relationship between Batoni and Reynolds by way of the Roman-trained Allan Ramsay (1713–84), the only writer of the period explicitly to question the assumption that ideal beauty is the proper object of painting. In Ramsay's *Dialogue on Taste* (1755) the purpose of art is quite simply to copy reality. Custom (or fashion) supplies notions of beauty, which may be followed by the painter but not 'believed in' by the philosopher. For Ramsay, the absolute notion of 'ideal beauty' was not only un-philosophical nonsense in theory, but also dreary to behold in practice. Such ideas would seem anathema to Italian artistic theory and yet seem to describe the practice of many Italian artists, like Canaletto, who were avidly collected by the English. Similarly, Batoni's portraits, for all their classical posturing, display an attention to detail that is highly realistic, even Dutch. For this reason, Shawe-Taylor explains, it was possible for Batoni to appear as a realist sheep in idealist clothing. Exploring the sustained attack on 'Batonismo' in the *Discourses*, Shawe-Taylor concludes that Reynolds's opposition to Batoni led him to a new conception of ideal beauty. Reynolds believed (like everyone) that grand-style painting should be the result of thought; but he also believed that it should *look like* thought, and for this reason should appear as summary in the details as is the human memory.

WENDY WASSYNG ROWORTH focuses on an artist who embodies the cosmopolitanism of the second half of the eighteenth century, Angelica Kauffman (1741–1807). The Swiss-born Kauffman, who was neither British nor Italian yet was recognized as both a member of the British School and a prominent artist in Italy, provided a unique link between artists and patrons in London and Rome. She was instrumental in bringing neoclassical history painting from Rome to England in the 1760s, and when she returned to Rome in 1782 with her Venetian husband, Antonio Zucchi (1726–95), she maintained ties with British printmakers and patrons, especially George Bowles, while cultivating new relationships with Italian artists, including Antonio Canova (1757–1822), Giovanni Volpato (1740–1803) and Giovan Battista Dell'Era (1765–99), and a broader international clientele. Poems written on the occasion of her departure from London by George Keate (1729–97) and by James Fordyce (1720–96) (*To Angelica Kauffman, at Rome: an Elegy*, a work not previously noted in Kauffman studies) lament Britain's loss and Italy's good fortune. Ippolito Pindemonte (1753–1828) expressed the opposite sentiment in a poem that celebrated the artist's triumphant return to the Tiber from 'Tamigi invidioso'. He extolled Kauffman's work, which was inspired by Italian art, and bemoaned the loss of Francesco Bartolozzi (1727–1815), Giovanni Battista Cipriani (1727–85) and Giovanni Locatelli (1735–1805) to England. Roworth analyses the language and views articulated in these poems, along with additional literary and pictorial evidence, in order to illuminate attitudes regarding cultural exchange, as well as Kauffman's real and symbolic role as a cultural intermediary in Rome.

Finally, KEVIN SALATINO examines another Swiss-English artist, Henry Fuseli (1741–1825), who devoted himself obsessively to making erotic sketches in Rome from 1770–8. By tracing the rich history of erotica in Italian art, and tying Fuseli's knowledge of this material to his intellectual interests in the Greek as well as Roman sources, Salatino offers concrete examples of the artist's deep interest in pre-Christian culture. Analysing a large group of previously unpublished pen-and-ink sketches, Salatino demonstrates that Fuseli's misogynistic depiction of women engaged with, on the whole, submissive men, was probably fuelled initially by his own introduction to a debauched lifestyle easily accessible to visitors to Rome. More significantly, Salatino argues that the moral laxity of Fuseli's Roman drawings was, in part, a reaction to the artistic culture of the city at the time of his residency there. 'In an age that felt more comfortable with the easy classicism of Raphael', writes Salatino, and that was dominated by the neoclassical aesthetic of Johann Joachim Winckelmann (1717–68), Fuseli's passionate interest in the 'excesses of Michelangelo's exuberant style' ultimately paved the way toward a modern sensibility of emotional turmoil and what a contemporary recognized as an 'unbridled license of imagination'. 'Ironically', observes Salatino, 'it was his experience of Rome, that most ancient of cities, that helped make Fuseli modern' (pp. 309 and 312).

Notes

1. R. Lassels, *The Voyage of Italy or a Compleat Journey through Italy. In Two Parts* ... (London, 1670), unpaginated preface, 'point 7': 'no man understands Livy and Caesar, Guicciardini and Monluc, like him, who hath made exactly the Grand Tour of France, and the Giro of Italy'.
2. J. Fleming, *Robert Adam and His Circle in Edinburgh and Rome* (London, 1962), 16–17, with note on p. 326.
3. J.M. Wright, *Ragguaglio della solenne comparsa fatta in Roma, gli otto di gennaio MDCLXXXVII* ... (Rome, 1687). Illustrated with engravings by A. van Westerhout, mostly after drawings by G.B. Lenardi. English edition 1688 (see caption to Fig. 1.1).
4. From the diary of David Nairne, Melfort's secretary: 'Diary of David Nairne', National Library of Scotland, MS 14266, fols 12r–30r.
5. A. Wilton and I. Bignamini (eds), *Grand Tour: the Lure of Italy in the Eighteenth Century* (London, 1996), 33: 'Now, in the autumn of 1763, Albani did his best to persuade the Duke to visit Rome, a death-blow for the Catholic Stuarts; the Hanoverian Duke of York did stay in Rome from 15 to 28 April, which caused the Stuart Duke of York and cardinal to move for sometime to his bishopric in Frascati'.
6. D. Szechi, 'The image of the court: idealism, politics and the evolution of the Stuart court 1689–1730', in E. Corp, *The Stuart Court in Rome. The Legacy of Exile* (Aldershot, 2003), 49–64, esp. p. 51.
7. Szechi, 'Image of the court' (above, n. 6), 50.
8. Cf. the remarks of Cardinal Giovanni Battista Patrizi (1658–1727) on hearing that Maria Clementina Sobieska (1702–35) had visited his villa in Rome.
9. F. Arisi, *Gian Paolo Panini e i fasti della Roma del '700* (Rome, 1986), 416–17, cat. 371 bis.
10. Cf. Chracas, *Diario ordinario* no. 775, 18 July 1722: 'Quella sera si vidde Roma tutta illuminata, e precisamente la gran Cupola del Vaticano, il Palazzo della Maestà del Rè d'Inghilterra, de' Sig. Cardinali, de' Regj Ministri, e di tutta la Nobiltà Romana' (That evening one saw Rome all illuminated, and specifically the great cupola of the Vatican, the palace of his Majesty the King of England, [the palaces of] the Cardinals, of the Royal Ministers, and of all the Roman nobility).
11. Cf. Francis Russell's remarks, referring to the portrait-painter Antonio David (1684–1737) — 'the qualities of a key figure in Roman portraiture of the second quarter of the Settecento, and the pattern of patronage it implies offers a hint that the development of Grand Tour portraiture owed more to the Jacobite presence in Rome than is generally admitted' (F. Russell, 'Notes on Grand Tour portraiture', *The Burlington Magazine* 136 (1994), 438–43, esp. p. 438). The Jacobite presence in Rome and contemporary portraiture has been explored in a series of publications by Edward Corp: E. Corp, *The King over the Water: Portraits of the Stuarts in Exile after 1689* (Edinburgh, 2001); E. Corp (ed.), *The Stuart Court in Rome. The Legacy of Exile* (Aldershot, 2003); E. Corp, *The Jacobites at Urbino: an Exiled Court in Transition* (Basingstoke/New York, 2009). See also his contribution to this volume.
12. C.M.S. Johns, 'The entrepôt of Europe: Rome in the eighteenth century', in E.P. Bowron and J.J. Rishel (eds), *Art in Rome in the Eighteenth Century* (London/Philadelphia, 2000), 16–45, esp. p. 19.

VISUAL CULTURE AND THE TRIUMPH OF COSMOPOLITANISM IN EIGHTEENTH-CENTURY ROME

Christopher M.S. Johns

Among the myriad adjectives traditionally used to describe the eighteenth century, cosmopolitan must be very near the top of the list. In an era that witnessed unprecedented levels of travel for pleasure, self-improvement and increased social visibility, among other motivations, cultural and artistic collision, confrontation and cooperation helped to fashion a new society in large part based on internationalist assumptions. The most conspicuous examples of this phenomenon occurred in the realm of visual and material culture. For example, in Settecento Italy one would not have had to look very far to find an English gentleman wearing French clothes, buying books published in Venice, on his way south to purchase Roman pictures and Neapolitan porcelain. Many important Grand Tour studies rightly have underscored the eighteenth century's obsession with material consumption and luxury in all forms, and there can be little doubt that neoclassicism, in all its facets, was born and disseminated largely through these essential forms of commodity exchange.[1] Arguably the last truly international aesthetic, neoclassicism's visual and political deployment by regimes as diverse as the papacy and the constitutional monarchy in Great Britain is evidentiary of eighteenth-century Europe's obsession with a shared past.[2] Rome was the epicentre of this pan-European movement, but whether or not the cosmopolitan character of Settecento Rome was responsible for this, or rather Europe's adaptation of Roman visual culture to its own particular purposes, is subject to debate.

Historians have long recognized the fact that *ancien régime* political systems failed at the end of the century partly because they were usually organized on dynastic, rather than national, principles. In almost all cases, the national interest gave way to dynastic concerns when they were in competition. Dynastic governments' inability to engage the rising tide of bourgeois nationalist sentiments and to overcome the culture of aristocratic privilege as the eighteenth century progressed doomed them to obsolescence or, in several cases, extinction. In many places, especially Spain, Naples, Tuscany, Lombardy, Parma, Flanders and parts of Poland, an enormous gulf opened between the people and their non-native rulers. As awareness of shared cultural identities dramatically increased among a rapidly expanding and socially ambitious middle class, a surge of enthusiasm for a national political identity could not be far behind.[3] This phenomenon engendered a wave of national particularism, and non-native dynasts could neither effectively control nor politically exploit it. In sum, the bond between the regnant cosmopolitan culture of dynastic government and aristocratic élites broke down in the face of largely middle-class challenges to the status quo fomented by national and political particularism.

The British component of this European equation, however, offers a unique and paradoxical success story in the eighteenth century's quest to reconcile dynastic politics and national identity. Unsurprisingly, the city of Rome and the role of Rome in the European imaginary were essential components of Britain's brilliant negotiation of the widespread destruction of the *ancien régime*'s institutions and the rise of the modern nationalist tradition from their ashes. Even though its reigning dynasty was German Hanoverian after 1714, by the accession of George III (1738–1820) in 1760 the vast majority of Britons thoroughly identified their nation with their king, or, perhaps more accurately, their king with their nation, especially as unhappy memories of Jacobite rebellion began to fade, at least in England and Wales, if not to the same degree in Scotland and Ireland. How did Great Britain escape the fate of most of its continental counterparts that were victims, to varying degrees, of the demise of the cosmopolitan age of Enlightenment? Geography, the political system and a religion defined nationally, instead of universally, doubtless were major factors, but I would argue that

Rome also played an important part in the relatively peaceful *ancien régime* nationalistic definition of what it meant to be British in the modern world.[4] Ironically and paradoxically, Great Britain successfully appropriated the mantle of world empire inherited from ancient Rome, a legacy that the papacy and the Holy Roman Empire had long contested and that would be claimed ephemerally by Napoleonic France.[5] Britain was to wear this garment unchallenged for most of the nineteenth century.

It is no accident that British Grand Tourism increased with the island nation's initial achievement of world empire, from the end of the War of Spanish Succession in 1713–14 to the conclusion of the Seven Years' War in 1763, and flowered in its aftermath. In a broad range of cultural media, Britons were not slow to identify their emerging empire with the greatest empire of antiquity: Rome. Educated people of all classes and both genders were as familiar with Graeco-Roman history as they were with their own national narratives, and the wish to see the monumental ruins of the ancient imperial capital and walk in the footsteps of its senators, cultural luminaries and emperors quickened the impulse to travel.[6] The popularity of the work of Giovanni Battista Piranesi (1720–78) in Britain is important evidence of the phenomenon, but we also might consider the impact of the audience's expectations, as the artist understood them, on Piranesi's enterprise, although the British were certainly not the only consumers of the printmaker's images.[7] In a similar fashion, the designs of John Flaxman (1755–1826) for the ceramic wares of Josiah Wedgwood (1730–95) not only helped to create a mania for antique forms and designs, but these very objects were deeply influenced by public expectations and perceptions that were created and nurtured by an international aesthetic in part created by Piranesi. Wedgwood's Etruria factory in the British Midlands has long been characterized as a prominent example of nationalistic, physiocratic enterprise, but few now think of Grand Tour Italy when they see or purchase Wedgwood products, so thoroughly has this brand of 'china' become anglicized (Fig. 2.1).[8] Eighteenth-century consumers, on the other hand, were at least intuitively aware that these objects were conceptual hybrids: such commodities were both classical, in the cosmopolitan sense, and quintessentially national, in the British sense. Thus, it could be argued that Piranesi's prints and Wedgwood's vases are cultural exemplars of the duality of British identity in the Georgian era — a construction that used the materials of the international neoclassicism whose capital was Rome for the purpose of national self-identification.

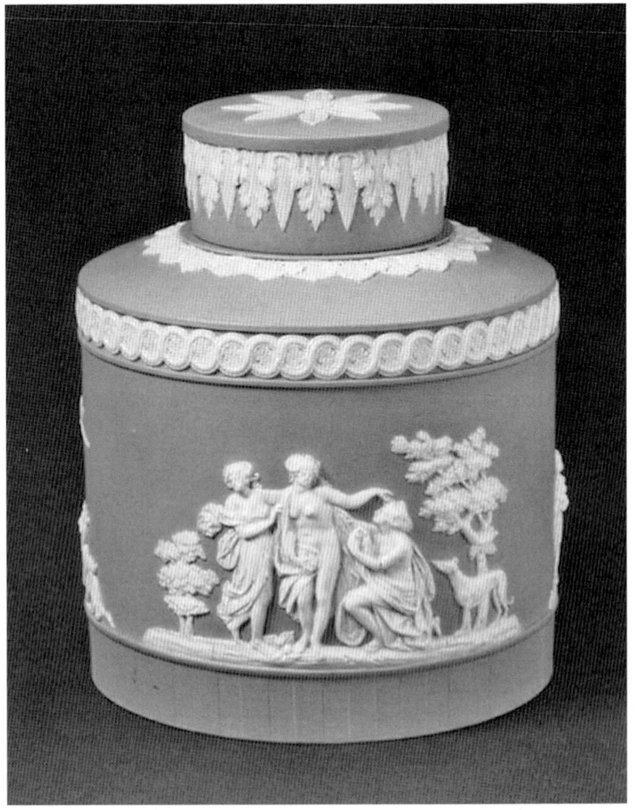

FIG. 2.1. Josiah Wedgwood and Sons, Ltd., *Tea Canister, Jasper with Blue Stain and Applied Relief of Diana and Nymphs*, c. 1795–1800. 10.16 × 8.09 cm. London, Victoria and Albert Museum, J.A. Tulk Bequest. *(© V&A Images/Victoria and Albert Museum, London.)*

In part, the dualities and seeming contradictions everywhere evident in eighteenth-century British national identity construction are present in different forms and to different degrees in most of *ancien régime* Europe, but, unlike the continental countries, Great Britain resolved the problem to its advantage. In the present context, Rome, ancient and papal, provided both positive and negative models for the construction of national identity based on a cosmopolitan, imperial and spiritually universalizing model. In order to understand this phenomenon better, above all in the realm of aesthetic and cultural politics, it is necessary to examine both the innovations and the continuities from the past of the long eighteenth century. My inquiry here is based on two assumptions; that imitation is the sincerest form of flattery, and that the burning desire of many influential Britons to acquire ancient and modern works of art and material culture while in Rome was an expression of an often unspoken, but none the less firmly-held, belief that Britons, not

Italians, were the truer and more worthy successors to the grandeur that was Rome. Concomitantly, the continuities between Roman art and culture and its ancient, Renaissance and Baroque past, and especially the latter, were the aspects of the Italian experience that Britons found especially distasteful, barbarous, superstitious, illogical, unreasonable and inferior.[9] Indeed, the constant negative comments found almost everywhere in British travel literature, which trumpets the unworthiness of modern Romans to their splendid inheritance from a halcyon past, begs the question: if the Romans are not worthy of the imperial legacy, then who is? The answer, often tacit, is the British themselves.[10]

An obvious place to look for the British appropriation of the Roman imperial past is in the portraits commissioned by visitors to Rome from resident painters and sculptors, who were only too happy to oblige the deep-pocketed milordi.[11] Most of the painted portraits place the sitter in close proximity to a wide variety of antique objects — some famous, some obscure and some imaginary. Pompeo Batoni's *John Staples* of 1773, casually dressed and posed with his dog and in easy communion with the *Ludovisi Mars*, is a case in point.[12] Even more representative of British 'antico-mania' is *Thomas Dundas, Later 1st Baron Dundas* (Fig. 2.2).[13] Thomas Dundas (1708–87) was the son of a wealthy merchant from Yorkshire, and commissioned his portrait from Pompeo Batoni (1708–87) in 1763. Nattily elegant in his red velvet suit, Dundas stands in an imaginary ancient building surrounded by celebrated painted replicas of antique statues, including the *Laocoön* and the *Apollo Belvedere* in the background and the Vatican *Cleopatra*, now identified as the *Sleeping Ariadne*, in the right foreground. All of these statues appear in other Grand Tour portraits, by Batoni and others, but my point here is the easy familiarity with which the British moderns interact with the faux-marble ancients. If the British are indeed the most worthy inheritors of ancient Roman civilization and its impressive empire, why should a future English baronet hesitate to ask an Egyptian queen conquered by Roman arms to dance?

Two portraits of Grand Tourists by Anton Raphael Mengs (1728–79), Batoni's friendly rival, also shed light on different aspects of the British appropriation of the ancient Roman inheritance. Painted in Rome in 1758, *John Brudenell-Montagu, Later Marquess of Monthermer* (Plate 2.1) depicts the learned aristocrat seated at a desk covered with books and papers in the company of a faithful dog.[14] The portrait's formula is more typical of Batoni than of Mengs, and, indeed, Batoni executed a portrait of John Brudenell-Montagu (1735–70) shortly before in possible emulation of Mengs's manner.[15] As Peter Bowron and Steffi Roettgen have suggested, it may be that both painters were consciously working in the Grand Tour portrait style of the other to demonstrate their proficiency in one another's personal idiom. Be that as it may, I am here concerned with the painted bust of the Roman orator Cicero atop the sitter's desk, an object that seems to be the presiding deity of the portrait's intellectual apparatus. As a British Grand Tourist, Brudenell-Montagu was rather unusual in his proclivities for Greek art and architecture, as opposed to the more dominant and popular Roman art promoted by Piranesi, and spent only about a month in the Eternal City. His tour of south Italy and Sicily, both with a rich heritage of west Greek architecture, lasted about eighteen months. I believe the painter's inclusion of the bust of Cicero is more than a generic antique reference in this particular case, and sheds light not only on Brudenell-Montagu's Hellenophilia specifically, but on the British attitude towards Graeco-Roman antiquity generally.

As a brilliant rhetorician and astute legal mind, Cicero's pride of place was universally acknowledged in the eighteenth century, and his image was an important signifier of the British political class. Widely read by schoolboys in Britain and elsewhere, familiarity with Ciceronian legal arguments and *bon mots* was essential for success in the public sphere, above all in Parliament. In the case of Brudenell-Montagu, however, one text of Cicero stands out as the key to his interests and the interpretation of Mengs's portrait: *The Verrines*.[16] On 5 August 70 BCE, Marcus Tullius Cicero initiated a prosecution of Gaius Verres, former Roman governor of Sicily, that was so eloquently persuasive and damning of Verres's nefarious activities that the defendant immediately left the city and went into exile. *The Verrines* is a series of study orations written as if they had actually been delivered in the Forum. While the case against Verres was that he had grossly abused his position as Roman governor to loot Sicilian public spaces, including temples, as well as private collections, of any work of art or material culture that struck his fancy, their interest to Brudenell-Montagu would have been their detailed descriptions of the cultural geography of Sicily and south Italy. It is almost impossible to imagine that plans for a serious tour of southern Italy and Sicily would not have included careful study of *The*

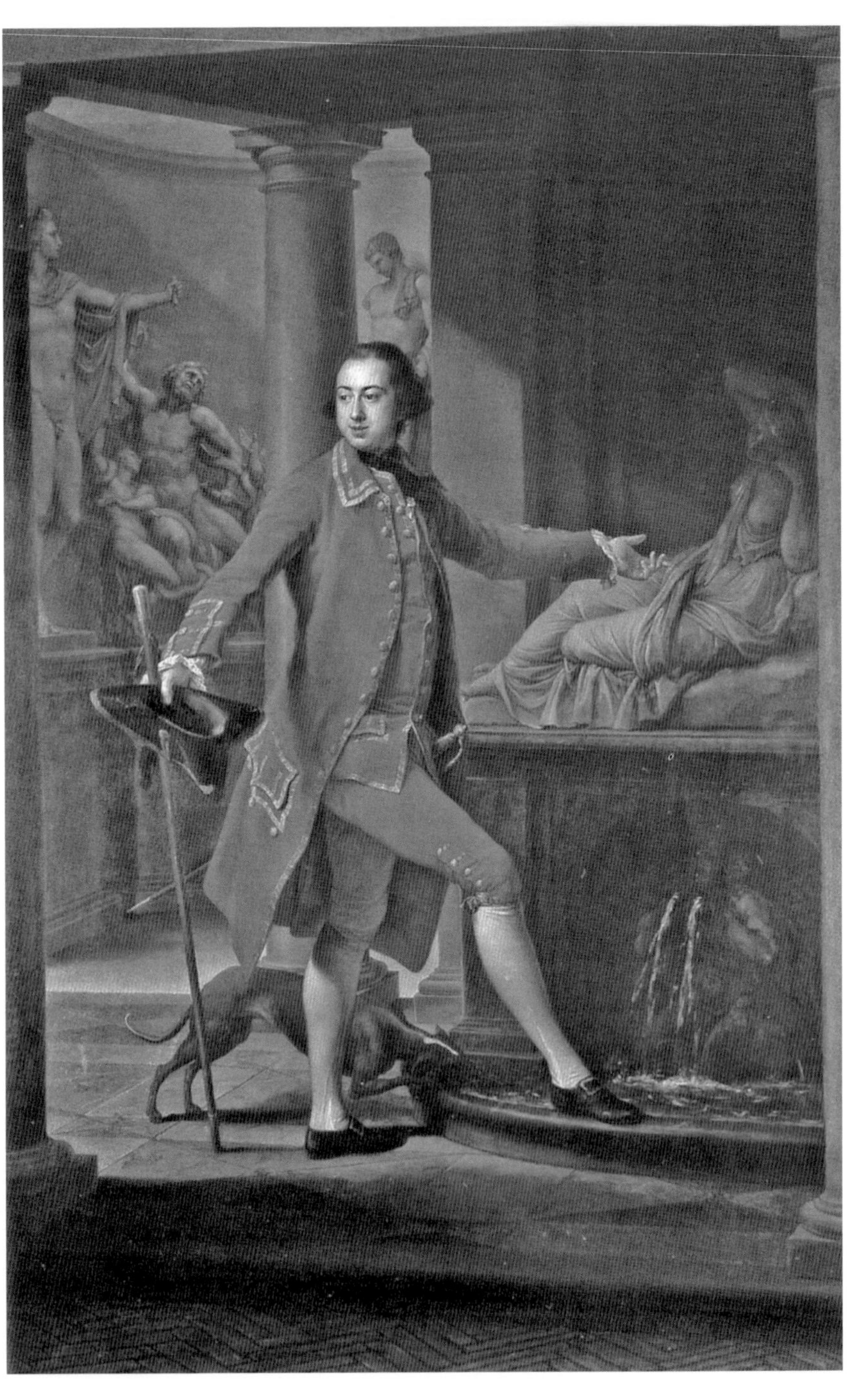

FIG. 2.2. Pompeo Batoni (1708–87), *Thomas Dundas, Later 1st Baron Dundas*, 1763–4. Oil on canvas. The Marquess of Zetland, Aske Hall, North Yorkshire. *(Photo: Jerry Hardman-Jones. Reproduced courtesy of the Earl of Ronaldshay.)*

Verrines.[17] A contemporary also obsessed with the antiquities of the Kingdom of Naples, the Abbé de Saint-Non (1727–91), certainly consulted Cicero's text in conjunction with his tour of the south.[18] A canonical ancient text whose main purpose was to denounce an individual for cultural spoliation of what may be termed a national patrimony certainly has some irony for a notable British Grand Tour portrait, although I think it unlikely that Brudenell-Montagu or any of his British peers would have looked at it in quite this way.

Another Grand Tour image by Mengs, the *Allegorical Portrait of James Caulfield, Lord Charlemont* (Fig. 2.3), painted in Rome in 1755–6, visualizes some different aspects of the British appropriation of the heritage of the Roman empire.[19] Although the actual identity of the sitter is still debated, the fact that he is British is the crucial point for my argument. This strange and curiously unappealing historical portrait may not be unique in Settecento Roman production, but it must be close to being so. Stylistically advanced for

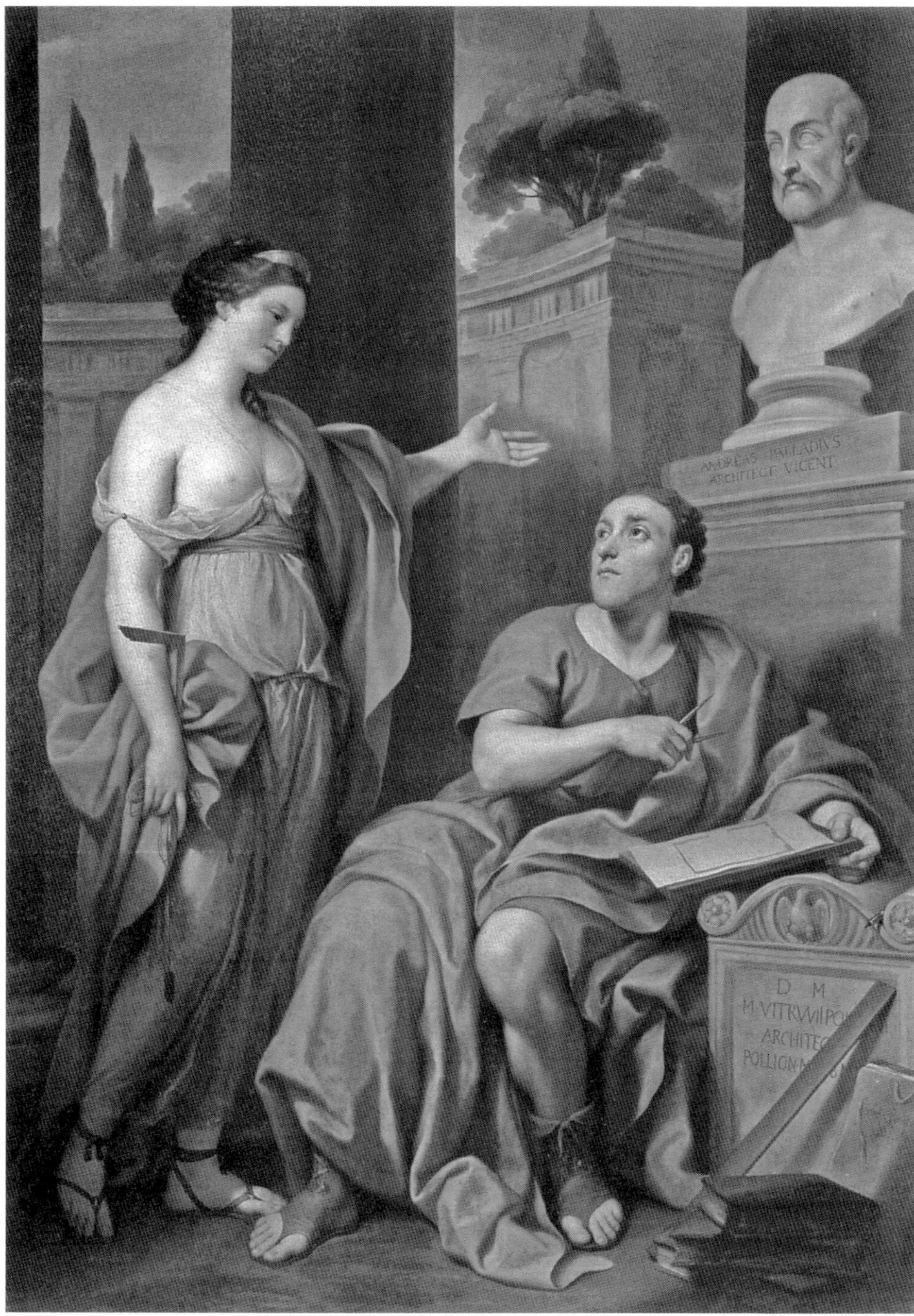

FIG. 2.3. Anton Raphael Mengs (1728–79), *Allegorical Portrait of James Caulfield, Lord Charlemont*, 1755–6. Oil on canvas. *(Prague, National Gallery.)*

the date and conceptually sophisticated, Roettgen rightly has characterized it as 'a seminal work for Roman Neoclassicism'.[20] Seated beneath a painted bust of the Renaissance architect Andrea Palladio (1508–80) and next to an inscribed tablet of Vitruvian inspiration, the pose of Lord Charlemont (1728–99) is based on the fresco by Raphael (1483–1520) of the Prophet Isaiah in the Roman church of Sant'Agostino. He is approached by a female personification of architecture, who recommends the bust to his consideration, and the conceit recalls Baroque examples of the 'Inspiration of the Poet' theme by Poussin and others. Charlemont is shown working on a quadrangular floor plan when he is interrupted by reified architecture, and the portrait conceit must refer to the keen architectural enthusiasms of the sitter.[21] Indeed, as some scholars have suggested, Charlemont's change of interests from the study of architecture and its history to actual building may be responsible in part for his ultimate refusal to give the financial support he had promised to Piranesi's *Antichità romane*, an act of bad faith that is well-documented in Piranesi studies.[22]

Interest in the portrait in the present context is confined largely to its allegorical conceit and the pose of the sitter. If one sees Palladio as a modern inheritor of the ancient architectural heritage of Vitruvius, it is not much of a leap to understand Charlemont's identification with the classical tradition in terms of his own appropriation of it to construct a personal identity and, by extension, a national one. This cultural/political territory had been traversed earlier in the century by Lord Burlington (1694–1753) and William Kent (1685–1748), whose Burlingtonian Palladian classicizing architecture was readily identified with a British, Whig sensibility that had definite nationalistic overtones. If I may so express it, the true architectural style was to come to live in Britain, shuddering in horror at the 'bizarre excesses' of modern Roman architectural practice, as many visiting Britons noted. The captious comments of Robert Adam (1728–92) about most modern Roman architects and, from a rather different point of view, the complaints of John Soane (1753–1837) about the smallness of modern buildings, generally are characteristic, and were shared by many, but certainly not all, potential patrons.

The position occupied by Palladio in the canon of eighteenth-century architecture compares favourably to the unchallenged pre-eminence of Raphael in painting. Mengs's admiration for Raphael, whom he considered the greatest of the moderns, is well-documented, and the selection of the Sant'Agostino *Isaiah* as the source for Charlemont's pose may have been suggested by the artist. Given Charlemont's artistic interests, however, it seems likely that he understood the reference as appropriate for a portrait programme that aimed to link modern achievement to ancient authority. I would argue that one of the major themes of this complicated image is cultural and intellectual inheritance — engaging the legacy of past greatness to promote contemporary worth —, but in an emulative, rather than an imitative, manner. To be emulous in the eighteenth-century sense of the word is complimentary. It indicates a thorough knowledge of, and respect for, tradition, while simultaneously seeking to create something new, modern and worthy of the emulated tradition. Great Britain's engagement with and appropriation of ancient imperial grandeur was a right of inheritance. As the leading global imperial power, the ancient empire had to be appropriated. The classical tradition and the antique were the bedrock of the lingua franca of cosmopolitan Europe. I think there is little doubt that the British thoroughly understood the cultural politics of their situation and acted accordingly.

In addition to Grand Tour portraiture, another prominent site of the British appropriation of the legacy of ancient Roman imperial authority was in the collecting of antiquities. Many British tourists acquired, or attempted to acquire, antique marble statues while in Italy, these artefacts of ancient Rome being privileged in the contemporary imagination beyond all other forms of visual expression. Henry Blundell of Ince (1724–1810), Charles Townley (1737–1805) of 7 Park Street, Westminster, and the Duke of Northumberland (1714–86) at the Robert Adam-designed Syon House are only three of the most celebrated British aesthetes who amassed impressive collections of Roman antiquities for domestic display. The *Charles Townley's Library at 7 Park Street, Westminster* of 1781–3 (Plate 2.2), by John Zoffany (*c.* 1733–1810), is the most familiar image of the British mania for collecting antiquities; copies, variants, pastiches and almost certainly outright forgeries populate the imaginatively arranged Park Street library.[23] The genuine admiration for antique statuary and the fervent desire to build collections of it for both domestic pleasure and public edification that are characteristic of eighteenth-century Britain in no way negates the absolute fact of patrimonial displacement. Cultural artefacts had been physically removed from their habitual context of display or had been excavated from Roman soil to inhabit a new, different space, far removed, at least geographically, from Italy. These objects, once on display in Britain, necessarily created a new context — aesthetic, cultural and political. The country-house destination of so many antiquities acquired by the British in Italy, seen in the present context, is yet another form of appropriation. Many of the landed élite who collected antiquities for their rural mansions must have understood that they were continuing the tradition of ancient Roman villas. Excavations at Tivoli and at Horace's villa had demonstrated to everyone the artistic wealth and splendour of privileged rural life in antiquity.[24]

If the adage that history is told by the victors is true, there can be little doubt that the construction of an imperial national identity in eighteenth-century Great Britain based on the precedent of ancient Rome was wildly successful. Deeply versed in classical literature, especially embracing the Plutarchian model of the virtuous leader and the antique notion of empire as a responsibility of an advanced civilization, British élites discovered in Rome what they knew was there all along — their own destiny. The British triumph, however, was not complete. The only conspicuous failure of the British co-option of the legacy of Rome was the former's inability to transplant the latter's artistic eminence from the Tiber to the Thames (or north of the Tweed, for that matter). Since the appropriation of ancient grandeur, culturally speaking, was based on demonstrable knowledge of the classical tradition in the arts and in possession of at least some of its prized objects, where did this leave the emerging British school of art? Why were many British patrons eager to commission works from artists living in Rome, Italian and foreign alike, when their relative neglect of native British practitioners aroused outrage and envy back home? Seventeenth-century English art had been dominated largely by foreigners, Nicolas Hilliard (1547–1619), William Dobson (1611–46), Robert Walker (1595/1610–1658) and a few others notwithstanding, but the dramatic rise in wealth, self-confidence, ambition and the impetus to empire should have witnessed the transfer of artistic primacy from Rome to London. But this did not happen. Indeed, some of the best commissions awarded to British artists by their compatriots were given in Rome rather than in Britain, portraits largely excepted.[25] Reynolds's disparaging remarks about the leading lights of the eighteenth-century Roman school — Agostino Masucci (*c.* 1691–1758), Mengs and especially Batoni, as discussed by Desmond Shawe-Taylor in this volume — could be interpreted as bitter reflections on the preferences of many British patrons, although it certainly is more complicated than that.[26] The necessity of an extended visit to Italy, especially to Rome, to complete one's artistic education was still unquestioned by most leading British artists, although Thomas Gainsborough (1727–88) and, later, John Constable (1776–1837) saw no need to follow their fellows southwards. After learning the lessons of antiquity and the classical tradition at the source, British artists wanted to be considered equal or even superior to their continental competitors. There are many reasons for the disconnection in Britain between artistic expectations and realities, and possibly the ancient view that Greek artists were superior to Roman ones, an aspect of ancient taste well known in the eighteenth century, is in play here. One particular case-study, however, reveals both what was at stake in this one-sided rivalry and helps to document the gap in perception between political and artistic empire in eighteenth-century Britain.

In 1771, Mengs completed an altarpiece for the chapel of All Souls' College at Oxford for which he was paid over 300 pounds.[27] The painting, *Noli Me Tangere*, reveals the artist's study of Raphael, Correggio (*c.* 1489–1534) and the *Apollo Belvedere*, all perfectly proper things for an academically inclined artist to do. Exhibited in both Rome and London before its delivery to Oxford, the altarpiece elicited both praise and blame, and almost everyone commented on such a high price being paid for a painting with only two figures. Commissioned in Florence and executed in Rome, *Noli Me Tangere* is one of the artist's finest religious pictures. That did not stop the British artist James Barry (1741–1806) from bitterly complaining about the high profile and well-remunerated commission going to a non-British artist working in Rome. In a letter to the 3rd Duke of Richmond (1735–1806), written in 1773, Barry's jeremiad concludes: 'Mengs and other natives of foreign countries where art and human mind have been long since in a vitiated, sickly and dying state, are employed without scruples in pictures for the churches of our universities'.[28] Barry's outrage on behalf of British artists is understandable, but his reference to art being produced in a 'vitiated, sickly and dying state' should be considered, since it returns us to the idea that modern Italians (or representatives of their culture in Mengs's case) are unworthy of the inheritance of ancient Rome.

One reason why the mantle of empire was not shared with British artists, I believe, may be the notion that British élites largely viewed art as an expensive and high-quality form of colonial import. Imperial centres imported luxuries from their provincial peripheries. They produced the things necessary to maintain control over an empire — technology, high-end manufacturing and a powerful military. *Roma Britannica*, then, could also be reversed — *Britannia Romana* —, since all western models for empire originated there. National destiny was formulated on a model that necessarily appropriated a shared, cosmopolitan past, but to make it work, the British had to make it their own. All empires, including Rome's and Great Britain's, are historically ephemeral, but their most positive legacies are their cultural and artistic production. That is why the museum is the most potent institutional link to a past that is still a crucial site of interpretative negotiation and ideological definition. It is highly logical that the first truly public museum in the western world, the Capitoline Museum, was established in Rome in 1734 by Pope Clement XII Corsini (1652–1740) (Fig. 2.4). The founding of a museum is an

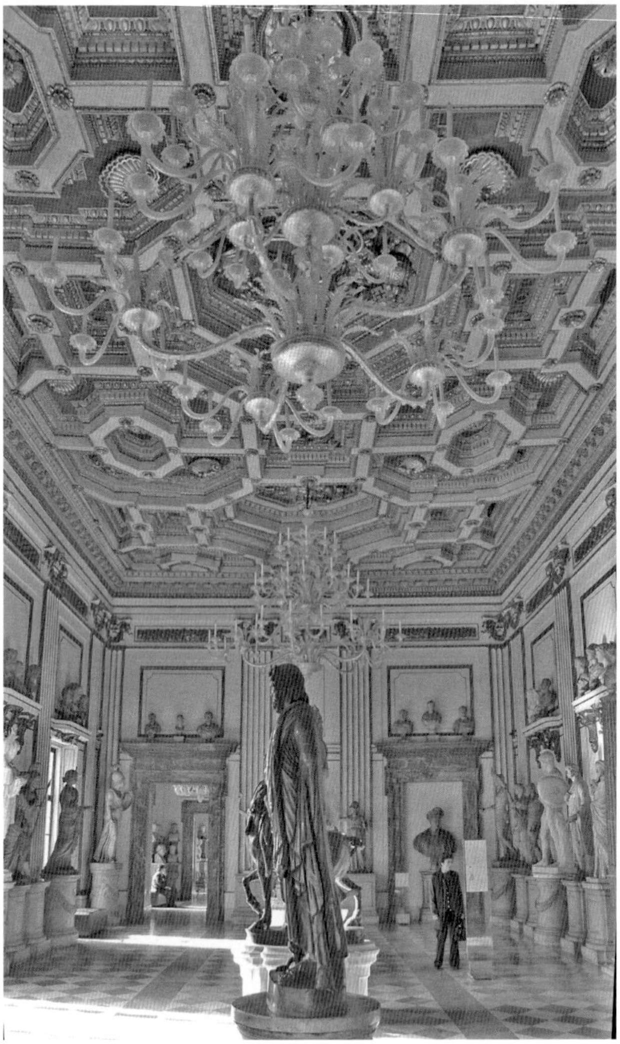

FIG. 2.4. **Capitoline Museum. View of the interior.** *(Photo: © David R. Marshall, 2009.)*

admission that the link with the past has been broken forever, and that the relationship of the present to its history will never be the same.

NOTES

1. The literature on the Grand Tour is vast. For a useful introduction, see J. Black, *Italy and the Grand Tour* (New Haven/London, 2003), esp. pp. 46–67, 174–202. For the British in Rome and the relationship of the Tour to eighteenth-century cosmopolitanism, see C. de Seta, *L'Italia del Grand Tour: da Montaigne a Goethe* (Naples, 2001), 75–9, 130–53 for numerous splendid colour plates. The magisterial study remains A. Wilton and I. Bignamini (eds), *Grand Tour: the Lure of Italy in the Eighteenth Century* (London, 1996), with extensive bibliography.
2. The historicist aspects of European neoclassicism in relation to the Grand Tour have been discussed in D. Irwin, *Neoclassicism* (London, 1997), 11–63, and the still indispensable H. Honour, *Neoclassicism* (Harmondsworth, 1977), chapter two: 'The vision of antiquity', pp. 43–67.
3. For an extensive discussion of the role of Rome in the British imagination, based on cultural and political commonalities, see P. Ayres, *Classical Culture and the Idea of Rome in Eighteenth-century England* (Cambridge, 1997), especially chapter one, 'Oligarchy of virtue', pp. 1–47, with extensive bibliography.
4. An alternative definition of 'British' in the context of English nativism is explored in L. Colley, *Britons: Forging the Nation, 1707–1837* (New Haven/London, 1992), 105–17.
5. For Bonapartist attempts to appropriate the legacy of ancient Rome, see C.M.S. Johns, *Antonio Canova and the Politics of Patronage in Revolutionary and Napoleonic Europe* (Berkeley/London, 1998), 88–122.
6. While the intellectual and high cultural context of the Grand Tour has received the lion's share of scholarly attention, its practical aspects should be considered also. See the innovative new study by A. Brilli, *Il viaggio in Italia: storia di una grande tradizione culturale* (Bologna, 2006), especially chapters 2–6, pp. 75–246, with extensive bibliography.
7. M. Craske, *Art in Europe, 1700–1830: a History of the Visual Arts in an Era of Unprecedented Urban Economic Growth* (Oxford/New York, 1997), 220–1.
8. For Wedgwood's place in the marketing of neoclassicism in Britain, see V. Coltman, *Fabricating the Antique: Neoclassicism in Britain, 1760–1800* (Chicago/London, 2006), 85–96, with additional bibliography. See also B. Nolan, *Josiah Wedgwood: Entrepreneur to the Enlightenment* (London, 2004).
9. Black, *Italy and the Grand Tour* (above, n. 1), 166–73, with additional bibliography.
10. The negative view of modern Romans held by the vast majority of British visitors is a central theme of much eighteenth-century travel literature. Sloth, a certain sexual challenge sensed by male visitors from Roman women, street violence, petty theft, the relentless demand for tips, the freedom permitted aristocratic women, and general insolence are among the myriad complaints registered against the *Popolo Romano*.
11. For a general discussion of British Grand Tour portraiture, see especially E.P. Bowron, *Pompeo Batoni (1708–87) and His*

British Patrons (London, 1982), and S. Roettgen, *Anton Raphael Mengs, 1728–1779, and His British Patrons* (London, 1993), both with full bibliographies.

12. A.M. Clark, *Pompeo Batoni. A Complete Catalogue of His Works*, edited and prepared for publication by E.P. Bowron (New York, 1985), 329.
13. Clark and Bowron, *Pompeo Batoni* (above, n. 12), 296–7.
14. S. Roettgen, *Anton Raphael Mengs, 1728–1779: das Malerische und Zeichnerische Werk*, 2 vols (Munich, 1999–2003), I, 264–5.
15. Clark and Bowron, *Pompeo Batoni* (above, n. 12), 270–1.
16. Roettgen, *Mengs and His British Patrons* (above, n. 11), 48–50, where the bust is identified as Cicero.
17. For *The Verrines* and their connection to the Sicilian cultural patrimony, see M.M. Miles, *Art as Plunder: the Ancient Origins of Debate about Cultural Property* (New York, 2008).
18. Saint-Non's travel account is one of the most ambitious and informative guides to the cultural geography of Sicily ever produced. In addition, it is illustrated lavishly by some of the era's leading artists, including Jean-Honoré Fragonard (1732–1806) and Hubert Robert (1733–1808). See P. Lamers, *Il viaggio nel sud dell'Abbé de Saint-Non* (Naples, 1995), with hundreds of illustrations and extensive bibliography.
19. Roettgen, *Mengs and His British Patrons* (above, n. 11), 52–5. A.M. Clark's identification of the subject of the portrait as Lord Charlemont, discussed and supported with additional evidence by Roettgen, is convincing.
20. Roettgen, *Mengs and His British Patrons* (above, n. 11), 52.
21. These interests are discussed in Roettgen, *Anton Raphael Mengs* (above, n. 14), I, 271–2.
22. The literature on Piranesi is vast. See especially J. Wilton-Ely, *The Mind and Art of Giovanni Battista Piranesi* (London, 1978); J. Scott, *Piranesi* (London/New York, 1975). Both books have extensive bibliographies.
23. For a stimulating discussion of this fascinating painting and its rather eccentric patron, see Coltman, *Fabricating the Antique* (above, n. 8), 165–75.
24. Townley's interests in excavations in and around Rome are documented in B.F. Cook, 'Charles Townley's collection of drawings and papers: a source for eighteenth-century excavations, the market and collections', in I. Bignamini (ed.), *Archives & Excavations. Essays on the History of Archaeological Excavations in Rome and Southern Italy from the Renaissance to the Nineteenth Century* (*Archaeological Monographs of the British School at Rome* 14) (London, 2004), 125–34. The magisterial study on the Emperor Hadrian's villa at Tivoli is W.A. MacDonald and J.A. Pinto, *Hadrian's Villa and its Legacy* (New Haven/London, 1995).
25. A notable example is John Flaxman's *Fury of Athamas*, commissioned in 1790 by the Earl of Bristol (1730–1803), who was in Rome on the Grand Tour. The large four-figured marble group, still at Ickworth, Bristol's country house in Suffolk, is a neoclassical emulation of the *Laocoön*. The acclaim accorded this sculpture led to another commission given in Rome, by Thomas Hope (1769–1831) of *Cephalus and Aurora*. See D. Bindman, 'John Flaxman: art and commerce', in D. Bindman (ed.), *John Flaxman* (London, 1979), 27–8.
26. Reynolds's condemnation of the leading painters of the Roman school is recorded in R.R. Wark (ed.), *Discourses on Art* (New Haven/London, 1981), XIV, 248–9, lines 52–8. The text reads: 'I will venture to prophecy, that two of the last distinguished Painters of that country, [Italy or Rome — it is unclear] I mean Pompeio Battoni, and Raffaelle Mengs, however great their names may at present sound in our ears, will very soon fall into the rank of Imperiale, Sebastian Concha, Placido Constanza, Massuccio, and the rest of their immediate predecessors; whose names, though equally renowned in their lifetime, are now fallen into what is little short of total oblivion'.
27. Roettgen, *Anton Raphael Mengs* (above, n. 14), I, 105–11, with additional bibliography.
28. Barry was a relentless critic of Mengs, Batoni and the entire modern Roman school, although his debt to Mengs's reductive, distilled version of Bolognese classicism is obvious. See W.L. Pressly, *The Life and Art of James Barry* (New Haven/London, 1981), 9.

ART FOR RELIGION:
CATHOLIC BRITAIN AND
JACOBITES IN ROME

Andrea Pozzo and the Venerable English College, Rome

Carol M. Richardson

Like British tourists who seek out a pub on the Costa Brava, visitors to Rome have always sought out the familiar. Throughout the seventeenth and eighteenth centuries the English College and its hospice were accessible to all English and Welsh visitors and residents in Rome. Bona fide pilgrims with references could stay for eight days at the hospice, an important part of the Venerable English College.[1] Established in 1362, the practice of receiving pilgrims at the hospice continued well into the eighteenth century and the pilgrim book was kept until 1767. Occasionally Protestants pretended to be Roman Catholics so they could enjoy its facilities, but such subterfuge was not strictly necessary, as ties of nationality often overcame those of religious division. In the middle of the seventeenth century the poet John Milton (in 1638–9) and the diarist John Evelyn (in 1644), both Protestants, dined at the College.[2] They probably attended one of the banquets that marked important feast-days, such as that of Saint Thomas of Canterbury (29 December), to which all the English resident in Rome were invited. But most of the visitors to the College were poor pilgrims who had travelled a long way and were hungry and sick. As scholars such as Edward Chaney and Judith Champ have pointed out, pilgrims, who endured in Rome much longer than Grand Tourists, often have been overshadowed by cultural travellers in recent literature.[3] At the same time, the separation of England from the continent and the absence of an indigenous Catholic culture perhaps has been overemphasized by Catholic historians.[4] The Venerable English College stands as an important case-study of cultural relations between Britain and the papacy.

One visitor who was motivated by both religion and antiquarian culture to travel to Rome and Italy was Dr Richard Rawlinson, an Anglican priest and Jacobite, who visited Rome in the early 1720s and made several visits to the English College during his stay.[5] He first went to the College on 15 December 1720, ten days after he had arrived in Rome, and he and his party were shown some of the paintings in the church and College, among them portraits of 'the Chevalier', the exiled heir to the throne of Britain, James Francis Edward Stuart, known as the Old Pretender, and his youngest sister, Louisa Maria Theresa, who had died in 1712. (The Stuart court had been resident in Rome since 1719.) On 8 January 1721 the Rawlinson party returned to the English College and saw the chapel, oratory and refectory (Figs 3.1 and 3.2). He and his party were 'very civilly received by one of the priests'.[6] On 14 and 15 January Rawlinson was back in the College, recording inscriptions, presumably of the monuments of the English community dating back to the fourteenth century in the College church. On 13 April he and his party visited the church, oratory, library and gardens and 'were treated to a glass of wine'.[7]

Through the Cardinal Protector, the College sometimes assumed a more official role. When, in 1686, Lord Castlemaine arrived in Rome as the first English ambassador there for 150 years, his host in the city was Philip Howard, Cardinal Protector for England and a supporter of the Stuarts, who met him and took him back to his new palace attached to the College. But, when the Jesuit rector and Castlemaine were found whispering together, the arrangement ended and the ambassador was removed to a safe distance at the Palazzo Doria Pamphilj, on Piazza Navona.[8]

Much of the hospice for English pilgrims was converted into a college in 1579, to train priests to send them back to England to face possible martyrdom. It is in the heart of the historic centre of the city, near Campo de' Fiori, which in the second half of the sixteenth century was effectively handed over to the reformed religious orders by the papacy to form a 'third pole' of papal influence and religious vigour in Rome, alongside Saint Peter's and Saint John Lateran.[9]

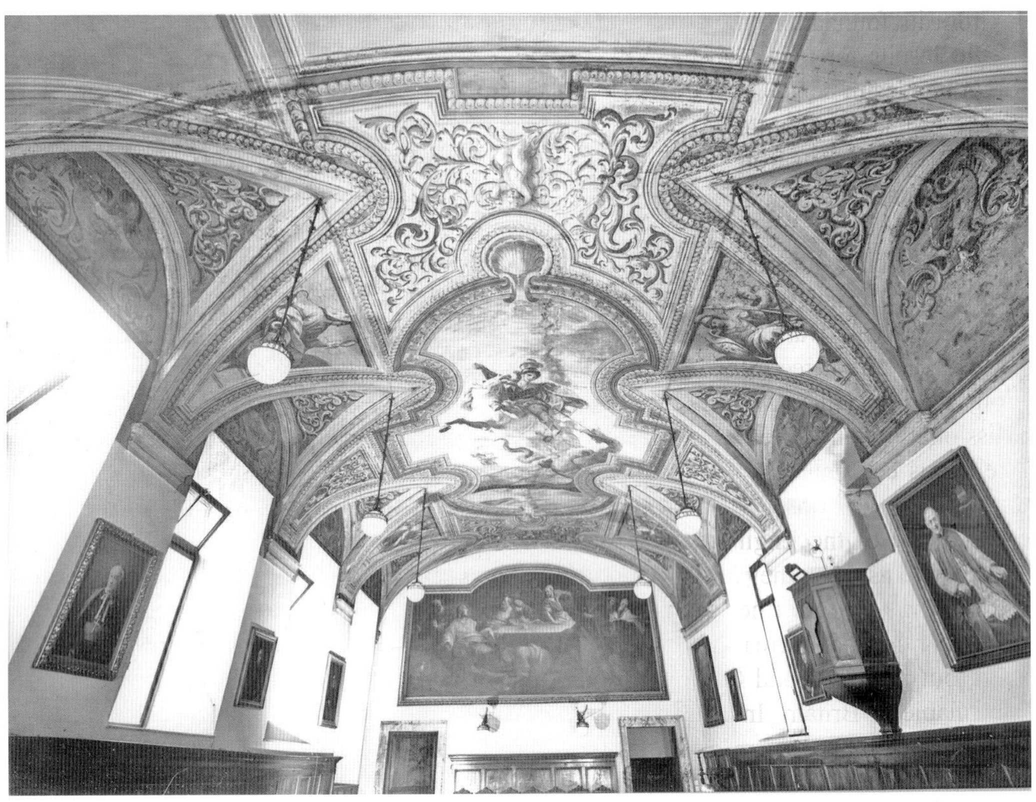

FIG. 3.1. View from the entrance of the refectory of the Venerable English College, Rome, with Andrea Pozzo's *Pharisee's Supper* on the rear wall, and a fresco of *Saint George and the Dragon* on the ceiling. Ministero per i Beni e le Attività Culturali, Istituto Centrale per il Catalogo e la Documentazione, Rome, no. E 56942. *(Photo: Ministero per i Beni e le Attività Culturali, Istituto Centrale per il Catalogo e la Documentazione, Rome.)*

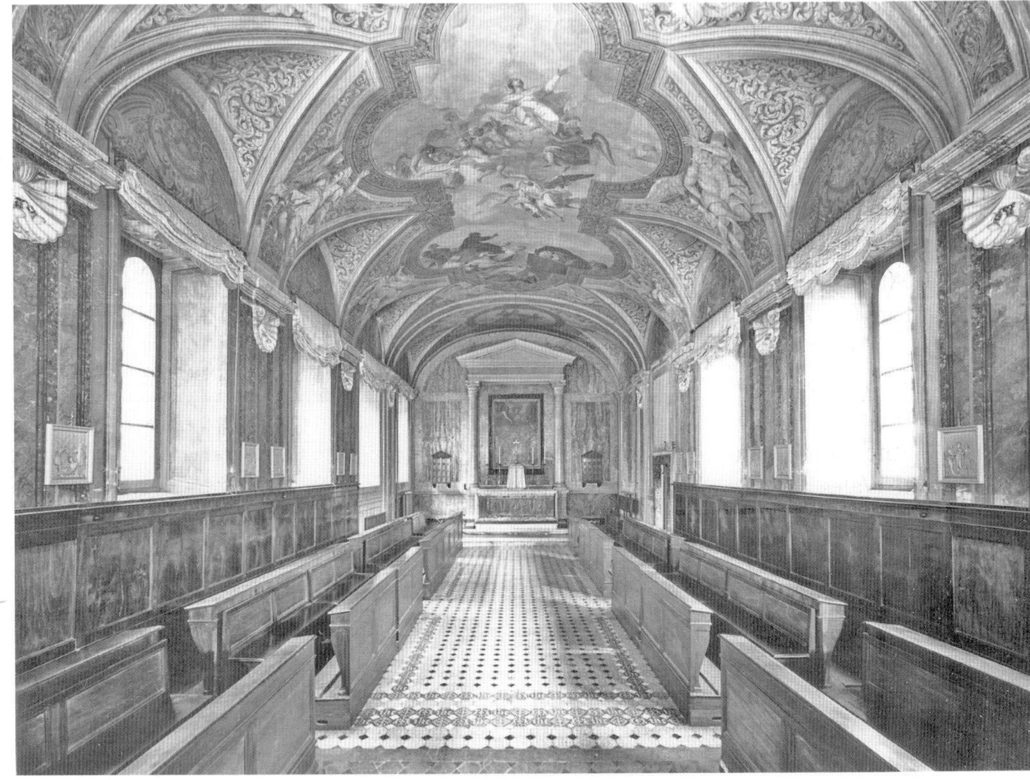

FIG. 3.2. View from the entrance of the Martyrs' Chapel of the Venerable English College, Rome, with Andrea Pozzo's fresco of the *Assumption of the Virgin* on the ceiling. Ministero per i Beni e le Attività Culturali, Istituto Centrale per il Catalogo e la Documentazione, Rome, no. E 56941. *(Photo: Ministero per i Beni e le Attività Culturali, Istituto Centrale per il Catalogo e la Documentazione, Rome.)*

From its foundation, the College was administered by the Jesuits for two centuries (though it was never formally a Jesuit house), and therefore the art and architecture of the complex make most sense in the context of their patronage in Rome. However, while all of the rectors from 1579 until the suppression of the order in 1773 were Jesuits, they were also English.

The students attended classes in the Collegio Romano, the Jesuit central seminary, and at the English College, but care was taken to ensure that the College did not become a recruiting ground for the Jesuits.[10] From its foundation in 1579 the students took the 'Missionary Oath', swearing that they would not join a religious community while they were in Rome, for this would have wasted the investment made in them for the sake of the English mission. However, many of the students when they arrived and stated their intentions in the *responsa* (the official entry questionnaire) were clear that they were not there to train for the priesthood, but to get a good Catholic education of a kind unavailable in Britain. In 1652, for example, three of the eight students who arrived to begin their studies declared that they had no intention of becoming priests.[11] Throughout its long history the College has been beset with problems of identity and jurisdiction.

Financial problems, as well as the precarious position of English Catholics, meant that little was done to improve the fabric of the College and hospice complex, which seems to have remained a ramshackle accumulation of properties until the middle of the seventeenth century. In a report of the 1660s it was described as 'old, with neither convenience nor architectural merit, with narrow and inconvenient stairs; only ten rooms to serve to accommodate the scholars ... and a few others for the rector, the other ministers and officials'.[12] All that soon changed. In the 1650s the neighbouring Corte Savella, the old papal prison, was bought and rebuilt as a palazzo to be rented out for income. In the 1680s the palace and College were extended to make a coherent, commodious and modern institution.

In 1688 the introduction of Vicars Apostolic for England and Wales added another element of jurisdictional tension to the ongoing struggle for authority over the College between the Cardinal Protectors and the Jesuits. When Cardinal Howard died in 1694 the anomalous position of the College and its properties was exposed further. Howard had been a Dominican and he made the order his universal heirs. Although in his will he left the palace to the College for a year, thereafter whose was it, whose were all the contributions he had made, and who should finish paying for them? Between 1694 and 1706 the Jesuit administrators enjoyed a period of relative freedom at the College, as the position of Cardinal Protector for England remained vacant, meaning that there was no one who could interfere in Jesuit business and remind them of their subordinate role at the institution.[13] The result was a period of intense engagement of the English College with the Jesuit campaign to celebrate its saints and missions through the magnificent embellishment of its churches. The main protagonist of this movement in Rome between 1681 and 1703 was Andrea Pozzo.[14]

ANDREA POZZO

Andrea Pozzo (1642–1709), a Jesuit brother from Trento, had been called to Rome from Milan in 1681 by the Jesuit General, Giovanni Paolo Oliva (General from 1664 to 1681), on the recommendation of the artist Carlo Maratti.[15] In the 1680s and '90s Pozzo was busy working in Jesuit circles in Rome, ably demonstrating Oliva's ideas about the glorification of the Christian and Jesuit message through the lavish decoration — both permanent and ephemeral — of churches.[16] Pozzo's first works were stage designs for the Carnival plays held in the Gesù in 1682, from which he earned a reputation for his innovative use of perspective. His illusions were ideal for solving the problems of restricted or irregular sites (as at the Casa Professa) or unfinished buildings (as for the famous dome for Sant'Ignazio, 1684–94). In the 1690s he was busy painting altarpieces and frescoes with his workshop, and at the same time moved into architecture.[17] In 1695 Pozzo won the most prestigious Jesuit commission of all, for an altar to Saint Ignatius in the Gesù. Throughout the period he also ran courses on painting and architecture at the Collegio Romano, where students from the English College went to study subjects that included natural philosophy, geometry and perspective. He left Rome for Vienna in 1703, to work for Emperor Leopold.

The Pozzo whirlwind also reached the English College. Brigitte Kuhn uncovered documents in the College archive demonstrating Pozzo's contact with the College. In December 1700 a gold frame was provided for a large painting made for the refectory by the 'reverend father Pozzo'. The *Pharisee's Supper* survives in the refectory, its subject — the learned discourse of Christ and the Pharisees pictured above the table and the repentant Mary Magdalen in the middle foreground beneath — appropriate for its

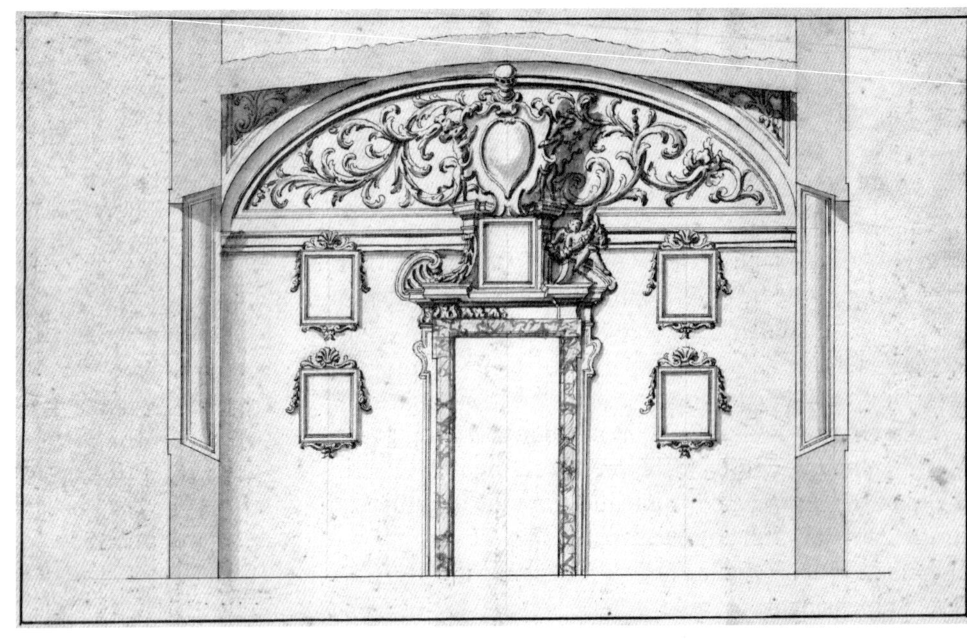

FIG. 3.3. Andrea Pozzo(?) (1642–1709), *Design for the Inside of the Entrance Wall of the Refectory or the Martyrs' Chapel, Venerable English College, Rome*, c. 1700. Pen and ink on paper. Venerable English College. *(Reproduced courtesy of the Venerable English College.)*

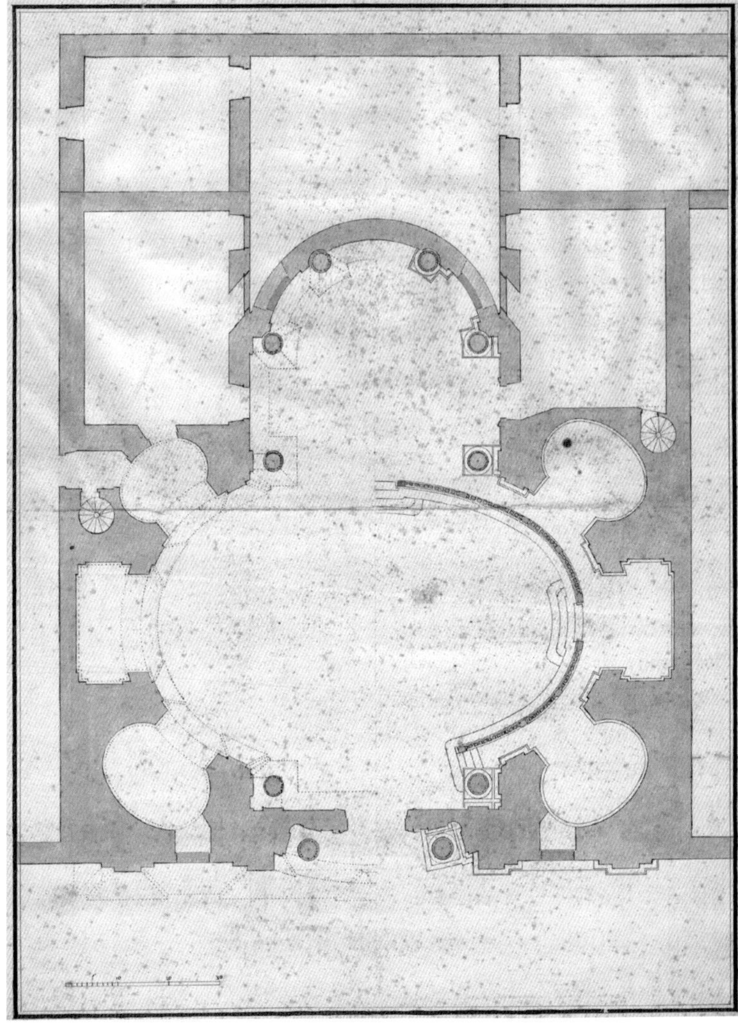

FIG. 3.4. Andrea Pozzo (1642–1709), *Plan for the New Church of the Venerable English College*, 1701–3. Pen and ink wash on paper. Venerable English College. *(Reproduced courtesy of the Venerable English College.)*

setting (Fig. 3.1). In February and again in September 1701 Pozzo was paid a total of 62 scudi for 'diverse works of painting' in the rooms of the Jesuits.[18] These were presumably paintings for the refectory and the Jesuits' Martyrs' Chapel, large rooms that were added to the College in the same period (Figs 3.1 and 3.2). The ceiling of the chapel was painted with a scene of the Assumption of the Virgin, while the refectory bears a powerful image of Saint George on his horse, slaying the dragon — the patron saint of England, but also symbol of the Catholic Church militant. Both ceiling paintings are depicted in such a way as to have maximum impact on the viewer entering the space. In addition, a drawing preserved in the College archive may show Pozzo's intentions for the decoration of the entrance walls of either room (Fig. 3.3).

In the 1690s Pozzo moved increasingly from two- to three-dimensional representations, from painting to architecture, compelled to do so by his experiments with perspective. He made a number of designs for the façade of Saint John Lateran, but his plans were only executed outside Rome, reflecting the international reach of his order, as well as the competitiveness of Rome's art market. He designed a Jesuit church for Dubrovnik and a cathedral for Ljubljana (1699–1700), and in 1701–2 the Jesuit church in Montepulciano. Around the same time he also designed a new church for the English College.

In the second volume of his treatise on perspective, published in 1700, Pozzo suggested that he would have liked to have built a college or conventual complex in Rome, and included plans and elevations for a small number of projects.

> I felt it timely to put forward to you these three examples, in which the interior, exterior and elevation of a temple devised by me are contained together with a plan, for a work which was not begun at Rome because of the excessive expense. I have done so to sharpen your mind through its consideration and so that you too may devise similar things both for building and for painting according to optical principles . . .[19]

One of the three examples is for a religious house or college big enough for 25–30 people, designed to fit on a triangular plot, with a triangular church in the middle consisting of three large apses at each corner, surmounted by a large dome, so that the space would have been lit from above.[20]

Preserved in the English College archive are plans that describe another set of conventual buildings to add to the Pozzo collection (Figs 3.3 and 3.4; Plates 3.1 and 3.2). These offer an innovative solution to the problem of building a church on the restricted site at the English College. The arms of Clement XI (r. 1700–21) that are used on the roofline and above the door — the three *monti* and the star behind the cross above the entrance — date the plans to the same time as Pozzo's documented contact with the College in 1701 and before he left Rome in 1703 (Plate 3.1). This would suggest also a very early date in Clement's pontificate, an early indication of the campaigns of restoration and preservation that characterized his papacy. As Christopher Johns has shown, although Clement XI was a true heir to the urban vision of Alexander VII (r. 1655–67), which sought to integrate the ancient Christian and classical monuments into the urban fabric, political circumstances diminished his achievement.[21] Moreover, with specific regard to the English College, throughout his papacy the Albani pope was a supporter of the Stuart cause to reclaim the throne of Britain, and it would not have been surprising if he had been particularly keen to support the mission to reconvert England that was the *raison d'être* for the College. Around 1715 Clement XI gave the Old Pretender Giuseppe Chiari's painting, *Allegory of the Church*. The painting shows Saint Peter steering a boat that holds the theological virtues, guided by the Trinity. In the background is a coastline that Johns has interpreted as the white cliffs of Dover, where two bishops (Canterbury and York?) stand waiting for the return of their rightful sovereign.[22] Although it is often known as the church of Saint Thomas of Canterbury, the first dedication of the church of the Venerable English College was to the Most Holy Trinity.

When parts of the English College complex were remodelled in the last decades of the seventeenth century the old church added to the complex in the fifteenth century was apparently left untouched. Presumably some thought was given to its restoration, however, as the floor had collapsed in 1687, suggesting that major work was necessary.[23] Money was almost certainly the reason why the plans were never executed, as Pozzo suggested. Funds were even scarcer in the eighteenth century: while the Visitation report published in 1739 praised the College buildings — they were spacious, light and of good air — the church was still the ancient structure and the College accounts were in a terrible state.[24] Nevertheless, Pozzo's plans for the English College represent a bold initiative to construct a church that was distinctively Jesuit in character.

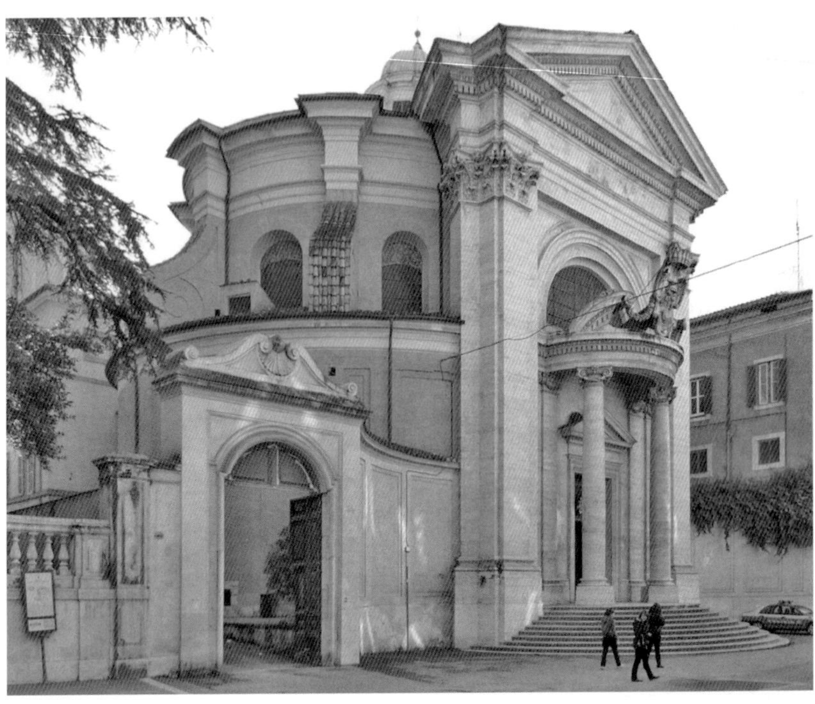

FIG. 3.5. **Gianlorenzo Bernini, Sant'Andrea al Quirinale, begun 1658.** *(Photo: Carol M. Richardson.)*

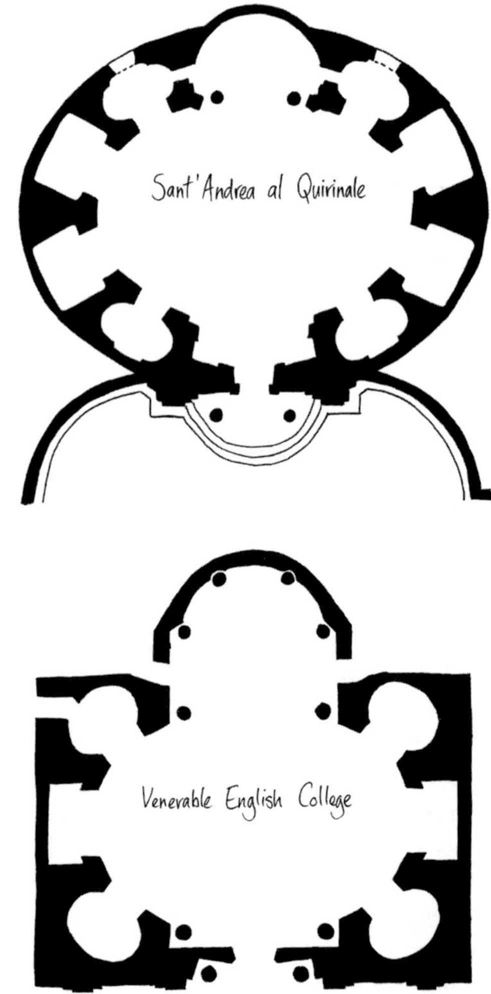

FIG. 3.6. **Plan of Bernini's Sant'Andrea al Quirinale and of Pozzo's new church for the Venerable English College.** *(Drawing: Carol M. Richardson.)*

Pozzo's plans for the church of the English College demonstrate interaction with the designs for Sant'Andrea al Quirinale (begun 1658), by Gianlorenzo Bernini, for both its innovative architectural design and its significance for the order as the church of the Jesuit novitiate (Fig. 3.5). Both buildings had to be designed around a restricted site in which the entrance from the street to the back is the shallowest dimension.[25] Like Bernini, Pozzo employed an oval plan but overcame the shallowness of the resulting nave with an extended chancel (a choir for the resident community), framed by a triumphal arch that would have echoed the arched recess over the entrance on the exterior (Figs 3.4 and 3.6).[26] The plan is pushed out at the sides to fill the rectangular space by replacing Bernini's two smaller rectangular chapels on either side with a single one on the transverse axis. This also means that the width of the 'nave' into these spaces is almost the same as the distance from the entrance to the high altar. Pozzo no doubt would have planned a theatrical effect to greet visitors to his church — possibly incorporating the high altarpiece in the old church, the *Martyrs' Picture* by Durante Alberti (Fig. 3.7), of 1581 — comparable with Bernini's Sant'Andrea, where the visitor is confronted by the high altar on entering.

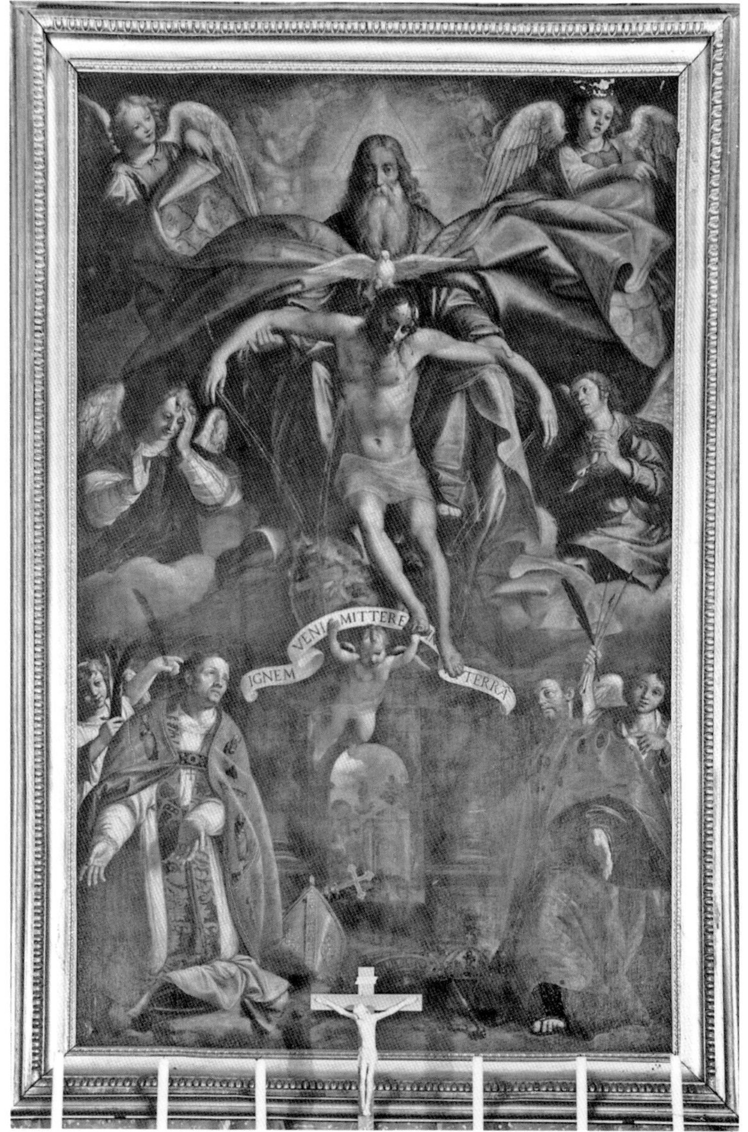

FIG. 3.7. Durante Alberti (1538–1613), *Martyrs' Picture*, 1581. Oil on canvas. Venerable English College. Ministero per i Beni e le Attività Culturali, Istituto Centrale per il Catalogo e la Documentazione, Rome, no. E 56932. *(Photo: Ministero per i Beni e le Attività Culturali, Istituto Centrale per il Catalogo e la Documentazione, Rome.)*

The site at the English College would not have allowed for the extension into the street of the exedra, which serves as a counterpoint to the sides of the church at Sant'Andrea. Like Sant'Andrea, however, Pozzo's church lacks a proscenium, with the entrance being straight into the church. Nevertheless, a portico is included that is remarkably like that at the novitiate, although it is enclosed within the central arch of the main façade, an appropriate Jesuit correlation between the two buildings. The façade would have been a particularly exciting composition of light and shade, recesses and projecting members, all carefully framed within the enclosed site. Huge buttresses stretch back and forth between the drum that supports the staggered vault within and the side chapels and portico, suggesting from the outside a conventional façade for a nave and two side aisles. The height of the building, designed to take in Pozzo's staggered vault, also would have made the most of the site at the English College, which the present church, which follows the orientation of the original fifteenth-century church, being orientated parallel to the street, does not (Fig. 3.8). The unfinished section of wall still visible at the top edge of the College buildings today adjoining the College seems to have been left at the time, awaiting the addition of the new church.[27] Had it been built, Pozzo's church would have risen over the College buildings, breaking out of the confined space, as it is taller than it is wide (unlike Bernini's more squat Sant'Andrea). The bell-tower probably also dates from the same period, as one of the three bells in the tower bears the date 1704 (Fig. 3.9).[28] Was

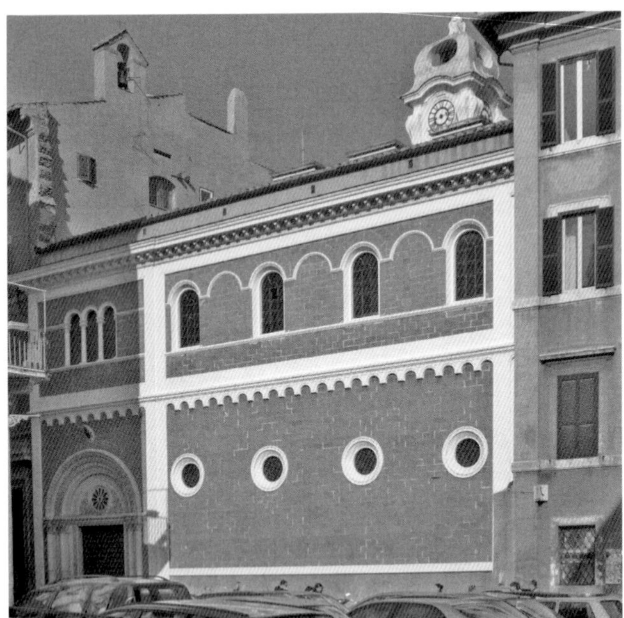

FIG. 3.8. **Venerable English College, view from Piazza Santa Caterina della Ruota.** *(Photo: Carol M. Richardson.)*

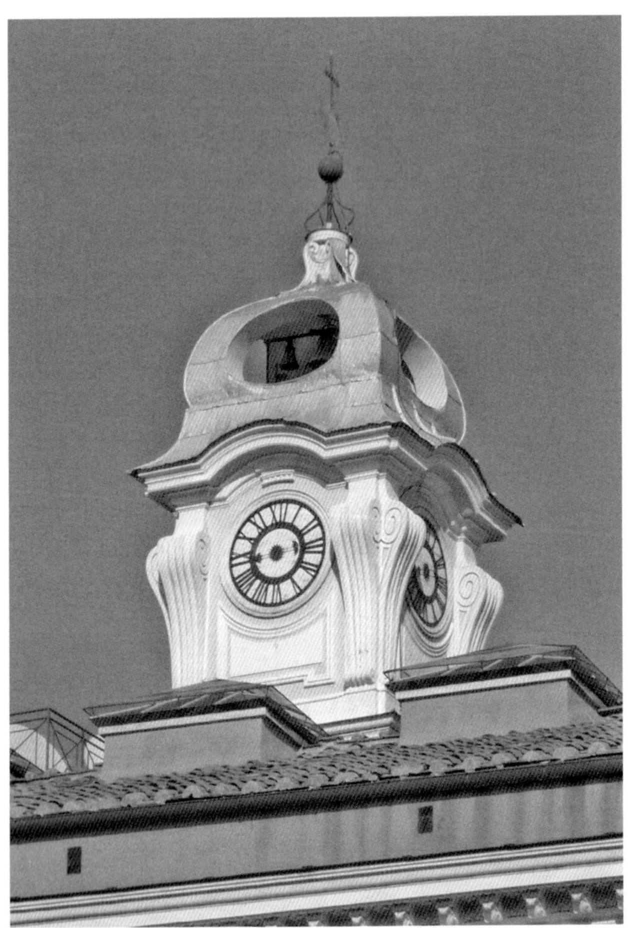

FIG. 3.9. **Bell-tower, Venerable English College.** *(Photo: Carol M. Richardson.)*

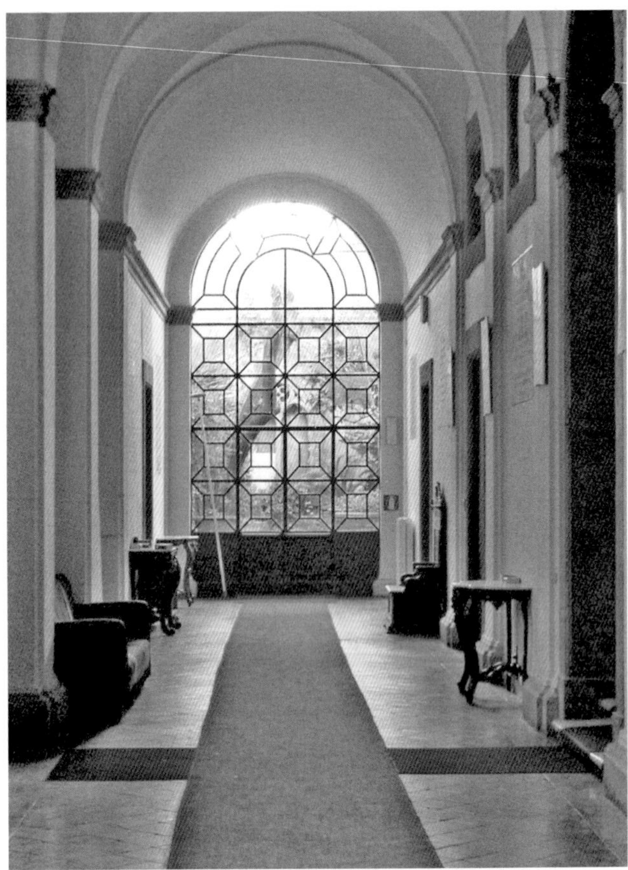

FIG. 3.10. **Entrance corridor, Venerable English College.** *(Photo: Carol M. Richardson.)*

this most visible and distinctive part of the College the only architecture designed by Pozzo actually built in Rome?

Bernard Kerber called the English College plans Pozzo's most significant draft because they represent a link between Rome and German Baroque churches designed by the Asam brothers who visited Rome between 1711 and 1714.[29] Pozzo seems to have presented similar designs to the Jesuit community in Montepulciano around 1702. Certainly by 1712 the English College plans were well known in Rome.[30] In particular the Asam church at Weltenburg closely follows the English College plan. The most innovative feature of the design is the double dome — a kind of staggered vault, with direct lighting from oval windows and indirect lighting behind a balcony in the uppermost part that would have imbued the space with, as Kerber has put it, 'an other/over worldly' effect, a floating glimpse of heaven.[31] Pozzo had used light in his painting for the vault at Sant'Ignazio to represent the founder of the Society as, in Evonne Levy's words, 'the heavenly illuminated point of origin of a vast number of missionaries'.[32] Kerber also suggested that the design for the English College church would have included a painted dome, as was done at Weltenburg, which would have been subtly illuminated by the diffuse light.

THE GARDEN FRESCO

Andrea Caprara, Cardinal Protector of the English College between September 1706 and June 1711, had cause to write to the rector complaining that a fresco in the College garden had been damaged by some works carried out on the wall.[33] In his letter Caprara described the fresco as designed to be seen from the main entrance corridor (Fig. 3.10). Comparison of what remains of the fresco with a design for a stage-set in Pozzo's *Prospettiva* makes it clear that it is another aspect of the College's interaction with the artist and his ideas.[34]

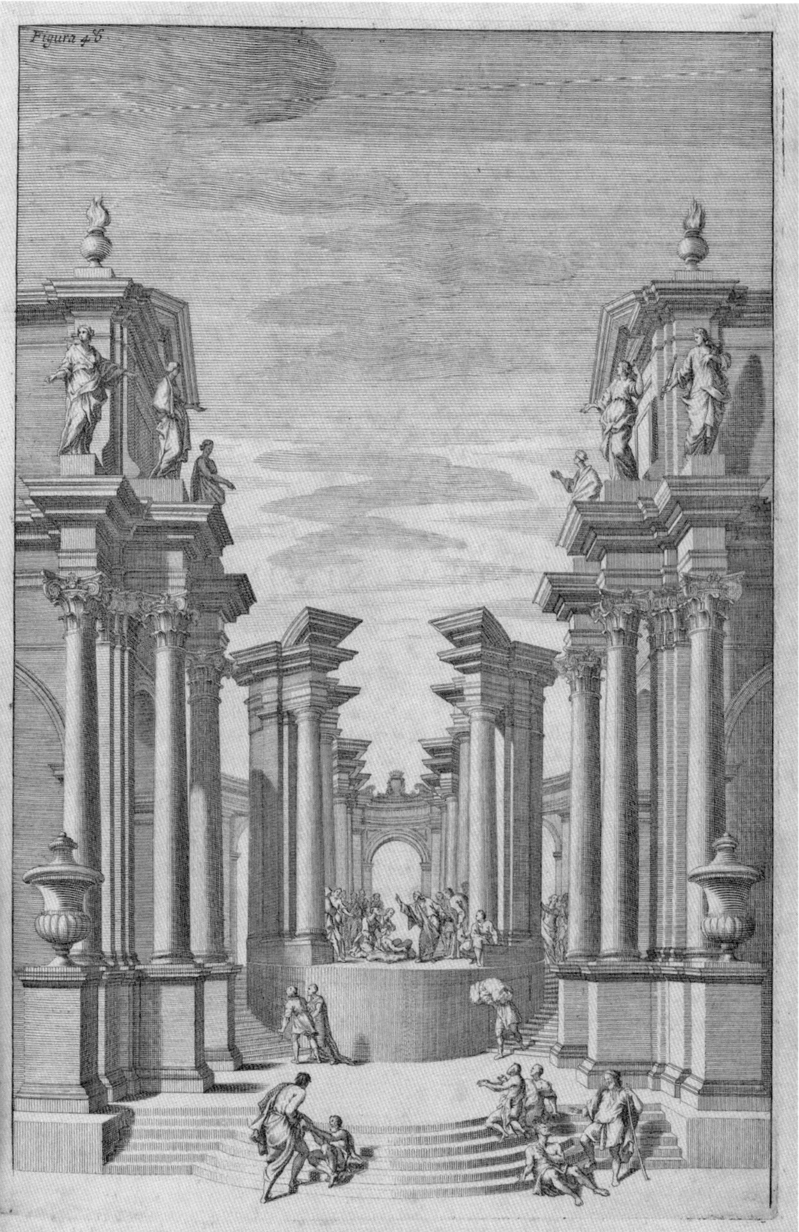

FIG. 3.11. Andrea Pozzo (1642–1709), *Christ Healing the Lame Man*, from *Prospettiva de' pittori e architetti* (1693–1700), II, fig. 46. (Photo: © *The British Library Board 747.d.25 pt 2 figure 6.*)

When the College was rebuilt in the 1680s the only part that was untouched was the garden. But while the old complex had allowed access to the garden through the loggia adjoining the refectory and along its long axis to the fountain fed by the Aqua Vergine at the opposite end, in the new building the entrance was switched to the other side. Visitors entered through a door on the left-hand side of the church and would have been faced with a view of the garden in front of them — but at its narrowest point (Fig. 3.10). This was a good place for an illusionistic fresco to make up for the disappointing view.

Pozzo's earliest works in Rome were for theatre designs, some of which he reproduced in his *Prospettiva de' pittori e architetti*, the first volume of which was published in 1693 and sold to pay for the decoration of Sant'Ignazio.[35] These included 'designs for sacred theatre in the Gesù', the 'fusion of real and fictive architecture' in Pozzo's words.[36] The first example included in the treatise, therefore, is the 'theatre for the Marriage Feast at Cana in Galilee, done in the Church of the Gesù in Rome in 1685 for the 40 hours' devotion'. These stage-sets are not mere geometric exercises: the vanishing-point of the perspective, or the 'true point of the eye, is the divine glory' — in the case of the Marriage Feast at Cana, Christ. Another design depicts a stage-set of columns with jagged entablatures and pediments that frames a scene of Christ healing the lame man (Fig. 3.11).[37] The tiny figures in the foreground of the scene help one another to their feet and up the steps to Christ, and the flames of charity burn in urns at the top. In

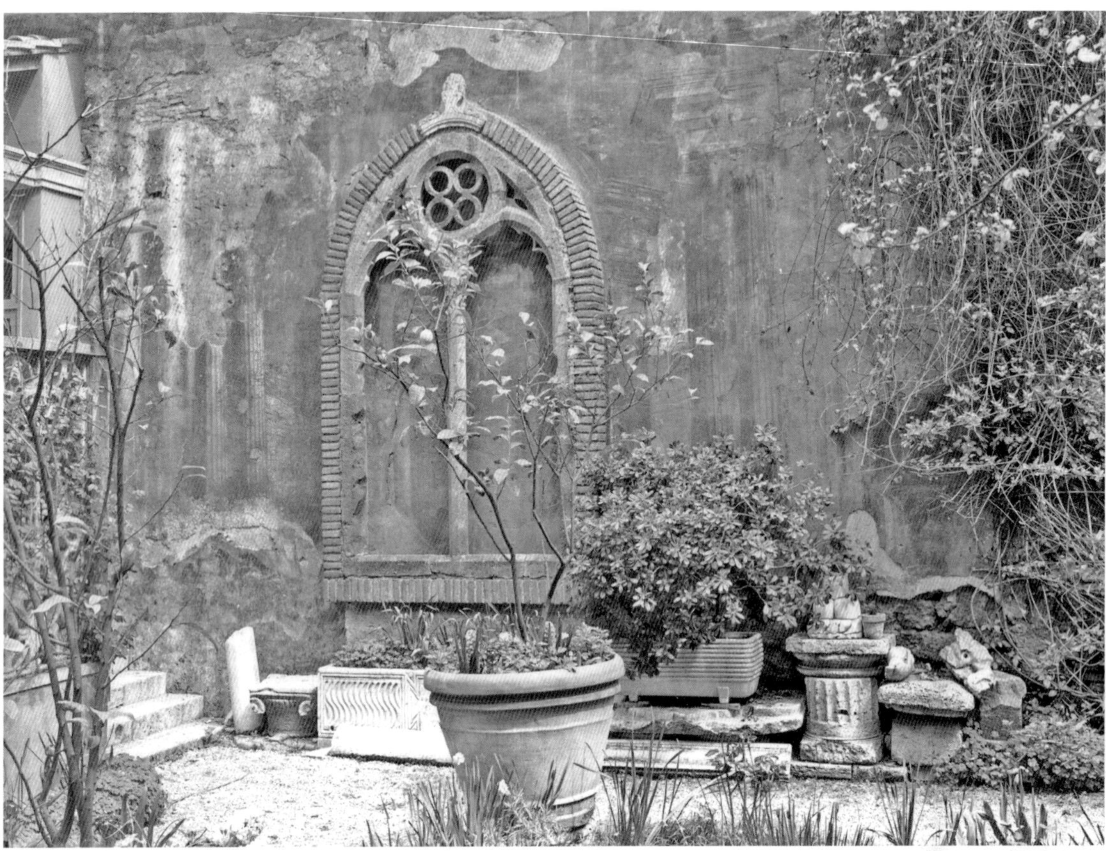

FIG. 3.12. After Andrea Pozzo (1642–1709), garden fresco, Venerable English College, *c.* 1700. Ministero per i Beni e le Attività Culturali, Istituto Centrale per il Catalogo e la Documentazione, Rome, no. E 56919. *(Photo: Ministero per i Beni e le Attività Culturali, Istituto Centrale per il Catalogo e la Documentazione, Rome.)*

the text accompanying the print Pozzo described it as an 'architectural invention that could serve as a Theatre for the 40 hours. Or for some other place where it might be seen from a distance, such as at the end of a garden, or a cortile of a large palace'.[38] Comparison of photographs taken of the fresco in the College garden, before it was covered over at the start of the twentieth century with one of the windows from the old church, and Pozzo's *Prospettiva* design is incontrovertible (Figs 3.12 and 3.13). Even if it was not painted by Pozzo and his workshop, it certainly comes from the *Prospettiva*. It is a particularly suitable image for the English College, where pilgrims came from far and wide to Rome, the city of Christ's vicar, the pope, and visited the English hospice in search of charity and care.

Could there be any connection with the garden fresco, one of Pozzo's stage-sets, and the Jesuit plays performed at the College? There was a long tradition of Jesuit plays at the College, best documented in the first half of the seventeenth century, to which the British community resident in Rome was usually invited. Records of the number of programmes printed suggests that as many as 300 visitors attended, so many that guards had to be hired to control the crowds.[39] While the records of any plays around 1700 do not survive, there are regular entries for the *feste* for College and Jesuit feasts. The plays — at the English College not always, as the Jesuit regulations laid down, religious — served a number of roles. Some of them were not theatrical performances as such, but viva voce examinations at which students finishing their studies were questioned by members of the ecclesiastical hierarchy. These events could be broken up with musical interludes and short theatrical pieces.[40] Other performances took the form of longer plays designed to edify and entertain audiences, but also designed as part of the curriculum, for the students to practice their skills of communication and persuasion.

CONCLUSION

From the end of the sixteenth century the Venerable English College in Rome existed to train priests who

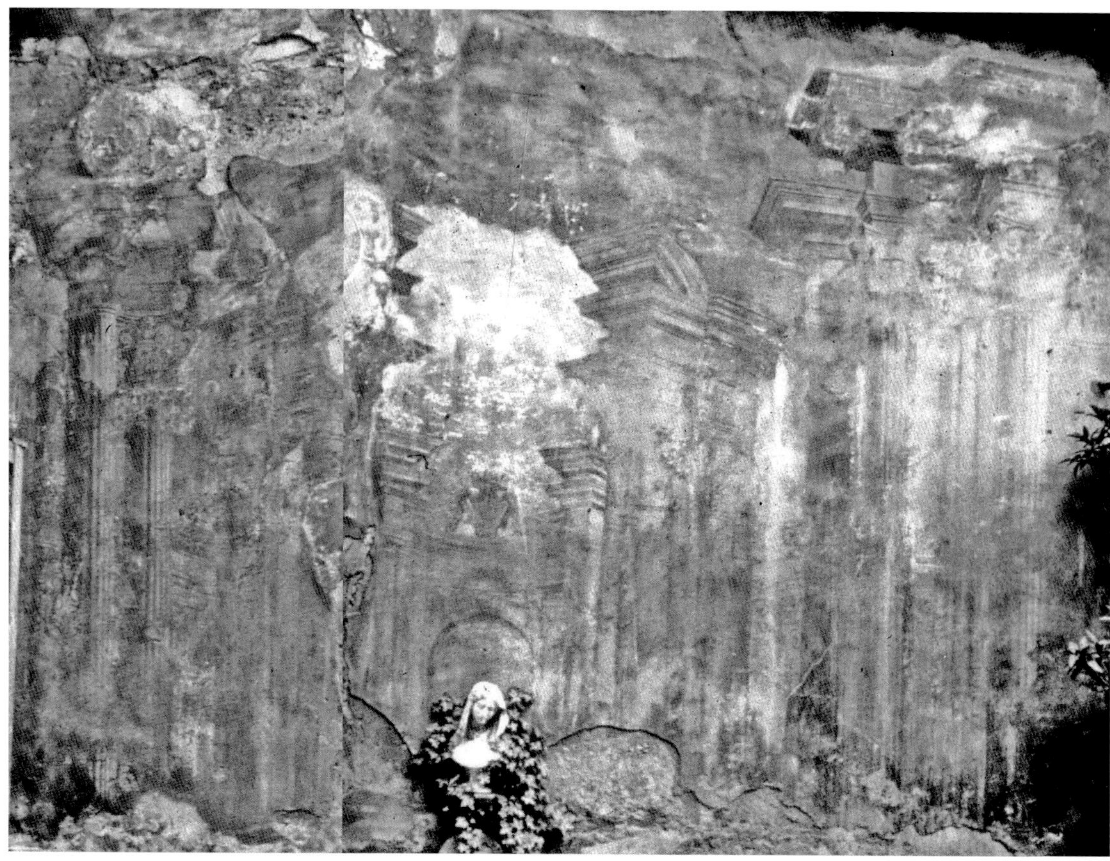

FIG. 3.13. After Andrea Pozzo (1642–1709), garden fresco, Venerable English College, c. 1700. Photomontage of frescoes in the first half of the twentieth century. *(Reproduced courtesy of the Venerable English College.)*

could go back to Britain to bring the country back into the Catholic fold. Its much longer standing role as a hospice for pilgrims continued, however, and as Grand Tourists joined pilgrims, they were all granted access to the College. The cultural influences they experienced at the College were Italian and Jesuit, which filled the void in the absence of overtly British expressions of Catholicism. But national identity seems to have overcome religious bias at times when the English College opened its doors to Protestant and Catholic visitors to Rome. Perhaps, then, it is not surprising that, just after Pozzo's contact with the College, his designs were welcomed in Protestant Britain by its most celebrated architects, who overlooked the more unpalatable aspects of their author's identity.

An abridged English version of Pozzo's treatise on perspective, *Rules and Examples of Perspective Proper for Painters and Architects*, was published in 1707. Its subscribers included Sir Christopher Wren (who refused to visit any Catholic country), Nicholas Hawksmoor and John Vanbrugh, who even added an approbation: 'At the request of the engraver, we have perused this volume of Perspective and judge it a work that deserves encouragement, and very proper for instruction in that art'.[41] In 1716 and 1717 William Kent, the architect, wrote from Rome to his patron Burrell Massingberd that he was avidly reading Pozzo's treatise and that he had managed to purchase copies to take back to Britain with him.[42] The full set of engravings from the *Prospettiva* seems to have been available in Britain by the 1720s, when James Gibbs was showing signs of their influence in his work.

It is somewhat ironic that Andrea Pozzo's very Jesuit and Roman Catholic designs took off so quickly in Britain so soon after the artist had worked at the English College, where he had helped reinforce the identity of the institution as a centre for Catholic mission. But the years immediately after 1700 were something of a watershed for British religious, cultural and political identity. The advent of the Stuart court in Rome in 1719 offered a new, exciting and much grander focus for English speakers resident in and visiting Rome.[43] The English College became its satellite.

Notes

1. J. Champ, *The English Pilgrimage to Rome: a Dwelling for the Soul* (Leominster, 2000), 95.
2. E. Chaney, *The Evolution of the Grand Tour* (London/Portland, 1998), 134 n. 22, 226–38.
3. Chaney, *Evolution of the Grand Tour* (above, n. 2), 203; Champ, *English Pilgrimage* (above, n. 1), 109.
4. Champ, *English Pilgrimage* (above, n. 1), 104.
5. Bodleian Library, Oxford, MS Rawl. 1180, 171–3, 214, 225, 1561. I am grateful to Rosemary Sweet for furnishing me with these references. On Rawlinson in Italy, see B. Ford and J. Ingamells, *A Dictionary of British and Irish Travellers in Italy, 1701–1800. Compiled from the Brinsley Ford Archive* (New Haven/London, 1997), 801–3.
6. Bodleian Library, Oxford, MS Rawl. 1180, 214.
7. Bodleian Library, Oxford, MS Rawl. 1180, 1561.
8. Champ, *English Pilgrimage* (above, n. 1), 92.
9. T.M. Lucas, 'The saint, the site, and sacred strategy: Ignatius, Rome and the Jesuit urban mission', in T.M. Lucas (ed.), *Saint, Site and Sacred Strategy: Ignatius, Rome and Jesuit Urbanism* (Vatican City, 1990), 41; E. Guidoni and A. Marino, *Storia dell'urbanistica: il Cinquecento* (Rome, 1982), 614.
10. G.A. Bailey, *Between Renaissance and Baroque: Jesuit Art in Rome, 1565–1610* (Toronto, 2003), 115; C.M. Richardson, 'Durante Alberti, the *Martyrs' Picture* and the Venerable English College, Rome', *Papers of the British School at Rome* 73 (2005), 248, 252.
11. M. Williams, *The Venerable English College, a History 1579–1979* (London, 1979), 58.
12. Williams, *Venerable English College* (above, n. 11), 199; Archive of the Venerable English College [henceforth VEC], *Scritture* 31.5.1.
13. Williams, *Venerable English College* (above, n. 11), 54–6.
14. On the embellishment of Jesuit churches in Rome, including the Gesù and Sant'Ignazio, in the last two decades of the seventeeth century, see E. Levy, "A noble medley and concert of materials and artifice': Jesuit church interiors in Rome, 1567–1700', in Lucas, *Saint, Site and Sacred Strategy* (above, n. 9), 54–9.
15. F.S. Baldinucci, *Vite di artisti dei secoli XVII–XVIII. Prima edizione integrale del Codice Palatino 565*, ed. A. Matteolo (Rome, 1975), 321. For a brief biography, see J. Pinto, 'Andrea Pozzo', in E.P. Bowron and J.J. Rishel (eds), *Art in Rome in the Eighteenth Century* (Philadelphia, 2000), 145.
16. On Oliva's influence on the decoration of Jesuit churches, see F. Haskell, 'The role of patrons: Baroque style changes', in R. Wittkower and I. Jaffe (eds), *Baroque Art: the Jesuit Contribution* (New York, 1972), 51–62.
17. Pozzo's reputation as an architect was somewhat controversial. See E. Levy, *Propaganda and the Jesuit Baroque* (Berkeley/Los Angeles/London, 2004), 97–8.
18. VEC, Liber 73, *Rubricella del Libro Mastro 1691–1703*, fol. 435; Liber 978, *Conti e obblighi di artisti e bottegari dall'anno 1701–1709* (unnumbered slips). See also B. Kuhn, 'Ein unbekanntes Gemälde von Andrea Pozzo in Rom', *Römische Historische Mitteilungen* (*Verlag der Österreichischen Akademie der Wissenschaften*) 26 (1984), 427; Williams, *Venerable English College* (above, n. 11), 201.
19. A. Pozzo, *Prospettiva de' pittori e architetti* II (Rome, 1700), 88–90; façade, fig. 91: 'Opportunum sensi tria haec exemplaria vobis proponere, quibus una cum vestigio continentur interior, exteriorque orthographia Templi a me excogitate, quod in opus deductum non est Romae prae nimio sumptu; ut vobis considerantibus mentem exacuat, ut et vobis similia adinveniatis tum ad aedificanda, tum ad opticè pingenda'.
20. N. Carboneri, *Andrea Pozzo Architetto (1642–1709)* (*Collana artisti trentini* 29) (Trent, 1961), 44–6.
21. C.M.S. Johns, *Papal Art and Cultural Politics. Rome in the Age of Clement XI* (Cambridge/New York, 1993), 171–94. On Alexander VII, see R. Krautheimer, *The Rome of Alexander VII, 1655–1667* (Princeton, 1985); and, more recently, D.M. Habel, *The Urban Development of Rome in the Age of Alexander VII* (Cambridge/New York, 2002).
22. Johns, *Papal Art and Cultural Politics* (above, n. 21), 4, characterized 'the beautification of Rome with an eye to foreign audiences' and the 'promotion of culture' as 'the most conspicuously effective political endeavour of Clement XI's pontificate'. The pope supported the Stuart claim to the throne of Great Britain and enabled the Old Pretender to move to the Papal States in 1716 and finally to Rome in 1719. As early as 1687 Albani had written a short tract on James II, whom he had encountered as a member of the court of Queen Christina of Sweden (Johns, *Papal Art and Cultural Politics* (above, n. 21), 6–7). For Chiari's *Allegory of the Church*, *c.* 1715, see Johns, *Papal Art and Cultural Politics* (above, n. 21), fig. 2 (incorrectly captioned as Chiari's *Allegory of the Reign of Clement XI*).
23. VEC, *Scritture* 81.2.24.
24. VEC, *Liber* 324, *1739 Visitation Report*, fols 25–7; Williams, *Venerable English College* (above, n. 11), 51.
25. On Sant'Andrea al Quirinale, see J. Connors, 'Bernini's S. Andrea al Quirinale: payments and planning', *Journal of the Society of Architectural Historians* 41 (1982), 15–37.
26. H. Hibbard, *Bernini* (Harmondsworth, 1965), 144.
27. Williams, *Venerable English College* (above, n. 11), 200.
28. Williams, *Venerable English College* (above, n. 11), 198.
29. B. Kerber, 'Ein Kirchenprojekt des Andrea Pozzo als Vorstufe für Weltenburg?', *Architectura. Zeitschrift für Geschichte der Architektur/Journal of the History of Architecture* 1 (1972), 42; on Cosmas Damian Asam in Rome, see H. Trottman, *Cosmas Damian Asam 1686–1739. Tradition und Invention im Malerischen Werk* (*Erlanger Beiträge zur Sprach- und Kunstwissenschaft* 73) (Nuremberg, 1986), 26–61, and on his encounter with Andrea Pozzo, 43–4.
30. M. Russo, *Andrea Pozzo a Montepulciano* I. *La Chiesa del Gesù, Montepulciano* (Montepulciano, 1979); R. Bösel, *Jesuitenarchitektur in Italien 1540–1773. Die Baudenkmäler der Römischen und der Neapolitanischen Ordensprovinz* I (Vienna, 1985), 114–23; R. Bösel, 'Le opera viennesi e i

loro riflessi nell'Europa centro-orientale', in V. De Feo and V. Martinelli (eds), *Andrea Pozzo* (Milan, 1995), 225.

31. Kerber, 'Kirchenprojekt' (above, n. 29), 37–9.
32. Levy, "A noble medley" (above, n. 14), 55, 58.
33. VEC, *Scritture* 8.2: 'Quando li Padri Gesuiti del Collegio Inglese remurino il Cancello aperto nel mio muro divisorio con il loro Giardino, e si dichiarino, che il Cappello del istesso muro voltato a loro favore, per far prospetto alla Portaria, al quale hanno anche appoggiato un poco do muro nuovo, lo godono in tal maniera per mia permissione con patto di ridurlo in pristino ad ogni mia richiesta, e de futuri possessori e successori a miei bene; come anesse di voltare le grandare di tetto sopra il loro terreno e di chiudere le fenestre aperte nella farica nuova, di stanze, scale, e loggie, aperte sopra li miei siti, non faro altra instanza, altrimente saro necessitato di venire alle scommuniche, e farli confessore le verità che occultano col p..sto che in antiquis, quando l'aggrario fatto'mi e froschissimi, a quasi tutti nostrio, e specialmente a tutto il Collecgio, et altri habitanti vicini e confinanti. Al P. Rettore del Collegio Inglese, che referisca A. Card. Caprara Protettore'.
34. The earliest attribution of the garden fresco to Pozzo was made by Cardinal Nicholas Wiseman in his autobiography, and he also noted that the scene was taken from 'his celebrated work on perspective': *Recollections of the Last Four Popes and of Rome in their Times* (London, 1858), 9–11.
35. E.L. Goldberg, *After Vasari. History, Art and Patronage in Late Medici Florence* (Princeton, 1988), 179; Levy, "A noble medley" (above, n. 14), 55.
36. Carboneri, *Andrea Pozzo* (above, n. 20), 21; J. Pinto, 'Andrea Pozzo's *Prospettiva de pittori e architetti*: architecture as a system of representations', in C. Anderson (ed.), *The Built Surface* I. *Architecture and the Pictorial Arts from Antiquity to the Enlightenment* (Aldershot, 2002), 231.
37. V. Martinelli, "Teatri sacri e profane' di Andrea Pozzo nella cultura prospettico-scenografica barocca', in De Feo and Martinelli (eds), *Andrea Pozzo* (above, n. 30), 111.
38. Pozzo, *Prospettiva* II (above, n. 19), fig. 46: 'Questa inventione d'architetture potrebbe servire altresi per un Teatro di quarant'ore, ò per qualche altro luogo, onde potesse vedersi da lontano, come sarebbe nel fondo d'un giardino, o pure nel cortile di un gran palazzo ...'.
39. S. Gossett, 'Drama in the English College, 1591–1660', *English Literary Renaissance* 3 (1) (1973), 71–4.
40. Gossett, 'Drama in the English College' (above, n. 39), 62.
41. A. Pozzo, *Rules and Examples of Perspective Proper for Painters and Architects*, trans. J. James (London, 1707); M. Carta and A. Menichella, 'Il successo editoriale del Trattato', in De Feo and Martinelli, *Andrea Pozzo* (above, n. 30), 230–3; Pinto, 'Andrea Pozzo's *Prospettiva*' (above, n. 36), 228. On the development of Wren's ideas on perspective, see L.M. Soo, *Wren's 'Tracts' on Architecture and Other Writings* (Cambridge/New York, 1998), 137, 155–6, 200–3.
42. C. Blackett-Ord, 'Letters from William Kent to Burrell Massingberd from the Continent, 1712–1719', *Walpole Society* 63 (2001), 94–5.
43. On some of the ambiguities of the Stuart court in Rome, see D. Szechi, 'The image of the court: idealism, politics and the evolution of the Stuart court 1689–1730', in E. Corp (ed.), *The Stuart Court in Rome. The Legacy of Exile* (Aldershot, 2003), 49–64.

The Stuart court and the patronage of portrait-painters in Rome, 1717–57*

Edward Corp

The Stuart court in exile was established in Rome in 1719, and remained there with only one short break until the death of James III at the beginning of 1766. For over 40 years it provided an important British presence in Rome, and thereby encouraged more British and Irish people to visit the city during the 1720s, 1730s and 1740s, and perhaps even later, than otherwise might have done so.

The fact that the court was in Rome is of course well known, but its nature and importance have consistently been misrepresented by political historians. As a result, the role it played as a cultural forum between Great Britain and Rome during the eighteenth century has tended to be underestimated by art historians. This article will reconsider briefly the importance of the court for British and Irish tourists in Rome, and then examine its patronage of portrait-painters.[1]

It needs to be emphasized that the position of the Stuart court in Rome was not necessarily linked to the reality of the political situation in Great Britain. The court in exile, in Italy as previously in France,[2] was locally of considerable interest and significance, regardless of the importance of the Jacobite movement back in England and Scotland. What really mattered was what the popes, the cardinals, the princely families and the people in general thought in Rome, not what the Tory party in England or the Lowlanders in Scotland might (or might not) have wanted. So long as James III was given the full honours of a legitimate Catholic king, and so long as enough people in Rome believed that a restoration might eventually take place, the Stuart court remained influential. In August 1747, well over a year after the decisive Battle of Culloden, James III wrote to one of his French friends: 'There can no longer be any question of our ever being restored to England. The Italians will never understand this, but it is nevertheless true'.[3]

We cannot appreciate the influence of the court on the patronage of portrait-painters unless we begin by considering the reality experienced by British people who visited Rome during the first half of the eighteenth century. They were a long way from home, and many of them were still relatively young. It is hardly surprising that under these circumstances national and linguistic affinities eroded the political and dynastic differences that divided British people when they were in England or Scotland. The fact of being surrounded in Rome by a much more significant and indeed overwhelmingly dominant 'other' — by the Italians and the other foreigners living in the papal city — forged a sense of national identity among Britons on the Grand Tour.

For this reason the Stuart court was able, in some respects, to take on the role of a surrogate British embassy. It has to be remembered that there were no formal diplomatic relations between England and the papacy during the eighteenth century. The Stuart court therefore filled an obvious gap, and was never threatened in Rome, as it had been at Saint-Germain-en-Laye, by the presence of a rival or real British embassy. Also, the purpose of an embassy in Rome was primarily to influence the distribution of benefices and the nomination of cardinals, things that James III did all the time, but which no Protestant embassy could have achieved.[4]

Nevertheless, the Stuart court was not merely a centre of ecclesiastical patronage. It was also a place where British and Irish people obtained passports and diplomatic protection. Moreover, and perhaps surprisingly, it was of particular importance for Protestants. It contained Protestant chaplains, and provided access to the new Protestant cemetery beside the pyramid of Cestius, already open by 1723 at the special request of James III.[5] It also contained English-speaking doctors, and English-speaking wine merchants, who provisioned the court but also supplied wines to British visitors. In addition, the Stuart court effectively controlled the English, Irish and Scottish Colleges in Rome.

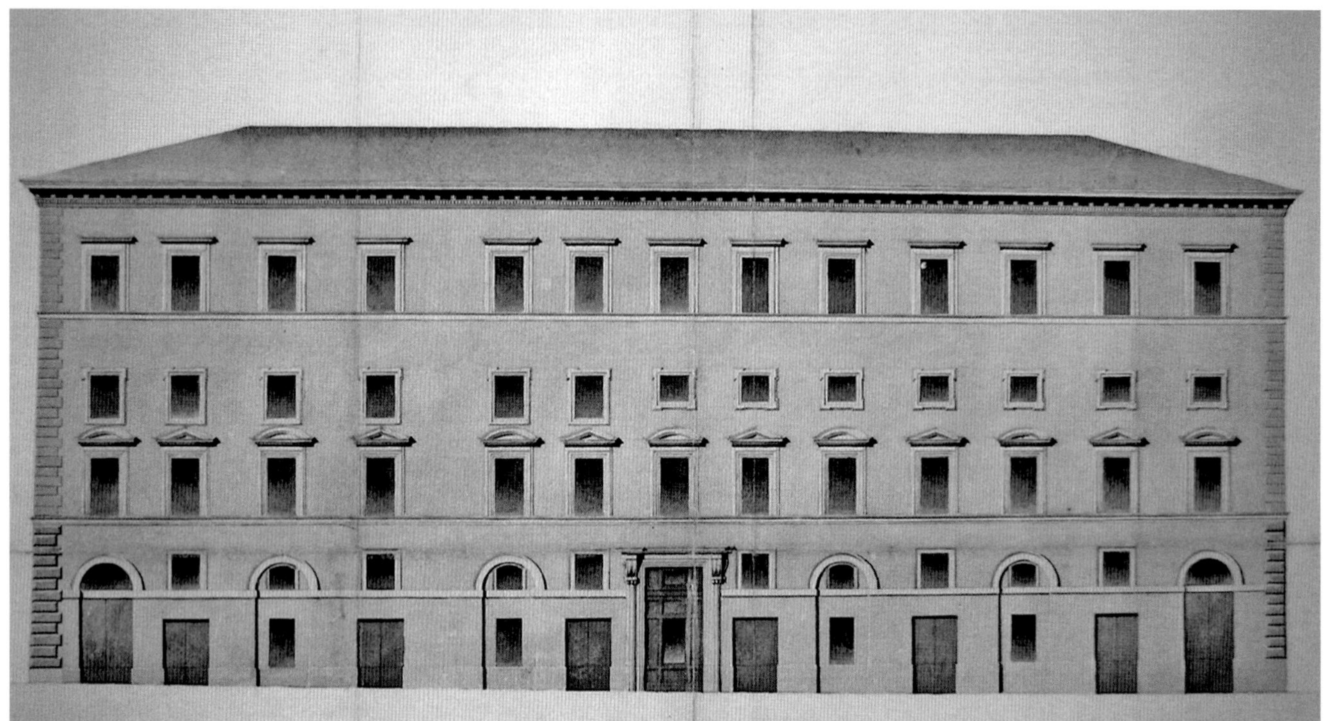

FIG. 4.1. Rome, 'Palazzo del Re', now Palazzo Balestra, façade on Via di San Marcello. Archivio di Stato di Roma, Collezione Disegni e Piante I, c. 87, n. 562, tipo VII. *(Photo: Archivio di Stato. Reproduced by permission of the Ministero per i Beni e le Attività Culturali, ASR 17/2009.)*

It could provide introductions to Italian *ciceroni*, but also could provide English-speaking guides and antiquarians from among the members of the court and colleges. The best known of these are the King's doctor, James Irwin; the King's Anglican chaplain, Thomas Wagstaffe; and the resident agents of the Catholic clergy, the Englishman Lawrence Mayes and the Scotsman Peter Grant. Hanoverians consulted Jacobites from the Stuart court; Protestants consulted Catholics from the colleges and agencies. It was not until the 1750s, when the court was in decline, that the well-known antiquarian guides Thomas Jenkins and James Byres offered an independent service. And even then, the king's assistant private secretary, Andrew Lumisden, continued to provide introductions for young Scottish painters.[6]

It is necessary to specify in which buildings the Stuart court was housed, because there has been considerable confusion concerning them. The court was primarily in a building known as the Palazzo del Re, which was beside another one called the Palazzo Muti. Originally both palazzi had been owned and occupied by the Muti family, and the plots of land on which they stood had then been referred to as the *insula maior* and the *insula minor*. The *insula maior* was in Via di San Marcello, off the north end of the Piazza dei Santi Apostoli. This was the one occupied by the Stuart court, and called the Palazzo del Re (Plate. 4.1). The *insula minor* was in the Piazza della Pilotta. It was never occupied by the Stuart court, and was called the Palazzo Muti (see Chapter 5, Fig. 5.5). The Palazzo del Re was connected on one side by an arch on the second floor to a so-called *palazzetta*.[7] Both buildings, the palazzo and the *palazzetta*, and also two adjacent houses that contained the King's stables, were rented for James III from the Muti family by the Camera Apostolica.[8]

The Palazzo del Re was a medium-sized Roman palazzo. It was not a particularly impressive one, but it was all that was available in 1719 when James III arrived, and it was large enough for his court. Moreover, it was occupied exclusively by the court, with no rooms or apartments rented to other people and no parts of the ground floor rented out as shops. It had three entrances. The main one was in the centre of the principal façade in Via di San Marcello (Figs 4.1 and 4.2). That street, however, was too narrow to allow carriages to turn and enter, so a decorated side entrance for carriages had been created in the façade overlooking the Piazza dei Santi Apostoli. The third entrance was at the back of the palazzo, in Via dell'Archetto. It provided access for the lower

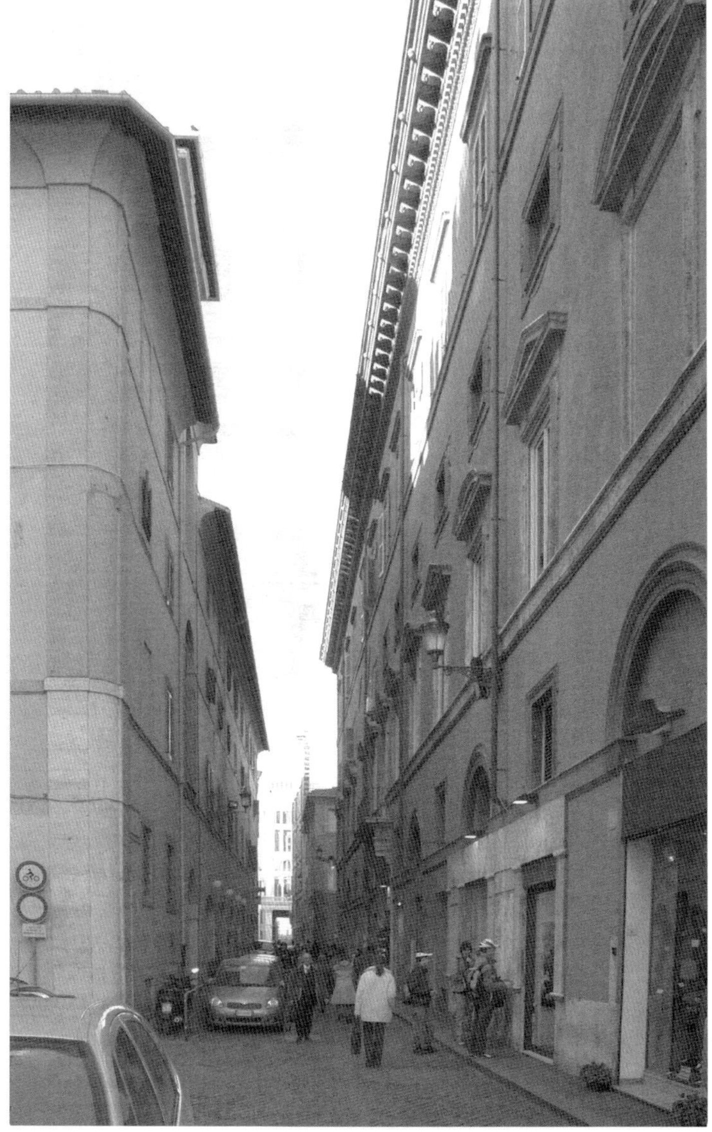

FIG. 4.2. **Rome, 'Palazzo del Re', now Palazzo Balestra, façade on Via di San Marcello.** *(Photo: © David R. Marshall, 2009.)*

household servants, and allowed horses and carriages to be brought into the courtyard from the stables.[9]

The king's apartment was on the first floor, overlooking Via di San Marcello and the Piazza dei Santi Apostoli. It consisted of a guard chamber, four antechambers, a bedchamber, a gallery and a cabinet, arranged by the architect Alessandro Specchi in 1719 (**Fig. 4.3**). The first two antechambers were really corridors, with low ceilings because there was a mezzanine floor above, so the staterooms effectively began with the third and fourth antechambers, which served as presence and privy chambers. They, like the bedchamber, had ceilings decorated in 1628–31 by Charles Mellin (**Fig. 4.4**), and overlooked Via di San Marcello. Beyond them, and overlooking the Piazza dei Santi Apostoli, were the gallery, decorated in 1719 by Giovanni Angelo Soccorsi, and the king's cabinet.[10]

When James III took up residence in the Palazzo del Re he was disappointed to find that there was no secret staircase, and that no one could visit him privately or incognito without going up the grand staircase and then passing through his guard chamber, all four antechambers and his bedchamber. He therefore had a new secret staircase built in 1724, immediately beside the side entrance for carriages in the Piazza dei Santi Apostoli. It gave direct access to his gallery, and then to his cabinet, thus bypassing all the rooms up to and including the bedchamber.[11] It allowed British and Irish tourists in Rome to make visits to the king, or his private secretaries, without being observed, and numerous Jacobites are known to have used this secret staircase.

The court was much smaller than it had been at Saint-Germain-en-Laye, but it was large enough to dominate the transitory British and Irish community in Rome. It employed about 135 people, of whom a little over 100 received salaries, and more than 30 received pensions. Fifty of these 135 people lived in the palazzo with their own families, children and servants. The remaining 85 lived in the surrounding districts of Rome, particularly near the Piazza di Spagna.

The court contained servants of several different nationalities, but James III made it as English as possible. At first the servants were mainly English and French, but then increasingly Italian. This is important because people have assumed that the court was mainly Scottish. In fact, it contained very few Scots. In the 1720s there were only six Scots out of 83 servants receiving salaries, and only thirteen Scots out of 33 receiving pensions. By 1730 there were only seven out of 102 with salaries, and only ten out of 34 with pensions. From then on the proportion of Scots went steadily down, and by the 1750s there were only three Scots with salaries, and two Scots with pensions.[12] When considering the cultural patronage of the court, it would be a mistake to think that English and Irish tourists regarded it as mainly Scottish.

This raises the question as to why so many historians have associated the Stuart court in exile with Scottish

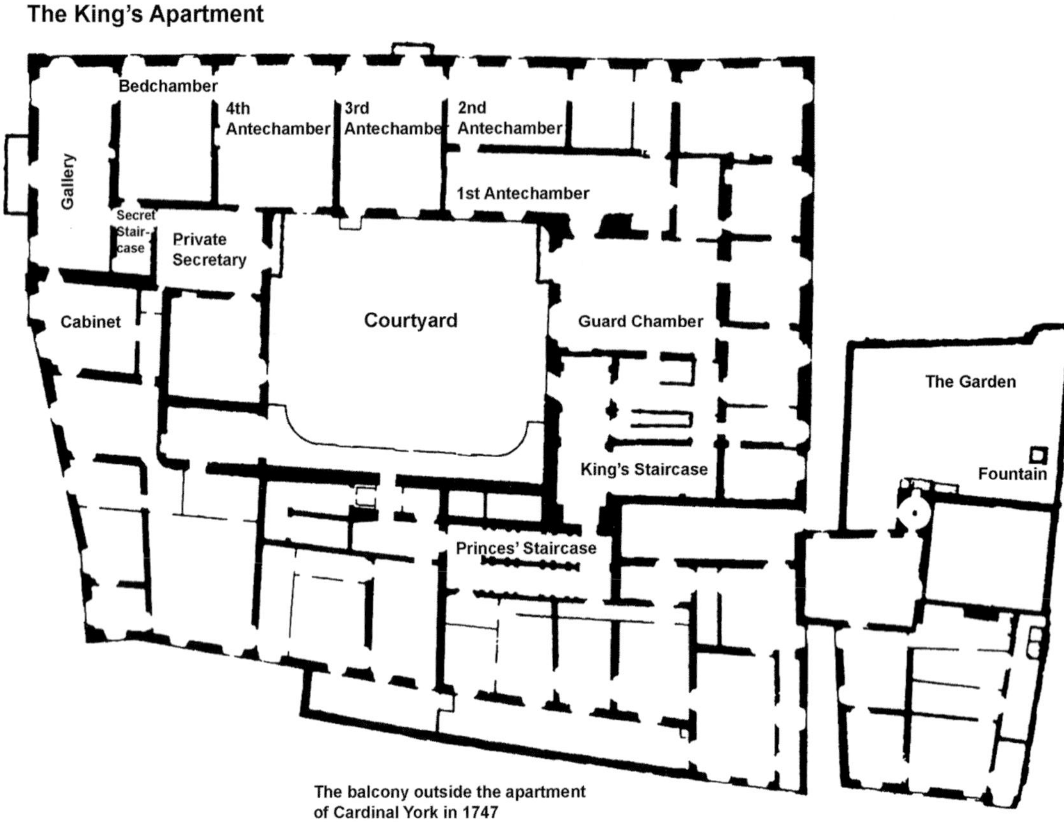

FIG. 4.3. Plan of the first floor of the Palazzo del Re, showing the apartment and balcony of Prince Henry in the east wing, and the apartment of James III in the west and south wings. Author, based on Archivio di Stato di Roma, Collezione Disegni e Piante I, c. 87, n. 562, tipo II (Archivio di Stato di Roma) and Royal Archives at Windsor Castle, Stuart Papers 98/131 and 106/79, two inventories of the Palazzo del Re, dated October 1726 and April 1727.

Jacobites. The answer is surprisingly straightforward. James III, like his father, liked to employ Scots in his political secretariat, so virtually all the surviving correspondence from the exiled court, and in particular the great collection of Stuart Papers at Windsor Castle, was dictated to, or written by, or received by, the tiny minority of Scots who *were* at the court. Moreover, the Scots at the court were very active in helping their fellow countrymen who visited the city. One important link between them seems to have been Freemasonry. It is interesting to note that by the 1730s virtually all the Scots in the court were Freemasons. The minutes of the Jacobite Lodge show that approximately one-third of the Freemasons were members of the court (such as Irwin), and that approximately two-thirds were tourists (such as Sir Thomas Twisden) or Scottish painters (such as Allan Ramsay).

In 1738 James III asked Pope Clement XII to condemn Hanoverian Freemasonry. Jacobite Freemasonry was not included in the papal condemnation, but the Jacobite Lodge nevertheless changed its name to become the Society of Young Gentlemen Travellers in Rome. In 1739–40 nine members of the Society were painted by Domenico Dupra. Two of them were members of the court, and seven were tourists (six of whom were Scottish).[13]

These Young Gentlemen, like most British tourists, lived mainly in and around the Piazza di Spagna, which was dominated by the Jacobites.[14] This means that the Palazzo del Re was very well situated and easily accessible. It was half way between the Piazza di Spagna and the Forum, on an approximately direct route. It was beside the Palazzo Colonna, occupied by James III's cousins, where the annual *Festa della Chinea* was held throughout the 1720s and until 1733. And it was two minutes from the Fontana di Trevi, which was constructed from 1733 to 1762.

Those tourists who did not wish to visit the court had plenty of other opportunities to see James III and his two sons. They often passed through the Piazza di Spagna, and they took frequent walks in the Borghese gardens, and elsewhere in Rome, offering opportunities for allegedly accidental meetings. They could be seen also in all the opera houses during the carnival seasons,

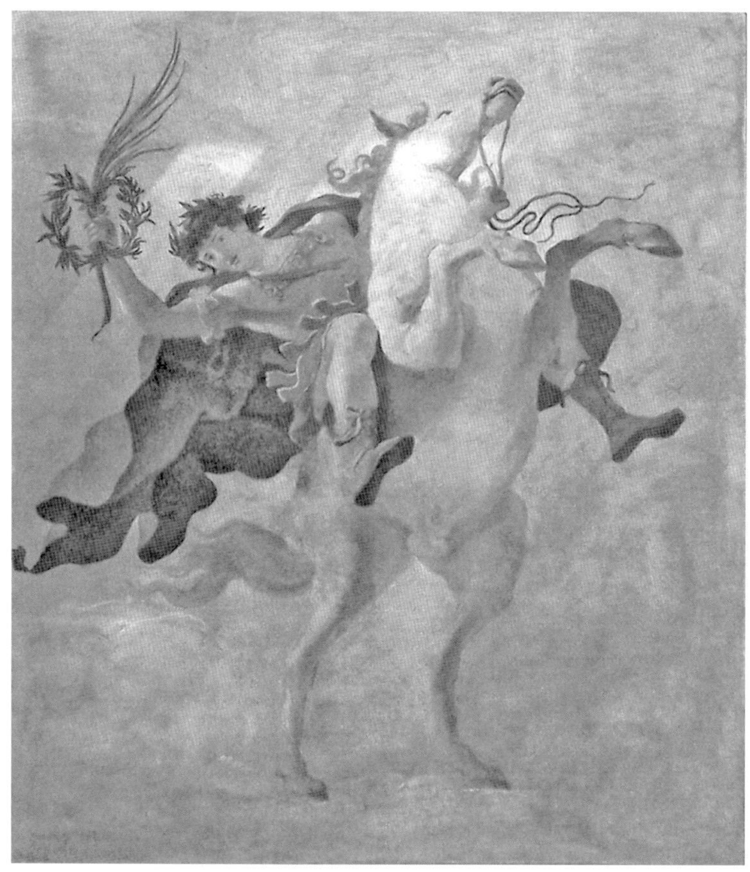

FIG. 4.4. Charles Mellin (c. 1597–1649), *Marcus Curtius*. Fresco. Rome, 'Palazzo del Re', now Palazzo Balestra, bedchamber. *(Photo: E. Corp.)*

and at several of the *conversazioni* in the palazzi of the aristocratic families. British and Irish tourists in Rome could hardly avoid seeing the Stuarts and meeting the Jacobite courtiers, even if they wanted to do so. The evidence suggests that they did not want to avoid them. They were naturally curious to see the exiled royal family and to take advantage of the presence in Rome of what would today be called the 'ex-pat community'. It is unrealistic to suggest that political differences within the British Isles took precedence over practical considerations in a far away and foreign city. The fact is that the British and Irish visitors to Rome socialized and dined together, whether they were Whigs, Tories or Jacobites. It is this that has to be borne in mind when considering the influence of the Stuart court on the patronage of portrait-painters.[15]

The portraits of the Stuarts themselves used to be the subject of much confusion. The basic facts have now been established. We know who the painters were, when they produced portraits, roughly how many copies they made, and how much they were paid. In addition, the Italian portraits have now been distinguished from the earlier French ones with which they were often confused. We have about 50 original portaits of James III, Queen Maria Clementina, Prince Charles and Prince Henry, painted during a period of 35 years. With multiple copies and miniatures (originals as well as copies), James III probably commissioned over 200 paintings.[16] That fact alone made him one of the most important patrons in Rome at the time.

The portrait-painters employed by the Stuarts in Rome may conveniently be listed in tabular form, with the official or semi-official court painters in italics (Table 4.1). The dates refer to the years in which the painters are known to have been employed by the Stuarts. This list does not include a number of painters whose Stuart portraits were commissioned by other patrons, or whose portraits (generally copies) were painted for private commercial transaction.[17] Nor does it include the painter who recorded the *facciata* erected on the Palazzo del Re in 1747 to celebrate Prince Henry's appointment to be a cardinal, which will be discussed below (pp. 47–9; and see also pp. 55–69).

This list provokes two questions. First, why and how did the Stuarts select their painters?

TABLE 4.1. Portrait-painters employed by the Stuarts in Rome.

Painter	Years employed by the Stuarts
Antonio David	1717–35
Francesco Trevisani	1719–20
Girolamo Pesci	1721
Martin van Meytens	1725
Agostino Masucci	1735
Jean-Etienne Liotard	1737–8
Louis-Gabriel Blanchet	1737–9, 1741, 1748, 1752
Pompeo Batoni	1738, 1744
Domenico Dupra	1740–2
Veronica Telli	1743–5, 1748
Domenico Corvi	1747–8
Anton Raphael Mengs	1748

Second, and more important, to what extent did the choice of painters by the Stuarts influence British and Irish tourists when commissioning their own portraits in Rome? Put another way, what evidence is there that British and Irish tourists asked the court to recommend painters?

It is not possible to explain why all the Stuart portraitists were selected, because the necessary documentation has not survived. We might guess that Pesci, who had been a pupil of Trevisani, was recommended by his master, that Liotard came to the attention of James III because of his portrait of Pope Clement XII, and that Telli was recommended by her brother, Lodovico Stern, who copied Meytens's portrait of Queen Maria Clementina so that it could be reproduced in mosaic for the Queen's monument in Saint Peter's. But we know nothing about the original choice of Meytens, nor about those of Masucci, Corvi and Mengs.

We do, however, know why David, Trevisani, Blanchet, Dupra and Batoni were selected, and an examination of the relations between the Stuarts and these painters sheds new light on the role of the exiled court in helping them find their British and Irish patrons.

Antonio David had established his reputation in Rome by painting the portraits of cardinals, and was chosen by Cardinal Gualterio during James III's first visit to Rome in 1717.[18] The king liked his work, made him his official painter in March 1718,[19] and regularly employed him for the next seventeen years (Plate 4.2). So, too, did some of the Jacobite courtiers, five of whose portraits by David have survived. But these portraits did not meet with general approval at the court, so alternative painters were looked for, particularly by David's chief critic, the Duke of Mar. It was Mar who selected Trevisani, whose British patronage will be the subject of a later essay in this volume, by Karin Wolfe (pp. 83–101).

It is tempting to assume that Trevisani's reputation as one of the leading painters in Rome was sufficient in itself to attract the attention of the Stuart court. It is probably true that James III had seen some of his pictures in the collection of Louis XIV. However, Mar was not necessarily aware of Trevisani when he sought an alternative to David, and Trevisani's pictures in France were not portraits, so a more positive explanation is needed. The man who in fact recommended Trevisani seems to have been David Nairne, the king's private secretary.

Nairne had been in Rome from 1689 to 1691 as a member of the embassy of the Earl of Melfort, who was Trevisani's first British patron. Nairne's diary contains many references to Trevisani, whose studio he visited on several occasions, and whom he evidently knew quite well. It also reveals that Trevisani painted a portrait of Lady Melfort. It is likely that Nairne recommended Trevisani to Mar.[20]

Mar visited Rome in April 1718, while the Stuart court was still at Urbino, and commissioned Trevisani to paint his portrait. He was so pleased with it that he ordered a miniature copy.[21] When the court moved to Rome at the beginning of 1719 he not only commissioned another portrait, this time of his wife and daughter, but also persuaded James III to commission his own portrait, in which he is shown wearing his Garter robes. Trevisani made at least two extra copies of the latter portrait, and then painted portraits of Queen Maria Clementina when she arrived in Rome later the same year. Before recommending Pesci at the end of 1720 (if he did), Trevisani had painted at least three other Jacobite portraits.[22]

The experience of Domenico Dupra was the reverse, in that he painted several portraits of British people in Rome before he was commissioned by the Stuarts. It was the success of his nine portraits of Jacobite Freemasons, the members of the Society of Young Gentlemen Travellers in Rome, which brought him to the attention of James III in 1740, and earned him several commissions in the following two years.[23]

Despite the success of these portraits, Dupra never became the official painter to the Stuart court, and seems to have stopped receiving (or accepting) British commissions. It was Louis-Gabriel Blanchet who instead became the semi-official court painter, and who is the portraitist most associated with the court from the end of the 1730s to the 1750s. This requires some explanation, because Blanchet was French, not Italian. An examination of how and why Blanchet was discovered by James III provides the necessary context to further our understanding of the relations between the Stuart court, the British and Irish tourists, and Giovanni Paolo Panini.

Blanchet was one of the first *pensionnaires* at the Académie de France, which had been opened in the Palazzo Mancini on the Corso in 1725 under the direction of Nicolas Vleughels.[24] James III had exceptionally friendly relations with the then French ambassador, Cardinal de Polignac, and in December 1729 was invited with his two sons to attend a performance of Molière's *L'Avare*, given by all the *pensionnaires*.[25] At that time they included both Blanchet and Pierre Subleyras, and this was probably the first time that James III came into contact with the two painters. Their performance was part of a series of entertainments organized by Polignac to celebrate the birth of the Dauphin, of which the most spectacular was a fête in the Piazza Navona. Polignac commissioned Panini to produce a painting of the temporary structures erected in the Piazza, and specified that it should include James III and his two sons.[26]

James did not apparently return to the Académie until 1732,[27] but in the meantime Vleughels, its director, married Panini's sister-in-law, thus strengthening the links between Panini and the French.[28] This was to be important because in 1732 one of James III's childhood friends, the duc de Saint-Aignan, was appointed to succeed Polignac as the French ambassador.[29]

Until 1732 the French embassy had been in the Palazzo Altemps, at the north end of the Piazza Navona. It was now transferred by Saint-Aignan to the Palazzo Bonelli, which was immediately opposite the Palazzo del Re in the Piazza dei Santi Apostoli.[30] As the Académie de France on the parallel Corso was situated midway between the Stuart court and the French embassy, a small triangle was thus created, linking James III and Saint-Aignan with the *pensionnaires* (like Blanchet and Subleyras) and friends (like Panini) of the Académie de France. It was noted that James III and his sons now began very regularly to visit the Académie.[31]

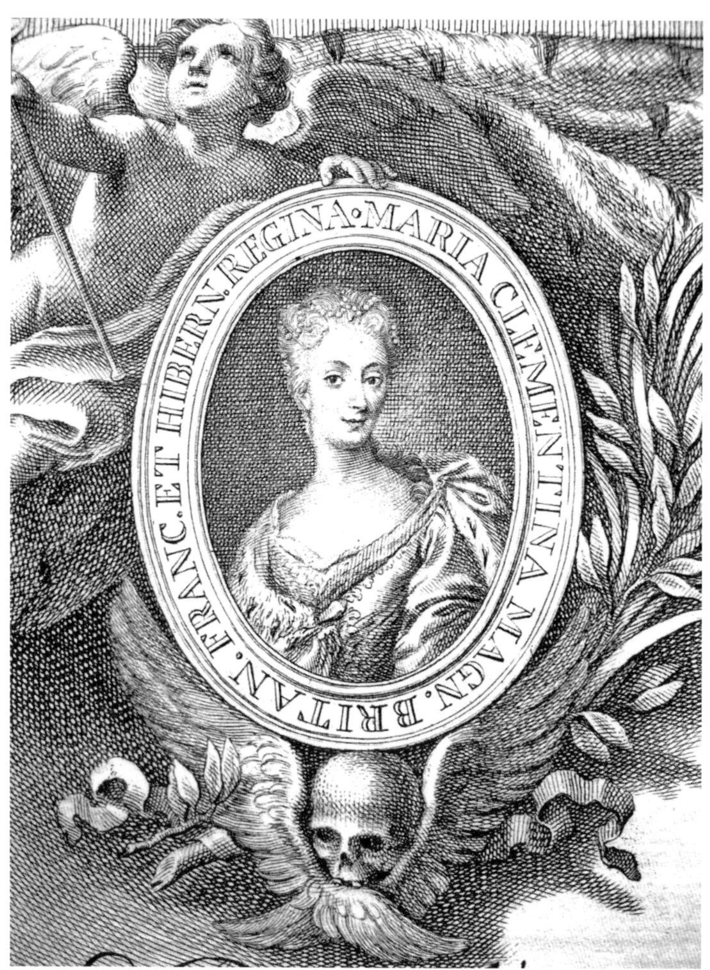

FIG. 4.5. Giovanni Girolamo Frezza (1659–after 1741), after Giovanni Paolo Panini, engraved frontispiece for *Parentalia Mariae Clementinae Magn. Britan. Franc., et Hibern. Regin Iussu Clementis XII Pont. Max.* (1735), detail. *(Photo: E. Corp.)*

One result of this was to bring Panini into contact with the British in Rome. As Alastair Laing points out below (p. 114), Panini's British patronage started in 1734, when he received commissions from three British tourists. One of them was Sir Thomas Twisden who, as already noted, was not only a Freemason but actually a member of the Jacobite Lodge in Rome.[32]

In the following year Panini was given two commissions connected with the death in January 1735 of Queen Maria Clementina. The first was to design and supervise the engraving of two very large prints, showing the interior of Santi Apostoli with the lying-in-state of the Queen, and her funeral procession from Santi Apostoli to Saint Peter's. The second was to design the frontispiece of an illustrated book describing the funeral. Panini included in it a portrait that he copied from the one by Meytens, and which would later be copied by Stern as the model for the mosaic in the monument to Maria Clementina in Saint Peter's (Fig. 4.5).[33] These three important engravings, which were widely circulated in Rome and elsewhere, brought Panini into direct contact with the Stuart court, and also brought his name to the attention of British and Irish patrons.[34] In the years that followed, Panini painted four more portraits of James III, all of them within large canvases commissioned by successive French ambassadors.[35]

The other result of the regular contact between James III and the Académie de France was the commissioning of several Stuart portraits from Blanchet. In 1736 Blanchet graduated from the Académie, but decided to remain in Rome, in lodgings shared with Subleyras, rather than return to Paris. Of the *pensionnaires* who had performed in *L'Avare*, he and Subleyras were by then the only ones still in Rome.[36] When, therefore, Antonio David died in July 1737, both Blanchet and Subleyras were known to James III and were possible candidates to replace him. We do not know why Blanchet rather than Subleyras was the painter selected. The two men were friends, and perhaps they settled the matter between them. Or perhaps it was because Blanchet had just painted his successsful portrait of Panini.[37] In any event, while Blanchet was painting his first Stuart portraits for James III at the end of 1737, Panini was painting a large canvas for Saint-Aignan, with James III and his two sons shown in a prominent position in the church of San Luigi dei Francesi.[38]

Virtually all the artists who painted the Stuarts in Rome also painted portraits of British and Irish tourists. It is therefore appropriate to consider to what extent these tourists were influenced by the court in their choice of portrait-painters, and to what extent they asked the court to provide introductions and make recommendations.

These questions are difficult to answer, mainly because of an absence of documentary evidence, but in part because there are relatively few portraits of British and Irish tourists — as distinct from Jacobite courtiers — painted in Rome before 1750. We know that David painted at least eight portraits of tourists, who were young men of all political persuasions.[39] Most of these pictures were painted late in David's career, at a time when the engravings of his Stuart portraits had been distributed widely in Great Britain and Ireland. Whether the tourists knew of David because of these engravings, or whether they were told about him after they had arrived in Rome, the fact is that they employed the man who was well known to be the official painter to the Stuart court, and it therefore seems reasonable to assume that it was the court that influenced their choice. In fact, if we are careful to distinguish between tourists and Jacobite courtiers, there are about as many Grand Tour portraits by David painted from 1717 until his death, as there are by all the other painters in Rome put together, which suggests that the Stuart court must have been important in this aspect of art patronage. One of David's portraits was of Lord Andover, the Master of the Jacobite Masonic Lodge.[40] It was only after David's death that the Freemasons in the Society of Young Gentlemen Travellers in Rome turned to Dupra.

The most important and prolific of all the Grand Tour portraitists in Rome was Pompeo Batoni. Although Batoni is not normally associated with the Stuart court, his career nevertheless provides a good illustration of how the role of the Stuart court has been neglected as a possible influence on the patronage of Roman painters by British and Irish tourists.

There is a letter of 1744 written by Prince Charles in Paris to his father's secretary in Rome, in which he asks him to send him portraits in miniature of his father, mother and brother. In this letter he specifies that he would like the portraits to be painted by Batoni.[41] This letter merits attention because at that time Batoni was not yet known as a portrait-painter. In fact, as far as we know, he had only ever painted two portraits, one British in 1740 and one Italian in 1743.[42] How, then, did Prince Charles know about Batoni? Why did he make this specific request? The answer lies in the fact that Batoni had links with the Stuart court that have been overlooked so far, and that it was the court that helped him to establish contact with his first British patrons.

Batoni, as we know, was helped at the beginning of his career in Rome by Francesco Fernandi, who adopted the name Imperiali in honour of his patron, Cardinal Imperiali. The latter was Cardinal Protector of Ireland, and in very close contact with James III. At this early point in his career, Batoni made drawings of classical sculptures in the private collection at Tivoli belonging to Count Giuseppe Fede. The latter's uncle, Innocenzo Fede, had served as Master of the Music at the Stuart court for many years.[43] Moreover, Batoni's work shows the influence of the English portraits painted by Van Dyck. He may, of course, have seen engravings elsewhere, but the Stuart court actually contained two of Van Dyck's original pictures.[44]

The first foreigner to commission an oil painting from Batoni was Captain John Urquhart of Cromarty, in 1733. As James Holloway explains below (p. 103), Urquhart was a Jacobite with very close links to the Stuart court, who also commissioned David to paint copies of his portraits of the Stuart princes during the same year.

Until 1740 Batoni lived in the parish of Santi Apostoli, and worshipped with members of the Stuart court in that church, which was immediately beside the Palazzo del Re. In particular, two of his children were baptized there. One of them was baptized at the same time as a child born to a man who was French and his German wife. The Frenchman was James III's *valet de chambre*; and the German was a daughter of Queen Maria Clementina's *valet de chambre*. We therefore have Batoni standing around the font with Jacobite courtiers before he had painted a single original portrait.[45] He had, however, already copied a Stuart portrait. Jean-Etienne Liotard testified in 1738 that

Batoni had made a miniature copy of his portrait of Prince Henry.[46]

Batoni also had links with the Jacobite Freemasons. For example, he knew Ramsay, who was a member of the Jacobite Masonic Lodge and in direct contact with members of the Stuart court, such as Irwin.[47] Another Jacobite Freemason was Lord Elcho, who visited Batoni's studio and also acquired an important subject painting by him before he had painted any known portraits. Elcho was one of the members of the Society of Young Gentlemen Travellers in Rome painted by Dupra, and is the man who has left us with the best description of the secret staircase in the Palazzo del Re.[48]

Finally, Batoni's earliest portraits to have survived were commissioned by certain Irishmen, who were included in Joshua Reynolds's *Parody of the School of Athens*. That painting also includes Irwin, another member of the Society of Young Gentlemen Travellers in Rome painted by Dupra. Batoni's next known portrait is of Thomas Barrett-Lennard, with his wife and recently deceased daughter. Barrett-Lennard came from a Jacobite family that had had extremely close links with the Stuart court in exile ever since 1689.[49]

Given all these facts, it is reasonable to suppose that Batoni was in close contact with the Stuart court, and that it was mainly the court, rather than Imperiali, that launched his career as a portrait-painter of British and Irish tourists. Here, therefore, is an explanation of why Prince Charles asked for portraits by him in 1744.

Of course Batoni's early patrons were not mainly Jacobites. On the contrary, they were mainly Whigs, and virtually all loyal Hanoverians. His career therefore provides a perfect example to support the argument of this essay, that in the first half of the eighteenth century the court served as cultural forum as well as surrogate embassy for many British and Irish people in Rome, regardless of their political loyalties.

The important artistic role of the Stuart court in Rome continued long after the prospects of a Stuart restoration had collapsed. This can be observed in a significant episode that took place later in Batoni's career, and that apparently has remained unknown until now. In the autumn of 1756, at a time when Prussia was allied to Hanoverian Great Britain, and when there were no doubt other and more politically suitable channels of communication, the court was used by Frederick the Great when he wanted to commission a painting by Batoni. Frederick requested Field Marshal James Keith to contact James III's private secretary (James Edgar) and to ask him to approach the painter. When, a little later, he decided that he would like a painting by Placido Costanzi also, to make a pendant with that of Batoni, he again asked Keith to approach James III's secretary.[50]

It is true that anyone in Rome could have contacted Batoni and Costanzi to commission paintings for a prestigious royal patron like Frederick the Great, but the point was that both artists were known to have links with the Stuart court. Those of Batoni have been examined already, but those of Costanzi were equally significant. Placido Costanzi's younger brother Carlo, a gem engraver, had engraved several portraits of James III,[51] and actually owed his life to James's protection. In 1729 he had killed the son of a Roman bourgeois, and escaped punishment thanks to the intervention of James III.[52] In or soon after 1731, when Carlo Costanzi had engraved his second portrait of James III, his brother Placido had painted a portrait of Field Marshal Keith's brother George, the 10th Earl Marischal, who was then living in the Palazzo del Re as James III's principal minister.[53] It was therefore natural that Frederick the Great and Field Marshal Keith should have wanted to use the Stuart court as a way of contacting the painters.

In February 1757, when James III's secretary sent the paintings by Batoni and Costanzi to Berlin, Frederick the Great was preoccupied with the Seven Years' War, which he was waging in alliance with his Hanoverian uncle, King George II. Despite this, he then decided not only to commission a second painting from Batoni, but also to invite him to leave Rome and move permanently to the Prussian court. Once again it was James III's secretary who was asked to approach the painter and try to persuade Batoni to accept Frederick's offer.[54]

The need to revise our understanding of the Stuart court is particularly well illustrated by the large painting, now in the Scottish National Portrait Gallery, which shows James III and members of his court greeting Prince Henry in front of a temporary *facciata* in July 1747 (**Plate 5.1**).[55] During that year Pope Benedict XIV decided that, as with other celebrations, a decorated false façade, or *facciata*, should be erected for 40 days on the palazzo in which each newly-created cardinal lived.[56] This posed a problem for the Stuarts because the main entrance to the Palazzo del Re was situated in a narrow street, where there was no room, and because the side entrance from the Piazza dei Santi Apostoli was too small. Moreover, any *facciata* erected there would have obscured the king's gallery and cabinet. It used to be assumed, therefore, that the

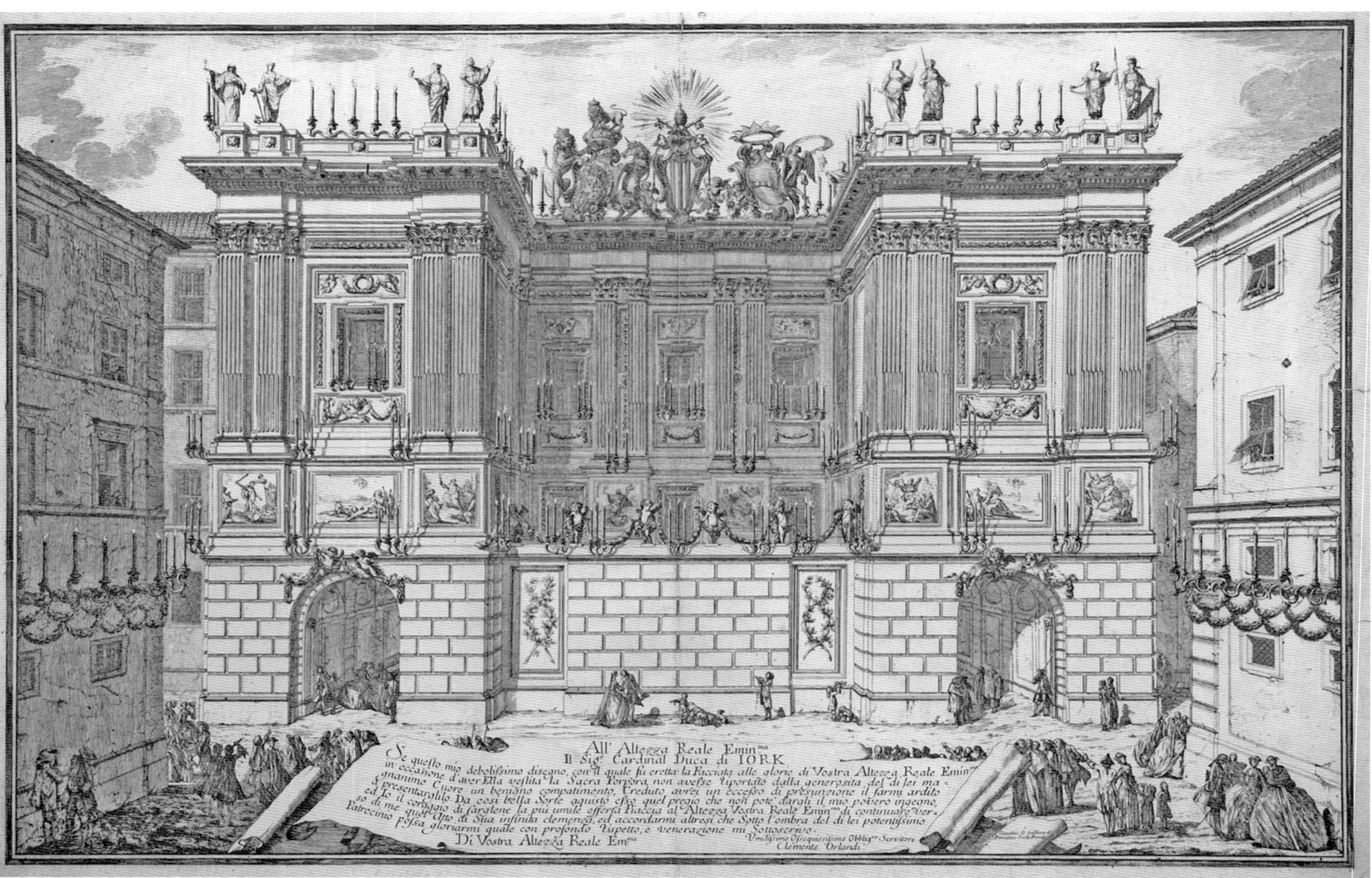

Fig. 4.6. Claude-Olivier Gallimard (1718–74), *The Temporary 'Facciata' Erected in Front of the Apartment of Prince Henry in the East Wing of the Palazzo del Re to Celebrate His Promotion to Cardinal in August 1747*, 1747. Engraving. *(Reproduced courtesy of the owner.)*

facciata was erected on the neighbouring Palazzo Muti. If the Stuarts had also occupied that building, as was once believed,[57] that might have been a credible solution, but we now know that they did not. As David R. Marshall conclusively demonstrates below (pp. 62–5), the *facciata* was actually erected on another part of the Palazzo del Re itself.

We know that the *facciata* was designed by Clemente Orlandi, that it took nineteen days to build and decorate, that it cost 4689 scudi, that it was paid for by Cardinal York rather than James III,[58] and that it remained in place from July to September 1747. We also know what it looked like, because it was engraved by Claude-Olivier Gallimard (**Fig. 4.6**).[59] There is, however, a problem that has yet to be resolved. At some point Cardinal York commissioned someone to paint a large picture based on the engraving, which he displayed in his first antechamber in the Palazzo della Cancelleria until his death in 1807.[60] We do not yet know the identity of the painter, or the date of the painting, and unless some documentary evidence emerges we might never discover them (*pace* Marshall, below, pp. 55, 66–7).[61] But perhaps we should look to the *pensionnaires* of the Académie de France, or the pupils of Panini to whom it used to be attributed. Gallimard, who made the original engraving, was at that time a *pensionnaire* of the Académie.[62] And the anonymous painter, whoever he was, added various figures that were copied directly from some engravings based on paintings by Vleughels.[63] It seems clear that the painter, like the Stuart court itself, had close links with the Académie de France.

Whatever the identity of the artist, the painting is important because it underscores the need to reconsider the reality of the Stuart court in Rome during the first half of the eighteenth century. No British or Irish tourist in Rome during the summer of 1747 can possibly have been unaware of the lavish Stuart fête in the Piazza della Pilotta. Yet it is not apparently mentioned in any of their surviving correspondence with their families and friends at home. This is a particularly revealing silence. The tourists who asked the Stuart court to recommend art dealers and portrait-painters, and socialized with the Jacobites in Rome, did not admit the fact in incriminating letters, which might have been opened by the agents of the Whig government. On the contrary, they made a point of claiming that they had absolutely nothing to do with the court, or with the Jacobites employed there. Historians have been too ready to take these protests at face value. We need to look beyond their façade, and to try to rediscover the reality that confronted British and Irish tourists when they visited Rome. Only then shall we be able to appreciate the importance of the exiled Stuart court in the patronage of portrait-painters in Rome during the first half of the eighteenth century.

Notes

* Much of the research on which this article is based was carried out while I was the Paul Mellon Centre Rome Fellow at the British School at Rome during the academic year 2004–5. It is therefore a great pleasure to record here my appreciation of the generous support I have received from the Paul Mellon Centre for Studies in British Art.

1. I am currently writing a book on the Stuart court in Rome, which will provide a radical reassessment of its nature, composition and importance, with a detailed description of the buildings in which it was based, and the significant role it played in the musical and artistic life of the papal city. Footnotes in the first half of this preliminary study therefore have been kept to a minimum.
2. For the Stuart court in France, see E. Corp, *A Court in Exile: the Stuarts in France, 1689–1718* (Cambridge, 2004).
3. Windsor Castle, Royal Archives, Stuart Papers [henceforth RA, SP], 287/4, James III to Cardinal de Tencin, 29 August 1747: 'il ne pourroit plus etre question d'Angleterre ni pour lui ni pour moy. Voila ce que les Italiens ne comprendront jamais, mais il n'est pas moins vrai pour cela'. I am very grateful to Her Majesty Queen Elizabeth II for gracious permission to quote from the Stuart Papers in the Royal Archives.
4. E. Corp, 'Maintaining honour during a period of extended exile: the nomination of cardinals by James III in Rome', in M. Wrede and H. Carl (eds), *Zwischen Schande und Ehre: Erinnerungsbrüche und die Kontinuität des Hauses* (Mainz, 2007), 157–69.
5. According to Carl Nylander, 'the first *known* burial at the Pyramid is that of Sir William Ellis ... and it took place on August 4, 1732' ('The people at the Pyramid: notes on the Protestant Cemetery in Rome', in T. Hall, B. Magnusson and C. Nylander (eds), Docto Peregrino*: Roman Studies in Honour of Torgil Magnuson* (Stockholm/Rome, 1992), 221–49, esp. p. 225). I am aware of several earlier burials, the first being those of James Graham and the 5th Earl of Linlithgow in March and April 1723 (London, National Archives, State Papers [henceforth NA, SP], 85/14/fol. 310, Stosch to Carteret, 3 April 1723; Bodleian Library, Rawlinson MS D.1183, p. 1555, Rawlinson's diary, 6 April 1723).
6. These people are all included in B. Ford and J. Ingamells, *A Dictionary of British and Irish Travellers in Italy, 1701–1800. Compiled from the Brinsley Ford Archive* (New Haven/London, 1997).
7. G. Marinelli, *L'architettura palaziale romana tra Seicento e Settecento. Problemi di linguaggio. Un approccio filologico: la testimonianza delle incisioni dello 'Studio d'Architettura Civile'; una verifica sistematica: il palazzo Muti Papazzurri alla Pilotta* (Università di Roma 'La Sapienza', doctoral thesis, no date shown but after 1990); A. Antinori, 'Il Palazzo Muti Papazzurri ai Santi Apostoli nei secoli XVI e XVII: notizie sull'attività di Giovanni Antonio de Rossi, Carlo Fontana e Carlo Francesco Bizzaccheri', in M. Caperna and G. Spagnesi (eds), *Architettura: processualità e trasformazione. Atti del convegno internazionale di studi, Roma, Castel Sant'Angelo, 24–27 novembre 1999* (*Quaderni dell'Istituto di Storia dell'Architettura*, 1999–2002, nos. 34–9) (Rome, 2002), 439–46.
8. Historical Manuscripts Commission [henceforth HMC], *Calendar of the Stuart Papers ... Preserved at Windsor Castle* VII (London, 1902–23), 662, Marchese Giovanni Batista Muti to the Camera Apostolica, 22 December 1718. The building was sometimes called the Palazzo Reale or the Reggio Palazzo. Not even Baron von Stosch, the Hanoverian spy, called it the Palazzo Muti. (He referred to it as the 'Palais du Prétendant', and occasionally the 'Palais Royal'.)
9. The relative importance of the three entrances is made very clear in the descriptions given of them in the Archivio Segreto Vaticano and the Archivio Storico del Vicariato di Roma, and in the deployment of the Swiss guards.
10. For the decoration of what became the king's apartment, see R. Pantanella, 'Palazzo Muti a piazza SS. Apostoli residenza degli Stuart a Roma', *Storia dell'Arte* 84 (1995), 307–28.
11. Archivio Segreto Vaticano, Palazzo Apostolica Computisteria [henceforth ASV, Pal. Ap. Comp.], 983, 'pagamenti fatti ... per la Maesta di Giacomo 3e Rè d'Inghilterra', no. 63/10 and no. 64/10, 15 October and 15 December 1724.
12. This statistical information is based on the numerous lists in RA, SP, and on the *Stati d'anime* in the Archivio Storico Vicariato di Roma.
13. E. Corp, 'La Franc-Maçonnerie jacobite et la bulle papale *In Eminenti* d'avril 1738', *La Regle d'Abraham* 18 (December 2004), 13–44. The minutes of the Jacobite lodge were published by William James Hughan in *The Jacobite Lodge at Rome in 1735–37* (Torquay, 1910). The nine members of the Society painted by Dupra were Dr James Irwin, William Hay, Bellingham Boyle, James Carnegie, Sir Hew Dalrymple, Lord John Drummond, Lord Elcho, James Stuart Mackenzie and Sir James Steuart.
14. Stosch described the Jacobites as 'les Maitres' of 'la place d'Espagne' (NA, SP, 98/32/fol. 31, Stosch to Newcastle, 2 March 1730).
15. This paragraph is based on the weekly letters from Stosch to Newcastle in NA, SP, 85/15, 16 and 98/32, 37. For a typical example, see NA, SP, 98/32/fol. 303, 23 November 1731: 'les Voyageurs Anglois ... converser avec les Domestiques du Prétendant sans aucune contrainte, qu'il devient a cet heur impossible de distinguer les sujets affectionés au Roy [Georges II] parmi ceux qui sont Partisans du Prétendant. Parce qu'il a peine arrive't'il un Etranger que le Chapelain Hamilton, le D. Orvien et Cap Hay l'attacherta luy, lesquels le conduisent chez le jeune Ratlif ou dans peu de jour il font amitiez avec tous les domestiques actuels du Prétendant. On me nomme des personnes don't je connois les principes d'etre entierement Wiggs, qui ensemble avec les autres ont été entrainés'. Ezekiel Hamilton was the Anglican chaplain at the Stuart court, 'D. Orvien' was Dr James Irwin (James III's doctor), 'Cap Hay' was William Hay of Edington

(groom of the bedchamber), and 'le jeune Ratlif' was Charles Radcliffe, 5th Earl of Derwentwater. Irwin, Hay and Derwentwater were all Freemasons. Derwentwater later went to Paris, where he became Grand Master of the *Grande Loge de France*. Irwin and Hay remained, and were two of the members of the Society of Young Gentlemen Travellers in Rome painted by Dupra (see above, n. 13).

16. Unless otherwise shown, information about the Stuart and Jacobite portraits is taken from E. Corp, *The King over the Water: Portraits of the Stuarts in Exile after 1689* (Edinburgh, 2001). James III also commissioned many engravings and medals, which are not discussed here.
17. The first group includes Giuseppe Maria Crespi, Antonio Gionima, Corrado Giaquinto and Domenico Muratori. The second group includes John Smibert and Cosmo Alexander. James III also commissioned portraits from Lucia Casalini Torelli and Giovanna Fratellini in Bologna, and from Rosalba Carriera in Venice, but they are not discussed here.
18. A. Spiriti and S. Capelli (eds), *I David: due pittori tra Sei e Settecento* (Milan, 2004); Bodleian Library, Carte MSS 208, 'Journal du Séjour de S.M.B. à Rome', 2 July 1717, fol. 355: 'David, estimé le meilleur peintre de Rome pour les portraits et pour bien attraper la ressemblance'.
19. RA, SP, Misc 20, p. 77, warrant of 21 March 1718 appointing Antonio David 'to be one of Our Painters'; HMC, *Stuart Papers* VI, 280, David to Nairne, 9 April 1718.
20. National Library of Scotland MS 14266, the Journal of David Nairne. Nairne visited Trevisani in his studio on at least seventeen occasions between 16 January and 1 September 1691. Trevisani's portrait of *Thomas Coke* (Holkham Hall) was painted in 1717 just before James III's first visit to Rome. James was then accompanied by Nairne, but not by Mar (who was in France). For the details of the king's visit to Rome in 1717, see E. Corp, *The Jacobites at Urbino: an Exiled Court in Transition* (Basingstoke/New York, 2009), chapter 2.
21. HMC, *Stuart Papers* VI, 517, Alexander to Mar, 11 June 1718; HMC, *Stuart Papers* VI, 517, Ramelli to Mar, June 1718.
22. In addition to the portraits of James III and Queen Maria Clementina commissioned and paid for by James III himself, copies were commissioned by Cardinal Ottoboni (A. Schiavo, *Il Palazzo della Cancelleria* (Rome, 1963), 196).
23. See above, n. 13. It is not clear to what extent Domenico Dupra was assisted by his brother Giuseppe in painting these nine portraits and his later Stuart portraits. One receipt for a Stuart portrait refers to 'i due Pitori Dupra' (RA, SP, 259/32, receipt by Edgar, 4 September 1744).
24. Blanchet joined the Académie de France in 1728. The list of *pensionnaires* is given in O. Michel and P. Rosenberg (eds), *Subleyras, 1699–1749* (Rome/Paris, 1987), 116–17.
25. NA, SP, 85/16/fol. 608, Stosch to Newcastle, 1 December 1729.
26. The original of 1729 is in the Musée du Louvre. Panini's copy of 1731 is in the National Gallery of Ireland.
27. NA, SP, 98/32/fol. 343, Stosch to Newcastle, 23 February 1732.
28. Michel and Rosenberg, *Subleyras* (above, n. 24), 123, 126.
29. Saint-Aignan's elder half-brother was the duc de Beauvilliers, who had been the governor of the three grandsons of Louis XIV, the ducs de Bourgogne, Anjou and Berri, with whom James III had been brought up almost as a younger brother. See Corp, *A Court in Exile* (above, n. 2), chapter 6.
30. For the French ambassadors and embassies, see A. Pialoux, 'Rome, théâtre des relations diplomatiques au XVIIIe siècle', *Revue d'Histoire Diplomatique* 118 (3) (2004), 251–80, esp. pp. 254–5. The duc de Saint-Aignan was asked by the Governor of Rome not to occupy the Palazzo Bonelli because it would pose problems for the *sbirri* guarding the Piazza dei Santi Apostoli, but he insisted on going there (NA, SP, 98/32/fol. 309, Stosch to Newcastle, 8 December 1731).
31. For example, he visited the Académie three times in eleven days in February 1733 (NA, SP, 98/32/fols 486, 488 and 490, Stosch to Newcastle, 14, 21 and 28 February 1733), and five times in ten days in February 1736 (NA, SP, 98/37/fols 317, 319 and 321, Stosch to Newcastle, 11, 18 and 25 February 1736).
32. Corp, 'La Franc-Maçonnerie jacobite' (above, n. 13), 20. When Twisden left Rome in October 1735, having been there for over a year, it was noted that he had passed 'presque tous les jours avec les Domestiques actuels' of James III (NA, SP, 98/37/fol. 283, Stosch to Newcastle, 29 October 1735).
33. ASV, Pal. Ap. Comp. 1007, 'Ristretti de Pagamenti fatti all'infratti p. carisa del Funerale ... della Maesta di Maria Clementina Subieschi Regina d'Inghilterra'. The payments to the engravers are nos. 54, 55 and 63. Panini's bill for all three works, written by himself, signed and dated 2 June 1736, is no. 65.
34. The three engravings are nos. 197–9 in R. Sharp, *The Engraved Record of the Jacobite Movement* (Aldershot, 1996), 109–10, where only the first two are illustrated. There is a copy of the book, entitled *Parentalia Mariae Clementinae Magn. Britan. Franc., et Hibern. Regin Iussu Clementis XII Pont. Max.*, with Panini's frontispiece reproducing Meytens's portrait of the queen, in the library of the British School at Rome. It was generally believed at the time to have been written by Cardinal Vincenzo Gotti (NA, SP, 98/37/fol. 251, Stosch to Newcastle, 23 July 1735), but it was actually written by Sir Thomas Sheridan (RA, SP, 192/85, James III to Innes, 16 December 1736).
35. *The Duc de Saint-Aignan Giving the Cordon of the Saint-Esprit to Prince Vaini in November 1737* (Caen, Musée des Beaux Arts); *The Performance of a Serenata in the Teatro Argentina in July 1747*, for Cardinal de la Rochefoucauld (Musée du Louvre); and both *A Ball* and *The Performance of a Serenata in the Palazzo Farnese*, in November 1751 for the duc de Nivernais (Waddesdon Manor, kindly communicated to me by Bent Sørensen).
36. Michel and Rosenberg, *Subleyras* (above, n. 24), 116, 120.
37. Blanchet's portrait of Panini was painted in 1736.
38. See above, n. 35.
39. Edward Finch (1723), Lord Cranstoun (1728), Charles Hamilton (1732), Stephen Fox (1732), Henry Fox (1732),

Lord Andover (1735), George Lewis Coke (1735) and William Perry (1736).

40. Now in Ranger's House, Blackheath.
41. RA, SP, 257/60, Charles to Edgar, 25 May 1744. The miniatures were copied from originals by Dupra (James III and Prince Henry) and Meytens (Maria Clementina), but only the one of Prince Henry was actually copied by Batoni. The other two were copied by Telli (RA, SP, box 1/98, Henry to Charles, 28 August 1744). Batoni's receipt for 20 scudi, 'per una mignature fatta da me rapresentate il ritratto di S. Altezza Reale il Sig. Duca di Yiorche' is RA, SP, 259/103, dated 21 September 1744.
42. The basic information about Batoni in the following paragraphs is taken from E.P. Bowron, *Pompeo Batoni (1708–87) and His British Patrons* (London, 1982), 7–20; and A.M. Clark, *Pompeo Batoni. A Complete Catalogue of His Works*, edited and prepared for publication by E.P. Bowron (London, 1985).
43. For Fede's career at the Stuart court, see Corp, *A Court in Exile* (above, n. 2), chapter 8.
44. The pictures were a portrait of Charles I and a copy by Van Dyck himself of *The Three Children of Charles I*. The former had been given by James II to Cardinal Philip Howard, and was acquired in Rome by James III's secretary, James Edgar (Ford and Ingamells, *Dictionary of British and Irish Travellers* (above, n. 6), 906). The latter, which had once belonged to Cardinal Mazarin, had been acquired by James II at Saint-Germain and brought to Rome by James III. For its provenance, see T. Yoshida-Takeda and C. Lebrun-Jouve (eds), *Inventaire dressé après le décès en 1661 du Cardinal Mazarin* (Paris, 2004), 185, no. 1003. It was described in the inventory drawn up for Cardinal York after the death of the Duchess of Albany in November 1789 as 'un Quadro della Famiglia Reale dipinto dal famoso Wandick essondo uno simile in Inghilterra, ambedue originale' (Archivio Storico di Propaganda Fide, Stato Temporale Eredita del Card. Duca de York: Inventario Contessa [sic] d'Albany vol. 5, no. 83/49).
45. Archivio Storico Vicariato: Santi Dodici Apostoli vol. 13, Battesimi, 1733–51, p. 60v, 22 March 1738: Joseph Maria Clement, son of François Decelles and Catherine (daughter of Gottfried) Rittel; and Anna Maria Bernardina, daughter of Pompeo Batoni and Francesca Satti.
46. In his study in four volumes of *La miniature en Europe aux 16e, 17e, 18e et 19e siècles* (Graz, 1964), Leo R. Schidlof recorded that 'je connais dans une collection suisse une miniature sur ivoire, portrait du prince Henry Benedict Stuart, plus tard Cardinal de York (1725–1807), avec l'inscription de l'artiste [that is, Liotard] au revers 'Prin.^e^ Henrico Benedetto Stuard a Roma', da ortola urbani. Sotto Pompeo Batoni an^o^ 1738' (vol. I, 522). Batoni also painted a lost portrait of Queen Maria Clementina at around this time. It is listed in the inventory of Conte Manfredo Benvenuti dated 1748, and in a second inventory of the Benvenuti family dated 1794. See L. Carubelli, 'Palazzo Benvenuti di Porta Ripalta a Crema e i suoi oggetti d'arte nei documenti d'archivio', *Bollettino Storico Cremonese*, nuova serie X (2003), 139–52, see p. 146 for 1748 and p. 152 for 1794. Manfredo Benvenuti also owned a painting of *La Beata Vergine* by Batoni (p. 146), and the portrait of Abate Cesare Benvenuti by Subleyras (now in the Louvre: p. 152). I am very grateful to Licia Carubelli for drawing this portrait of Queen Maria Clementina to my attention.
47. Corp, 'La Franc-Maçonnerie jacobite' (above, n. 13), 20. Batoni also knew William Mosman, another member of the Jacobite Masonic Lodge.
48. The painting acquired by Lord Elcho was *The Sacrifice of Iphigenia*, now in the National Gallery of Scotland. Lord Elcho's description of the secret staircase can be found in B. Lenman and J. Gibson, *The Jacobite Threat* (Edinburgh, 1990), 189–90. The painting was originally commissioned for Lord Mansell by Dr John Clephane, who 'played a part ... in its subsequent sale to David Wemyss, Lord Elcho' (E.P. Bowron and P.B. Kerber, *Pompeo Batoni: Prince of Painters in Eighteenth Century Rome* (New Haven/London, 2007), 48). Clephane's father, Colonel William Clephane, had for many years been a member of the Stuart court in Rome (Corp, *The Jacobites at Urbino* (above, n. 20)); RA, SP, 123/21, pensions paid in Rome by James III, 1729.
49. Thomas Barrett-Lennard (later 17th Lord Dacre) was the nephew of Barbara Lennard, who joined the Stuart court at Saint-Germain in 1689 and married Charles Skelton, whose father Bevil was Comptroller of the Household. He inherited from them the portrait of *James II* (1698) by François de Troy, which is still in the Barrett-Lennard Collection.
50. J. Preuss (ed.), *Oeuvres de Frédéric le Grand* XX (Berlin, 1852), 263–5, nos. 9 and 10, Frederick II to Keith, 17 (November) 1756; and to Marischal, 21 (November) 1756; RA, SP, 368/164, Edgar to Keith, 11 February 1757, in reply to a missing letter from Keith to Edgar, 22 November 1756. Edgar's detailed instructions for the sending of the pictures to Berlin, dated 2 February 1757, are RA, SP, 368/163. The letters from Frederick include the dates but not the months to which they refer. The editor of the *Oeuvres* suggested that they were written in March 1756, but the letter in the Stuart Papers makes it clear that they were really written in November of that year.
51. For Carlo Costanzi's first two engraved portraits, NA, SP, 85/15/fol. 456, Stosch to Newcastle, 3 November 1725; and NA, SP, 98/32/fol. 215, Stosch to Newcastle, 19 June 1731. Two others were sent to Prince Charles in 1750 (RA, SP, 310/70, Charles to Edgar, 25 August 1750).
52. NA, SP, 85/16/fol. 586, Stosch to Newcastle, 15 September 1729.
53. Lord Marischal lived in the Palazzo del Re from July 1731 to March 1733. The portrait is in the National Portrait Gallery in London.
54. RA, SP, 369/87, Keith to Edgar, 7 March 1757. The two letters in the Stuart Papers, read in isolation, seem to imply that Frederick the Great had asked for portraits of James III by

Batoni and Costanzi. The two letters in the *Oeuvres de Frédéric le Grand*, however, make it clear that Frederick actually wanted subject paintings by Batoni and Costanzi. I am very grateful to Peter Kerber for drawing to my attention these letters from Frederick, and thus for enabling me to correct this mistake (which I included in Corp, *King over the Water* (above, n. 16), 90, 109). Frederick did, however, acquire a portrait of James III by Jacob van Schuppen a little later. It was reproduced, for the first time, as an illustration to E. Corp, 'Jacobite books in Toulouse', *The Journal of the Edinburgh Bibliographical Society* 1 (2006), 71–85 (fig. 1, on p. 9).

55. The painting was first exhibited, after restoration, in the exhibition *The King over the Water* at the Scottish National Portrait Gallery in 2001.
56. RA, SP, 285/187, James III to Cardinal de Tencin, 25 July 1747: 'Le Pape a reveillé une ancienne coutume don't je ne scais pas trop ni l'origine ni l'utilité qui est que toute les nouveaux Cardinaux doivent mettre ce qu'on appelle une Fassade peinte à leurs maisons, et qui doit y rester 40 jours après avoir reçü le Chapeau. Celle du Duc ne vient que d'être fini'.
57. The origin of this belief seems to be R. Marshall, *Bonnie Prince Charlie* (Edinburgh, 1988), in which a photograph of the Palazzo Muti in the Piazza della Pilotta is described as the building that contained the Stuart court. It was accepted and repeated in E. Corp, *The Stuart Court in Rome. The Legacy of Exile* (Aldershot, 2003), 13–15.
58. RA, SP, 288/164, a list of Cardinal York's expenses, 24 July to 31 December 1747: 'Per la Facciata 4689:80'. James III commented (in the letter cited in n. 56): The *facciata* 'du Duc … ne laissera pas d'etre majeur de depense, et en verité je n'aurois jamais pu croire que les depenses memes necessaires du Cardinal eussent pü monter si haut'. Eight days later Pope Benedict XIV commented that 'la seule chose qui nous ait fait peine dans cette affaire-ci, c'est que le roi ait dépensé plus de quatre mille écus pour illuminer et décorer la façade de son palais, laquelle regarde celui où demeurait le feu Cardinal Cinfuegos. Si on nous avait parlé, nous aurions dit qu'il ne fallait pas faire cette dépense. La maison où habite le cardinal d'York étant, ou bien au pape, ou bien au roi son père et ne devant point être illuminée dans l'un ou l'autre cas' (E. de Heeckeren (ed.), *Correspondance de Benoît XIV* (Paris, 1912), I, 342, Benedict XIV to Cardinal de Tencin, 2 August 1747). As Cardinal Cinfuegos lived on the east side of the Piazza della Pilotta, directly opposite the Palazzo Muti, but not the Palazzo del Re, this letter seemed to support the belief, now discredited by David R. Marshall in his contribution to the present volume, that the *facciata* was erected on the Palazzo Muti. According to Chracas, the *facciata* was created between Thursday 6 July and Tuesday 25 July (*Diario ordinario* 4674 of 8 July 1747, 17; and 4683 of 29 July 1747, 20).
59. I am grateful to Richard Sharp for drawing this engraving to my attention, and for giving me a facsimile.
60. Archivio di Stato di Roma, Misc. famiglia: Stuart, b.171, fol. 5, 'copia dell'Inventario de Beni Ereditari della … Duca di York esistenti nel palazzo della Cancelleria', 18 July 1807: 'Stanze situata nel secondo Appartamento, Prima Anticamera, Un quadro grande rappresentante la facciata fatta per la creazione al Cardinalato di S.A.R. Em.a con cornice'. It is described later in the same inventory as 'un quadre grande di misura di Palmi otto, e dodici per traverso'.
61. Perhaps it was painted by Giuseppe Paladini, or by Giovanni Angeloni, both artists associated with the Stuarts. Paladini was a pupil of Sebastiano Conca: 'C'est d'ailleurs en visitant l'*Academia* [de Conca] que le Cardinal d'York découvrit le talent du jeune artiste et lui acheta ses premiers dessins'. By the mid-1760s Angeloni was the most successful decorative artist in Rome: 'Il peint, sous la direction de Paolo Posi, l'apparat funêbre de Jacques III aux Saint-Apôtres' (O. Michel, *Vivre et peindre à Rome au XVIIIe siècle* (Rome, 1996), 275, 459).
62. Michel and Rosenberg, *Subleyras* (above, n. 24), 117. Gallimard had left the Académie by 1748.
63. They are reproduced in B. Hercenberg, *Nicolas Vleughels, peintre et directeur de l'Académie de France à Rome, 1668–1737* (Paris, 1975), plates XC–XCIII, figs 137–40, cat. nos. 124–7. It was Alastair Laing who first identified these figures, and very generously drew them to my attention.

The cardinal's clothes: the temporary façade for the investiture celebration of Cardinal York in 1747

David R. Marshall

On 3 July 1747 Henry Benedict Stuart (1725–1807), Duke of York, second son of the Young Pretender, James III, was created cardinal by Benedict XIV. To celebrate his elevation to the purple, a temporary façade was erected on the palace occupied by the Stuarts. This façade and the associated decorations are recorded in a painting recently acquired by the Scottish National Portrait Gallery (Plate 5.1).[1] It came from the collection of the Dukes of Hamilton, and had been acquired in the nineteenth century from the Villa Muti at Frascati, the country residence of Cardinal York.[2] It was commissioned by Cardinal York and appears in an inventory of his collection in the Palazzo della Cancelleria in 1807.[3] It is either based on, or executed concurrently with, a corresponding engraving by Claude-Olivier Gallimard (Fig. 4.6).[4] It traditionally, and perhaps inevitably, has been attributed to Giovanni Paolo Panini, but is now catalogued as being by an unknown artist.

The painting shows the fictive façade to have represented a palazzo with a U-shaped top storey, articulated with windows framed by paired pilasters, relief decorations, and crowning statues and coats of arms. A mezzanine forms a supporting plinth, while the ground floor is rendered as drafted marble with inset reliefs and arched passageways on either side. The central part of the ground floor is set back less than the upper storeys, implying a courtyard behind. To the left and right are indications of a piazza and a narrow street, while in front, the same width as the palace façade, is another piazza, with buildings placed symmetrically on either side.

Where was this temporary façade located? When James III and his new wife Maria Clementina Sobieska arrived in Rome in 1719, Pope Clement XI rented for them one of two adjacent palazzi owned by the Muti Papazzurri family. One, usually known today as the Palazzo Balestra, had its main façade on the Piazza dei Santi Apostoli, and I will call it the Santi Apostoli palace for clarity (see below, 'A' in Fig. 5.3). The other was adjacent and had its main façade on the Piazza della Pilotta, and is today occupied by the Pontificio Istituto Biblico, and I will call this the Pilotta palace (Fig. 5.1; and, below, 'B' in Fig. 5.3).[5] The two palazzi belonged to different branches of the Muti Papazzurri family: in 1685 the Pilotta palace belonged to Marchese Pompeo Muti and his brothers,[6] and in 1644 the Santi Apostoli palace belonged to Marchese Giovanni Battista Muti Papazzurri. Although matters are complicated by relationships and changes of ownership across the two branches of the family, usually the Pilotta palace was referred to as the Palazzo Muti,[7] and the Santi Apostoli palace as the Palazzo Muti Papazzurri.[8]

Alessandro Antinori has published a documented study of the Santi Apostoli palace,[9] drawing on the family archive now in Forli, but the Pilotta palace has been little studied. Most Roman palazzi began as clusters of simple *case*, or houses, often with a single doorway, an internal staircase, and two windows or so on each floor. These would then be developed, both internally and externally, into noble palazzi during the seventeenth century, with more or less unified façades. This is what happened to the buildings that now form the basis of the Santi Apostoli palace. Its condition in 1625 can be seen in Giovanni Maggi bird's eye view (Fig. 5.2). In 1638 it was turned by the Muti Papazzurri into a noble palazzo, and early in this process it acquired significant frescoes by Charles Mellin. As was often the case, it made better financial sense for the family to let the best part of the palace to a cardinal needing a residence in Rome, while taking up residence in other, less grand, parts of the block. From 1660 it was rented to various cardinals, and the Muti Papazzurri moved into the corner closest to the Pilotta palace and Santi Apostoli. So things stood until the palace was rented for

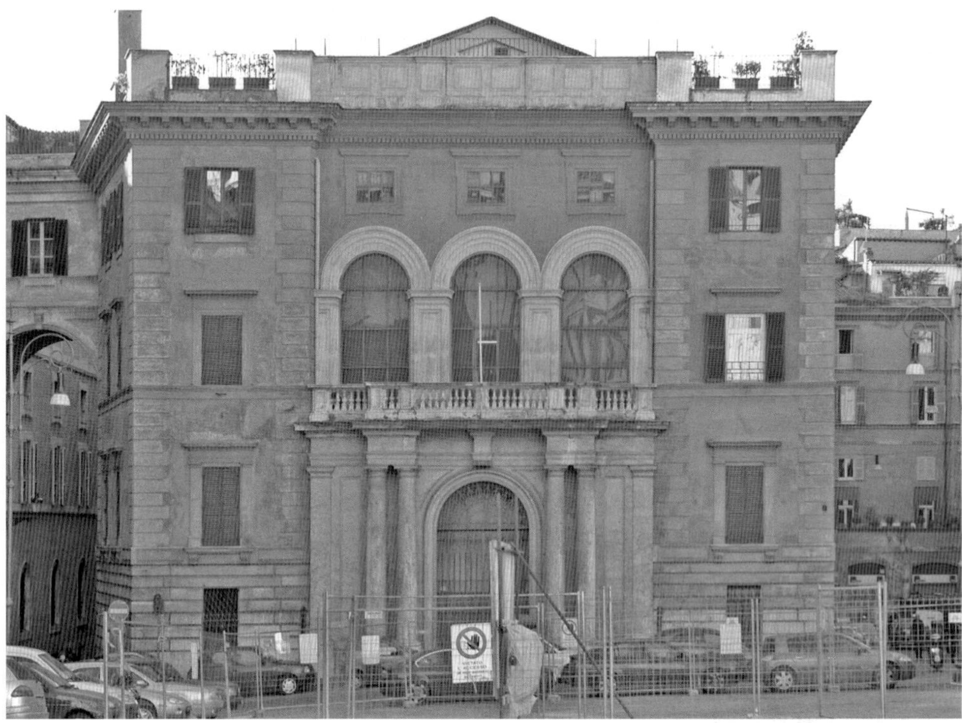

Fig. 5.1. Rome, Palace of the Pontificio Istituto Biblico ('Pilotta palace') from the north. *(Photo: © David R. Marshall 2009.)*

the Stuarts, who occupied it all, and Clement XI spent a certain amount of money refurbishing it to be suitable for its Royal occupants.[10]

The Santi Apostoli palace has its principal façade facing down the Piazza Santi Apostoli. To its left is the palazzo of the Frati Minori Conventuali ('E' in Fig. 5.3, a detail from the plan of Giovanni Battista Nolli), followed by the church of Santi Apostoli (Nolli 283) and Palazzo Colonna (Nolli 281). To its right is the Palazzo Chigi-Odescalchi (Nolli 284), which in 1747 was owned by the Odescalchi, Dukes of Bracciano. At first sight, the logical place for the Stuart temporary façade would be here, as it is the main façade of the palazzo occupied by James. Yet the façade shown in the painting clearly would not have fitted, as the actual façade is narrow — only three bays wide — and proportionately tall. Moreover, there are good political reasons why it would be unsuitable. The Piazza dei Santi Apostoli was the site of the temporary structures erected to celebrate the ceremony known as the

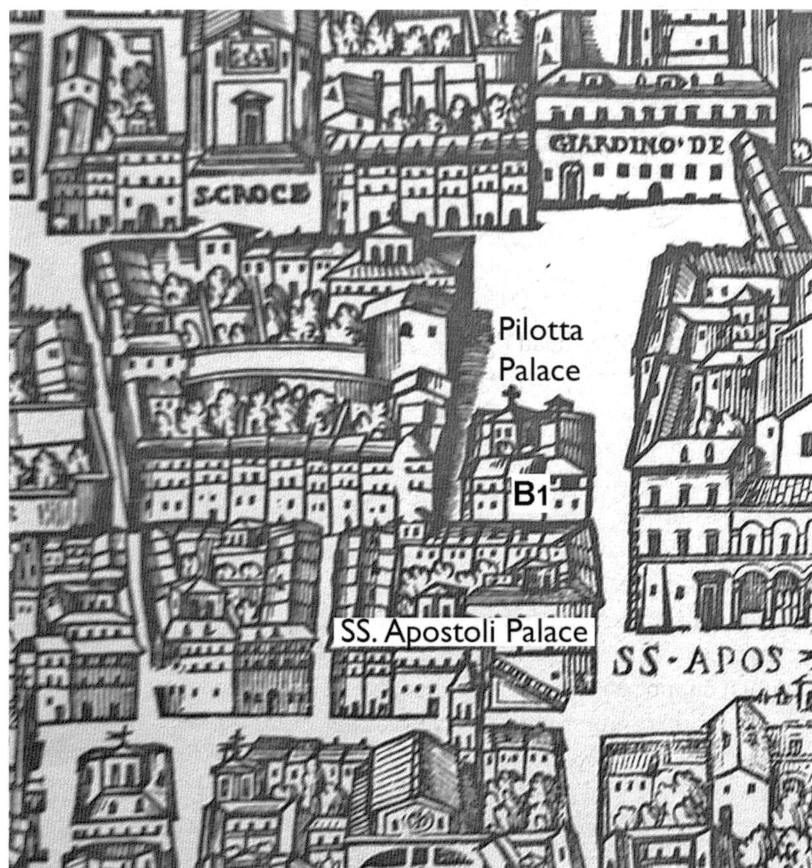

Fig. 5.2. Giovanni Maggi (1566–1618), *Perspective Plan of Rome*, 1625. Detail, Santi Apostoli palace. *(Photo: David R. Marshall.)*

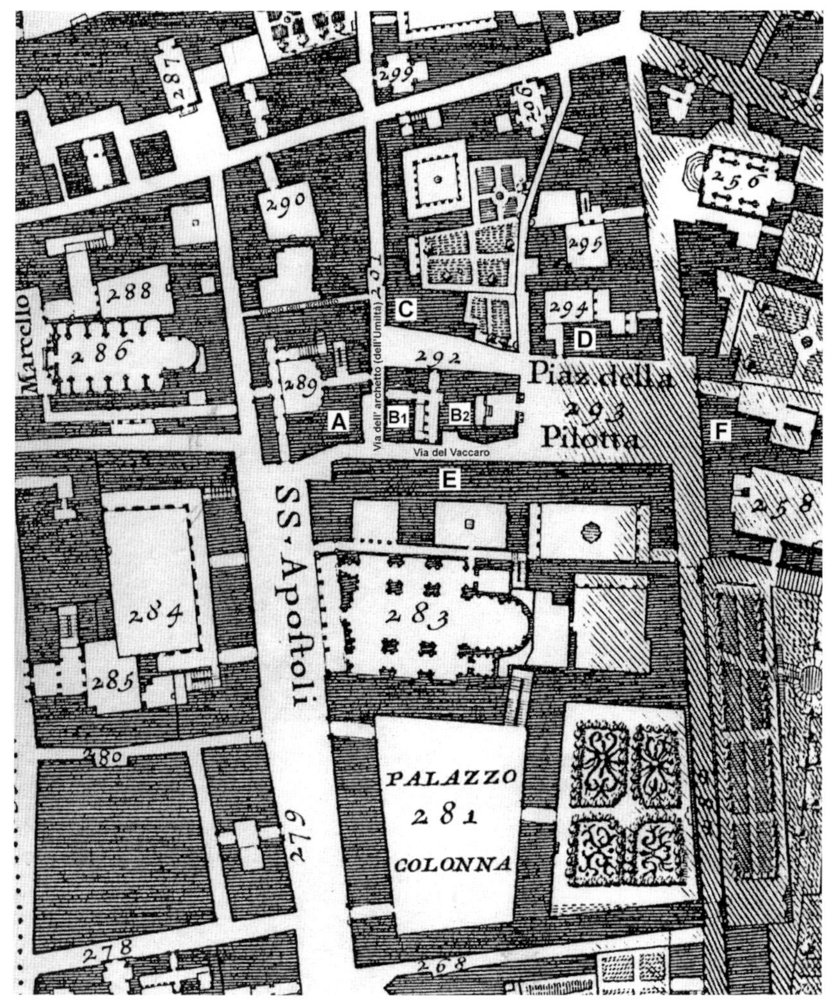

FIG. 5.3. Giovanni Battista Nolli (*c.* 1692/1701–1756), *Plan of Rome*, 1748. Detail of the area around Santi Apostoli, with labelling by the author. *(Photo: © David R. Marshall, 2009.)*

Chinea, in which the head of the Colonna family, who was hereditary Constable of the Kingdom of Naples, paid a tribute on behalf of the King of Naples to the papacy on the Feast of Saints Peter and Paul (28–9 June). In fact, the *Chinea* was celebrated here two weeks before the Stuart festival. Since the Piazza dei Santi Apostoli was dominated ceremonially by the Colonna and the Bourbon King of Naples, Charles III, it would have been problematic for the Stuarts to have muscled in on their territory, even though the Colonna supported them.[11]

The façade of the Pilotta palace, facing Piazza della Pilotta, was, however, not associated with temporary festivities (Nolli 292, 'B' in Fig. 5.3). In 1747 it had on one side the convent of Santa Maria dell'Umiltà ('C') and the Palazzo Ciogni ('D'), and on the other side the palazzo of the Frati Minori Conventuali ('E'). At the far end of the piazza was the Palazzetto Colonna (Nolli 258, 'F'), destroyed to make way for the Gregorian University in the 1920s.

The façade on the Pilotta palace facing the piazza is five bays wide, and has the right proportions for the temporary façade (Fig. 5.1). This façade, however, has been altered, most of all in 1909 when the building was adapted for use by the Istituto Biblico. What was it like in 1747? According to Angela Negro, the Pilotta palace was constructed in two phases, the older part at the back facing Via dell'Archetto, which runs between the Santi Apostoli and Pilotta palaces (Fig. 5.3, 'B1'), and the newer built by Mattia de' Rossi in the later seventeenth century oriented to Piazza della Pilotta (Fig. 5.3, 'B2'). In old maps and bird's eye views it looks like the greater part of the building had been here for some time (Fig. 5.2), so that de' Rossi's project would have involved building two wings into the Piazza della Pilotta to form the courtyard visible in the Nolli plan. Certainly the building line along the Santi Apostoli façade implies a complex earlier history.[12]

Negro dated the remodelled front of the building to *c.* 1660 on the basis of the frescoes attributed to Giovanni Francesco Grimaldi and others in the gallery on the *piano nobile* on the north side of the courtyard, which are linked to a Muti Papazzurri marriage in 1660. Yet the small bird's eye view by Giovanni Battista Falda of 1667 (the 'small Falda') still shows an irregular Piazza della Pilotta façade, while that of 1676, the 'large Falda' (Fig. 5.4), shows the remodelled palazzo, with the courtyard, screen wall and parapet statues clearly shown. The bulk of the rear of the building has been contracted, shifting attention to the front, presumably because, being new, it was more important. The Falda maps imply limiting dates for this new construction of 1667–76, but it is possible that the small Falda was not up to date. We have a good representation of the Piazza della Pilotta façade as it was in 1699 in an engraving by Alessandro Specchi of 1699 (Fig. 5.5).

Is this, then, where the temporary Stuart façade went, as the literature has begun to assume?[13] In

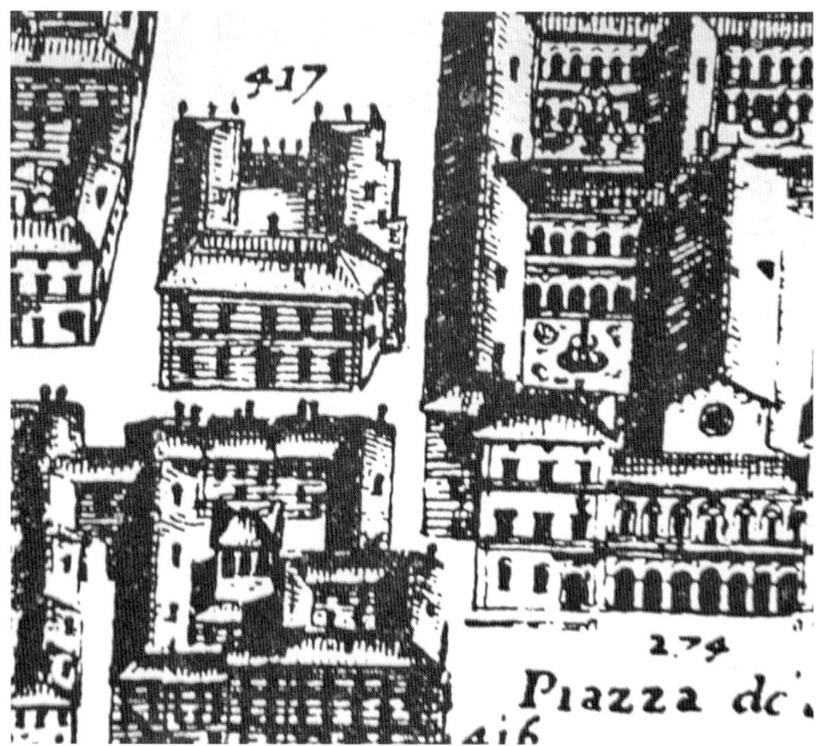

Fig. 5.4. Giovanni Battista Falda (1640s–1678), *Perspective Plan of Rome* ('the large Falda'), 1676, detail of the Pilotta palace. *(Photo: David R. Marshall.)*

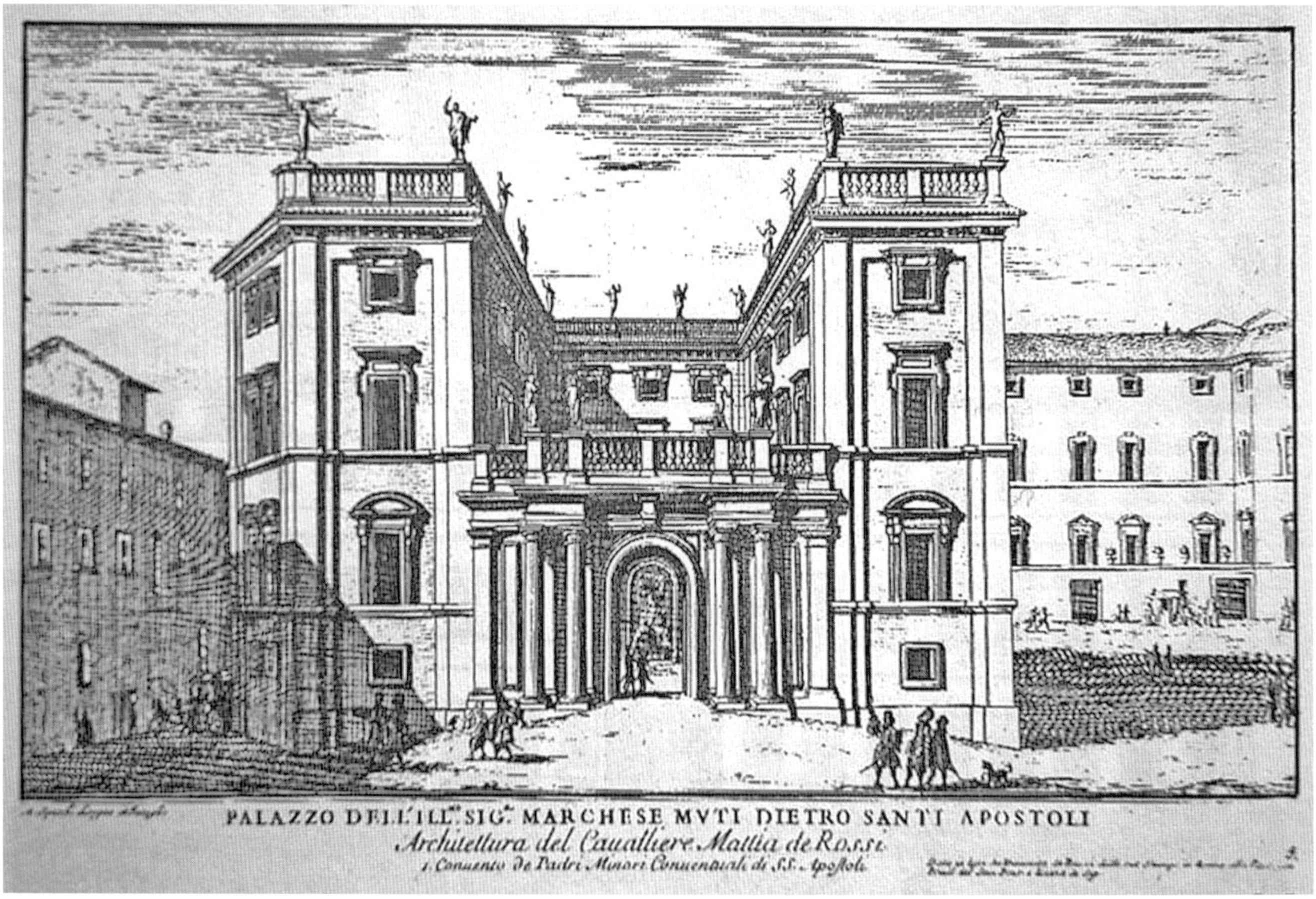

Fig. 5.5. Alessandro Specchi (1668–1729), *Palazzo dell'Ill.mo Sig.r Marchese Muti dietro Santi Apostoli*, 1699. Engraving. *(Photo: David R. Marshall.)*

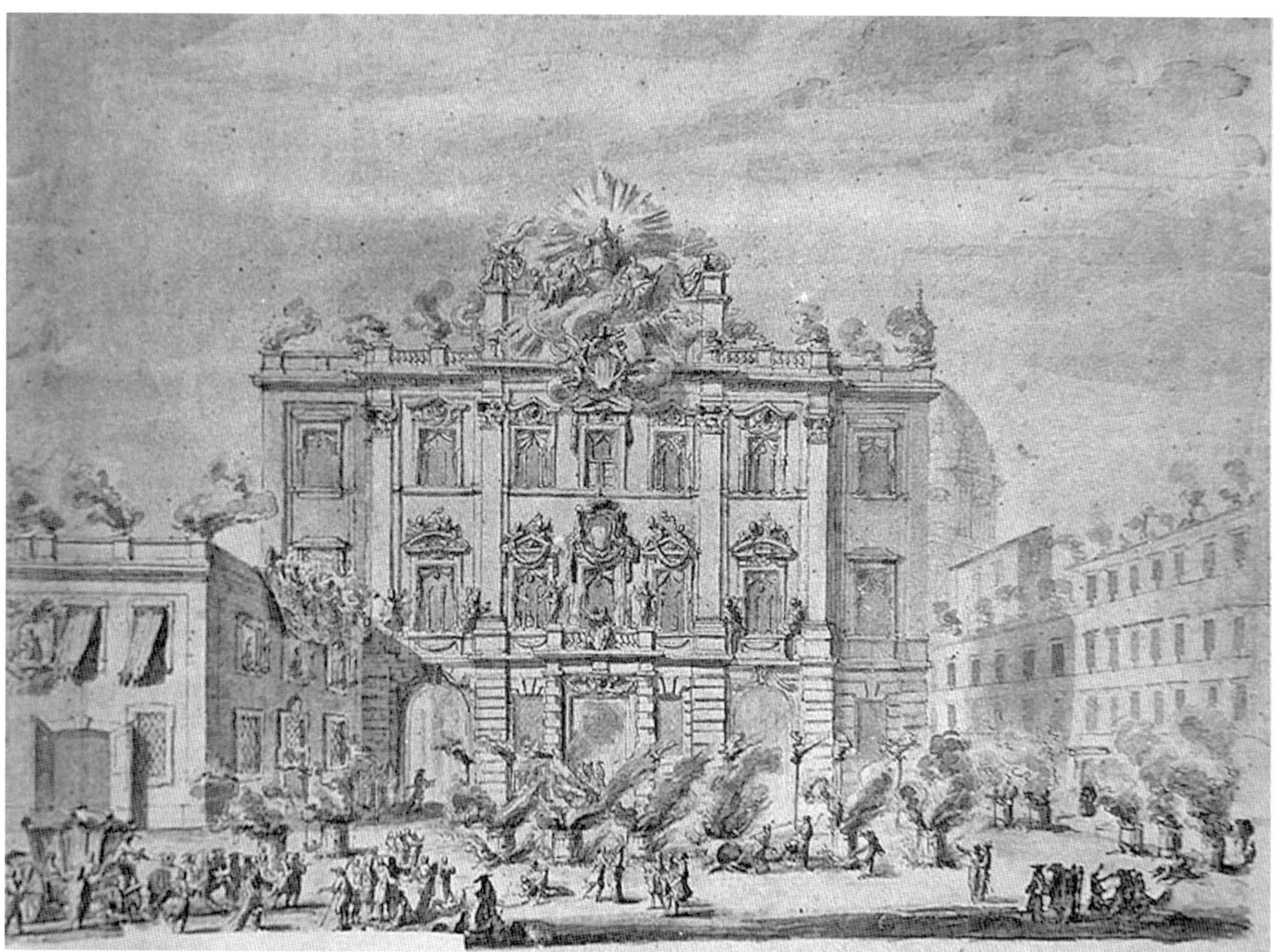

FIG. 5.6. Carlo Marchionni (1702–86), *Festa for the Nomination as Cardinal of Carlo Vittorio Amedeo delle Lanze*, 1747. Drawing. Rome, Istituto Nazionale della Grafica, FN 8847. *(Photo: Istituto Nazionale della Grafica. Reproduced with the kind permission of the Ministero per i Beni e le Attività Culturali.)*

order to resolve the issue we need to be aware that the painting in Edinburgh is a fiction on several levels. As a painting it is necessarily a fiction; and what it purports to represent was a temporary fiction; moreover, the palace that lay behind it has since changed. In order to negotiate these layers of illusion, it is useful to have some comparative data about what we might expect the relationship between a temporary façade and the building it covers to be like.

Such comparative data is ready to hand. Henry Benedict was created cardinal on Benedict XIV's third creation, which was for York alone (rather than a group, as was usual), on 3 July 1747; and his temporary façade was begun five days later, on 8 July, and finished on 25 July. Some months earlier, on 10 April 1747, Carlo Vittorio Amedeo delle Lanze was created cardinal by Benedict XIV, along with ten others.[14] Delle Lanze was in Turin at the time, so his *festa* was delayed until after his arrival in Rome shortly before 11 July, and was held on Saturday 22 July. It consisted of a temporary façade erected on the Palazzo della Valle, which delle Lanze was renting. In short, the two ephemeral façades are exactly contemporary, both celebrate elevations to the purple, and both were decorations of the façades of rented palaces.

Cardinal delle Lanze's façade was designed by Carlo Marchionni, and is recorded in an autograph drawing (Fig. 5.6).[15] That this was erected on the rear façade of the Palazzo della Valle is self-evident, as this façade has changed little since the eighteenth century. To judge from the rooflines today (Fig. 5.7), the Palazzo della Valle is composed of at least four *case*, but this rear façade was never regularized by a major Renaissance or Baroque refacing. Marchionni's façade thus provided, albeit temporarily, what the rear of Palazzo della Valle desperately needed: a proper façade.

There is a straightforward relationship between the façade we see today and that drawn by Marchionni.

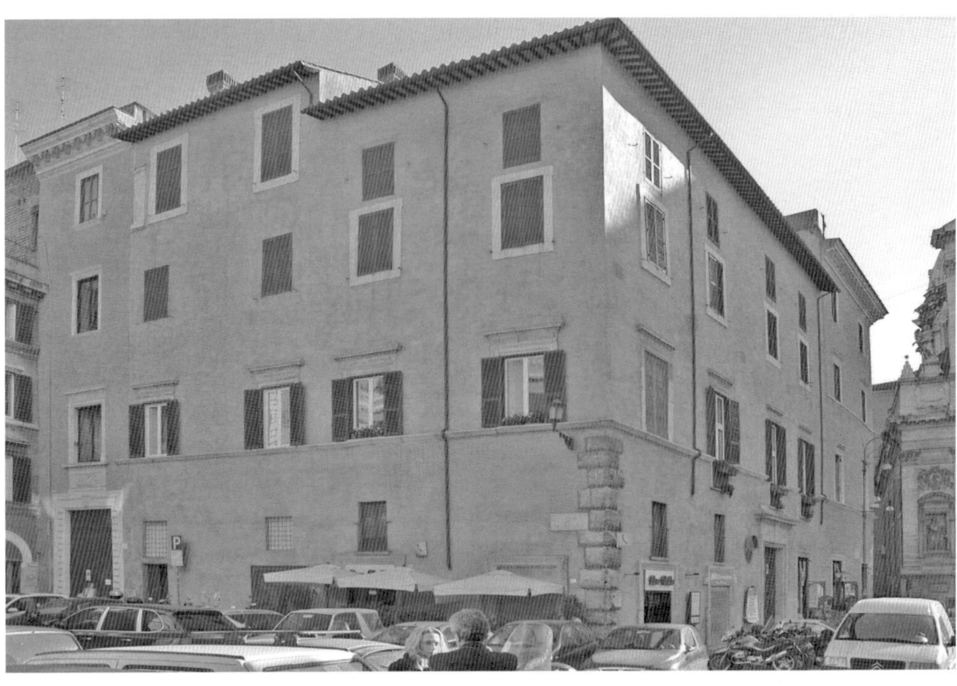

FIG. 5.7. Rome, Palazzo delle Valle, rear façade. *(Photo: © David R. Marshall 2009.)*

The low building that overlaps the first bay of the façade is still there, though it has acquired two additional floors. The second bay contains the entrance to the *cortile*, which passes through to the main façade on the Via Papale (now Corso Vittorio Emmanuele II). In the temporary façade it consequently functions as an entrance. The next component building has two vertical columns of windows with a space between, equivalent to the three central bays of Marchionni's façade, which explains why they are grouped so tightly in the drawing. The next building contains two more bays, and there are corresponding bays in Marchionni's façade.

Marchionni's façade steps forward in three planes. The rearmost plane was presumably created with a wooden frame attached directly to the wall surface to which a canvas fictive façade was attached. The stepping-out of the next two planes was presumably

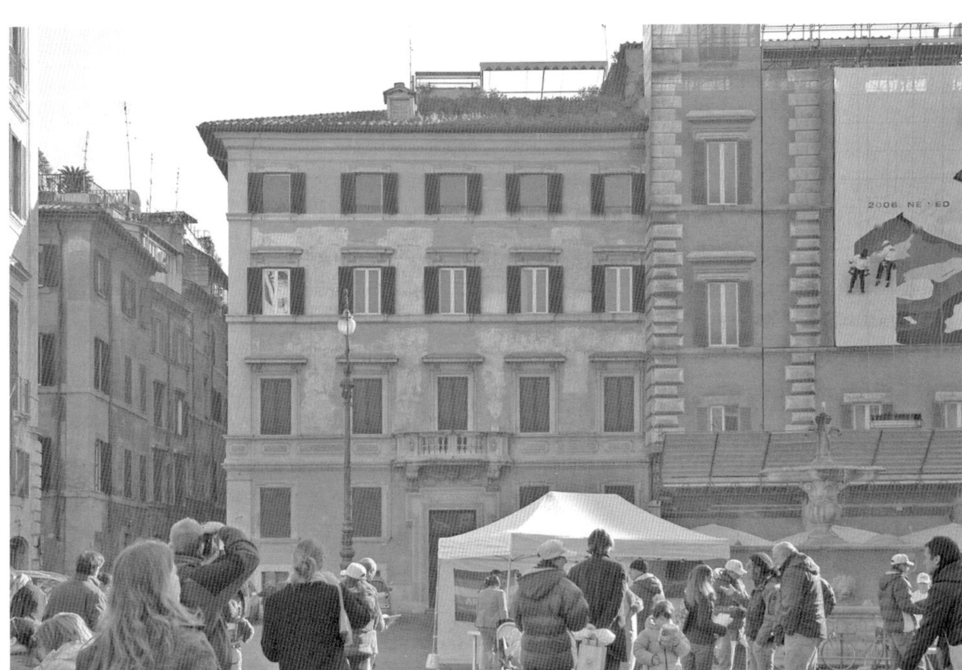

FIG. 5.8. Advertisement forming a temporary façade in the Piazza Farnese, 2006. *(Photo: © David R. Marshall, 2009.)*

real, implying a more elaborate scaffolding-like structure, although how deep the projections were cannot be established from the drawing, which might well exaggerate effects of relief. We can get a sense of what was going on by the temporary façades that are erected today on buildings under restoration, which have photographs of the building underneath printed onto fabric (Fig. 5.8). These usually bear advertisements: the difference is that in the eighteenth century the façade *was* the advertisement, whereas today the advertisement is inserted clumsily into the fictive façade and competes with it.

In the Palazzo della Valle the string-course found today at the base of the *piano nobile* windows probably corresponded to the base of the windows shown in Marchionni's drawing. The outermost of these windows may have functioned as real windows, from which people inside the palace could look out, as we see them looking out from the window of the bay to the left of centre, which, like its counterpart on the other side, also might have continued to function, but through the additional depth created by the temporary façade. There is no window today in the central bay, but the balcony in front of it, on which Marchionni placed figures, presumably would have been reached by a kind of gallery made possible by the separation of the projecting central sections of the fictive façade from the wall of the palace. Marchionni's fictive *piano nobile* windows are taller and grander than the Renaissance windows of the actual palace, while the wildly irregular second-floor windows abandon any attempt to correspond to the actual windows on the upper levels.

The dome of Sant'Andrea della Valle shown in the drawing behind and to the right of the façade, although not visible when the façade is viewed frontally in the confined space of the piazza, is placed in the correct topographical relationship to the palazzo (cf. Fig. 5.7, where Sant'Andrea della Valle is just visible at the right). Drawings like these were constructed, rather than being quasi-photographic views taken from a fixed point. In this case it is built around an elevation of the façade, to which topographical indicators have been added. Because these additions exist to situate a constructed elevation in a real place, we have every reason to expect a reasonable degree of topographical accuracy from such additions: the users of the drawing would have expected these buildings to be recognizable. Hence the buildings at the right, though now gone, were probably something like this, as the carriage house at the left would have been, since it clearly does not partake of the façade fiction.

If we now return to the Stuart ephemeral decoration and the Piazza della Pilotta façade of the Pilotta palace, the two do not correspond in the same neat way. Aligning the façades vertically, the overall height of the fictive façade comes out too low (Fig. 5.9). Aligning them horizontally, the fictive façade extends too far laterally, with no space for the structure on the inside and too much on the outside (Fig. 5.10). If we assume that the artist got the proportions wrong and stretch it vertically, it can be made to fit overall, but the second-floor windows do not correspond with the fictive windows, which, on the basis of the Palazzo della Valle façade, we might expect them to do.

What emerges from these experiments is the fact that, whatever we do, the grand portal of the real building, designed by Specchi, extends well above the basement and plinth levels of the fictive building. This, like the real building, shows a recessed bay, but one that is only one bay deep, not the two deep bays shown in Nolli's plan. In the painting some of the most significant decoration, including the coats of arms, is placed at the back of this recess. If this corresponded to the back of the courtyard, these features would not have been visible from the ground unless the viewer were a long way back in the piazza. For them to be fully visible the recess of the fictive façade would have had to have been as shallow as it appears, which means that the back of this recess would have to be physically in front of the portal. In other words, if the fictive façade went on the Pilotta façade, it must have been a U-shaped temporary structure of quite significant depth, erected against the front of the façade, and hiding it completely. Such a structure would indicate a quite different approach from that adopted at the Palazzo della Valle. Whereas the latter made economical use of the existing form of the façade, here the façade would have been much more expensive, and have denied the façade behind while at the same time representing its U-shaped form when it could have taken almost any form.

If we look at the surrounding buildings there are further difficulties. The buildings on either side do not make sense as topographical indicators. The building at the right corresponds to the Palazzo Ciogni, but appears to be a convent, not a palace, as there are nuns at the window. The space glimpsed beyond it could be construed as a loose representation of the extension of the Piazza della Pilotta down the side of the Pilotta palace, but it doesn't work very well. On the left, the situation is even worse. Here there is, and always has been, a continuous wall

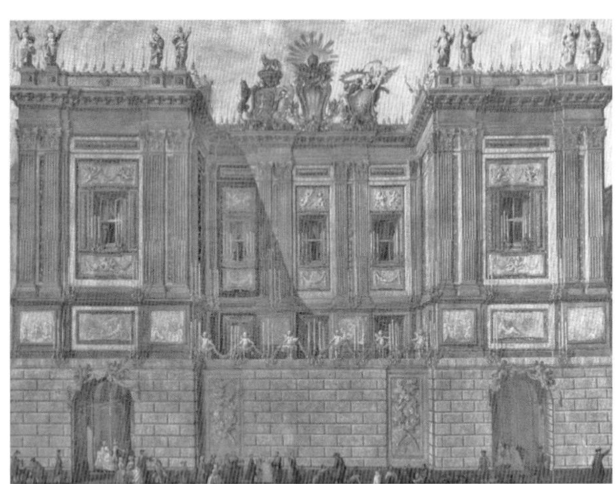

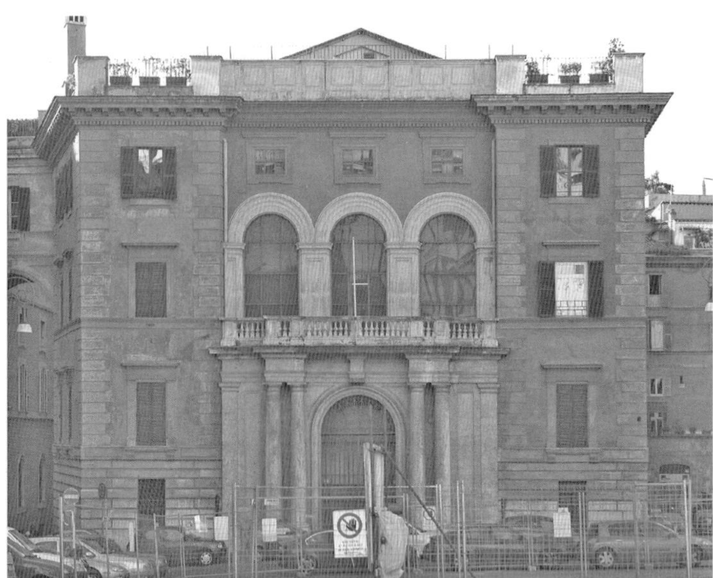

With the outer edges of the temporary facade aligned vertically (right) the temporary facade is too low to cover the real facade (top)

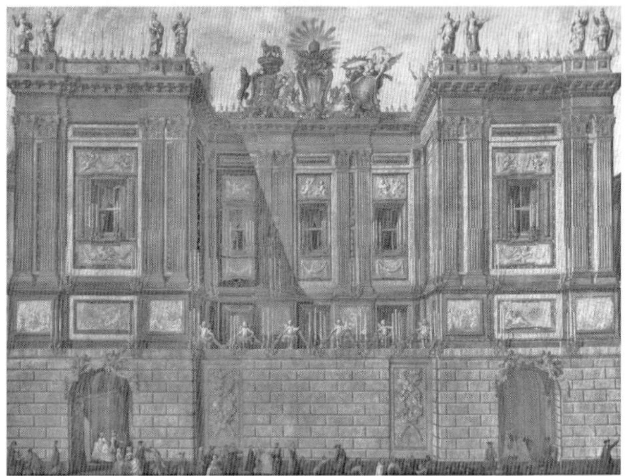

Fig. 5.9. Façade of the Pilotta palace compared to *Prince James Receiving His Son, Prince Henry, in Front of the Palazzo del Re* (Plate 5.1), aligned vertically. *(Photo: © David R. Marshall, 2009.)*

along Via del Vaccaro from the Piazza dei Santi Apostoli to Via della Pilotta: the outer wall of the palazzo of the Frati Minori Conventuali. There was no piazza in the position shown by the painter, as we can see from Specchi's engraving (Fig. 5.5).

These observations leave only two possible conclusions. The first is that the temporary façade was a free-standing structure that fully screened the Piazza della Pilotta façade and that the painter has not attempted to surround it with the topographical indicators usual in such representations. The second is that we have got it all wrong, and the façade did not go here at all.

We have already ruled out the Piazza Santi Apostoli façade of the Santi Apostoli palace. Are there any other options?

The answer is provided by Chracas. He described the temporary façade as being 'affixed to his Royal Palazzo, specifically on the part opposite Palazzo Muti'.[16] At first sight, this description seems confusing, if we consider both palazzi to have constituted the Stuart royal palace. But the *Stati d'anime*, the Easter parish censuses, at this period identify the Santi Apostoli palace as the 'Palazzo del Rè', and the Piazza della Pilotta palace as the 'Palazzo Muti'; indeed, the latter was still occupied in part by the Muti. Hence Chracas is referring to a façade of the Santi Apostoli palace opposite the Pilotta palace. The only part of the Santi Apostoli palace that fits this description is the façade along the Via dell'Archetto, which separates the two palazzi.

Can we, then, fit the temporary façade here? Using the same principles employed before, we can begin

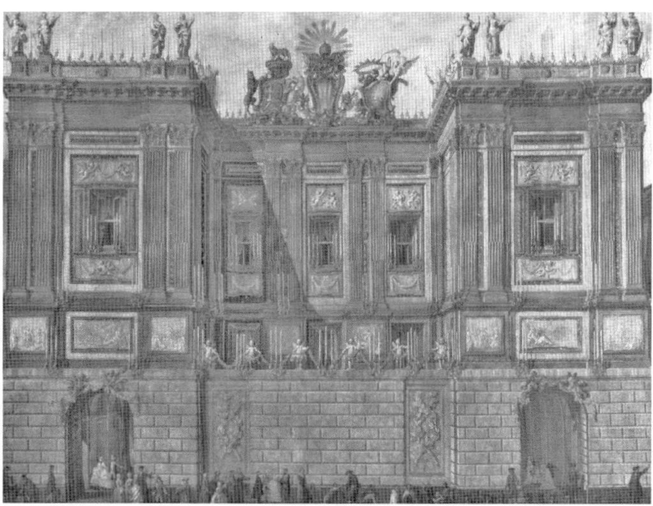

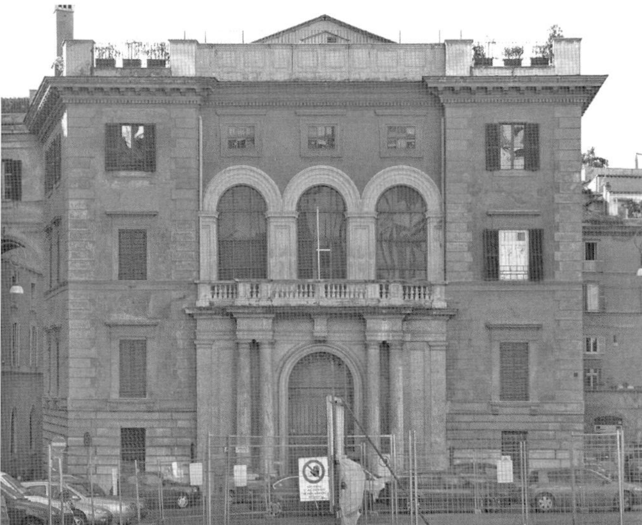

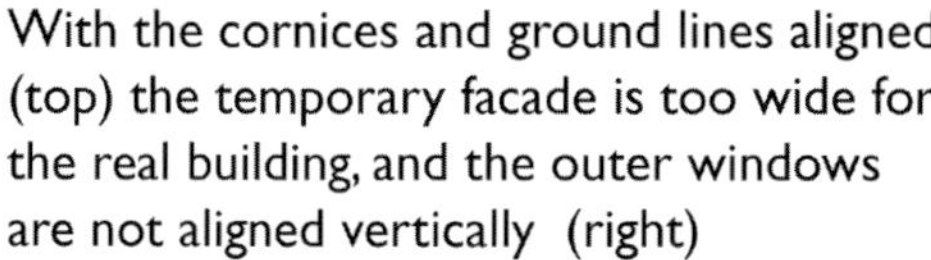

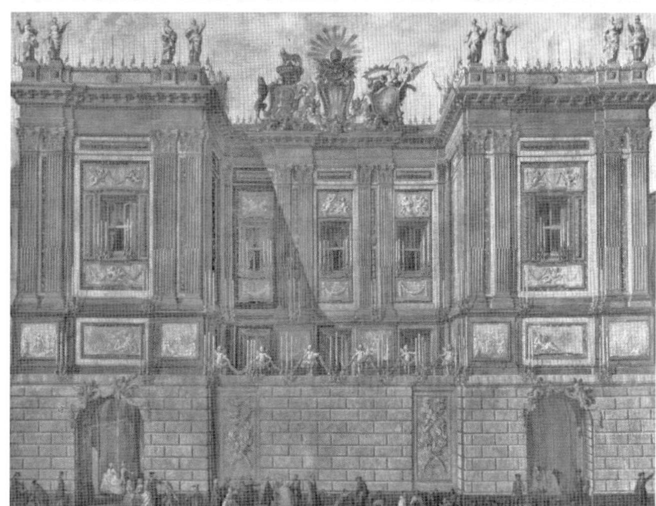

FIG. 5.10. Façade of the Pilotta palace compared to *Prince James Receiving His Son, Prince Henry, in Front of the Palazzo del Re* (PLATE 5.1), aligned horizontally. *(Photo: © David R. Marshall, 2009.)*

by aligning the horizontal elements, beginning with the ground level and the top cornice of the recess (Fig. 5.11). If we do this, it turns out that the top of the terrace aligns with the top of the fictive basement, the top of the first tier of windows aligns with the top of the first tier of widows in the painting, and the top of the third tier of windows aligns with the top of the *piano nobile* windows in the painting. Keeping the size of the painting the same, we can now look at the vertical alignments. If we align the corner of the projection with the left edge of the right wing of the painting, the first three columns of windows align, more or less, with the windows in the recess in the painting. I say more or less, because the real windows are not regular in their spacing, the centre column being shifted to the left (Fig. 5.11).

These correspondences are too consistent for them to be by chance. In particular, the existing structure explains the high plinth, as well as the shallow depth of the recess. If we now look at a photomontage (Plate 5.2), we see a view of the *palazzo* at the end of the piazza, with the side bays partially obscured. Moving closer to the façade, these bays would have come into view.

Looking at what happens in the parts that are out of sight, it is possible to align the façade with Nolli's plan (Fig. 5.12). It would make sense for the façade to run from the Vicolo dell'Archetto at the right to the corner where the façade breaks at the left.[17] The central bay would correspond to the width of the piazza, and the left fictive passageway would correspond to the real passageway, just as it

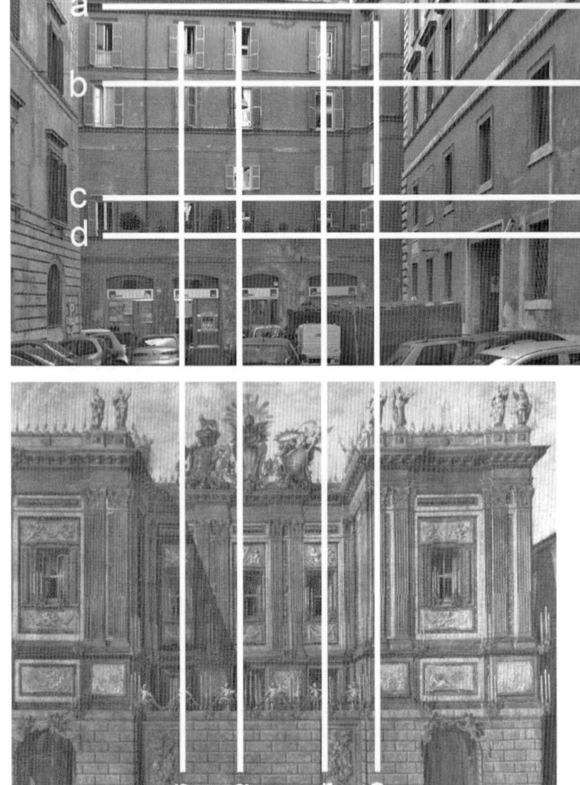

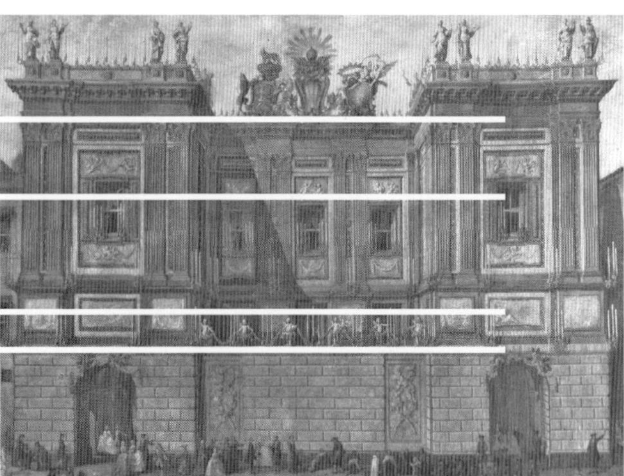

FIG. 5.11. Rear façade of the Santi Apostoli palace compared to *Prince James Receiving His Son, Prince Henry, in Front of the Palazzo del Re* (PLATE 5.1), aligned vertically and horizontally. *(Photo: © David R. Marshall, 2009.)*

did in Marchionni's façade. This makes for a rather large façade, but not impossibly so, and with rather more of the side wings obscured that in the earlier photomontage.

If we now look at the surroundings, the problems we faced with placing the temporary façade on the Pilotta façade dissolve (**Plate 5.2**). The road leading to the left and right is the Via dell'Archetto. The narrow alley at right angles is the Vicolo dell'Archetto. The plain façade to the left is the rest of the Via dell'Archetto façade of the Santi Apostoli palace. The troublesome buildings on either side now make sense. The building at the right, with the nuns, is the convent of the Umiltà. This façade today has two upper levels of windows above a broad string-course, with two tiers of windows below, which corresponds as far as the basic forms are concerned, if we allow the painter a tendency to heighten the lowest zone. The rustication of the corner on the ground floor is the same, although that on the upper part is simpler. In the painting, though, there are two round-headed windows in the upper storeys of the second bays. These look like windows at the end of corridors of conventual buildings, such as the Servite monastery at the back of San Marcello on the other side. The view by Falda (**Fig. 5.4**), and an eighteenth-century view of uncertain date published by Edward Corp,[18] however, show a palace-type building, which indeed it was. It was the original Ciogni palace that was acquired by the Dominican convent of Santa Maria dell'Umiltà in 1735–7 in exchange for the building further up.[19] There was building work along this line a little further up in 1737, and possibly the nuns made the changes we see here, though the absence of any trace of them in

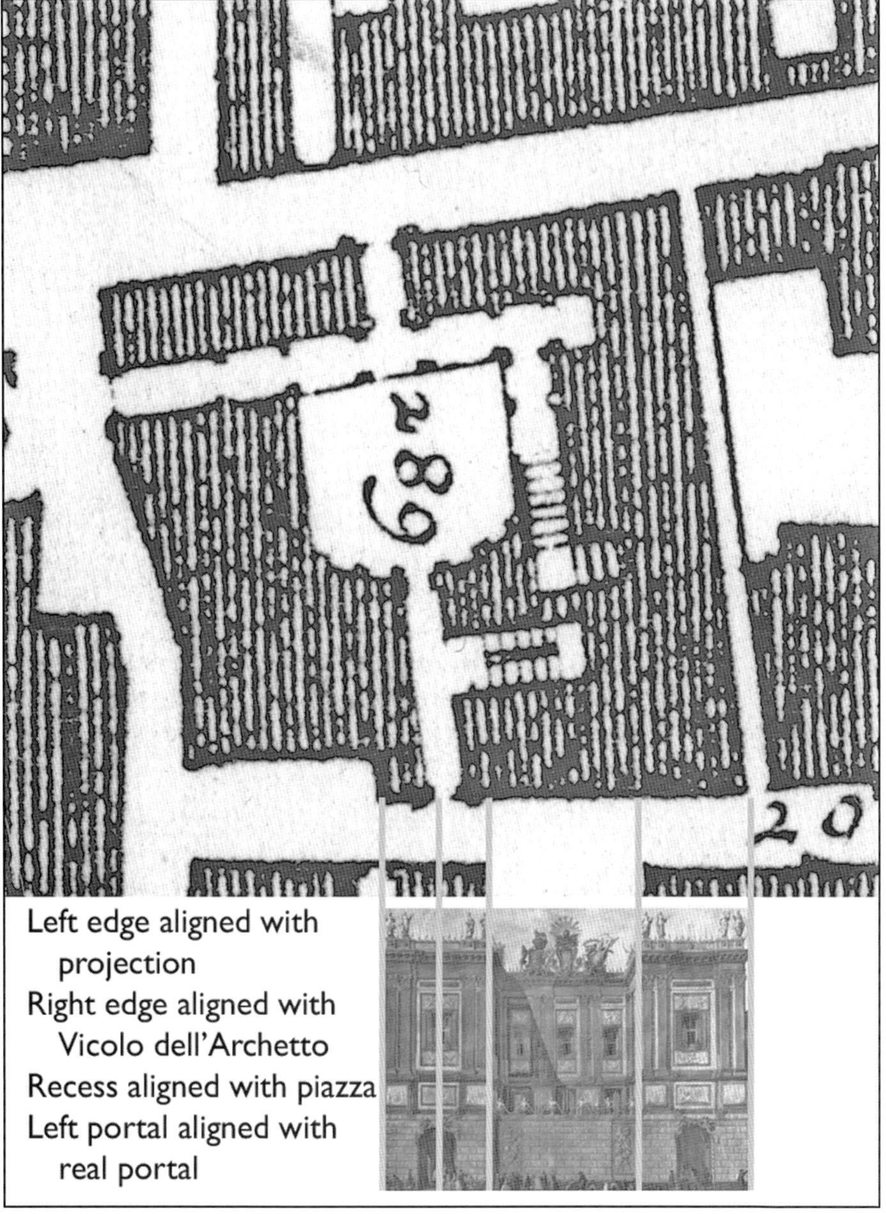

FIG. 5.12. Photomontage of *Prince James Receiving His Son, Prince Henry, in Front of the Palazzo del Re* (PLATE 5.1) with the rear façade of the Santi Apostoli palace in relation to Nolli's plan. *(Photo: © David R. Marshall, 2009.)*

these old views or in the fenestration of the building today forces me to conclude, somewhat reluctantly, that in this respect the painter is not correct topographically.[20]

The building on the other side of the piazza in the painting is, as we have seen, a palazzo, and can now be recognized as the southwest corner of the Pilotta palace. Today this has a top-storey window, a more noble second-storey window on a string-course, and a *piano nobile* window, all of which are found in basic form in the painting. The lowest zone in the painting, though, is again exaggerated in height compared to the actual building, with a mezzanine window.

In short, the buildings in the painting correspond well enough to the basic forms of the buildings today, which would go back to the eighteenth century and earlier, even allowing for subsequent remodellings.

CONCLUSIONS

There are a number of conclusions that can be drawn from this investigation. The first is that the examples of the façades of the Palazzo della Valle and Palazzo Muti Papazzurri (Santi Apostoli palace) show that they were intended not to compete with monumental façades, but to complement them. Hence they were erected on undistinguished parts of the building. Second, such façades took their cue from, and made best use of, the form of the façade that presented itself to the architect. Third, and the corollary of the first two, is that such façades were economical in construction. The greater part of both façades could have been created by canvases attached to simple frameworks attached directly to the wall, with only some parts being built as free-standing structures. Fourth, the ceremonial territory of the Stuarts was this side arm of the Piazza della Pilotta, which one is tempted to name, without historical justification, 'Piazza Stuard'.

INTERPRETATION

This now enables us to interpret the Stuart façade more fully. To begin with, it was no more elaborate than that for Cardinal delle Lanze; indeed, physically, it was quite similar. The nature of the response to these façades is indicated by Chracas. Chracas's description focuses on enumerating the design, which is understood primarily in terms of the fictive marbles of which it was composed. The same is true of the delle Lanze façade, even though Marchionni's drawing gives no indications of the materials. Chracas also described the response of the public. It is worth comparing his accounts of the two *feste*.

For delle Lanze he wrote:

> The invention and design of so magnificent a work was by the Architect Carlo Marchionni, and the paintings were by Signor Antonio Bicchieriari. They knew how to express the Lordly idea of His Eminence, so that deservedly they received much praise, and with the Cardinal received great applause for this, one of the most beautiful, majestic, and noble [works] yet seen, and a representation of great distinctiveness.[21]

For Cardinal York's temporary festival apparatus he wrote:

> The architect and inventor of so magnificent a structure was Signor Clemente Orlandi Romano, who beside having expressed so well the Royal soul of the Cardinal, has received great applause.[22]

Delle Lanze's façade gets a longer and more enthusiastic account than Cardinal York's. In both, though, the façade is said to express in some way the nature of the person it celebrates; in Cardinal York's case it is his 'Royal soul' (*animo Regio*). But to what extent does it express his ideas about architecture? In order to explore this idea further, we need to try to unravel the factors that conditioned the design. One is the physical site, which we have considered already: it seems to have dictated one projecting wing, and therefore the other wing, the recessed centre, and the basement.

The second factor is the architect. Clemente Orlandi was a Roman architect who emerged under the Corsini, and worked for Alessandro Galilei on the Lateran.[23] His style, as demonstrated by his considerably later church of San Paolo Primo Eremita (1767–75), owes much to Bernini. He was, therefore, an embodiment of the tendency sometimes called 'late Baroque classicism'. Galilei had worked in England, but this connection is unlikely to be of much relevance, as he worked mainly for Whigs, which would not have recommended him to the Stuarts. More significant is the connection with papal patronage through the work with the Corsini Lateran project.

The third factor is, of course, the input of Cardinal York and James III. If the façade was seen by Chracas to respond, in some way, to York's 'Royal soul', the Stuarts must have been thinking along the same lines. So was this façade seen by them to be Roman; something that befitted a cardinal of the Roman Catholic church? Or did they see it as something quintessentially royal, which, for a family that had spent 26 years in France, would mean Versailles? Probably the latter: the rusticated lower storey with a pilaster order on the *piano nobile* is broadly similar to Jules Hardouin-Mansart's *Enveloppe* at the palace at Versailles, not to mention other Royal palaces, such as Inigo Jones's designs for Whitehall Palace or Filippo Juvarra's for the Royal Palace in Madrid. And Orlandi's colour harmonies seem richer and more gilded than those of the Marchionni project, which, to judge by the description, seem to be somewhat cooler and more subtle.

ATTRIBUTION

Finally, who painted the picture (Plate 5.1)? Architectural paintings are often difficult to attribute, as the technique can be quite anonymous sometimes, and there are not many names to play with. Panini can be ruled out, although there are connections with his style.[24] Whereas in the case of the Palazzo della Valle façade Chracas mentioned both the architect who designed the whole and the painter who painted the figurative components, in the case of the Stuart façade he only mentioned the architect. Given that Orlandi designed stucco reliefs for San Marco, it

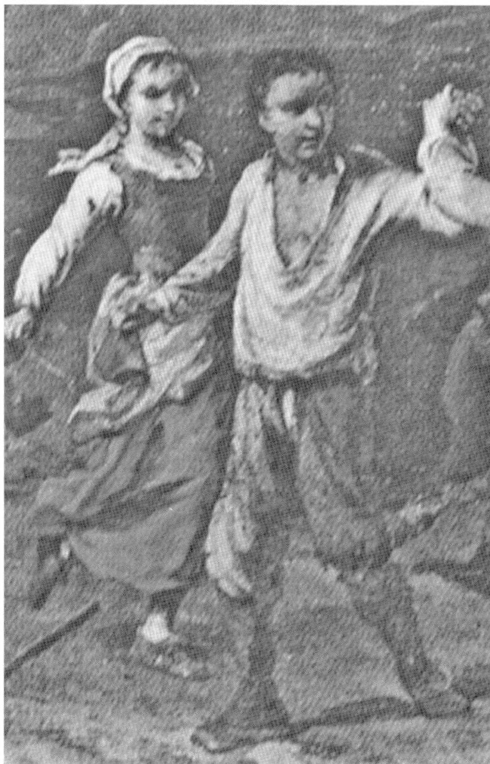
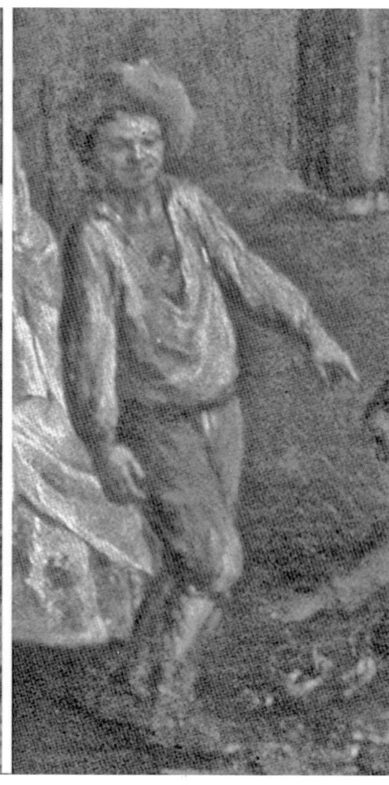

FIG. 5.13. *Bamboccianti* figures in *Prince James Receiving His Son, Prince Henry, in Front of the Palazzo del Re* (PLATE 5.1) (left), compared to a detail of Paolo Anesi (*c.* 1700–*c.* 1769) (landscape) and Paolo Monaldi (1720–99) (figures), *Fantasy Landscape in Lazio with the Saltarello*. Milan, Alemagna Collection. After A. Busiri Vici, *Trittico paesistico romano del '700: Paolo Anessi, Paolo Monaldi, Alessio De Marchis* (Rome, 1976), figs 112, 138. *(Reproduced courtesy of Ugo Bozzi Editore.)*

seems that his skills extended to the more graphic arts, so that he may have designed both the architecture and the painted reliefs. It is possible that he, or an artist under his direction, was responsible for the painting as well: some of Panini's projects for temporary festivals involved both designing the *festa* and producing a depiction of it.

The painter of the architecture need not have been responsible for the figures. There seem to be two hands involved: the nobler figures are undistinguished, but the *bamboccianti*-style figures are more distinctive, with dark, smoky modelling. One of these, a woman seen from the back, is based on an engraving by Edme Jeaurat after Nicolas Vleughels of 1734.[25] One possible, albeit speculative, identification of this hand is Paolo Monaldi.The cheeky boy with the loose shirt recalls a dancing peasant in the *Fantasy Landscape in Lazio with the Saltarello* (Fig. 5.13)[26] painted for the Villa Chigi in Via Salaria in collaboration with Paolo Anesi, who did the landscapes. Monaldi's work at the Villa Chigi dates from 1767, and his earliest dated work dates from 1753, so that if these figures are indeed by Monaldi they would be among his earliest works. This is not impossible: he was born *c.* 1724 and would have been 23 in 1747, old enough to have developed a style similar to that which he was employing twenty years later.

NOTES

1. *Prince James Receiving His Son, Prince Henry, in Front of the Palazzo del Re*, *c.* 1747. Oil on canvas, 195.58 × 297.18 cm (framed: 226.00 × 330.00 cm). Edinburgh, Scottish National Portrait Gallery, accession no. PG 3269. Purchased with the support of the Heritage Lottery Fund and The Art Fund 2001. See also G. Coccioli, 'Festa per la nomina di Enrico Benedetto Stuart, duca di York', in M. Fagiolo, *Corpus delle feste a Roma* II. *Il Settecento e l'Ottocento* (Rome, 1997), 138–9; G. Sestieri, *Repertorio della pittura romana della fine del Seicento e del Settecento* (Turin, 1994), fig. 847; and E. Corp, *The King over the Water: Portraits of the Stuarts in Exile after 1689* (Edinburgh, 2001).
2. G. Evans, 'The acquisition of Stuart silver and other relics by the Dukes of Hamilton', in E. Corp (ed.), *The Stuart Court in Rome. The Legacy of Exile* (Aldershot, 2003), 131–48, esp. pp. 139–40. It was bought by William, 11th Duke of Hamilton, in 1845 from Robert Macpherson, who moved to Rome in 1840–1 and became its leading photographer. He offered the painting to Hamilton in a letter dated 29 August 1845. Macpherson had purchased it from 'Macbean the Banker in Rome', and it had been in the Villa Arrigoni-Muti at Frascati.
3. See Corp, above, p. 49, nn. 58, 60.
4. See Corp, above, p. 49, text to n. 59.
5. A. Negro, *Guide rionali di Roma. Rione II. Trevi. Parte quarta* (Rome, 1992), 102–10.
6. A. Antinori, 'I palazzi Muti Papazzurri nel rione Trevi', in M. Caperna and G. Spagnesi (eds), *Architettura: processualità e*

trasformazione. Atti del convegno internazionale di studi, Roma, 24–27 novembre 1999 (*Quaderni dell'Istituto di Storia dell'Architettura*, 1999–2002, nos. 34–9) (Rome, 2002), 444.

7. In the *Stati d'anime*, the Pilotta palace is described as: 'The Palazzo of the Signori Muti, or *isola minore* of the Signori Muti' (Palazzo de Signori Muti, ò sia isola minore de Signori Muti) (Archivio Vicariato di Roma [henceforth AVR], *Stati d'anime*, Santi Apostoli, 57, 1720, fol. 35v).
8. In the *Stati d'anime* the Santi Apostoli palace is described as: 'The Palazzo of illustrissimo Signor Marchese Giovanni Battista Muti with the whole block, called the *isola maggiore* of the Signori Muti, which surrounds the whole of that palazzo, that is from the alleyway facing the small portico of San Marcello, and returning to the said *vicolo*. This *palazzo* is presently occupied by their Majesties the King and Queen of England with their retinue, together with some apartments beyond the said street, which, however, are united in perfect communication to the aforesaid *isola*' (Palazzo dell' Illustrissimo Sig.r Marchese Gio. Batta. Muti con tutta l'isola, chiamata l'Isola Maggiore de Muti, quale circonda tutto il detto palazzo, cioè dal vicoletto in faccia alla porticella di S. Marcello, e ritornando al detto vicoletto. Qual palazzo presentemente è abitato dalle Maestà del Rè, e Regina d'Inghilterra con la loro fameglia assieme con alcuni appartamenti di là dal detto vicolo, quali però sono uniti con perfetta communicazione alla predetta isola) (AVR, *Stati d'anime*, Santi Apostoli, 57, 1720, fol. 36r).
9. Antinori, 'Palazzi Muti Papazzurri' (above, n. 6), 439–46.
10. R. Pantanella, 'Palazzo Muti a piazza SS. Apostoli residenza degli Stuart a Roma', *Storia dell'Arte* 84 (1995), 307–28.
11. On relations between the Colonna and James III, see E. Ciletti, 'Corsini Rome, regency Florence, and the last Medici facade for San Lorenzo', *Mitteilungen des Kunsthistorisches Museum in Florenz* (1988), 479–518, esp. n. 63 on p. 511.
12. The bird's eye view of Tempesta (1693) shows a simple squarish block with a courtyard.
13. E. Corp, 'Introduction', in Corp, *Stuart Court in Rome* (above, n. 2), 15; and the contribution by Corp to this volume, n. 57.
14. These included Frédéric-Jérôme de la Rochefoucauld de Roye, archbishop of Bourges. Rochefoucauld had a *festa* beginning on the day of his creation in Piazza Farnese, but this involved a free-standing temporary festival apparatus (*macchina*) in Piazza Farnese, and so is not so useful in this context. The others were Álvaro Eugenio de Mendoza Caamaño Sotomayor, patriarch of the West Indies; Daniele Delfino, patriarch of Aquileia; Raniero Felice Simonetti, titular archbishop of Nicosia; Armand de Rohan-Soubise-Ventadour, titular bishop of Tolemaida, coadjutor with right of succession of Strasbourg; Ferdinand Julius von Troyer, bishop of Olomütz; Giovanni Battista Mesmer, treasurer general of the Apostolic Chamber; José Manuel da Câmara d'Atalaia, *primarius principalis* of the cathedral church of Lisbon; Gian Francesco Albani, cleric of the Apostolic Chamber; and Mario Millini, dean of the Sacred Roman Rota.
15. E. Kieven, *Ferdinando Fuga e l'architettura romana del Settecento. I disegni dalle collezioni del Gabinetto Nazionale delle Stampe. Il Settecento* (Rome, 1988), 192–3; Coccioli, 'Festa per la nomina' (above, n. 1), 139.
16. 'apposta al suo Regio Palazzo, e propriamente dalla parte dirimpetto al Palazzo Muti': Chracas, *Diario di Roma* 4683 (29 July 1747), 20.
17. There was building activity in this area in 1705, with minor adjustments to the street alignments at the corner of Vicolo dell'Archetto and Via dell'Archetto following the acquisition by the Muti Papazzurri of a house owned by the confraternity of Santi Apostoli. See the entry by T. Manfredi in P. Micalizzi (ed.), *Roma* 3. *Roma nel XVII secolo* II (Rome, 2003), 30, no. 42.
18. Corp, 'Introduction', in Corp (ed.), *Stuart Court in Rome* (above, n. 2), 15, fig. 5.
19. A. Cicinelli, *S. Maria dell'Umiltà (Via dell'Umiltà 30) e la Cappella del Collegio Americano del Nord (Via del Gianicolo 14)* (*Le chiese di Roma illustrate* 111) (Rome, 1970), 130–1; T. Manfredi, 'Designs by Filippo Juvarra for the convent of S. Maria dell'Umiltà, Rome', *The Burlington Magazine* 142 (2000), 101–3; G. Vasi, *Delle magnificenze di Roma antica e moderna. Libro ottavo che contiene i monasteri e conservatori di donne* (Rome, 1758), no. XXIV.
20. Manfredi, 'Designs by Filippo Juvarra' (above, n. 19), 103 and n. 13.
21. 'L'invenzione, e disegno di tal magnifica opera è dell' Architetto Sig. Carlo Marchionni, e le pitture del Sign. Antonio Bicchieriari, quali hanno saputo così bene secondare la Signorile idea di Sua Eminenza, che meritamente ne hanno riportato molta lode, come pure il Sig. Cardinale tutto l'applauso, per esser questa una delle vaghe, maestose, e nobili, che fin'ora vedute, e di una rappresentanza particolare'. Chracas, *Diario di Roma* 4680 (22 July 1747), 7–8.
22. 'Architetto, & inventore di si magnifica struttura è stato il Sig. Clemente Orlandi Romano, che oltre l'aver secondato così bene l'animo Regio del Sig. Cardinale, ne ha riportato tutto l'applauso.'
23. On Orlandi, see E. Kieven, *s.v.* 'Orlandi, Clemente', in B. Contardi and G. Curcio (eds), *In Urbe Architectus. Modelli, disegni, misure. La professione dell'architetto Roma 1680–1750* (Rome, 1991), 412; P. Guerrini, 'Clemente Orlandi architetto e sue opere inedite per Niccolò Maria Pallavicini', in *Architettura città territorio. Realizzazioni e teorie tra illuminismo e romanticismo. Studi sul Settecento romano* (Rome, 1992), 93–129.
24. Corp, in this volume, nn. 61, 62, suggests a *pensionnaire* of the Académie de France in Rome, a pupil of Panini, or Giuseppe Paladini or Giovanni Angeloni, two artists associated with the Stuarts.
25. This forms one of a set of six engravings by Edme Jeaurat and François-Auguste Moitte of women of Rome and its environs after paintings by Nicolas Vleughels. This plate represents a 'femme du peuple de Rome'. See the contribution by Corp in this volume, n. 63; B. Hercenberg, *Nicolas Vleughels, peintre et directeur de l'Académie de France à Rome, 1668–1737* (Paris, 1975), cat. 125, 103–4 and fig. 138.

26. Paolo Anesi (landscape) and Paolo Monaldi (figures), *Fantasy Landscape in Lazio with the Saltarello*, Milan, Alemagna Collection. See A. Busiri Vici, *Trittico paesistico romano del '700: Paolo Anesi, Paolo Monaldi, Alessio De Marchis* (Rome, 1976), figs 112, 138.

THE ART OF CATHOLIC RECUSANCY: LORD ARUNDELL AND POMPEO BATONI*

Peter Björn Kerber

In five decades of serving English, Irish, Scottish and Welsh clients, Pompeo Batoni (1708–87) received only a single commission for a religious history picture from a British patron.[1] The fact that the painter was a devout Catholic is mentioned frequently in contemporary sources, and religious subjects inspired him in a way that portrait commissions rarely did.[2] In terms of emotional intensity and elegant refinement, *The Appearance of the Angel to Hagar in the Desert*, 1774–6 (Plate 6.1), has few equals in Batoni's *oeuvre*.[3]

It was no accident that the patron who commissioned the work was a devout Catholic himself: Henry, 8th Baron Arundell (1740–1808), the scion of a recusant Catholic family from Wiltshire who had succeeded to the title at the age of sixteen (Fig. 6.1). His taste had been formed during a three-year Grand Tour that included a meeting with Batoni in Rome in 1760.[4] Arundell travelled with a Jesuit governor, Charles Booth (1707–97), and their piety was such that it 'would not permit them to continue their journey yesterday out of respect to All Souls', as an astonished Sir Horace Mann (1706–86) informed Horace Walpole (1717–97).[5]

With a substantial family fortune at his disposal, Lord Arundell started to build the spectacular new Wardour Castle in 1768, and began to fill it with an art collection that eventually included more than 200 works acquired from Italy.[6] As his agent in Rome, the young nobleman engaged Father John Thorpe (1726–92), his former tutor at the English Jesuit College at Saint-Omer. Thorpe, a Jesuit priest, worked as an English penitentiary at Saint Peter's. Even after the suppression of the Society of Jesus in 1773, Father Thorpe remained in Rome as a secular priest and continued to serve as Arundell's art agent.[7] More than 400 extant letters, shipment lists and accounts sent by Thorpe, in conjunction with records kept by his patron, permit a detailed reconstruction of Lord Arundell's patronage.

When the 28 year old aristocrat initially enquired after the merits of the painters 'most in vogue' in Rome, Thorpe answered the question unequivocally: 'Pomp. Battoni is without dispute the first Painter in Rome, and if Mr. Mencks at Madrid be excepted, he is the most eminent in Europe'.[8] The only 'cause why some great personnages employ other pencils, is because they cannot be served by his'.[9] The novice patron was as naive and inexperienced as he was rich and enthusiastic. As his first commission, in 1768, Lord Arundell asked Batoni to copy two ancestral portraits.[10] The following year, he attempted to commission copies of Raphael's *Madonna della Sedia* and Van Dyck's *The Three Eldest Children of King Charles I* from Batoni.[11] The Van Dyck was in the collection of Charles Edward Stuart (1720–88) at the Palazzo Muti, and Father Thorpe obtained permission for it to be taken down for copying, but Batoni evidently did not want to work outside his studio and declined.[12] In the event, Thorpe turned first to Ann Forbes (1745–1834), then to Philip Wickstead (fl. 1763–86) for the copy.[13]

Batoni did agree to copy the two family portraits, but demanded the steep price of 512 scudi for the pair, making the copies 28 per cent more expensive than his going rate for new half-length portraits from the life — even though the copies would be largely executed by studio assistants, as Father Thorpe cautioned his patron.[14] When Arundell tried to bargain, Batoni retorted that he had already lowered his demands from the original 600 scudi and that one of the portraits contained an additional figure, a page boy.[15]

Over the course of the next five years, Lord Arundell's Roman agent periodically reported in various permutations that Batoni 'has begun nothing: there is no doing any thing with him'.[16] In the pecking order of Batoni's patrons, the English baron was nowhere near the top:

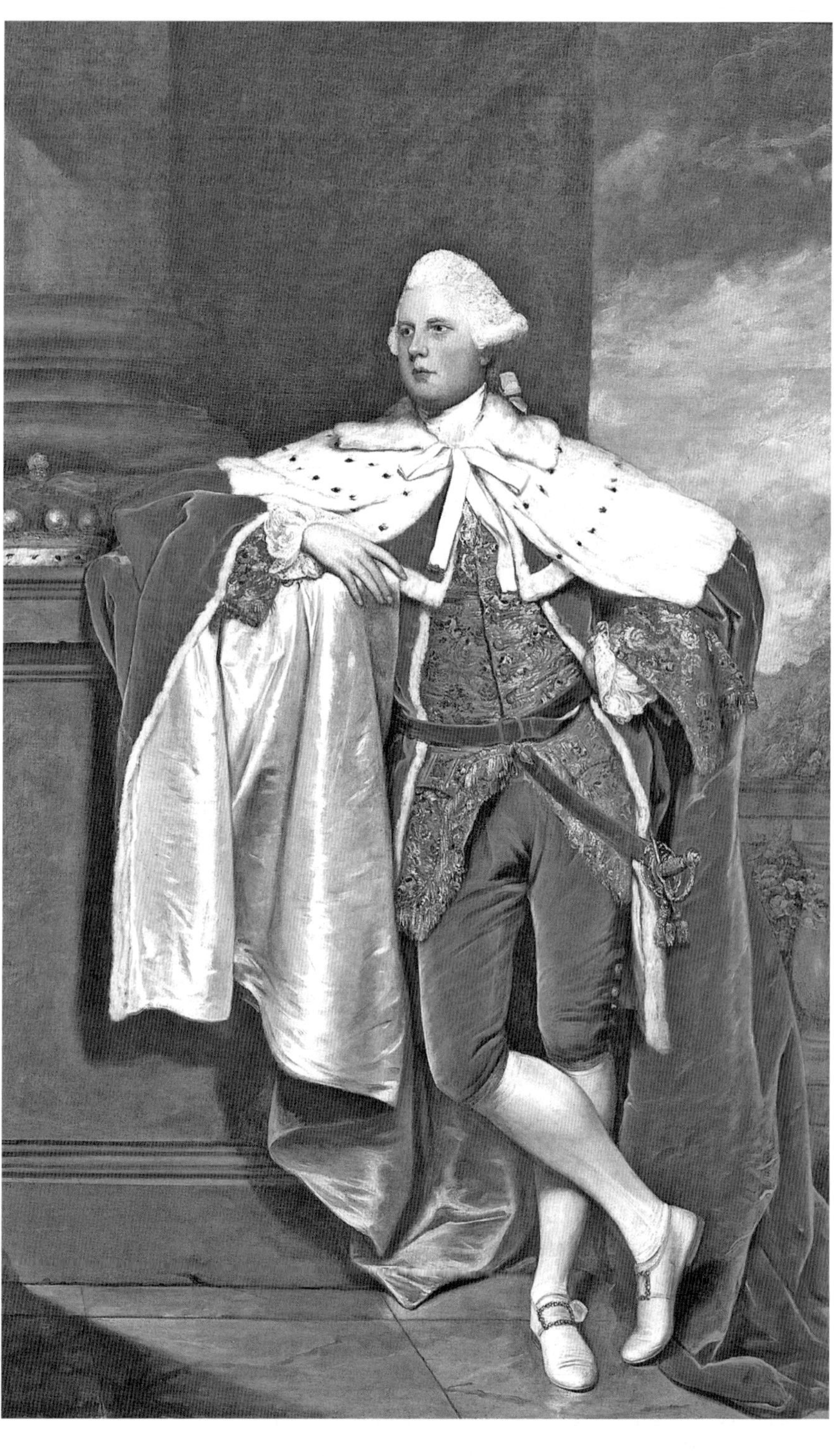

FIG. 6.1. Sir Joshua Reynolds (1723–92), *Henry, 8th Lord Arundell of Wardour*, c. 1764–7. Oil on canvas, 239 × 147 cm. Dayton, Ohio, The Dayton Art Institute, Gift of Mr and Mrs Harry S. Price, Jr (1969.52). *(Reproduced courtesy of the Dayton Art Institute.)*

> Pompeo's pencil is at present all busy in a grand portrait of the Emperor and his brother; but he has again assured me that he will serve You ... The Emperor has shewn a very extraordinary regard for his merit ... He has given Pompeo a large gold chain and medal of himself, and an elegant gold Snuffbox, besides the payment of the picture (five hundred Zequins) ... What Charles V.th did for the celebrated Titian, does not come up to what Joseph II.d has done and said to Pompeo Battoni.[17]

Soon the painter was angling for much more than snuffboxes: 'Pompeo ... is again employed by the Court of Vienna, for which he finishes every thing in a masterly manner, in hopes of a large estate or some very considerable pension'.[18]

Thorpe tried to console Arundell by telling him that even the highest-ranking clients were often left hanging: 'Pompeo will ... perhaps begin the pictures, & then leave them unfinished for many years: it is thus he treats Souvereign princes & the first gentry in England & France'.[19] Repeated promises notwithstanding, Batoni never did paint the two Arundell family portraits, which in the end were executed by François-Louis Lonsing (1739–99) in 1774 and Pietro Labruzzi (1739–1805) in 1775.[20]

This outcome should not have surprised Lord Arundell, who had been warned that Batoni was:

> unwilling to give back his commissions, tho' as dilatory as ever in fulfilling his promises: he would be glad to receive part of the money before he begins, several do advance one third or one half of the prices & they are commonly the soonest served. Perhaps there will be no other way of dealing with him.[21]

But the discouraging experience with the portraits failed to spoil Lord Arundell's appetite for Batoni's work. Undaunted, the agent tried a different tack, sidestepping delays and squabbles over payment schedules. In February 1771, Thorpe purchased *The Presentation in the Temple*, 1735–6 (**Plate 6.2**), Batoni's modello for the high altar of the Oratorian church of Santa Maria della Pace in Brescia, out of the estate of Cardinal Filippo Maria Pirelli (1708–71).[22] The accounts show that the Batoni modello was acquired in a single lot, presumably from the same source, with a small *Head of the Virgin* by Carlo Dolci (1616–86) and a 6 × 6 feet *Holy Family with the Infant Saint John the Baptist* by Luca Giordano (1632–1705), priced at 106 scudi for all three.[23] The underlying value of *The Presentation in the Temple*, on the other hand, was more than four times higher than the purchase price, as Thorpe proudly emphasized:

> Pompeo would not paint a companion for what You already have of his pencil, for less than two hundred Zequins, & I know Your Lordship would give it, but the piece You have does not stand you in more than one hundred Crowns & is as well painted as he paints now.[24]

How well Lord Arundell's agent had come to know Batoni's style and sources is demonstrated by the description given in the shipment list: 'A very pleasing composition somewhat borrowed from Barocci, & well painted in the author's first manner'.[25] Thorpe was referring to *Presentation of the Virgin* (1593–1603), by Federico Barocci (1535–1612), in Santa Maria in Vallicella, a painting much admired by the young Batoni.[26] Francesco Benaglio (1708–59), his early biographer, noted that for the Brescia altarpiece Batoni made 'disegni, modelli, studi senza fine, e tutto dal vero'.[27] But when painting what must have been the final modello submitted for approval, Batoni was still making significant changes to the composition. The modello shows a major pentimento of an arch above the figure of Joseph, suggesting a completely different architectural background that cannot have included the round tempietto. Cardinal Angelo Maria Querini (1680–1755), the bishop of Brescia who commissioned the altarpiece from Batoni, may have requested these changes at a very late stage, with the artist altering the finished modello and resubmitting it.[28]

After the small *Presentation in the Temple* entered his collection, Lord Arundell continued to hanker after a major history picture by Batoni and was prepared to pay an exorbitant price. Father Thorpe had by now become a frequent visitor to Batoni's house at 25 Via Bocca di Leone. The close relationship between the cleric and the painter cannot be explained through the significance of Arundell's commissions, which was negligible compared to the prestige and financial rewards Batoni obtained during these years from patrons such as Empress Maria Theresa (1717–80), Empress Catherine II of Russia (1729–96) and King Frederick II of Prussia (1712–86).[29] It may well have been his status as a priest, rather than as a client, that endeared Thorpe to the pious artist and helped him to gain Batoni's trust.

In spite of this familiarity, or perhaps precisely because he knew Batoni's ways only too well, Father Thorpe continued to recommend secondary market acquisitions: 'I am perpetually upon the enquiry for something of Mengs, and Pompeo. Either of them would undoubtedly engage to do such a piece as Your Lordship describes for two hundred Guineas', but Thorpe felt that 'it is more advisable to wait for some opportunity of getting two or three pieces of their work than to give them an extravagant sum for executing a particular commission'.[30] Lord Arundell, however, would have none of it; he insisted on commissioning a new painting. Apart from the issue of prestige, the kind of picture he had in mind in fact would have been extremely hard to come by on the secondary market. Instead of one of the profane historical or mythological canvases more prevalent in Batoni's output, the devout Catholic patron wanted a biblical history painting as the centrepiece of the Grand Saloon at Wardour Castle.

The episode of Hagar in the Desert was selected as the theme, and Lord Arundell's agent dutifully entered into negotiations with Batoni, who was steadfast in demanding a down payment of 40 per cent: 'There is no other way of dealing with [Batoni], & I think that he will repay it by painting more chearfully'.[31] The deal was struck:

> Pompeo has begun a sketch of the Agar; & according to contract is to finish the Picture within the term of eight months ... His agreement is to paint a picture representing Agar, her son & Angel in a country scene of ... 4 1/2 feet by 3 ... for the sum of Two hundred Zequins ... I told him that if he would exert himself & finish it within the due time, Your Lordship would then order him to paint a companion to it.[32]

The initial progress gave rise to optimism: 'Pompeo will for this time, be as good & perhaps better than his word; he wants already to have the other subject; he is a very devout man, & his late sickness has made him, or seems to have made him, more than ever inclined to paint sacred figures'.[33] After only a few weeks, Batoni began colouring the canvas.[34] Soon the discussion was turning to the pendant, for which Thorpe had proposed the Return of the Prodigal Son to the artist:

> He likes it & it is a subject in which he has excelled ... To make it a more suitable companion to the Agar, I propose to have it taken in that moment, wherein the Father having seen his son returning at a distance, & being gone out of doors to meet him, tenderly embraces him. Thus a country scene may be introduced, & be free of servants, musicians &c. who would only serve to augment the painter's demands, who requires as much for a piper, as for the good Pater familias.[35]

What a piper and a *pater familias* had in common was Batoni's painstaking and costly method of studying every figure from life, not only when making sketches, but also during the execution of the final painting: 'Il mio costume nell'ultimazione di ogni quadro è tenere sempre il vivo d'avvanti agl'occhi'. Perpetually in need of a good excuse for his interminable delays, the artist once wrote to a patron that the unseasonably cold weather in Rome was to blame, since it meant that his models refused 'di star l'ore intiere nudi in un freddo così attroce'.[36] As the number of figures in a composition was the key factor in determining its price, one of the other options for the pendant, Jacob's Bargain with Laban for his Daughter Rachel, had a distinct disadvantage: 'As there must be four whole figures besides sheep &c. in this picture, Pompeo would scarce undertake it for less than double his price for the Agar'.[37]

The Prodigal Son agreed upon as the subject, patron and painter entered into a tug of war about the composition. There were serious reservations against Batoni's proposal 'for the Prodigal Son, whom he throws flat upon the ground before his good father, who is coming to raise him up. He has not yet done anything upon this thought, nor would I have him begin to put it on canvas untill you approve of it'.[38] Instead, the agent insisted that the artist 'must be brought to Your Lordship's idea of the Prodigal Son, which is the most beautiful as well as the most interesting point of time; he shall not certainly make it as he pretends'.[39]

Meanwhile, *The Appearance of the Angel to Hagar in the Desert* was far from finished. At the end of November 1774, Father Thorpe was still convinced that the picture would be completed on time, but after Christmas all bets were off, because Batoni was giving priority first to a portrait of Charles Theodore (1724–99), Elector Palatine, then to *Alexander and the Family of Darius*, a painting for Frederick II that he had been working on for more than ten years.[40] In the newly-elected Pope Pius VI (1717–99), the hierarchy of patrons reached its pinnacle: 'Your Agar yet weeps unfinished, & if Pompeo go[es] to the Vatican to paint the Pope, she may prolong her weeping, for he will then have an excuse for neglecting her, which admits of no reply'.[41] In November 1775, Batoni was still busy with the papal portrait, and the following May, the painter gave the exasperated priest a new promise to finish *The Appearance of the Angel to Hagar in the Desert* by the end of the summer.[42]

The breakthrough came in July 1776, when Lord Arundell's agent finally hit upon the right method of dealing with the obstinate artist:

> Pompeo once again has not kept his promise of finishing Agar before the end of June; however there is strong assurance of his doing it before August be at an end; because now he is to paint some part of it every week, on condition of receiving 30 or 40 Crowns each week that he does so. He hitherto keeps his word, & the picture begins to come on admirably.[43]

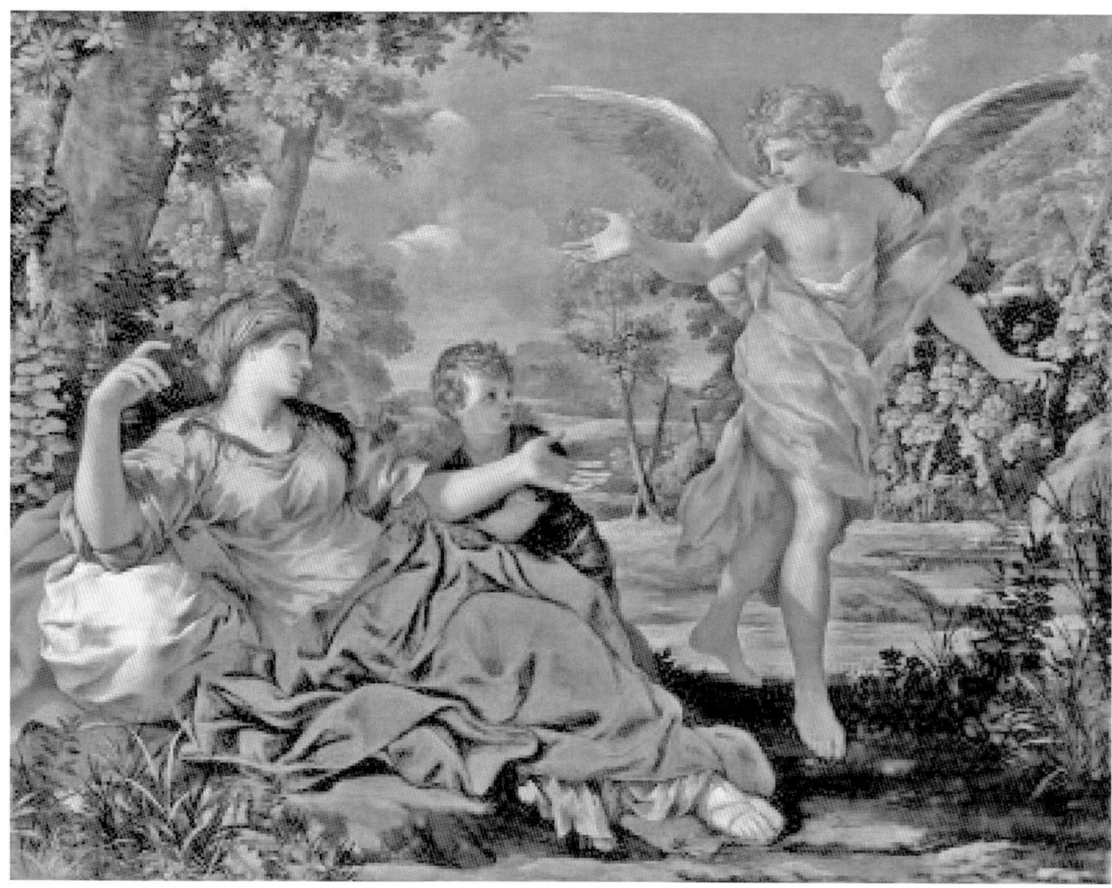

FIG. 6.2. Pietro da Cortona (1596–1669), *The Appearance of the Angel to Hagar in the Desert*, c. 1637–8. Oil on canvas, 114 × 149 cm, SN132. Bequest of John Ringling, Collection of The John and Mable Ringling Museum of Art, the State Art Museum Florida, Florida State University. *(Reproduced courtesy of the John and Mable Ringling Museum of Art.)*

The change was swift and marked:

> Pompeo, who has been so infamously dilatory now maintains his promises, & to keep him in this good humour I every week endeavour to be even better than my word to him. His painting will not be the worse for it, & in all appearance will be finished about the middle of next month.[44]

Only a week later, Thorpe was able to report that 'Pompeo ... will soon give the last finishing stroke to his Agar, & now would willingly engage to paint a companion: but I tell him that he can not be relied on, & that Your Lordship will not expose yourself to new disappointments'.[45] After another fortnight, the agent sighed with relief: 'Agar is at length finished, & admired as one of Pompeo's most pleasing pictures'.[46]

Father Thorpe's concerns about Batoni's unreliability were overridden by Lord Arundell, who evidently felt that by applying the drip-feed payment method again he could make the artist more malleable the second time around, and decided to commission a pendant before *The Appearance of the Angel to Hagar in the Desert* had even been shipped to England.[47] Alas, the argument about the subject flared up again:

> Pompeo objects against the Prodigal as a companion to his Agar, because the Son must be an emaciated figure, & meanly clad. The drapery of the old father must also be grave & serious: the whole scene affords him no place for brilliancy of colouring: he proposes the Sacrifice of Abraham, or Pharaoh's daughter finding Moses.[48]

But even Arundell's enthusiasm when he received *The Appearance of the Angel to Hagar in the Desert* could not keep the negotiations from foundering over the price:

> Your opinion of the picture of Agar will highly flatter Pompeo, ... but [he] will not paint a companion to it for less than the hundred pounds. He pretended to oblige me by doing what he has done for Your

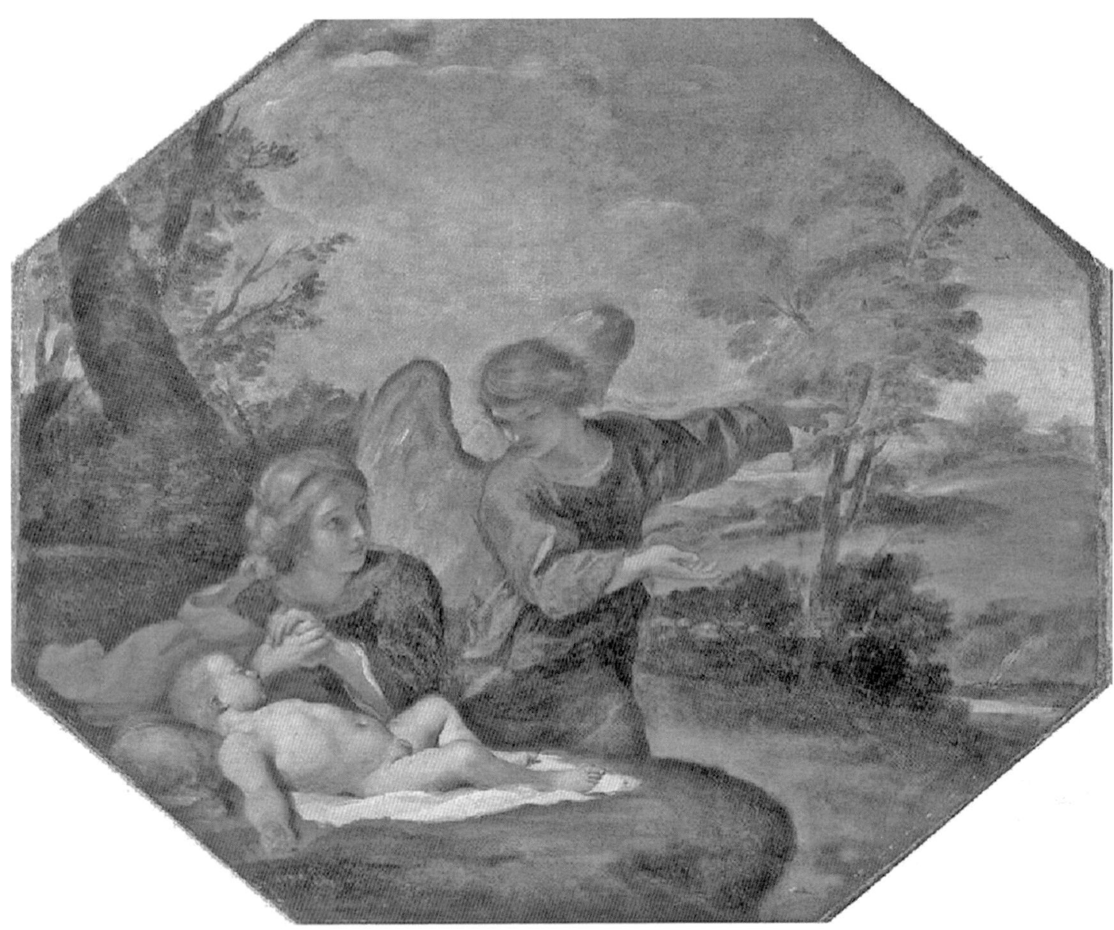

FIG. 6.3. Andrea Sacchi (1591–1661), *The Appearance of the Angel to Hagar in the Desert*, early 1630s. Oil on canvas, 76 × 92 cm. Cardiff, National Museum Wales (NMW A 9). *(Reproduced courtesy of the National Museum of Wales.)*

> Lordship at that price: he demands three times that sum or six hundred Zequins, for his Peace & War, tho' the size be the same as Agar, & the figures be only down to the knees.[49]

In the end, the plans for the much-discussed pendant picture came to nothing.[50]

When Batoni's *The Appearance of the Angel to Hagar in the Desert* arrived at Wardour Castle, it was given pride of place in the Grand Saloon.[51] Like other recusant Catholics such as Charles Townley (1737–1805) and Henry Blundell (1724–1810), Lord Arundell aggressively collected art as a form of over-compensation for the fact that he was barred from making his mark in most other areas of public life because of his religion.[52] But in marked contrast to Townley and Blundell, who devoted the lion's share of their resources to the acquisition and display of antiquities, Arundell's collection was an expression not only of his wealth and taste, but of his faith, a crucial factor in his patronage.[53]

Most contemporary British collectors purchased religious paintings merely as examples of a particular artist's work, without much regard for — and often in spite of — their subject-matter.[54] Lord Arundell, however, was motivated by his Catholicism to get involved in the creative process, debating biblical narratives and iconographies with the artist through his agent. The correspondence does not discuss the specific thinking of Arundell and Thorpe, but the parallels between the story of Hagar in the Desert and contemporary events are striking.[55] In July 1773, under immense pressure from the Bourbon courts, Pope Clement XIV (1705–74) suppressed the Society of Jesus.[56] Arundell had been a staunch supporter of the Society since his days as Father Thorpe's pupil at a Jesuit college. The chaplaincy at Wardour was occupied by a succession of Jesuit priests, who would have acted as a constant reminder to Arundell of the calamity that had struck their brethren on the continent.[57] Batoni, having painted the celebrated image of the *Sacred Heart of Jesus* for Il Gesù in Rome, also had close ties to the order.[58] An undated note in Lord Arundell's hand suggests that he was at least planning to commission a 'Madonna SS. del Sacro Cuor di Gesù by Pompeio'.[59]

The Jesuits saw themselves as suffering the same fate as Hagar and Ishmael — innocent victims banished to the wilderness at the instigation of jealous enemies. Abraham, called by God to be 'the father of all them that believe' (Romans 4.11), symbolized the pope, forced into rejecting an order devoted to serving him. *The Appearance of the Angel to Hagar in the Desert*, *c.* 1637–8 (**Fig. 6.2**), by Pietro da Cortona (1596–1669), provides an instructive comparison to Batoni's treatment of the subject.[60] Whereas the latter's figures of the mother and the angel are quite reminiscent of their earlier counterparts, Cortona's cherubic little Ishmael has grown up into a muscular adolescent.

In many other treatments of the scene by artists of the Roman school, Ishmael is also a small boy. He has yet to lose his baby fat in the depiction by Giuseppe Chiari (1654–1727) of *c.* 1705, listed in the inventory of Marchese Nicolò Maria Pallavicini (1650–1714) in Rome (**Plate 6.3**).[61] In the painting of Andrea Sacchi (1591–1661) from the early 1630s, Ishmael is still an infant (**Fig. 6.3**).[62] While Sacchi, Cortona and Chiari all show Abraham's son as a child, emphasizing his vulnerability, Batoni's Ishmael looks barely younger than his mother. Once given a refreshing drink, this athletic young man seems quite capable of picking himself up and going off to found a great tribe.[63] Genesis 21.20 recounts that Ishmael was to become an archer, making him a fitting image for the Jesuits, an order not lacking in military connotations.

In 1774, when Arundell commissioned *The Appearance of the Angel to Hagar in the Desert*, the Society's leaders were imprisoned in the Castel Sant'Angelo.[64] Hagar and her offspring are described as 'in bondage' in Galatians 4.25. While Batoni was working on the picture, Cardinal Giovanni Angelo Braschi (1717–99), reputed to be sympathetic toward the Jesuit cause, was elevated to the Chair of Saint Peter as Pius VI (r. 1775–99), creating (ultimately futile) hopes for an impending restoration of the Society.[65] Through their choice of subject, Lord Arundell and Father Thorpe articulated the expectation that the Jesuits would be rescued from their wilderness, whether by divine intervention or political reversal of fortune. The resulting painting stands as eloquent testimony to a meeting of the minds of a British recusant and a Roman painter, united in their Catholic faith.

Notes

* For their generous help with various aspects of this article, I would like to offer heartfelt thanks to Liliana Barroero, Annette Hojer, Elisabeth Kieven, Anna Lo Bianco, Steffi Roettgen, Edgar Peters Bowron, Jeffrey Collins, Steven Hobbs, the Rev. Geoffrey Holt SJ, Christopher Johns, Todd Longstaffe-Gowan and the Rev. Thomas McCoog SJ.

1. A *Holy Family with Saint Elizabeth and the Infant Saint John the Baptist* (untraced), acquired by Thomas Dundas (1741–1820) in 1763, appears to have been a finished painting Dundas saw in Batoni's studio rather than a commission. See E.P. Bowron, *Pompeo Batoni and His British Patrons* (London, 1982), 20, 24, n. 83; A.M. Clark, *Pompeo Batoni. A Complete Catalogue of His Works*, edited and prepared for publication by E.P. Bowron (Oxford, 1985), 296, 368.
2. See J.G. Puhlmann, *Ein Potsdamer Maler in Rom. Briefe des Batoni-Schülers Johann Gottlieb Puhlmann aus den Jahren 1774 bis 1787*, ed. G. Eckardt (Berlin, 1979), 27; H.W. Tischbein, *Aus Meinem Leben*, ed. K. Mittelstädt (Berlin, 1956), 246; M. Missirini, *Memorie per servire alla storia della Romana Accademia di S. Luca fino alla morte di Antonio Canova* (Rome, 1823), 221; O. Boni, *Elogio di Pompeo Girolamo Batoni* (Rome, 1787), 69.
3. Rome, Galleria Nazionale d'Arte Antica, Palazzo Barberini. Signed and dated 'pompeo de batoni/ p romæ 1776' on the rock at the lower right. See Clark and Bowron, *Pompeo Batoni* (above, n. 1), 341–2, cat. no. 396; E.P. Bowron and J.J. Rishel (eds), *Art in Rome in the Eighteenth Century* (London/Philadelphia, 2000), 319–20, cat. no. 174; E.P. Bowron and P.B. Kerber, *Pompeo Batoni: Prince of Painters in Eighteenth-century Rome* (New Haven/London, 2007), 50, fig. 48.
4. See B. Ford and J. Ingamells, *A Dictionary of British and Irish Travellers in Italy, 1701–1800. Compiled from the Brinsley Ford Archive* (New Haven/London, 1997), 29–30; Trowbridge, Wiltshire and Swindon Record Office, Arundell MSS 2667 [henceforth WSRO], and private collection, letters from Father John Thorpe to Henry, 8th Baron Arundell [henceforth cited as Thorpe Letters], 21 October 1780.
5. Sir Horace Mann to Horace Walpole, Florence, 3 November 1759. Transcribed in H. Walpole, *The Yale Edition of Horace Walpole's Correspondence*, ed. W.S. Lewis (New Haven, 1960), XXI, 339.
6. See C. Hussey, 'Wardour Castle, Wiltshire, II', *Country Life* (29 November 1930), 676–82.
7. See P.B. Kerber, 'Holy orders: a Jesuit art agent in Settecento Rome. Father John Thorpe and his acquisitions of religious paintings', in C. Frank (ed.), *Rome and the Constitution of a European Cultural Heritage in the Early Modern Period. The Impact of Agents and Correspondents on Art and Architecture. Papers of the Conference, Rome, Bibliotheca Hertziana, 2005* (forthcoming).
8. Thorpe Letters, 2 October 1768, referring to an earlier letter from Lord Arundell of 6 September 1768.

9. Thorpe Letters, 2 October 1768.
10. Thorpe Letters, 22 December 1768; WSRO, 2667/20/22/11, 5 June [1769], 'Comissions to Mr. Thorpe', in Lord Arundell's hand: 'My Great Uncle kill'd at ye battle of Boyne, to be copied by Pompeio, a half length to ye knees, the black [page boy] to be holding his helmet'; 'My great uncle to be copied by Pompeio, to be in armour, his helmet on a table by him'. Each picture was to be copied 'from a small original' apparently sent to Rome for the purpose; see J. Rutter, *An Historical and Descriptive Sketch of Wardour Castle and Demesne, Wilts* ... (Shaftesbury, 1822), 31, nos. 35, 39. F. Russell, 'The Stourhead Batoni and other copies after Reni', *National Trust Year Book* 1 (1975–6), 109–11, at p. 111, has suggested that one of the originals was by John Michael Wright (1617–94), the other possibly by John Riley (1646–91). However, the portrait by Wright formerly in the Arundell family collection does not match either of the two descriptions above; see S. Stevenson and D. Thomson, *John Michael Wright. The King's Painter* (Edinburgh, 1982), 70, cat. no. 15.
11. WSRO, 2667/20/22/11, 13 March 1769, 'Orders to Mr. Thorpe'.
12. For the Van Dyck (1635; Royal Collection), see S. Barnes, N. De Poorter, O. Millar and H. Vey, *Van Dyck. A Complete Catalogue of the Paintings* (New Haven, 2004), 479, cat. no. IV.61; E. Corp, *A Court in Exile: the Stuarts in France, 1689–1718* (Cambridge, 2004), 200.
13. Thorpe Letters, 9 December 1769: 'An Englishman (Wicksteed) who has been brought up in the stile of Vandyke is esteemed to be as proper a hand as any for copying the Original of that author in the palace of the Dodici Apostoli, where leave has been graciously given for taking it down as soon as ever the Master goes into the Country'; 19 May 1770: 'Wicksted [is preparing] to copy the little children from the Original at SS. Apostoli; for the master of that Palace is going to Albano untill the feast of St. Peter and Paul'; 29 September 1770: 'Wickstead is abroad, a Miss Forbes whose pencil is admirable in such performances is now copying the little Family from Vandyke'; 15 December 1770: 'The copy of the little children at the SS. Apostoli comes on to admiration, & will realy be a fine piece; the young Lady who paints it . . . cannot fail of having a great reputation when she returns [to England]'; 29 June 1771: 'Wicksted has begun the little Family at S. Apostoli, for Miss Forbes would not leave in other hands what she had begun for You, but has taken it to finish at London on her own account'. The copy was shipped to England in August 1772; see WSRO, 2667/20/22/11, list of paintings shipped to Lord Arundell 1770–6, p. 5. For Forbes, who returned to Britain in March 1771, see Ford and Ingamells, *Dictionary of British and Irish Travellers* (above, n. 4), 367; for Wickstead, in Rome 1768–73, see Ford and Ingamells, *Dictionary of British and Irish Travellers* (above, n. 4), 998.
14. Thorpe Letters, 9 December 1769, 'Note of the Expences': 'Pompeo Battoni demands for the two half-length portraits 512″50 [scudi]' '; 10 October 1769.
15. Thorpe Letters, 10 January 1770: 'Pompeo Battoni insists upon having a hundred & twenty five Zequins for making each of the two Portraits . . . , and will not touch them for less: in his own writing, which I have, he had first required 150 each: the figure of the black Page holding a helmet is one reason that he brings for heightening his demands'.
16. Thorpe Letters, 30 June 1770. For similar statements, see: 27 May 1769; 10 January 1770; 22 September 1770; 20 April 1771; 1 January 1774.
17. Thorpe Letters, 15 April 1769. As Thorpe was not yet closely acquainted with Batoni at this point, his source may have been Chracas's *Diario ordinario* of the same day (no. 8049), which listed the gifts. See Associazione Culturale Alma Roma, *Chracas Diario ordinario (di Roma). Sunto di notizie e indici* II (Rome, 1998), 170.
18. Thorpe Letters, 25 May 1771.
19. Thorpe Letters, 13 March 1771. See also 2 February 1771: 'The present vogue for [Batoni] keeps up his extravagant demands, & makes gentlemen please & vex themselves with expectations of getting some picture from him, but he is perpetually occupied for Vienna'.
20. WSRO, 2667/20/22/11, list of paintings shipped to Lord Arundell 1770–6, pp. 9 and 11; WSRO, 2667/20/22/11, accounts, May 1775: 'Portrait of Hon.ble Arundell with a Moor by P. Labruzzi [scudi] 41'. The two portraits were listed in 1822 as hanging in the dining-room at Wardour Castle; see Rutter, *Historical and Descriptive Sketch* (above, n. 10), 31 nos. 35, 39. Russell, 'Stourhead Batoni' (above, n. 10), 111, erroneously stated that 'the pictures in question were in fact never painted'. For Lonsing, in Rome 1761–78, see O. Michel, 'L'apprentissage romain de François Joseph [sic] Lonsing', *Mélanges de l'École Française de Rome. Moyen Âge, Temps Modernes* 84 (1972), 493–509, esp. p. 497, rejecting the claim that Lonsing was himself a pupil of Mengs, but connecting him to several of Mengs's pupils in Rome; 'Lonsing, François-Louis', in J. Turner (ed.), *Dictionary of Art* XIX (London, 1996), 643. For Labruzzi, see A. Busiri Vici, 'Pietro Labruzzi. Pittore romano di ritratti', *Strenna dei Romanisti* 18 (1957), 248–52; A. Busiri Vici, 'Addenda alla ritrattistica del romano Pietro Labruzzi', *L'Urbe* 38 (1975), 27–30.
21. Thorpe Letters, 20 March 1771.
22. Private Collection. Signed 'POMPEO BATONI PINS' on the bottom step. See Clark and Bowron, *Pompeo Batoni* (above, n. 1), 211, cat. no. 4, erroneously giving the signature as on the reverse of the canvas, and the location at Wardour Castle as 'The Saloon', citing the Musgrave Lists, which in fact specify the location as 'Lord Arundell's Dressing Room'. See W. Musgrave, 'Papers relating to the portraits of distinguished persons in public buildings and family mansions' [Wardour Castle list dated 1797], London, British Library, MS Add. 6391, fol. 235v. The purchase was first mentioned in Thorpe Letters, 23 February 1771; 2 March 1771: 'I bought it out of the Collection of the deceased Card.l Pirelli. It represents the B.d Virgin offering the Holy Infant to the High Priest at the

entrance to the Temple, there are several angels & other figures in it. The size is about thirty inches high by fifteen broad. The Painter has wrote his name on it & would now require above fifty Guineas for such a painting; it does not cost Your Lordship half that sum'. Cardinal Pirelli had died suddenly, after a fever, on 10 January 1771; see G. Moroni, 'Filippo Maria Pirelli', in *Dizionario di erudizione storico-ecclesiastica* LIII (Venice, 1851), 250. Batoni had painted Pirelli's portrait in 1767; see Clark and Bowron, *Pompeo Batoni* (above, n. 1), 307–8, cat. no. 308.

23. The price of 106 scudi for all three pictures is recorded in WSRO, 2667/20/22/11, accounts, August 1771, matching the converted amount of £26 for the same pictures in WSRO, 2667/20/22/11, undated list of pictures purchased, in Lord Arundell's hand.
24. Thorpe Letters, 20 July 1771. See also 28 August 1771: the modello 'did not cost [that is, cost less than] fifty Zequins'.
25. WSRO, 2667/20/22/11, shipment list [August 1771], entry 'Presentation of the H. Infant in the Temple by Pompeo Battoni'.
26. For Barocci's altarpiece, see A. Emiliani, *Federico Barocci (Urbino 1535–1612)* II (Bologna, 1985), 346–59.
27. F. Benaglio, 'Abbozzo della vita di Pompeo Batoni pittore' (written *c.* 1757), in A. Marchesan (ed.), *Vita e prose scelte di Francesco Benaglio* (Treviso, 1894), 15–66, at p. 59. A sketch sold as by Francesco Trevisani in the Bossi sale in Munich in 1917 may have been a sketch, in reverse, for the composition of *The Presentation in the Temple*. See Clark and Bowron, *Pompeo Batoni* (above, n. 1), 211, cat. no. 5. This possibility is supported by a study for the legs of the Christ Child and the head of the acolyte (Edinburgh, National Gallery of Scotland, inv. no. D 2146), which shows the child's legs in a position suggesting that Mary is presenting the Infant Jesus from the left to the priest at the right, reversing the final composition, with the acolyte's head also reversed. For an illustration of the drawing, see Bowron, *Pompeo Batoni and His British Patrons* (above, n. 1), 85, cat. no. 59. An additional drawing (Besançon, Musée des Beaux-Arts et d'Archéologie, inv. no. D 1421) was published by C. Legrand, 'A propos de l'exposition du Louvre 'La Rome baroque de Maratti à Piranèse'. Pompeo Batoni (1708–1787) ou la recherche de la perfection', *Revue du Louvre et des Musées de France* 40 (1990), 502–3, at p. 503, fig. 4.
28. For Querini as the work's patron, see A. Sambuca, *Lettere dell'abate D. Antonio Sambuca scritte al Signor abate D. Andrea Bacci Canonico* (Brescia, 1745), 24.
29. See Bowron and Kerber, *Pompeo Batoni* (above, n. 3), 92–111.
30. Thorpe Letters, 26 October 1771; 19 February 1774.
31. Thorpe Letters, 11 May 1774. For the negotiations, see also 9 March 1774; 12 March 1774.
32. Thorpe Letters, 26 March 1774.
33. Thorpe Letters, 2 April 1774. See also 23 April 1774.
34. Thorpe Letters, 7 May 1774.
35. Thorpe Letters, 25 June 1774.
36. 'My custom in the final execution of each painting is to have the life model in front of me'; '... to be nude for hours in such atrocious cold conditions'. Both quotations from a letter by Batoni to Lodovico Sardini, 21 April 1742. Lucca, Archivio di Stato, Archivio Sardini, filza 143, no. 885. Transcribed in I. Belli Barsali (ed.), *Mostra di Pompeo Batoni* (Lucca, 1967), 272.
37. Thorpe Letters, 26 March 1774. The fourth figure is Laban's elder daughter Leah (Genesis 29.16–19).
38. Thorpe Letters, 14 September 1774.
39. Thorpe Letters, 5 November 1774.
40. WSRO, 2667/20/22/11, 'Note of divers Articles not mentioned in the Acc.ts that were sent 26th Nov.r 1774': a list of paintings 'now finished or to be so before Xtmas' includes 'Angel & Agar by Pompeo'; Thorpe Letters, 24 December 1774; 11 February 1775. For the portrait of Charles Theodore and *Alexander and the Family of Darius*, see Clark and Bowron, *Pompeo Batoni* (above, n. 1), 334–5, cat. no. 381; 335–6, cat. no. 382; Bowron and Kerber, *Pompeo Batoni* (above, n. 3), 114–15, 95, figs 104, 86.
41. Thorpe Letters, 18 March 1775. For the portrait of Pius VI, see Clark and Bowron, *Pompeo Batoni* (above, n. 1), 339–40, cat. no. 391; Bowron and Kerber, *Pompeo Batoni* (above, n. 3), 116, fig. 107.
42. Thorpe Letters, 11 November 1775; 11 May 1776.
43. Thorpe Letters, 13 July 1776. There was a notable precedent for this method: 'The Empress of Russia is glad to engage [Batoni] to finish two or three pieces, at the rate of thirty Crowns a week' (Thorpe Letters, 4 August 1770).
44. Thorpe Letters, 31 July 1776.
45. Thorpe Letters, 7 August 1776.
46. Thorpe Letters, 21 August 1776.
47. Thorpe Letters, 31 August 1776; WSRO, 2667/20/22/11, shipment list, [November 1776], entry 'Agar & the Angel by Pompeo Batoni': 'The principal figure & the Landscape part universally admired'.
48. Thorpe Letters, 20 November 1776.
49. Thorpe Letters, 12 July 1777. For the *Allegory of Peace and War*, see J. Gedo, 'Pompeo Batoni's Allegory of Peace and War', *The Burlington Magazine* 144 (2002), 601–5; E.P. Bowron, 'Pompeo Batoni's 'Allegory of Peace and War' and other subject pictures', in M.G. Bernardini, S. Danesi Squarzina and C. Strinati (eds), *Studi di storia dell'arte in onore di Dennis Mahon* (Milan, 2000), 356–60; Bowron and Kerber, *Pompeo Batoni* (above, n. 3), 138–40, fig. 122.
50. Thorpe Letters, 29 November 1777.
51. W. Musgrave, 'Papers relating to the portraits of distinguished persons in public buildings and family mansions' [Wardour Castle list dated 1797], London, British Library, MS Add. 6391, fol. 234r.
52. See V. Coltman, *Fabricating the Antique. Neoclassicism in Britain, 1760–1800* (Chicago, 2006), 189, 196; G. Vaughan, 'Henry Blundell's sculpture collection at Ince Hall', in P. Curtis (ed.), *Patronage and Practice. Sculpture on Merseyside* (Liverpool, 1989), 13–21, esp. p. 17. For Townley's collection,

see V. Coltman, 'Representation, replication and collecting in Charles Townley's late eighteenth-century library', *Art History* 29 (2006), 304–24. See also C. Haydon, *Anti-Catholicism in Eighteenth-century England, c. 1714–80. A Political and Social Study* (Manchester, 1993), 164–92, esp. p. 181, for the general situation of English Catholics at the time.

53. The size and decoration of the chapel Arundell built at Wardour Castle clearly indicate the fact that it functioned not only as a private chapel, but as the unofficial parish church for the area's diaspora Catholics, more than 100 of whom were supported by work on the Wardour estate. See A. Rowan, 'Wardour Castle Chapel, Wiltshire', *Country Life* (10 October 1968), 908–12; R. Haslam, 'Wardour Park, Wiltshire', *Country Life* (25 February 1993), 56–9, esp. p. 58. In 1767, the vicar of Fonthill Gifford, asked by the Anglican bishop of Salisbury to comment on the high number of Catholics in his parish, explained that 'we are situated too near Lord Arundell', while his counterpart at Tisbury noted that the locals were 'following [Lord Arundell] for Loaves and Fishes'. Salisbury, Diocesan Archives, Returns of Papists, box 1; Tisbury and Fonthill Gifford reports, 1767. Cited in J.A. Williams, *Catholic Recusancy in Wiltshire 1660–1791* (London, 1968), 82.
54. See N. Llewellyn, ''Those loose and immodest pieces'. Italian art and the British point of view', in S. West (ed.), *Italian Culture in Northern Europe in the Eighteenth Century* (Cambridge, 1999), 67–100, esp. pp. 76–7; C. Haynes, *Pictures and Popery. Art and Religion in England, 1660–1760* (Aldershot, 2006), 77–9.
55. See Genesis 21.9–20. Scripture passages are cited from the Douay-Rheims translation in Richard Challoner's revision of 1749–50, that is, the text that Lord Arundell and Father Thorpe would have used.
56. For a summary of these events, see O. Chadwick, *The Popes and European Revolution* (Oxford, 1981), 368–74.
57. See Williams, *Catholic Recusancy* (above, n. 53), 156–63.
58. See C. Johns, ''That amiable object of adoration'. Pompeo Batoni and the Sacred Heart', *Gazette des Beaux-Arts* 132 (1998), 19–28.
59. WSRO, 2667/20/22/11, untitled and undated note, in Lord Arundell's hand, in a format similar to the 'Comissions to Mr. Thorpe' list. There is no evidence that this commission was ever executed.
60. Sarasota, John and Mable Ringling Museum of Art, inv. no. SN 132. See A. Lo Bianco (ed.), *Pietro da Cortona 1597–1669* (Milan, 1997), 350, cat. no. 43. The painting was in England by 1763, when it was sold in London.
61. Formerly attributed to Carlo Maratti (1625–1713); whereabouts unknown. See S. Rudolph, *Niccolò Maria Pallavicini. L'ascesa al Tempio della Virtù attraverso il mecenatismo* (Rome, 1995), 129, fig. 101; 228, no. 372. For the autograph version illustrated in **Plate 6.3** (Paris, Louvre, inv. no. R.F. 1997-35), see S. Loire (ed.), *La collection Lemme. Tableaux romains des XVIIe et XVIIIe siècles* (Paris, 1998), 120–2.
62. Cardiff, National Museum Wales, inv. no. NMW A 9. See A.S. Harris, *Andrea Sacchi. Complete Edition of the Paintings with a Critical Catalogue* (Oxford, 1977), 63, cat. no. 22. During a visit to Rome in 1752, John Northall, *Travels Through Italy* (London, 1766), 320, noted 'a small piece of Hagar, Ismael, and the angel by And. Sacchi' in the Palazzo Corsini.
63. See Genesis 17.20 and 21.18.
64. Thorpe Letters, 27 August 1774.
65. J. Collins, *Papacy and Politics in Eighteenth-century Rome. Pius VI and the Arts* (Cambridge, 2004), 12.

CULTURE FOR SALE: BRITISH PATRONS, COLLECTORS, AGENTS AND THE ROMAN ART MARKET

Acquisitive tourism: Francesco Trevisani's Roman studio and British visitors[*]

Karin Wolfe

In a passage of his manuscript biography of *c.* 1736, dedicated to the painter Francesco Trevisani (1656–1746), which he later inexplicably crossed out, Lione Pascoli (1674–1744) described the artist's approach to his profession:[1]

> He has had very little luck with his pupils; either because they were not able to imitate him, or because he alone paints in a manner so refined, so delightful, and so enticingly that to this date few have been able to master his style in a manner worthy of his name. Even searching both within and outside his studio it is difficult to find someone who can pleasingly copy him; and I speak from experience, as I desired to have a copy made of a beautiful painting of a Magdalene that I received from Trevisani many years ago, and as I couldn't find anyone of his ability, I had to bring a copy I had had made of this Magdalene back to the painter to have him retouch it. And certainly Trevisani excels in this very activity, because aside from correcting the pose and expression and colouring of the copy, from the innumerable versions that he painted of this same subject (measuring four *palmi* [*c.* 89 cm]), you won't find one that is exactly like another. And the same can be said about Madonnas and many other images, of which he keeps duplicates in canvas in more or less the same size.

This passage helps explain the confusing nature of Trevisani's *oeuvre*, with its multiplicity of versions of uncertain date and authorship.[2] Not having pupils who could adequately copy his works,[3] he produced multiple replicas, with slight variations, of his own compositions, certainly with studio assistance in laying out the composition (as was the usual practice), and he was prepared to retouch copies sourced from outside his own workshop.[4]

The fact that Pascoli used his own *Magdalene* to discuss what he considered to be Trevisani's painterly virtuosity not only reflects his pride as a discerning collector, but also demonstrates the importance of this subject in the artist's repertory. A selection of paintings of the *Penitent Magdalene* attributed to Trevisani bears this out (Figs 7.1 and 7.2; Plate 7.1). After having perfected the basic iconographic representation, composition and palette, with help from his studio, initially probably with the assistance of his younger brother who was also a painter, the artist worked up replicas ready for sale. When he had a buyer he would retouch the painting himself, making minor variations in order to showcase his exceptional technical ability and to guarantee his products' originality. While retouching was traditionally employed to correct errors — and Trevisani sometimes had to do this[5] — it also served, as Richard Spear has pointed out, to 'provide a quite good studio work or copy with the precious patina of the 'divine hand', with the appearance of the master's inimitable and unsurpassable *ingenium*'.[6] The information Pascoli supplied about the artist's ready-prepared stock also sheds light on the commercial aspect of Trevisani's activity, which fed the flourishing market for devotional cabinet pictures in the papal city at the beginning of the eighteenth century.[7] In addition, Pascoli leaves little doubt as to what types of paintings both local patrons and tourists, including British visitors of all political persuasions,[8] could best expect to find hanging on the walls in Trevisani's Roman studio.

Research undertaken in Roman archives shows that Trevisani arrived in the papal capital from Venice in September 1679 and confirms that, upon his arrival, he established a small family *bottega* (workshop) in rented accommodation.[9] His first assistant was surely his brother Pietro, described as 'pittore' in the census ledgers, but another painter soon joined the studio. Over the next twenty years Trevisani's family expanded, causing him to move his apartments and studio on two occasions,

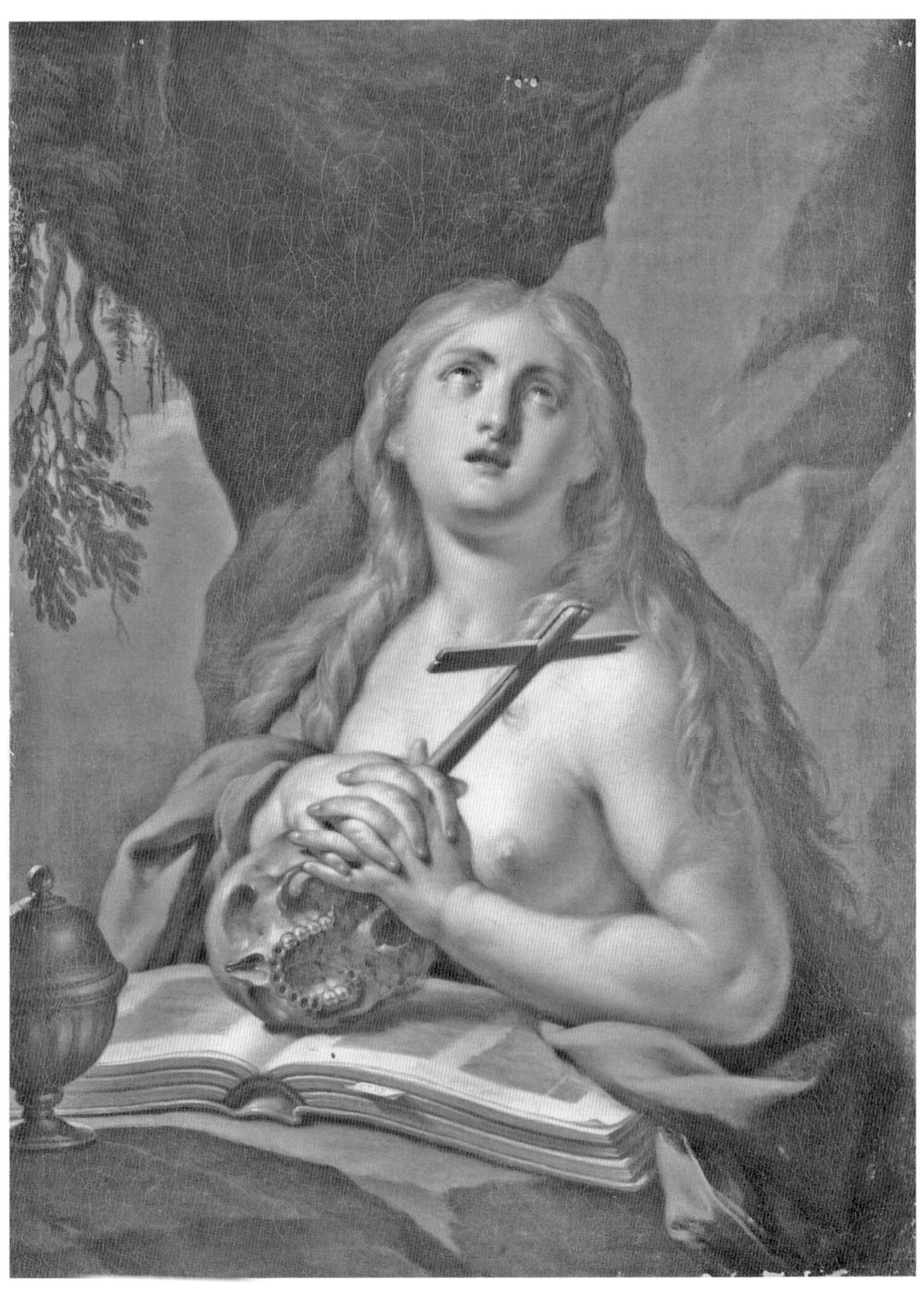

FIG. 7.1. Francesco Trevisani (1656–1746), *Penitent Magdalene*, dated 1727 on the bookmark. Oil on canvas, 97.6 × 73.6 cm. Finarte, Rome, 11 December 2008, lot 48. *(Reproduced courtesy of Finarte.)*

although he remained in the same area, adjacent to the Via del Corso between the church of San Girolamo degli Schiavoni and the church of San Carlo al Corso, where he had first lodged, a choice that may have been dictated by his Istrian heritage, as the church of the Schiavoni served that community. A Scottish travel journal of 1689–91 informs us that already during those years Trevisani's *bottega* was frequented by British visitors, in this case the Jacobite ambassador to Rome, John Drummond, Lord Melfort (1650–1714).[10] Melfort commissioned a portrait of his wife from Trevisani and also apparently purchased a painting that featured 'Belizar' (Belisarius), but neither of these works has been identified.[11] In 1697, when Trevisani joined the court of Cardinal Pietro Ottoboni (1667–1740), Vice-chancellor to the papacy, he settled with his family 'in considerable distinction' at the Palazzo della Cancelleria, where he was given the use of a large top-floor studio, along with other rooms, and he also received a regular stipend from the Cardinal.[12] Although the Cardinal apparently had first refusal on Trevisani's artistic output, the painter continued to exhibit his stock of ready-prepared paintings for sale as he had done earlier, and he accepted at least as

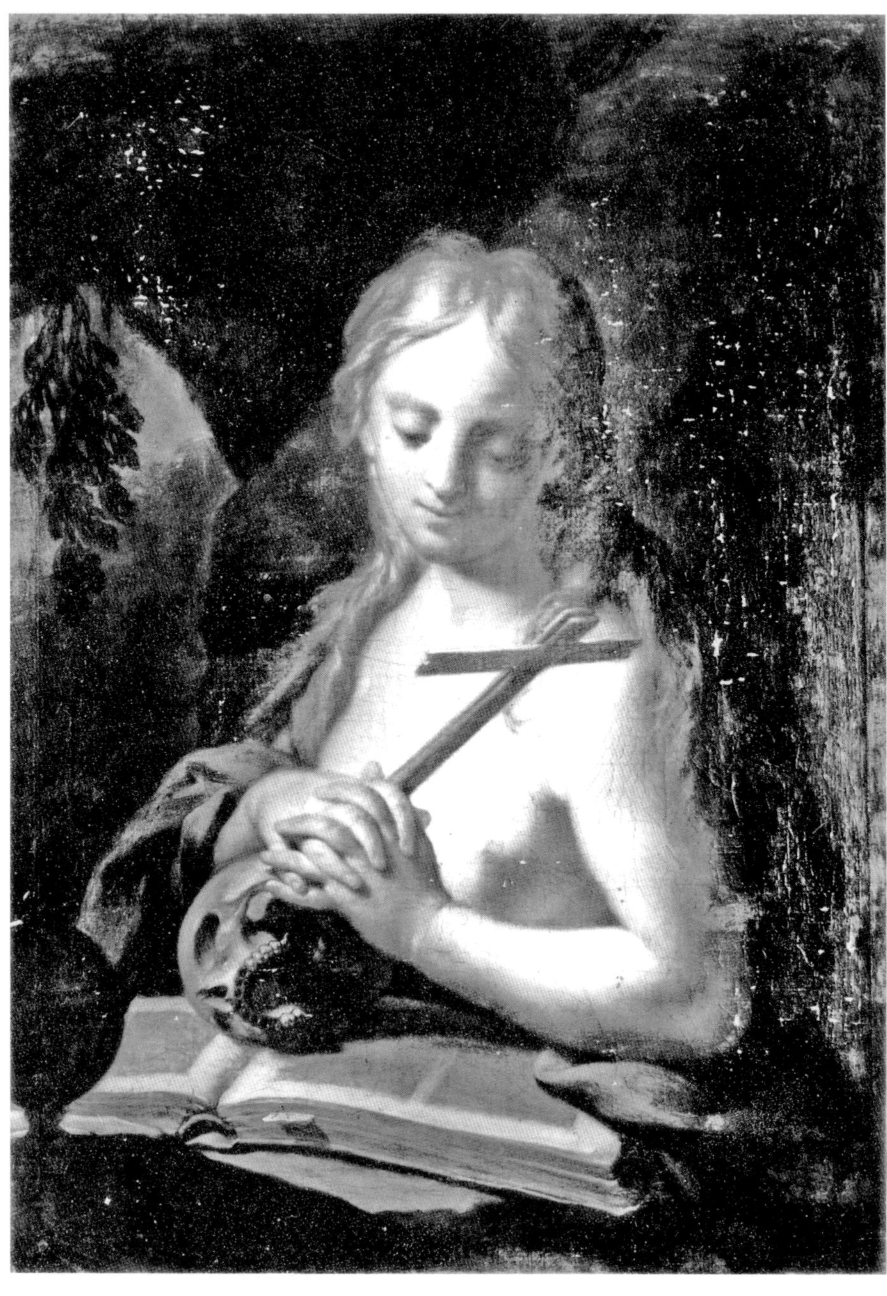

FIG. 7.2. Francesco Trevisani (1656–1746), *Penitent Magdalene*, signed 'F.T.' on the bookmark, and inscribed on the reverse 'an original by Fran. Trevisani Rome 1739 / bought by my son / James Clerk'. Oil on canvas, 99 × 76.2 cm. Private Collection. *(Reproduced courtesy of the owner.)*

many commissions from other patrons as he did from Ottoboni himself.

TREVISANI'S DEVOTIONAL PICTURES

Throughout his lengthy career, spanning over 70 years, British visitors to Rome were among Trevisani's best clients for three categories of paintings: devotional cabinet pictures representative of his popular repertory; sketches and replicas after his public altarpieces that he produced as souvenirs; and portraits.[13] Where devotional cabinet pictures are concerned, it was for his elegant and superbly finished *Magdalene*s and *Madonna*s that the painter became renowned throughout Europe. The Trevisani *Magdalene* that belonged to Pascoli may now be identified with a painting that recently came to light at Christie's, New York (Plate 7.1).[14] In another passage in the *Vite,* the biographer (Pascoli) returned to the subject of this picture, noting that 'for me Trevisani painted a *Magdalene* in oval format of four *palmi*, which is one of the most beautiful he has ever made, even if they are all memorable and all dissimilar and all utterly graceful'.[15] Of the known versions of the subject, the Christie's picture not only conforms to the measurements provided by Pascoli, but is also of oval format. It is an exquisite example of the artist's exceptionally fine and delicate brushwork and shimmering glazes; the Magdalene's skin appears flushed, translucent and porcelain-like, while a tear cascades like a small light-reflecting crystal down her cheek.

Another *Penitent Magdalene*, which appeared at Finarte, Rome, in 2008, is close in conception to Pascoli's and is dated 1727 (Fig. 7.1).[16] Writing the artist's biography around 1736, Pascoli noted that he had received his *Magdalene* from Trevisani 'many years ago'. Whether the 1727 date is indicative of the date of Pascoli's painting is not known, but the fact that the biographer had a copy of his painting retouched by the artist at a considerably later date than when he acquired it demonstrates the difficulty of establishing a chronology for Trevisani's work.

Where British patronage is concerned, of the remaining *Magdalenes* for which photographic documentation exists, the picture that is most close to the painting here proposed as the one owned by Pascoli has a well-established Scottish provenance. It is signed with the artist's initials and retains an old label on the back describing it as 'an original by Fran. Trevisani Rome 1739 / bought by my son / James Clerk', and is still today in the Clerk family collection at Penicuik House, Scotland (Fig. 7.2).[17] James Clerk (1709–82), a distinguished amateur architect, accomplished draughtsman and heir to a Scottish family at the forefront of the cultural renaissance that had been underway in Edinburgh since the end of the seventeenth-century, visited Italy in 1732–4, intending 'to see some of the best things in the way of Virtù'.[18] He was encouraged in his travels and in his activities as a collector by his father, Sir John Clerk (1676–1755), who had visited Rome in 1697–8, had spent time studying painting in the studio of Carlo Maratti (1625–1713) and associating with the violinist and composer Arcangelo Corelli (1653–1713), and who later wrote evocatively about his youthful passion to visit Italy in his *Memoirs*.[19] While in the papal city, the younger Clerk associated with a group of Scottish artists and collectors also actively involved in Roman artistic circles, including the painter William Mosman (*c.* 1700–71), an apprentice in the studio of Francesco Ferdinandi, called Imperiali (1679–1740).[20] Not only did this group frequent artists' studios in Rome to view and acquire contemporary paintings, but they also toured the city's famed private art collections, such as those of the Barberini and Pamphilj, in order to study 'old master' and Baroque pictures, of which they also commissioned copies.[21]

Mosman remained in Rome until at least 1738, acting as an agent purchasing and shipping art-works on behalf of Clerk and other Scottish collectors. By this date Trevisani's fame had long been firmly established — as we have seen, he had already received British clients at his *bottega* in 1691 — and, as Pascoli explained: '[i]t is unnecessary to publicize his work, because all Rome knows very well that he does not need more commissions, as he is already inundated with them, both old and new, and that he daily refuses contracts for church altarpieces, cabinet pictures, small private works and gallery pictures'.[22] As the correspondence of 1733–5 between Mosman and another Scots collector, the Jacobite Captain John Urquhart of Cromarty and Craigston (1696–1756) shows, it was at that time difficult to commission work from Trevisani because of his full schedule, his advanced age (in 1733 he was 77 years old) and because he had been unwell for most of the summer of 1733.[23] Urquhart, who was as determined a personality as he was newly rich, finally managed to acquire seven Trevisani paintings, although probably only the portrait of himself (cf. Fig. 8.1) and a large *Resurrection* (Plate 8.2), which he specifically ordered for his family chapel and which surely was intended to allude to the resurrection of the Stuart cause politically, were commissioned from the artist, while the other works (two *Madonnas*, a *Holy Family*, a *Saviour* and a *Saint John the Evangelist*) were subjects typical of Trevisani's repertory.[24] Clerk's acquisitions, on the other hand, were more modest, and he may have secured the Trevisani *Magdalene* for his family collection on the advice of Mosman. Whatever the true circumstances, Clerk's *Magdalene* was certainly a work of earlier design that the artist had kept in his studio, and may even be the first version of this subject in this pose.

Along with the discovery of the location of Trevisani's house and studio at the Lungara (in the Via dei Riari, adjacent to the Palazzo Corsini, formerly the Palazzo Riario), properties that he had acquired from 1733, there have now emerged a series of inventories of the contents of the artist's estate, including his library and paintings.[25] These sources reveal the breadth of Trevisani's cultural interests, which surely played a role in his relations with foreign clients, particularly British visitors, many of whom, like Sir John Clerk and later Thomas Coke, future Earl of Leicester (1697–1759), also shared similar musical interests with the artist.[26] Trevisani's inventories document his dedication to his profession and are revealing about his approach to his work: the inventories of paintings list 265 pictures, of which 124 are identified as 'originali' by Trevisani. The *originali* make up a unique group, as they include examples of almost all the artist's known works, but also some subjects that have not been recovered yet. They range from initial sketches to fully-finished replicas, including even the artist's earliest commissions for his first important Roman patron, Cardinal Flavio Chigi (1631–93), which are listed as 'nella prima maniera del Trevisani'. Ninety-one paintings are described as 'copies', and, significantly, of these the majority is subjects from Trevisani's popular repertory (Madonnas, Magdalenes and various saints), suggesting they were works by assistants, prepared to be given a final retouching by Trevisani himself. Lastly, fourteen paintings are identified as by other named artists, mostly contemporaries of Trevisani.[27] Although no drawings are inventoried, many are known, and at least one case can be documented of a Trevisani drawing that almost certainly was acquired by a British tourist from the artist in Rome and still remains in the same collection.[28] In almost all instances the inventory entries list the measurements, subject titles and prices of the works. The assessors were two artists who knew Trevisani well, his apprentice and best pupil, Andrea Casali (1705–84), and his lodger for many years, the little-known Roman painter Vincenzo Lupi (b. 1710).

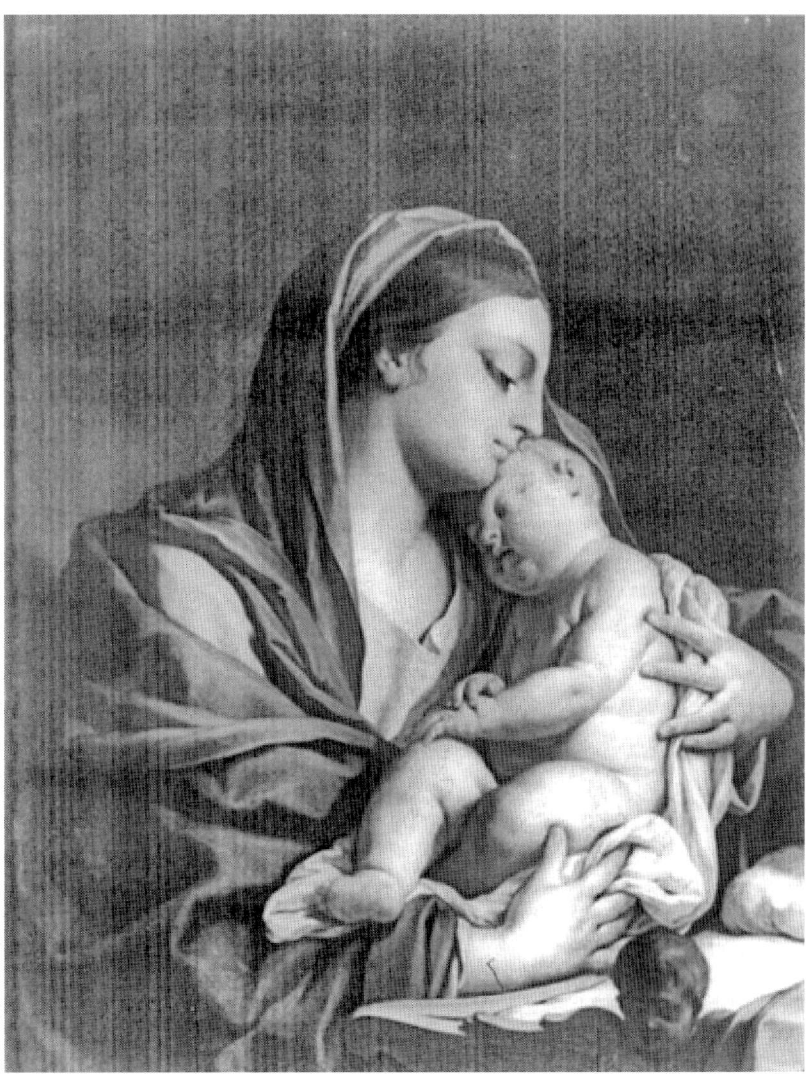

FIG. 7.3. Francesco Trevisani (1656–1746), *Madonna and the Sleeping Christ Child*, before 1700. Oil on canvas, 84.5 × 65.5 cm. Stourhead, The Hoare Collection (The National Trust), cat. 462. *(Reproduced courtesy of the Photographic Survey, Courtauld Institute of Art.)*

As I have argued, one of Trevisani's most beautiful paintings on the theme of the Madonna, the *Madonna and the Sleeping Christ Child*, today at Stourhead, originally belonged to the artist's friend, the musician Corelli (Fig. 7.3).[29] Trevisani would have met Corelli at the Palazzo Riario, which was occupied by Queen Christina of Sweden (1626–89, in Rome from 1655), to whom the composer was court musician. Trevisani was a frequent visitor to the Palazzo Riario, where he studied and copied paintings from the Queen's collection.[30] Corelli, moreover, was a passionate collector of paintings, and at his death in 1713 owned almost 150 works by his contemporaries, including 22 pictures by Trevisani, four of which represented the Madonna.[31] Trevisani's considered interpretations of the theme of the Madonna and Child (the most frequently occurring subject in the inventories and the subject of the majority of surviving cabinet works by the artist) may have been stimulated by Corelli's interest in this popular subject, as the musician possessed eight other paintings of the Madonna, including original works by such celebrated painters of the subject as Carlo Cignani (1628–1719), Maratti and Giovanni Battista Salvi (1605–85), called Il Sassoferrato.

While Trevisani may have used his wife as a model for his first paintings of Madonnas — her distinctive features appear as the Virgin in a series of *Mater Dolorosa* pictures, one of which can be related to the early period of his career when he was patronized by Cardinal Chigi[32] —, eventually he refined the physical characteristics for his Virgin types to a near-abstract perfection, creating a genre of flawlessly executed and idealized devotional cabinet picture for which he was unrivalled in his lifetime. The Stourhead *Madonna*, inspired by the meticulous academic models of Cignani that the artist probably studied in Bologna,[33] as well as by the example of Maratti, begins this process. Her chiselled profile an exercise in classicizing severity, her large and deeply-set eye is drawn so far from the bridge of her nose in order to elevate her beauty to an otherworldly realm and to emphasize her status as an icon. The sleeping Christ Child, by contrast, is a voluptuous, fleshy putto modelled on Baroque sculptural prototypes, such as those by François Duquesnoy (1597–1643) or Gian Lorenzo Bernini (1598–1680). The contrast between the aloof bearing of the Madonna and the realistic softness of the Child (cleverly highlighted by the way the artist repeats His head in the head of the carved putto at the foot of the crib, playing off the sleeping, but 'life-like' Christ, against the wide-awake, but wooden putto) signals a pivotal moment in Trevisani's career. The artist was balancing the academic restraint that dominated contemporary Roman painting against a taste for heightened naturalism, probably in accordance with a new aesthetic promoted by the Arcadian Academy, for which he felt a natural affinity and to which he would be elected in 1712.[34]

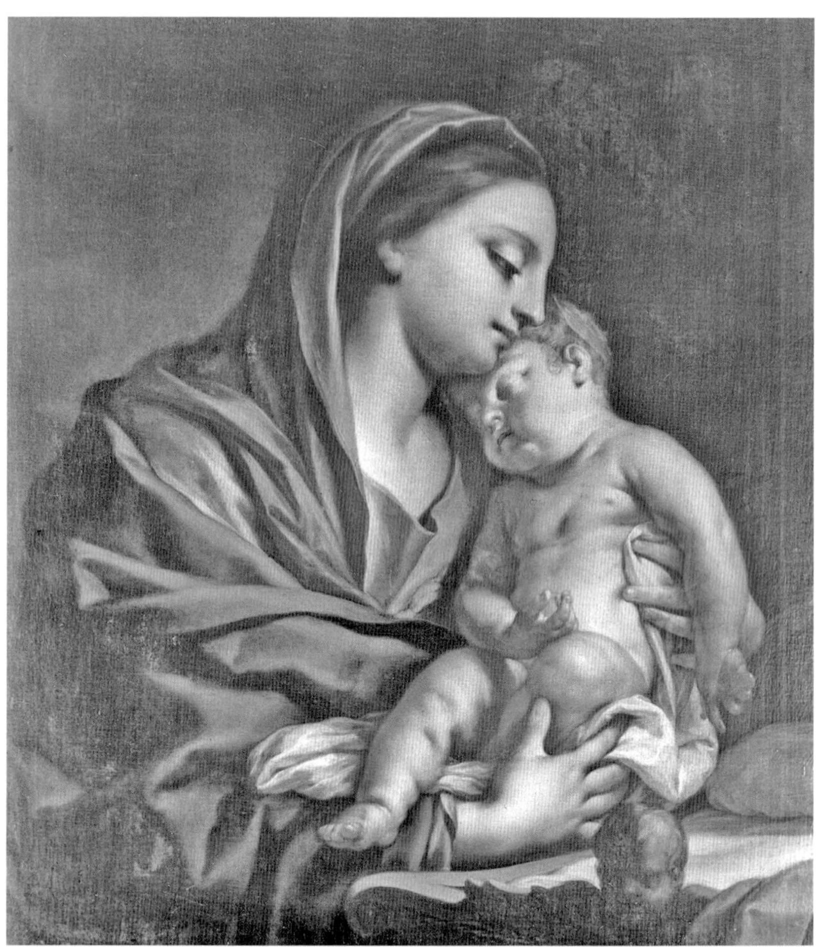

FIG. 7.4. Francesco Trevisani (1656–1746), *Madonna and the Sleeping Christ Child*, c. 1700. Oil on canvas, 82.5 × 69.8 cm. Burghley House Collection, Stamford. *(Reproduced courtesy of the Photographic Survey, Courtauld Institute of Art.)*

While it is not known exactly when the Stourhead *Madonna and the Sleeping Christ Child* was acquired for the Hoare Collection, and the picture apparently did not enter the collection during the artist's lifetime,[35] another *Madonna and the Sleeping Christ Child* in a British collection, that of the Marquess of Exeter, Burghley House, was almost certainly acquired directly from Trevisani in Rome in 1700, if not earlier, by John Cecil, 5th Earl of Exeter (1648–1700) (Fig. 7.4).[36] The Burghley *Madonna* allows us to study physically the practices decribed by Pascoli, since clearly visible underneath a thin layer of overpainting is the same composition as the Stourhead *Madonna*, and the dimensions are almost the same.[37] Trevisani reworked minor aspects of the composition: deftly altering the pose of the Christ Child's arms and legs; slightly changing the position of the fingers of the Virgin's left hand; painting out her veil, which in the Stourhead picture is draped over the Child's head; and painting out the wisp of hair in front of the Virgin's ear. There are also minor changes to the winding cloth with which the Virgin cradles her Child. The Burghley painting is therefore a copy of the Stourhead picture that has been reworked by Trevisani, just as Pascoli described in the case of the copy of his *Magdalene*. Whether the Burghley version was initially blocked in by an assistant surely did not matter to Trevisani's buyers, since the artistry of the picture consisted both in its trademark recognizability as a 'Trevisani' composition, as in the final reworking and finishing that made it unique. As Pascoli noted with praise about Trevisani's repertory subjects: 'you won't find one that is exactly like another'.[38]

A third version of the *Madonna and the Sleeping Christ Child*, also acquired for a British collector, but at a far later date, and that never arrived in England, has recently been identified and attributed to Trevisani.[39] While the painting presents anomalies of handling and style that have yet to be addressed, the composition closely follows the Stourhead model (and it is of similar dimensions), with slight variations to the pose of both the Madonna and the Christ Child. The Madrid *Madonna* was almost certainly acquired by George Legge (1755–1810), Viscount Lewisham (later 3rd Earl Dartmouth, 1801) (**Fig. 13.3**) at some time during his visit to Italy in 1777–8 for his family's collection. (His father, William Legge (1731–1801), 2nd Earl Dartmouth, had visited Rome in 1752–3.[40]) Unfortunately, by the date of Viscount Lewisham's visit the whereabouts of the contents of Trevisani's studio can no longer be traced in the archives. In the inventory made ten years after Trevisani's death in 1746, when his heirs put part of his remaining stock of pictures up for sale, Lewisham's painting cannot be identified.[41] A fourth *Madonna and the Sleeping Christ Child*, attributed to Sebastiano Conca (1680–1764) but clearly dependent on the Stourhead prototype, survives in poor condition in the Hermitage Museum.[42] Upon his arrival in Rome in 1707, Conca at first came under the influence of Trevisani, and the Hermitage picture (which formed part of the collection of Sir Robert Walpole (1676–1745)) attests not only to the popularity of Trevisani's invention among tourists, but also demonstrates that the taste for his devotional subjects was not limited to Jacobite visitors to Rome.

Together with the *Madonna and the Sleeping Christ Child*, Lord Exeter acquired five other paintings by Trevisani, which are today at Burghley House.[43] Not only does this nucleus of the artist's paintings attest to the 5th Earl's extraordinary activity as a collector at this early date,[44] but it is particularly interesting from the standpoint of Trevisani studies as the pictures record the major public works of his career in Rome, before he joined Cardinal Ottoboni's *famiglia* (household). Four of the paintings relate directly to Trevisani's first public commissions and are representative of the sketches and replicas he produced as souvenirs relating to his altarpieces. Two of these are similarly-sized, small-scale works. The first is based on the artist's 1687 altarpiece for Siena Cathedral, the *Martyrdom of the Four Crowned Saints* (**Fig. 7.5**), commissioned by Cardinal Chigi and exhibited to great praise in Rome before it was installed in Siena.[45] The second, the *Saint Andrew Placed on the Cross* (**Fig. 7.6**), relates to the painting in the apse of Sant'Andrea delle Fratte, which probably dates to 1688–90, and which is certainly Trevisani's first public work in Rome, as Ursula Fischer-Pace recognized.[46] These small, intensely azure-coloured and dramatically composed oil sketches are bursting with the Venetian artistic motifs that excited Trevisani. These include the pseudo-antique architectural colonnade and faux-historical throne that set the backdrop for the *Martyrdom of the Four Crowned Saints*, which is copied from his master in Venice, Antonio Zanchi (1631–1722);[47] and the dramatic scene unfolding at the foot of Saint Andrew's cross, consisting of a barking hunting dog (Trevisani was a keen hunter), a scrum of figures trying to raise the Saint and a voluptuous woman clutching an infant, reminiscent of the crowded canvases by Jacopo Tintoretto (1518–94) for San Rocco. These picturesque genre elements contend forcefully with the painter's newly-discovered Roman monumentality, which is apparent in the statuesque poses and gestures of the figures. While these sketches may have formed part of the preparatory phase of planning for the altar paintings, they are finished with such wonderful painterly details and carefully picked-out highlights that it is more likely that Trevisani painted them as mementoes to advertise his new-found public fame.

Also at Burghley are two large replicas with variations of Trevisani's slightly later pictorial cycle in the Crucifixion Chapel in San Silvestro in Capite of 1695–6, the *Mocking of Christ* and the *Flagellation of Christ*.[48] This cycle of paintings, in which Trevisani melded his Venetian origins as colourist and highly expressive narrator with the example of the works of Guido Reni (1575–1642) he had seen in Bologna, and with the Renaissance and Baroque models he had studied in Rome, copper-fastened the artist's reputation in the papal city, leading to his nomination to the Accademia di San Luca a year later, in 1697. Trevisani enthusiastically capitalized on the success of this project, producing multiple versions of the chapel paintings in different sizes and formats for various patrons, including not only the 5th Earl, but also Corelli, who owned two sketches related to the chapel,[49] and Cardinal Carlo Colonna (1665–1739), who acquired a large variant of the *Mocking of Christ* that is still today in the family palace at the Piazza

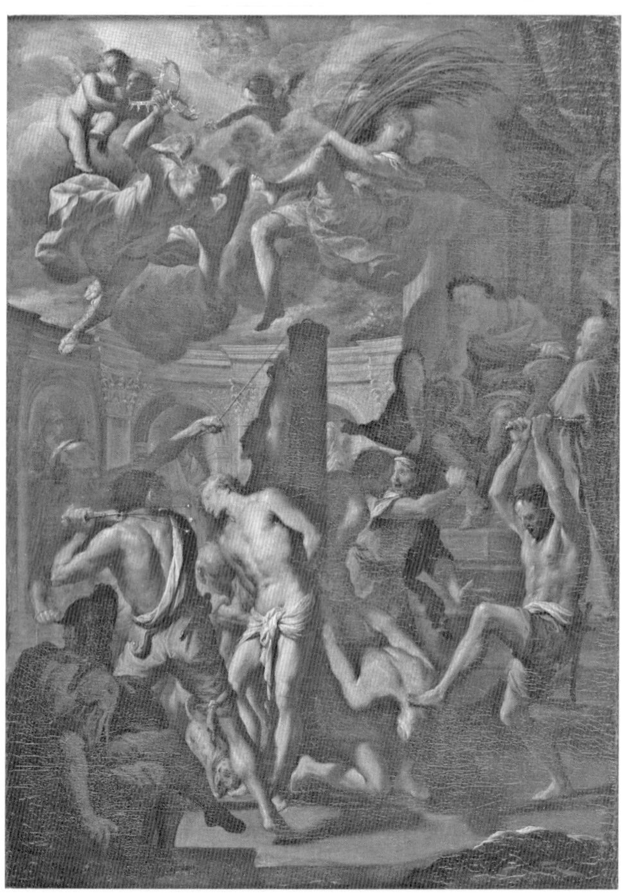

FIG. 7.5. Francesco Trevisani (1656–1746), *Martyrdom of the Four Crowned Saints*, c. 1700. Oil on canvas, 50.8 × 35.5 cm. Burghley House Collection, Stamford. *(Reproduced courtesy of the Photographic Survey, Courtauld Institute of Art.)*

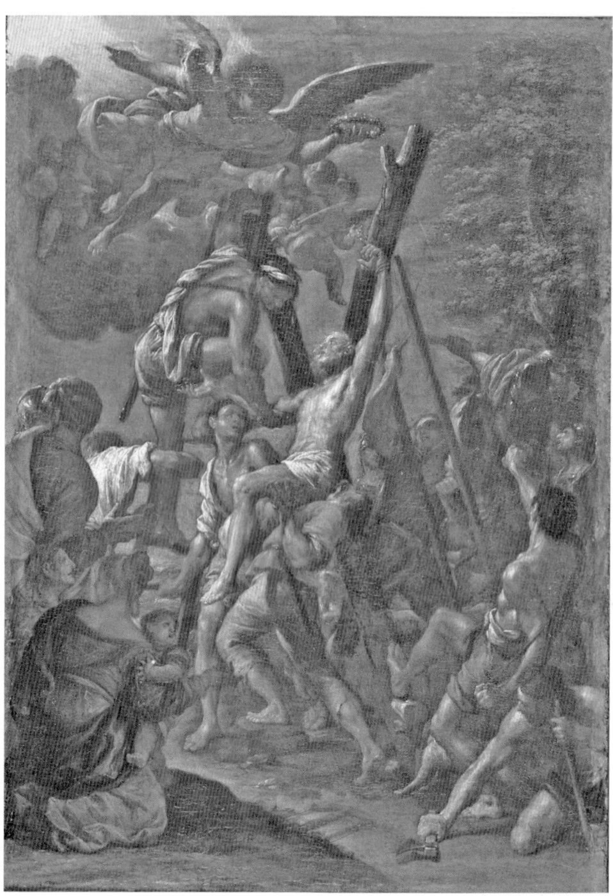

FIG. 7.6. Francesco Trevisani (1656–1746), *Saint Andrew Placed on the Cross*, c. 1700. Oil on canvas, 52.1 × 36.8 cm. Burghley House Collection, Stamford. *(Reproduced courtesy of the Photographic Survey, Courtauld Institute of Art.)*

Santi Apostoli in Rome.[50] DiFederico observed that the Burghley *Flagellation of Christ* has weak passages, which may be further evidence of Trevisani's studio practice of having assistants block out his most popular compositions, before touching them up himself.[51] None the less, it is difficult to believe that he did not exercise a strong control over what issued from his studio, especially regarding paintings destined for such an important patron.

While in Rome, the 5th Earl also acquired Trevisani's magnificent *Noli Me Tangere,* a painting that displays an especially delicate sensibility in the relation of its natural setting to the poignancy of the subject, and which features a startlingly huge swathe of costly ultramarine blue for the fabric wrapped around the Risen Christ, painterly ingredients perfectly attuned to the refined taste of an extremely sophisticated and wealthy collector (**Fig. 7.7**).[52] The 5th Earl and his party, including his wife, Lady Anne Cavendish (1643–1703), were invited by Cardinal Ottoboni to a musical evening at the Palazzo della Cancelleria orchestrated by Corelli, and something of the opulent atmosphere and cosmopolitan flavor of the ambient of the cardinal's court can be gleaned from a diary entry of an officer in the 5th Earl's service:

> Cardinall Ottabone invited ye Quene of Poland [Maria Casimira Sobieska (1641–93)]; & her 3 sones; and all ye Cardinalls to a fine Musick; their were: 26 cardinalls their; & a great maney strangers & a sermon in ye middle of ye musick; Cardinall Ottabone is a rich & great cardinall & keepes in his house Corelle ye famosest man in ye world for ye Violin & [blank space] a very good painter.[53]

The blank space almost certainly was left for Trevisani, court painter to Ottoboni by this date and resident in the Cardinal's 'house'. As the *Noli Me Tangere* is one of

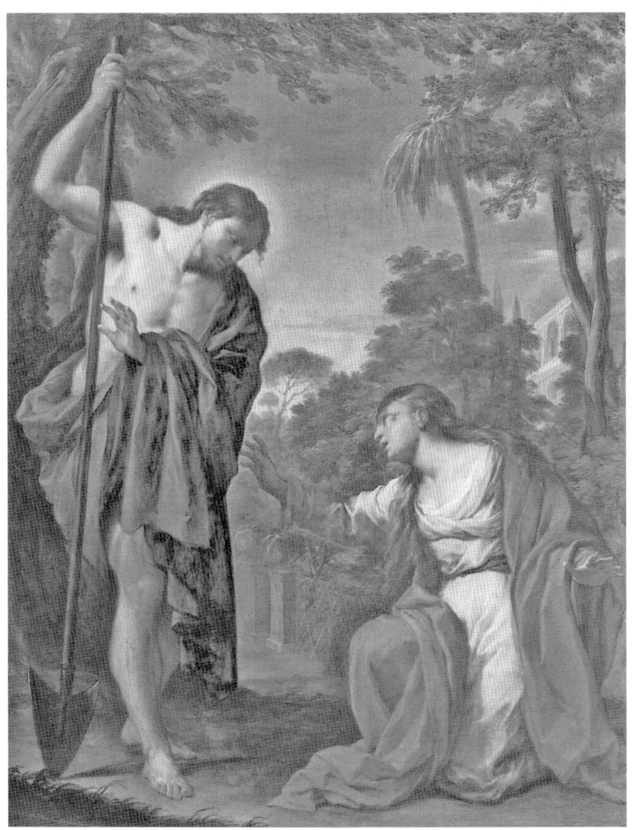

FIG. 7.7. Francesco Trevisani (1656–1746), *Noli Me Tangere*, c. 1700. Oil on canvas, 97.8 × 72.4 cm. Burghley House Collection, Stamford. *(Reproduced courtesy of the Photographic Survey, Courtauld Institute of Art.)*

the few Trevisani pictures for which no replicas have emerged (a smaller version of this same subject is listed in Trevisani's inventories, but it is impossible to know if this has the same composition) it was almost certainly a special commission from the 5th Earl; the composition is based on the well-known Correggio of the same subject (in reverse). Significantly, Lady Anne particularly admired devotional pictures with penitential themes, with which she decorated her apartments,[54] and this painting was surely intended for her, and may even have been commissioned by her.

Apart from the Burghley *Noli Me Tangere* and *The Resurrection* ordered by Captain Urquhart, both commissions that directly reflected their patrons' particular interests, no large-scale religious or historical paintings by Trevisani have emerged that were commissioned by British visitors.[55] Rather, the British seem to have acquired mainly devotional cabinet pictures consistent with the artist's existing repertory, or purchased souvenirs by him after his public altarpieces or later bought Trevisani paintings already in other collections when they became available.[56] On the other hand, more British visitors sat to Trevisani for portraits than did Italians, and the artist's activity as a portraitist cannot be separated from the British presence in Rome.[57]

TREVISANI AND THE GRAND TOUR PORTRAIT

Trevisani's own self-portrait, decribed in his inventory as 'Trevisani, opera dello stesso Trevisani', which hung in the front hall of his house at the Lungara, was a variant of a work he painted on at least seven occasions throughout his life. The example illustrated here (Fig. 7.8), previously unpublished, is one of the largest and most beautiful of the series. In each he assumes the same pose and wears the same Istrian costume of fur hat and fur-lined coat, but his features gradually age.[58] There is, however, greater variety, and a considerable degree of originality, in the series of more than twenty portraits of British visitors attributed to the artist. The felicitous pairing of the painter's obsessive interest in the accurate recording of a likeness, together with the deeply considered interest of the British visitor in portraiture, as testified by the series of likenesses produced by Maratti for British visitors beginning in 1678, contributed to the birth of the genre of the Grand Tour English portrait. That this was a recognized genre is established by the fact that, in 1767, Casali, who compiled the inventory of Trevisani's house, described an anonymous portrait hanging in the hall next to a series of likenesses of well-known popes, princes and cardinals as a 'Ritratto d'un Inglese'. That Trevisani kept a portrait of an anonymous British visitor in his gallery of famous faces demonstrates that he himself considered it to be an instance of a type or genre from his painterly repertory.

Beginning with the commission from Lord Melfort for a likeness of his wife in 1691, British visitors to Rome regularly stopped at Trevisani's studio to sit for their portraits.[59] These included Christopher Vane (1653–1723), 1st Lord Barnard, Whig Member of Parliament for County Durham from 1675 to 1679, and for Boroughbridge from 1689 to 1690.[60] Lord Barnard visited the papal capital as part of his Grand Tour in 1701, when he was 48 years old, rather older than the usual age for touring milordi, probably because of his political obligations. He rented lodgings in the Strada Felice, above the Piazza di Spagna, together with 'Monsú de Villard' and 'Monsú Brun', all three of whom are identified in the archives of the annual

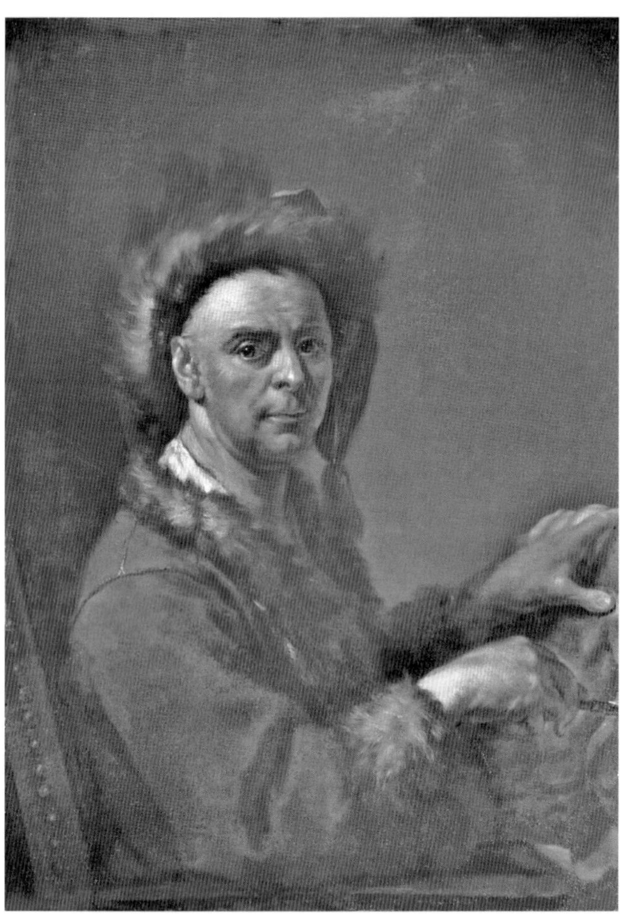

FIG. 7.8. Francesco Trevisani (1656–1746), *Self-portrait*, before 1700. Oil on canvas, 95.5 × 71 cm. Private Collection, UK. *(Reproduced courtesy of the owner.)*

Lent census as 'Heretici'.[61] This previously unpublished, three-quarter-length portrait of Barnard (Fig. 7.9), today still in the family collection, was drawn to my attention by Francis Russell.[62] Although no documents relating to the painting have come to light, the picture exhibits stylistic affinities with other Trevisani portraits, notably the *Cardinal Ottoboni* in the Bowes Museum (which probably dates to *c.* 1692–6), while the carved and gilt marble-topped table is the same as that in the later *Portrait of Thomas Coke*, discussed below.[63] The painting shows Barnard wearing his fur-lined peer's robes over a magnificent velvet coat with golden buttons, embroidered button-holes and wearing an impressive high-crowned *perruque*, and resting his right hand beside his baron's coronet (he was created Baron Barnard of Barnard Castle by William III (1650–1702) on 8 July 1699).[64] The formality of his pose, together with the deeply saturated cobalt blue of his coat and the deep teal colour of the velvet drapery glinting with a hint of gold fringe hung as a backdrop, perfectly convey the first Lord's social prominence, just as the marble column behind his left shoulder reminds us that he was a political 'pillar' of society, a feature that Trevisani invested with connotations of Roman imperial authority.

In the first months of 1717 Trevisani painted a glamorous full-length portrait of the young Thomas Coke, also sumptuously robed, seated on an impossibly ornate carved figural throne on which he rests his arm, while he pats his mastiff with his other hand, surrounded by luxurious accoutrements (Fig. 7.10).[65] Trevisani was surely reaching deep into his own Venetian heritage for the brilliant range of shades employed for Coke's embroidered oriental gown and the mauve swathe of drapery swagged up behind him. We know from his inventories that the artist had kept a copy he had made of a Veronese from Queen Christina's collection in his studio, and we know that he borrowed a painting by Paolo Veronese (1528–88) from the Pio collection in 1715 for inspiration.[66] The Coke portrait features a classicizing architectural background representing a gallery, with niches containing two well-known Roman statues, the Farnese Hercules and the Venus de' Medici. While Coke was interested in antique statuary and purchased important sculptures in Rome for his ancestral seat in Norfolk at Holkham Hall,[67] thus justifying Trevisani's decorative invention, the artist's pseudo-antique prop would spark a succession of similar visual topoi that would become the hallmark of Grand Tour imagery. While at first sight this background seems unmistakably Roman, it surely derives from Trevisani's memories of the grand tableaux of Veronese and of Tintoretto, which are set before splendid classicizing architectural backdrops, as well as the works of Zanchi, who set his narrative scenes before architectural colonnades. Trevisani had experimented with such architectural props already, in the 1691 portrait of Carlo Colonna (Fig. 7.11),[68] a distinguished Roman rather than a Grand Tourist, which employs the device of an arcade with statues in niches, although the perspective and modelling is handled less well than that in the Coke portrait. In both cases the architecture provides a noble theatre for the sitter to stage his persona. Colonna subsequently would commission set designs from Trevisani, attesting to their mutual interest in the theatre.[69]

During the same period that he was at work on the Coke portrait, Trevisani was contacted by James III's Secretary of State, the Earl of Mar (1675–1732), who,

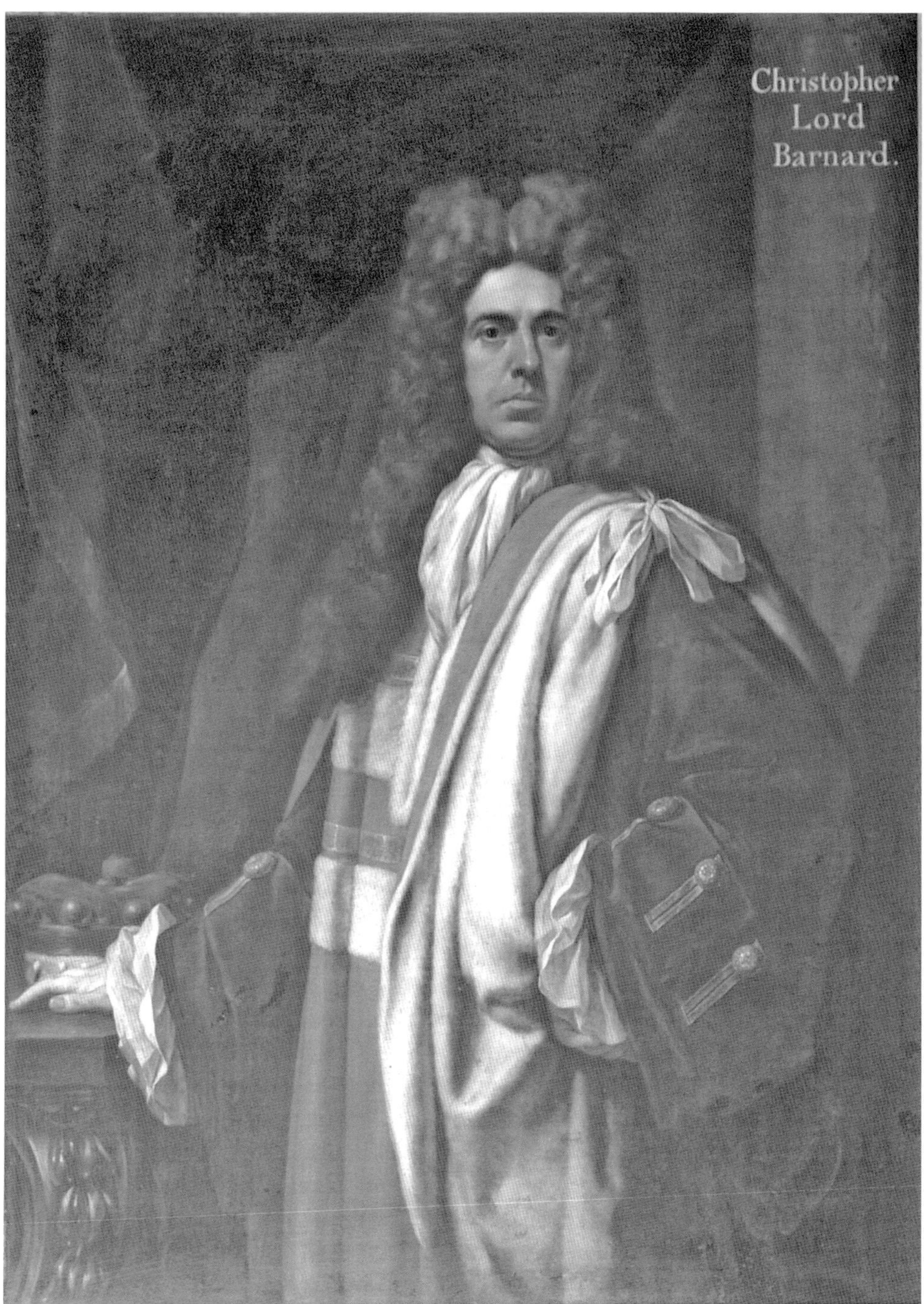

FIG. 7.9. Francesco Trevisani (1656–1746), *Portrait of Christopher Vane, 1st Lord Barnard*, 1701. Oil on canvas, 135.5 × 99 cm. Private Collection, UK. *(Reproduced courtesy of the owner.)*

among more pressing political concerns, was scouting out the Roman cultural scene in 1717 for the Pretender, who was about to arrive.[70] Mar engaged Trevisani to paint portraits of James and his future wife, Maria Clementina Sobieska (1702–35),[71] both of which are today in Scotland, and commissioned the charming likeness of his own second wife, Lady Frances Pierrepont (–1761), with their daughter, which was painted by Trevisani in 1719.[72] These prestigious commissions surely benefited Trevisani's reputation, but he did not allow himself to get drawn into the serial production of Stuart portraiture, which was what the exiled court desired. He was slow to finish his portraits and was overtaken by Antonio David, who took up the slack in this niche market.[73] Nevertheless, Trevisani did paint a series of bust-length and half-length portraits of British visitors either directly employed by James III or sympathetic to the Stuart cause, but these display a certain lacklustre sameness that makes them less interesting than his other portraits.[74]

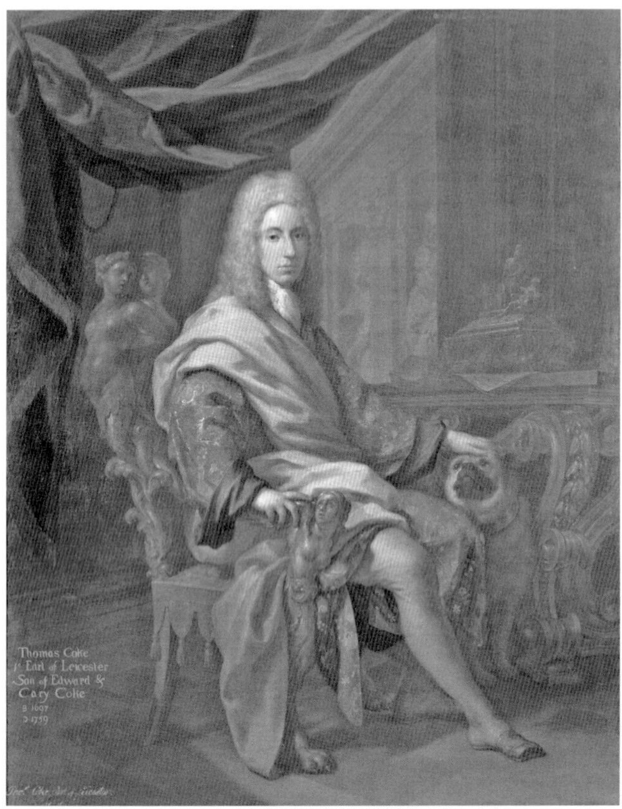

FIG. 7.10. Francesco Trevisani (1656–1746), *Portrait of Thomas Coke (b. 1698) 1st Earl of Leicester (of the First Creation)*, 1717. Oil on canvas, 200.7 × 161.3 cm. Viscount Coke and the Trustees of the Holkham Estate, Holkham Hall, Norfolk. *(Photo: © Collection of the Earl of Leicester, Holkham Hall, Norfolk/The Bridgeman Art Library.)*

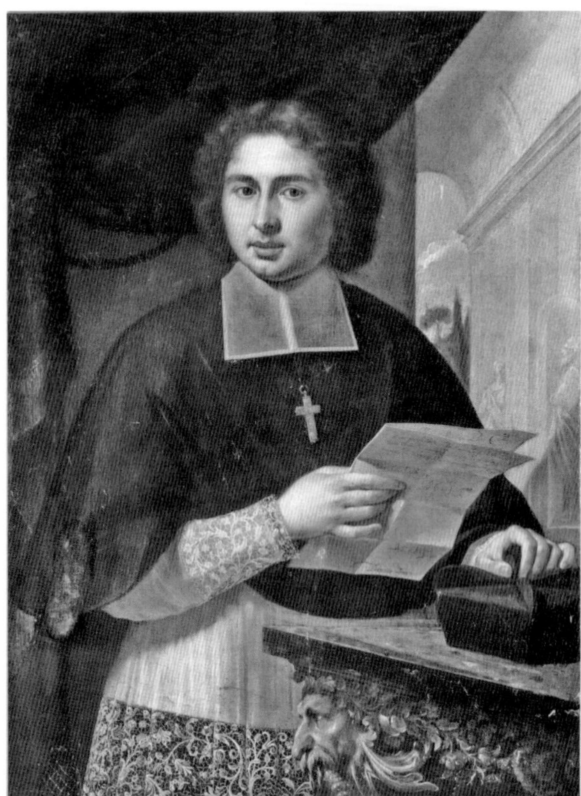

FIG. 7.11. Francesco Trevisani (1656–1746), *Portrait of Abate Carlo Colonna*, signed and dated 'Rome 1691'. Oil on canvas, 96.5 × 71 cm. Sotheby's London, 6 December 1972, lot 57. *(Reproduced courtesy of Sotheby's.)*

For his most important patrons, Trevisani produced truly memorable likenesses. This is the case with portraits of two of the most significant Jacobites, of which Trevisani kept versions in the foyer of his house. The first was Maria Clementina Sobieska (Plate 7.2), consort of James III, whose charmingly feminine and decorous portrait of 1719 was immortalized in engravings that circulated throughout Europe in a strategy aimed at keeping the Stuart cause fresh in sympathizers' thoughts and alive as a political issue.[75] The second was Henry Somerset, 3rd Duke of Beaufort (1707–45), who was painted in both half- and full-length portraits (Fig. 7.12).[76] The versions today at Badminton are the original works for which he sat to Trevisani, while the artist retained a head study of the 3rd Duke in his studio. Notwithstanding his immense wealth, and the fact that he employed a Scottish painter, as well as a cardinal, to aid him in his art acquisitions, and even though he frequently visited James III's private rooms when he was in Rome in 1725–6 and had access to every art collection in the city, apart from a series of portraits, the 3rd Duke acquired only two devotional pictures from Trevisani, which appear, from photographic evidence, to be inferior versions of repertory subjects.[77] But while he may have been manipulated by his advisers in his acquisitions, Trevisani painted a splendid full-length portrait of the 3rd Duke employing the faux-Roman colonnade replete with antique statuary that presents him as a modern-day descendant of a Roman statesman, regal in stance and imperious in expression. This portrait, in which the sitter is dressed in modern costume but is surrounded with antique references, and which combines Venetian colouring and theatricality with Roman gravitas and British aplomb, signals the beginning of the full-blown Grand Tour style. It was Trevisani's own cosmopolitanism that produced this example of aristocratic hauteur, which set the standard for the Grand Tour portraits that followed.

With the portrait of 1725 of Sir Edward Gascoigne (1697–1750) (Plate 7.3), a British visitor who took a deep interest in antiquarian and architectural studies,

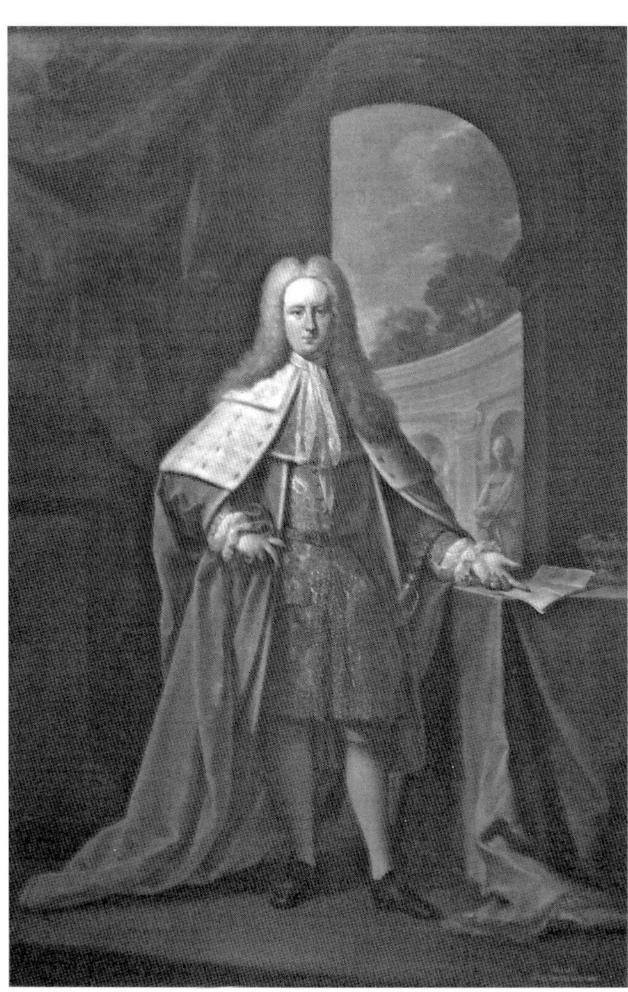

FIG. 7.12. **Francesco Trevisani (1656–1746), *Henry Somerset, Third Duke of Beaufort*, 1725–6. Oil on canvas, 236 × 145 cm. The Duke of Beaufort, Badminton House, Gloucestershire.** *(Reproduced courtesy of the Duke of Beaufort.)*

Trevisani formulated a model suited both to the sitter's learning and to his concern with presenting himself as the protagonist of a universal culture, a concern that would become the norm for British visitors to Rome.[78] Sir Edward, wearing a brilliant green damask dressing gown and seated on an upholstered chair in cardinal red, stares boldly out at the viewer. His erudition is signalled by his fingers buried deep in his guidebook, a volume of Horace nearby, and he appropriates Rome's glorious past by balancing the Colosseum in the palm of his hand. For British visitors to his Roman studio who posed for their portraits, Trevisani offered the unforgettable experience that Jonathan Richardson (1665–1745) described in his contemporary theoretical writings:

> Upon the sight of a Portrait, the Character, and the Master-Strokes of the History of the Person it represents are apt to flow in upon the Mind, and to be the Subject of Conversation: So that to sit for one's Picture, is to have an Abstract of one's Life written, and published, and ourselves thus consign'd over to Honour, or Infamy. I know not what Influence this has, or may have, but methinks 'tis rational to believe that Pictures of this kind are subservient to Virtue: that Men are excited to imitate the Good Actions, and persuaded to shun the Vices of those Whose Examples are thus set before them.[79]

Notes

* I would like particularly to thank Jane Cunningham, formerly of the Photographic Survey, Courtauld Institute, for her generous help with her knowledge of British patrons and collections; Alastair Laing, Christopher Johns, David R. Marshall and Susan Russell for their great enthusiasm and expertise in organizing the *Roma Britannica* conference; and especially Tommaso Manfredi, whose profound understanding of life in Rome in the eighteenth-century has immeasurably enriched my own.

1. Pascoli's manuscript draft is in Perugia — L. Pascoli, 'Vita di Francesco Trevisani', in *Vite de' pittori scultori ed architetti viventi,* MS 1383, Biblioteca Comunale 'Augusta', Perugia, fols 88–101. Fortunately, Frank DiFederico copied Pascoli's manuscript *in toto*, including all emendations and changes that the author had made: F. DiFederico, *Francesco Trevisani, Eighteenth-century Painter in Rome* (Washington, 1977), 86–98, esp. p. 93. The later critical edition of Pascoli by L. Salerno ('Vita di Francesco Trevisani (*c.* 1736)', in L. Pascoli, *Vite de' pittori, scultori ed architetti viventi, dai manoscritti 1383 e 1743 della Biblioteca Comunale 'Augusta' di Perugia* (Treviso, 1981), 25–57, esp. p. 38) makes no mention whatsoever of the passages that Pascoli altered or struck out, thus leaving out important information. I am indebted to Dott.ssa Angela Iannotti, Ufficio Fondo Antico of the Biblioteca Comunale 'Augusta', who kindly checked the original manuscript and provided me with the following transcription. MS 1383, fol. 94r: 'Poca fortuna però ha avuto cogli scolari; perchè o che essi non abbiano saputo imitarlo, o che egli solo in così rara, vaga e saporita maniera sappia dipingere, pochi ve ne sono stati fin ora che l'abbian presa, e che degni siano di averne il nome. Tanto che da questi in fuori si stenderà anche a trovar chi sappia ben copiare l'opere sue; ed io parlar posso per isperienza che avendo dovuto far fare una copia di certa bellissima Maddalena che anni sono ebbi da lui, non trovai alcuno che mi desse nel genio, e la miglior mi convenne farla tutta da lui rimpastare. Ed è certamente stato mirabile in questa, perchè oltre alla correzione, attitudine, espressione, e colorito d'innumerabili che ne ha fatte in tela di quattro palmi non sie ne trova nessuna simile all'altre. E lo stesso è seguito della Madonna e d'altre innumerabili immagini, che ha in tele della stessa misura o poco meno o poco più duplicate'.
2. I am preparing a monograph on Trevisani, including the publication of his inventories. See also K. Wolfe, 'The artist as collector: Francesco Trevisani's last years in Rome and unpublished inventory', unpublished conference paper, *American Society for Eighteenth-century Studies (Colorado Springs, Colorado, 4–7 April 2002)*; K. Wolfe, 'Il pittore e il musicista: il sodalizio artistico tra Francesco Trevisani e Arcangelo Corelli', in G. Barnett, A. D'Ovidio and S. La Via (eds), *Arcangelo Corelli tra mito e realtà storica. Nuove prospettive d'indagine musicologica e interdisciplinare nel 350° anniversario della nascita. Atti del congresso internazionale di studi, Fusignano, 11–14 settembre 2003* (Florence, 2007), 169–88.
3. Pascoli, in DiFederico, *Francesco Trevisani* (above, n. 1), 93, named Trevisani's pupils as 'Claudio Bomont Piemontese, Girolamo Pesce, il Cav. Andrea Casali, Gregorio Guglielmi Romani, Francesco Bertosi Fulignato, e Filippo Palazzeschi Maceratese'. See also V. Caprara, 'Documenti per gli artisti veneti del Seicento e del Settecento', in *Pittura veneziana dal Quattrocento al Settecento. Studi di storia dell'arte in onore di Egidio Martini* (Venice, 1999), 151, who published the census records for another Trevisani pupil, 'Antonio Ruperti da Udine, pittore che studiava sotto la guida del Trevisani, San Lorenzo in Damaso 1712'. Even after residing in Rome for over 30 years, Trevisani kept in contact with artists from his birthplace (Istria).
4. On copies see J. Richardson, *Two Discourses* I. *An Essay on the Theory of Painting.* II. *Of the Goodness of a Picture. Of the Hand of a Master, and* III. *Whether 'tis an Original, or a Copy* (London, 1725), 180–1: 'There are certain Arguments made use of in determining upon one, or more of these Questions, which are to be rejected; If there are two pictures of the same subject, the same Number of Figures, the same Attitudes, Colours, etc. it will by no means follow that One is a Copy; for the Masters have frequently repeated their Works either to please Themselves, or Other people, who seeing, and liking One have desired Another like it'. See also H. Brigstocke, cat. no. 40, in H. Brigstocke and J. Somerville (eds), *Italian Paintings from Burghley House* (Alexandria (VA), 1995), 116, who explained, with reference to a painting by Pier Francesco Mola (1612–66), that it was a normal studio practice for pictures to be laid in by the artist's assistants and then retouched by the artist, and that this also may explain the appearance of *pentimenti* (visible underpainting). For the most complete overview of the question of copies, see R.E. Spear, 'Di Sua Mano', in E.K. Gazda (ed.), *The Ancient Art of Emulation. Studies in Artistic Originality and Tradition from the Present to Classical Antiquity* (*Memoirs of the American Academy in Rome, Supplementary Volume* 1) (Ann Arbor, 2002), 79–98.
5. For example, a painting of *Maria Aegyptica* that Trevisani painted for Prince-Bishop Johann Philipp Graf von Schönborn (1655–1729) was returned to the artist because an agent for von Schönborn had criticized the anatomy of an arm and Trevisani was required to repaint it. See DiFederico, *Francesco Trevisani* (above, n. 1), 49–50, cat. no. 40, pl. 32.
6. Spear, 'Di Sua Mano' (above, n. 4), 90: 'Traditionally retouching was prompted by the need to correct something: the drawing or modeling of some form, a passage of color, the subtlety of expression, and so forth. In this sense, retouching is closely connected to mimesis and the quality of the hand. But it could also provide a quite good studio work or copy with the precious patina of the 'divine hand', with the appearance of the master's inimitable and unsurpassable ingenium. This sort of retouching points less to the labor invested than to its maker. That was explained quite clearly in 1633 by the Florentine-born Spanish court painter and theorist, Vincencio Carducho. He said that, 'after the assistant considers his work finished, the master retouches the painting again and perfects it. This is the last

step and the refinement which breathes spirit into a painting. Here, in these brushstrokes and fine finishing touches, the true master is revealed'. On the complex subject of 'retouching', see also M. O'Malley, 'Late fifteenth- and early sixteenth-century painting contracts and the stipulated use of the painter's hand', in E. Marchand and A. Wright (eds), *With and Without the Medici: Studies in Tuscan Art and Patronage 1434–1530* (Cambridge, 1998), 155–66.

7. For Trevisani's activity as a painter of popular devotional images, see K. Wolfe, 'Francesco Trevisani and landscape: *Joseph Sold into Slavery* in the National Gallery of Victoria', in D.R. Marshall (ed.), *Art, Site and Spectacle: Studies in Early Modern Visual Culture* (*Melbourne Art Journal* 9–10) (Melbourne, 2007), 53–4.
8. Trevisani's British patrons were primarily Catholic sympathizers or Jacobites: R. Sharp, *The Engraved Record of the Jacobite Movement* (Aldershot, 1996). See also E. Corp, 'Melfort: a Jacobite connoisseur', *History Today* 45 (10) (1995), 40–6; E. Corp, *The King over the Water: Portraits of the Stuarts in Exile after 1689* (Edinburgh, 2001); E. Corp (ed.), *The Stuart Court in Rome. The Legacy of Exile* (Aldershot, 2003); E. Corp, *A Court in Exile: the Stuarts in France, 1689–1718* (Cambridge, 2004); E. Corp, *The Jacobites at Urbino: an Exiled Court in Transition* (Basingstoke/New York, 2009). See also his contribution to this volume (pp. 39–53). For Scottish visitors to Rome, see J. Holloway, *Patrons and Painters: Art in Scotland 1650–1760* (Edinburgh, 1989); J. Holloway, 'John Urquhart of Cromarty: an unknown collector of Italian paintings in Scotland and Italy', in *Papers Presented at the Fourth Annual Conference of the Scottish Society for Art History, Scottish Arts Council* (Edinburgh, 1989), 1–13; and his contribution in the present volume (pp. 103–12).
9. For the date of Trevisani's arrival in Rome, see F. Petrucci, *Pittura di ritratto a Roma: il Seicento* II (Rome, 2008), 422. On Trevisani's early career, see Wolfe, 'Francesco Trevisani and landscape' (above, n. 7), 58–9.
10. The travel journal is that of David Nairne (1655–1740), Melfort's secretary, and has been discussed by Corp, 'Melfort' (above, n. 8): see, 'Diary of David Nairne', National Library of Scotland, MS 14266, fols 12r–30r; and esp. fol. 22r, 1691 Janvier mardi 16: 'Mil. acheta quelques petites pieces d'un vieux Antiquaire. Travisani commença le portrait de M.e'; fol. 22v, 1691 Janvier vendr. 19: 'Travesani travailla pour la 2da fois au portrait de M.e'; fol. 25r, 1691 Avril mecr. 25: 'et puis avec Mel. a St. Carlo et chez Travesani. Mil. acheta son tableaux de Belizar'.
11. Pascoli noted that Melfort also commissioned a painting of a 'Furio Cammillo' from Trevisani: see DiFederico's transcription of Pascoli (DiFederico, *Francesco Trevisani* (above, n. 1), 88).
12. N. Pio, 'Vita di Francesco Trevisani', in N. Pio, *Le vite di pittori, scultori et architetti: (cod. ms. Capponi 257)* (*Studi e testi, Biblioteca Apostolica Vaticana* 278), edited and with an introduction by C. Enggass and R. Enggass (Vatican City, 1977), 38: 'È huomo ameno e sincero e vive felicemente con somma gloria appresso il sudetto cardinale [Ottoboni] nel palazzo della Cancelleria in Roma'. While Trevisani's name does not appear in the Cardinal's household accounts (the *computisteria*), Johann Georg Keyssler (1693–1743), a visitor to Rome *circa* 1729, wrote that Trevisani received 'an allowance of fifty scudi a month from the cardinal, on condition that he will let him have the first refusal of his pieces': see J.G. Keyssler, *Travels through Germany, Bohemia, Hungary, Switzerland, Italy, and Lorrain: Giving a True and Just Description of the Present State of Those Countries, Their Natural, Literary, and Political History, Manners, Laws, Commerce, Manufactures, Painting, Sculpture, Architecture, Coins, Antiquities, Curiosities of Art and Nature, &c., Illustrated with Copper-plates, Engraved from Drawings Taken on the Spot, by John George Keyssler, Carefully Translated from the Second Edition of the German*; in four volumes, London; printed for A. Linde … and T. Field … (1956–7), II, p. 227. I would like to thank E.P. Bowron for very kindly pointing out to me the Anthony Clark transcription of this passage.
13. Trevisani's important activity as a portraitist, whether of Grand Tourists to Rome, of Italian patrons, or even of self-portraits, so far has only been touched upon. See DiFederico, *Francesco Trevisani* (above, n. 1), 20–4 and cat. nos. P1–P20. For the Jacobites, see Corp, *King over the Water* (above, n. 8), esp. pp. 105–9, an extremely useful catalogue of known Stuart portraits, and Corp's contribution in this volume (pp. 39–53). For Trevisani's self-portraits, see E. Spaccini, 'Gli autoritratti di Francesco Trevisani: un'aggiunta al catalogo', in G. Barbera, T. Pugliatti and C. Zappia (eds), *Scritti in onore di Alessandro Marabottini* (Rome, 1997), 289–92. Trevisani's talent as a portraitist was well-recognized by his contemporaries such as Pascoli. See DiFederico, *Francesco Trevisani* (above, n. 1), 94: 'É singolare nel fare li Ritratti e particolarmente per ornarli d'abiti e di ricchi abbigliamenti gli esprime così al vivo che non vi è chi l'uguali …'. See also the biography of Trevisani by Francesco Moücke, transcribed in DiFederico, *Francesco Trevisani* (above, n. 1), 101: 'Non passava personaggio per Roma, che non lo visitasse, e nol ricercasse per farsi ritrarre al naturale …'.
14. Christie's, New York, 28 January 2009, lot 239, *Penitent Magdalene*, signed 'F.T.' on the bookmark. Oil on canvas, oval, 70.8 × 65.7 cm. This painting I believe is the same as that illustrated in the catalogue of the Messinger Collection: see P. D'Achiardi, *La Collection Messinger* (Rome, 1910), 59, cat. no. 24, fig. 41.
15. DiFederico, *Francesco Trevisani* (above, n. 1), 90, citing Pascoli, fol. 91v: 'e mi fece … una Maddalena in ovale di Quattro palmi, che è delle più belle che abbia mai fatte, benchè immemorabili siano e tutte dissimili e graziosissime'.
16. Francesco Trevisani, *Penitent Magdalene*, dated 1727 on the bookmark. Oil on canvas, 97.6 × 73.6 cm. Finarte, Rome, 11 December, 2008, lot 48.
17. The picture is signed 'F.T.' on the bookmark and measures 99 × 76 cm, oil on canvas. A black and white photograph of

this painting is in the Trevisani file, Witt Collection, Courtauld Institute, London. The mount is inscribed: 'No. 24 in the undated Mavisbank Inventory'. For the Mavisbank inventory, see T. Clifford, 'Imperiali and his Scottish patrons', in *Pittura toscana e pittura europea nel secolo dei lumi. Atti del convegno (Pisa, Domus Galilaeana, 3–4 dicembre, 1990)* (Florence, 1993), 41–59, esp. p. 43.

18. B. Ford and J. Ingamells, *A Dictionary of British and Irish Travellers in Italy, 1701–1800. Compiled from the Brinsley Ford Archive* (New Haven/London, 1997), 216. See also Holloway, *Patrons and Painters* (above, n. 8).
19. J. Fleming, *Robert Adam and His Circle in Edinburgh and London* (London, 1962), 16–17, note on p. 326: 'the vast desire I had to see a country so famous for exploits about which all my time had been hitherto spent in reading the classics, likeways a country so replenished with Antiquities of all kinds and so much excelling all other countries in painting and music, I say these things created such a vast desire in me to see it that I am sure nothing in life had ever made me happy if I had denied myself this great pleasure and satisfaction'.
20. For the complex relationships between the various Scottish patrons and painters, see Holloway, *Patrons and Painters* (above, n. 8), 85–97; Holloway, 'John Urquhart of Cromarty' (above, n. 8); Clifford, 'Imperiali' (above, n. 17).
21. Holloway, 'John Urquhart of Cromarty' (above, n. 8), 5, 10–12. A listing of Urquhart's pictures for sale after his death reveals that he owned contemporary copies of paintings by Caravaggio (1571–1610) (from the Palazzo Barberini) and by Guido Reni (1575–1642) (from the Vatican), among others.
22. Pascoli, in DiFederico, *Francesco Trevisani* (above, n. 1), 92 (fol. 94v): 'Né si fatta mia voglia deriva dal far servizio a lui conforme per avventura sarà a taluno passato pel pensiero, perché tutta Roma sa molto bene ch'egli non ha bisogna di lavori e avendone innumerabili fra mano per vecchi, e nuovi impegni contratti, e che giornalmente ricusa di contrarre per tavole di chiesa, e di gabinetti, e di camere, e di gallerie'.
23. Holloway, 'John Urquhart of Cromarty' (above, n. 8), 3–5; and see also his contribution in this volume (pp. 103–12).
24. Holloway, 'John Urquhart of Cromarty' (above, n. 8), 1–6. The Resurrection is not a common subject in Roman churches, nor in Roman private collections. It is otherwise unknown in Trevisani's *oeuvre*, aside from an unfinished replica that must be related directly to the Urquhart commission (Phillips, London, 8 December 1992, lot 128, 134 × 98 cm). However, the *Resurrection* that has emerged and that shares the measurements of the one recorded in Urquhart's inventory (Colnaghi's New York, Ltd) has been discovered to be inscribed 'Francesco Trevisani Pinxt. Romae 1721', making the question of Urquhart's commission problematic. A painting by Trevisani of *The Young Saint John the Evangelist Adoring the Crucifixion* has appeared recently and almost certainly can be identified with the painting of the same subject catalogued in Urquhart's collection. See K. Wolfe, 'San Giovanni evangelista testimonia la Crocifissione', in F. Petrucci (ed.), *Le Collezioni Ferrari, Laschena ed altre donazioni a Palazzo Chigi in Ariccia* (Rome, 2008), 86–8, cat. no. III.2.
25. See n. 2.
26. Not only did Trevisani design stage-sets and act in amateur skits with his friends at the Palazzo della Cancelleria, he also owned and played musical instruments, notably a clavicembalo, the very instrument illustrated in the frontispiece he designed for his friend and fellow courtier at the Ottoboni court, Corelli, for Corelli's *Concerti Grossi* (Opera VI). See Wolfe, 'Il pittore e il musicista' (above, n. 2).
27. These include six landscapes by Alessio de Marchis (1675–1729); a *Still Life of Fruit* by Giovanni Paolo Spadino (documented 1687–1703); two landscapes by François Simonot called Monsù Francesco Borgognone (*c.* 1660–1731); a *Saint Anthony* by Carlo Dolci (1616–86); *Vulcan's Forge* (well-finished) and *The Fall of Paul* (*bozzetto*) by Luca Giordano (1632–1705); and a *Madonna with Christ Child and Saint John the Baptist* by Giuseppe Passeri (1654–1714).
28. A black chalk drawing of *David and Bathsheba*, probably acquired by Thomas Coke (1697–1759) in Rome *c.* 1717, is in the portfolios at Holkham Hall. See A.W. Moore, *Norfolk and the Grand Tour, Eighteenth-century Travellers Abroad and their Souvenirs* (Norwich, 1985), 115, cat. no. 45, n. 1.
29. Stourhead, Wiltshire, Hoare Collection (The National Trust), no. 462, oil on canvas, 84.5 × 65.5 cm, formerly attributed to Carlo Cignani. See Wolfe, 'Il pittore e il musicista' (above, n. 2), 183, n. 69.
30. Pascoli related that upon his arrival in Rome, Trevisani copied the Queen's Correggio. See DiFederico, *Francesco Trevisani* (above, n. 1), 87, citing Pascoli, fol. 88v: 'e studio molto in quelle de'Caracci nella galleria Farnese, ed in quelle del Coreggio negli appartamenti della Regina di Svezia'. Trevisani's inventories include a copy after the Queen's *Danae* by Correggio, as well as copies of paintings after Veronese and Rubens from her collections. See n. 2.
31. A. Cametti, 'Arcangelo Corelli i suoi quadri i suoi violini', *Roma* 9 (1927), 412–23. See also Wolfe, 'Il pittore e il musicista' (above, n. 2).
32. See the Trevisani *Self-portrait* (Musée des Augustins-Musée des Beaux Arts de Toulouse, RO 425, oil on copper, 15 × 12 cm), which shows the artist at his easel painting a portrait of a woman, almost certainly his wife, Girolama Riva. For the *Mater Dolorosa*, in which the Virgin shares the similar features of a long oval-shaped face and the pronounced nose of Riva, see DiFederico, *Francesco Trevisani* (above, n. 1), cat. 72, pl. 60 (oil on canvas, 99 × 74 cm; Rome, Palazzo Corsini). DiFederico, however, dated the picture to 1715–20. Two further copies of this subject have appeared, one with a Chigi provenance, thus supporting the proposal of an early dating for the formulation of this type and certainly from before 1693, the year of Cardinal Chigi's death. This picture, measuring 105 × 75 cm, is on the Italian art market in Rimini with Filippo Gaffarelli. Another, today in a private collection in the UK, passed through Philipps, London, on 11 December 1998, lot 81, as 'studio of Trevisani' (oil on canvas, 100 × 73.7 cm).

33. Pascoli said that Trevisani left Venice before his 22nd birthday (that is, in 1678), wishing to visit other cities in Italy (DiFederico, *Francesco Trevisani* (above, n. 1), 86, citing Pascoli, fol. 88v). Since it has not been possible to trace Trevisani in the Roman archives before September 1679, this leaves an interval of more than a year unaccounted for, during which time the artist most probably visited Bologna. A portrait by Trevisani of the Bolognese painter Ercole Graziani the Elder (1651–1726) has come to light recently, and Trevisani's paintings show a marked interest in this Bolognese master, as well as in Reni's Bolognese works (especially the Capuchin altarpiece of *The Crucifixion*).
34. C.M.S. Johns, 'Francesco Trevisani', in E.P. Bowron and J.J. Rishel (eds), *Art in Rome in the Eighteenth Century* (London/Philadelphia, 2000), 441–2.
35. As Louise Newstead, House Steward at Stourhead, has informed me, the painting does not appear in the 1742 inventory, but only in that of 1800.
36. *Madonna and the Sleeping Christ Child*. Oil on canvas, 82.5 × 69.8 cm. Marquess of Exeter, Burghley House Collection, Stamford. See DiFederico, *Francesco Trevisani* (above, n. 1), 55, cat. 62, pl. 50, who, however, dated the picture much later, to *c.* 1710. The 5th Earl (1648–1700) visited Rome on at least three occasions, in 1681, 1683–4 and 1700. A newly-discovered travel journal that Edward Chaney has kindly shared with me, written by a half-pay officer who accompanied the 5th Earl and his family on their last tour, may suggest that the 5th Earl's Trevisani acquisitions date from this visit. See R. Creed, *Journal of the Grand Tour 1699–1700* II (transcribed with modern spelling from the original two volumes by A. Thomas) (Corby, 2002); H. Brigstocke, 'The Fifth Earl of Exeter as Grand Tourist and collector', *Papers of the British School at Rome* 72 (2004), 331–56. See also Wolfe, 'Il pittore e il musicista' (above, n. 3), for a discussion of the *Madonna and the Sleeping Christ Child* in the context of Trevisani's artistic rapport with Corelli.
37. The Stourhead and Burghley *Madonna*s measure 84.5 × 65.4 cm and 82.5 × 69.8 cm respectively.
38. See p. 83 and n. 1.
39. *Madonna and the Sleeping Christ Child*. Oil on canvas, 97 × 79 cm. Museo de la Real Academia de Bellas Artes de San Fernando, Madrid, inv. no. 527. The painting, which ended up in Madrid after various vicissitudes, was described as a 'copy of Maratti' by Antonio Ponz in 1784. See A.M. Suárez Huerta, cat. no. 68, in *El Westmorland Recuerdos del Grand Tour* (Madrid, 2002), 330, which, however, includes outdated information about Trevisani.
40. I am indebted to Francis Russell for pointing out to me that it was the 3rd Earl who surely acquired this picture. For Viscount Lewisham, see Ford and Ingamells, *Dictionary of British and Irish Travellers* (above, n. 19), 600; for the 2nd Earl Dartmouth see p. 277. The second Earl's agent was, for a period from 1753–4, Thomas Jenkins (1722–98).
41. A *Madonna and the Sleeping Christ Child* is listed in the inventory of pictures for sale, but the measurements (3 *palmi*) do not coincide with the measurements of the Madrid painting (97 × 79 cm). For the inventories, see n. 2.
42. *The Madonna and the Sleeping Christ Child*. Oil on canvas, 31.5 × 24.5 cm. St Petersburg, Hermitage Museum, inv. no. 2256. See L. Dukelskaya and A. Moore (eds), *A Capital Collection: Houghton Hall and the Hermitage* (New Haven/London, 2002), 123, cat. no. 29.
43. Alongside the *Madonna and the Sleeping Christ Child* (see n. 36), the Trevisani pictures at Burghley House are: (all oil on canvas) *Martyrdom of the Four Crowned Saints* (50.8 × 35.5 cm); *Saint Andrew Placed on the Cross* (52.1 × 36.8 cm); *Mocking of Christ* (85.3 × 109.5 cm); *Flagellation of Christ* (116.8 × 72 cm); and *Noli Me Tangere* (97.8 × 72.4 cm). See DiFederico, *Francesco Trevisani* (above, n. 1), cat. nos. 5, 28, 21, 22 and 34 respectively. For the *Mocking of Christ* and the *Noli Me Tangere*, see also Brigstocke and Somerville (eds), *Italian Paintings* (above, n. 4), 142, cat. nos. 54, 144, 55.
44. While Francis Haskell called the 5th Earl 'inconsistent' in his taste because of the wide-ranging nature of his acquisitions (F. Haskell, *Patrons and Painters: a Study in the Relations between Italian Art and Society in the Age of the Baroque* (New Haven/London, 1980), 197), Edward Chaney has argued for an interpretation in terms of 'a more pluralist collecting environment . . . [that] now compared itself favourably with the more monolithic (and monopolistic) cultural agenda set across the channel by the likes of Richelieu, Mazarin and Louis XIV . . . Exeter may have been the most extravagant but he was not the last to commission and collect Italian Baroque pictures, which Whigs and Tories alike continued to do': E. Chaney, 'The Italianate evolution of English collecting', in E. Chaney (ed.), *The Evolution of English Collecting: the Reception of Italian Art in the Tudor and Stuart Periods* (New Haven/London, 2003), 74–5.
45. Wolfe, 'Francesco Trevisani and landscape' (above, n. 7), 53, n. 49. For the date of the *Martyrdom of the Four Crowned Saints*, see the catalogue entry by Margherita Anselmi Zondadori, cat. no. 330, in A. Angelini, M. Butzek and B. Sani, *Alessandro VII Chigi (1599–1667). Il papa senese di Roma moderna* (Siena, 2000), 494–5 (reproduced in reverse).
46. U. Fischer-Pace (ed.), *Disegni del Seicento romano* (Florence, 1997), 209–11, cat. no. 139. A beautiful small *pensiero* (oil on canvas, 47 × 33 cm) is in a private collection in Biarritz, France. See A. Brejon de Lavergnèe and P. Rosenberg, 'Francesco Trevisani et la France', *Antologia di Belle Arti* 7–8 (1978), 265–76, esp. p. 276, n. 86.
47. For Zanchi, see A. Riccoboni, 'Antonio Zanchi, pittore veneto (1631–1722) nel secondo centenario della morte', *Rassegna d'Arte Antica e Moderna* (1922), 109–19.
48. For the paintings, see DiFederico, *Francesco Trevisani* (above, n. 1), 44, cat. nos. 21–2; Brigstocke and Somerville (eds), *Italian Paintings* (above, n. 4), 142, cat. no. 54.
49. See Cametti, 'Arcangelo Corelli' (above, n. 31), nos. 43–4. See also G. De Marchi (ed.), *Mostre di quadri a San Salvatore in Lauro (1682–1725)* (Rome, 1987), 154. A very fine variant of

the chapel altarpiece depicting the Crucifixion, which may be that painting owned by Corelli and exhibited at San Salvatore in Lauro in 1701, is in a private collection in Biarritz, France (98 × 60 cm, oil on canvas, signed with the monogram 'F.T.').

50. DiFederico, *Francesco Trevisani* (above, n. 1), 44, cat. no. 23, oil on canvas, 221 × 171 cm; Wolfe, 'Il pittore e il musicista' (above, n. 2), 178, n. 42.
51. DiFederico, *Francesco Trevisani* (above, n. 1), 44, cat. no. 22.
52. Brigstocke and Somerville, *Italian Paintings* (above, n. 4), 144, cat. no. 55; Brigstocke, 'The Fifth Earl of Exeter' (above, n. 36), 349.
53. Creed, *Journal* (above, n. 36) II; no specific date is recorded, but the page is headed March 1700. I wish to thank Edward Chaney for sending me this excerpt.
54. J. Somerville, 'Burghley: the house and the Cecil family, a history', in Brigstocke and Somerville (eds), *Italian Paintings* (above, n. 4), 15–27, esp. pp. 17–19.
55. This situation may change as Trevisani pictures continue to appear regularly at auction, and as more research on British collectors is published. Andrew Moore noted that 'two subject pictures by Trevisani' were to be sent back to England for Coke by Matthew Brettingham (1699–1769) (Moore, *Norfolk and the Grand Tour* (above, n. 28), 115, cat. no. 45, n. 2), while a small painting of a *Saint Catherine Receiving the Palm of Martyrdom* (46 × 35.5 cm, perhaps from the 'Sale of fine pictures brought from abroad by Mr. Andrew Hay' (Hay was a member of the Jacobite family that served James III (1688–1766) in Rome) at Cock's in Poland Street, on 19 February 1725/6, lot 33, bought by the 2nd Duke of Devonshire for £22), was sold at Christie's, London, 21 May 1976, lot 59. This subject is not known in any other collections. See also p. 84 and note 11 for Melfort's commissions to Trevisani.
56. See Wolfe, 'Francesco Trevisani and landscape' (above, n. 7), 45, for the *Joseph Sold into Slavery* from the Pallavicini Collection that ended up in the Westminster Collection, at Grosvenor House. For the *Baptism of Christ*, today at Temple Newsam, Leeds, see DiFederico, *Francesco Trevisani* (above, n. 1), 60, cat. no. 78. Also, see the painting attributed to Trevisani, *Mary Magdalene Receiving Water from the Angels*, oil on canvas, 289.6 × 193 cm, on loan to Scunthorpe Museum and Art Gallery from Lindsey County Council.
57. As Francis Russell noted, referring, however, to the portrait-painter Antonio David (1684–1737), 'the qualities of a key figure in Roman portraiture of the second quarter of the *Settecento*, and the pattern of patronage it implies offers a hint that the development of Grand Tour portraiture owed more to the Jacobite presence in Rome than is generally admitted' (F. Russell, 'Notes on Grand Tour portraiture', *The Burlington Magazine* 136 (1994), 438–43, esp. p. 438). The David family was closely associated with Trevisani (Wolfe, 'Francesco Trevisani and landscape' (above, n. 7), 52, n. 35). No catalogue exists of Trevisani's British sitters, although the majority was Jacobites (see n. 9). Aside from the photographs filed under the artist's name at the Witt Library, in the Courtauld Institute and the archives in the National Portrait Gallery, London, see DiFederico, *Francesco Trevisani* (above, n. 1), 74–7, cat. nos. P8–19, plates 102–12; Sharp *The Engraved Record* (above, n. 8); and the writings of Corp cited in n. 8.
58. The *Self-portrait* in Figure 7.8 (oil on canvas, 95.5 × 71 cm, before 1700; Private Collection, UK), may well be the picture that Trevisani kept in his house. However, as it was one of the few paintings for which no measurements were given in the inventory, it is impossible to know for sure. The dating of this *Self-portrait* is based on a comparison with the variant that the artist presented to the Medici Gallery of artists' self-portraits in Florence in 1710, which measures 81 × 64 cm. See DiFederico, *Francesco Trevisani* (above, n. 1), 74, cat. no. P7, pl. 101. For the vexing problem of the various Trevisani self-portraits, see, in the first instance, Spaccini 'Gli autoritratti di Francesco Trevisani' (above, n. 13).
59. Trevisani's biographer, Francesco Moücke, wrote with slight overstatement 'that no-one visited Rome without stopping by Trevisani's studio and once there, wanted to have their portrait painted from life'; see n. 13.
60. For Lord Barnard in Italy, see Ford and Ingamells, *Dictionary of British and Irish Travellers* (above, n. 18), 52.
61. Archivio del Vicariato, Rome, Sant'Andrea delle Fratte, Stati delle anime, 1701, fol. 13.
62. Francesco Trevisani, *Christopher Vane, 1st Lord Barnard*, 1701. Oil on canvas, 135.5 × 99 cm. Private Collection, UK. The owner of the portrait kindly informed me that Oliver Millar first suggested an attribution to Trevisani.
63. For the Ottoboni portrait, see Johns, 'Francesco Trevisani' (above, n. 34), 443, cat. no. 291.
64. A. Ribeiro, *Fashion and Fiction: Dress in Art and Literature in Stuart England* (New Haven/London, 2005), 307–8.
65. *Portrait of Thomas Coke (b. 1698) 1st Earl of Leicester (of the First Creation)*, 1717. Oil on canvas, 200.7 × 161.3 cm. On Coke, see Moore, *Norfolk and the Grand Tour* (above, n. 28), 115, cat. no. 45.
66. For the Veronese from the Pio collection, see P.G. Baroni, *Il cardinale Pietro Ottoboni: un conformista del diciottesimo secolo* (Bologna, 1969), 117, n. 36: 'E. 9 febbraio 1715 — Francesco Trevisani (detto il Romano) nativo di Capo d'Istria (1656–1746)'. Letter of 20 April 1715: 'Il mio pittore Trevisani, che oggi ha il primo luogo tra quelli che vivono, vorrebbe per una settimana poter portare nelle sue stanze un piccolo quadretto di Paolo Veronese di grandezza di tre palmi che rappresenta Marte, Venere, che sta con gli altri in una casa che tiene qui il principe Pio con il rimanente della sua galleria'. Trevisani's request was granted (letter of 18 May 1715). Moreover, Queen Christina also owned portraits by Titian (*c.* 1490–1576) and Anthony van Dyck (1599–1641), and Trevisani also surely knew and exchanged ideas with her court painter, the Swede, Michael Dahl (1656–1743), who spent several years in Rome, later travelling to England and establishing himself as a highly accomplished portraitist.

67. F. Haskell and N. Penny, *Taste and the Antique: the Lure of Classical Sculpture 1500–1900* (New Haven/London, 1981), 62.
68. *Portrait of Abate Carlo Colonna*. Oil on canvas, 96.5 × 71 cm. The picture is signed and dated 1691 on the letter, and traditionally has been identified with Carlo Colonna, created cardinal in 1706. See DiFederico, *Francesco Trevisani* (above, n. 1), 72, cat. no. P3, pl. 98.
69. Wolfe, 'Francesco Trevisani and landscape' (above, n. 7), 45, n. 12.
70. For Mar, see in the first instance Ford and Ingamells, *Dictionary of British and Irish Travellers* (above, n. 18), 638–9. For Mar as a patron, see Corp, *King over the Water* (above, n. 8), 58–9.
71. Corp, *King over the Water* (above, n. 8), 57–60.
72. For the picture (oil on canvas, 134.6 × 96.5 cm), which is at Alloa House, The Earl of Mar and Kelly, see the Trevisani files at the Witt Library, Courtauld Institute (neg. no. B/3931).
73. On David's career in Rome, see S. Capelli, 'I David a Roma', in A. Spiriti and S. Capelli (eds), *I David: due pittori tra Sei e Settecento* (Milan, 2004), 67–89. For David's portraits of the Stuarts, see Corp, *King over the Water* (above, n. 8), 107. See also the contribution by Corp to this volume (pp. 39–53).
74. See nn. 8 and 57.
75. For the *Portrait of Maria Clementina Sobieska* (oil on canvas, 98 × 73 cm; Edinburgh, Scottish National Portrait Gallery, no. 886), see Corp, *King over the Water* (above, n. 8), 56–61. For the engravings, see Sharp, *The Engraved Record* (above, n. 8), 22, 104–10.
76. DiFederico, *Francesco Trevisani* (above, n. 1); for the half-portrait see pp. 76–7, cat. no. P18, pl. 111; for the full-length portrait see p. 77, cat. no. P19, pl. 112. The full-length one is illustrated here (Fig. 7.12). Oil on canvas, 236 × 145 cm. Badminton House, the Duke of Beaufort.
77. For one of the pictures, a *Holy Family*, see DiFederico, *Francesco Trevisani* (above, n. 1), 55, cat. no. 63, who noted the Badminton variant; for the other painting, the *Three Maries at the Sepulchre*, oil on canvas, 40 × 50 cm, cat. no. 124, see the photograph in the Trevisani file, Witt Collection, Courtauld Institute. On the 3rd Duke's collecting activities, see Ford and Ingamells, *Dictionary of British and Irish Travellers* (above, n. 18), 67–9, with Stosch reporting (p. 68) that Beaufort 'is said to have spent over 30,000 scudi on pictures and marbles, which, with the exception of eight or ten pieces, the majority are of little importance'.
78. *Sir Edward Gascoigne, 6th Baronet*. Oil on canvas, 96.5 × 80 cm. Lotherton Hall, Leeds, City Art Galleries. DiFederico, *Francesco Trevisani* (above, n. 1), 74, cat. no. P10, pl. 103. On Gascoigne, see Ford and Ingamells, *Dictionary of British and Irish Travellers* (above, n. 18), 393.
79. J. Richardson, *An Essay on the Theory of Painting. Second Edition. Enlarged and Corrected* (London, 1725), 13–14.

John Urquhart of Cromarty: a Jacobite patron in Rome

James Holloway

The purpose of this paper is to present a hitherto little-known collector and patron of Italian paintings, Captain John Urquhart of Cromarty and Craigston who lived between 1696 and 1756 (Fig. 8.1).[1] He was the direct descendant of the famous Sir Thomas Urquhart, the colourful translator of Rabelais, and Captain Urquhart's own life might, without embellishment, pass for a work of fiction itself. He was a Jacobite who at the age of nineteen fought at Sherrifmuir with the Earl of Mar. He then escaped to France, became a Captain in the Spanish Navy when he was wounded by an English cannon-ball at the Siege of Gibraltar. Subsequently he made a fortune in privateering and became a Roman Catholic.

It was the money that he made in trade with the Americas, which his Hanoverian enemies branded as piracy, that enabled him to buy back his great ancestral castles of Cromarty on the Black Isle and Craigston in Banffshire, and to embark on an ambitious spending spree on the Italian art market. He could do this because he was able to call on the services of a fellow Aberdonian, the artist William Mosman who, between 1732 and 1738, was in Rome working in the studio of the painter Francesco Fernandi, better known as Imperiali. While Mosman was learning the skills of history painting, he was also employed by Urquhart's cousin, Patrick Duff of Premnay, who in 1729 had bought Culter House at Peterculter and, with the aid of Mosman's copies after Guido Reni and Imperiali himself, was busy making it 'one of the most beautiful and best finished gentleman's seats in the North'.[2]

As a loyal Jacobite, Urquhart wanted to buy portraits of the exiled Stuart royal family. He commissioned the very famous pair of portraits of Bonnie Prince Charlie and his brother Prince Henry from Antonio David (Fig. 8.2; Plate 8.1).[3] Mosman wrote anxiously to Urquhart:

> I beg you'l advise me some time befor you give me orders to send off the pictures of P & D [Prince and Duke] because I have begun copies of them for my Lord Marishal for whom I have to do the K & Q [King and Queen] half length from Trevisani's originals. But my master willing I should continue drawing this summer from Rafael have delayed finishing them till winter so if befor that time you incline to have them sent off pray advise me — I shall likewise beg to know if you design them for Scotland because if you do I would not spend time here to coppy them for myself presuming you will let me have them to coppy there but if you design them for Spain would not loose such an opportunity.[4]

That letter, written on 25 September 1733, was the first of a long correspondence from Mosman to Urquhart keeping him informed of his commissions.[5] Captain John Urquhart had been in Rome with Mosman the previous year, when they had visited artists and drawn up their shopping list. Like many other eighteenth-century collectors, Urquhart was as interested in good copies of old masters as originals, and ordered both. Trevisani was his favourite artist, as indeed he was of the Jacobite Court, and Urquhart's portrait by Trevisani still hangs at Craigston.

Already in his seventies when Urquhart and Mosman were in Rome, Trevisani was commissioned to paint a large *Resurrection of Christ* (Plate 8.2),[6] but his age was a problem. 'I have frequently visit[ed] Trevisani this summer on acct of your picture', wrote Mosman to the Captain in the same letter of 25 September 1733, 'was with him two days agoe he has al this summer been uncapable of working by reason of a weakness in his eye but is now almost recovered & says he will begin your picture verie soon & promises he will have it finished by the first of Jan^{ry}'. Three months later:

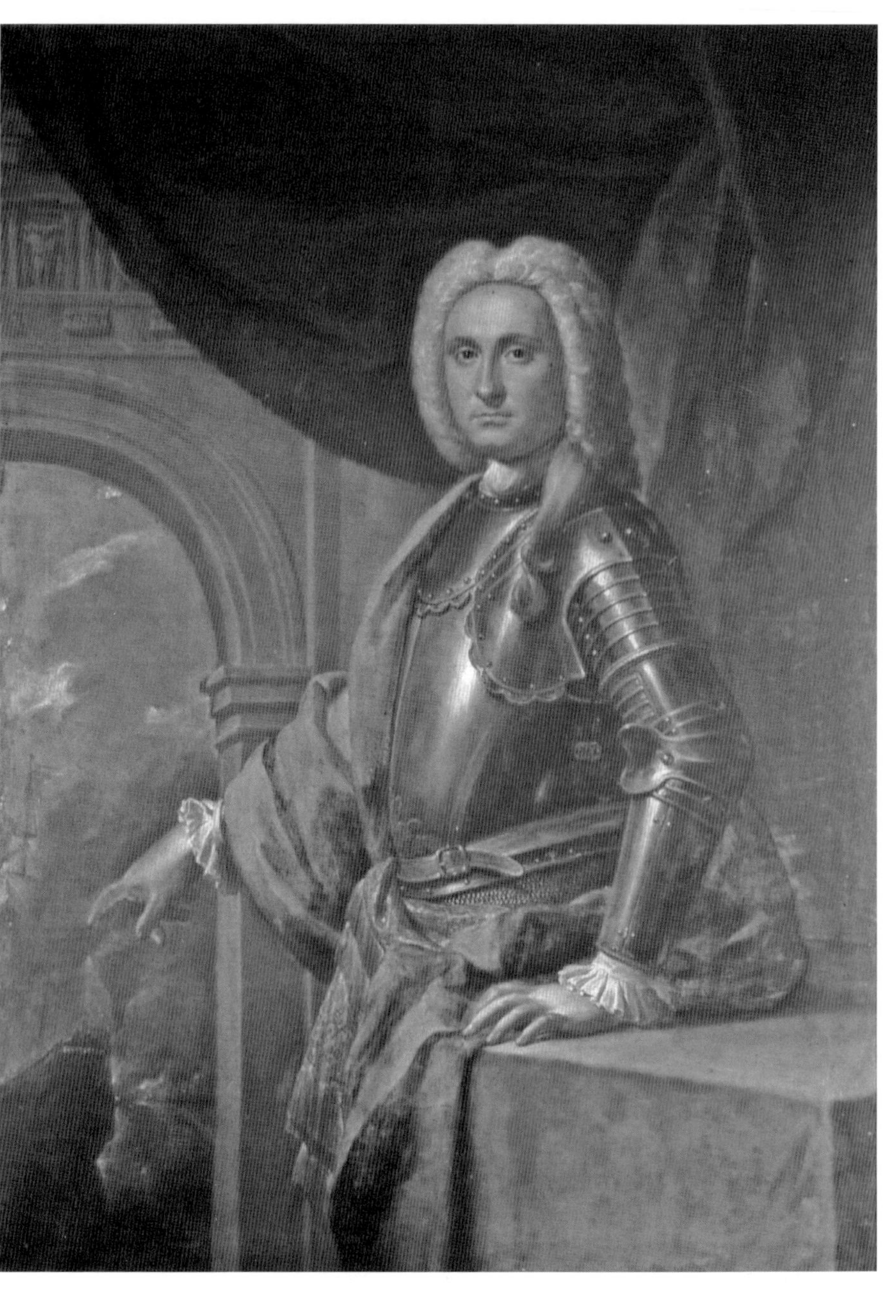

FIG. 8.1. Francesco Trevisani (1656–1746), *Portrait of John Urquhart of Craigston and Cromarty (1696–1756)*, 1732. Oil on canvas, 134 × 98 cm. Craigston Castle, Banffshire. *(Photo: Eric Ellington. Reproduced courtesy of William Pratesi Urquhart.)*

> I have at present to inform you that Trevisani has dead coloured your picture and I have carried some friends to see it who agrees with me that the invention is good. How he may be able to finish it time can only show his constitution is by age so weak that he cannot promise exactly on the time when it will be finished but promises to use all diligence to give it you soon which he says may perhaps be in two months and perhaps not in four.[7]

Writing the following April:

> Trevisani has as yet proceeded no further in your picture tho' he promises every week to sett about it. I should be glade you would if you can inform me about what time you intend to be here that I may endeavour to prevail with Trevisani to advance if not finish the picture that you may be able to determine in that affair your self.[8]

In September 1734 Trevisani had still not produced the picture, and Mosman was despairing:

> I have visit[ed] Trevisani almost every week who gives me fair promises to begin to finish your picture every other day but as yet nothing more is done & if the information I have be just I doubt if you ever get it

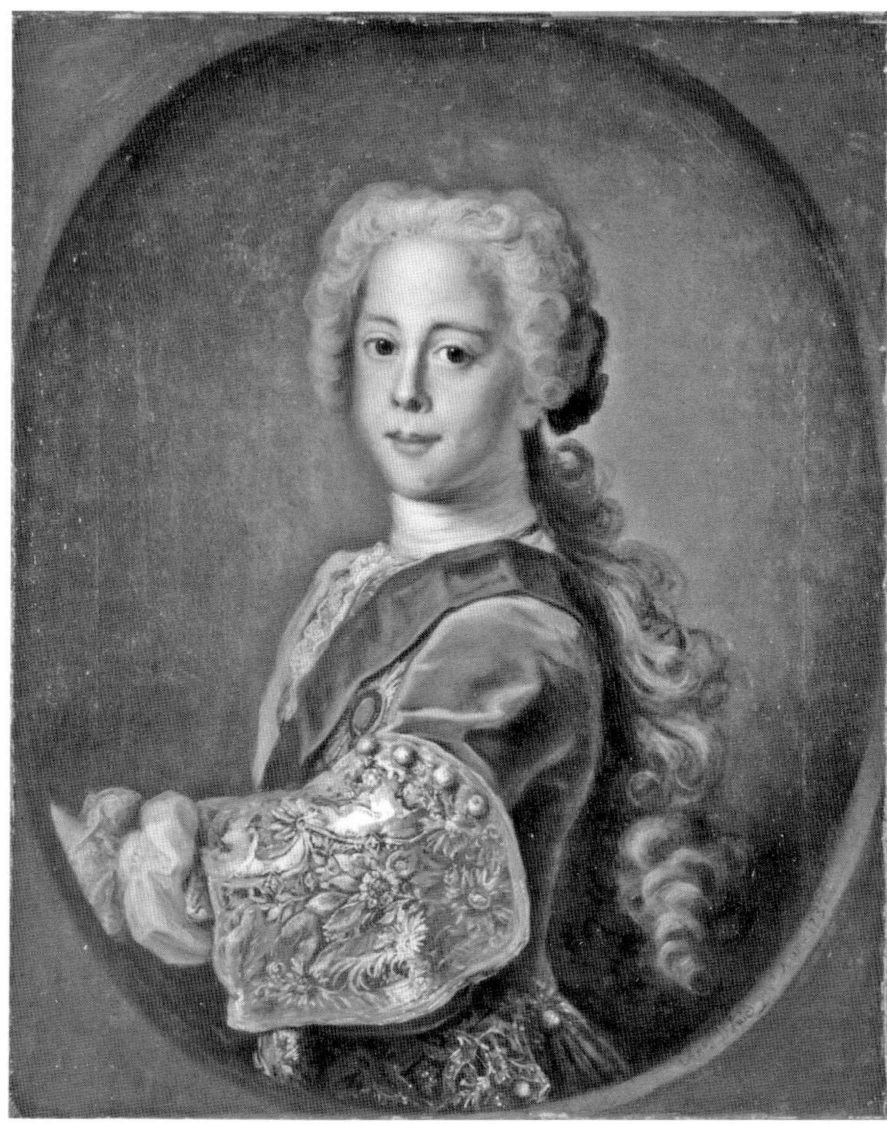

FIG. 8.2. Antonio David (1684–1737), *Prince Henry Benedict Clement Stuart, 1725–1807. Cardinal York; Younger Brother of Prince Charles Edward*, 1732. Oil on canvas, 73.4 × 60.6 cm. Scottish National Portrait Gallery, acc. no. PG 888, purchased 1918. *(Photo: National Galleries of Scotland.)*

> or at least for some years being informed he has ten years work on hand a great part of which was bespoken before yours.[9]

At last, on 12 March 1735, Mosman was able to write that 'Trevisani has been as good as his word & has brought your picture to the last stroaks which will not take above four days'; but ominously he added 'I am of the same opinion I was that old age is plainly seen in it tho' I think in honour you cannot leave it on his hand — since to my certain knowledge he left very considerable works to serve you'.[10] Final payment was made on 16 July 1735, 30 months after the contract was signed.

If the problem with Trevisani was his extreme old age, Pompeo Batoni was equally tiresome, but for a different reason. Urquhart appears to have been the first foreigner to have commissioned oil paintings from the young Italian artist. In the late 1720s, newly-arrived in Rome from Lucca, Batoni had come under the guidance of Imperiali, and it was at the latter's suggestion that Mosman and Urquhart approached the fledgling artist. Urquhart wanted Batoni to copy three paintings: Reni's ceiling of the *Ascension of Christ* in the Vatican, Reni's *Christ on the Cross* in San Lorenzo in Lucina and Federico Barocci's *Rest on the Flight into Egypt* in the Pamphilj Palace. Contracts for all three copies were signed on 20 January 1733, and a *capara*, a deposit, was paid to Batoni for the *Ascension*.

From the beginning this particular commission was jinxed. There were difficulties in getting papal permission to erect scaffolding in the Vatican. When that was resolved and Batoni had started work, he fell ill with a fever that lasted three months. On his recovery Batoni, like Byron after *Childe Harold*, awoke one morning and found himself famous. His altarpiece for San Gregorio al Celio had been exhibited publicly at the Palazzo San Marco in August 1733, and from then on Batoni was the coming man. Writing a year later, on 3 September 1734, Mosman's irritation with the Italian artist is apparent:

> Pompeo on whom we depended most has also failed so far that had we not forced him under a new obligation to deliver the picture within such a time or return his capparo we had not got the Ascension from Guido begun above a year ago perhaps for a year to come which at last I have received & is a good copy. He found on his exposing the original picture you saw begun for S. Gregorio several other original pictures to do which he judges will be more for his advantage than copying. He grasps at interest without any regard to former engagements positively refusing to coppy the other pictures. He has served another English gentleman the same way likewise recommended to him by Imperiali which has so irritate[d] Sig^{r} Francesco [Imperiali] that he has quite abandoned him.[11]

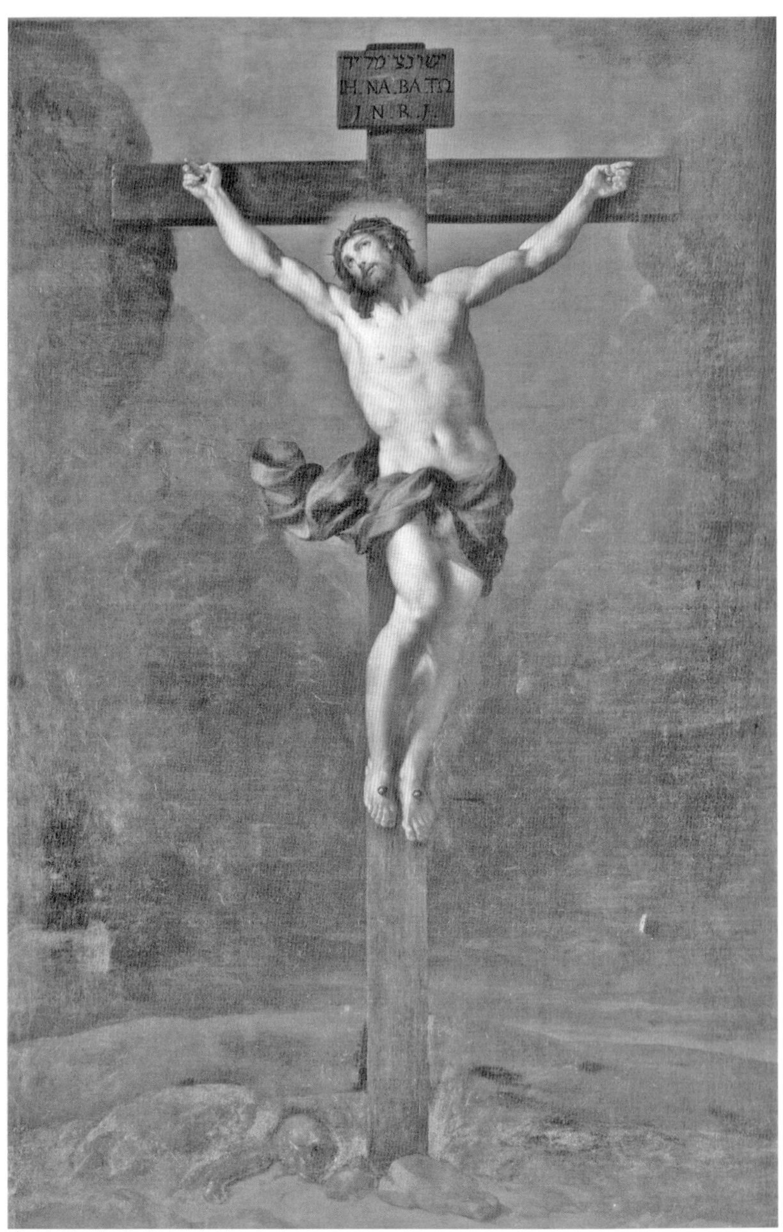

FIG. 8.3. **Francesco Fernandi, called Imperiali (1679–1740), *Crucifixion*. Oil on canvas, 300 × 200 cm. The Earl of Wemyss and March, Gosford House, East Lothian.** *(Photo: AIC Photographic. Reproduced courtesy of the Countess of Wemyss.)*

Worse was to come. When Batoni's ceiling arrived in Scotland, Urquhart did not like it. Mosman wrote in March 1735:

> I am surprised you seem to like the Ascension the worst . . . Tho I am sure you will be of a quite different opinion when you put it in a roof wher you mentioned you designed it for on which acc^{t} Pompeo justly imitated the manner of the original and was the reason of his having a scaffold. The blew I assure you is the best tho' a light colour being to us the original.[12]

As well as works by Trevisani and Batoni, Urquhart commissioned original compositions from Imperiali, Pietro Bianchi, Chiari, Paolo Monaldi, Orizzonte (Jan Franz van Bloemen) and others. The good natured Imperiali, embarrassed at the failure of his protégé to produce more than one of his copies, agreed to paint Urquhart a *Crucifixion* as a substitute for Batoni's copy of Reni's San Lorenzo in Lucina altarpiece. This painting (**Fig. 8.3**) is an original composition, although Imperiali followed Reni's altarpiece very closely in lighting and design.[13]

In 1738, back in Scotland, Mosman was arranging for frames to be made by the Aberdeen frame-maker Patrick Barron, so that 41 of Urquhart's paintings could be

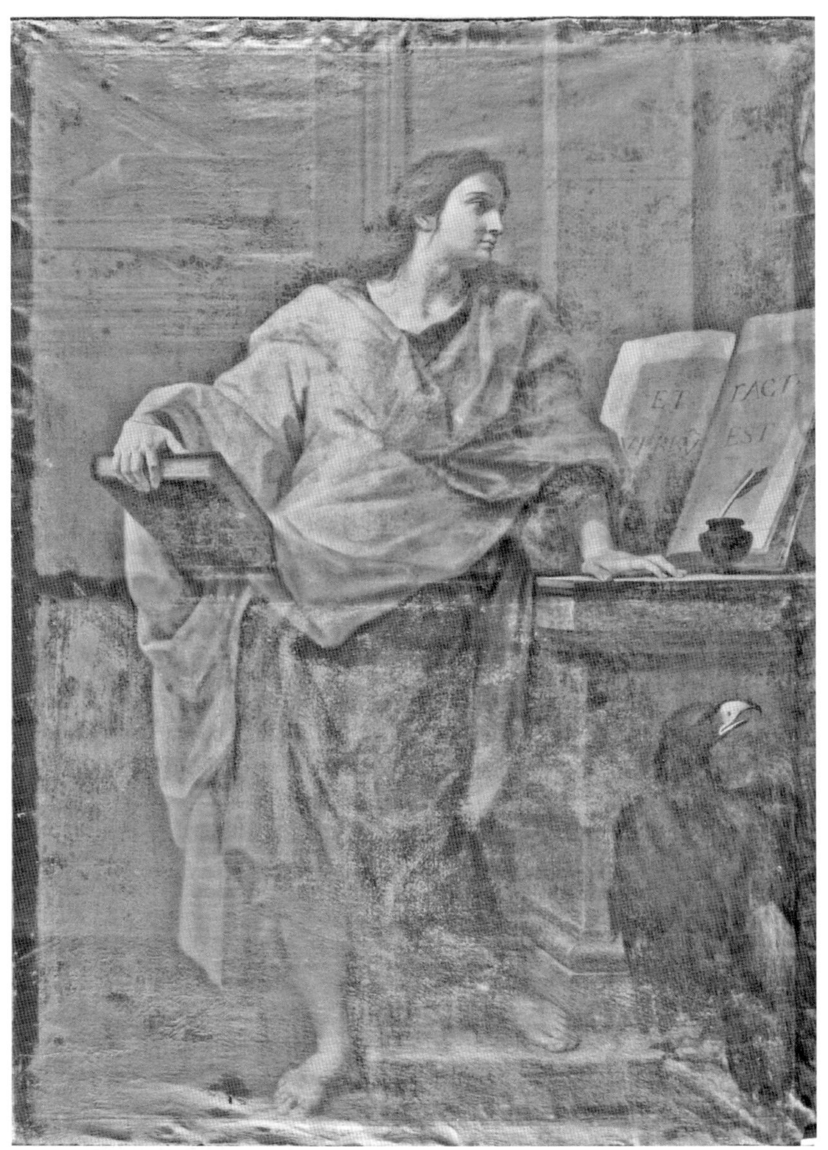

FIG. 8.4. Stefano Pozzi (1699–1768), after Carlo Maratti (1625–1713), *Saint John the Evangelist*. Oil on canvas, 197.2 × 164.0 cm. Thirlestane Castle, Lauder, Berwickshire. *(Photo: AIC Photographic. Reproduced courtesy of the Thirlestane Castle Trust.)*

exhibited at the newly-completed Robert Gordon's hospital. The following year that other great Scottish admirer of contemporary Roman painting, Sir John Clerk of Penicuik, was in Aberdeen, and on 21 May 1739 he met Urquhart, mentioning him in his journal:

> I dined this day with the above named gentleman Captain Urquhart who had been 15 years in the Spanish service. He had been likewise in Italy and as he was a lover of pictures he showed me 2 fine original pictures as large as the life one with several figures by Trevisani and another being a crucifix by Imperiali, he had likewise several other little originals & many good copies after the Roman Masters.[14]

The collection remained together until Urquhart's death, when it was sold at auction in Edinburgh in January 1757, with Mosman arranging the sale.

The Trevisani *Resurrection* was the most expensive picture, at £90. It was bought by John, 2nd Earl of Hopetoun, for the green drawing-room at Hopetoun House.[15] He also bought an Imperiali of *Our Saviour in the Garden* for £25 for the green bedroom at Hopetoun, 'a pair of pictures of Game' by Baldassare de Caro, and Stefano Parrocel's copy of Andrea Sacchi's *Martyrdom of Saint Andrew*.

Imperiali's *Crucifixion* was bought by Francis Charteris of Amisfield and is today in the collection of his descendant, the Earl of Wemyss, at Gosford House, East Lothian. Sir James Clerk, whose father had admired the collection twenty years earlier, bought Chiari's *Madonna and Child*, still at Penicuik House, Midlothian. Still at Thirlestane Castle is Stefano Pozzi's excellent copy of Carlo Maratti's *Saint John the Evangelist*, for which the Countess of Lauderdale paid £16 (**Fig. 8.4**). Lord Elibank bought two paintings by Trevisani, a *Madonna* and a *Saint John the Evangelist*, of similar size and probably companions.[16] He also bought Batoni's ceiling, but that, like many of the other 49 lots in the sale, has disappeared.

APPENDIX

A
CATALOGUE
OF
VALUABLE PICTURES[17]

Collected by the deceas'd JOHN URQUHART, Esq;
of Cromarty during his long Residence abroad;
CONSISTING OF

Several Capital Pictures, by the most eminent Italian and Flemish Masters;
Together with a very Curious Collection of Italian Prints, finely
pasted, and bound in Twenty one Volumes;
As also Some Valuable Basso-Relievo's:
To be exposed to Sale, at the ABBEY of Holyroodhouse, on Monday
the Tenth of January 1757, and the Three following Days;
To begin at Eleven o' Clock Forenoon precisely.
The Lowest Prices are affixed to each Article.
If two or more Persons claim the same Article, it is to be put to
Auction; and he that bids most, shall be the Purchaser.
The Collection will be shown for Four Days before the Sale, from
Ten o' Clock Forenoon, to Two o' Clock Afternoon.

		L.	s.	d.
1	A Dutch Conversation-Piece, an Original, length 1 foot 4 inches, breadth 1 foot,	1	10	0
2	Two Ditto Companions, length 1 foot 5 inches, breadth 1 foot 2½ inches,	3	3	0
3	Our Saviour by Fran. Trevisani, length 2 feet 1 inch, breadth 1 feet 7 inches,	3	10	0
4	A Madonna by Ditto, and Ditto Measure,	3	10	0
5	A Copy of Guido Reni's famous Picture of St Peter weeping, by Cavaliero Costanzi, Ditto Measure,	4	10	0
6	The Annunciation, a Copy of Stephano Pozzi, from the famous Picture of Barrocci, length 6 feet 6 inches, breadth 4 feet 10 inches,	10	10	0
7	St. John the Evangelist, copied by Ditto from Carlo Maratti's Picture in the Barbarin Palace at Rome, Ditto Measure,	10	10	0
8	A Mary Magdalene, sow'd with Silk, which comes nearest to Painting of any perhaps of the kind, finely fram'd and glass'd,	15	15	0
9	The Resurrection of our Saviour, an Original, by Fran. Trevisani, Ditto Measure,	90	0	0
10	The Apostles beholding our Saviour's Ascension, copied from the famous Picture of Guido Reni in the Vatican, by Pompeo Girolomo Battoni, being round The Diameter 6 feet, proper for the Roof of a Chapel or Library,	30	0	0
11	Our Saviour on the Cross, an Original, by Fran. d'Imperali, length 9 feet 6 inches, breadth 6 feet 6 inches,	30	0	0
12	Our Saviour in the Garden, an Original by Ditto, length 2 feet 2 inches, breadth 1 foot 5 inches,	25	0	0
13	A Madonna with our Saviour a Child in her Arms, by Gioseppo Chiari in his best manner, Ditto Measure,	25	0	0
14	Another Madonna, an Original, by Pietro Bianchi, Ditto Measure,	8	0	0
15	An Oval Portrait, copied from Gioseppo Chiari,	0	5	0

		L.	s.	d.
16	Our Saviour a Child, and St. John Baptist, in Conversation, by a Flemish Master, length 4 feet 1 inch, breadth 3 feet 6 inches,	3	3	0
17	Our Saviour led to his Crucifixion, by Titian, finely framed, length 2 feet 3 inches, breadth 2 feet,	3	3	0
18	The Nativity, painted on Wood, by Albert Durer, length 3 feet 1 inch, breadth 2 feet 5 inches,	4	4	0
19	Mary Magdalen, an Original, on Wood, highly finished and framed, length 2 feet 1 inch, breadth 1 foot 7 inches,	4	4	0
20	A Conversation, on Wood, an Original, by Teniers, length 1 foot 9 inches, breadth 2 feet 5 inches,	6	6	0
21	A Copy of Michael Angelo de Carravaggio's famous Picture of the Gamesters in the Barbarin Palace at Rome, by Camillo Paderni, same Size with the Original,	9	9	0
22	A Head of St Paul, on Wood, an Original, by Titian, finely framed, length 1 foot 10 inches, breadth 1 foot 3 inches,	8	8	0
23	A Boy reposing himself, an Original, by Amarosi, length 2 feet 4 inches, breadth 3 feet 2 inches,	4	4	0
24	A Sacrifice, an Original, on Wood, highly finished and framed, length 2 feet 3 inches, breadth 1 foot 8 inches,	4	4	0
25	Two Original Pictures, Companions, by Paulo Monaldi; one represents Narcissus, the other Angelica and Medoro, the Back Grounds of both by Horizonti, each in length 2 feet 5 inches, breadth 2 feet,	12	12	0
26	Two Heads, Companions, copied by Bartolomeo Nazari of Venice from Rembrant, finely framed, each in length 1 foot 10 inches, breadth 1 foot 5 inches,	12	12	0
27	Lucretia stabbing herself, by a Flemish Master, length 3 feet 1 inch, breadth 2 feet 4 inches,	3	0	0
28	A Piece of Fish and Roots, an Original, length 3 feet 3 inches, breadth 2 feet 7 inches,	3	0	0
29	Two Fruit Pieces, Companions, Originals, by Peter Sneers, length 16 inches, breadth 13 inches,	5	5	0
30	Two Views on Copper, Companions, Originals, by Fruen Brook, fram'd,	6	6	0
31	An original Portrait, finely painted on Copper and fram'd,	3	3	0
32	The Resurrection of our Saviour, cut in Ivory, by the famous Pozzi, glass'd and fram'd,	4	4	0
33	Two Ovals, the medallion Size, cut in Ivory, by ditto glass'd and fram'd,	5	5	0
34	A three quarter Picture of Mary Queen of Scots when a Widow, copied from the famous Original in the Scots College at Paris,	4	4	0
35	Two Pieces of Game, Companions, Originals, by Baldasar Caro, on half-length Cloths,	10	10	0
36	Two Pictures in miniature, copied by the famous Bereton from the Originals of An. Caracci in the Farnese Gallery at Rome, finely fram'd and glass'd,	10	10	0
37	Two Night Pieces, Companions, on Copper, Originals, by Fruen Brook, the one representing Mount Vesuvius, the other the Burning of Troy,	6	6	0
38	Two Landscapes, Companions, Originals, by Lucatelli, length 2 feet 2 inches, breadth 3 feet, in black Frames,	12	12	0
39	Moses and the Burning Bush, an Original, by one of the Bassan's, length 2 feet 8 inches, breadth 3 feet 7 inches,	4	4	0
40	An original Landscape, by Gio. Baptista Buseri, the Figures by Cava. Costanzi, length 2 feet 2 inch, breadth 3 feet,	7	7	0

		L.	s.	d.
41	A Landscape, by Horizonti, in his best manner, the Figures by Gioseppo Chiari, ditto measure,	8	8	0
42	A Madonna, by Fran. Trevisani, length 2 feet 1 inch, breadth 1 foot 7 inches,	3	10	0
43	St John the Evangelist, by ditto, ditto measure,	3	10	0
44	A Holy Family, by ditto, length 3 feet 1 inch, breadth 2 feet 5 inches,	6	0	0
45	St John Baptist, an Original, by Cavaliero Costanzi, the Landscape or back Ground by Horizonti, length 4 feet 5 inches, breadth 3 feet 3 inches,	10	0	0
46	Mary Magdalene, copy'd from Guido Reni's Picture in the Barbarin Palace at Rome, length 6 feet 6 inches, breadth 4 feet 10 inches,	10	10	0
47	The Nativity, copy'd from Romanelli's Picture in the Vatican by Camillo Paderni, ditto measure,	10	10	0
48	St Andrew's Martyrdom, copied from And. Sacchi's Picture in the Pope's Palace, by Stephano Parocell, ditto measure,	10	10	0
	Twenty one Volumes of Italian Prints, to be put up if in one Lot at	105	0	0
	But if in single Volumes, at an additional Price.			

CATALOGUES may be had at the Shop of Mess. HAMILTON & BALFOUR, Booksellers in Edinburgh.

LIST OF BUYERS AND PRICES PAID AT THE SALE OF THE PICTURES COLLECTED BY JOHN URQUHART OF CROMARTY.[18]

		£.	s.	d.
1				
2	Captain Murray	2	0	0
3	Mr Gavin Hamilton	3	0	0
4	Mr Gavin Hamilton	3	0	0
5	Sir Alexander Ramsay of Balmain	4	10	0
6	Mr Millar	10	10	0
7	Lady Lauderdale	16	0	0
8				
9	Lord Hop[e]ton	90	0	0
10	Lord Elibank	20	0	0
11	The Honble Mr Francis Charteris	52	10	0
12	Lord Hop[e]ton	25	0	0
13	Sir Names Clark	25	0	0
14	Mr Alexander	6	0	0
15	Baillie Hamilton	0	5	0
16	Mr Brookbanke	3	3	0
17	Mr Millar	4	15	0

		£.	s.	d.
18				
19				
20	Sir Alexander Ramsay of Balmain	6	6	0
21	Lord Elibank	11	0	0
22	Honble Mr Charteris	12	17	0
23				
24	Honble Mr Weems	8	8	0
25	Mr John McGowan	14	0	0
26	Mr Alexander Sheriff	12	17	0
27	Mr Millar	2	10	0
28				
29	Baillie Simpson	6	0	0
30	Sir Alexander Ramsay	6	6	0
31				
32				
33				
34	Doctor Mackenzie	4	4	0
35	Lord Hop[e]ton	13	13	0
36				
37	Mr Alexander	6	11	0
38	Sir Alexander Ramsay	12	12	0
39	Mr Garden of Troup	4	4	0
40	Mr John MacHowan	7	17	6
41	Mr MacGowan	8	8	6
42	Lord Elibank	5	10	0
43	Lord Elibank	5	10	0
44	Mr Alexander	12	12	0
45	Mr Millar	9	0	0
46				
47	Mr Millar	10	0	0
48	Lord Hop[e]ton	17	17	0
49	Mr Philp	105	0	0
	Sum Total	£567	16	0

Notes

1. This paper originally appeared in another version: J. Holloway, 'John Urquhart of Cromarty: an unknown collector of Italian paintings in Scotland and Italy', in *Papers Presented at the Fourth Annual Conference of the Scottish Society for Art History, Scottish Arts Council* (Edinburgh, 1989), 1–13. It is included in the present volume with new documentary research on recusant patronage and with new facts regarding paintings from Urquhart's collection.
2. For Mosman's work for Patrick Duff, see J. Holloway, *Patrons and Painters: Art in Scotland 1650–1760* (Edinburgh, 1989), 93–7.
3. Antonio David (1684–1737), *Prince Charles Edward Stuart, 1720–1788. Eldest Son of Prince James Francis Edward Stuart*, 1732. Oil on canvas, 73.4 × 60.3 cm (framed: 92.07 × 80.01 × 7.62 cm). Scottish National Portrait Gallery, acc. no. PG 887, purchased 1918. Antonio David, *Prince Henry Benedict Clement Stuart, 1725–1807. Cardinal York; Younger Brother of Prince Charles Edward*, 1732. Oil on canvas, 73.4 × 60.6 cm. Scottish National Portrait Gallery, acc. no. PG 888, purchased 1918.
4. Craigston papers, NRA(S) 2570, bundle 72.
5. The letters are still owned by the Urquhart family at Craigston Castle, and it is with the permission of the late Major Bruce Urquhart that I quote from them.
6. The choice of the *Resurrection of Christ* as the subject for Trevisani's commission, as Karin Wolfe has suggested in her contribution to this volume (p. 86), was surely prompted by Urquhart's Jacobite sympathies. While the Resurrection is an uncommon subject for Trevisani, for Urquhart it presented an ideal opportunity to allude allegorically to the restoration of the Stuart monarchy. See also the contribution in the present volume by Peter Björn Kerber (pp. 71–80), on the recusant allusions in a Pompeo Batoni picture commissioned from the artist by Henry, 8th Baron Arundell. Additionally, a few years earlier (1718) another Scottish artist, John Alexander, wrote to his Jacobite patron, John Erskine, 6th Earl of Mar, resident with the exiled Stuart court in Urbino, 'I received your letter, while I was busy about the drawings of the two little ovals, which I shall send in a letter next post … I hope the stories will please you, if my weak performance and ideas answer your bon gusto … One represents Perseus cutting off Medusa's head and the other Perseus delivering Andromeda. I had a genio to do these two stories, because I found them applicable to your Grace in the last conjuncture you had in Scotland'. (This is a reference to the 1715 Jacobite Rising, which was led by the Earl of Mar.) Moreover, in *c.* 1715, when Pope Clement XI Albani commissioned Giuseppe Bartolomeo Chiari to paint an altarpiece for the Stuarts, the subject chosen was an allegory of the Church with Faith, Hope and Charity in a small boat steered by Saint Peter through a dangerously high sea. In the distance a rainbow and dry land suggest a safe harbour, and thus a return of the royal family from exile.
7. Craigston papers, NRA(S) 2570, bundle 72.
8. Craigston papers, NRA(S) 2570, bundle 72.
9. Craigston papers, NRA(S) 2570, bundle 72.
10. Craigston papers, NRA(S) 2570, bundle 72.
11. Craigston papers, NRA(S) 2570, bundle 72.
12. Craigston papers, NRA(S) 2570, bundle 72.
13. Francesco Fernandi, called Imperiali (1679–1740), *Crucifixion*. Oil on canvas, 300 × 200 cm. The Earl of Wemyss and March, Gosford House, East Lothian.
14. Clerk of Penicuik papers, SRO GD18/2110.
15. The Urquhart *Resurrection* may be the painting of the same subject by Trevisani sold from the collection of Sir Billy Butlin at Phillips, London, 10 May 1983, lot 45 (79½ × 58½ inches (202 × 149 cm)), as the measurements almost exactly match those given in the sale catalogue of Urquhart's picture ('length 6 feet 6 inches, breadth 4 feet 10 inches' or 78 × 58 inches (198 × 147 cm)). However, the purchasers of the Butlin picture, Colnaghi USA Ltd, discovered when they relined the painting that the original lining canvas was inscribed 'Francesco Trevisani Pinxt. Romae 1721', a date clearly not congruent with Urquhart's commission, rendering a conclusive connection with his patronage difficult, until more facts emerge. Another, smaller and unfinished replica of the same subject attributed to 'the studio of Francesco Trevisani' has also appeared (Phillips, London 8 December 1992, lot 128, 134 × 98 cm). Whether this picture is autograph or by an assistant of the artist, it was probably prepared as a *ricordo*, either for Trevisani to keep in his studio to record the larger composition or to be sold as a cabinet painting to a collector.
16. The *Saint John the Evangelist* has been identified recently: see K. Wolfe, 'San Giovanni Evangelista testimonia la Crocifissione', in F. Petrucci (ed.), *Le Collezioni Ferrari, Laschena ed altre donazioni a Palazzo Chigi in Ariccia* (Rome, 2008), 86–8.
17. Lord Hopetoun's annotated copy of the Sale Catalogue can be found amongst the Hopetoun papers, NRA(S) 888, bundle 1525.
18. John Urquhart's collection was sold on behalf of his son William by William Mosman between 10 and 13 January 1757. This list of buyers and the prices fetched is amongst the Craigston papers, NRA(S) 2570, bundle 72.

Giovanni Paolo Panini's English clients*

Alastair Laing

It is evident from the number of works by Giovanni Paolo Panini (1691–1765) — the real as opposed to the supposed ones[1] — in Ferdinando Arisi's *catalogue raisonné* that have a British provenance that he was a particular favourite with the British. Not to the same degree as Canaletto, nor so exclusively as the latter, but to a considerable extent, none the less. His popularity is all the more striking when one contrasts it with the lack of taste for the comparable paintings of Hubert Robert: by whom there is not one even in the collection of those Paris dwellers and Francophiles, the Marquesses of Hertford and Sir Richard Wallace, the Wallace Collection. Nor was it some anti-French prejudice that militated against the collecting of capriccios of Rome and ruins by Robert; many of his fellow-countryman Joseph Vernet's earliest and most enthusiastic collectors were English or Anglo-Irish. In both his case and in Panini's, it is more likely to have been their smooth finish, their lack of obvious and visible brushwork — in contradistinction to the evident painterliness and artifice of Hubert Robert — that appealed to their British clientele.

With both Canaletto and Vernet, we have a pretty good idea of who those clients were, and — in the case of Canaletto — how he came to their notice. With Canaletto, we have several pieces of correspondence concerning his early work for British clients, and we know the successive roles of Owen MacSwiny and — crucially — Consul Smith.[2] For Vernet, we have the artist's own lists of commissions and receipts — and we know that his wife was the daughter of the English antiquary and Captain of the Papal Galleys, Mark Parker.[3] When it comes to Panini, we are in the dark as to how he made contact with his earliest clients, and as to who his intermediaries were.

The first record that I have found of an Englishman buying a painting by Panini, surprisingly, antedates what was until recently his first surviving securely documented work, the ruin-piece with *Alexander Visiting the Tomb of Achilles*, his reception piece for the Accademia di San Luca, presented in November 1719.[4] In 1716 that great collector, Edward Harley, 2nd Earl of Oxford, bought from the dealer Andrew Hay: 'A fyne piec of Architectur by Chisolfi', and 'A Companion to it by S^r^. Jo[hn] Pabolo'.[5] The pairing of this earliest recorded English purchase of a Panini with a Ghisolfi might have led one to expect that the two pictures would have been ruin-pieces. Somewhat surprisingly, therefore, we find that in Lord Oxford's posthumous sale in 1742 Giovanni Ghisolfi's picture was called *View of a Church*, and Panini's again, *Its Companion*.[6] Arisi's *catalogue raisonné* contains no view of a church (or of a subject that would make a suitable pair to a view of a church) by Panini this early in his career — nor, indeed, any view of an actual building, as opposed to capriccios of ruins and the like, so soon.

It was Andrew Hay again — a Scottish portrait-painter turned dealer, who, according to George Vertue, became a 'great dealer in pictures, marble busts, books &c., & bronzes — had been 6 times in Italy on that account — he walked there once or twice afoot' (although we have records of only three sojourns in Rome, in 1716, 1718 and 1721–2) — who is first recorded as putting a Panini into an auction in London, in his own sale of 1724/5.[7] This was called *Curtius Jumping into the Lake*, but its real title should obviously have been *Marcus Curtius Leaping into the Flaming Gulf*. It would be fascinating if this were to have been the upright version of the subject that subsequently belonged to Sir Joshua Reynolds, which reappeared on the art market in 1980.[8] It is the only painting of this subject that Arisi dated to before 1724/5. The oblong pictures in the Fitzwilliam Museum in Cambridge and in the Smith College Museum of Art, Northampton, Massachusetts[9] — each of which may have an eighteenth-century English provenance — he dated to around 1730.

Hay also put a Ghisolfi into his sale, but the two were not paired.[10] From that time on — but with any regularity only from the 1740s — both Paninis and Ghisolfis appeared in London auctions. Helen

Wyld very kindly on my behalf has gone through that fascinating manuscript compilation of catalogues for sales at London auctions between 1711 and 1759 made by Richard Houlditch Jr, now in the National Art Library in the Victoria and Albert Museum, noting all the pictures by Panini, Ghisolfi and Canaletto that were sold. Intriguingly, there were no less than 60 Paninis, as against 47 Ghisolfis, and only 26 Canalettos. Not only does this highlight the extraordinary popularity of Panini with English collectors already before 1760; it also suggests that, by comparison with Canaletto, who painted almost exclusively on commission, at least until after his visits to England, Panini painted a considerable number of pictures directly for the market, since many of them feature in the sales of dealers such as Hay, Robert Bragge, Samuel Paris, Rongent, William Kent and John Blackwood. What is also striking about all three artists is that, more often than not, their paintings were sold in pairs, or even sets of four.

With Panini, therefore, there does not seem to have been any single figure who, like Consul Smith, acted as intermediary between the artist and his clients. It was not until later that the Abbé Peter Grant, Father John Thorpe, Thomas Jenkins and James Byres came to fulfil that role for other artists and clients in Rome.[11] Panini's clientele was also much more diverse than Canaletto's, with an initial and robust local Roman and Italian element, a strong French element, and with commissions even from the King of Spain, in addition to his English ones. Panini thus never felt the compulsion, as Canaletto did when the flow of English tourists to Venice dwindled because of the War of the Austrian Succession, actually to go to England, to get commissions at first hand.

We are thus, for the most part, reduced to examining Panini's *oeuvre*, to see which of his paintings have an English provenance, and which of those are already recorded in eighteenth-century inventories, or can be presumed to have been in their first recorded collections since the eighteenth century, because of the character of those collections. Even then, as we have seen, that may not mean that they were commissioned or bought directly from the artist: they may have been simply bought at a dealer-importer's auction. One cannot be sure that the 'two views of Rome' acquired, along with 'two views of Venice' by Henry II Hoare of Stourhead from Arthur Pond, as recorded by the latter's receipt dated 15 January 1727/8, were by Panini;[12] but Horace Walpole recorded a *Constantine's Arch & Other Ruins* by Panini on his visit to Stourhead in July 1762, as well as an *Inside of Saint Peter's* and no less than 'Three views of Venice, by Caneletti'.[13] The Paninis sound, from their subjects, to have been later acquisitions, however, and the 'two views of Rome' may instead have been the 'Ruins of Rome, over doors by Paolo Anesi'.

The painting that appears to be the earliest identifiable surviving acquisition for an English collection is the little *Ruin-piece with Banditti and a Naked Philosopher* at Wilton House.[14] This is already named in the catalogue of the collection of Thomas, 8th Earl of Pembroke by Count Carlo Gambarini of Lucca, which was published in 1731 — the first such catalogue of any English collection of pictures. Dated by Arisi to around 1720, this is in the by then well-tried idiom of the ruin-piece, and was probably simply picked up on the London market by Lord Pembroke, who had never made the Grand Tour, and who was to die two years after publication of the catalogue, in 1733, at the age of 77. He had succeeded his brother at Wilton as early as 1683, and was a major collector not only of paintings, but of drawings, coins, books and antique sculpture — including from the Mazarin and Giustiniani Collections —, employing agents on the Continent to obtain them. Even so, according to Gambarini: 'This Lord has not increased the number [of paintings], he has only changed many Jerman and Flanders, to make a greater variety of Italian Painters' — of which this little picture was evidently a modest instance.[15]

After this one little picture, of traditional type, acquired sometime before 1731, I can find no surviving picture certainly acquired by an English collector, until suddenly, in 1734, there are three pairs of paintings of quite a different character, all signed and dated, or documented as commissioned in, that year. This is evidently the year in which British patronage of Panini took off: what had happened to occasion this? There is no obvious connection between any of the three people commissioning these pairs or sets of pictures, so the explanation cannot reside in them. A contributory factor — but not one that supplies a clue to the precise year, 1734 — was that of the changes that had occurred in the character of Panini's paintings themselves: his first securely datable pair of views of actual buildings appear to be the two *Views of the Castello di Rivoli*, commissioned from him by King Vittorio Amedeo II for the Castello di Racconigi in 1723;[16] and the first of his dated agglomerative capriccios of actual, as opposed to imaginary, Roman buildings appears to be the *Capriccio with the Temple of Minerva Medica and the Arch of Constantine*, formerly in the collection of Pietro Candiani in Busto Arsizio, which is signed and dated 1730.[17] Two of the pairs of pictures acquired by English clients that are signed and dated 1734, or commissioned in that year, are or were of contemporary sites in Rome; the other pair, apparently survivors from a larger set of uncertain character, are capriccios of existing antique Roman buildings in imaginary settings.

It is possible that one reason for this sudden flurry of commissions from the English in 1734 was that Panini had found a middleman who had put him in touch with English tourists, as Smith did for Canaletto. If so, we have no clue as to who that was. It is too early for the Abbé Grant's activities in this respect, nor were any of the three clients, like him, either Scotsmen or Catholic — though one of them, Sir Thomas Twisden, was, like the abbé, a Jacobite. I am intrigued by the fact that Panini's second wife, the Rome-born French woman, Catherine or Caterina Gosset (sister of Marie-Thérèse, wife of the Director of the Académie de France in Rome, Nicolas Vleughels),[18] whom he married in 1722, bore the same surname as the two French Huguenot wax modellers and carvers who made their careers in England, Matthew and Isaac Gosset,[19] and I wonder whether they may not have been related; but there is no evidence for any such link, nor for Isaac Gosset (who, like other members of his family, carved picture frames) ever even having made a frame for a Panini.

A more vital reason for the commissions that now started to flow to Panini was the change that was coming over English domestic architecture at this period. Palladianism had swept everything before it, and, though neither of its idols, Andrea Palladio himself and Inigo Jones, had left clear models for the decoration of the interiors of their buildings, Palladian, and Palladian-influenced, architects — Giacomo Leoni, Colen Campbell, William Kent, Roger Morris, James Gibbs and others, aided by Italian stuccadors such as Artari and Bagutti —, had devised a way of giving Roman gravitas to their interiors, by way of a system of rectangular plaster panels, and of rectangular overdoors and overmantels, that were intended to be filled either with classicizing marble or plaster reliefs, or with paintings that were often evocative of that same antique past. Thus Panini was faced with a demand not only for his representations of Roman ruins and buildings, whether singly, or combined in capriccios, but also with a demand for pairs, or even sets, of them.

The three pairs of pictures painted for English clients in 1734 were as follows. In 1734, Henry, Duke of Kent ordered two pictures, the *Interior of Saint Peter's, Rome*[20] and the *Interior of the Pantheon*.[21] These have long since been sold, and are now in the Kunsthaus, Zurich, and in a private collection respectively. We do not know for certain for which house they were commissioned. It might have been for Wrest Park, which Leoni had made designs for rebuilding in 1715, but it is more likely that they were for the Duke's town house, 4 Saint James's Square, which was built for him by Edward Shepherd between 1726 and 1728, and doubtless continued to be fitted out thereafter. Walpole only mentioned one, unspecified 'Large Paolo Panini' at the latter, but 'nothing valuable' in the former, but Francis Russell has kindly informed me that the de Grey/Lucas papers reveal them to have constantly been hung in 4 Saint James's Square.

The second pair, of two very fine pictures, entitled *A Capriccio of Roman Buildings and Sculpture*, is in the Maidstone Museum and Art Gallery (**Fig. 9.1**).[22] Each is signed and dated 1734. They were bequeathed to the museum by Julius Lucius Brenchley in 1873, but the curator at the time noted that they had been bought by an ancestor of his at the sale of Sir John Twisden, 8th and last Baronet of Bradbourne. We have no direct documentation of Sir Thomas Twisden, 4th Baronet, who had spent nearly four years in Italy, between 1733 and 1736, before his untimely death in Spain in 1737,[23] having commissioned these pictures from Panini, but a drawing by Panini from his collection is now in the Royal Institute of British Architects,[24] and William Angus's *Seats of the Nobility and Gentry* recorded no less than six Paninis at his seat, Bradbourne House, in 1787 — and no subsequent member of the family had made the Grand Tour between 1737 and that year.[25] The only awkward thing is that Brenchley bequeathed three other supposed Paninis to Maidstone in 1873 — but all three are imitations.[26] There is nothing to say that his ancestor had bought these too at Sir John Twisden's sale. If he did, it is possible that only two of the six purported Paninis at Bradbourne were acquired by Sir Thomas Twisden, and were genuine, and that the others were pastiches commissioned after his death.

1734 was also the second and last year of the Grand Tour made by William Holbech of Farnborough Hall, Warwickshire. It seems to have been then that he commissioned the first two of what were ultimately to be five Paninis for his family seat.[27] One of these was

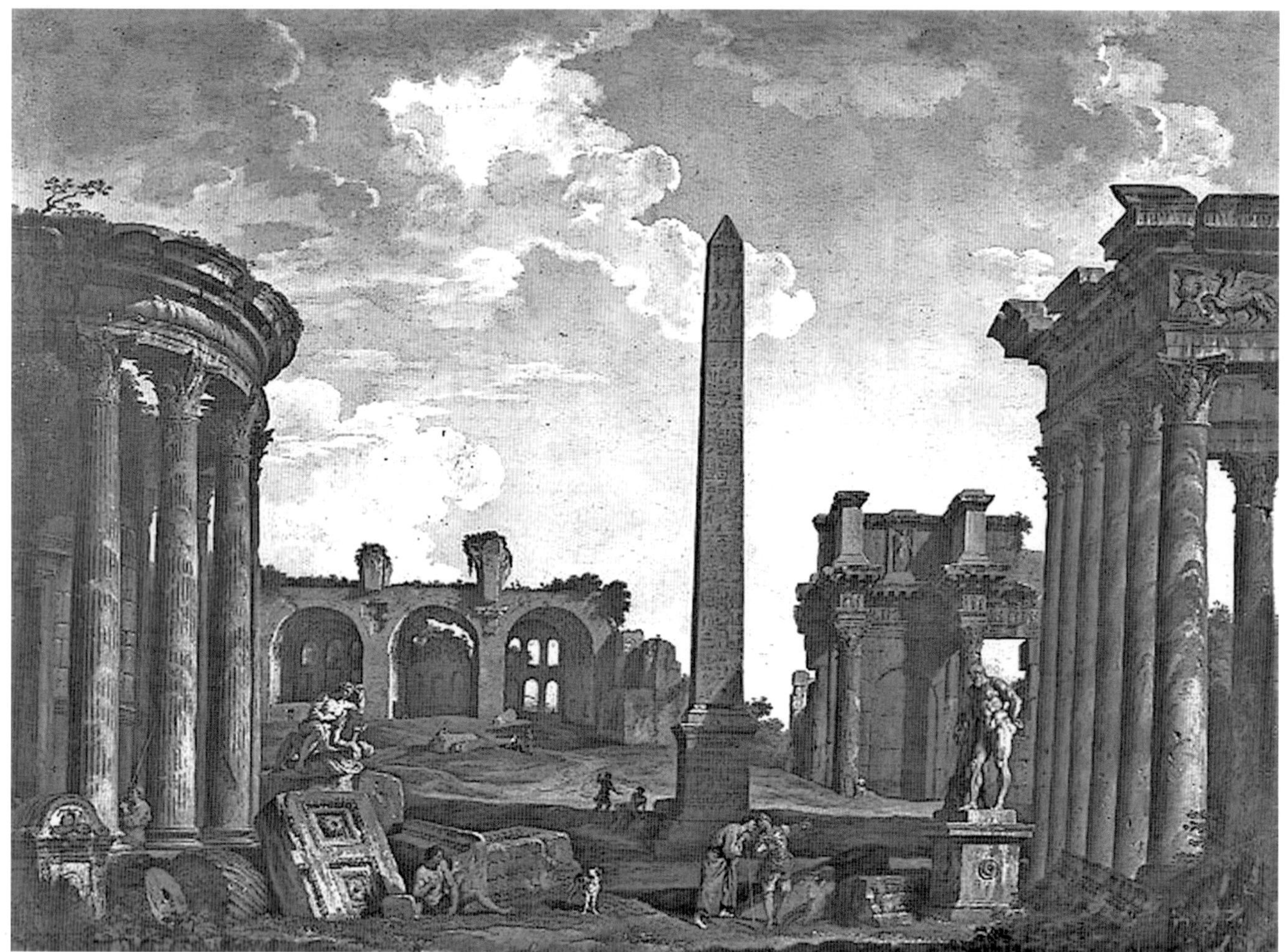

FIG. 9.1. Giovanni Paolo Panini (1691–1765), *A Capriccio of Roman Buildings and Sculpture*, signed and dated 'I.P. Panini/Roma 1734'. Oil on canvas, 97.2 × 134.6 cm. Maidstone Museum and Art Gallery, inv. 00-1873-4. *(Photo: © The Maidstone Borough Council. Reproduced courtesy of Maidstone Museum and Bentlif Art Gallery.)*

the *Interior of the Pantheon*, signed and dated 1734,[28] which is now in the collection of Asbjorn Lunde in New York (Fig. 9.2). I have not yet succeeded in identifying the second, but the two were mentioned by an unknown antiquary whose journal survives in the British Library, and who visited Farnborough Hall in 1746.[29] After listing the most interesting antique busts in the house, the antiquary goes on to say that they were: 'all brought back from Rome with two pictures, one of the Rotunda [by which the Pantheon was meant], and the other of diverse buildings, by Panino'.

Now it just so happens that we do know the compositions of three other Paninis that were once at Farnborough Hall, from copies still at the house (Plate 9.1). This is because, in the late 1740s, Holbech took the decision not only to remodel the Entrance Hall, Staircase and Saloon (now Dining Room) at Farnborough, and to have these and the Library stuccoed with glorious Rococo Palladian stucco-work by William Perritt of York, but also to have his chief purchases in Italy — his antique busts, marble reliefs and paintings — not just by Panini, but also by Canaletto — incorporated into his schemes, with the paintings let directly into the stucco-work. Not content with that, he ordered additional paintings from Canaletto and Panini, to make his schemes symmetrical. The final payment to the stuccador Perritt was made in November 1750.[30]

If only all this had survived, it would have made the interiors at Farnborough Hall some of the most beautiful and remarkable in the United Kingdom. They are still striking, but now only because of the stucco and the incorporated classical sculpture. For, soon after succeeding in 1812, Holbech's great-grandson, William Holbech IV, removed the rococo stucco-work — and with it, probably, the two Paninis, the *Interior of the*

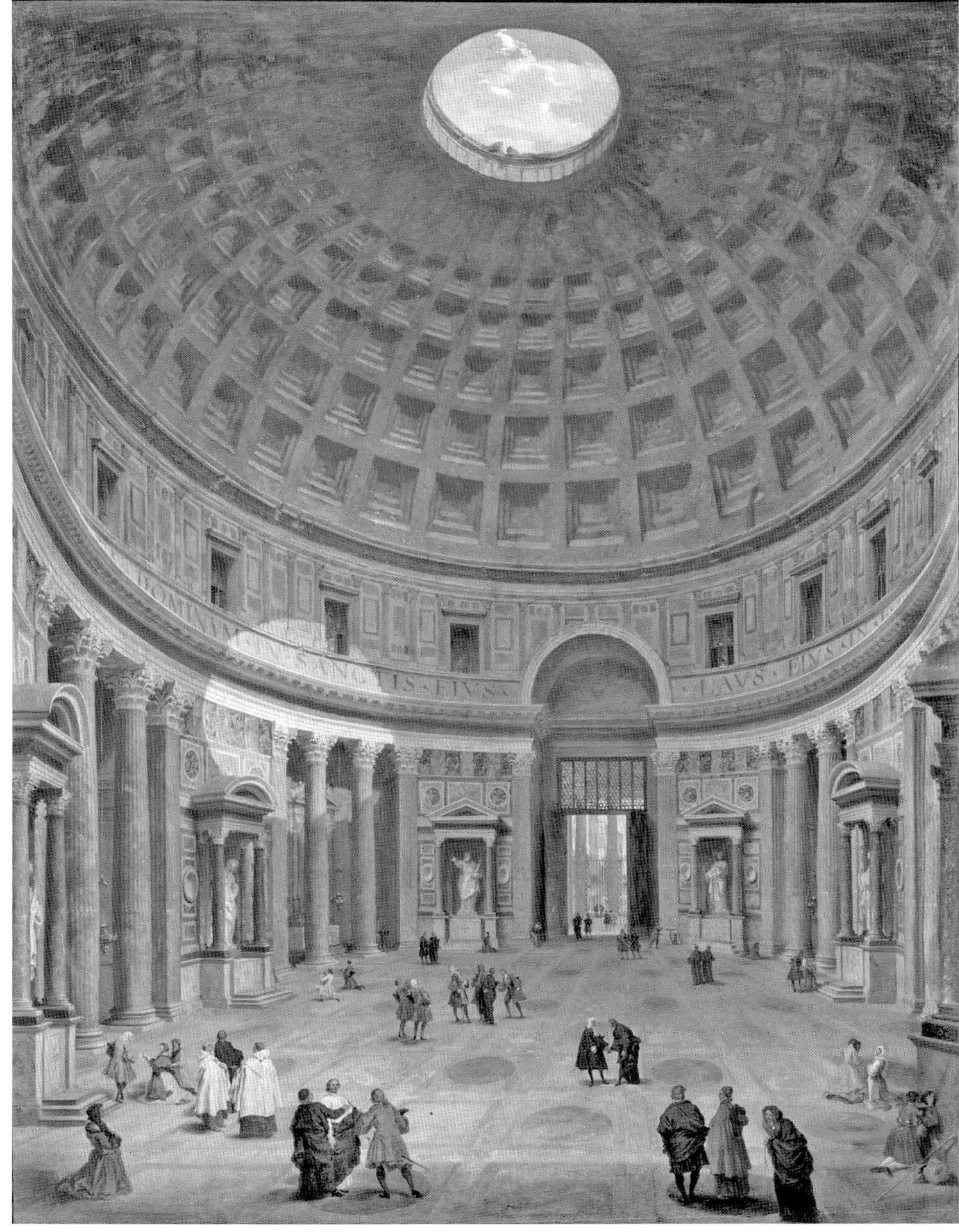

FIG. 9.2. Giovanni Paolo Panini (1691–1765), *Interior of the Pantheon*, 1734. Oil on canvas, 122 × 98 cm. New York, Asbjorn Lunde Collection. *(Reproduced courtesy of Asbjorn Lunde.)*

Pantheon and *Diverse Buildings*, from the Library.[31] But in 1929, much worse occurred: not only these two Paninis, but all of the still inset paintings, consisting of the four Canalettos and two Paninis in the Saloon — by now the Dining Room — and a third Panini serving as the overmantel in the Entrance Hall, were removed and sold. Copies of the inset paintings were commissioned from an Indian artist, called Mohammed Ayoub, but the two Paninis that must have been removed from the Library previously, soon after 1812, and so would have been free-hanging, were not copied. Since the pictures removed were not sold at auction, but privately, for a long time it has been difficult to identify some of them with certainty. It is symptomatic of the state of Panini studies, as compared with those of Canaletto, that, whereas all four of the Canalettos have been identified, and their current whereabouts are known, only two of the Paninis have been identified with certainty and published. Even in the case of these two, however, you will look in Arisi's book in vain for any mention of Farnborough Hall.[32] They are the already-mentioned *Interior of the Pantheon*, signed and dated 1734, in Lunde's collection in New York (Fig. 9.1), and the *Interior of Saint Peter's, Rome*, signed and dated 1750, in the Detroit Institute of Arts (Plate 9.2). In the latter, the lopsided view of the interior, as compared with those of other views of Saint Peter's, strongly suggests that it was commissioned specifically for the place that it was to occupy at Farnborough Hall.[33] Of the remaining two Paninis formerly at Farnborough Hall — the *Piazza di S. Pietro* and the *Campidoglio* — I know little.[34] They are not in Arisi's *catalogue raisonné*, nor have I ever seen them.

It is particularly sad that the installation of Canalettos and Paninis at Farnborough Hall has been broken up, as I do not know of any other surviving combination of the two that goes back to the eighteenth century. We know that Henry, Duke of Kent owned five Canalettos, in addition to his two Paninis; but not only have all these been long since dispersed, we also do not know how they were disposed originally, or even in which house of his they were, though it is probable that they too were in 4 Saint James's Square.

The next Paninis painted for an English client that I can identify with certainty were executed four years later than those for Holbech, Sir Thomas Twisden and Henry, Duke of Kent. In this short paper they make an appropriate note on which to end, since together they form the most striking set of Paninis *in situ* in England, and their reconstitution as a set *in situ* is little short of miraculous.

The Paninis in question are four capriccios of Roman buildings and sculpture, and one imaginary ruin-piece (Plate 9.3) All five are signed and dated 1738. They are inset as overdoors and an overmantel in the Great Room of Marble Hill House, Twickenham (Plate 9.4). This is one of the earliest and purest Palladian buildings in England, and one of the few survivors of the villa retreats that used to line the Thames upstream from London.[35] The original design, of around 1724, was probably due to the pioneering Scottish Palladian, Colen Campbell. It was modified by the architect-earl, Henry, 9th Earl of Pembroke — the Great Room was inspired by the Single Cube Room of his seat, Wilton House —, and executed by Roger Morris. Construction was completed in 1729. It was built for Henrietta Howard, Countess of Suffolk, the English mistress of the Hanoverian King George II. It was not, however, until her first husband had died and she had retired from court in 1734, marrying her second husband, the Hon. George Berkeley, the next year, that she had the resources and leisure fully to furnish and enjoy Marble Hill House.

Once again, we lack hard and fast documentation for the Paninis. Neither the Countess of Suffolk nor Berkeley made the journey to Italy, and we can only guess at how the commission came to Panini. It may, however, have been the knowledge that she was the mistress of George II (he may not have known that the relationship was actually over) that persuaded Panini to complete the whole commission in one year. It also may have been the fact that a Panini ruin-piece was already serving as an overmantel in the Octagon Room of the neighbouring house, now called Orleans House, that inspired the Countess to commission the set of five pictures, including an overmantel, from him.[36] The Orleans House ruin-piece, which can be seen in old photographs of the interior,[37] was regrettably stolen from the Octagon before it was opened to the public in 1972.[38]

The Marble Hill House paintings also suffered an unhappy history. By the beginning of the twentieth century Twickenham had become a suburb of London. After the death of the last private resident in 1887, the house stood empty for fifteen years, and it was on the point of being demolished (and it and its park turned into a housing estate), when the London County Council stepped in and rescued house and park. Some time between 1900 and 1902, the interior of the house had been stripped bare, including the removal of the five Paninis. It was only in the 1980s, when a campaign of restoring the interiors of the house to what could be discovered of their original condition began, that serious attempts were made to locate the Paninis that had served as overdoors and overmantel in the Great Room.[39] In 1981 two, then belonging to the British Rail Pension Fund, were identified while on loan to the Bowes Museum, Barnard Castle, and were lent to Marble Hill House, and then acquired for it.[40] In 1984 the overmantel appeared at auction in New York, and was successfully bid for.[41] And in 1988 the remaining two capriccios were tracked down to a private collection in the South of France, and purchased.[42] The refulgent result of their reinstallation in the Great Room makes one fervently wish that the same could be done at Farnborough Hall. All but one of its Canalettos are now in public institutions, and can never be recovered. But two of the Paninis that were in fixed positions as overmantels are still in private hands: if the will — and enough money — were there, it should still be possible to recover at least those, when they leave their present owner's hands, so as to put them back, and give at least a partial idea of how their rooms looked, when they were a shining memorial to the taste for Canaletto and Panini in England in the eighteenth century.

Notes

* Dedicated to the memory of Sir Brinsley Ford (1908–99), who has done more than anyone to explore and promote knowledge of the links between Britain and Rome in the eighteenth century, and who himself inherited a pair of early Paninis from his ancestor, Benjamin Booth (1732–1807). See L. Herrmann (ed.), 'The Ford Collection – I', *Walpole Society* 60 (1998), i–xii, 1–396, cat. nos. BB2 and BB3, 10 and pl. 8.

I should like to express my gratitude to David R. Marshall for checking references and pursuing illustrations on my behalf. Any errors are, however, of course my own.

1. Cf. the 'Not Panini' appendix to D.R. Marshall. 'The architectural piece in 1700: the paintings of Alberto Carlieri (1672–*c.* 1720), pupil of Andrea Pozzo', *Artibus et Historiae* 25 (no. 50) (2004), 120–2.
2. See F. Haskell, *Patrons and Painters: Art and Society in Baroque Italy* (New York/London, 1971), 287–91, 299–310, 391–4; F. Vivian, *Il Console Smith: mercante e collezionista* (*Saggi e studi di storia dell'arte* 14) (Vicenza, 1971).
3. L. Lagrange, *Les Vernet: Joseph Vernet et la peinture au XVIIIe siècle* (Paris, 1864).
4. F. Arisi, *Gian Paolo Panini e i fasti della Roma del '700* (Rome, 1986), no. 114; F. Arisi, *Gian Paolo Panini* (Soncino, 1991), no. 14.
5. R.W. Goulding, *Catalogue of the Pictures Belonging to His Grace the Duke of Portland, K.G.* (Cambridge, 1936), xxx.
6. Auctioneer Cock, the Piazza, Covent Garden, Lord Oxford's Sale, from 8 March 1741/2, 4th Day, lots 49 and 50.
7. G. Vertue, 'The notebooks of George Vertue, volume III', *Walpole Society* 22 (1934), 125; B. Ford and J. Ingamells (eds), *A Dictionary of British and Irish Travellers in Italy, 1701–1800. Compiled from the Brinsley Ford Archive* (New Haven/London, 1997), 475, *s. v.* 'Hay, Andrew'; [Richard Houlditch, Jr], *Sale Catalogues of the Principal Collections of Pictures (One Hundred & Seventy-one in Number) sold by Auction in England within the Yeares 1711–1759 . . .*, manuscript volumes in the National Art Library, Victoria & Albert Museum, London, Pressmark 86.00.18 and 19, vol. II, p. 46, lot 49.
8. Arisi, *Panini e i fasti* (above, n. 4), no. 116.
9. F. Arisi, *Gian Paolo Panini* (Piacenza, 1961), no. 115; Arisi, *Panini e i fasti* (above, n. 4), no. 191.
10. [Houlditch], *Sale Catalogues* (above, n. 7), II, 45, lot 36.
11. Ford and Ingamells, *Dictionary of British and Irish Travellers* (above, n. 7), *s.vv.*
12. K. Woodbridge, 'Henry Hoare's paradise', *The Art Bulletin* 47 (1965), 89 and no. 43.
13. H. Walpole, 'Journals of visits', *Walpole Society* 16 (1928), 41–2. There is no record in Arthur Pond's surviving accounts (cf. L. Lippincott, 'Arthur Pond's journal of receipts and expenses, 1734–1750', *Walpole Society* 54 (1988[1991]), 220–333) of his later selling more than a couple of Paninis, one to Mr Smart in July 1738 (p. 241), and 'a small Panini' to Mr Mister (?) in May 1747 (p. 287), each time for 7 guineas; but he regularly sold copies to his clients, the first recorded being 'Mr. Foot for a picture of Rotunda from Pannini', for 15 guineas, in November 1734 (p. 223), and between 1744 and 1747 he published a set of four engravings by J.S. Muller after Panini, three of them in the collection of George Lewis Coke, and the fourth in that of Humphrey Edwin. The set of three strongly suggests that they were after two overdoors and an overmantel in Coke's house in Soho Square (see in the index to Lippincott, 'Arthur Pond's journal' (above), 331).
14. Sidney, 16th Earl of Pembroke, *A Catalogue of the Paintings and Drawings in the Collection at Wilton House, Salisbury, Wiltshire* (London/New York, 1968), no. 214; Arisi, *Panini e i fasti* (above, n. 4), no. 127.
15. Pembroke, *Catalogue* (above, n. 14), 6. Since this paper was first given in Rome, Andria Derstine has suggested that Panini's early painting of *Ruins of a Triumphal Arch in the Roman Campagna*, now in the Detroit Institute of Arts, which he has dated to *c.* 1717/19, and which is traceable by a label to the ownership of Sir Compton Domvile, 1st Baronet of the 2nd creation, in 1847, was acquired in Rome by the latter's great-uncle, who left him his estate, Sir Compton Domvile, 2nd Baronet of the 1st creation, who was in Rome between 1717 and 1719. That would make it the second earliest acquisition of a Panini so far known (Lord Oxford's having been the first).
16. Arisi, *Panini e i fasti* (above, n. 4), nos. 158, 159.
17. Arisi, *Panini e i fasti* (above, n. 4), no. 207.
18. B. Hercenberg, *Nicolas Vleughels: peintre et directeur de l'Académie de France à Rome, 1668–1737* (Paris, 1975), 25, 49, 57–8, fig. 14.
19. See E.J. Pyke, *A Biographical Dictionary of Wax Modellers* (Oxford, 1973), 56–9, s.*vv.*
20. Arisi, *Panini e i fasti* (above, n. 4), no. 217; C. Klemm, *Die Gemälde der Stiftung Betty und David M. Koetser* (Zurich, 1988), no. 61.
21. Arisi, *Panini e i fasti* (above, n. 4), no. 218.
22. S. Legouix, *Maidstone Museum and Art Gallery: Foreign Paintings Catalogue* (Maidstone, 1976), 36–8; Arisi, *Panini e i fasti* (above, n. 4), nos. 226, 227; *Oil Paintings in Public Ownership in Kent* (London, 2004), 152.
23. Ford and Ingamells, *Dictionary of British and Irish Travellers* (above, n. 7), 958–9.
24. Ford and Ingamells, *Dictionary of British and Irish Travellers* (above, n. 7), 959.
25. W. Angus, *The Seats of the Nobility and Gentry in Great Britain and Wales* (Islington, 1787), text to pl. 46.
26. Legouix, *Maidstone Museum and Art Gallery* (above, n. 22), 38–9; *Oil Paintings in Public Ownership in Kent* (above, n. 22), 151–2.
27. G. Jackson-Stops, revised by J. Haworth, *Farnborough Hall* (London, 1999); Ford and Ingamells, *Dictionary of British and Irish Travellers* (above, n. 7), 507–8.
28. Arisi, *Panini e i fasti* (above, n. 4), no. 221, as from the collection of R.H.A. Holbeck [*sic*].

29. British Library, *Hypnomnemata*, Add. MSS 6230.
30. Jackson-Stops, *Farnborough Hall* (above, n. 27), 4.
31. Jackson-Stops, *Farnborough Hall* (above, n. 27), 16.
32. I gratefully acknowledge the help of David R. Marshall and Andria Derstine in identifying them.
33. Andria Derstine, in R. Ward Bissell, D. Miller and A. Derstine, *Masters of Italian Baroque Painting: The Detroit Institute of Arts* (London, 2005), no. 46.
34. This is because they belong to a collector in New York highly protective of her privacy.
35. *Marble Hill House, Twickenham: the Short Account of its History and Architecture* (London, 1982).
36. It was built originally for Secretary Johnson in 1702 to 1710, the Octagon having been added in 1720. See P.A. Cooper, *The History of Orleans House, Twickenham* (London, 1984; second edition 1994).
37. It resembled Arisi, *Panini e i fasti* (above, n. 4), no. 195.
38. C. Hussey, *English Country Houses: Early Georgian, 1715–1760* (London, 1955; revised edition 1965), 44, fig. 42.
39. J. Bryant, *London's Country House Collections* (London, 1993), 56–83.
40. Arisi, *Panini e i fasti* (above, n. 4), nos. 253–4; Bryant, *London's Country House Collections* (above, n. 39), 64–5.
41. Arisi, *Panini e i fasti* (above, n. 4), no. 257; Bryant, *London's Country House Collections* (above, n. 39), 68.
42. Arisi, *Panini e i fasti* (above, n. 4), nos. 255–6, as 'Ubicazione ignota'; Bryant, *London's Country House Collections* (above, n. 39), 66–7.

John, 3rd Earl of Bute and James Byres: A Postscript

Francis Russell

John Stuart, 3rd Earl of Bute (1713–92), is in many ways an elusive figure (Fig. 10.1). As I hope I have established elsewhere, he was one of the most effective collectors and patrons of eighteenth-century England.[1] Much is known about the Italian tour — or rather tours — he undertook in 1768–71, partly to escape from political opprobrium at home, and partly to recover his health, which had been undermined by the strains resulting from his withdrawal from office in 1763. Bute had not been on the Grand Tour — perhaps because of the presence of an uncle in the Old Pretender's court — and Italy clearly galvanized his artistic, architectural and literary interests in equal measure. Moreover, while abroad he was actively considering the decoration of the great mansion Adam was working on for him at Luton.

Bute left London on 2 August 1768, travelling by way of Barèges in France: in Venice by mid-November, he arrived in Rome on 28 December, and was at Naples from 14 February until 1 March 1769, returning to Rome, before heading north, spending three days in Florence, and visiting Leghorn (Livorno), Lerici, Genoa, Turin, Milan and Venice, arriving in London on 31 July. Less than four months later, on 5 November, he set out from Dover, making for the waters of Valdagno and then, in January 1770, for Venice. By mid-May he was back in Valdagno, later settling in Consul Smith's villa at Mogliano: he had returned to Venice by 8 October 1770 and remained there until 15 April 1771, when he set out on his way home.[2]

Despite an endeavour to avoid attention, travelling as the Chevalier Stuart, Bute's advent inevitably caused a stir in the ranks of those diplomats and *ciceroni* who catered for British visitors to Italy. Such information as was available in 1993, when the text of my study on Bute began to be set on metal, appears in that work, eventually published in 2004. Some information came to light after 1993, including references from the unpublished diaries of General Pattison, commander of the Venetian forces, which it was frustrating not to be able to use. Ironically, a few months after the publication of the book, a cache of papers relating to Bute's Italian transactions turned up in an Edinburgh lawyer's office. These generously have been brought to my attention by Andrew Maclean, the archivist at Mount Stuart.[3]

The new documents record Bute's purchases in Italy in considerable detail: the material concerning his Venetian transactions will be published elsewhere,[4] but the series of letters to Bute covering the period 1769–71 from James Byres, as well as related schedules and accounts, deserves to be known more widely.

James Byres of Tonley (1734–1817), as a Scot who was at once an artist and a connoisseur, was exactly the sort of man to win Bute's confidence (Plate 10.1). A list annotated by Bute, 'Things of Mine left with Mr Bires', establishes what was purchased during his visit to Rome.[5] Fifteen pictures are listed — of which *The Holy Family* (Fig. 10.2) and a *Madonna*, both by Sassoferrato, remain in the collection, as do some of the eight landscapes variously given to Rosa and the Poussins.[6] There were, among other things, also 1,400 'sulphers' (volcanic specimens) and two vases.

On 12 May 1769, when the Earl was on his way back to England, Byres wrote to Bute's confident, John Symonds, referring to the packages despatched with the scholar Richard Paul Joddrell, and with Laurence Oliphant, and stated that Lord Exeter would bring another box.[7] The copyists Bute employed were being slow: 'You know how difficult it is to get Artists to keep their time'. Byres ends with further messages and his 'Compliments to M^r^. Charles his portrait is known by every body and much admired'. No portrait done in Rome of Bute's adored son Charles is known, but

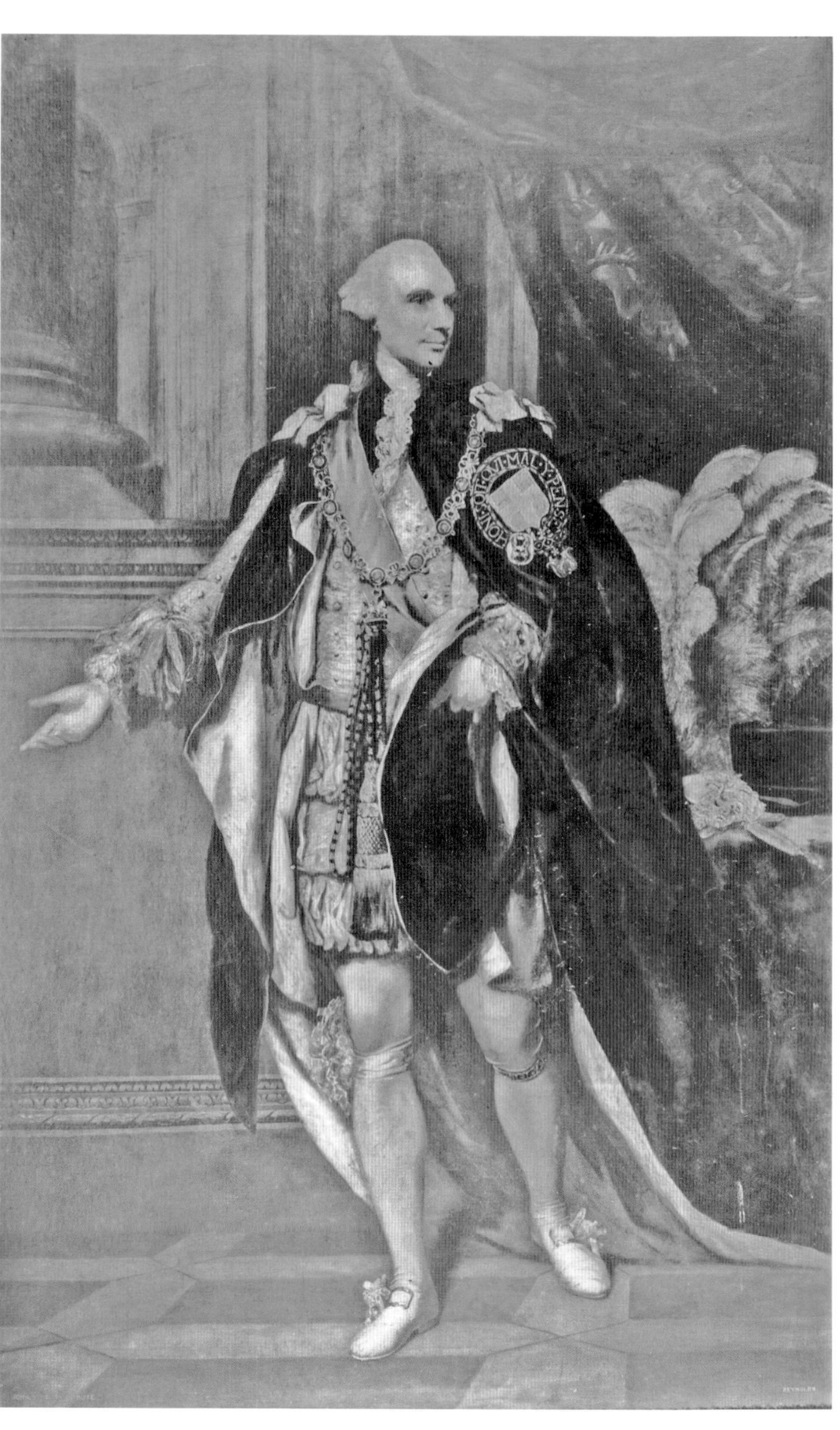

FIG. 10.1. Sir Joshua Reynolds (1723–92), *John, 3rd Earl of Bute*. Oil on canvas. The Mount Stuart Trust, Mount Stuart House, Isle of Bute. *(Reproduced courtesy of the Mount Stuart Trust.)*

Byres's aside must surely mean that, like his elder brother Mountstuart — who had been in Rome in 1764–5 —, he was painted by Batoni.

On 20 May Byres wrote at much greater length to Bute himself.[8] The Earl had written saying that a copy by the Scottish painter, Anne Forbes, had met with his approbation, and Byres had reported this to the artist and her mother. He explained that Giuseppe Manocchi, who had done a book of copies after the Raphael *loggie*, had gone to England with 'M^{r}. Adams' (spelt with an s) but 'ran away and left him. he is now under Engagements with Piranesi but has some hours of the day to himself'. Byres detailed the progress of other copyists, including Magnani,

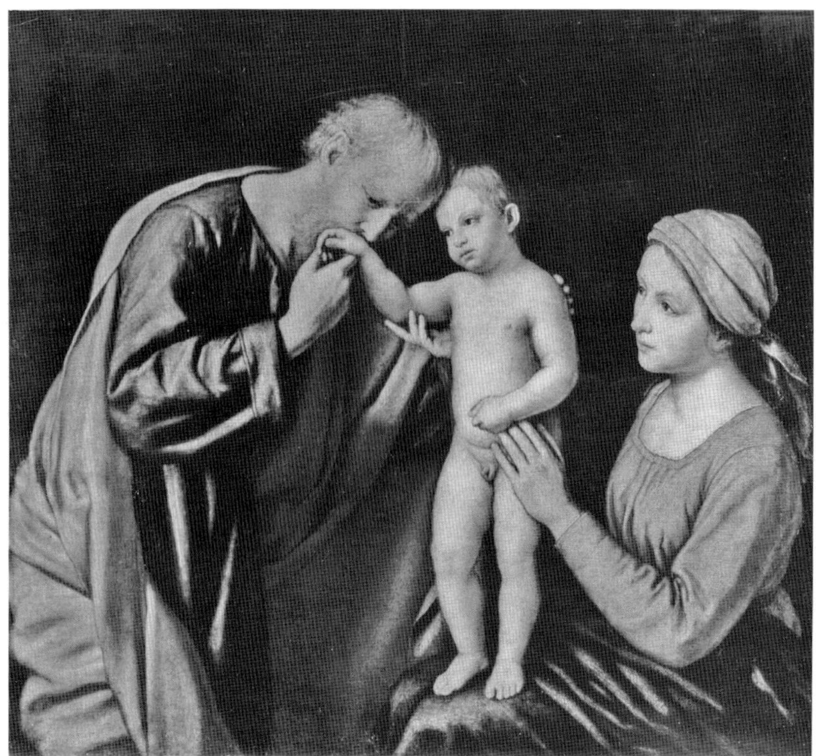

FIG. 10.2. Giovanni Battista Salvi (1605–85), il Sassoferrato, *The Holy Family*. Oil on canvas, 49.5 × 57.2 cm. Private Collection. *(Reproduced courtesy of the owner.)*

George Robertson, Felice Batoni and Franciszek Smuglevitz. He evidently had a free hand in purchases and had acquired two views by 'a German lately come from France ... I think them amongst the finest things in that way I ever saw and on that account sent Your Lordship these two as a Specimen': the German was the young Philip Hackert. Byres reported on work on vases, on Giuseppe Clause's progress with models for sculptures and on the cork-cutter Giuseppe Altieri's progress with cork models of classical buildings, of which Bute ordered two duplicate sets.

Byres clearly understood Bute's requirements, as a reference in that same letter to a book of drawings shows: 'the Books spoke of by Pompeio [that is, Batoni], I have got, and paid forty Zequins for. but do not think, Your Lordship would like it, altho' it contains several good drawings'. Byres wrote again on 10 June, with news of work on numerous commissions.[9] He was sending drawings after pictures attributed to Claude and Rosa that were for sale, and again implied that he understood his patron's taste: 'the best Picture I have got since Your Lordship left Rome is what you will not like, — the Original Sketch by Hanibal Carrach painted on Copper of his fine Picture in the Pamphili Chapel'. He touched, too, on wider news. He hoped that the new pope, Clement XIV, would 'at least restore Quiet to this decay'd State'; and then turned to a topic that would have interested Bute's elder son, in view of his close friendship with James Boswell, who was an eloquent advocate of General Paoli, the Corsican patriot who resisted the French occupation of the island: 'O my Lord poor Corsica and worthy Paoli's defeat, has given a sad damp to our Spirits here'.

On 14 August Byres wrote again.[10] After discussing shipping and the copies, he turned to the work of 'Hackert the Prussian' (Philip Hackert), whose charges for large drawings Byres now felt to be too high. On 26 September Byres reported further progress, although he and Felice Cettomai ('the worker in Tapestry') had disagreed over prices.[11] Moreover, the copyist Ludovico Tesi was not available to work on chiaroscuro copies for Bute, as he had 'been so entirely taken up with repeated Copies of the Emperours and Grand Dukes Portraits for his Master Pompeio Battoni'.

Byres was no doubt informed of Bute's departure for Italy in the following November. The subsequent hiatus in the correspondence is explained by the schedule of goods despatched to Venice that Byres submitted. On 29 December he himself 'carried' a consignment of drawings to Bute in Venice — and clearly the two settled many matters between themselves then.

The next extant letter is of 7 April 1770.[12] A week earlier Bute had written with orders for chimney-pieces for Luton, two for the Saloon, to be of the size of that already supplied for the Library, three for the 'Drawing Room and two oval rooms' of the size of those for the side rooms of the Library.[13] This reference is of interest as it clarifies the order of the fitting up of the house. Byres himself supplied the designs. The Earl's decision to order chimney-pieces for the main rooms at Luton through Byres suggests how impressed he was by the quality of Roman workmanship. It also demonstrates how far he himself was concerned with the interior decoration of the house. Bute's interest in Italian poetry had led to his asking if Byres knew of busts of Italian poets that were for sale: Byres rejoined with details of prototypes that could be copied.

On 12 May Byres wrote again.[14] Bute had offered 'two Hundred' for a chimney by Giovanni Battista Piranesi, but Byres was not sure whether that was in pounds or sequins: Piranesi's charge would be 500 sequins, to include a relief that Byres considered dispensable: 'the Chimney Piece is realy beautifull altho' perhaps too luxuriant'. More copies were on the way, drawings by Felice Batoni and others. Byres had also costed busts of poets: twenty sequins a piece for bronzes, 23 for marbles.

On 23 June Byres wrote again, responding to a letter from Bute, who was evidently pleased with the drawings brought to Venice by yet another traveller who was induced by Byres to act as courier, Frederick Barnard.[15] Bute's offer of £200 for Piranesi's chimney-piece had been refused, but half-size bronze busts of Italian poets had been ordered from an unnamed sculptor. Byres had also secured two landscapes by Giovanni Battista Busiri and the portrait of Pope Innocent X, signed by Pietro Martiri Neri but which he believed to be by Velázquez (Fig. 10.3).[16] Bute apparently asked for these to be sent to him in Venice, but Byres outlined the risks of overland travel and a list of cases shows that they were shipped from Leghorn.

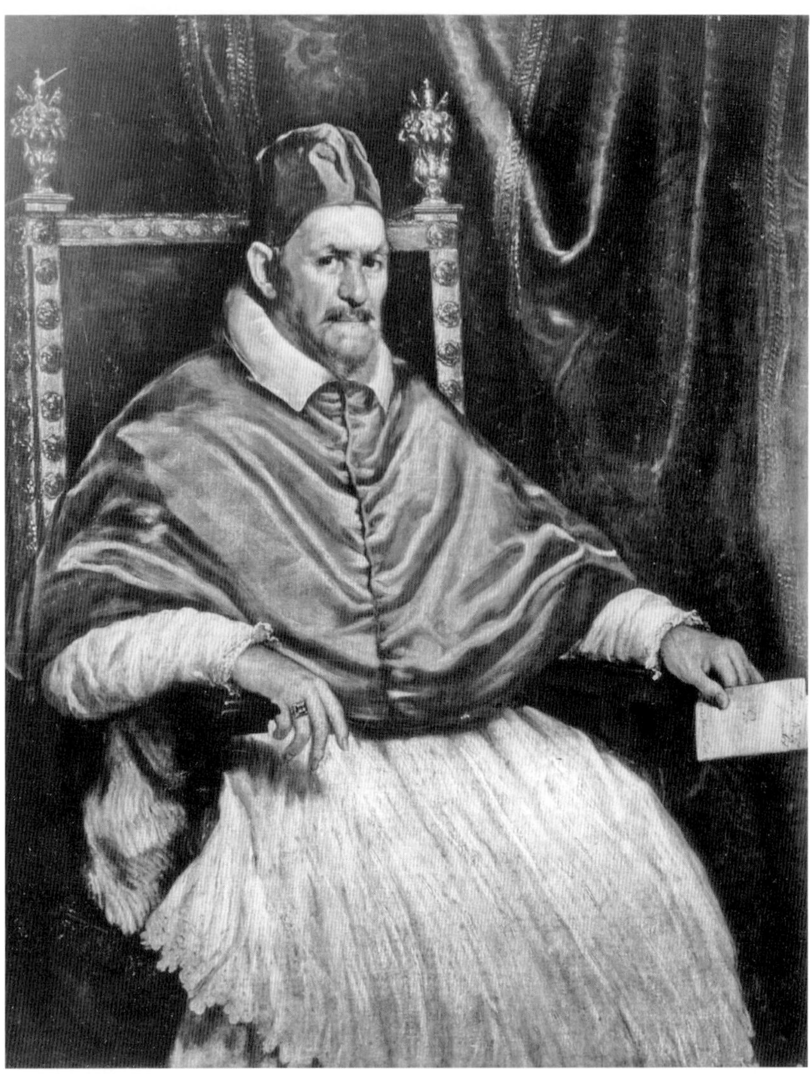

Fig. 10.3. Pietro Martire Neri (1591–1661), *Pope Innocent X*, after Velázquez. Signed. Oil on canvas, 137 × 114 cm. The Mount Stuart Trust, Mount Stuart House, Isle of Bute. *(Reproduced courtesy of the Mount Stuart Trust.)*

A letter of 21 July is lost, but on 11 August the correspondence continues.[17] Byres had sent a small package including a sample of 'Scotch Snuff' that he thought 'most delicious', two volumes of drawings by Manocchi and the second volume of Giuseppe Antonio Monaldini's Etruscan vases[18] — 'which I think but poorly executed and extravagantly dear' — at eight sequins. He also forwarded papers from 'M^r^. Hamilton the painter' (Gavin Hamilton), who had called on him.

In addition to his own commissions, Byres regularly forwarded material supplied by William Hamilton in Naples. On 5 January 1771 Byres wrote, announcing the despatch of a box with drawings of the 'Pallace of Pausilippo', the Palazzo Donn'Anna, which he thought 'very well executed', but at 150 ducats expensive.[19] These were intended for his collection of drawings recording Italian buildings, and are now in the Victoria and Albert Museum.[20] With them came more drawings by Tesi and by Byres himself.

On 16 February Bute wrote to Byres agreeing to two of the chimney-piece designs. Byres replied on 2 March, proposing an alteration to the detail of another chimney 'as Your Lordship, seem'd to disapprove of the Architraves breaking under the Tablet' — a characteristic example of the Earl's exactitude in such matters.[21] He explained the problems of securing flawless white marble, and also sent watercolour copies of three landscapes that were for sale, a Salvator Rosa of *Latona*, another of *Saint John Preaching*, and a *Venus and Adonis* given to Rubens.

From Byres's next letter, of 16 March, it emerges that he had forgotten to design a chimney-piece for

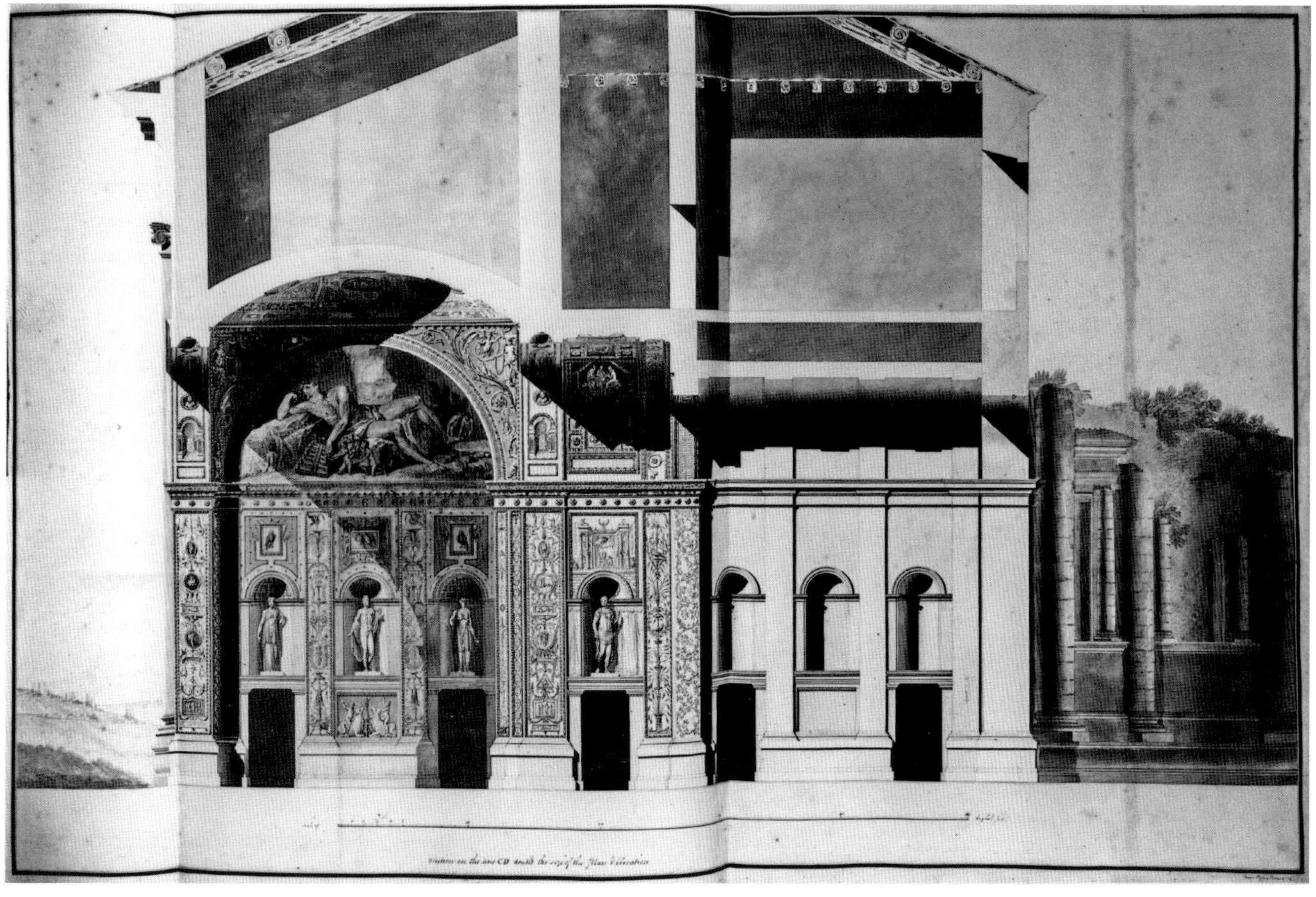

FIG. 10.4. James Byres (1734–1817), *The Villa Madama, section*. Pen and ink and watercolour on paper. London, Victoria and Albert Museum. *(Reproduced courtesy of the previous owner.)*

the Saloon at Luton.[22] Bute had evidently determined to buy the pictures offered in February, and Byres had had all his purchases 'Cased up': 'as there is no danger of a War for some time, I would fain delay sending them off until the Equinoxial winds are over'. Precisely a week later (23 March) Byres sent off two designs for the Saloon chimney-pieces — estimated at £57 and £65 respectively.[23] He despatched other trifles and was evidently rather busy with other visitors: 'The Town is full of English, I believe about sixty Travellers here at Present, seven or eight Ladies amongst them'.

Bute evidently wrote on the same day, Byres replying in another letter, perhaps mis-dated 23 March.[24] He listed the statues that had been ordered for Luton — only the *Marius* was as yet finished: the sculptor Mr Claus was working on models for the others. The Earl wanted to order another of a figure in armour and Byres suggested possible prototypes. Bute clearly had asked about preparing grounds for drawing paper, and Byres explained that, while clay was often used in Rome, he preferred chalk, because of the oiliness of the former.

Byres wrote again on 6 April.[25] Bute evidently had accepted the designs for the Saloon chimney-pieces, and these would be ready for despatch in October. Byres was now designing a less ambitious one for a small room. He had sent nine prints 'of the best Figures in Armour, in Rome' for Bute to select from, but recommended that the *Pyrrhus* would be the most suited for a niche, knowing that the proposed statue was intended for such a position on the garden front at Luton. It was characteristic of Bute to have sent Byres a thermometer — and tactful of the latter to send a 'register' of the weather, over a five-month period, with readings at 'eight O'Clock in the Morning, at Midday, at six in the Afternoon and at ten at night'.

The last of the 'new' letters is of 21 May 1771.[26] Byres had learnt that Bute had left Venice and reported on a number of commissions. He also enclosed a list of the contents of fourteen cases that were being shipped. In addition to the pictures already mentioned, these contained a landscape by James Forester, six vases — out of an order of fourteen[27] — supplied by a certain Signor Minelli, the bronze busts of the poets, 1,600 sulphers, the two sets of cork models, two alabaster table tops, three chimney-pieces, the *Marius* — and a case of lavas forwarded by William Hamilton from Naples.

In addition to Byres's letters, a detailed schedule in his hand of 'money laid out' for Bute survives.[28] By 16 May 1770 3,547 sequins had been spent, by 10 November of that year a further 2,391.97, by 21 May 1771 a final 1,837. The schedule duly records the cost of the copies commissioned from draftsmen already mentioned and also from William Mosman and Pierre Subleyras. It and associated documents establish that Bute bought four drawings and four pictures by Hackert. Although he failed to secure Piranesi's chimney-piece, Bute did buy two vases from him, one of serpentine, the other of red porphyry, when in Rome.[29] He bought an equally unidentifiable 'perspective View of Villa Albani by Pannini' — sent in the same case as large pictures and drawings, as well as miscellaneous objects and 'a dozen of Porcupine Quills'. As both his letters and his lists testify, Byres, like others, must at times have found Bute a demanding patron. But his letters, and those that continue the correspondence, explain why Byres was so successful in his role as *cicerone*-cum-agent. Alas, only three of the pictures he secured for the Earl can be traced.[30] But the drawings of the Villa Madama (Fig. 10.4) that Byres himself made for him are now in the Victoria & Albert Museum;[31] and although most of the Luton chimney-pieces were destroyed by fire after the 2nd Marquess's sale of the house, two that were retained and are now at Mount Stuart may well have been designed by Byres.[32]

APPENDIX

The following documents are in Byres's hand and unless otherwise indicated the letters and lists were addressed to Lord Bute: Bute's annotations are indicated in square brackets.

I.a

[Things of Mine left with Mr Bires.]

Things in the hands of James Byres. to be sent to the Right Honble the Earl of Bute accord.^{g} to his Lordships Directions ——

7 Cases already pack'd
15 Pictures viz.

- 3 large pictures	Gasparo Poussin Landskips	
- 1 large Landskip	Sal: Rosa	
- 2 small d.^{o} ________	Sal: Rosa	
- 2 small d.^{o} ________	M: Poussin	
- 1 Battle ___________	Borgognone	
- 1 Holy Family _____	Sassoferato	
- 1 Madonna ________	Sassoferato	
- 1 Holy Family _____	Franceschina di Bologna	
- 1 St Jerome ________	Guercino	
- 1 Still Life ________	Gio: de Udine	
- 1 Sybil ___________	Guido	
2 Setts Sulphurs _____	1000 one sett.	400 the other
2 Heads Giallo Antique		

2 Vases. 1 Serpentine 1 Porphyry
5 Shell Cameos
Agripina & Gypsy by Picler
Statues. Chimneypieces. Cork Temples, as mentioned in the other account unfinished
6 Fans. an Enameld Candlestick. an Etrusk Vase

I.b

Commissions to be executed for the Right Hon.[ble] the Earl of Bute

—— By James Byres –

6 Statues of white Marble about 5 feet high viz

—— the Apollo Belvedere
—— Marius at the Capitol
—— Agripina at the little Farnese
—— Sylla at the Villa Negroni
—— Gypsy at the Villa Borghese
—— Faustina at the Giustiniani

at 420 Crowns each of which is paid 200 Crowns. remains			2320.
2 Chimneys with trusses –	mark'd E		230.
2 Chimneys with Columns –	mark'd D		240.
a Chimney	mark'd F		140.
Copy of the Mosaic Pidgeons at 800 Crowns. 266 paid – remains		}	534.
for 2 Setts of Cork Temples & the 2 Setts 440 Zeq. – 20 Zeq. paid remains		Crown. P.. }	877..40
the Vestal Tuccia. to be work'd in tapestry at 5..50 the – Palm		}	71..50
			4412..90
a full Sett of Christiano's Sulphurs consisting .... —— of 1600. at a Paoli a Piece		}	160
	Roman Crowns –		4572..90

[Commissions left with Bires to be executed ——]

I.c

the Vases making for the Right Hon.ble the Earl of Bute.
at Minelli's are ——

2 of Oriental Alabaster fluted, the one transparent, the other flower'd
2 of Porphyry. 1 of Black, the other green
2 of Granate. form of Urns, the one red, the other green
2 of Basalte – form of Urns – the one black, the other green
2 of Jasper. the one Yellow, the other green
2 others of Jasper. the one red, the other varigated Brown & Crystaline
2 others. the one of Verde Antique, the other of Corscian green
______ ornamented with handles, foliage & fluting. –
these will cost his Lordship 20 Zeq.[s] a piece. –

II

Dear Sir

I had the satisfaction of receiving Your most obliging and kind letter from Genoa. had the honour of writing You a few lines to Milan, and was yesterday honour'd with Your most welcome letter from Venice, but am heartily sorry to find that My Lords health continues so indifferent. I was in hopes from Your letter to the Abbe [Grant] that he was quite recovered. Poor Paulino's Death likewise gave me great Concern it must have affected You very much. – The Frier at Reggio da Modena has been twice wrote to about the Book of Arabesks, I mention'd to my Lord but has answer'd neither of these letters altho' from his Superiours. they say that he his a most Whimsical odd sort of Man. however it does not signify much as I found here the other Book which I sent by M.r Joddrel, fully better than the Friers and much cheaper than he would have given it. in case my Lord likes it the Painter is here and will do more. I paid fortyfour Zequins for it which is at the rate of two Zequins a piece it contains twenty two Paintings, thirteen of which are from Raphaels Loggia, but You will find a list of the things contained in that Box inclosed with the prices I paid annexed to it, as also a list of the things contained in a Box I sent by M.r Oliphant. I shall send on Wednesday the 15.th another Box by Lord Exeter who will be at Venice by the 25 or 26th

—— I'm sorry it was not in my power to get all these things ready to send together, but You know how difficult it is to get Artists to keep their time, the three other Fans which his Lordship bespoke are not as yet near finished nor has Picler done the Zingara as yet nor Mosman the drawing of it and of the Agrippina, but I shall take care to send them home by some safe hand who will be in England by the time my Lord arrives there. I shall be able to send You in my next the size of the Landskips of which I have sent the Drawings, but have not had a moments leasure to Day to go and measure them, indeed ever since You left this I have been in a constant hurry, if my Lord likes the Drawing of Ornaments in Chiaro oscura such as that from Gio d'Udine, and that from the Antique in Villa Medici, I think the Man that does them is reasonable. —— and I have heard nothing from Naples either of the Snuff Boxes or Books; nor did I receive any Answer to a letter I wrote M.r Hamilton some weeks before he set out for Sicily if they be sent to me I shall take care to forward them with the other things. –

I forgot to get a direction from my Lord to whose care I should send the things he left in my hands. I'l be obliged to You if You'l send it me, and at the same time let me know when his Lordship would chuse that his Pictures should be sent home —— in the case by Lord Exeter I shall send some of the incrustations of the waters of S.t Phillipo, did my Lord come to any agreement with those people? –

— Don't scold me about Sicily You may Depend upon it that I shall write You as fully as I can on that head assoon as I have a moments leasure. –

— the Conclave is as yet come to no determination. Santa Bono is at present much talk'd of. all friends here are well.

Please make offer of my best Respect to my Lord and M.r Stuart and Compliments to M.r Charles his portrait is known by every body and much admired. the Tapestry Picture is near finished. the Mosaic Pidgeons, and the Chimney Pieces are begun.

if I can serve You in any thing I hope you will command me, let me know where I can direct to You after You leave Venice and believe me to be, with the most Respectful attachment and most sincere Esteem

My Dear Sir

Rome 12 May 1769 Your most Obliged and most hble Servant

James Byres

I hope You'l excuse my hurry

III

I had yesterday the honour of receiving Your Lordships letter of the 13th: am happy that the two Boxes arrived safe, and that Mrs Forbes Copy has met with Your approbation. I mentioned to her what Your Lordship was pleased to say which gives her and her Mother the greatest Satisfaction and they charged me to return Your Lordship their most grateful thanks, for the many favours you have been pleased to honour them with, they hope to profit of Sir James and Lady Wrights kind Offer and stay some time at Venice in their way home ——

— the Book of Arabesques I had the honour of sending Your Lordship was done by Gioseppe Manocchi, who went to England with Mr. Adams and workd there sometime for him. but I believe ran away and left him. he his now under Engagements with Piranesi but has some hours of the day to himself which he employs in Painting in that way. those I sent Your Lordship were all he had done but he promises to do the other Pilasters from Raphaels Loggia. I recommended to him to keep as exact to the Originals as possible, if he does them well and will part with them reasonable. in case Your Lordship chuses them I shall send them. he has studies of twelve Cielings in that way in different places and by different Masters which he proposes doing out fair. I told him that I would probably take them, and beg'd to have the refusal of them. he is the cleverest in this way I have ever saw, but very little to be depended upon so I would enter into no engagements with him but take the things if I liked them when finished. for thats by far the cheapest and surest way with such people, the thirteen first paintings in the Book are from Raphaels Loggia, Painted by Gio. d'Udine, the other nine are in different Places and I think mark'd on them where and by whom. — I paid forty four Sequins for it which I thought realy cheap. I did not know of this Man when Your Lordship was here ——

the large Arabesque sent in the last Box is from the Ceiling in Villa Magnani on the Palatine hill / formerly Villa Spada / done under Raphaels direction by his scholars which You know Abbe Grant and me had so much difficulty to procure the Lycence from the Marquese. it is done by Gioseppi Sublerass son to the Paintress in Miniature. altho' exact it's not quite so well as I could have wished, and I think rather dear having paid him fifteen Zequins for it but he affirms that it was upwards of two Months constant work ——

— there were three other Arabesque Drawings. two in Chiaro scuro and one in Colours. by a Scholar of Pompeio Battoni. those in Chiaro scuro pleased me much. the Colour'd one is not so well. I don't know the mans name but shall get it and send it: I paid five Zequins for these three Drawings ——

— in the first Box there were five Landskip Drawings. one from Bott in the Barbarini Palace, two from Salvator Rosa in the Grilli Palace by the son of Pompeio Battoni, the sizes of which I shall send Your Lordship. and two from the two Salvator Rosa's belonging to Your Lordship, by George Robertson ——

— in the second Box there were two Drawings from Claude Lorrain. the one in the Colonna palace by Pompeio's Son, the other by M.[r] Robertson from a Picture I have. I paid four Zequins a piece for these Drawings. Pompeios Son Felice Battoni has been constantly employ'd for Your Lordship since the very first, and is at present doing the two famous Claude's in the Altieri Palace, which shall be sent as soon as finished. M.[r] Robertson shall do no more. I was not at all pleased with the last he did, which was certainly very slovenly but having employ'd him was obliged to take it. ———

— in the last Case, there was likewise a waterColour View of Monte Mario and Villa Madama taken from near Ponte Molle by a Soldier whose name I shall send Your Lordship in my next. I don't think that it's so well as it might be, but I believe by a little practice, he would come to do very well in that way I paid him two Zequins for it, as also for another I sent Your Lordship by Lord Exeter. a view of the same hill taken from the River side near the Porto del Popoli. Your Lordship will judge by these specimens if You would choose to have any more done by him. —— I had the honour of sending Your Lordship by Lord Exeter who left this the 15.th a tin Case which contains two small waterColour Paintings by a German lately come from France. the one is a View of the Temple of Minerva Medica here, the other is a View which he says he took between Florence and Rome, I asked him where but he could not tell me exactly. his name is on each of them. I think them amongst the finest things in that way I ever saw and on that account sent Your Lordship these two as a Specimen. he had no more finished by him and indeed stay'd somedays from going into the Country to finish these two, for all the others he had were bought up before I heard of him. his price is six Zequins a piece, he is to stay here some years for his Study. in case You choose any more You'l be pleased to let me know and I'l endeavour to pick out the most Interesting Views and got them done by him. in the same Box is the two drawings of Boys from Domenichino & Guido by Alexander Finney. they are fix'd by Mosman and cannot spoil but Red chalk does not fix so well as black. the Landskip fan from Claude Lorrain in the Altieri Palace. A Watercolour view of Monte Mario by the Soldier, eight Architectonic drawings of the Villa called Papa Giulio, built by Vignola which come to twenty Zequins. a View by Francesco Smugglewitz I think of Foligni with the Original sketch by M.[r] Robinson this is what was contained in the tin Case. Lord Exeter has also a small wooden Box for Your Lordship containing five Specimens of the Incrustations of the waters of S.[t] Philipo, the only tolerable ones which remain'd with the Abate Vigni these are address'd to M.[r] Symonds as usual. and Your Lordship will have them by the 26.th or 27.th if the Election of the Pope does not bring Lord Exeter back to Rome. if it does I shall forward them by the Post with whatever else may be ready.

— I hope the other three fans will be done in time to send before Your Lordship leaves Venice. I am afraid of hurrying the Painters too much for fear of their slighting them, but they shall certainly do nothing else till they are finished. –

seeking for a good Stone for Your Lordships Cameo has prevented it's being done Pichler has shewn me several but none that I could approve of no diligence shall be omitted in search of one, and when found will be immediately cut. — seven of Your Lordships Vases are finished. two of Alabaster. two of Green & Black Porphyry. two of Granate the red and the Grey, and one of Jasper. the others are at work upon. – Giuseppe Clause the Sculptor is modeling in Clay for Your Statues. the Marble for them is not yet arrived from Carrara. — I have got three Models from the Corkcutter Giuseppe Aldieri. two of the Temple at Tivoli and one of the Egerian Grotto. The Tuccia in Tapestry is well advanced and will be finished by the end of June. the Mosaic Pidgeons are begun. as

soon as possible I shall send Your Lordship the two Drawings by Nicholas Mosman of the Agrippina and Gypsey, but it will be impossible to begin them until the middle of next week. whatever is sent from Naples I shall carefully forward, and Your Lordships directions shall be carefully observed in whatever is sent, if any thing realy good falls into my hands Your Lordship shall have the refusal of it. I shall send a sketch, the price, and as nearly as I can, describe, it's state, Colouring and preservation, and in case You choose it You'l let me know, and if upon seeing it You don't like it I'l take it back ——
—I wrote M.[r] Symonds last week that the Frier at Reggio, had never answer'd the letters wrote to him relative to the Book of Drawings, which does not signify much for as near as I can recollect they were much the same as those by Manocchi –
— the Books spoke of by Pompeio, I have got, and paid forty Zequins for. but do not think,Your Lordship would like it, altho' it contains several good drawings. they are studies for Pictures by different Old Masters, only one Drawing in it by Gio: d'Udine. in M.[r] Symonds letter was inclosed a list of the things contain'd in the two first Boxes. by M.[r] Jodrel and M.[r] Oliphant. –
— I shall not attempt to return Your Lordships thanks for the many favours You have been pleased to honour me with. it would be impossible for me either to express my sentiments of Gratitude, or the satisfaction I feel in having the honour of being known to Your Lordship, so can only pray that You may enjoy health and happyness and have the honour to remain with the most Respectful Attachment

Your Lordships
Most Obliged
and most humble Servant
James Byres

Rome 20.th May 1769. —

P.S: I shall send the drawings of the Chimney Pieces before Your Lordship leaves Venice ——

IV

My Lord

Words are insufficient to express the joy that the happy news of Your Lordships recovery, gave to the few who have the honour of being known to You here. I really felt an unusual lightness about me, for several days after the receipt of Your most welcome letter, I hope the waters near Valdagna will fully answer our ardent Wishes, in confirming Your Lordships health for many years. —— I delay'd writing last post in hopes of receiving by this weeks Couriers the things that were to come from Naples, but they are both arrived and brought nothing, nor has M[r]. Leigh wrote Barazzi or me about them. M.[r] Hamilton is not yet returned from Sicily. ——
— the fans are not yet done. two of them will be finished in about ten days. the third in three weeks, this is not owing to any neglect of the Painters, for I have found them at work upon them at six o'clock in the Morning, and I really believe they have done nothing else. —— I have at last got a good Stone of three Colours for Your Cameo, it will come very well and will be finished in ten or twelve days. ——
— its true L[d] Exeter desired Mosman to do the two Drawings for Your Lordship. but a few days before he left this he set him to work upon a holy Family by Guercino, in the Giovenazza Collection, which he was very desirous of having done immediately, it is now finished and on Monday he begins Your Lordships, which he supposes will take him about sixteen or eighteen days work, so that they will be finished about the same time with the last four I am heartily sorry that Your Lordship is disapointed in not having those things done so soon as You wished but it was realy impossible to get the fans and Cameo, without serving You ill. if You will let me know whether these things should be sent by the Post, and where they can meet You on the Road, or if You would rather Charge that they should go home with Your other things or by any Gentleman that's going straight to England. ——
— thing go from here to Leghorn in about ten days but they are sometimes much longer. there is commonly in the Summer time every six weeks Ships from Leghorn to London, their Passage may be reckon'd from six weeks to two Months, so that from Rome to London things ought to go in about three Months. but I have had things sometimes six Months on the way. ——
— I am glad the Book of Arabesques met with Your approbation I never saw any thing in that way better done. with this days Courier I have the honour of sending Your Lordships nine other which I think most beautiful. they are by the same hand, he had done the six Ceilings some time ago for Piranesi but finding that I was desirous of having every thing he did in that way bought them back and let me have them for three Zequins and half each, which is wonderfully cheap. the two Pilasters from the Loggi of the Vatican he did for Your Lordship at two Zequins each. —— I took the liberty of writing You his Character in my last, and have not as Yet mention'd anything to him of going to England. indeed I suppose he dares not go, as he was engaged in articles to M. [r]

Adams for four Years. from whom I hear he run away immediately after the commencement. but in case Your Lordship chuses it I shall speak to him, and let you know his terms. ––
–– Lodovico Tesi who did the Chiaro scuro Drawings seems to be a worthy Man it's him I have employ'd to do Your last fan. /the Rape of Helen/ which I believe will do the best of them all, he accidentally told me that he had done Fans, so I immediately employ'd him to do that which was the only one not begun. his doing that prevents me sending you more of his chiaro scuro.

I wrote Your Lordship in my last about the Vases, there are none finished since. –– The Tapestry Picture is going on particular care shall be taken in packing it up ––
–– the Antique Cameo I return restored by Pickler. it's well worth what You paid for it. the Sculpture is good, the Stone singular, and the Subject I fancy rare. for it is the only Melpomone with the Tragick Mask on her head, I ever saw in Cameo. ––
my Cameo which You are pleased to inquire about, is certainly the finest I ever saw. I have sent Your Lordship a Drawing of it just double the size of the Original. which is better than any description I can give of it. one part of the ground was fragmented, I have got it restored by Pickler. it has also a slight crack on one side. the restoration is indicated in the Drawing by a line over the head and Arm of the women and Faun next her. all the four figures are wonderful for the excellence of the Sculpture, Elegance, expressions and beauty of the Stone the Young Mans nose is a little damaged. I have asked three hundred Pounds for it but the real price that I'l part with it for is two hundred and fifty Pound. ––
–– the Picture of which I sent Your Lordship a Drawing by Robertson is a good picture, altho' the Drawing was bad. I believe it to be by Claude Lorrain, but I am not certain. it's on wood in excellent preservation and well colour'd. the price is fifty five Pound.
–– I send in this box a Drawing by Felice Battoni of a Salvator Rosa, I have got, well preserved but not high finished. rather slight and free. the price is thirty Pound. but the best Picture I have got since Your Lordship left Rome is what you will not like, – the Original Sketch by Hanibal Carrach painted on Copper of his fine Picture in the Pamphili Chapel representing a dead Christ with the Virgin and two little Angels. as soon as possible I shall send You a slight sketch of it. the Price is sixty Pound.
–– I have not been able to hear of any Collection of Medals, such as Your Lordship wants, if any such thing be to be disposed of I shall immediately let you know. ––
–– the New Pope seems to give universal satisfaction we are in great hopes that he'l at least restore Quiet to this decay'd State.
–– O my Lord poor Corsica and worthy Paoli's defeat, has given a sad damp to our Spirits here. Yesterdays letters from Leghorn and Corsica give us some hope that he may reestablish his Affairs ––
Miss [Margaret] Murray is married and seems very happy she is gone to the Country with her Husband [Marchese di Accaromboni] and good Abbe Grant who charged me before he went to present his Comp.^{ts} in the most Respectful Manner to Your Lordship. may I beg leave to present mine to Mr Stuart, Mr Symonds and Mr Charles. I shall have the honour of writing Mr Symonds next Post. the following is a list of the things in the Box which I this day consign'd to the Courier of Venice directed to Sr James Wright I have the honour to be with the most Respectful Attachment

Your Lordships
Rome 10.th June 1769–– Most Obliged and most humble Servant

James Byres

			S	B
6 Arabesk Ceilings	at 3 Zeq for each		43..	10
1 Arabesk Facciata	by Monochi	3 Zeq for - - - -	7..	17½
2 Pilasters from Raphaels Loggi	at 2 Zeq		8..	40
½ Sheet cont.^{g} 2 Arabesks from Raphael and 1 from Sansovino	Lod.^{o} Tesi	1 Zeq ½	3..	7½
2 Drawg.^{s} from Claude, in the Altieri 1 from Sal. Rosa – in Posess.^{n} of J: Byres	Felice Battoni at	4 Zeq	25..	20
1 Landskip in waterColours by the Soldier		2 Zeq	4..	10
1 Drawing of the Cameo in Posess.^{n} of J: Byres				
4 Chimney Pieces belong.^{g} to your L.^{d}Ship				
2 heads of the Pope which though badly done are thought like				
a small Box cont.^{g} 1 Ring and a Col.^{d} Head of the Emperor by Picler - in Gos – – retouch.^{g} the Cameo 1 Zeq the Col^{d} Gesi 50^{B}			2..	55

the foll.^{g} is list of the sizes of the Pictures from which F. Battoni has made
– Draw.^{gs} ——

	inches	
1 Landskip by Poussin – ..	3 feet by 4.. 1 –	Barbarini Palace
2 D.^{o} – by Bott -	3.. 9 by 5.. 3	
2 Landskips by S: Rosa –	3.. 9 by 5.. 3	Grilli Palace
1 Landskip by Claude Lorrain	1.. 10½ by 2.. 7	Colonna Palace

V

My Lord

I received the letter Your Lordship was pleased to honour me with from Venice the 24.th June, but having nothing particular to say delay'd troubling You, until I received the Bills of Lading from Leghorn, which I have the honour of sending Enclosed. by which Your Lordship will observe that Your twelve Cases were embark'd the 7.th Instant onboard the Juno Captn Robt Woolcombe; which I am inform'd is one of the Best Ships in the Leghorn Trade, and is under Contract to sail the 15.th Current, weather permitting Your Lordship will likewise find Enclosed a list of the things contain'd in the Cases pack'd up by me, as also an Account of the Money laid out. – when they arrive at the Custom House /which I hope will be in the Month of Sept.^{r}/ it will be necessary that Mr Foot, or some intelligent Person, attends to see the Cases properly open'd and repack'd with care, that nothing may be lost or spoil'd. —— Altho' Your Lordship did not Order it, for the greater Security I got the five Cases, pack'd up by me Embaled, the eight Cases sent to me pack'd up I got half embaled, joining that Mark'd N.º 6 & 7 as they are small together, and Mark'd it N.º 6. that which was mark'd N.º 8 is now mark'd N.º 7 —

the four Arabesque Drawings by Monocchi complete Raphaels Loggi at the Vatican, the Ornaments of the other Pilasters being entirely defaced. he is now doing the two Antient Cielings on the Palatine hill, for Your Lordship. I had no Chiaro Scuro Drawings to send. Lodovico Tesi having been entirely occupy'd in finishing Your Lordships last Fan /which will be sent by first opportunity/ he is now doing a Picture for the Duke of Northumberland which was bespoke before I receiv'd Your Lordships Letter, as soon as that is finished the Capitals and Ornaments You order shall be done. the two Water Colour Paintings by Hackert the Prussian are very Correct Views. they are the same size with those You had before. he demands sixteen Zequins for Views of about double that size, which appear'd to me to be so much, that I did not bespeak any until further Orders from Your Lordship. however on his return from Tivoli if any of the Views he is doing there, are extraordinary Well, I shall take them for Your Lordship ——

The Zingara in Cameo, the Tapestry Picture, the Fan representing the Rape of Helen, two Cork Models of the Temple of Concord, the two Chimney Pieces from the design Mark'd D for the East & West Rooms of the Library and four Vases, two of Jasper, one of antient, and another of Corsican Green, are finished and shall be sent the first Opportunity. ——

——— the Black and Green Porphyry, the Red and Green Granate Vases, I got ornamented with gilt Bronze, as I thought they look'd rather dull, the ornamenting the four, only cost twenty Crowns. if Your Lordship approve of these I shall get the others that require it Ornamented. —— I shall have the honour of sending as soon as possible some Sketches of the Pictures, I have met with since Your Lordship left this.

—— the Drawing by Sal. Rosa on board I got accidentally some time ago and have taken the liberty of sending it to Your Lordship, which I hope you will be so good as to accept. ——

—— I have heard no more of the Jesuits Picture nor the Books of Shells, but I am sure You offer'd fully enough for both, and do not imagine that they will meet with such another Offer ——

——— I was happy to see in the Press (?) that Your Lordship was save return'd to England, and hope to God that Your health continues to improve. I have the honour to be with the Most Profound Respect.

Your Lordships

Most Obliged

Rome 14.th August 1769—— and most humble Servant

James Byres

VI

My Lord

I had the honour of writing Your Lordship the 14.th Augt in which was Enclosed a Bill of Lading for twelve Cases, with a list of their Contents, and an Account of the Money I had laid out. I hope by this time they are safe Arrived, for we have had fine weather and southerly Winds ever since they Sail'd.

Some weeks ago Mr Hamilton of Naples sent me four Snuff Boxes and four setts of Fansticks of white TortoiseShell inlaid with Gold. they arrived here safe, and I sent them off last week to Leghorn with several other things of which Your Lordship will find a list Enclosed. these seven Cases are Mark'd E B as usual and directed to Mr Foot in Durham Yard. as soon as I receive the Bills of Lading from Leghorn, I shall have the honour of forwarding them to Your Lordship. ——

— As Felice Cettomai's /the worker in Tapestry/ Account does not exactly tally with the Estimate I gave Your Lordship, I have sent Enclosed his receipt, the difference is owning to his insisting on the selvage which turns down being paid at the same rate as the rest, which I had not thought of, measuring the Picture ——

Your Lordship left sixteen Zequins in my hands to pay Young Pickler for the Zingara in Cameo. I paid him fifteen Zequins for the cutting and paid six Zequins for the Stone, so there remains five Zequins which the Stone is mark'd at in the Enclosed Account of Money laid out on this Cargo which Amounts to five hundred & eighty Crowns thirty Baiochi. if Your Lordship pleases You may send me Bills to the Amount of two Hundred & fifty or three hundred Pounds. for as these Bills are only payable about three Months after Date, the remainder of that Money will probably be expended before they become due. it will be necessary that the Banker who buys these Bills Insures them /which I believe they do for half p.^{r} Cent/ for otherways if the Merchant upon whom they are drawn should break Your Lordship would lose the Money ——

— Monocchi on account of the Damp in the Vaults of the Palatine hill during the Summer has not been able to finish the Drawings of the Antient Arabesques that are there but will do them this Winter. Lodovico Tesi has been so entirely taken up with repeated Copies of the Emperours and Grand Dukes Portraits for his Master Pompeio Battoni, that it has not been in my power to get him to do any thing for Your Lordships or the Duke of Northumberland. and he is the only person that I know of in Rome capable of pleasing Your Lordship in these Chairo Scuro Drawings, but he promises that in about a fortnight he'l be able to work entirely for me.

— I last Post received the letter Your Lordship was pleasd to honour me with the 22.^{d} Augt and am most heartily sorry to see that You have reaped so little benefit from Your long Journey. but would fain hope that Your Lordships health is reestablished before now. if You come to Recovaro in the Spring I shall certainly have the honour of waiting on Your Lordship there. and have the honour to be with the most Respectful Attachment

Your Lordships

Rome 26.th Sept.^{r} —— Most Obliged and most humble Servant

James Byres

P:S: the Mosaic worker at St Peters was with me Yesterday to let me know that he would take the three hundred and Eighty Crowns Your Lordship offer'd for the head and Rabbit. I shall wait Your Lordships Orders before I take them ——

J:B

VII

(Estimate for chimney-pieces for Luton sent to Lord Bute and Byres's record of instructions sent by the Earl, 10 March 1770)

The Estimate of the expences, of executing the Chimneys, in the best Statuary Marble. with their slabs of the same and insides line'd with Black Marble. ——

				£
that mark'd Letter	A	160 Roman Crowns wch is	ab.^{t}	38. –
– the Cariatides for the same		400 Crowns	about	95. –
that mark'd	B	150 Crowns	ab.^{t}	35..10 –
– the two Busts for the same		50	ab.^{t}	12.. –
that mark'd	C	145 Crowns	ab.^{t}	34. –

that mark'd	D	140 Crowns	ab.[t]	32..15 –
– the tablet for the same		130 Crowns	ab.[t]	31.. –
that mark'd	E	135 Crowns	ab.[t]	32. –
– the tablet for the same		210 Crowns	ab.[t]	50. –
that mark'd	F	160 Crowns	ab.[t]	38. –

the expence of the Slabs, and lining of the Chimney, will be 20 Crowns

the expence of Case Packing Embaling & Freight to Leghorn.

	£		£
expence there, & Freight to London will be from	12..	to	15. –

[English Estimate of chimneys with the Italian Prices]

Note of the Chimney Pieces

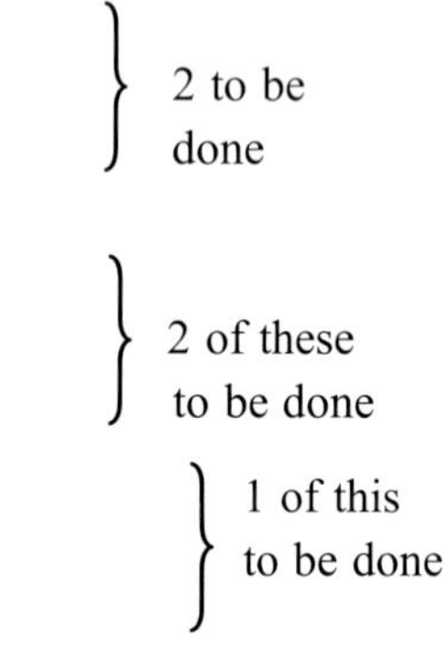

the Chimney with Columns mark'd D. for – the East & West rooms of the Library to have the entire Frieze of the Chimney with .... mark'd A	2 to be done
the Chimney with trusses mark'd E for the East & West parts of the Center Room of the Library to have an Elegant Frieze of ornament chose from it from the Herculaneum –	2 of these to be done
the Chimney Piece mark'd F for the bow window drawing Room to be executed according to the drawing	1 of this to be done

VIII

My Lord,

I had the honour of receiving Your Lordships letter of the 10.th Ult.[o] and shall have the honour of obeying the distinct order You favour'd me with therein, relative to the Orders of Architecture as soon as I have a little leasure in day light to work which I hope will be soon after Easter, for I cant trust any part of a Commission that requires this exactness,. to the Young Men that work with me. ——

I was honourd last week with Your Lordships order relative to the five Chimney Pieces, two for the Salon of the size of those of the middle Room of the Lybrary, which is four feet four Inches wide, by four feet high. the other three for the drawing Room and two Oval Rooms of the size of those of the lesser Rooms of the Library, which is four feet six inches wide, by four feet two inches high. this I should think rather large for the Oval Rooms. on this account I have done all the ten Sketches, I have now the honour of sending You of the size of the Chimney, of the middle Room of the Library, that is four feet four inches wide, by four feet high, and the enclosed Estimate has been made according to that size. if Your Lordship should approve of any of them, and chuse to diminish or augment the size the price to the Marble cutter, will diminish or augment accordingly but to the Sculptor. I mean for the Figures a little larger or smaller makes no odds. had I had a little more time these Sketches would perhaps been a little more correct, and better drawn, and I should have kept outlines of them which I have not had time to do. I should have also made another Drawing of a Chimney for the Frieze of the Dancing hours, for that with the Cariatides does not thoroughly satisfye me, and they come dear. I think the two Friezes for the Chimneys of the Salon will come well, the one representing the pleasures of the River and the other of the Wood. all the figures in them are taken from the Antiques. I only brought them together. the Effect they would have in Sculpture is best seen in the Chiaro Scuro Drawings of them. —— in case Your Lordship determines to have any of these Chimneys executed or alter'd I must beg You to send them back as I have no duplicates of them. ——

—— I had yesterday the honour of receiving Your Lordships letter of the 31st. I never saw any Busts or Figures of the Italian poets to be sold. there is a good Bust of Dante at the little Farnese, and a Bust of Tasso at his Tomb in the Church of S.[t] Onofrio. altho' I don't remember to have seen, there may probably be Busts of Ariosto and Petrarch in Town. I shall make it my business to enquire about them, at Naples there is a Bust of Sanazarius at his Tomb, what size would Your Lordship chuse to have them of. I have the honour to be with the most respectful Attachment

My Lord
Your Lordships most Obliged
And most humble Servant

Rome 7.th April 1770 James Byres

IX

My Lord

I had the honour of receiving Your Lordships letter of the 5.th am most conscious of the inattention I was guilty of, shall be more punctual for the future, and am infinitely obliged to Your Lordship for Your kind reprimand. ——

——The Measures You give of the opening of the Chimneys shall be exactly followed. ——

I shall have the honour of sending as soon as possible another Idea for the Drawing room Chimney Piece. I do not apprehend that there will be any difficulty of extending that Freize to six feet long. for it must not only cover the opening of the Chimney but also the bredth of the Ribbets, which for an opening of five feet can't be less than six Inches each, but in case, extending the nine figures to the length of six feet, should make them appear too Sprawling, it's only adding another Figure in the same stile, of which we have many examples in Rome. the five figures in the middle of this Frieze is all that are in the Original at Villa Borghese. the other four were added to make out Sir Laurences Frieze. ——

Your Lordship says that You will give two Hundred for Piranesi's Chimney Piece. but I am not certain whether it be Pounds Sterling or Sequins. I talk'd to him to day about it. he says that he will give the Chimney for four hundred Sequins which is less than two Hundred Pounds, but without the Basso Relievo representing the Feast of Trimaltian which comes above the Cornish, but that with the Basso Relievo, his last price is five hundred Sequins. —— I think it would be a better bargain, and as compleat a thing without the Basso Relievo. which I reckon the worst part of it. the Chimney Piece is realy beautifull altho' perhaps too luxuriant ——

——I left a Commission at Florence relative to Gilli's Grammar and shall know next week whether it has been sent to M.r Richie, if it cannot be found at Florence I shall again see if it be possible to find it here. ——

I had the honour of sending Your Lordship by M.r Barnard who left this the 5.th Current. the Drawings sent by M.r Hamilton from Naples as also nine Drawings by Felice Battoni from pictures by Gasparo Poussin on the ground floor of the Colonna Palace, which are amongst the best things of that Master and I believe were never before copied. I likewise sent two collourd Drawings from Pictures of Gian Battista Busiri, six feet six inches long by five feet eight inches high to be sold here for Sixty Sequins. I think that they are well worth the money but they are too large for me to buy. they might perhaps do for Your Library on which account I sent Sketches of them. ——

The heads of the Italian Poets which Your Lordship wants of the size of half life, will cost in Bronze twenty Sequins each and in Statuary Marble twenty three Sequins each. ——

I beg'd M.r Barnard in case he did not find Your Lordship at Venice to leave the Case of Drawings with M.r Richie to be forwarded to Your Lordship at Valdagna immediately. where I hope you will reap the desired benefit from the Waters, and have the honour to remain with the most respectful Attachment

Your Lordships
Most Obliged and
Most humble Servant

Rome 12.th May 1770 James Byres

X

My Lord

I had yesterday the honour of receiving Your Lordships letter of the 15.th and am grieved to see that You have received no benefit from the waters, in which I had great hopes. ——

I am glad that the Drawings sent by Mr Barnard are agreable to Your Lordship. I suppose Mr Richie has before now sent You Gilli's Grammar, and the few Prints that are come out, of the Florentine Collection of Pictures, as a friend of mine wrote me from Florence the 17.th May, that he had got them, and would deliver them to Mr Richie in a few days as he was going immediately to Venice.

According to Your Lordships Orders I offer'd Sig.^{r} Piranesi two Hundred Pounds for his Chimney Piece, but he will not take it.

I have ordered four Busts of the Italian Poets, vizt Dante, Petrarch, Ariosto and Tasso. of half the size of life, in bronze with low Pedestals of the same, on which their Names may be engraved, as their heads are little known out of Italy. they will cost twenty Sequins each, if you choose to have the Busts of any of the others done, they shall be immediately order'd if Portraits of them can be found. ——

I have received from Messrs Coutts on Your Lordships Account Bills of Exchange on Leghorn for three Hundred Pounds Sterling, of date the 27.th of April when they become due I shall negotiate them to the best Advantage, and inform You of it. ——

I have this day order'd a migniature of the Aldobrandini Marriage, in the form of a Picture, which will be finish'd in about two Months at the same price as the Fan, twenty five Sechins ——

When Mr Hamilton sends the 2^{d} Vol. of the Etruscan Vases, and the other things, they shall be immediately forwarded to the care of M^{r}. Richie. ——

Sig.^{r} Domenico to whom the Landskips by Busiri belongs is at present out of town, as soon as he returns I shall get them and have them Cased up with the Pope by Diego de Velasquez. and if Your Lordship does not order to the contrary, shall send them to Venice, but that will be attended with a very great Expence, both for the long carriage by land, and the Duty going in, and out of Venice, as also with some danger, as Cases of that size if a Cart should oversett is liable to burst and the Pictures to be ruin'd, and in the way that these carts travel. You may count about forty Days from the time they leave this before they arrive at Venice. I should think it by far a safer, Quicker & Cheaper way to send all the large and heavy things, from here to Leghorn, and from thence to London. but whatever Your Lordship Orders shall be punctually obey'd. ——

I send to Mr Richie by this nights Courier two small Cases for Your Lordship, of which I gave him notice along with this. enclosed is a note of their Contents, as also an Estimate of the Chimney Pieces, the drawings of which you will please to return, as I have no Duplicates of them. ——

——I am ashamed to tell Your Lordship, that the Drawings of the Orders are not yet quite finish'd, but will be ready to send off saturday next. the reason of this delay is that the best of my young people, has been for these six weeks confin'd with a disorder in his Bowels, and I have been sadly tormented with head achs for some time. so that the few hours of the day I have to my self, I have scarce be able to apply seriously to any thing, but I shall send them Saturday night without fail. ——

Mr Grant is well and desires his best Respects to Your Lordship and I have the honour to be with the most Respectful Attachment

Your Lordship
Most Obliged and most humble Servant

Rome 23 June 1770

James Byres

Estimate of the Chimney Pieces

N.º 1&2—	to the Marble Cutter		190		
	to the Sculptor for the Frieze		300		
	to the Goldsmith for the Bronze, gilt		50		£ s
		Roman C.^{n}		540	about 130..10 Sterling
N.º 3&4—	to the Marble Cutter		101		
	For the Frieze		300		£ s
		Roman Crowns	401	about 114..10 Sterling	
N.º 5&64—	to the Marble Cutter		165		
	For the Frieze		300		£ s
		Roman Crowns	465	about 110..15 Sterling	

Contents of the 2 Small Boxes sent the 23.rd June 1770

1 Drawing from Salvator Rosa by Felice Battoni
2 D.^{o} ornaments by L: Tesi
2 setts of the 2^{d} Publication of the Arabesques from the Loggi of Raphael
6 Sketches of Chimney Pieces, on three half sheets.
a Small Box with 2 lb of the best Green Tea. –

XI

My Lord

I have the honour of sending You by this nights Courier, a small Box to the care of Mr Richie it contains the second Volume of Monaldini's Etruscan Vases,/which I think but poorly executed and extravagantly dear, eight Sechins is the price/,two Arabesque cielings by Monocchi, and a Tortoiseshell Snuff Box sent me by Mr Hamilton for Your Lordship. I got lately some Scotch Snuff from Aberdeen which I think most delicious[.] I have taken the liberty of sending You a taste of it. if it be to Your Lordships liking I have got a Couple of Pound at Your Service. —

I am happy to hear from Mr Richie, that Your health is better then it was, when Your Lordship left Valdagna God grant that it may daily continue to improve. —

I had the honour of writing Your Lordship the 21.st of last Month and should have wrote last Post, but had not got the Arabesque Cielings. —

there is no News of any Consequence here. Abbe Grant begs to make Offer of his best Respects. I have the honour to remain with the most Respectful Attachment

Your Lordships
Most Obliged and
most humble Servant
James Byres

Rome 11.th Augt 1770

P.S. since writing the above, M^{r}. Hamilton the Painter call'd on, to desire that I would forward the enclosed Papers to Your Lordship.
I have seen some of the Drawings, they are very well done in red Chalk.– —

[account to March 1771 and list of things orderd but not yet finished also account of each parcel sent home —]

Commissions to be executed for the Right Honble the Earl of Bute

– By James Byres –

6 Statues of white Marble about 5 feet high viz

– the Apollo Belvedere
– Marius at the Capitol
– Agripina at the little Farnese
– Sylla at the Villa Negroni
– Gypsy at the Villa Borghese
– Faustina at the Giustiniani
at 420 Crowns each of which is paid 200 Crowns. remains 2320

2 Chimneys with trusses –	mark'd E	230
2 Chimneys with Columns –	mark'd D	240
a Chimney	mark'd F	140
Copy of the Mosaic Pidgeons at 800 Crowns. 266 paid – remains		534

for 2 Setts of Cork Temples & the 2 Setts 440 Zeq. – 20 Zeq paid ______ remains___________	Crown. P..	877..40
the Vestal Tuccia. to be work'd in tapestry at 5..50 the – Palm		71..50
		4412..90
a full Sett of Christianos Sulphurs consisting .... – of 1600 at a Paoli a Piou		160
	Roman Crowns –	4572..90

XII

My Lord

I was in hopes of sending You tonight, an account of all that has been done for Your Lordship since You left Rome but I find that it is impossible to finish it in time for the Post, so must delay until next Week. I have this night Consign'd to the Courier four Sketches of Chimney Pieces for the Drawing Room. —

that Mark'd N°. 1. will cost two hundred Crowns _______		about 48 £
that Mark'd N°. 2. ______	one hundred & seventy five Cro:	ab.^{t} 42 £
that Mark'd N°. 3. ______	three hund^{d}. & twenty Crowns	ab.^{t} 76 £
that Mark'd N°. 4. ______	one hundred & fifty Crowns	ab.^{t} 36 £

if any of these should meet with Your Lordships approbation, I beg You'l be so good as send them back, as I have no Copies of any of them.

The Wax Models and the Molds are finish'd for the four heads of the Italian Poets, Your Lordship order'd, but they are not yet cast in Bronze. I cannot say that I think any of the other Portraits of Poets we have in Rome, are either sufficiently ascertain'd, or good enough work, for Your Lordship to get Copies of them. —

The Aldobrandini Marriage is orderd and will be finish'd in two months. —

You know the Ionick Capital at Terracina, was drawn by Mr Kirby. he did it on his way from Naples. I never had a Copy of it. if I can find any Archictect going to Naples I shall get it done. I think Mr Kirby said he had another Drawing of it. —

The Man that makes the Sulphurs is going to publish a printed Catalogue of them, with Historic remarks as he lives by selling his Sulphurs to the British Travellers[.] he wants in Gratitude to Dedicate his Catalogue to the King[.] I could not tell him whether it would be agreable or not, and on that Account take the liberty to ask Your Lordship. —

I hope the Milk Diet continues to agree with Your Lordship and that Your Health continues to improve, and have the honour to remain with the most respectful Attachment

Your Lordships

Most Obliged and most humble

Rome 8.th Octr 1770—

Servant

James Byres

XIII

My Lord

I have this night Consign'd to the Courier, a small Box for Your Lordship, directed to the care of Mr Richie, whom I have inform'd of it. this box contains, twenty five Drawings, eleven of the Pallace of Pausilippo sent me by Mr Hamilton. I have examined these Drawings, I think that they are very well executed, but that the Price demanded is most Extravagant. I don't pretend to Tax, and should be very sorry to undervalue any Artists work, but all I can say is this, that had I done them and I believe I could have done them just as well, I should not have expected above fifty Zechins for them. Mr Hamilton writes me, that he has already advanced a Hundred & fifty Ducats /which is something more that sixty Zechins/ for them, so they are certainly fully paid.

There are eleven Drawings in Chiaro Scuro by Lod.^{o} Tesi, from different Ornaments in Rome, as is wrote under each, and three Drawings by me. the Dorick Capital in Villa Borghese, with its Plan. the Composite Capital in Villa Albani, and that in the Noviciate of the Jesuits adjusted. I have done this in two ways, so that Your Lordship may chuse which You like best, and a sketch from which the Friezes of the Chimney Pieces have been done. from the note I have of Your Lordships Commissions, I found it mention'd from some Elegant Frieze in the Herculaneum, and interlined over that ornamented with Goats, I lookd over the work of the Herculaneum but did not find any thing exactly to my mind, so endeavour'd to mix Goats that I found there, with Foliage to make out a frieze. —

I yesterday had a letter from Mr Coutts, with a Bill on Leghorn enclosed for three Hundred Pounds, on Your Lordships Account which I shall negotiate as soon as it becomes due, and inform You of it. I have the honour to be with the most Respectful Attachment

Your Lordships
most Obliged and most humble Servant
James Byres

Rome 5.th Jany 1771.

XIV

[Venice March 30 1771

This day I sent Bires a commission for five chimneys all of white marble; two for Saloon of number Seven, only one to have the frieze

of number Nine,		about 57 each	4-6 high 5 f wide
number one for the small Drawing Room.	about	23 – 10	4 – high 4-4 wide
and such another varied for my Dressing Room —		23 – 10	
number 3 for Drawing room. ________	about	76 ——.	4-6 high, 5f wide]
	in all	180 – 0	

My Lord

I had last week the honour of receiving Your Lordships letter of the 16.th February, and am most heartily glad that You have got the better of Your violent Cold. I have this night consign'd to the Courier directed to the care of Mr Richie a tin Case for Your Lordship, containing five Drawings of Chimney Pieces. the two You already approved of. N.º 1 all of white Marble, which will cost about 23£..15s Sterling. N.º 4 incrusted with Corsican green which will cost £45..5 Sterl.^{g} the other three Drawings are different Ideas for N.º 3 as Your Lordship, seem'd to disapprove of the Architraves breaking under the Tablet, as it is in the first Idea of this Chimney Piece. in the second the Tablet is made narrower, and only comes down to the underfillet of the Architrave. in the third it rises to the Corona of the Frieze but of these three, I must own, I would prefer the first, and cannot think of any other way of adjusting it. the execution will come to about seventy six Pounds. —

Your Lordship may believe that I take all the possible care to examine the Marble, and to recommend to the Sculptor who knows more of it than I do, to chuse the best, and without spots but it is impossible from the outside appearance, to be certain that some small spots may not appear in cutting it, and they will not undertake to do them absolutely free from spots, under an advanced price, for they say that they may be obliged to throw aside several pieces, after they are half wrought

there is in the same Case three water Collour Drawings of the Landskips I mentioned to Your Lordship. N.º 1 is from a Picture by Sal: Rosa 3^{ft}..9 Broad by 2^{ft}..10^{i} high. the picture is good, and in excellent preservation, it represents the Lydian Peasants turn'd to Frogs. the value of it is £40. N.º 2 is also from Sal: Rosa 4 feet broad by 5^{ft}..7 high. has been an excellent Picture, but is turn'd a little black. it repres.^{ts} St John preaching in the Wilderness. the value of it is £25. N.º 3 is from Rubens. five feet Broad, by three feet eleven Inches high, represents Venus and Adonis, is in tolerable preservation but has never been a first Rate Rubens. the Value of it is twenty five Pounds. I believe them all three originals.

I have according to Your Lordships directions wrote Mr Hamilton, concerning the Drawings, and shall forward then assoon as they arrive, and have the honour to remain, with the most Respectful Attachment

Your Lordship
Most Obliged and most humble Servant
James Byres

Rome 2.^{d} March 1771

XV

My Lord

I had yesterday the satisfaction of receiving the letter Your Lordship was pleased to honour me with of the 9.th I am really ashamed of my unaccountable forgetfulness. I was surprised in reading Your Lordships letter, and can not to this Moment concieve how a thing that You had order'd so particularly, and that I had thought of so much, as the Chimney Pieces for the Salon, could escape my Memory. I hope Your Lordship will pardon this. I have sett about them to day, and shall certainly have the honour of sending them this day sevenight with the Courier so that Your Lordship will have them the 27.th Cur.^{t} I shall also send along with them the Medals and Prints of the Pope. —

I am infinitely obliged to Your Lordship; for the Specimens of the Bones, You have been so good as to send me, as also for mentioning me to a Man of Mr Stranges knowlege. I have heard much of Him, and I shall be happy to have the honour of serving him in any thing that lies in my Power.

Your Lordships things are all Cased up but as there is no danger of a War for some time, I would fain delay sending them off until the Equinoxial winds are over. the Statue of Marius is finish'd, and will go along with the other things, as Mr Claus is so very tedious, and has broke his agreement in not finishing in time, if Your Lordship approves of it I shall get other Artists to do those of which Mr Claus has not yet done the Models. he is now at work on the Gypsy. —

The large Landskip by Sal: Rosa has been lined and Clean'd. I am affraid that it will be impossible to make it clearer than it is. — I am happy to hear that Your Lordship is considerably recovered, and hope You will find the Roads tolerably good. we have had charming weather here for these six weeks past. I have the honour to remain with the most Respectful Attach.^{t}

Your Lordships,

most Obliged and most humble Servant

Rome 16.th March 1771—— James Byres

XVI

My Lord

I had the honour of writing Your Lordship the 16.th Curr.^{t} and have this Night consign'd to the Courier a small Box for Your Lordship, directed to the care of Mr Richie, Containing the two Drawings for the Chimney Pieces for the Saloon mark'd N.º 7 and N.º 9. The executing that Markd N.º 7 all of white Marble will come to two Hundred and forty Crowns, which is about fifty seven Pounds Sterling. N.º 9 will come to two Hundred seventy four Crowns, about sixty five Pounds Sterling. ——

In the same Case is a small box containing five Silver, and four Copper Medals of the present Pope. —— of the late Pope sixteen of silver and nine of Copper. —— some of the Dyes being broke, it was not possible to make a Compleat Collection of each. —— there are three Prints of the present Pope and one of the late Pope. with an Arabesque Cieling by Monocchi which is wrote on the Margin from whence taken. — in the same Box, I have taken the liberty to send some Ermine which Mr Symonds by a letter from England desired me to send to Mr Richie for Him ——

I have not as yet had any Answer from Mr Hamilton, concerning the Drawings which Your Lordship mention'd, if they arrive by next Saturday, I shall forward them by the Courier to Venice, but if they don't come in time shall send them with Your other things to England ——

our Weather continues good here. The Town is full of English, I believe about sixty Travellers here at Present, seven or eight Ladies amongst them. Mr Abbe Grant /who is well/ begs to make offer of his most Respectfull Compliments to Your Lordship. I hope in God that Your health continues to improve and that You'l find no inconveniency from the Fatigue of the Journey and have the honour to remain with the most Respectful Attachment ——

Your Lordships

most Obliged and most humble Servant

Rome 23 March 1771 —— James Byres

(Enclosures)

[These papers contain the Estimates of the chimneys order'd March 30 1771, for Saloon, Drawing Room, antyroom & Morning Room.]

Estimate of the Expences of the executing, the Following Chimney Pieces according to the Designs. —

+N.° 1 ____ all of white Marble Rom: Crowns __ 100——
which is about £23..15. ——

N.° 2 ____ with the Giallo Antique Ground 182——
about £ 43. ——

3 ____ with the ground of Egyptian Red 165——
about £39..6. ——

\+ 4 ____ with the ground of Paragonian Black, or any other colour 190 ——
the Medalion of the Frieze costs 40 Crowns of this sum –
about £45..5. ——

\+ 5____ with the ground of Verd Antique or Corsican. 195——
about £46..10. ——

6 ____ all of white Marble 250——
the Frieze comes to 150 Crowns of the sum. –
about £59..10. ——

\+ 7____ all of white Marble, with the same Frieze 240——
2 of these about £57.. ——

8 ____ all of white Marble 280——
the Frieze cost 280 of the sum. ——
about £66..13 ——

9 ____ all of white Marble with the same Frieze 274——
about £65. ——

[So I have orderd no 5 for the 2 small rooms and of N.° 7 or 9 for the Saloon. NB. these were estimated of 4 feet & the Chimneys are 4½ & Saloon 5 f –
I have desird another plan of the Drawing Room chimney & offered Piranezi 200 . . . for his, all the 4th of May 1770 ———]

N.° 10 ____ all of white Marble Rom: Crowns __ 898 ——
the Frieze comes to 300 Crowns
the Cariatides to 500 Crowns
the Ribetts & Cornish to 98 Crowns
______ about £214. ——

there is likewise a Drawing of a Chimney piece lately finishd by Cav.r Piranesi which he brought some days ago begging I would shew it to the English Gentlemen. he values it a six hundred Zechins which is something less than three Hundred Pounds. the Bass Relievo above representing the Feast of Trimalchien, is partly Antique but very much restored. the faun with the Goat in the entablature of the Frieze. the Meleager and faun with the Tyger are likewise partly Antique partly restored. the two round Medaglions, are I believe of the 15.th Century. they are realy pretty. these five Basso Relievos are of Red Egyptian. all the rest is of white Marble extremely well executed. the whole has a Magnificent and rich Effect, and I suppose would give it for less than he asks, in case Your Lordship has any thoughts of it.

[N. 3. with double Comp: fluted Columns with a Row of leaves, & a tablet of a Sacrifice (?) is the one I chuse, but I do like [?] the lower member of the architrave coming down to go round the bottom of the tablet. –]

XVII

My Lord

I had yesterday the honour of receiving Your Lordships most Obliging letter of the 23.d am glad that You approve of keeping the things here until the weather settles. we had about ten days ago, a Storm of wind and some Boats lost between this and Leghorn.

the six Statues Your Lordship order'd Copies of were
the Apollo at the Belvedere. — which shall be omitted,

Marius at the Capitol, which is finished /He is in the Consular Robe/
Agrippina at the little Farnese. a sitting Figure
Sylla, at the Villa Negnoni. – a sitting Figure
the Gypsy at the Villa Borghese. ——
Faustina, the younger, at the Guistiniani. –

I scarce know of any very excellent figure in Armour, perhaps the Pyrrhus, King of Epirus at the foot of the Capital Stairs is the best we have in Rome. what is Antient of it, is very fine, but the legs and Arms which are Modern are but poorly restored, but might be corrected in a Copy. — the Bronze Statue of Septimius Severus, in Armour at the Barbarini Pallace is entirely Antient and is perhaps the next best. the Antoninus Pius, at the Villa Mattei, and the Marcus Aurelius at the Capital are both tolerably good. I shall send Your Lordship Prints or Sketches of these figures by next Post it was impossible to get them today. ——

the Models that M.r Claus has made are of the Sylla, the Aggripina and the Gypsy. he has begun to work the Gypsy in Marble. –

the third publication of the Arabesques at the Vatican, are promised for the beginning of June. I shall endeavour to get a full Sett well collour'd for Your Lordship. –

the Picture of Sal: Rosa I mention'd being lined and Clean'd is one of the three last, that which represent S.t John preaching in the wilderness. Your other must have arrived in England soon after Your Lordship left it.

They often make use of Clay here, to stain paper but I prefer the Chalk to it, as the Clay has an Oyliness in it, which I think has a bad Effect and does not take the Chalks so well. but the great Art is to put the proper quantity of Size. if too much sized, it makes the Work shine and will not receive the Chalk. if too little size the Colour rubs of.

I have the honour to remain with the most Respectful Attachment

Your Lordships
most Obliged and
most humble Servant
James Byres

Rome 23d March 1771 –

XVIII

My Lord

I had the honour of receiving Your Lordships letter of the 30.th Ult.o Your Orders relative to the Chimney Pieces shall be punctually observed and the Measures exactly attended to. I have this day talk'd to the workmen, they promise to sett about them immediately. that the whole shall be finish'd by the beginning of Oct.r, those that are finish'd before shall be directly forwarded to England. I shall next week do a Drawing of that for the small Room, all of white Marble and to come to about twenty three Pounds ——

I have this night consignd to the Courier a tin Case for Your Lordship, containing nine Prints of the best Figures in Armour, in Rome. I was mistaken when I said that the Bronze Statue of Septimius Severus in the Barbarini Palace was in Armour. however as I mention'd it I have sent the Print of it. — if Your Lordship intends that this figure should Stand in a Nich, I think that the Pyrrhus will do the best; as the Arms are not much detach'd from the Body so that the lines of the Figure will correspond to that of the Nich but if it be to stand on a Pedestal, whichever pleases Your Lordship best in the Print will be the thing. for the goodness of the Sculpture is nearly the same in them all, none of them first Rate, but whichever of them Your Lordship pitches on, as far as possible the Defects shall be conceiled in the Copy. ——

in the Case with the Prints is the Register of the Weather for this five Months past, observed on Your Lordships Thermometer, at eight O'Clock in the Morning, at Midday, at six in the Afternoon, and at ten at night. ——

As soon as Your Cases are Embark'd at Leghorn, I shall have the honour of forwarding the Bills of Lading to Your Lordship at London. and in wishing You most heartily a good journey, and a happy meeting with Your Family and friends, and all the Felicity this world can afford, have the honour to remain with the most Respectful Attachment

Your Lordships
Most Obliged and
Most humble Servant
James Byres

Rome 6.th April 1771 ——

P:S: hitherto I have not received any Drawings from M.r Hamilton

XIX

My Lord

I had the honour of writing Your Lordship last, the 6.th April to Venice, and at the same time consignd to the Courier a tin Case, with nine Prints of the best arm'd Statues in Rome which I hope Your Lordship has received, but altho' I wrote Mr Richie a line at the same time, have not as yet heard from him, so don't know exactly when Your Lordship left Venice nor what Rout you took, but hope that by this time, you are safely arrived in England, and found no inconvenience from the Fatigue of the Journey, nor change of Climate. –

Enclosed I have the honour of sending Your Lordship a Bill of Lading for fourteen Cases. thirteen are Mark'd E^B N.º 1 to 13. N.º 14 is Mark'd QQ as Your Lord.^{p} order'd — Enclosed is also a list of the things contain'd in each Case as also a Note of the State of Your Lordships Acc.^{t}

the Mosaic Pidgeons will be finish'd in about three Months. Sig.^{r} Claus is working on the Gypsy of the Borghese Villa, and the Chimney Pieces are going on with all possible Expedition. I have the honour to remain with the most respectful Attachment

Your Lordships
most Obliged and
most humble Servant
James Byres

Rome 21.st of May 1771

Contents of fourteen Cases. sent to the Right Honourable
The Earl of Bute. by the Duke of Savoy. Capt Harman

	Case	
E^B	N.º 1	A Landskip ___ by Rubens
		D^{o} __________ by Sal: Rosa
		D^{o} __________ by Sal: Rosa
		D^{o} __________ by James Forester
		2 D^{o}. ________ by J: Batt: Busiri
		Portrait of Pope Innocent y^{e} 10.th by Diego de Velasquez.

	Case		
E^B	N.º 2	A Vase of Cyprian Jasper	
		A Vase of Oriental Jasper	
		A Vase of Verde Antique	
		A Vase of Black Paragonian	
		A Vase of Green Basalto	
		A Vase of Black Basalto	
		Bust of Petrarch	in Bronze
		Bust of Dante ________	d^{o}
		Bust of Ariosto _______	d^{o}
		Bust of Tasso ________	d^{o} –
		1600 Sulphurs. _______	

	Case	
E^B	N.º 3	2 Cork Models of the Arch of Constantine
		2 d.^{o} Arch of Septimius Severus

	Case	
E^B	N.º 4	2 Cork Models of the Arch of Janus. ——
		2 Tables of Oriental Alabaster

	Case	
E^B	N.º 5	1 Cork Model of the Capo de Bove

	Case			
E^B	N.° 6	1 Cork Model of the Capo de Bove		
		2 d.° of the Temple of Giove Tonnans		
	Cases			
E^B	N.° 7 X 8 X 9 10	2 Marble Chimney Pieces	letter E	
	Cases			
E^B	N.° 11 12	1 Marble Chimney Piece		letter F
	Case			
E^B	N.° 13	A Marble Statue of Marius	70	
	Case			
QQ	14	A Case of Lavas. from Naples		

Notes

1. F. Russell, *John, 3rd Earl of Bute, Patron and Collector* (London, 2004).
2. Russell, *John, 3rd Earl of Bute* (above, n. 1), 82–101.
3. I am grateful to Johnny Bute for permission to publish the documents in question. They are referred to here as Bute MSS.
4. In a forthcoming note in *The Burlington Magazine*.
5. Document Ia.
6. Russell, *John, 3rd Earl of Bute* (above, n. 1), 194–6.
7. Document II.
8. Document III.
9. Document IV.
10. Document V.
11. Document VI.
12. Document VIII.
13. Document VIII.
14. Document IX.
15. Document X.
16. The Busiris cannot be traced, but the Neri is at Mount Stuart: Russell, *John, 3rd Earl of Bute* (above, n. 1), 192, 195, pl. 91.
17. Document XI.
18. Monaldini was the publisher of *Picturae Etruscorum*, issued in three volumes 1767–75.
19. Document XIII.
20. V&A 6.E.8-2001 to E.22-2001.
21. Document XIV.
22. Document XV.
23. Document XVI.
24. Document XVII.
25. Document XVIII.
26. Document XIX.
27. Document Ic.
28. This is headed 'Acct. of money laid out for the Right Hon.ble the Earl of Bute', Bute MSS.
29. Cf. 'Account of things sent to England', Bute MSS.
30. Two Sassoferratos and the Neri mentioned above remain in the Bute Collection.
31. See Russell, *John, 3rd Earl of Bute* (above, n. 1), 101; and, for a relevant letter from Byres, p. 213.
32. I am indebted to Andrew McLean, archivist at Mount Stuart, to Kay Sutton, to David R. Marshall for his editorial patience, and to those responsible for the Roma Britannica conference.

CONFRONTATIONS WITH THE ANTIQUE: THE BRITISH RECEPTION OF EGYPT AND ROME

Roma Britannica and the Cultural Memory of Egypt: Lord Arundel and the Obelisk of Domitian

Edward Chaney

Thomas Howard, 14th Earl of Arundel (1585–1646), sometimes known as 'the Collector Earl', has been much studied, not least for the pioneering Grand Tour he undertook with his family and an entourage that included Inigo Jones between 1613 and 1614 (Plate 11.1).[1] More than any other, this tour advanced the appreciation of Renaissance art and architecture in England, which manifested itself in the so-called 'Golden Age' of Charles I. Appreciation of the Renaissance led to an enhanced understanding of both 'modern' art and of antiquity, hence the 'Roma Britannica' phenomenon that is the subject of this volume.[2] I would argue that Arundel's discreet loyalty to Roman Catholicism was of a piece with his collecting activities and with his crucial role in maintaining continuity between the past and posterity, epitomized by the eighteenth-century collections of antiquities accumulated by his direct descendant, Charles Townley, and fellow Catholic, Henry Blundell.[3]

It had been James I's 1604 peace treaty with Spain, which dominated most of Italy, that facilitated direct access to the Italianate taste that was comparatively familiar to the élites of the rest of Europe. At the beginning of the previous century Henry VII had begun to show an interest in contemporary Italian art, Cardinal Wolsey consolidating this with his patronage of Pietro Torrigiano, Giovanni da Maiano and Benedetto da Rovezzano. Even when Henry VIII's bellicose and increasingly isolationist policies prompted the return home of the Italians, the arrival of Hans Holbein at least enabled portraiture to flourish for long enough to establish some sort of tradition in England. The iconoclastic devastation confirmed during Edward VI's reign, however, was such that, despite the best efforts of Queen Mary and King Philip of England, who was at one point importing Titians to London, their successor, Elizabeth, could hardly have convinced an English parent that the visual arts represented a promising career path, even had she been so inclined.[4] Until the age of Sir Joshua Reynolds and Thomas Gainsborough, most artists would be imported if and when required. Due partly to his Roman Catholic family's historic connections with Flanders, Spain and Italy, Lord Arundel grew up more conscious of England's cultural isolation than most of his contemporaries.

In what follows, I wish to highlight Arundel's imaginative originality by focusing beyond his expertise in modern art, Italianate and otherwise, upon his ever-deepening interest in antiquity. The relevant cultural memory here combines the classical one, dating back to Caesar's arrival in Britain and its consequent relationship with Rome, with the Christian revival of the Roma–Britannica connection effected by Saint Augustine and his Gregorian missionaries at the end of the sixth century. At the deepest level, Arundel's classicizing collecting was motivated by a sense of loss, of mourning both for his aristocratic antecedents, the Fitzalans, Howards and Lumleys, epitomizing what Lord Clarendon called 'the primitive nobility', and for the visual arts with which his family was so involved and which, like his family, suffered during the Reformation and then again during the Civil Wars and Interregnum.[5]

But rather than allow a tendency to introspection to prevail, Arundel travelled widely and sent his agents in search of art and antiquities beyond Christian Europe far into the Ottoman Empire, not only to ancient Greece but as far, geographically and chronologically, as Egypt. Though he looked forward to establishing a Shakespearean 'brave new world' (or Baconian 'New Atlantis'?) in Madagascar, it is clear from the bronze head of 'a Macedonian King' (later thought to be Homer and then Sophokles) and the bust of Minerva or Apollo he included in Van Dyck's *Madagascar* portraits, that this island's cultural climate would have been a classical as well as Catholic one.[6] As well as Greek ingredients it might have included cultural memorials even of ancient Egypt. Arundel's interest in the latter is by British standards a pioneering manifestation of an expanding, Europe-wide, appreciation and acknowledgement of Egyptian culture by post-medieval Christianity, which had retained more than it realized of the civilization it had been primarily responsible for destroying. It was not merely the motif of the motherly Isis with Horus on her lap that the fundamentalist Copts and Byzantines (followed by their Muslim conquerors) failed to obliterate from the memory of the Roman Empire. The polytheistic dimension that re-emerged in medieval Roman Catholicism, in the form not just of Mariolatry, but in the cult of saints and their relics and images, along with the practice of pilgrimage and sale of indulgences, eventually provoked another round of fundamentalism that insisted on the application of the second commandment, in the form of the Protestant Reformation.[7]

The longing of folk to go on pilgrimages, so vividly celebrated by Chaucer, was too deep-seated to be eliminated by a mere change in religion, so that new, secular justifications for travel were evolved, eventually to be dominated by the quest for artistic heritage.[8] Northern Europeans almost always first encountered the material culture of Greece and Egypt, then regarded by readers of Hermes Trismegistus or Herodotus as the ultimate source of western civilization, during their visits to Rome.[9] To the extent to which Arundel, as the King's Commissioner for Buildings, aspired that London should become the new Rome and thus a repository of representative artefacts from an equivalent Empire, his aspiration was disrupted by the Civil War.[10] Even in the eighteenth century this early Stuart aspiration remained somewhat diffused, the great country houses of the purportedly Whig oligarchy epitomizing the classical culture imbibed during the Grand Tour more coherently than the crowded, industrial and, for the most part, improvised capital city. Only in the nineteenth century, with the classical style by this time alternating with nationalist neo-Gothic, did London really rival Rome as a world-class cultural centre. From this perspective, Arundel's collection may be seen as the prototypical British Museum; his 1617 will indeed requested that it should be accessible to 'all gentlemen of Vertue or Artistes which are honest men …'.[11]

Despite his obsession for collecting, often a symptom of social dysfunction, Arundel had a genius for employing and usually befriending both artists and scholars, including those scholarly agents who travelled throughout the Mediterranean world 'ad conquirenda Monumenta antiqua' — the phrase used in an entry in the *Pilgrim Book* of the English College in Rome to describe the mission of that most enterprising of all his agents, William Petty.[12] Thus, as well as Rubens, Van Dyck, Jones, Wenceslaus Hollar, Clemente Coltreci, François Dieussart, Francesco Fanelli, Hendrik van der Borcht and Lucas Vorsterman, Arundel sponsored the scholarship or travel of (as well as collaboration between): John Borough, John Burberry, William Camden, Thomas Coke, Robert Cotton, William Dugdale, John Evelyn, Peter Fitton, William Frizell, George Gage, John Greaves, Richard Greenbury, Samuel Harsnett, William Harvey, Franciscus Junius, Jerome and Nicholas Lanier, Michel le Blon, William Lisle, John Markham, Tobie Matthew, Edward Norgate, William Oughtred, Henry Peacham, Edward Pococke, John Price, John Selden, William Smith, John Speed, Henry Spelman, Henry and Robert Spiller, Anthony Tracy, Francesco Vercellini and Edward Walker (at least six of whom also tutored his children or grandchildren).[13]

ARUNDEL AND THE OBELISK

Due to Imperial Rome's extraordinary enthusiasm for Egyptian culture and its obelisks in particular, there are more obelisks in this city than anywhere else in the world including Egypt. The Ptolemys had already moved ancient obelisks down the Nile to confirm the imperial status of Alexandria. Between the reigns of Augustus and Constantius in AD 357 more than 40 obelisks were shipped down the Nile, across the Mediterranean and up the Tiber to Rome, the last being transported to the new Rome of Constantinople and erected by Theodosius in the hippodrome in 390.[14] Described by Pliny as symbolizing the rays of the sun (whose temporarily exclusive worship by Akhenaton may have inspired Moses to introduce monotheism to the world), all but one of those in Rome had, by the eleventh century, collapsed or been pulled down.[15] (Later references to 'Egyptian spires' encourage my belief that the medieval spire, particularly associated with north European churches, originated in the obelisk, but that is too obscure a discussion for this paper.[16]) Despite the fact that only one or two were still standing, partly because of the hieroglyphs with which most were adorned, obelisks were a focus of increasing attention throughout the Renaissance, and featured prominently in fifteenth- and sixteenth-century Latin and Italian publications, including Andrea Fulvio's *Antichità … di Roma* and Sebastiano Serlio's

Architettura — both of which Jones later owned — and even in English in William Thomas's *Historie of Italie* of 1549 and Jan van der Noot's *Theatre of Wordlings* of 1569.[17] Though proposals to move the great obelisk from the southern flank of Saint Peter's to the front of the Basilica had been made as early as the mid-fifteenth century by Pope Nicholas V (who also sponsored the translations into Latin of the Egyptophile Herodotus, Strabo and Diodorus Siculus), this was not achieved until 1586 by Sixtus V, who, even more extraordinarily, re-erected three other obelisks in key locations during his relatively brief papacy.[18] As well as being publicized throughout the world by Domenico Fontana's lavish publications, the four obelisks dominate the engraving on the title-page of the very popular compilation, *Le cose maravigliose dell'alma città di Roma*, the 1588 edition of which Jones also owned (Fig. 11.1). Followed by later popes, cardinals and city authorities, most of the fallen obelisks were re-erected during the next two and a half centuries, their vaguely monotheistic anticipation of the true religion being rendered more specifically Christian by surmounting each with a cross or other relevant symbol.[19]

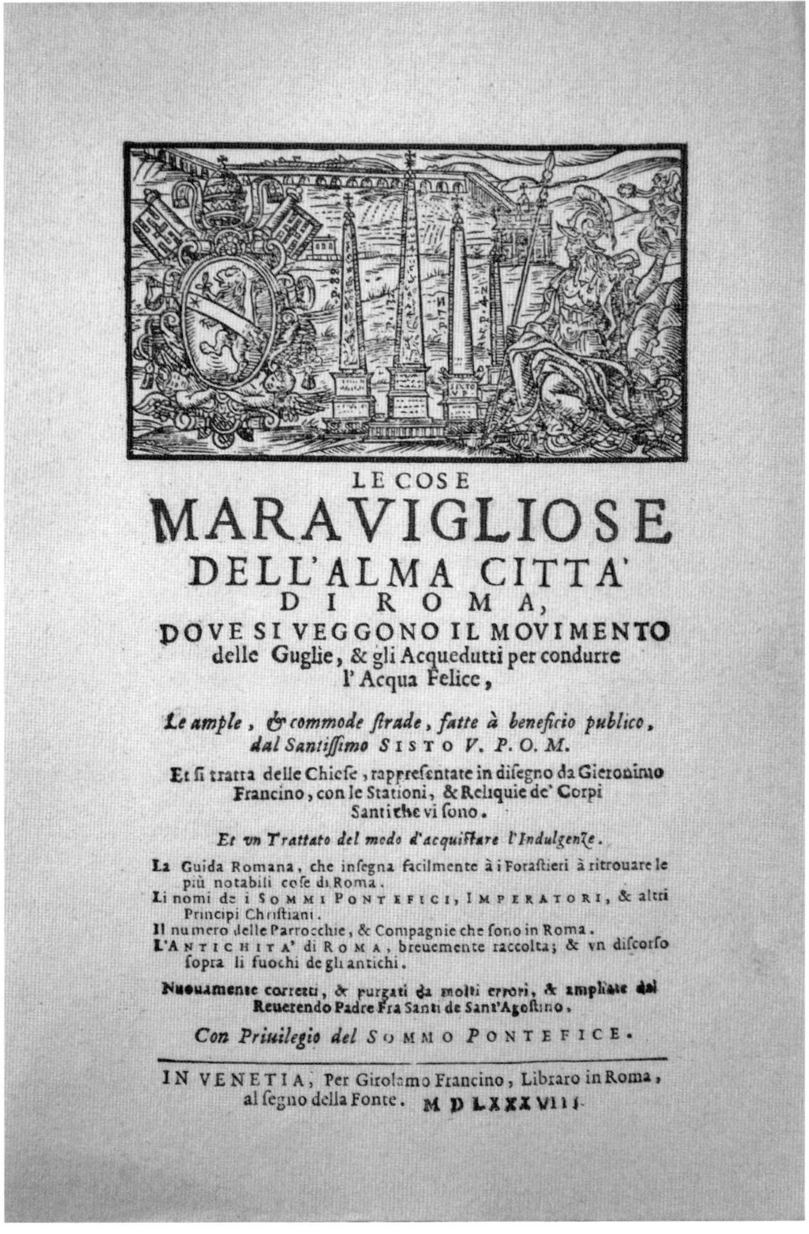

LE COSE
MARAVIGLIOSE
DELL'ALMA CITTA'
DI ROMA,
DOVE SI VEGGONO IL MOVIMENTO
delle Guglie, & gli Acquedutti per condurre
l'Acqua Felice,

Le ample, & commode strade, fatte à beneficio publico, dal Santissimo SISTO *V. P. O. M.*

Et si tratta delle Chiese, rappresentate in disegno da Gieronimo Francino, con le Stationi, & Reliquie de' Corpi Santi che vi sono.

Et vn Trattato del modo d'acquistare l'Indulgenze.

La Guida Romana, che insegna facilmente à i Forastieri à ritrouare le più notabili cose di Roma.
Li nomi de i SOMMI PONTEFICI, IMPERATORI, & altri Principi Christiani.
Il numero delle Parrocchie, & Compagnie che sono in Roma.
L'ANTICHITA' di ROMA, breuemente raccolta; & vn discorso sopra li fuochi de gli antichi.

Nuouamente corretti, & purgati da molti errori, & ampliate dal Reuerendo Padre Fra Santi de Sant'Agostino.

Con Priuilegio del SOMMO *P*ONTEFICE.

IN VENETIA, Per Girolamo Francino, Libraro in Roma, al segno della Fonte. M D LXXXVIII.

FIG. 11.1. Title-page of *Le cose maravigliose dell'alma città di Roma* ... (Venice, 1588). *(Photo: © Edward Chaney.)*

In the engraving with which he introduced chapter I of Jean-Jacques Boissard's *Theatrum Vitae Humanae* of 1596, Theodore de Bry depicted an obelisk as the centrepiece, connecting earth to heaven, of a tragic setting compatible with Shakespeare at his 'All the world's a stage' gloomiest (Fig. 11.2).[20] The Latin inscription confirms that 'the life of man is like a circus or great theatre', in case we were in any doubt. Collaborating with Boissard again in the last year of his life, de Bry also, in the most detailed guide to Rome of the period, went on to depict specific obelisks, including what is now known at the Obelisk of Domitian (Fig. 11.3).[21]

The first, full-size Egyptian obelisk to leave its native land since antiquity was brought back from Philae by William Bankes and erected in his garden at Kingston Lacy in Dorset in 1821 (Plate 11.2).[22] This was followed, later in the nineteenth century, by the so-called Cleopatra's Needles, France transporting and erecting her gift from Mohamed Ali more than half a century before the British shipped their obelisk from Alexandria to the new Thames embankment, after a full-scale wooden model in Parliament Square prompted the vetoing of that more prominent location (Fig. 11.4).[23] It was Arundel, however, inspired above all by Sixtus V's re-erected obelisks, who had first attempted to import an obelisk to this country.[24] An intermediate inspiration, but one seen prior to his

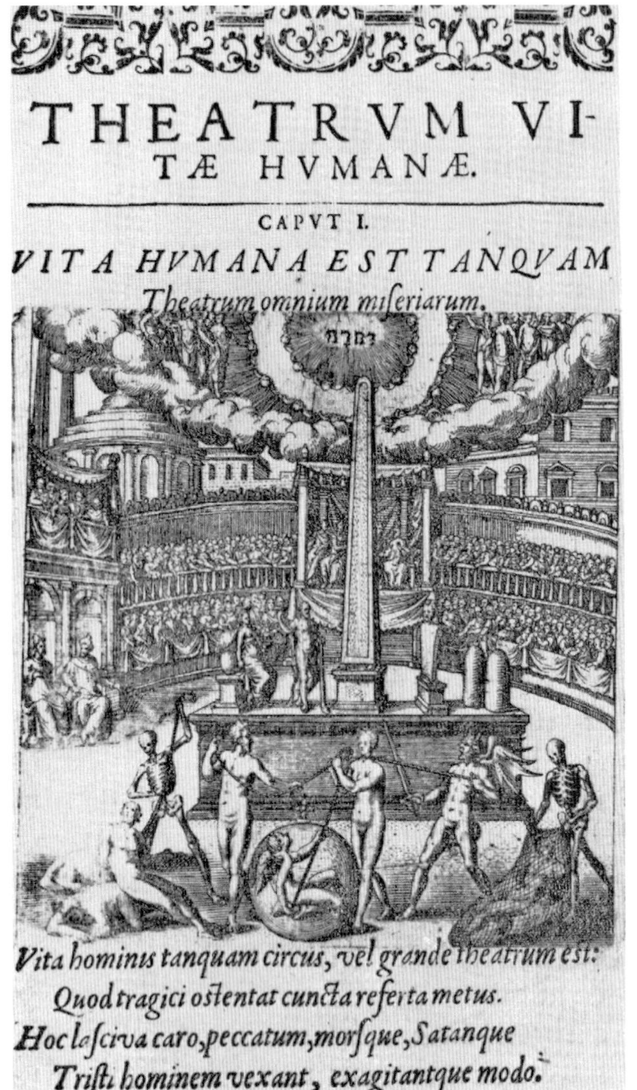

FIG. 11.2. Theodore de Bry (1528–98), *The Theatre of Human Life*. Engraving. From J.-J. Boissard, *Theatrum Vitae Humanae* (Metz, 1596). *(Photo: Edward Chaney.)*

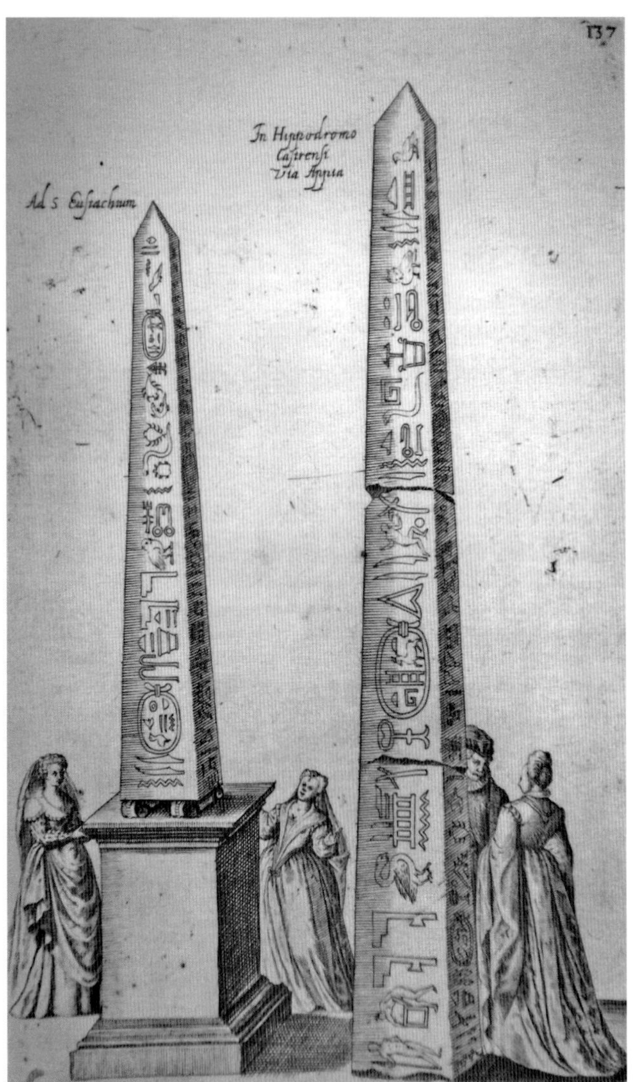

FIG. 11.3. Theodore de Bry (1528–98), *Obelisk at S Eustachio* (left) and *Obelisk of Domitian* (right). Engraving. From J.-J. Boissard, *I–VI Pars Romanae Urbis Topographiae et Antiquitatum* (Frankfurt, 1597–1602), I, pl. 137. *(Photo: Edward Chaney.)*

journey to Rome, would have been the large obelisk that his great uncle, Lord Lumley, erected at Nonsuch, which is surely later than usually thought in being likewise inspired by the example of Sixtus V and therefore post-1585, just as the variety of smaller obelisks to be found on and around great houses such as Montacute and Burghley no doubt were.[25]

Due to the Arundels' ever-more generous patronage and collecting activities and to Jones's subsequent development as an architect, the consequences of their 1613–14 tour were immense. In 1624, Selden, already celebrated as a comparative orientalist for his *De Diis Syriis* of 1617, published *Marmora Arundelliana*, thereby announcing to the learned world that a major collection of Mediterranean antiquities and inscriptions had for the first time been accumulated in London. By 1629, when Rubens also came and enthused about Arundel's collection, a cosmopolitan Dutch visitor praised the Earl as 'a great lover of paintings and antiquities — against the nature of most Englishmen'.[26] After admiring Arundel's riverside garden, with its 'very antique statues and other carved figures', Abram Booth entered the west wing of the great house: 'In a very long gallery standing below and opening on to the Thames, one sees an extraordinary number of very ancient statues, epitaphs in Greek and Latin on square and other antique gravestones, which were brought here from every corner of Christendom at the expense of the aforementioned Earl. Yes, even from Egypt and Greece'.[27]

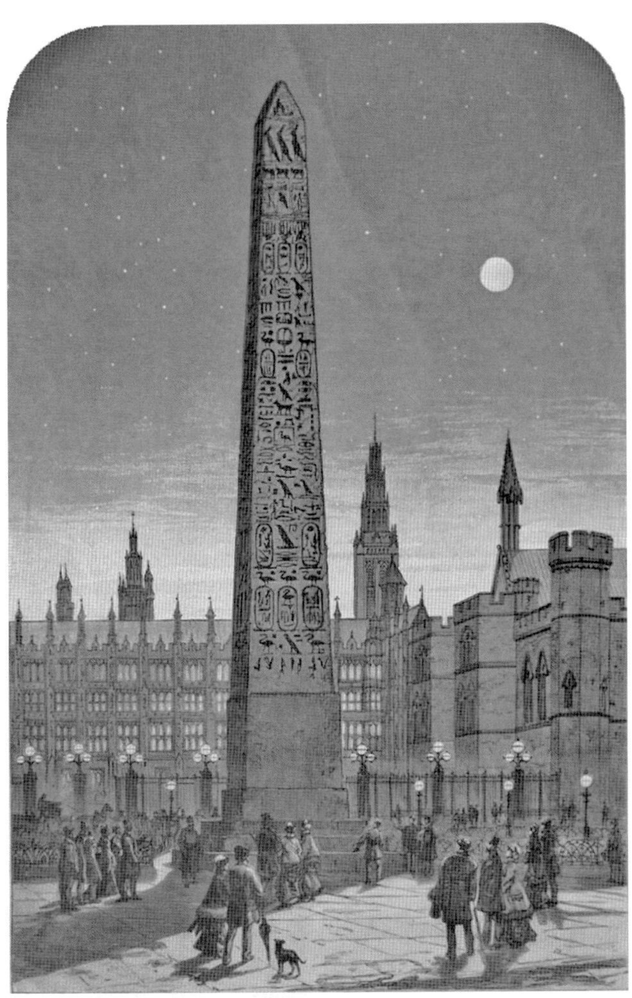

FIG. 11.4. Wooden model of Cleopatra's Needle in its proposed location in front of the palace at Westminster. Coloured engraving. From *Extra Supplement of the Illustrated London News*, 26 January 1878. *(Photo: © Edward Chaney.)*

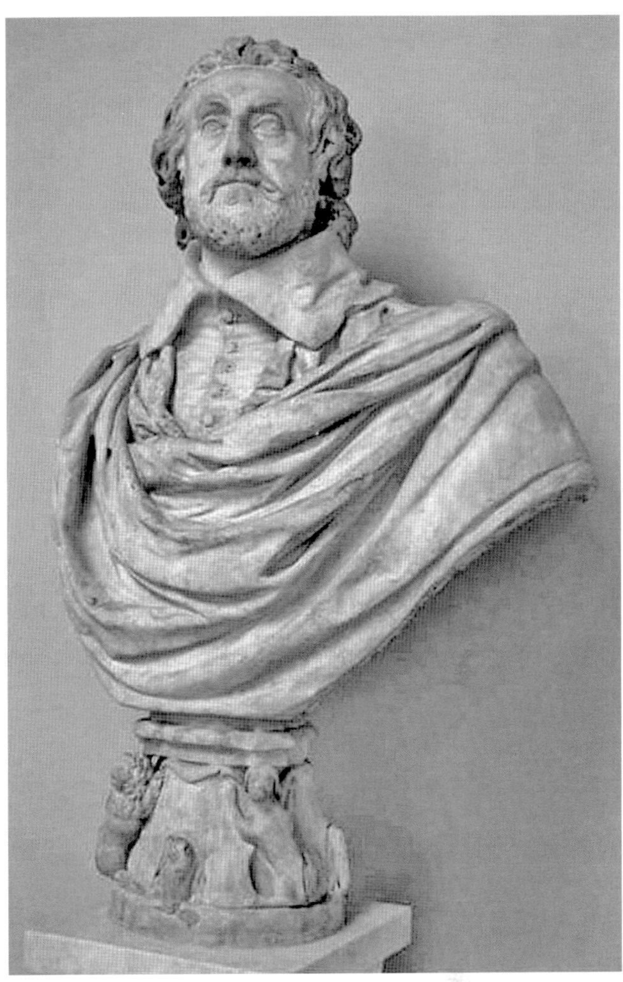

FIG. 11.5. Francois Dieussart (*c.* 1600–61), *Bust of the 14th Earl of Arundel*, *c.* 1635. Ashmolean Museum, Oxford. *(Photo: © Edward Chaney.)*

Apart from the little shabti brought back from Egypt by George Sandys in 1611 and given to John Tradescant, the reference here to Egyptian antiquities is exceptional in England and uncommon even in early seventeenth-century Italian collections.[28] Given the unconvincing Arundelian provenance of the Egyptian column at Wilton, the Roman sphinx (with its later companion), now in the Ashmolean Museum, is the only surviving artefact that could illustrate Booth's account.[29] One turns instead to the portrait that best epitomizes the neoclassical grandeur achieved in the two decades after Daniel Mytens painted him, Dieussart's *c.* 1635 bust of the Earl, now appropriately in the Ashmolean Museum, presiding over most of what remains of his sculpture collection (Fig. 11.5).[30]

Disappointed in his plans to travel to Egypt itself by the requisition of the ship he had planned to sail in, as the next best thing, from a boat moored off Venice, where he had been visiting collections with Arundel's son, Henry, Evelyn acquired what he called an Egyptian stone:

> lately brought from *Gran[d] Cairo* ... from the Mumy-pitts, full of *Hieroglypics*, which I designd on paper, with the true dimensions & sent in a letter to Mr. Henshaw, to communicate to Father Kircher, who was then setting forth his greate work *Obeliscus Pamphilius*, where it is described, though without mentioning my Name at all.[31]

In his indignation at not being acknowledged by Athanasius Kircher, whom he had met and heard lecture on Euclid, and whose books on magnetism and Coptic he had acquired already, Evelyn confused Kircher's two most important later publications, for it

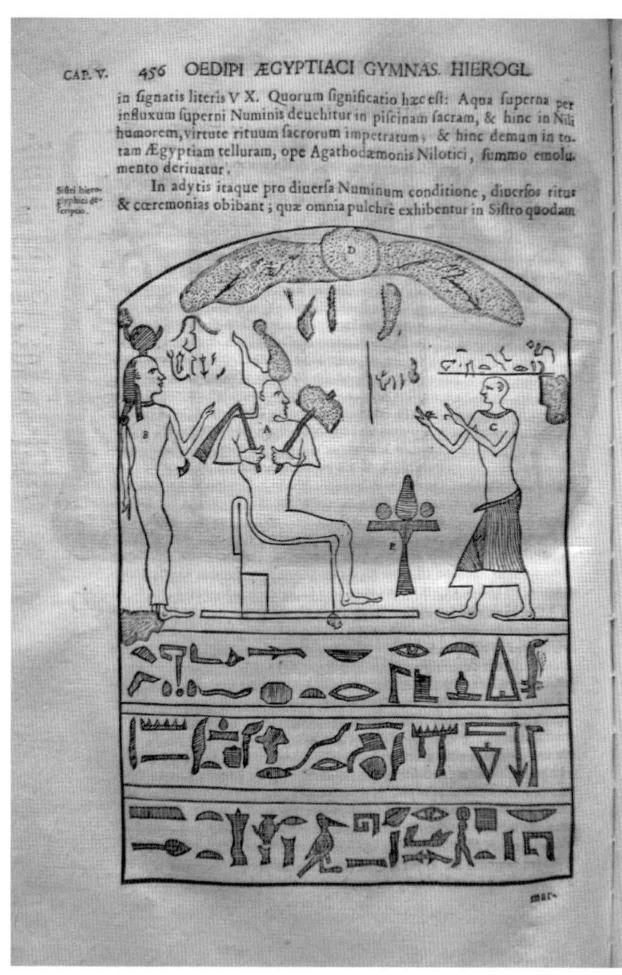

FIG. 11.6. Engraving after John Evelyn's drawing of his stele, credited to 'eruditissimo vir Thomas Henschau Anglus'. From A. Kircher, *Oedipus Aegyptiacus*, 3 vols (Rome, 1650), II, 456. *(Photo: © Edward Chaney.)*

is in fact in the slightly later, three-volume *Oedipus Aegyptiacus* (in which Kircher argued that Hermes Trismegistus was Moses) that we find an engraving of Evelyn's inscribed stele, complete with his elaborately-recorded dimensions, all credited to 'eruditissimo vir Thomas Henschau Anglus', with no mention of poor Evelyn (Fig. 11.6).[32] A measure of how strongly Evelyn must have felt about this is shown by the fact that on 16 March 1654 (more than two years before he claims to have seen the offending copy of *Oedipus Aegyptiacus*) he presented to the Bodleian Library his richly illustrated copy of Herwart von Hohenburg's *Thesaurus Hieroglyphicorum*, complete with a version of the inadequately acknowledged drawing, which looks suspiciously like he has copied it from the engraving in Kircher.[33] Ironically, according to information already recorded in an earlier diary entry by Evelyn himself, a far more significant credit was omitted in *Obeliscus Pamphilius*, that otherwise massively documented account of the obelisk Bernini erected in the Piazza Navona, and that is a credit to Lord Arundel.[34] Having participated in the relevant negotiations in Rome with Greaves and Petty, and with the young van der Borcht in tow, no doubt Harvey would have noticed this omission when he received his copy of *Obeliscus Pamphilius* from Cassiano dal Pozzo a decade after Arundel's death.[35]

Evelyn's earlier diary entry of 15 February 1645, when he was still based in Rome, describes what he called the 'once famous *Circus Caracalla*', now known to be the Circus of Maxentius, off the Via Appia:

> In the midst of [this] there now lay prostrate one of the most stately & antient Obelisks, (full of Ægyptian Hieroglyphics) that is now in the World, twas it seemes broken in 4 pieces when o'rethrowne by the Barbarians, & would have been purchas'd & transported into England by the magnificent *Thomas Earle of Arundel*, could it have ben well removed to the Sea.[36]

Evelyn went on to write, incorporating material from guidebooks published long after his visit: 'This is since set together, & plac'd on the stupendous Artificial Rock, made by *Innocentius Decimus* & serving for a Fountaine in Piazza Navona, the worke of Cavaliere Bernini, the Popes Architect'.

In April 1645 Evelyn visited the Earl in Padua for the last time: 'I tooke my leave of him in bed, where I left that great & excellent Man in teares upon some private discourse of the crosses had befaln his Illustrious family', including 'the unkindnesse of his *Countesse*, now in *Holland*'.[37] Arundel's eldest surviving son and heir, Henry, Lord Maltravers, had joined him in Padua the previous summer, but his younger son, William, Lord Stafford, eventually executed for his religion, remained with his more overtly Catholic mother, though after the Earl's death he wrote that Arundel had been: 'the best father and friend to his children that ever lived'.[38] Maltravers's sons, including the two future Dukes of Norfolk and two Dominican novices (one of whom became a cardinal), were also based in Italy with Arundel at this time.

Almost four years after his death, Arundel's perhaps remorseful widow was presented with a commemorative print designed by one of Rubens's less talented pupils, Cornelius Schut, etched by Hollar and published by van der Borcht (Fig. 11.7).[39] Unremarked

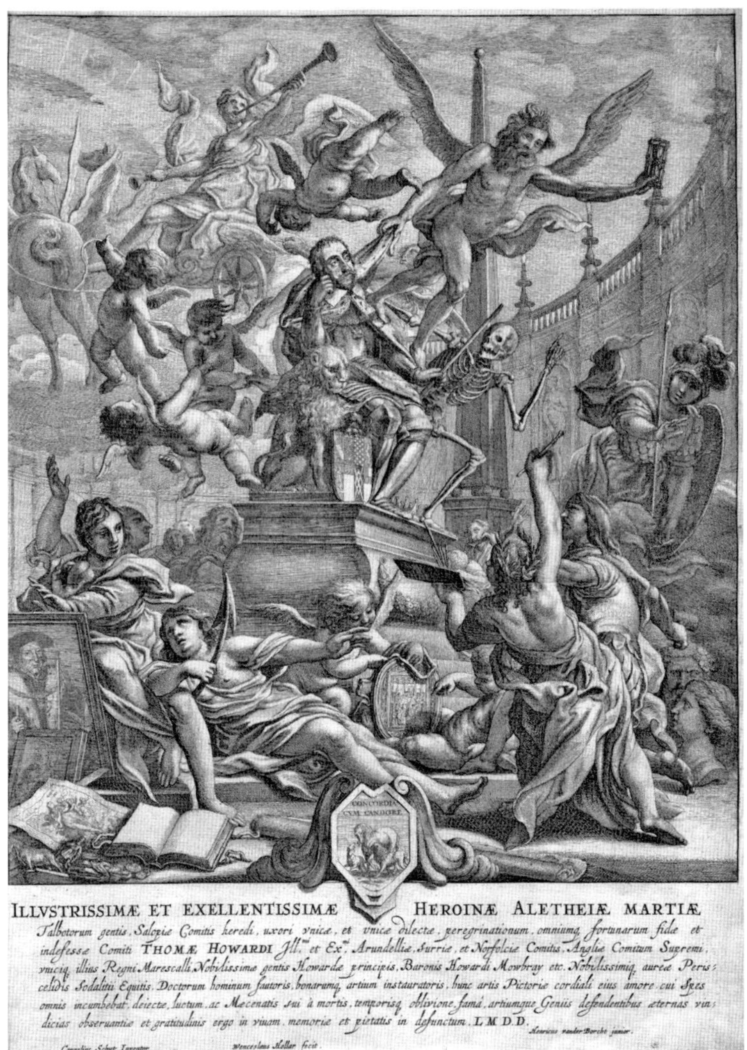

FIG. 11.7. Wenceslaus Hollar (1607–77) (engraver), Cornelius Schut (1597–1655) (designer), Hendrik van der Borcht the Elder (1583–1651), *Commemorative Etching of the 14th Earl of Arundel*, c. 1650. The British Museum, Prints and Drawings, Q,6.142AN47482. *(Photo: © Trustees of the British Museum.)*

upon by previous commentators, but providing Arundel with a uniquely vertical element of stability in the background of all this Baroque chaos, is a monument suggestive of even greater permanence and antiquity than all the Graeco-Roman statues to which Arundel had once so proudly pointed, that is, a large obelisk.[40] Its symbolism is as cryptic as it is inclusive, and in this respect renders the total effect of the design reminiscent of de Bry's allegory of human life (Fig. 11.2) rather than Correggio's allegory of virtue, as has been suggested.[41]

In the early sixteenth century, the widely-travelled Gentile Bellini had painted a far more realistic obelisk that played a similarly supportive visual and symbolic role behind Saint Mark preaching in Alexandria.[42] Soon after this in France, in *Les heures de Dinteville*, the obelisk seems to function as an eternal symbol of the Resurrection (possibly of Lazarus) among otherwise crumbling ruins.[43] But for all such connotations, given the personal nature of most of the other objects surrounding him, this obelisk surely also references the real obelisk Arundel almost acquired, not least because van der Borcht, who probably devised the print's iconography, was in Rome assisting Petty at the time he was negotiating to export it to England.[44] Soon after Hollar produced this testamentary etching, Jones wrote his own will, setting aside £100 for a marble tomb-chest on top of which would be a carved bust of himself, no doubt also looking suitably melancholic, flanked by two large obelisks of a similar type to the one in the Arundel print, each likewise set on four balls and a plinth, which is how the obelisk in the Circus of Maxentius was set.[45] Unfortunately this impressive tomb in the old Saint Benet's, Paul's Wharf, was ruined in the Great Fire of 1666, and we depend on John Aubrey's crude sketch for our knowledge of its appearance.[46] The type of obelisk is very similar to the colossal pairs Jones had placed on either side of the triangular pediments on the façade and north and the south entrances of Saint Paul's Cathedral, likewise lost in the Fire.[47]

The obelisk in the Schut/Hollar image no doubt would have been depicted more accurately had Arundel pulled off what would have been his greatest collecting coup and transported a genuine obelisk to his Thames-side garden two and a half centuries before Cleopatra's Needle was placed a few hundred yards down-river. George Vertue, Britain's first art historian (and like fellow antiquaries John Talman and Thomas Hearne, another Catholic), may have had this etching in mind, which he included in his catalogue, when he engraved the prominent vignette for the first page of his *Description of the Works of the Ingenious Delineator and Engraver Wenceslaus Hollar* in 1745 (Fig. 11.8). This, too, features Arundel in armour in the centre of the composition, albeit here, in the manner of Jones's tomb, in the form of a bust, surrounded by books, medals, an etcher's tools, copper plates and prints:

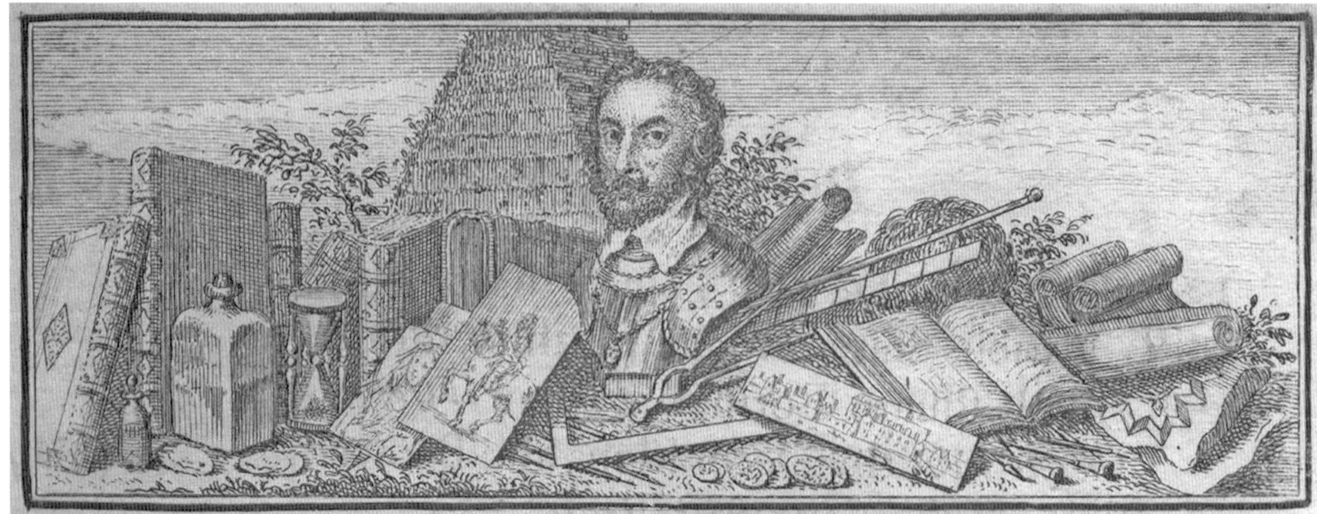

FIG. 11.8. George Vertue, Vignette on page 1 of *Description of the Works of the Ingenious Delineator and Engraver Wenceslaus Hollar* (London, 1745). *(Photo: © R. Harding.)*

'especially', as Vertue's dedication to the Duchess of Portland reads, 'from those belonging to that Maecenas, Thomas Earl of Arundel, the foremost of English Noblemen who cultivated those rare and valuable Monuments of Antiquity, from all parts of the Learned world into this Nation'.[48] As if epitomizing these 'Monuments of Antiquity', and hinting perhaps at the ancient religion they shared, behind Arundel, Vertue has placed a pyramid.[49] Like Schut's obelisk, this is not very convincingly Egyptian, inspired as it was by the more familiar Roman Pyramid of Cestius, itself the product of circa 12 BCE Roman Egyptomania. Richard Symonds sketched a similarly overgrown version of this pyramid in 1651 in a notebook used by Vertue.[50] Even when genuine Egyptian pyramids were depicted, their representation tended to be influenced by the more pointed and thus obelisk-like Pyramid of Cestius. Despite carrying a relatively clear, written account by Marco Grimani, Serlio's 1545 *Architettura*, which elsewhere depicted a page of obelisks very accurately, illustrated the Great Pyramid of Giza in pointy Cestius style, complete with alluring female Sphinx.[51] To his or his engraver's credit, Sandys improved on both pyramid and sphinx in his *Relation of a Journey*, originally published in 1615 (Fig. 11.9). Interestingly, partly because it documents familiarity with Sandys's account of Egypt in the Arundel circle, when Hollar came to etch his emblematic *Civilis Seditio* (or Civil Discord) early in the Civil Wars, he copied this engraving as an appropriately timeless and unchanging background to the 'Amphisbaena', the two headed snake representing the commonwealth being torn apart by opposing factions (Fig. 11.10).[52]

In fact the first scientific account of the Egyptian pyramids was published in London by another of Arundel's protégés a matter of weeks before the Earl died in Padua.[53] In his *Pyramidographia* of 1646, Greaves not only described, measured and depicted the pyramids of Giza; in a notebook that survives in the Bodleian Library he did the same for Arundel's obelisk at the very time he was assisting in its acquisition (Fig. 11.11).[54] Greaves enthused about the hieroglyphs on 'Mr Petties Agulia [without] at Rome', thus referring to Arundel's agent, with whom he had been liaising on this and other matters since Petty's return to Italy from Greece in October 1636.[55] In February 1637 Petty tried to persuade Greaves to go with him to Athens on Arundel's behalf, but Greaves returned to England and then travelled via Livorno to Constantinople, where he rejoined that other distinguished Arundel protégé and orientalist, Pococke.[56] In the late summer, Greaves then journeyed to Egypt, thus remaining within what he called 'the greatest Monarchy upon earth', the Ottoman Empire.[57] His late arrival in Alexandria after being delayed at Rhodes means that it cannot have been he who sent Arundel what was probably the first complete mummy to be sent to England for artistic and archaeological, rather than medicinal, purposes (the English then being enthusiastic consumers of 'mumia', the tar-like substance consisting for the most part of Egyptian corpses).[58] The reception in London of this elaborately painted coffin was described in a report sent back to Cardinal Francesco Barberini on 28 February 1638 by

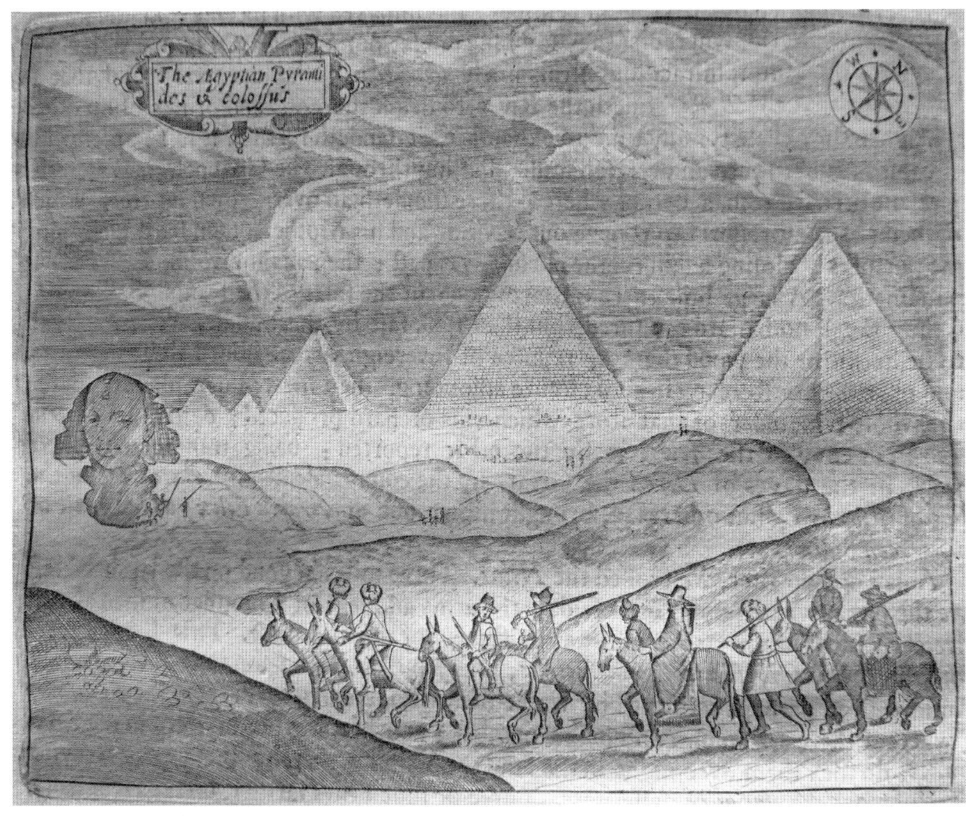

FIG. 11.9. ***Travelers Visiting the Pyramids and Sphinx***. Engraving. From G. Sandys, *A Relation of a Journey Begun An. Dom. 1610*, sixth edition (London, 1670), 100. *(Photo: © Edward Chaney.)*

the papal agent, George Conn, who despite having lived most of his life in Rome was very impressed with this acquisition, recommending that the Cardinal inform the great connoisseur and collector, dal Pozzo, about the event:

An English ship has brought from Egypt excavated from the grottos under the pyramids, a complete body with all the burial ornaments, a very curious thing and worth seeing. I went the other day with the Earl and Countess of Arundel and with the Countess

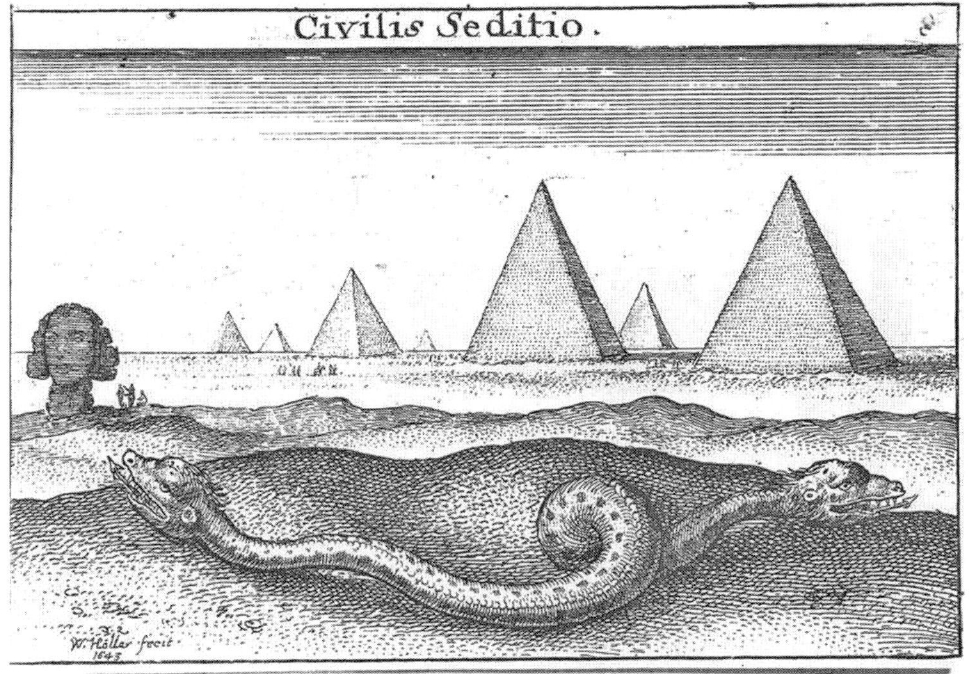

FIG. 11.10. Wenceslaus Hollar (1607–77), *Civilis Seditio*, 1643. Etching. *(Photo: © Edward Chaney.)*

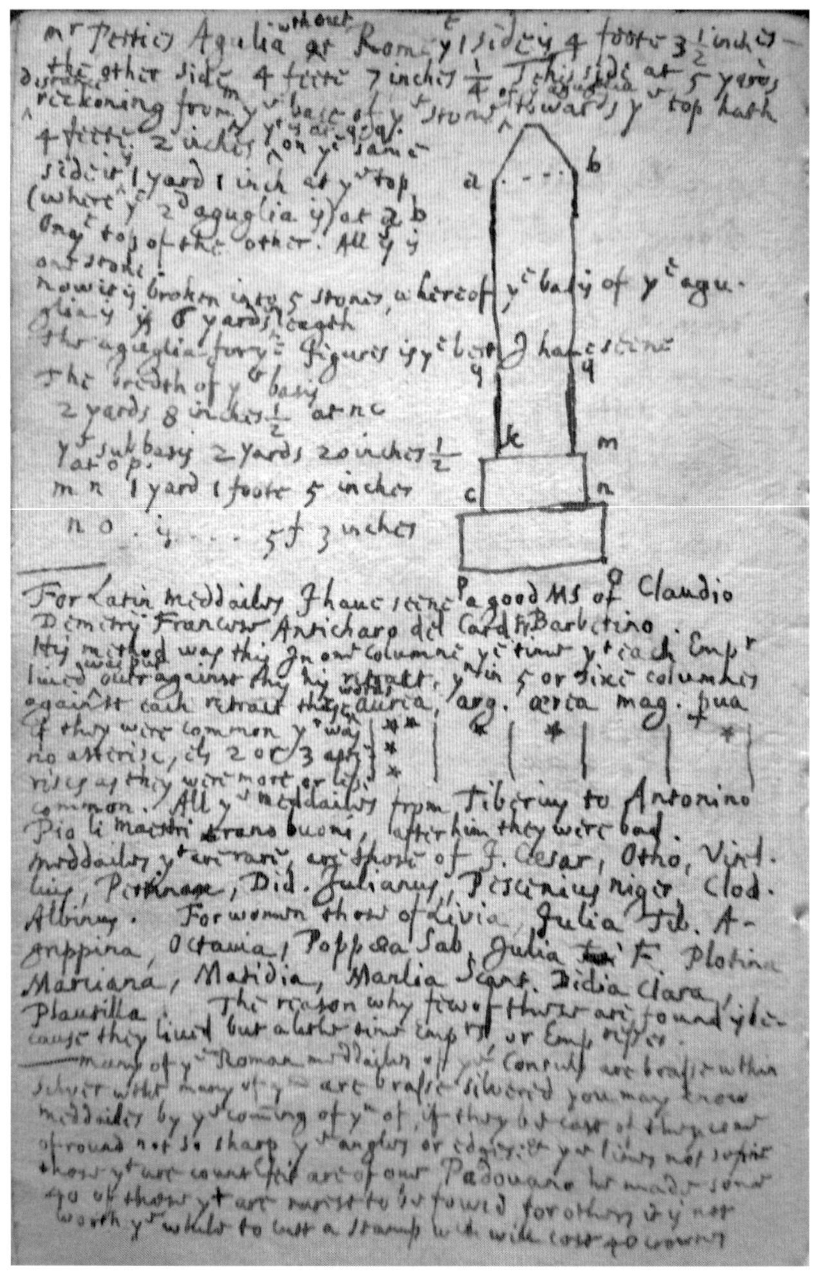

FIG. 11.11. John Greaves, 'Mr Petties Agulia [without] at Rome'. From John Greaves's almanac/notebook; Bodleian Library Savile MS 49, 1. *(Photo: © The Bodleian Library, University of Oxford.)*

> of Kent [Lady Arundel's scholarly sister] to see it and it was decided to convey it to the house of the said Earl, who will have it drawn and engraved in order to publish it. [John] Selden and others maintain that it is around three thousand years old, and yet the colours appear very fresh . . .[59]

It is interesting that Arundel's Thames-side, next-door neighbour, Henrietta Maria, seems to have acquired a mummy soon after this, later presenting it to Bacon's former amanuensis, Thomas Bushell, for his museum at Enstone.[60] Arundel's grandson, Henry, Duke of Norfolk, eventually presented a mummy, 'an entire one taken out of the royal pyraminds', to the Royal Society, which published it in 1681.[61] By the time Arundel's memorial was being etched and Jones was ordering his real tomb, Bernini was putting the finishing touches to his extraordinary Fountain of the Four Rivers in the Piazza Navona, a commission he had managed to wrest from his rival, Borromini. The crowning adornment of Bernini's papal fountain was 'Mr Petties Agulia', that which Arundel had been so close to acquiring. According to at least one account, it was indeed this distinguished foreigner's interest in the obelisk that prompted Urban VIII to forbid its export and his successor, Innocent X, to acquire it for the family piazza.

When the Catholic priest and author of the first Grand Tour guidebook, *The Voyage of Italy*, Richard Lassels, described the Basilica of Sant'Antonio in Padua, the modest marble plaque marking the spot beneath which Arundel's intestines are buried provided him with the opportunity to wax lyrical about his two favourite subjects, Italy and Roman Catholicism. Comparing the published version of 1670 with the 1664 manuscript, now in the Beinecke Library, we find that an interesting passage on Arundel was eliminated by the Protestant publishers: 'In this one thing', wrote Lassels, 'he was happyer than the other antiquarians of his country and time: that by loving *Antiquityes* so much as he did he fell in love with the best piece of antiquity, the ancient Faith'.[62]

When Lassels got to Rome and visited the Via Appia he returned to the subject of Arundel, whose career he clearly followed with interest, kept informed by Fitton, the fellow priest and connoisseur with whom he stayed in Rome and whom Arundel subsequently presented to Charles I as 'virtuoso rather than priest'.[63] Lassels was also connected with the Arundels via Lady Catherine

Whetenhall, née Talbot, whom he escorted to Rome in 1650 and who had an entrée to the Pope's sister-in-law, Donna Olimpia, at the Palazzo Pamphilj, in front of which the obelisk was being raised.[64] In the later, revised version of the aide-mémoire he wrote about that journey, Lassels described visiting the tomb of Cecilia Metella and returning home via the so-called Circus of Caracalla:

> In the midst of it stood that Gulia which now stands in Piazza Navona. I saw it lye here some four and twenty yeares ago [that is in the late 1630s], broken in three pieces and neglected until that the noble Earle of Arondel and Lord Marshal of England offering to buy it, and having given[65] threescore crownes earnest, made the Romans begin to think it a fine thing, and to stop the transporting of it into England . . .[66]

Lassels's account is partly confirmed by a letter written by Arundel to Petty of February 1637 (when Lassels was on his way to stay with Fitton in Rome), which also reveals that Charles I himself had initially been involved in trying to acquire the obelisk, an idea he abandoned in favour of a fine painting:

> For the Agulia His Matie thankes yu for yr care in it, but desires I should take it, saying he hath much more minde to some good picture, and meanes to employ yu to buy for him that of Brondzino wch yu mencioned but hath ordered mr Secretary Windebanke to write unto Sr Will: Hamilton to solicite any thinge for ye Aglulia [sic] or Statua, for me as if it were for him selfe . . .[67]

Kircher's *Obeliscus Pamphilius* account thus omits not merely Arundel's alleged role in making the Romans think it a fine thing, but Charles I's also. Confirmation that Arundel had indeed paid at least a deposit for the obelisk is the letter from Conn to Barberini, dated 9 February 1637, which ends: 'The Earl of Arundel tells me that Petty has bought a Guglia at Rome; and hopes for your Eminence's customary kindness, as much in this, as for the Adonis of Pichini, promising not to trouble you again regarding this sort of thing'.[68]

Pre-dating Lassels's *Voyage* was John Raymond's *An Itinerary Containing a Voyage Made Through Italy in the Year 1646 and 1647*, published in 1648. Raymond provides another reason for Arundel's failure to bring the obelisk home: 'Hard by [the Sepulcher of *Metella Crassus* his wife] is the *Cirque* of *Caracalla*, where lies the Pyramid that the old Earle of *Arundell* would have bought, but in regard of the vastnesse, could find no possibility of conveying it to the *Tyber*, tis said the present Pope after his Nephewes Pallace in Piazza Navona is finisht, will erect it there in *Circus Agonalis*'.[69]

Raymond was well informed on this matter as he had been in Rome in April 1647 when Innocent X formally inspected the obelisk, in the company of Kircher and probably then still Borromini (rather than Bernini), with a view to erecting it in front of the family church and palazzo.[70] But his account suggests that Arundel's project was less realistic than it was by writing of the difficulty of conveying 'it' to the Tiber for, as we have seen, the obelisk in fact lay in five separate and therefore more easily transportable pieces. Smaller pieces had gone in various directions and were even implanted into the Aurelian Walls, the damaged remains of the inscribed apex being replaced by Kircher with newly-carved replicas.[71] They were being further subdivided even as Raymond stood and admired the ruins, for in his notes, Raymond's travelling tutor, Dr John Bargrave, who helped his protégé write his guidebook, recalled, in his interesting account of the Roman obelisks, chipping a piece off 'the butt end' of this one in 1646 and having it polished for his cabinet of curiosities, which is still preserved, along with his riding boots, in Canterbury Cathedral Library.[72] Elsewhere, Bargrave catalogued 'Another thin piece of jasper stone, unpollished, it being sawn off of that piece of the *guglio*, pyramid, or obelisc that standeth now in the Piazza Navona at Rome' (Fig. 11.12).[73] The fact that Raymond, Bargrave, Lassels and Evelyn all referred to the obelisk lying in the Circus of Caracalla confirms that the right-hand obelisk in Serlio's engraving, described by him also as in the 'Circo di Antonio Caracalla' and depicted with four breaks in it, is not, as stated in the 1996 Hart and Hicks edition of the 1545 edition of the *Architettura*, the Campus Martius obelisk now in the Piazza Montecitorio, but the Piazza Navona one.[74] This and other evidence somewhat alters the perspective on Arundel's obelisk. Among *cognoscenti*, at least, this was not, as Lassels suggested, a forgotten object that the Romans only began to value when a foreigner threatened to expropriate it. In the interests of glorifying his own reputation, fellow foreigner Kircher gave himself an equivalently crucial role in its rediscovery. In fact this obelisk had been commented upon as early as the second decade of the fifteenth century, first by the Anonimo Magliabechiano, and soon after by Poggio Bracciolini, following his 1417 discovery of

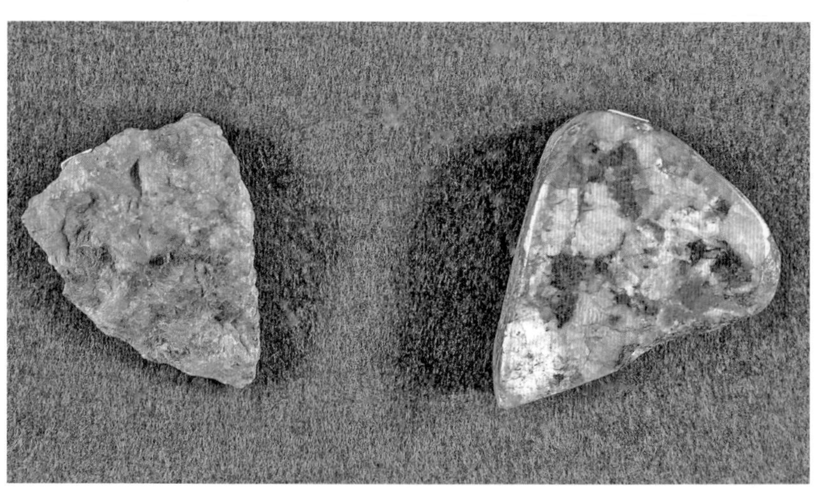

FIG. 11.12. Two fragments from the obelisk from the Circus of Maxentius, from the collection of curiosities of John Bargrave (c. 1610–80) in the Canterbury Cathedral Library. Right: a polished piece chipped off 'the butt end'. Left: 'Another thin piece of jasper stone, unpollished, it being sawn off of that piece of the *guglio*, pyramid, or obelisc that standeth now in the Piazza Navona at Rome' in 1646. *(Photo: Mark Bateson. © The Dean and Chapter of Canterbury Cathedral.)*

Ammianus Marcellinus and his reading of Horapollo.[75] Subsequently it was discussed by Filarete and Pius II, who admired the 'huge shattered obelisk' that had 'once served as a goal-post' for chariot races.[76] Throughout the sixteenth and early seventeenth centuries artists and scholars described the broken obelisk, the idea of its re-erection being visualized in drawings by Giuliano da Sangallo and Andreas Coner[77] prior to Serlio, while Pirro Ligorio, Etienne du Pérac and Aegidius Sadeler all depicted it lying in the Circus (Fig. 11.13).[78] In the wake of Sixtus V's campaign and his 'official obelisk scholar' Michele Mercati's 1589 book on *Gli obelischi di Roma*, which specifically suggested it should be re-erected, as also von Hohenburg's publication of unprecedentedly accurate engravings of all four sides in his *Thesaurus Hieroglyphicorum* of *c.* 1610, Arundel's near-acquisition may be seen therefore as a further catalyst to the completion of a project that had been considered for two centuries.

Since Jones, who owned at least two editions of Serlio,[79] also annotated Palladio's engraving of what he called the 'Tempio i cui vestigi si veggono vicino alla Chiesa di Santo Sebastiano sopra la via Appia', correctly deducing that a brick building of this type on the Appian Way was likely to be a tomb, it seems very likely that Jones and Arundel visited not just

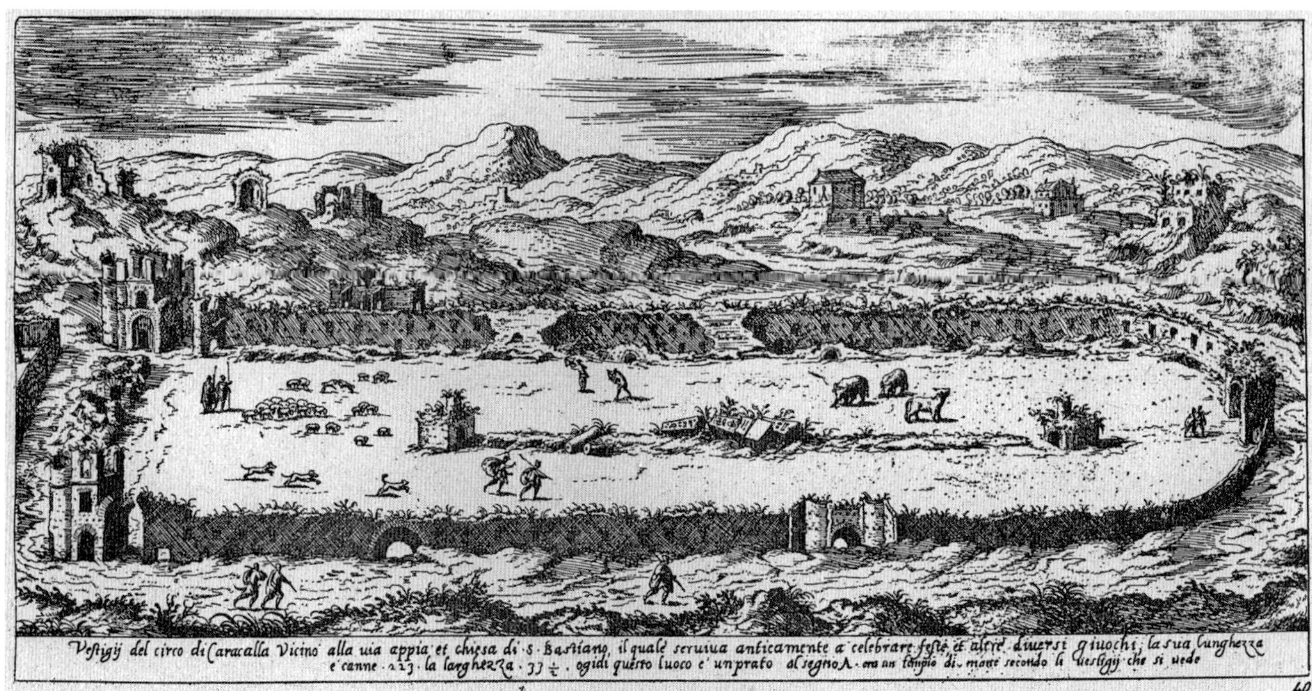

FIG. 11. 13. Etienne du Pérac, engraving of the 'circo di Caracalla' (actually the Circus of Maxentius); Rome, 1575. *(Photo: © Edward Chaney.)*

this, the mortuary temple of Romulus, but also the huge hippodrome that stretched out beyond it, built by Romulus's father, the Emperor Maxentius. Thus they would have inspected the broken obelisk of Domitian, which Maxentius had requisitioned as the centrepiece of the spina. A visit might have been encouraged further by the account in Palladio's earlier *Antichità di Roma*, which Jones was busy précising in his 'Roman Sketchbook', where this so-called Circus of Caracalla was described as the place where 'si celebravano gli giuochi Olimpici'.[80]

That Jones would have become the English Fontana, or indeed Borromini or Bernini where the re-erecting of this obelisk was concerned, whether for King or Earl Marshal, is suggested by his detailed remarks on the raising of obelisks in ancient Egypt and post-Renaissance Rome in his posthumously-published book on Stonehenge.[81] Quoting Herodotus as an eye-witness, Jones wrote:

> *In the Temple of* Latona (in *Ægypt*) *is a Chappell framed of one stone, whose walls being of equall height, are in length forty cubits, covered in like manner with one sole stone four cubits thick*. Those, which made this wonder would have much more admired, if they could have seen the *Obelisk* raised in times of old by King *Ramesis* at *Heliopolis*, in that part of *Aegypt* anciently called *Thebais*, in height one hundred twenty one Geometrical feet (which of our measure makes one hundred thirty six feet) of one entire stone ... Amongst the *Romans*, *Augustus Caesar* erected in the great Cirque at *Rome*, an *Obelisk* of one stone, one hundred and twenty foot, nine inches long: another also, was set up in *Mars* field, nine foot higher then it, by the said Emperour. And it seems also, neither they, nor *Camdens* self had ever seen that Obelisk, which even in these our days, in the year one thousand five hundred eighty six, *Sixtus Quintus* caused to be erected in the *Piazza* of S. *Peter* at *Rome*, one hundred and eight *Roman* palms high, and at the base twelve palms square, (according to our Assise, fourscore and one foot high, and nine foot square) of one entire stone also: *Dominico Fontana* being *Architect*.[82]

It is interesting that among the illustrations of the reconstructed Stonehenge, no doubt prepared for the press by John Webb, Jones included obelisk-like pillars within the larger stone circle. Webb's *Vindication* of his master's thesis that Stonehenge was a primitive Roman building reveals that he had inherited correspondence in which Arundel and Jones exchanged melancholy views on the declining state of art until shortly before the death of the Earl, who in happier days had planned a study of Roman Britain.[83]

Failing to obtain a genuine Egyptian obelisk for his riverside garden, Arundel and Jones persisted in persuading Henrietta Maria, living next door to Arundel House, to erect two massive modern obelisks to flank her Watergate at Somerset House. The drawings executed by Webb belong to a group dating from 1638 when Arundel was still negotiating for the obelisk and Jones still modernizing Somerset House, having recently completed its superb, double-cube Catholic chapel.[84] By the late 1650s, when Hollar produced his most brilliant, albeit unfinished, aerial view of west-central London, Sir Edward Ford had built his water-pump and tower at the southwest corner of the garden of Arundel House.[85] Its resemblance to an obelisk may or may not reflect the collector Earl's one-time aspiration to place a genuine obelisk in his garden, but it would have been a perfect location and in fact close to that eventually chosen for Cleopatra's Needle. Somehow symbolic of the state of England after the Interregnum is the state of this water tower soon after the Restoration, sketched by Thomas Wyck as if it were one of the Roman ruins he had studied with Pieter van Laer. The distant view of Jones's earlier obelisks, soon to be destroyed in the Great Fire along with the rest of his classicized Saint Paul's Cathedral, is a poignant reminder of the early Stuart campaign to Romanize London.[86]

As if epitomizing the Restoration response to the price that had been paid for the Puritan experiment, Isaac Beckett's amusing 1686 mezzotint, after Simon du Bois, portrays his learned friend and fellow-debauchee, Adrian Beverland, sketch-pad in hand, in front of a variety of obelisks, sphinxes and pyramids (Fig. 11.14). Most prominent, however, is the rear view of a less austerely antique Venus, exposing herself indeed more carelessly and completely than the Syracusan Aphrodite Kallipygos, on an altar pedestal.[87] A slightly later mezzotint of Beverland by Beckett, based on a painting by Ary de Vois, now in the Rijksmuseum, portrays the somewhat louche-looking author of the sexological *Peccatum Originale* (1678), smoking and drinking beside his quasi-topless mistress.[88] She is looking up from his scholarly treatise, *De Prostibulis Veterum* (Of Ancient Brothels), and somewhat ambiguously admonishing him.

No doubt Beverland suggested the domestic setting for this portrait to de Vois. Hitherto unnoticed is the

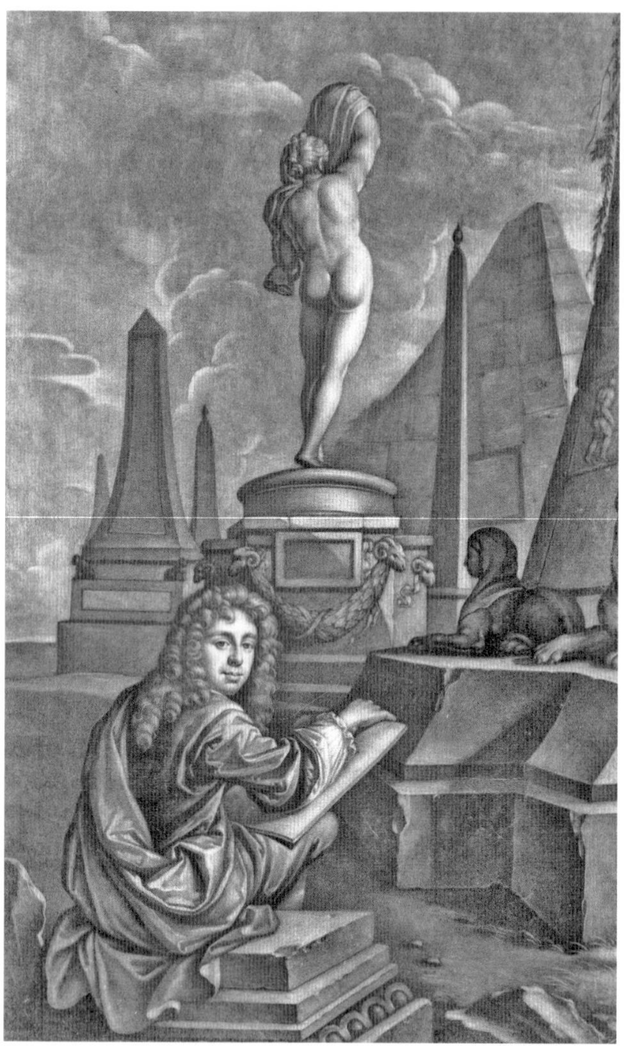

FIG. 11.14. Isaac Beckett, mezzotint after Simon du Bois, *Adrian Beverland drawing a Statue* (1686). The British Museum, Prints and Drawings, AN11873100I. *(Photo: © Trustees of the British Museum.)*

source for the setting he presumbly also chose, this time in discussion with du Bois, for his portrait of the artist sketching his Callipygian mistress among the Egyptian antiquities. In showing the spectator that there was another, even less modest side, to his mistress, he reminds one of Titian who, when sending his rear view of *Venus with Adonis* to King Philip of England in 1554, wrote: 'Because the *Danae*, which I have already sent your Majesty, was entirely of the front part, I have wanted in this other *poesia* to vary and show the opposite part, so that it will make the room in which they are to hang, more pleasing to see'.[89] Du Bois, Beckett and Beverland were all three print collector-dealers, so any of them could have suggested the source, which is clearly the engraved title-page of the 1670 edition of Pignoria's *Mensa Isiaca*, engraved by Abraham Blooteling (Fig. 11.15).[90] Where the

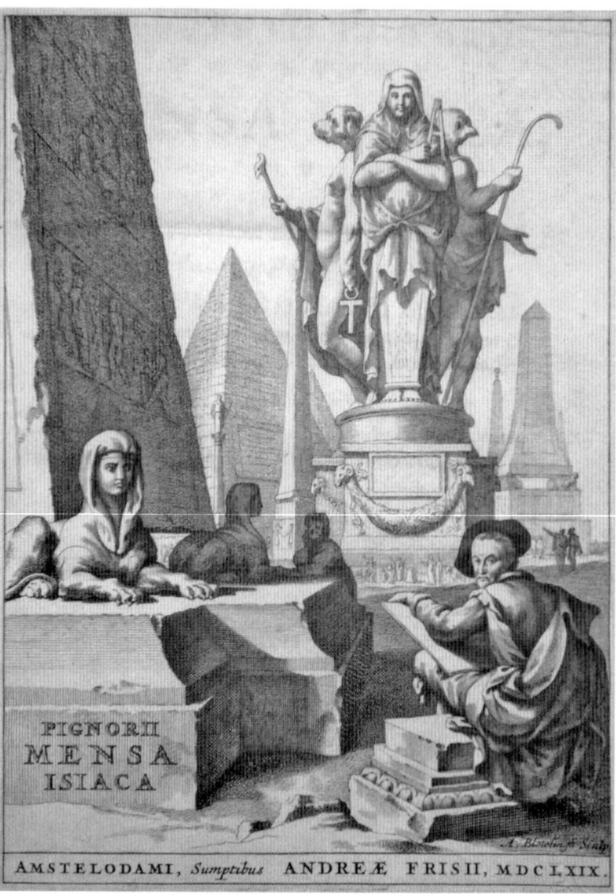

FIG. 11.15. Abraham Blotelingh (Blooteling) (1640–90), Title-page of Lorenzo Pignoria, *Mensa Isiaca* (Amsterdam, 1670). Engraving. Plate dated 1669. *(Photo: © Edward Chaney.)*

worthy Pignoria, whom Arundel and Jones would surely have met in Padua, who was certainly known to Price and whom Evelyn cited in his Bodleian donation, turns momentarily from his intense study of Egyptian civilization, of hieroglyphs protected by sphinxes and a colossal cluster of animal-headed gods, Beverland smiles at us in a leisurely manner, the formidable female sphinxes literally having been put in the shade and the worrisome gods on their altar having been reduced to the rear view of a woman who, surrounded as she is by obelisks, may or may not have needed Sigmund Freud to point up their phallic significance.

Although Bankes's Kingston Lacy obelisk ended up being the first to arrive in England, a scaled-down replica of the Piazza Navona obelisk and fountain, begun by Bernini himself and completed after his death by his workshop, was acquired by the 1st Duke of Marlborough for the gardens of Blenheim Palace in around 1710.[91] Nicholas Hawksmoor had designed an obelisk at Ripon, Yorkshire, in 1702, and together with John Vanbrugh built the Marlborough Obelisk at

Castle Howard twelve years later.[92] After Vanbrugh's dismissal at Blenheim, Hawksmoor designed an even grander one there, but it was never built.[93] Meanwhile, the Bernini fountain remained in pieces until William Chambers improvised its assembly at some distance from the Palace in the 1770s. It was not until 1927 that it was repaired and assembled in its present location, in the pool on the north terrace, by the Catholic 9th Duke.[94]

William Kent designed obelisks at Holkham and Shotover, while his patron, Lord Burlington, who had 'discovered' him in Rome, took the credit for designing the two at Chiswick. On the plinth of the one placed inside the Jonesian Burlington Lane Gate, in a position reminiscent of the obelisk erected by Sixtus V in the Piazza del Popolo, Burlington attached an antique relief of a Roman marriage scene (or perhaps a funeral) that had belonged to Lord Arundel.[95] Having in 1717 enthused over the obelisk in the Piazza del Popolo, which provides what he called a 'magnificent impression' to the traveller 'upon his first entrance' to Rome, Burlington's friend, George Berkeley, featured three strategically placed obelisks in his design for the city of Bermuda while he waited for government funding in America.[96] His Catholic friend, Alexander Pope, erected an obelisk as a memorial to his mother in his garden at Twickenham.[97] Prior to acquiring his middle name of 'Athenian', the Catholic James Stuart might have been known as 'Egyptian' on the basis of his scholarly publication of the Obelisk of Psammetikos II, a work that 'procured him the honour of being presented to His Holiness the Pope [Benedict XIV]' in 1750.[98] The restoration and preparations for its erection in the Piazza di Montecitorio were admired in 1765 by the fourteen-year-old future collector, Sir Richard Worsley, who in 1774 erected an obelisk in memory of his Grand Touring father on the Isle of Wight, on a hill above his great house of Appuldurcombe, in which he gathered one of the most important collections of Greek and Egyptian antiquities of the time.[99] Having returned to Rome after accompanying Worsley through Greece and Egypt, in September 1786 Willey Reveley described the erection of another obelisk at the Quirinale, ahead of the Obelisk of Psammetikos, which was not completed until after 1790.[100] The delay had enabled John Brown to feature this still prostrate obelisk in his conversation piece depicting a group of Grand Tourists with their *cicerone*, James Byres.[101]

Today, the Washington Monument is probably the best known obelisk in the world, although its very familiarity perhaps renders it invisible to many. When I originally gave this talk I ended by praising America in what I hoped would be provocative style. America is still America, but since the election of President Obama it is no longer considered as provocative to praise the heir to Egypt, Greece and Rome. Though funded largely by Freemasons, the Washington Monument survives to symbolize whatever people choose. It featured prominently in photographs of Martin Luther King when he gave his 'I have a dream' speech and, reminiscently, during the inauguration of the new president. Barnett Newman's 'Broken Obelisk', in front of the Rothko Chapel in Houston, was dedicated to the assassinated King but he is now to be more massively (albeit less metaphorically) memorialized by a Chinese-made (but Egyptian-style?) sculpture alongside the Mall. Literally 'Out of Africa', however, it is the 'sky-aspiring' Washington Monument that seems the most appropriately inclusive memorial, referencing is it does, via Greece, Rome and *Roma Britannica*, the profoundly creative legacy of ancient Egypt. Now some 4,000 years old, the obelisk has few rivals as a symbol of the past, present and future of humankind.

NOTES

1. M. Hervey, *The Life, Correspondence and Collections of Thomas Howard Earl of Arundel* (Cambridge, 1921); D. Howarth, *Lord Arundel and His Circle* (New Haven/London, 1985); E. Chaney, *The Grand Tour and the Great Rebellion* (Geneva, 1985); E. Chaney, *The Evolution of the Grand Tour: Anglo-Italian Cultural Relations since the Renaissance*, revised edition (London, 2000); E. Chaney, *Inigo Jones's 'Roman Sketchbook'*, 2 vols (London, 2006). See now also: G. Worsley, *Inigo Jones and the European Classicist Tradition* (New Haven/London, 2007); C. Anderson, *Inigo Jones and the Classical Tradition* (Cambridge, 2007).
2. Pompilio Totti sold two guidebooks in the late 1620s and 1630s, entitled *Ritratto di Roma moderna* and *Ritratto di Roma antica* respectively. Panini's two great mid-eighteeenth-century capriccios in Boston and Stuttgart perpetuated the same distinction; see J. von Schlosser, *La letteratura artistica: manuale delle fonti della storia dell'arte moderna*, ed. O. Kurz, third Italian edition (Florence, 1977); L. Schudt, *Le guide di Roma* (Vienna, 1930).
3. Townley's grandmother, Lady Philippa Howard, was the daughter of Henry, 6th Duke of Norfolk, Arundel's grandson; see G.E.C[ockayne], *Complete Peerage*, 13 vols (London, 1910–19) and the *Oxford Dictionary of National Biography* (Oxford, 2004 and on-line) [henceforth *ODNB*].
4. E. Chaney, 'The Italianate evolution of English collecting', in E. Chaney (ed.), *The Evolution of English Collecting: the Reception of Italian Art in the Tudor and Stuart Periods* (New Haven/London, 2003), 35–6.
5. For Arundel commissioning a painting of the Vatican cope of Saint Sylvester, embroidered with the seven sacraments, given by Henry VIII to one of the Medici popes (probably Leo X), see Chaney, *Grand Tour and the Great Rebellion* (above, n. 1), 306–7. In his *Voyage of Italy* (Paris, 1670), II, 52, the Catholic priest Richard Lassels drew attention to the fact that Arundel had 'it painted out, and so much the more willingly, because it had been given to the *Pope* by *King Henry VIII* a little before his schisme'.
6. For the bronze bust, see now R. Harding, "The head of a certain Macedonian king': an old identity for the British Museum's 'Arundel Homer'", *British Art Journal* 9 (2) (2008), 11–16. John Johnstone's 1632 account confirms that this head was 'found in a well at Smyrna [Izmir] by Petty, who spent five years there in his search for such things' (Harding (this note), 13).
7. To the extent to which Martin Bernal's *Black Athena* (New Brunswick, 1987) succeeds in persuading us that western civilization is rooted in (African) Egypt, it explains the irony of how the age of the fully-fledged Grand Tour, the eighteenth century and the increase of historical information, saw the decline of the acknowledgement of its indebtedness to ancient Egypt in favour of more exclusive credit to Greece. I believe Bernal could strengthen his case by highlighting the Protestant fundamentalist origins of the so-called Enlightenment, the ingredient that encouraged subsequent Positivism. His Marxism may, however, provide him with a problem here. For the best discussion, see J. Assmann, *Moses the Egyptian* (London, 1997).
8. Chaney, *Evolution of the Grand Tour* (above, n. 1), *passim*.
9. The early modern idea of ancient Egypt was conditioned by both the Bible and the Greeks, though the Protestant Casaubon's exposure of the extent to which the 'thrice-great' Hermes was a Graeco-Roman construction was both less effective and less justified than is often claimed, in that the neo-Platonic version of Hermes was ultimately derived from the 12th Dynasty *Book of Two Ways* associated with the Temple of Thoth in Hermopolis (*c.* 1800 BC); see E. Hornung, *The Secret Lore of Egypt: its Impact on the West* (Ithaca, 2001). For the persistence of Hermeticism in early Stuart Britain and beyond, both heavily influenced by Frances Yates, see V. Hart, *Art and Magic in the Stuart Court* (London, 1994), and the more enterprising M.K. Schuchard, *Restoring the Temple of Vision: Cabalistic Freemasonary and Stuart Culture* (Leiden, 2002). Both emphasize the role of James I as the temple-building Solomon (an ultimately Egyptian project), Schuchard in particular documenting James's eighteenth-century status as pioneering Freemason. For a more sober account, see H. Gatti, 'Giordano Bruno and the Stuart court masques', *Renaissance Quarterly* 48 (1995), 809–42.
10. For James I giving the go-ahead for the destruction of the houses around Saint Paul's Cathedral, see Hervey, *Life, Correspondence, Collections* (above, n. 1), 167. Jones would be prosecuted for his part in this after the Civil War; cf. J. Lubbock, *The Tyranny of Taste: the Politics of Architecture and Design in Britain: 1550–1960* (New Haven/London, 1995).
11. J. Newman, 'A draft will of the Earl of Arundel', *The Burlington Magazine* 115 (1980), 695; E. Edwards, *Lives of the Founders of the British Museum* (London, 1870), 282. In fact much of his ancient sculpture went to the Ashmolean Museum in Oxford.
12. H. Foley's published translation of *Pilgrim Book* (*Records of the English Province of the Society of Jesus*, 8 vols (London, 1875–1909), X, 612), has: 'to search for ancient documents' rather than 'monuments'; cf. the Latin original, *English College Pilgrim Book*, Liber 282, 115: 'Die 12. Decemb. [1635] Dns Petty missus per Italiam a Rege et Com. Arundelio ad conquirenda Monumenta antiqua ...'. Later, on 26 December, the Earl of Devonshire dined at the College with his tutor, Thomas Hobbes; see Chaney, *Grand Tour and the Great Rebellion* (above, n. 1), 301. Here 'Hobbes' was mistakenly abbreviated in the de-Latinized Foley version to 'Hobbs', thus disguising the philosopher's true identity. This was exacerbated by the misidentification of Lord Devonshire, Hobbes's young patron and tutee on this journey. For Petty, see now A. Lapierre, *Le voleur d'éternité. La vie aventureuse de William Petty, érudit, esthète et brigand* (Paris, 2004), which, despite being a fictionalized account, is well researched. Also relevant is H. Cools, M. Keblusek and B.

Noldus (eds), *Your Humble Servant: Agents in Early Modern Europe* (Hilversum, 2006), which includes a somewhat disappointing essay on 'A question of attribution: art agents and the shaping of the Arundel collection', by D. Howarth (pp. 17–28).

13. For most of these see the *ODNB*, but cf. E. Chaney, '*The Oxford Dictionary of National Biography*: a personal view', *British Art Journal* (Winter 2004), 88–94. In *Philip II: Patron of the Arts* (Dublin, 2004), 19, Rosemary Mulcahy cited Federico Zuccaro on Philip's unusually informal rapport with artists. For le Blon, who has the least obvious claim to be included here, see H. de la Fontaine Verwey, 'Michel le Blon, graveur, kunsthandlaar, diplomat', *Jaarboek van het Genootschap, Amstelodamum* 61 (1969), 103–25; and most recently, B. Noldus, 'Lealtà e tradimento. Due agenti-artisti e un cancelliere', *Quaderni Storici* (2) (2006), 385–400. For Selden's 1630 recommendation of Pococke and its result in the form of a letter from Consul Wandesford of Aleppo, see D. Howarth, *Lord Arundel as a Patron and Collector* (Ph.D. thesis, University of Cambridge, 1979), 114, citing Bodleian Lib. Selden supplementary, 108, fol. 25. Smith, a painter from Norfolk, dined at the English College, Rome, on 6 September 1616; Foley, *Pilgrim Book* (above, n. 12), 596 (Liber 282, 84). Howarth (*Lord Arundel* (this note), 231) noted Jones reporting on Smith, 'painter of burnisht worke', witnessing the removal of the bronze beams from the Pantheon in 1625. Howarth believed that this was the same Smith, now described as a trumpeter in Arundel's entourage, who was murdered near Nuremberg in 1636 (*Lord Arundel* (this note), 56).
14. E. Iversen, *Obelisks in Exile*, 2 vols (London, 1972), II, 11–12.
15. *Natural History* 37.66: 'this is the meaning for the Egyptian word for it'; D.E. Eichholz's note in the Loeb edition says: 'Pliny is right. *Tekhen* means both sunbeam and obelisk'; cf. the discussion, including on the shadowlessness of obelisks, in I. Kagis McEwen, *Vitruvius. Writing the Body of Architecture* (Cambridge (MA), 2003), 240–51. The gold or electrum cap that usually surmounted an obelisk was designed partly in order to reflect the first rays of the sacred sun. In *Moses and Monotheism* (London, 1939), Sigmund Freud argued that it was Akhenaton's exclusive worship of the sun that inspired Moses to promote the idea of a single god; see E. Chaney, 'Egypt in England and America: the cultural memorials of religion, royalty and revolution', in M. Ascari and A. Corrado (eds), *Sites of Exchange: European Crossroads and Faultlines* (Amsterdam/New York, 2006), 39–73.
16. See J. Webb, *A Vindication of Stone-Heng Restored* (London, 1725), 215–17, quoting Guillaume de Salluste du Bartas. Cf. p. 214 for an account of the pyramids.
17. 'Of Obeliskes', I, fol. 33v–34r, an account indebted to Fulvio; cf. Chaney, *Inigo Jones's 'Roman Sketchbook'* (above, n. 1), II, 125, 130. Fallen obelisks were described coherently as early as *c.* 1410 by the Anonimo Magliabechiano; see A. Roullet, *The Egyptian and Egyptianizing Monuments of Imperial Rome* (Leiden, 1972), 67–84; B. Curran, *The Egyptian Renaissance: the Afterlife of Ancient Egypt in Early Modern Italy* (Chicago, 2007), 53–4. They were depicted in E. du Pérac, *I vestigi dell'antichita di Roma* (Rome, 1575), and in the sketchbooks and publications of Filarete, Antonio da Sangallo, Andreas Coner, Pirro Ligorio, Onofrio Panvinio and others discussed below. Jones also owned and had read Herodotus thoroughly in Italian translation. In 1540 Serlio wrote: 'And what should we ourselves say of the absolutely extraordinary remains of Egypt, which seem more like dreams and visions than real objects' (V. Hart and P. Hicks (eds), *Sebastiano Serlio on Architecture,* I, *Antiquities*, Book III, CLIII, fol. 123v).
18. For the best recent account, see Curran, *Egyptian Renaissance* (above, n. 17); see also E. Iversen, C. D'Onofrio and J. Collins, 'Obelisks as artifacts in early modern Rome: collecting the ultimate antiques', in *Viewing Antiquity: the Grand Tour, Antiquarianism and Collecting*, special issue of *Ricerche di Storia dell'Arte* 22 (2000), 49–68. These remind us that part of the Vatican obelisk's status (perhaps why it had not been pulled down) was derived from the belief that Saint Peter is supposed to have been crucified in its shadow. Collins (in the article cited above) has tended to reject the notion that Sixtus also revered the obelisks generally due to their association with the Egypt of Hermeticism and the 'prisca religio' as advocated by G. Cipriani, *Gli obelischi egizi: politica e cultura nella Roma Barocca* (Florence, 1993).
19. Sixtus V surmounted each of the four obelisks he erected with a cross; see D. Fontana, *Della trasportatione dell'obelisco Vaticano et delle fabriche di nostro signore Papa Sisto V... libro primo* (Rome, 1590), from which (p. 18) Jones derived his Doric design for the windows at Somerset House, next door to Arundel House, in 1623; see the comparison illustrated in Worsley, *Inigo Jones and the European Classicist Tradition* (above, n. 1), 101. Jones also borrowed Fontana's design for Sixtus V's catafalque for the one for James I (J. Peacock, 'Inigo Jones's catafalque for James I', *Architectural History* 25 (1982), 1–5). Michele Mercati (*De gli obelischi di Roma* (Rome, 1589)) wrote, under 'Della religione secondo la quale gli Egizi facevano gli obelischi': 'Pare che in Egitto rimanesse cognizione del vero Iddio dal tempo che si compare tornar gli uomini sopra le terra ...'. Shakespeare's mention of 'pyramids built up with newer might' in *Sonnet* 123 probably reflects his awareness of Sixtus V's campaign to 'build up' the obelisks (the words 'pyramid' and 'obelisk' were more or less interchangeable in this period) but more specifically the family tomb of his patron, the Earl of Southampton, at Titchfield. According to Iversen it was in 1584, the year prior to Sixtus V's papacy, that Jacques Androuet du Cerceau published his *Livre des édifices antiques romains*, which included an engraving of the Vatican obelisk, albeit covered with invented hieroglyphs; see E. Iversen, 'Hieroglyphic studies of the Renaissance', *The Burlington Magazine* 100 (1958), 15–21; E. Iversen, *The Myth of Egypt and its Hieroglyphs in European Tradition*, third edition (Princeton, 1993). Du Cerceau also seems to be the source for the tomb design that features an

obelisk on each corner, as in the Stanley, Montagu and Southampton tombs.

20. For the influence of Thomas Lodge, the Catholic traveller, physician and author, see *ODNB*.
21. See F. Yates, *Theatre of the World* (London, 1987). For the de Bry engravings, see J. Boissard, *Theatrum Vitae Humanae* (Metz, 1596); J. Boissard, *I–VI Pars Romanae Urbis Topographiae et Antiquitatum* (Frankfurt, 1597–1602), I, pl. 137, illustrated in Curran, *Egyptian Renaissance* (above, n. 17), 52.
22. Iversen, *Obelisks in Exile* (above, n. 14), II, 62–85 (and for his qualification to this statement, pp. 51–61); P. Usick, *Adventures in Egypt and Nubia: the Travels of William John Bankes (1786–1855)* (London, 2003), *passim*.
23. 'Cleopatra's Needle in its proposed position at Westminster', *Extra Supplement of the Illustrated London News*, 26 January 1878. Cf. Iversen, *Obelisks in Exile* (above, n. 14), II, figs 92–3 for two related illustrations, and R. Hayward, *Cleopatra's Needles* (Buxton, 1978).
24. As early as 1589 an anonymous Venetian traveller, admiring the two great obelisks of the Temple of Luxor, wrote: 'Oh what a rare thing it would be to see them placed in a superb piazza such as the one in Venice ... Countless numbers of people would flock there to see these trophies installed'. See Curran, *Egyptian Renaissance* (above, n. 17), 283. Perhaps the Venetian had seen the magnificent *Saint Mark Preaching in Alexandria* by Gentile and Giovanni Bellini, which depicts a convincing obelisk to the side of a basilica.
25. Very early dates are suggested by, for example, J.S. Curl, *The Egyptian Revival. Ancient Egypt as the Inspiration for Design Motifs in the West*, third edition (London/New York, 2005), 151, and R. Barnes, *The Obelisk: a Monumental Feature in Britain* (Kirstead, 2004), 10 and dustjacket, which specifies that 'the first obelisk to arrive was brought to Nonsuch Palace in about 1570'. Though it is unlikely that Lumley ever visited Rome, his father-in-law, Henry Lord Arundel, had done so, and, as a Catholic and connoisseur-collector with one of the largest libraries in England, Lumley in any case would have been especially well informed on the Pope's regeneration of the city. *The Lumley Inventory*, first published by the *Walpole Society* (VI, 1917–18), is being republished in it entirety by James Stourton for the Roxburghe Club. It includes a colour illustration of the Nonsuch Obelisk, which also appears engraved, to a presumably exaggerated scale, to the left of the House in Speed's *Map of Surrey* of 1610. As Nonsuch was one of the courts of Prince Henry and a favourite hunting venue for his father, James I, the obelisk would have been well-known. In a 1650 survey, it is described as 'one piramide or spired pinnacle of marble set upon a basis of marble grounded uppon a rise of free stone'; see J. Dent, *The Quest for Nonsuch* (Sutton, 1970), 290. For Lumley's other collecting activities, see K. Barron, 'The collecting and patronage of John, Lord Lumley (*c.* 1535–1609)', in Chaney (ed.), *Evolution of English Collecting* (above, n. 4), 125–58.
26. Transcribed, with slight adjustments, from H.J. Booth, 'Some royal and other great houses in England: extracts from the journal of Abram Booth', *Architectural History* 26 (1984), 503–9; cf. the original in the 'Journal van Abram Booth', in A. Merens (ed.), *Een Dienaer der Oost-Indische Compagnie te Londen in 1629* (The Hague, 1942), 66.
27. Merens, *Een Dienaer der Oost-Indische Compagnie* (above, n. 26), 66: 'iae selffs vuyt Egypten ende Grieckenlandt alhier gebracht sijn, op coste van gem[elte] Graeff'.
28. Illustration in G. Sandys, *Relation of a Journey* (London, 1615), 104; H. Whitehouse, 'Egyptology and forgery in the seventeenth century: the case of the Bodleian shabti', *Journal of the History of Collections* 1 (2) (1989), 187–95, n. 9; cf. H. Whitehouse, 'Towards a kind of Egyptology: the graphic documentation of ancient Egypt, 1587–1666', in *Documentary Culture: Florence and Rome from Grand Duke Ferdinand I to Pope Alexander VII* (Bologna, 1992), 63–79. Thomas Platter saw an infant mummy in Sir Walter Cope's collection in 1599. Archbishop Laud gave the Bodleian Library 'unum Aegyptiorum votus' in June 1636; see Whitehouse, 'Egyptology and forgery' (this note), 193.
29. For William Stukeley's drawing of the column, see R. Guilding, *Marble Mania: Sculpture Galleries in England 1640–1840* (London, 2001), 25, but her account of its acquisition by John Evelyn for Arundel seems to be based on eighteenth-century guidebook literature to Wilton or the antiquarian wishful thinking of the 8th or 9th Earl of Pembroke. Evelyn's detailed documentation of himself and his relations with Arundel (see below), as also the fact that by the time Evelyn went to Rome Arundel had left England, never to return, makes also the story in the current Wilton House guidebook of the Venus that surmounts the Egyptian column being Evelyn's gift to Arundel highly unlikely. The column is in fact recorded by Stukeley in 1723 as being in the Great Court at Wilton, having been bought by the 8th Earl of Pembroke 'of Mr Talman'; see E. Chaney, 'Egypt in England' (above, n. 15), 52; cf. Howarth, *Lord Arundel* (above, n. 13), 252, citing the unreliable Kennedy on Wilton, pl. 66: 'The Column of Aegyptian Granite ye shaft of one piece — ye Earl of Arundel bought it from ye Ruins before the temple of Venus at Rome where Julius Caesar had set it up having first brought it from a Temple of Venus in Aegypt, it is also noted for having old Aegyptian letters on it'. For the sphinx, see M. Vickers, *The Arundel and Pomfret Marbles* (Oxford, 2006), 48.
30. Arundel recruited Dieussart from Rome in 1635, a fact that was obscured by a mistranscription of the Earl's name in Thomas Birch's translation of Cyprien de Gamaches's 'Memoirs' in the *Court and Times of Charles I* (London, 1838). The superior version of Gamaches, which gives Arundel's name correctly, is A. de Valence (ed.), *Memoires de la Mission des Capucins de Paris près la reine d'Angleterre depuis l'année 1630 jusqu'a 1669 par le Cyprien de Gamaches* (Paris, 1881); see E. Chaney, 'Thomas Howard, 14th Earl of Arundel by François Dieussart', *Apollo* 144 (*The Arundel Collection*) (1996), 49–50. Springell transcribed a 1636 letter from Arundel to Petty showing that Arundel

wanted Gianlorenzo Bernini or François Duquesnoy to sculpt his portrait standing next to his grandson (p. 262), which perhaps suggests that he thought these superior to Dieussart (F.C. Springell, *Connoisseur and Diplomat* (London, 1963)). In Holland, having fled the now more Puritan England, Dieussart would use the motif of a Hellenistic stele from Arundel's collection in a monumental wall tomb with free-standing figures; see F. Scholten, *Sumptuous Memories: Studies in Seventeenth-century Dutch Tomb Sculpture* (Zwolle, 2003), 112–41.

31. E.S. De Beer (ed.), *The Diary of John Evelyn: Now First Printed in Full from the Manuscripts Belonging to Mr. John Evelyn*, 6 vols (Oxford, 1955), II, 469 and III, 171. This has been noticed by P. Findlen, 'Un incontro con Kircher a Roma', in E. Lo Sardo (ed.), *Athanasius Kircher: il Museo del Mondo* (Rome, 2001), 44. Evelyn continued: 'The stone was afterward brought for me into England, landing at Wapping where before I could heare of it, it was broke into several fragments, & utterly defaced to my no small affliction'. He also acquired other artefacts from this boat, however.
32. See A. Kircher, *Oedipus Aegyptiacus*, 3 vols (Rome, 1650), II, ii, 456. The engravings in this book and the *Obeliscus Pamphilius* (Rome, 1650) were designed by Giovanni Angelo Canini, to whom Richard Symonds apprenticed himself in this period; see M. Beal, *A Study of Richard Symonds: His Italian Notebooks and Their Relevance to Seventeenth-century Painting Techniques* (New York, 1984), *passim*. Canini's brother, Marcantonio, a pupil of Bernini, carved replacement sections of the obelisk with hieroglyphs that Kircher considered too worn in the original fragments; see Iversen, *Obelisks in Exile* (above, n. 14), I, 86. In *The Look of Van Dyck* (London, 2006), 268–71, John Peacock noticed that Evelyn purchased a copy of Kircher's *Magnes sive de Arte Magnetica* ... (Rome, 1641) in Rome on 13 March 1645. Ironically, Kircher acknowledged contributions from Greaves in this (Z. Shalev, 'The travel notebooks of John Greaves', in A. Hamilton, M.H. van den Boogert and B. Westerweel (eds), *The Republic of Letters and the Levant* (Leiden/Boston, 2005), 94–5). In the same year Evelyn also acquired a copy of Kircher's book on Coptic, which had been dedicated to Francesco Barberini in 1636, the *Prodromus Coptus sive Aegyptiacus*; see *The Evelyn Library* (London, 1977), II, 132. In August 1655 Evelyn noted Archbishop Ussher's description of Kircher as 'a Mountebank' (De Beer (ed.), *Diary of John Evelyn* (above, n. 31), III, 156).
33. This rare collection of engravings after Fontana, Lorenzo Pignoria and others, mainly by Nicolaus van der Aelst, compiled and commissioned by Johann Georg Herwart von Hohenburg, was published *c.* 1609. It includes the most accurate engravings to date of the Obelisk of Domitian (illustrated in Whitehouse, 'Towards a kind of Egyptology' (above, n. 28), fig. 6). The Bodleian copy (Arch. Bodl. A111/Bb.2) has Evelyn's engraved portrait by Robert Nanteuil as its bookplate and an annotated drawing of the front and back of a shabti similar to those now in the Ashmolean Museum. Meanwhile, I found what appears to be a page of this item, the engraving of the whole Bembine Table of Isis, with Ursus Books America. It is annotated by Evelyn beneath. It was on the market together with a small sheet in Evelyn's hand and surmounted by an L and his Mercury logo listing a collection of books and prints relating to Roman antiquities. This has now been acquired by Maggs Brothers of London.
34. In the Kircher archives there is merely a reference to the obelisk having been discovered by an Englishman; I thank Alexandra Lapierre for this information. Kircher interpreted and published hieroglyphs that had been on the hidden side; see Findlen, 'Un incontro con Kircher' (above, n. 31), and now D. Stolzenberg, *Egyptian Oedipus: Antiquarianism, Oriental Studies and Occult Practices: the Work of Athanasius Kircher* (Ph.D. thesis, Stanford University, 2004). The Englishman who features most prominently in *Obeliscus Pamphilius* is John Dee, whose *Monas* Kircher connected with the Egyptian ankh, or symbol of life; see P. Tomkins, *The Magic of Obelisks* (New York, 1981), 94.
35. That is, by way of his friend, George Ent; see A. Cook, 'A Roman correspondence: George Ent and Cassiano dal Pozzo 1637–1655', *Notes and Records of the Royal Society* 59 (2005), I, 5–23. Interestingly, in 1638 Harvey had asked dal Pozzo for a Catholic catechism, reminding one that as a student in Padua he took a Catholic oath; see Cook, 'A Roman correspondence' (this note); Chaney, *Grand Tour and the Great Rebellion* (above, n. 1), 291. The Catholic poet and physician who conducted Evelyn around the hospital of Santo Spirito, Dr James Gibbes, wrote a eulogistic dedicatory poem for *Obeliscus Pamphilius.* Kircher likewise inscribed the engraved portrait of Gibbes by Pietro da Cortona. For Gibbes, see Chaney, *Grand Tour and the Great Rebellion* (above, n. 1), 232–9.
36. De Beer (ed.), *Diary of John Evelyn* (above, n. 31), II, 362.
37. De Beer (ed.), *Diary of John Evelyn* (above, n. 31), II, 479; cf. E. Chaney, 'Evelyn, Inigo Jones, and the collector Earl of Arundel', in F. Harris and M. Hunter (eds), *John Evelyn and His Milieu* (London, 2003), 50 and note. Due to using the incomplete, pre-De Beer edition of Evelyn's *Diary*, Mary Hervey (*Life, Correspondence and Collections* (above, n. 1)) omitted the phrase about the Countess from her transcription, as, following her, did J.M. Robinson in his edition of Arundel's *Remembrances* (London, 1987). There are references to Arundel's disappointment in not receiving letters from the Countess. Something of Henry's subsequent antagonism towards his mother may be explained by her behaviour in this period. For Symonds reporting Arundel planning to go to Italy 'to buy drawings and pictures' in 1644, see Chaney, 'Evelyn' (this note), 46.
38. S.N.D.[Sister Rose Meeres], *Sir William Howard, Viscount Stafford; 1612–1680* (London, 1929), 15. Arundel's profound human feeling for his family (and friends) is suggested in his correspondence with Evelyn's future father-in-law, Richard Browne, regarding the delicate health of his granddaughter, Katherine: 'I thanke our Lord our deare childe Katherine

goes on in her recovery, which gives a great deal of comfort amongst so many miseryes which wee doe endure …', BL Add. MS 78,193, fol. 19r. In his 1641 will he also asked for a suitable memorial to be built for his only sister, who died when she was fifteen. Further confirmation of the regard in which he was held is to be found in Junius's letters, for which see S. van Romburgh (ed.), *'For My Worthy Freind* [sic] *Mr Franciscus Junius: an Edition of the Correspondence of Francis Junius FF (1591–1671)*' (Leiden, 2004).

39. Van der Borcht named his daughter Aletheia after the Countess (Springell, *Connoisseur and Diplomat* (above, n. 30), 103), in whose house he was resident when she died.
40. The most detailed commentary on this image is to be found in the catalogue of the exhibition organized by Nicholas Penny and David Howarth at the Ashmolean Museum, Oxford, in 1985: *Thomas Howard, Earl of Arundel* (Oxford, 1985), 22–3. This included Schut's original oil on paper design, as well as the etching, thus making clear which details were added by Hollar: that is, the prints, inscriptions and small bronzes distributed in the foreground. He also improved the resemblance of the face to Arundel's. In his entry on Schut's design, Penny talks of the print being a feasible alternative to a grand funeral, which Arundel, 'a protestant dying in exile during the Civil War could not be given'. In fact, his will specifically vetoed any pomp at his funeral.
41. Howarth, *Lord Arundel* (above, n. 13), 188: 'A winged figure crowning Virtue in the Correggio is transformed in the Hollar print into Mars, while the female seated to the right in the Correggio becomes, in the print, an Allegory of the sea …'.
42. See D. Howard, *Venice and the East* (New Haven/London, 2000), 71–2. The *c.* 1504–7 picture, begun by Gentile and completed by Giovanni Bellini after his death, is in the Brera, Milan. The obelisk depicted is now in Central Park, New York. The British had finally taken its fallen twin in the same decade (the 1870s).
43. M.M. McGowan, *The Vision of Rome in Late Renaissance France* (New Haven/London, 2000), 151, pl. IV: 'Resurrection of Lazarus', Bibliotheque Nationale, MS lat. 10558, fol. 73v. The obelisk is thus here an abstract version of Francis Bacon's joking reference to Arundel's sculpture collection as 'the Resurrection'.
44. Van der Borcht was Arundel's servant, as he mentioned in his letter to Petty from Ratisbon of 28 October 1636: 'I hope yr servante Henry will continewe as faith[ful] & industrious as I conceive him to be …' (Springell, *Connoisseur and Diplomat* (above, n. 30), 257).
45. Chaney, *Inigo Jones's 'Roman Sketchbook'* (above, n. 1), 27, n. 47. For the attribution of the tomb to Edward Marshall, see A. White, 'A biographical dictionary of London tomb sculptors *c.* 1560–*c.* 1660', *Walpole Society* 61 (1999), 93. It also features carved reliefs of the Banqueting House and Jones's façade of Saint Paul's Cathedral, which was itself surmounted by two obelisks.
46. J. Harris, S. Orgel and R. Strong, *The King's Arcadia: Inigo Jones and the Stuart Court* (London, 1973), 209.
47. Jones boasted of his work at Saint Paul's in the passage in I. Jones, *The Most Notable Antiquity of Great Britain, Vulgarly Called Stone-heng on Salisbury Plain. Restored by Inigo Jones Esquire, Architect General to the Late King* (London, 1655), in connection with the ancient Egyptians' capacity to move obelisks and build pyramids (p. 35). The obelisks were added (very faintly) to the first design for the façade of Saint Paul's (in the RIBA), which, partly for this reason, I believe should be dated to more than a decade earlier than the 1633–4 dating given in J. Harris and G. Higgott, *Inigo Jones: Complete Architectural Drawings* (New York, 1989), 241–3 (where the obelisks are not mentioned). They were probably inspired by the smaller pair on the façade of Sant'Ambrogio, Genoa, as illustrated in P.P. Rubens, *Palazzi di Genova* (Antwerp, 1622), pl. xxiii. Interestingly, even when he incorporated them in his Worcester College design (Harris and Higgott, cat. no. 79), the obelisks are of a squatter, more pyramidal kind, compared with the slenderer variety eventually adopted here and on his tomb.
48. G. Vertue, *Description of the Works of the Ingenious Delineator and Engraver Wenceslaus Hollar* (London, 1745) p[1] and iv–v. This is cited (from the 1759 edition) in K. Aldrich, P. Fehl and R. Fehl (eds), *Franciscus Junius: the Literature of Classical Art* I. *The Painting of the Ancients:* De Pictura Veterum (Berkeley/Los Angeles/Oxford, 1991), n. 20, but the engraving is described as a frontispiece and the quotation given slightly differently.
49. A large, pyramidal garden structure is visible in the background to the portrait of Arundel at Welbeck.
50. Illustrated in Chaney, *Evolution of the Grand Tour* (above, n. 1), 336. In his notebook Greaves wrote: 'Sestius his Tomb or Pyramid is 26 yards broad at the base; within it is brick & mortar, without covered with a marble about 15 Inches thick, as in several places I tried'.
51. A sharp pyramid and traditional obelisk feature in Serlio's 'Tragic Scene', which no doubt influenced Jones. Serlio was published in English by Robert Peake as *The Five Books of Architecture* (London, 1611), dedicated to Prince Henry, and based on the 1606 Dutch edition. Peake's version of the pyramid and bare-breasted sphinx (book III, fol. 43v) includes the statement that 'of this pyramid and head, Peter Martir writeth, and hath also seene and measured them, which differ not much'.
52. R. Pennington, *A Descriptive Catalogue of the Etched Work of Wenceslaus Hollar 1607–1677* (Cambridge, 2002), 481. This is based on a crude broadside woodcut showing that 'if one draw too hard one way, and the other other, the whole Common-wealth must be in danger to be pull'd in sunder'; F.G. Stephens and D. George, *Catalogue of Political and Personal Satires* (London, 1870), 314.
53. That the *Pyramidographia* was published prior to Arundel's death is shown by a thank-you letter from John Hales published by Birch in the biography that prefaces his *Miscellaneous Works of Mr John Greaves*, 2 vols (London, 1737). Hales concluded his letter with a request for information

regarding the Sphinx, 'which is wont to be represented as a woman' (II, 455–6). The sphinx that may have belonged to Arundel looks female; Vickers, *Arundel and Pomfret Marbles* (above, n. 29), 48–9. A publication that may have inspired Greaves to visit Egypt and investigate the great pyramid, Henry Blount's *A Voyage into the Levant* (London, 1636), describes this correctly as 'a male head' (p. 47). It also provides the first English account of the two obelisks that became known as Cleopatra's Needles in Alexandria, now in New York and London (p. 34).

54. Bodleian Library Savile MS 49, 1. For Greaves and his travelling companions, see *ODNB*; Chaney, *Grand Tour and the Great Rebellion* (above, n. 1); G.J. Toomer, *Eastern Wisdom and Learning: a Study of Arabic in 17th Century England* (Oxford, 1996); Chaney, 'Egypt in England and America' (above, n. 15); Z. Shalev, '"Measurer of all things': John Greaves (1602–1652), the great pyramid, and early modern metrology', *Journal of the History of Ideas* 63 (2002); Shalev, 'Travel notebooks' (above, n. 32). For Greaves's later friendship with Junius, see van Romburgh (ed.), *'For My Worthy Freind'* (above, n. 38). Junius had been planning to go to Italy in October 1630.
55. Greaves added the word 'without' above the line, using a caret beneath, which effectively eliminates the word 'at', in the interests of a truer description of the obelisk's location outside the Roman walls, off the Via Appia.
56. Howarth, *Lord Arundel* (above, n. 13), 113, cited the slightly confusing account by John (not Thomas) Ward, *Gresham Professors* (London, 1740), which should be supplemented by Leonard Twells's in the life of Pococke (reprinted in 1816) included in his contemporary edition of *The Theological Works of ... Dr Pococke*, 2 vols (London, 1740), 9–10. Collating the two, which summarize a letter from Greaves to Pococke: 'While he was in Italy, Mr Petty proferred him in my Lord of Arundel's name £200 per annum, and such fortunes as that lord could heap on him if he would stay with him and go into Greece. In answer to which, Mr Greaves declared his purpose of returning first into England, to see Mr Pocock, after so long an absence; adding that if he returned back, he should rather think of going into Egypt, where few had been, and where besides searching after books and antiquities, he should make astronomical observations. Mr Petty very much approved his resolutions, and assured Mr Greaves, if he would undertake that Journey, as under his Lord's sending If he, Mr Greaves went into the East he should by the Archbishop's means go consul to Aleppo ...'. This is to some extent confirmed by a letter in the National Archives (SP 16,381, fol. 159) from Greaves to Peter Turner describing a meeting with Petty; see Shalev, 'Travel notebooks' (above, n. 32), 85.
57. Shalev, 'Travel notebooks' (above, n. 32), 98. For Nicholas Stone Jr reporting on William Paston's journey to Egypt and back in 1638–9, a journey from Livorno that he almost undertook himself but for 'the losse of my time and the great taxes that Christians pay entring the Grand Care and other parts of Egypt', see his Diary in *Walpole Society* 6 (1919), 167 and 172. Paston had been liaising with the merchant Samuel Boothouse, who in turn helped Petty raise large sums of money in Italy on Arundel's behalf. For the copy of a letter among Boothouse's papers in the Florentine archives from Petty to Arundel, see D. Howarth, 'Samuel Boothouse and English artistic enterprise in seventeenth-century Italy', *Italian Studies* 32 (1977), 92. Dated Rome 16 December 1636, it acknowledges receipt of 'the full some [sic] of three thousand crownes'.
58. In Alexandria, Greaves was shown a mummy case 'yt was broght from Cairo ye chest was faire handsomely painted'. Howarth quoted this (*Lord Arundel* (above, n. 13), 115) and concluded that it must have been Greaves who sent the mummy back to London. Alas his not arriving in Alexandria until after it was sent makes this unlikely; see below, n. 59. *Mumia* was the tar-like substance produced from a combination of the bodies of Egyptian mummies and the matter the ancient embalmers used to preserve them. In 1587 Sir John Sanderson 'broke of all parts of the bodies to see howe the flesh was turned to drugge, and brought home divers heads, hands, arms and feete for a shewe. We brought allso 60 lb. for the Turkie company in peces, and brought into Ingland in the Hercules ...'; P. Conner, *The Inspiration of Egypt* (Brighton, 1983), 7. Platter saw an infant mummy in Sir Walter Cope's collection in 1599. For Rubens's mummy and drawing, see his letter to Valavez dated 26 December 1624 in M. Rooses and C. Ruelens, *Correspondance de Rubens*, 6 vols (1887–1909), III, 315; cf. M. van der Meulen, *Rubens Copies after the Antique* (*Corpus Rubenianum Ludwig Burchard* 23) (London, 1995), I, 29, n. 12.
59. 'VS di favorita di significare al Sig Cav dal Pozzo che una nave inglese ha portato dall'Egitto cavato delle grotte sotto alla piramide, un corpo intiero con tutti gli ornamenti sepolcrali, cosa tuttavia curiosa, e degna d'esser vista. Io andai l'altro giorno col Sig Conte e Contessa di Arundale e con S Contessa di Kent per vederlo; e fo risoluta quali portate in casa di detto S Conte; il quale lo fara designare et intagliarsi per puoterlo communicare, il Seldano et altri tengono che ha di tre mill'anni in circa, e nondimeno li colori paiono freschisimi ...': Biblioteca Apostolica Vaticana, Barberini latini 8645, fol. 276. I am grateful to Roberto Cobianchi for correcting the reading of the manuscript cited by Howarth, *Lord Arundel and His Circle* (above, n. 1), 225, n. 11; beware the latter's identification of the letter-writer as Gregorio Panzani, Conn's predecessor as papal nuncio, on p. 138; cf. Chaney, *Evolution of English Collecting* (above, n. 4), 105, n. 283. For transcripts of most of Conn's letters to Barberini, see British Library Add. MSS 15, 389–92. According to Aubrey, Selden secretly married the Countess of Kent after her husband's death. She left him £40,000 in her will (*ODNB*). For Selden and others' use of Eutychius and other early Christian Egyptian writings, which to some extent perpetuated the idea of 'the ancient wisdom', see A. Hamilton, *The Copts and the West: 1439–1822. The European Discovery of the Egyptian Church* (Oxford, 2006).

60. According to Aubrey, 'When the Queen-mother came to Oxon to the King, she either brought (as I thinke) or somebody gave her, an entire Mummie from Egypt, a great raritie, which her Majestie gave to Mr. Bushell, but I believe long ere this time the dampnesse of the place has spoyled it with mouldinesse' (J. Aubrey, *Brief Lives*, ed. O.L. Dick (London, 1950), 44); Tim Knox ('The Vyne Ramesses: 'Egyptian monstrosities' in British country house collections', *Apollo* 147 (April 2003), 33) took this visit to be in 1635 (the King and Queen visited Bushell in Enstone in 1636), but from the phrasing 'to the King' I believe it more likely to be at the beginning of the Civil War, when Henrietta Maria joined Charles I in Oxford, meeting him at Edgehill in July 1644; S.R. Gardiner, *History of the Great Civil War*, 4 vols (London, 1904), I, 166.
61. L.L. Peck, *Consuming Splendor: Society and Culture in Seventeenth-century England* (Cambridge, 2005), 328–9.
62. Now in the Osborne Collection, Beinecke Library, Yale University, quoted at greater length in Chaney, 'Evelyn' (above, n. 37), 37. For the biography of Lassels, see Chaney, *Grand Tour and the Great Rebellion* (above, n. 1) and *ODNB*.
63. For Father Fitton being presented by Arundel 'a bacciar la mano del Re come virtuoso, non come sacerdote', in the spring of 1638, see Chaney, *Grand Tour and the Great Rebellion* (above, n. 1), 36 and 282.
64. The Whetenhalls were given a wedding present by Lady Arundel's sister, Lady Kent, and were entertained by the Pope's widowed sister-in-law, Donna Olimpia; see E. Chaney, *Richard Lassels and His European Travels* (M.Phil. dissertation, Warburg Institute, 1977), 74.
65. The published version of the *Voyage* says 'depositated' rather than 'given', which would explain the surprisingly modest sum of money.
66. *The Voyage of Italy* manuscript (*c.* 1664), now in the Osborne Collection, Beinecke Library, Yale University, 322–3; quoted in Chaney, *Grand Tour and the Great Rebellion* (above, n. 1), 407–8.
67. Springell, *Connoisseur and Diplomat* (above, n. 30), 267. *Pace* previous commentators, the earlier part of this letter, referring to the Fide Commissa, does not refer to the obelisk but to what Arundel correctly identified as Meleager ('Adonis'; see F. Haskell and N. Penny, *Taste and the Antique: the Lure of Classical Sculpture 1500–1900* (New Haven/London, 1981), no. 60); see Conn's letter to Rome in BL Add. MS 15390, fols 65v–66r: 'Il sudetto Conte mi ha detto di avere comprato ad istanze di V. Emza le disegni di Gadi, ed ora di essere intorno all Adone, o Meleagro come dice egli del Pichini, dicendo che Vra Emza avea commandato al Pette di trovare qualche cosa degna di essere portata in Inghilterra, e che l'Emza Vra avrebbe procura la licenza. Io risposi che la statua del Pichini era sottoposta a stretto fide commisso a che l'Emza Vra avrebbe procurata la licenza. Egli prega e supplica, a mi ha fatto parlare dalla Regina alla quale ho promesso di scrivere, ma con darle poca speranza, e rappresentare le grandissima difficolta ... Ho detto al Conte che tocca al Pichini d'ottenere il consenso del Popolo Romano, non convenando che Vra Emza apparisca in cosa simile ...'. For more detail on the exporting of works of art from Rome, including references to some of Arundel's previous difficulties, see A. Bertolotti, *Esportazioni di oggetti di belle arti da Roma nei secoli XVI, XVII, XVIII e XIX*, 4 vols (Rome, 1875–80).
68. My translation of the transcript in BL Add. MS 15390, fol. 90r (cf. Hervey, *Life, Correspondence and Collections* (above, n. 1), 399). 'Il Sig.r Conte d'Arundell mi dice che il Pette ha comprata una Gulia a Roma, e spera nela solita benignita di Vra Emza tanta per quella, quanto per l'Adone del Pigini [*sic* for Pichini], promettendo di non volerle piu di fastidio in simile materie'. Hervey, *Life, Correspondence and Collections* (above, n. 1), 399, supplied a version of this, with 'Giulia' for the manuscript's 'Gulia' (that is: guglia = needle or obelisk). Meanwhile, Arundel reminded Petty of his wish to acquire the Gaddi Torso from Jacopo Gaddi. This is clearly the same Gaddi mentioned in Greaves's almanac/notebook, Bodleian Library Savile MS 49, opposite title page. It seems not to have been noticed that this is the same Gaddi who founded the Svogliati Academy and hosted John Milton in July 1638; see G. Campbell and T. Corns, *John Milton: Life, Work and Thought* (Oxford, 2008), 109–11. Petty's mutual acquaintance with Gaddi lends further support to my hypothesis that he may be the author of the MS 'Of statues and antiquities', hitherto attributed to Milton; see E. Chaney, 'Review of A. MacGregor (ed.), *The Late King's Goods* (1989)', *English Historical Review* 103 (1993), 719–21.
69. J. Raymond, *An Itinerary Containing a Voyage Made Through Italy in the Year 1646 and 1647* (London, 1648), 115.
70. For Borromini's drawing of the obelisk on a fountain, whose water he was responsible for bringing to the Piazza Navona, see Iversen, *Obelisks in Exile* (above, n. 14), I, pl. 46; cf. M. Heimburger Ravalli, *Architettura, scultura e arti minori nel barocco italiano: ricerche nell'archivio Spada* (Florence, 1977), cat. no. X.7. I thank Kerry Downes for this reference.
71. Now in the Vatican; see Iversen, *Obelisks in Exile* (above, n. 14), I, pl. 39.
72. J. Bargrave, *Pope Alexander the Seventh and the College of Cardinals* (London, 1847), 118. Bargrave made no mention of Arundel's involvement, but referred to the obelisk's 'Egyptian hyeroglifficks; of which Father Kercherius, that eminent Jesuit, and of my acquaintance, hath writt a large folio'. On the same page, Bargrave referred to the role of 'Cavalier Bernino, that famous architect, my neighbour and friendly acquaintance'.
73. Bargrave, *Pope Alexander* (above, n. 72), 122. David Sturdy and Martin Henig provided mistaken catalogue numbers for this and the related item; see B23 (cf. B19) in *The Gentle Traveller: John Bargrave, Canon of Canterbury, and His Collection* (Abingdon, n.d.).
74. V. Hart and P. Hicks (eds), *Sebastiano Serlio on Architecture* (New Haven/London, 1996), 440.

75. *De Varietate Fortunae*, lib. 1. 20 as cited by Curran, *Egyptian Renaissance* (above, n. 17), 55–6; cf. Roullet, *Egyptian and Egyptianizing Monuments* (above, n. 17), 67–84.
76. Iversen, *Obelisks in Exile* (above, n. 14), I, 82; Curran, *Egyptian Renaissance* (above, n. 17), 152, citing the *Commentarii*.
77. Following Iversen (*Obelisks in Exile* (above, n. 14), I, fig. 41), Curran (*Egyptian Renaissance* (above, n. 17), 150–1) illustrated the Sangallo drawing (Biblioteca Vaticana, Barberini lat. 4424, fol. 70r, but, in brilliantly synthesizing the work of his predecessors, pointed up the resemblance between the hieroglyphics and cartouche on Poliphilo's elephant obelisk in the *Hypnerotomachia* and their representation in Sangallo's drawing of the Obelisk of Domitian. The *c.* 1512 Coner drawing in Sir John Soane's Museum also depicts this obelisk and is cat. no. 69 (55)c, in T. Ashby (ed.), 'Sixteenth-century drawings of Roman buildings attributed to Andreas Coner', *Papers of the British School at Rome* 2 (1904), 40. It is identified as being 'apud capitem bovis' (after the bucrania of the frieze of the nearby tomb of Cecilia Metella).
78. For the Ligorio, see T. Ashby, 'The Bodleian MS. of Pirro Ligorio', *Journal of Roman Studies* 9 (1919), 170–201 and plates X–XIV, esp. p. 188 (referring to fol. 75r of the manuscript). For du Pérac's 1575 engraving of the Circus of Maxentius (from the *Vestigi dell'antichita di Roma*), see Iversen, *Obelisks in Exile* (above, n. 14), I, fig. 40. I believe that Rudolf Wittkower's arguments for a pre-1575 date for du Pérac's drawings, first published by Thomas Ashby with the Roxburghe Club as dating from the early 1580s, are supported by the absence from this bound collection of his depiction of the Circus of Maxentius, which was thus an addition to his series; see R. Wittkower, *Le antiche rovine di Roma nei disegni di du Pérac* (Rome, 1960; reprinted 1990). Ironically, thanks to the fake back-dating of the title-page and earlier binding, when Sir Andrew Fountaine acquired the drawings he may, at least initially, have believed the drawings to date from 1450. Closer inspection of du Pérac's view of the Aventine (p. 66) would have disabused him, however, for, relevant to the topic of obelisk transport, there is a large boat laden with the column from the Baths of Caracalla that was given to Cosimo I and erected in the Piazza Santa Trinità in Florence in the early 1560s.
79. Jones's copy of the *Quattro libri* at Worcester College, Oxford, IV, 89 and *Le cose maravigliose dell'alma città di Roma* (Rome, 1588), fol. 111v. Jones's surviving copies of Serlio are in the Queen's College, Oxford, and the Canadian Centre for Architecture in Montreal, the 1559–62 and 1600 editions respectively.
80. For his précising of the Palladio (in English perhaps to help him guide Arundel and others), see Chaney, *Inigo Jones's 'Roman Sketchbook'* (above n. 1), II, 124–6. In the *Quattro libri*, Jones also commented on the use of the Romulus portico idea in the Palazzo Thiene in Vicenza, attributing this to Giulio Romano rather than Palladio, though the latter 'sets yt doune as his owne' (IV, 89).
81. Jones, *Most Notable Antiquity* (above, n. 47), 25–6.
82. Jones, *Most Notable Antiquity* (above, n. 47), 34–5. Jones's quotation of Herodotus in Latin (which he then appears to translate) adds to the impression that his notes, 'found ... long after his Death' were heavily edited, indeed entirely rewritten, by his protégé, John Webb, who was a superior linguist. This is adumbrated (as evidence of Jones's modesty) by Webb when he mentioned that Harvey and Selden encouraged him to publish it (Jones, *Most Notable Antiquity* (above, n. 47), 118). Jones owned Matteo Maria Boiardo's 1539 Venice edition of Herodotus, *Delle guerre de Greci & de Persi*, the first half of which is annotated thoroughly. He also owned a 1562 Italian edition of Strabo: *La prima parte della Geographia*; see Harris, Orgel and Strong, *The King's Arcadia* (above, n. 46), appendix III. The now-lost copy of Bordino's book on Sixtus V given him by Edmund Bolton was almost the only surviving book in Latin belonging to Jones.
83. *Mr. Webb's Vindication of Stone-Heng Restored* (London, 1725), 182: 'And have I not by me a Letter written to Mr. *Jones* from that never-to-be-forgotten Maecenas of all Learning, the Right Honourable Thomas Earle of Arundel and Surrey, not long efore his Death, saying that Italy was no more Italy; he then found such Decay of Architecture, Sculpture, Painting, and all that was good and virtuous, from what not forty Years before he had seen therein?'. Kevin Sharpe mentioned Arundel's plans for a study of Roman Britain, which would no doubt have encouraged Jones (BL Harl. MS 4840, cited by K. Sharpe in 'The Earl of Arundel, his circle and the opposition to the Duke of Buckingham, 1618–1628', in K. Sharpe (ed.), *Faction and Parliament: Essays on Early Stuart History* (Oxford, 1978), 239). Those advising Arundel would have known of the Egyptian ingredient in Roman religion and the fact that there were temples of Isis in Britannia. Edmund Spenser's *Fairie Queen*, for example, features a Temple of Isis. Camden hoped that an antique bronze he found soon after Arundel's return from Italy was a statue of Isis. He wrote to Franciscus Sweertius and Nicolas-Claude Fabri de Peiresc about the object, and they passed Camden's not very precise drawing on to Rubens and Lorenzo Pignoria, who opined that it was not Isis; see D. Jaffé, 'The Barberini circle: some exchanges between Peiresc, Rubens, and their contemporaries', *Journal of the History of Collections* 1 (2) (1989), 119–47. Peiresc visited Camden in England in 1606, when no doubt he would have communicated to him and others his enthusiasm for matters Egyptian, for which see S.H. Aufrère, *La momie et la tempête: Nicolas-Claude Fabri de Peiresc et la curiosité égyptienne en Provence au début du XVIIe siècle* (Avignon, 1990); P. Miller, 'History of religion becomes ethnology: some evidence from Peiresc's Africa', *Journal of the History of Ideas* 67 (October 2006), 675–96 (for contact with Pignoria).
84. J. Harris, *Catalogue of the Drawings Collection of the Royal Institute of British Architects* (London, 1972), cat. nos. 46–7 (figs 42–4).

85. Pennington, *Descriptive Catalogue* (above, n. 52), 1002, following Rhys Jenkins in *London Topographical Record* II (1903). Ford had been the Royalist commander who surrendered Arundel Castle in 1644. He built the tower in 1655, and it was dismantled a decade later; see *ODNB*.
86. See L. Stainton and C. White, *Drawing in England from Hilliard to Hogarth* (London, 1987), 118–19.
87. See A. Griffiths, *The Print in Stuart Britain 1603–1689* (London, 1998), 238–9, which is indebted to E.J. Dingwall, *Very Peculiar People: Portrait Studies in the Queer, the Abnormal and the Uncanny* (London, 1950); R. de Smet and A.E.C. Simoni, 'The realm of Venus Hadriani Barlandi [H. Beverland] De Prostibulis Veterum Ms Leiden BPL 1994', *Querendo* 17 (1) (1987), 45–58; R. de Smet, 'Hadrianus Beverlandus', *Verhandelingen van de Koninklijke Academie voor Wetenschappen, Letteren en Schone Kunsten van Belgie: Klasse der Letteren* 50 (1988), 5–187.
88. Dingwall, *Very Peculiar People* (above, n. 87), frontispiece.
89. Chaney, *Evolution of English Collecting* (above, n. 4), 35.
90. Blooteling probably worked in England in the early 1670s; see Griffiths, *Print in Stuart Britain* (above, n. 87), 224.
91. C. Avery, 'The Duke of Marlborough as a collector and patron of sculpture', in Chaney, *Evolution of English Collecting* (above, n. 4), 427–64.
92. See R. Hewlings, 'Ripon's Forum Populi', *Architectural History* 24 (1981), 39–52.
93. Hawksmoor's fine but unused design for an obelisk at Blenheim dates from 1727. He also wrote an 'Explanation of the Obelisk', still in Blenheim library; see K. Downes, *Hawksmoor* (London, 1959); K. Downes, *Hawksmoor* (London, 1969); K. Downes, *Vanbrugh* (London, 1977); K. Downes, *Sir John Vanbrugh: a Biography* (London, 1987). For a survey, see Barnes, *The Obelisk* (above, n. 25).
94. Avery, 'Duke of Marlborough' (above, n. 91), 458; *ODNB*.
95. According to the *Gentleman's Magazine* of July 1769, Burlington was given the relief in 1712 by a 'Mr Theobald'; see J. Harris, *The Palladian Revival: Lord Burlington, His Villa and Garden at Chiswick* (New Haven/London, 1994), 195, 223–5. This is likely to have been James Theobald or his father, Peter, the surgeon-cum-timber merchant who indeed acquired fragments of the Arundel Collection *c.* 1712. Today the relief has been replaced by a fibreglass facsimile. Interestingly, Henry Flitcroft's drawing for this obelisk has the correct proportions and sharp-pointed top but, despite the assertion in Flitcroft's hand, 'Earle Burlington Invenit', the final product is less elegant and capped with the flattened top familiar from innumerable later versions.
96. See Chaney, *Evolution of the Grand Tour* (above, n. 1), fig. 56. Berkeley praised Sixtus V for raising the obelisks and added: 'Most of these Obelisks are scribbled over with Hieroglypics [sic]. They are each of single piece of Granate. Nothing can give one a higher notion of the stupendous magnificence of the old Egyptian Monarchs who made these Obelisk than that the Roman Emperors in their greatest glory valued themselves upon bringing them from Egypt. And the most spirited of the Popes look'd on it as the greatest event of his life to be able to place one of them on it's pedestal'; see G. Berkeley, *Works*, ed. A.A. Luce and T.E. Jessop (London, 1955), VII, 250.
97. See his letter from Sherborne to Martha Blount in G. Sherburn, *Correspondence of Alexander Pope* (Oxford, 1956), II, 239, recommending memorial obelisks. For a later watercolour of Pope's obelisk, see M. Mack, *Alexander Pope: a Life* (New Haven/London, 1985), 549.
98. S.W. Soros (ed.), *James 'Athenian' Stuart: the Rediscovery of Antiquity* (New Haven/London, 2007), 67: 'a distinction', continued James Gandon, Stuart's assistant, 'perhaps, never before conferred on an artist who was a Protestant'. Stuart was, however, listed in the *state d'anime* of 1747 as 'Sign. Jiacobo Stuard Ingles Catol 30'; C. Arbuthnot, 'Life', in Soros, *James 'Athenian' Stuart* (this note), 91, n. 28 (cf. F. Salmon, 'Antiquary and archaeologist', in Soros, *James 'Athenian' Stuart* (this note), cf. 141, n. 10). Iversen (*Obelisks in Exile* (above, n. 14), I, 152) called Stuart's etchings 'the first reproductions of Egyptian hieroglyphs to reflect the beauty of the originals'. In London in 1769, Stuart presented a paper on Egyptian hieroglyphs to the Royal Society; Soros, *James 'Athenian' Stuart* (this note), 76. Pius VI's later obelisk-erecting campaign, the most intensive since Sixtus V, led Antonio Canova to comment, in response to a question about Roman tree planting: 'In Rome they plant obelisks'; cf. J. Collins, *Papacy and Politics in Eighteenth-century Rome: Pius VI and the Arts* (Cambridge, 2004).
99. D.W. Lloyd and N. Pevsner, *The Isle of Wight* (New Haven/London, 2006), 72. I thank Linda Bek for reminding me of Worsley's obelisk. Built of Cornish granite, it was nevertheless damaged by lightning in 1831 and further reduced by a storm five years later. Worsley travelled to Egypt with the artist-architect Reveley, who later compiled materials for a 'Journey through Italy, Greece and Egypt' (RIBA; cf. Lincolnshire Archives, Lincoln, Worsley MS 23 'Journal of a Tour, 1783–7'.
100. B. Ford and J. Ingamells, *A Dictionary of British and Irish Travellers in Italy, 1701–1800. Compiled from the Brinsley Ford Archive* (New Haven/London, 1997), 807. Iversen, *Obelisks in Exile* (above, n. 14), 158–9.
101. A. Laing, 'John Brown as a painter', in D. Adshead (ed.), *The National Trust Historic Houses and Collections Annual 2009* (London, 2009), 12–17. While the sitters are all identified, what some are seated upon is not, though very clearly the obelisk of Psammetikos is depicted perhaps with assistance from Stuart's engravings.

EGYPT, ROME AND THE CONCEPT OF UNIVERSAL HISTORY*

Elizabeth Bartman

Collecting antiquities ranked high among the pleasures of an Englishman's Grand Tour in the eighteenth century, and the pastime's popularity is attested by the hundreds of statues still displayed in English country houses and museums. Although they were later to be dethroned by the aesthetic 'purism' of the Elgin marbles, these statues epitomized classical taste for English viewers for more than a century. In view of this reception, the occasional appearance of an Egyptian object — as often an authentic pharaonic work as a Roman imitation (what we would call 'Egyptianizing') — in a Grand Tour collection calls for interpretation. Did the Egyptian objects enjoy special treatment or a privileged status? How much was known about ancient Egypt and to what extent were contemporary views accurate? Was Egyptian art viewed as 'classical' in the eighteenth century? As we shall see, the eighteenth century witnessed a major shift in attitudes towards Egypt; what had been regarded as exotic and alien became part of the mainstream of antiquity, absorbed into an all-embracing concept of universal history. Egyptian art may have been regarded by some aesthetes as inferior to Greek, but its discussion vis-à-vis the classical integrated it into the history of western civilization to a degree that it had not been before — and would cease to be in later scholarship.

EGYPT IN ENGLISH COLLECTIONS

No full accounting of the Egyptian works in British Grand Tour collections exists, and it is not my intent to provide an exhaustive treatment here.[1] Instead I shall present a selective corpus, intended to elucidate general trends by highlighting major objects from several of the most celebrated collections in Britain. Egyptian and Egyptianizing works appear in a number of collections whose owners, locations and dates range widely: that is, they conform to no single profile. Among the most impressive is the greywacke head of a sphinx purchased in the 1770s by Lord Shelburne for Lansdowne House (Fig. 12.1);[2] the head was acquired from Gavin Hamilton, one of the most active excavators and dealers of the period.[3] Although his correspondence to clients inevitably contains self-promotion and hyperbole, Hamilton's description of the head seems reliable: 'I have the liberty to send . . . a fine Erma of an Egyptian Idol in green basalto, which are so rare and valuable that the Cardinal Albano alone in Rome can boast of having a piece in his possession, and I may safely venture to say that this is the first that has ever been sent to England. I may add that this is truly Egyptian, whereas the [he mentions two other statues belonging to the Earl][4] . . . are done in the time of Hadrian in imitation of the Egyptian'.[5]

Dated 6 August 1772, Hamilton's letter suggests that in the latter part of the eighteenth century, despite decades of energetic collecting, authentic Egyptian monuments were rare in England.[6] Even so well-connected a connoisseur as Charles Townley, arguably the most influential British collector of the century, did not acquire a large-scale pharaonic antiquity until the 1790s, at the end of his collecting career (Fig. 12.2).[7] Like the Earl's head, Townley's was a fragment in dark stone whose colour, sharp carving and stereometric forms would have contrasted visually with the more familiar Graeco-Roman white marbles in the collection; today identified as a late king, it was then known as an 'Isis in basaltes'.[8]

Far more commonplace in English collections were works in dark stone or marble that looked Egyptian but actually were made in Roman times. Deified after he drowned in the Nile, Antinous, the Emperor Hadrian's lover, was frequently shown in an Egyptian mode; once again, Lord Shelburne secured one of the finest surviving examples, a marble portrait head wearing an Egyptian *nemes*

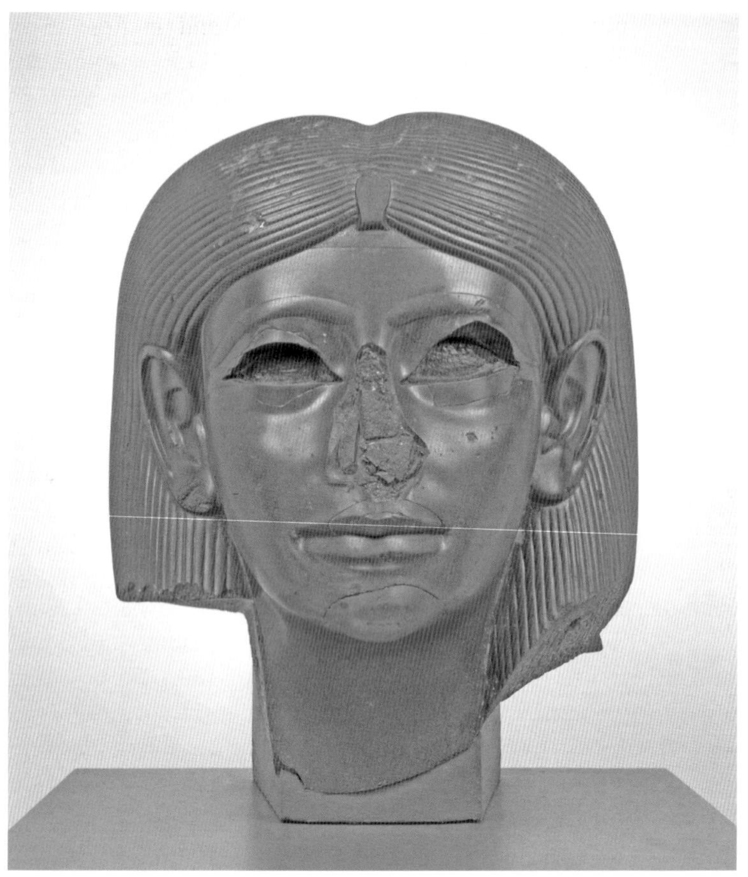

FIG. 12.1. *Head from a Female Sphinx*. Greywacke. Brooklyn Museum of Art 56.85, Charles Edwin Wilbour Fund. *(Reproduced courtesy of the Brooklyn Museum of Art.)*

head-dress (Fig. 12.3).[9] As a known historical personage — and one bearing racy connotations — Antinous appealed as a subject to English buyers. Moreover, unlike many Egyptianizing works, the life-size (or larger) scale at which the deified Antinous typically was represented made it an appropriate decoration for monumental sculpture galleries such as Shelburne installed in his London dining-room.[10]

EGYPT AND ROME

Because the excavator tells us its find-spot, the Lansdowne Antinous can be associated with Hadrian's Villa at Tivoli. Although the Villa was a prestigious 'address', sometimes cited falsely by unscrupulous dealers wanting to add cachet to objects, the discovery of many other comparable Egyptianizing works, both in the eighteenth century and more recently, makes it a more than plausible provenance.[11] Indeed, so many works of this style were discovered there that at the time scholars such as Johann Joachim Winckelmann dated almost all the surviving Egyptianizing sculpture known to Hadrian's reign.[12]

The two dark stone heads that belonged to Townley and Lord Shelburne, both officially without provenance, may likewise have come from Rome or its environs.[13] Yet, as we have seen, they are Egyptian works that date to the Pharaonic period: whether as spoils of war taken by Augustus to proclaim his victory over Cleopatra or as objects of devotion intended for the religious cults promoted by later emperors, they came to be familiar elements of the ancient city. Certain objects like obelisks and the pyramid-shaped tomb of Cestius (imitative of Egyptian forms) never lost their monumental presence, while others came to light only when the surface of the modern city was probed. (The central location in the Campus Martius of a vast temple complex dedicated to Isis and Serapis ensured a continuous reappearance of Egyptian artefacts.) As a result, virtually all the old aristocratic collections formed in early modern Rome included Egyptian works (Plate 12.1).[14] Like Old Master paintings and classical Graeco-Roman antiquities, these pieces were offered for sale to the visiting English buyers who dominated the market in eighteenth-century Italy.

Indeed, Rome was the primary source of Egyptian monuments at this time. Firstly, relatively few Englishmen travelled to Egypt itself in the eighteenth century.[15] (Some of those who did proudly commemorated the fact by having themselves depicted wearing Arab head-dresses; the practice was especially common for the portraits of members of the Society of Dilettanti commissioned from George Knapton to hang in the Society's headquarters in London.)[16] Secondly, those Englishmen who did explore the pyramids and sailed the Nile immortalized their exploits primarily through books and letters — they did not ship any large-scale antiquities back to England. As a result, eighteenth-century collectors with an interest in ancient Egypt had to content themselves with small, portable works such as mummified animals and papyri.[17]

Notwithstanding the still primitive understanding of Egyptian archaeology, the eighteenth-century visitor to Rome could not help but be struck by the foreign, non-Roman character of the Egyptian monuments he saw. To him, Rome was a kind of museum of antiquity; as the repository of Egyptian works she was confirmed in her status as universal *fons et origo*. Numerous paintings emphasized the seamlessness of ancient

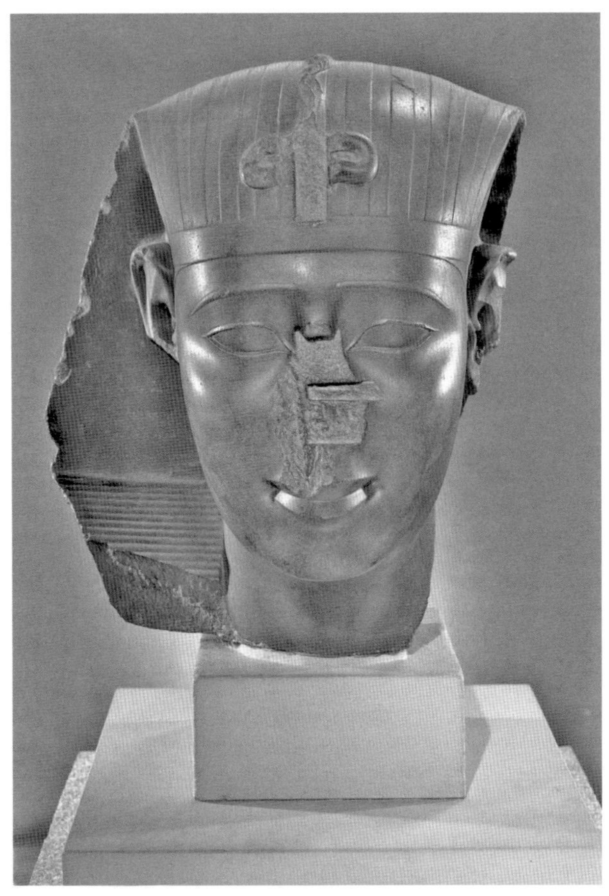

FIG. 12.2. *Portrait Head of a Pharaoh*, front view. Green siltstone. London, The British Museum EA 97 (ex-Townley Collection). *(Photo: © The Trustees of the British Museum.)*

history by displaying Egyptian works in juxtaposition with Roman; Giovanni Paolo Panini's *oeuvre* often conveys this theme,[18] but the message of cultural harmony occurs also in Johann Tischbein's celebrated portrait of the reclining Johann Wolfgang von Goethe (Fig. 12.4).[19] Here the poet reclines amidst a lapidary assemblage that includes a block carved with women of classical Graeco-Roman type and another with Egyptian hieroglyphs (presumably a broken obelisk). In assuming the imperial mantle by collecting, the British were fortunate in the attribution of so many Egyptian statues to the time of Hadrian. Hadrian's characterization as a 'good emperor' served to enhance the importance of the British inheritance — from ancient Egypt, to imperial Rome, to eighteenth-century Britain embodied a flattering historical trajectory.

EGYPT MISUNDERSTOOD

In view of the (relative) unfamiliarity of Egypt and the fact that hieroglyphics still remained untranslated, it is not surprising that errors of fact and interpretation occurred. Anton Raphael Mengs's 1759 painting of Octavian in the palace of his vanquished nemesis Cleopatra, one of the first attempts to recreate an archaeologically accurate Egyptian interior, represents a modest example (Plate 12.2).[20] By infusing the painting with an atmospheric gloom, Mengs strove to evoke the internal spaces of the labyrinthine temples that travellers recorded; in other respects, however, he simply depicted a generic ancient house.

Egyptian statues also inspired false readings. A draped male (today clasping a water jug; Fig. 12.5)[21] misled no less a scholar than Winckelmann. Owned by Henry Blundell of Ince, the water-carrier was acquired from the Villa Mattei in Rome in the late 1770s. Like the other works of Egyptian theme in Blundell's collection, the figure was an Egyptianizing statue of Roman date rather than a bona fide Egyptian work: its material — white marble — clearly conveys its status, although the piece conforms with pharaonic statuary by its static, frontal pose with one leg advanced and by its back pillar. The water-carrier wears a voluminous but light cloak draped, in a non-classical fashion, symmetrically around the neck and enveloping both hands in its pleated folds. Clasped in front of the belly, the hands and lower arms form a shelf-like support for a rotund jar; although what exists at present is modern, comparable ancient iconography certifies that the figure has been restored correctly as an Egyptian *naophoros*, or male water-carrier.[22] Almost certainly the eighteenth-century restoration was guided by a similar figure carved on a relief that was well known; also part of the Mattei Collection, it was engraved for *Monumenta Mattheiana*, published in Rome in the late 1770s, apparently to advertise the upcoming sale of the collection.[23]

Before its restoration, Blundell's statue caught the attention of Winckelmann, who discussed the Mattei figure in the *Geschichte der Kunst des Alterthums* (1764).[24] Winckelmann misinterpreted its forms completely, however, when he concluded from the figure's rotund mid-section that it represented a pregnant female. Winckelmann's assessment of the statue was negative, in keeping with an idealization of Greek art that essentially saw Egyptian art as but a primitive precursor.[25] In this particular case, however, the statue's implied female sexuality also may have triggered antagonism. (Elsewhere he disparaged statues of Egyptian women for their large breasts.)[26]

Winckelmann's error was quickly corrected by Ennio Visconti in an appendix to Blundell's *Account*

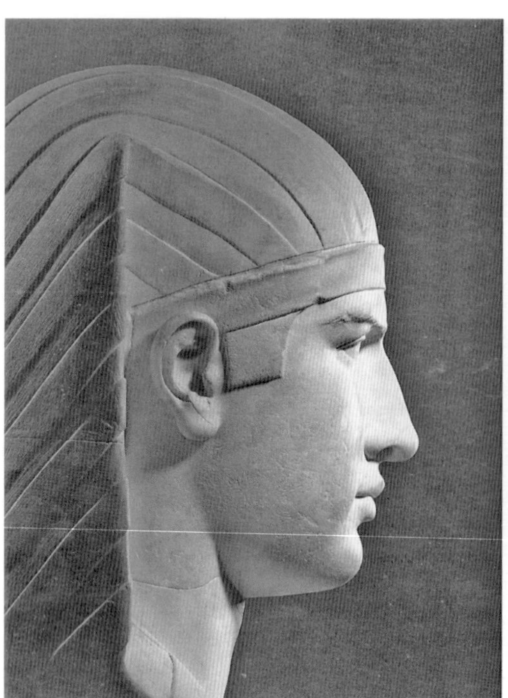
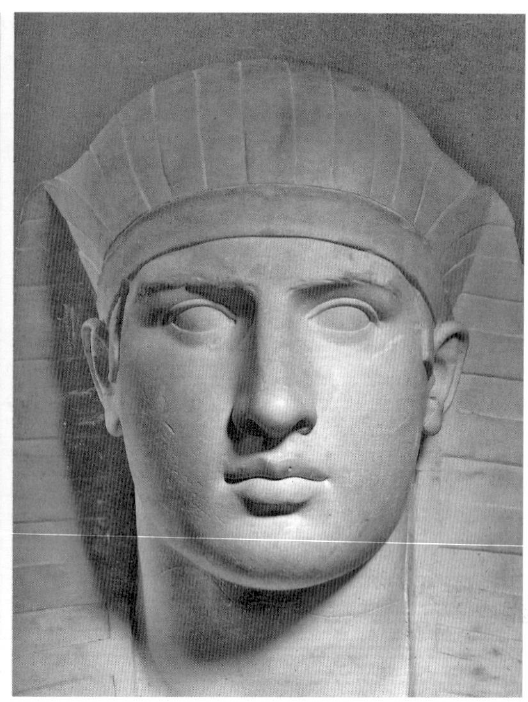

FIG. 12.3. *Head of Antinous* (restored as bust), front and side views. Marble. Whereabouts unknown (ex-Lansdowne Collection). *(Photo: Christie's Images Limited.)*

of 1803.[27] Notwithstanding this corrective — and the published acknowledgment that the statue depicted a male —, Blundell persisted in calling the statue by the name to which he had referred to it for decades: Isis. Indeed Isis appears to have been a verbal catch-all for anything looking vaguely Egyptian; according to Blundell, virtually all the female statues of Egyptian style in his collection were representations of Isis.[28] This nomenclature found a wide usage during the eighteenth century, even, as in the case of the Ince water-carrier, when the figure was male.

One of the most celebrated antiquities in England, Townley's so-called *Clytie* (Fig. 12.6),[29] also elicited a false 'Egyptian' reading, but in this instance the mistake seems willful. Townley bought the piece in Naples in 1772, and we know that *Clytie* was among his favorite works: tellingly, she is foregrounded in the well-known painting by Johan Zoffany depicting Townley in his library, joined by colleagues and surrounded by works from his collection (Fig. 2.2). In the painting (whose sculptural arrangements have been recognized to be fictive), *Clytie* sits nearly in the exact centre, atop the desk at which Townley's colleagues gather.[30]

In contrast to Blundell's water-carrier, *Clytie* has virtually no Egyptian features — its white marble, bust format and iconography (especially the hairstyle, with its back-swept tresses and coiled bun at the back) represent quintessentially Roman forms. Although many have called the bouquet of leaves in which the bust nestles the lotus, this identification is false.[31] Still ultimately Townley pronounced it an Isis;[32] late in life he wrote, 'The calm repose ... in which the Goddess is here represented, and placed upon the waters, which are symbolized by the Lotus, may relate to the temporary inaction of the productive germ in nature, which is personified by Isis, the *magna rerum parens*, the universal mother'.[33] Like his friend Blundell, Townley had a tendency to see Isis in various figures in his possession, especially those executed in hard dark stone.[34] In view of the rarity of such pieces in Britain, many collectors must have been tempted to identify works as the Egyptian goddess, although in Townley's case there may have been contributory forces. On his first trip to Italy in 1767–8, Townley had travelled to the bay of Naples and actually seen the Temple of Isis as it was being uncovered at Pompeii; at a time when archaeology was in its infancy, the excitement generated by such digging should not be underestimated.[35] But Townley's lapse of judgment probably stems as well from the influence of Pierre François Hugues, the self-styled Baron d'Hancarville. A brilliant but wildly idiosyncratic scholar, the Baron was supported financially by Townley for years (it is he who sits writing at the desk bearing *Clytie* in Zoffany's painting of Townley's library). Today d'Hancarville is largely ignored, but in the eighteenth-century, whether in Naples with William

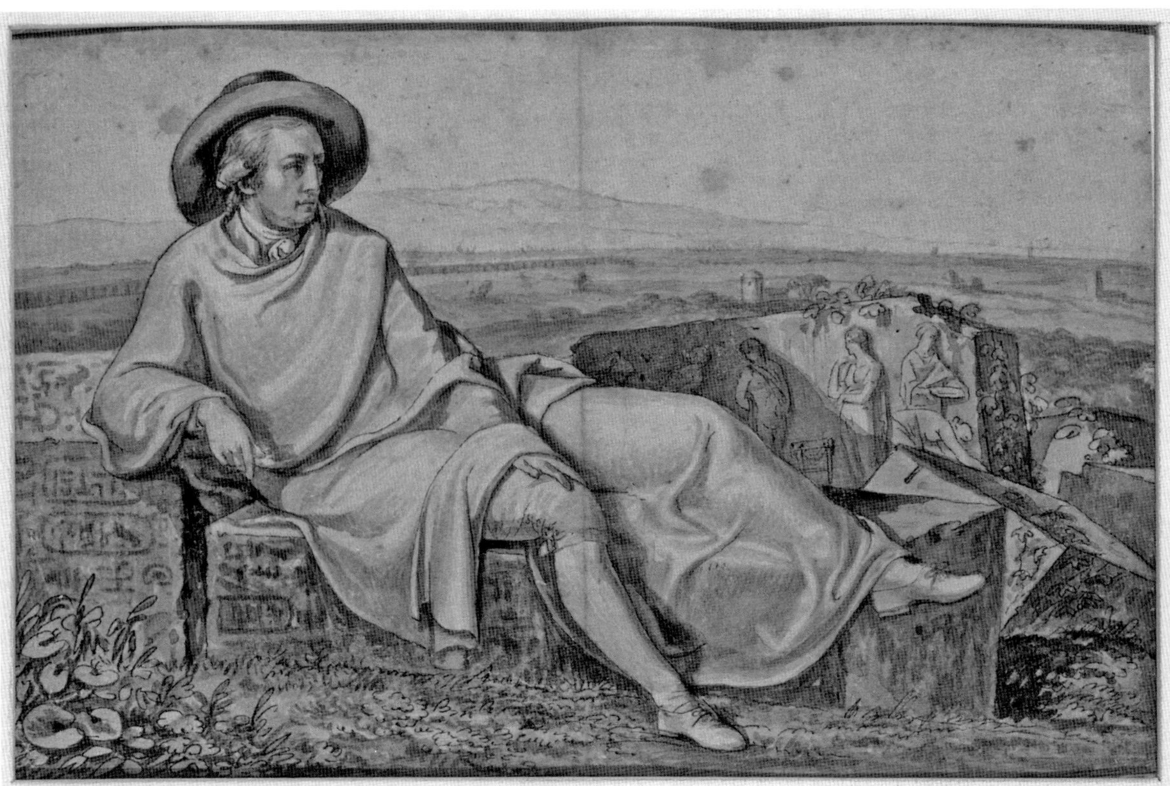

FIG. 12.4. Johann Tischbein (1751–1829), J. Schütz and F. Bury, *Goethe in the Campagna*, c. 1787. Watercolour. Weimar, Goethe-Nationalmuseum, Graphische Sammlung, Klassik Stiftung inv. KHz/00365. *(Reproduced courtesy of the Goethe-Nationalmuseum.)*

Hamilton or in London with Townley, he found receptive audiences.[36]

At the heart of all religions, d'Hancarville argued, was the cult of fertility,[37] and it is here that Isis assumed a central importance because of her connection with water and regeneration. Although d'Hancarville himself did not discuss *Clytie*, it is likely that Townley's final identification of the bust as Isis stemmed from his theories. To be sure, Townley dismissed some of d'Hancarville's ideas as chimeras (as did Blundell), but ultimately they both succumbed to the preaching of this seductive iconoclast. In the case of *Clytie*, the bare shoulder and partially exposed left breast, as well as the luxuriant foliage that encircles her body (Fig. 12.7), endowed the bust with a sensuality that is both rarely attempted and rarely achieved by Roman stone carvers. So unusual is it in the corpus of Roman portraits, in fact, that perhaps Townley can be excused for letting his enthusiasm overcome his scholarly sobriety. In the case of Blundell, the collector may be excused for naming his water-carrier Isis because, in a sense, the goddess does appear in the image, albeit not directly but symbolically via the water jug. In antiquity Isis was connected with water; in Egypt, water — in the specific form of the annual flooding of the Nile — ensured survival; the river's annual flooding, which changed a dry barren landscape into thriving green, connoted fertility. Isiac temple rites always included Nile water, and surely that is what was carried in the jug hoisted by the man. Thus the man is Isis's priest and, in a sense, a stand-in for the goddess herself.

Just as Blundell's female statues of Egyptian type were all named 'Isis', so the males were called 'idols'. By calling them idols, Blundell adopted a nomenclature that had been well established among European observers for at least a century — notwithstanding their varied burial styles, all mummies were 'idols', shabti figures were 'idols', and amulets were 'little idols'.[38] Despite the growing visibility of Egyptian and Egyptianizing monuments in Rome and elsewhere, and an increased scholarly treatment of the subject, many eighteenth-century collectors and observers continued to look at Egyptian art through a biblical lens.[39] Connoisseurs may have been able to quote Winckelmann on the aesthetic traits of Egyptian sculpture, but even those (like Blundell) who acknowledged its virtues assumed that all Egyptian art had a religious intent. Mistaking a male figure carved in red

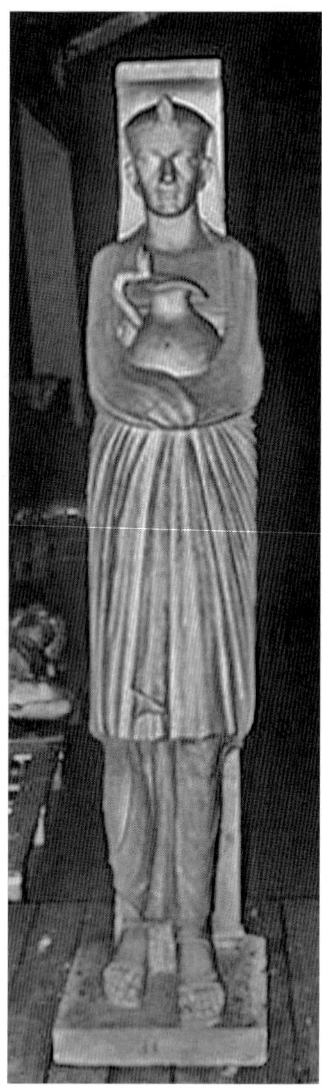

FIG. 12.5. ***Statue of a Water-Carrier***, front view. Marble. Liverpool Museums, Ince 11. *(Photo: Elizabeth Bartman. Reproduced courtesy of National Museums Liverpool, World Museum Liverpool.)*

granite as religious rather than the simple portrait it is, Blundell wrote that it was 'strange that such ridiculous figures should ever have been objects of adoration'; the baboon statue from his collection (**Fig. 12.8**) was a 'wonderful specimen of what absurd objects were formerly in veneration with the Egyptians'.[40] Of the baboon, Blundell also noted that antiquarians often called it Osiris for its generative capacity (whereas Egyptologists today associate the baboon, or *cyncocephalos*, with the god Thoth and the sun).

DEISM AND THE CONCEPT OF UNIVERSAL HISTORY

In a published appendix to Blundell's *Account*, a Walter Green M.D. provided an excursus on Bacchus in which he equated the Roman god with Osiris and noted that some also associated him with Noah. Connections between the Egyptian and Graeco-Roman gods were a commonplace of contemporary literature, with Bernard de Montfaucon making a similar argument in his multi-volume *Antiquité expliqué*; here, de Montfaucon conflated Osiris with a host of male gods such as Bacchus, Helios, Jupiter and Apollo, and saw Osiris's female counterpart, Isis, as synonymous with Ceres, Juno, Luna, Terra Minerva, Cybele, Venus and various other female deities: 'in short, all the goddesses', he wrote.[41] His equations owed much to the ancients themselves, for Herodotus and others who were read in the eighteenth century had noted parallels between the functions and domains of Egyptian and Graeco-Roman gods. Involving as they did deities worshipped in the distant past, these discussions could be seen as innocent antiquarian debates. When Osiris and Bacchus were likened to Moses, however, as a number of eighteenth-century theologians and writers argued,[42] the stakes were much higher; indeed, the fundamental tenets of Christianity came under attack. Here we move into the realm of Deism, an interpretation of Christianity that sought to strip it of its mystical, revelatory aspects.

Deists (and likewise Spinozists and Freemasons) regarded Egypt as the source of ultimate wisdom.[43] Others saw in Egypt the origins of Jewish law, Chinese writing, east Asian religion, even Druid circles![44] In 1761 John Turbeville Needham claimed that Egypt had founded China as a colony, while an anonymous tract of 1706 argued that the English system of weights and measures derived from the measurements of the pyramids. Today such notions are risible, but at the time they seemed to corroborate fundamental tenets of Enlightenment thought regarding the equality of man and the interconnectedness of all things. With the translation of hieroglyphic writing by Jean-François Champollion in 1824, however, the myth of Egyptian wisdom that had long enthralled Europeans was debunked.[45] With it went the many eighteenth-century theories that espoused universal history and promoted Egypt's centrality among world civilizations.

While modern perceptions of ancient Egypt have shifted dramatically, our critical assessment of its art still owes much to eighteenth-century observers such as Winckelmann and his patron in Rome, Cardinal Alessandro Albani. Not only their writings but also the way in which Egyptian art was displayed expressed new, if sometimes contradictory, attitudes. Rome was the intellectual epicentre, as the city was the only

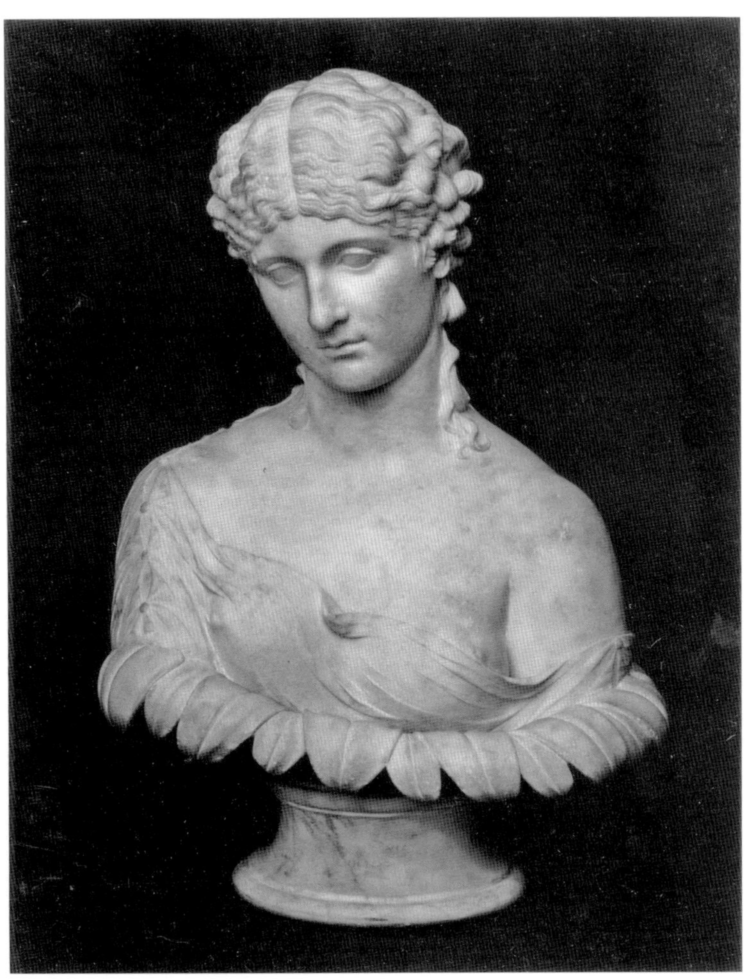

FIG. 12.6. *Portrait Statue of a Woman, 'Clytie'*, front view. Marble. London, The British Museum GR 1805.7-3.79. *(Photo: © The Trustees of the British Museum.)*

place outside Egypt that Egyptian art in any quantity could be seen. Although it had garnered considerable humanist attention from as early as the Renaissance,[46] it was not until the eighteenth century that scholars attempted a systematic treatment of the material. Within a short span of years at approximately the mid-century, two major surveys of ancient art were published — the multi-volume *Recueil d'antiquités* by the Comte de Caylus (1761), and the already-mentioned *History of Ancient Art* by Winckelmann.[47] Although Caylus disavowed a profound knowledge of Egypt, his comparison of Egyptian art, particularly architecture, to the ancient cultures in Italy attempted a pan-mediterranean synthesis that was overtly historical. Moreover, his aesthetic approach to Egyptian art paralleled the work of Winckelmann, whose near-poetic descriptions of many ancient statues earned him the nickname 'father of art history'. Winckelmann's inspired writing — not to mention his swift translation into Italian and French (an English translation did not appear until the mid-nineteenth century)[48] — ensured his wide reception by learned persons throughout Europe as well as the many British Grand Tourists who purchased works of art.

Given Winckelmann's well-documented aesthetic idealization of Greek art, his more negative assessment of Egyptian is not surprising. In his view, Egyptian artists were hindered by their customs, laws and 'modes of thought'; thus they never reached the heights of Greek art.[49] Yet within this overall critical judgment, Winckelmann found many works to admire; through close examination, he posited a chronological scheme by which he accounted for the artistic changes that occurred over the many centuries in which Egyptian artists worked. In addition, he was among the first to recognize that much surviving Egyptian statuary from Italy was in fact of Roman production, made in imitation of pharaonic monuments. Because his writings were read so widely, Winckelmann's evaluation of Egyptian art had an enormous impact on eighteenth-century intellectual thought.

To what extent Winckelmann's thinking was influenced by that of his patron, Albani, remains unclear. Albani had already formed two major collections before Winckelmann arrived in Rome,[50] and Egyptian works figured prominently in both. His final collection, acquired and installed in the Villa Albani with the guidance of Winckelmann, contained a mix of Roman, Greek and Egyptian works.[51] In many rooms of the large villa, these were displayed together in a kind of cross-cultural harmony; however, from contemporary renderings and the names historically associated with certain villa spaces (for example the Gabinetto Egiziano of 1765 and the Stanza del Canopo),[52] it appears that Albani also created rooms for the exclusive display of Egyptian works. In its museological construction, then, the Villa Albani seems to look in two contradictory directions — it both segregates and integrates Egyptian art vis-à-vis the more familiar classical. Shortly after, taste in Rome shifted towards segregation, as can be seen in Mengs's *Sala dei Papiri* of 1776 for the Museo Pio-Clementino and Antonio Asprucci's Egyptian room at the Villa Borghese (1779–82).

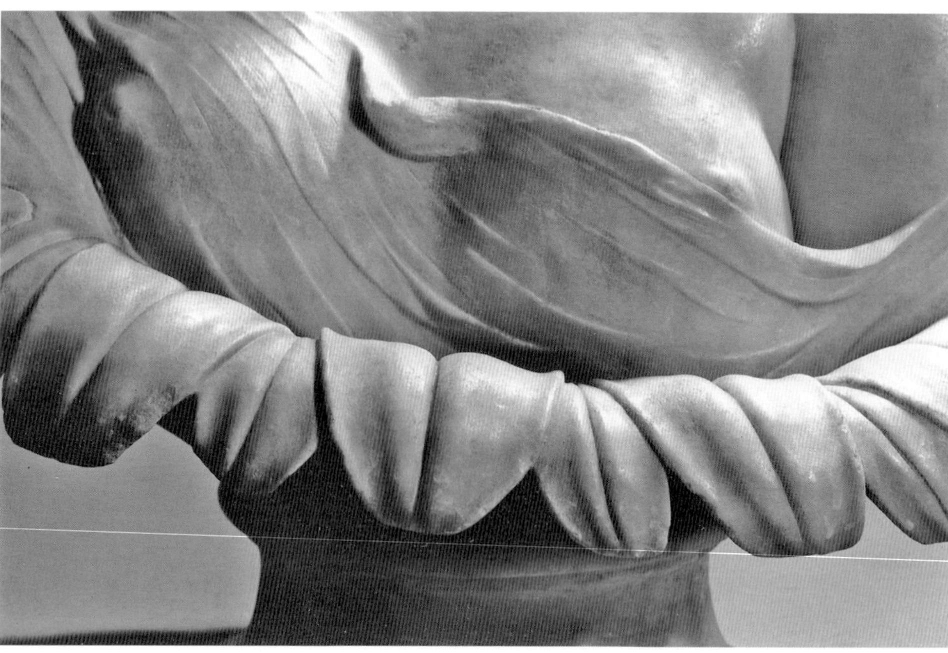

FIG. 12.7. ***Portrait Statue of a Woman, 'Clytie'***, detail of floral base. Marble. London, The British Museum GR 1805.7-3.79. *(Photo: © The Trustees of the British Museum.)*

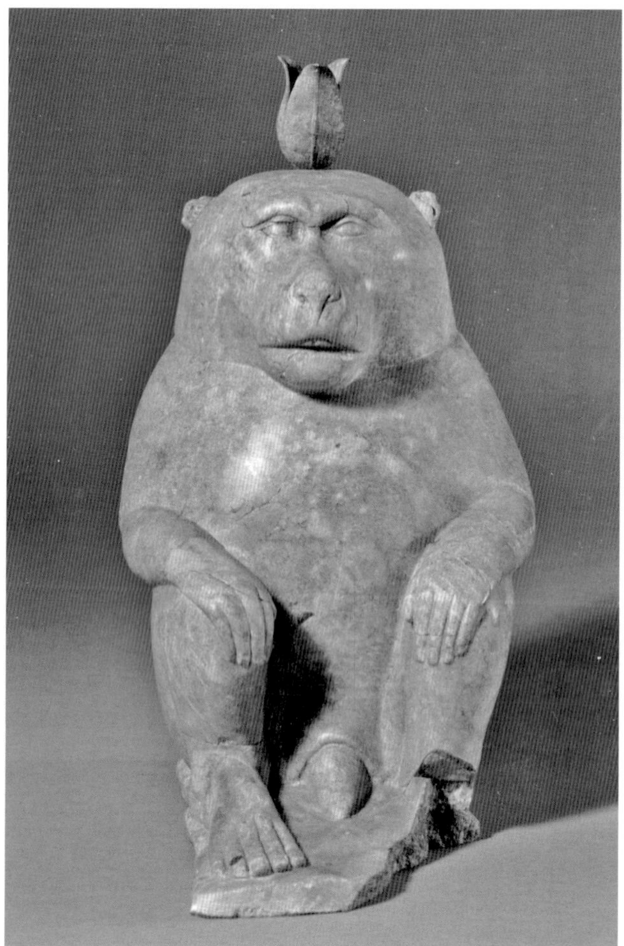

FIG. 12.8. ***Statue of a Baboon***. Grey hard stone. Liverpool Museums, Ince 78. *(Photo: David Flower. Reproduced courtesy of National Museums Liverpool, World Museum Liverpool.)*

In contrast, eighteenth-century British collectors combined ancient works from Egypt, Greece and Rome in arrangements dictated more by scale or iconography than ethnic source.[53] One might argue that their relative paucity would have made a segregated display rather sparse, but certainly both Townley and Blundell had enough Egyptian-looking works to create a separate tableau if they had so desired. Instead, they adopted the mixed approach that they had both seen in the old aristocratic and public collections in Rome, an approach that was endorsed implicitly by the reigning authors of the period. The interconnectedness of the ancients, as the Comte de Caylus would say, found visual expression in the salons and libraries of England, while the Roman provenance of so many works solidified its reputation as *caput mundi*.

NOTES

* This article forms part of a larger study of the ideal sculpture collected by Henry Blundell for Ince. I am grateful to the British School at Rome and to the organizers of *Roma Britannica* for the opportunity to locate some of Blundell's pieces in their broader intellectual context. As this study took me into much unfamiliar scholarly terrain, I relied upon the expertise of many colleagues. In particular I wish to thank Jeffrey Collins, Brian Curran and Christopher Johns for helping me navigate the post-modern period; and Sally-Ann Ashton and Richard Fazzini for aid on Egyptian matters. Sue Russell aided on many practical fronts, as did the staff of the Department of Egyptian Antiquities at the British Museum. I am grateful to Brian Cook for sharing his extensive archival research on Charles Townley, and Thorsten Opper for his assistance.

1. Some examples are included in the Society of Dilettanti's *Specimens of Ancient Sculpture* I (London, 1809) and II (London, 1835). Other scattered sources are the volumes *Antike Skulpturen in Englischen Schlössern*, published in the *Monumenta Artis Romanae* series (1986–), with the support of the Forschungsarchiv für Antike Plastik in Cologne. For a recent treatment of this general subject, see T. Knox, 'The Vyne Ramesses: 'Egyptian monstrosities' in British country house collections', *Apollo* 147 (April 2003), 32–8.
2. Now Brooklyn Museum of Art 56.85; A. Grimm and G. Mina Zeni (eds), *Winckelmann e l'Egitto. La riscoperta dell'arte egizia nel XVIII secolo* (Bern, 2004), 152–5, 158.
3. A. Smith, *A Catalogue of Ancient Marbles of Lansdowne House* (London, 1889), 36 no. 76b.
4. Figures of Antinous and Isis that were incorporated into the chimney-piece commissioned for the library at Lansdowne House (Smith, *Catalogue of Ancient Marbles* (above, n. 3), 36 no. 76a; sold Christie's, London 5 March 1930 (lot 70)). An eighteenth-century watercolour illustrated in another Lansdowne sale catalogue shows the chimney-piece (Christie's, London 5 July 1995, fig. 3).
5. Smith, *Catalogue of Ancient Marbles (*above, n. 3), 58. The letter introduces a number of themes to which I shall return later in this paper. Hamilton's erroneous characterization of the head as a herm must stem from the clean break and holes for piecing. By quoting the text in full, I hope to overturn the long-standing tradition of linking this head with the Albani Collection. It is unclear, however, to which Albani piece Hamilton was referring (possibly the statue of Isis now in Munich (Grimm and Mina Zeni, *Winckelmann e l'Egitto* (above, n. 2), 131–3 no. 105)).
6. The collector Henry Blundell wrote that Egyptian figures in dark stone were rare and 'much sought after by the antiquarians' (*An Account of the Statues, Busts, Bass-relieves, Cinerary Urns, and other Ancient Marbles and Paintings at Ince* (Liverpool, 1803), 138).
7. Now British Museum EA 97; B. Cook, *The Townley Marbles* (London, 1985), fig. 43; E. Russmann, *Eternal Egypt. Masterworks of Ancient Art from the British Museum* (London, 2001), 246–7 no. 135; J. Malek, *Topographical Bibliography of Ancient Egyptian Hieroglyphic Texts, Statues, Reliefs, and Paintings* 8. *Objects of Provenance Not Known Part* 1, *Royal Statues. Private Statues (Predynastic to Dynasty XVII)* (Oxford, 1999), 159–60. Both Amasis and Nectanebos I have been suggested as the subject. Some decades earlier, however, Townley had acquired some minor works such as statuettes (a figure of Bes, now British Museum EA 47973 and an 'Egyptian figure in Basalt', EA 989), as well as alabaster vases (EA 34875, EA 34876).
8. Catalogue of Ancient Marbles Collected in Mr. Townley's House, Park Street, Westminster 1804, MS now in the Department of Greek and Roman Antiquities, British Museum, no. 24. By 1809, the publication date of *Specimens of Ancient Sculpture* I (above, n. 1), pl. 3, its identification had shifted to 'Osiris'.
9. Present whereabouts unknown. Sold Christie's, London, 5 July 1995, pp. 18–21, lot 221; with earlier bibliography.
10. The large-scale Antinous owned by Thomas Hope did not suit the scale of Egyptian works installed in the 'Egyptian Room' he designed for his house at Duchess Street, London, of 1802. He reproduced the room in his *Household Furniture* of 1807. See D. Watkin and P. Hewat-Jaboor (eds), *Thomas Hope, Regency Designer* (New Haven/London, 2008), 34–6 and fig. 2-15. The Antinous is in Port Sunlight: G. Waywell, *The Lever and Hope Sculptures* (Berlin, 1986), 94 no. 52 fig. 24.
11. Hamilton told Lord Shelburne that the statue was found in 1769 (Smith, *Catalogue of Ancient Marbles* (above, n. 3), 52). For other Egyptianizing statuary from the villa, see J. Raeder, *Die Statuarische Ausstattung der Villa Hadriana bei Tivoli* (Frankfurt, 1983), *passim*; J.-C. Grenier, *La décoration statuaire du 'Serapeum' der 'Canope' de la Villa Adriana* (Rome, 1990); and the new finds connected to the 'Antinoeion' (Z. Mari and S. Sgalambro, 'The Antinoeion of Hadrian's Villa: interpretation and architectural reconstruction', *American Journal of Archaeology* 111 (2007), 83–104).
12. J. Winckelmann, *History of Ancient Art* I, trans. G. Lodge, 4 vols (Boston, 1849–73), I, 178; his views were picked up by: the Baron d'Hancarville (*Recherches sur l'origine, l'esprit et les progrès des arts de la Grèce; sur leurs connections avec les arts et la religion des plus anciens peuples connus; sur les monuments antiques de l'Inde, de la Perse, du reste de l'Asie de l'Europe et de l'Egypte* (Paris, 1785), II, 13), James Dallaway (*Anecdotes of the Arts in England* (London, 1800)) and the Society of Dilettanti (*Specimens of Ancient Sculpture* I (above, n. 1), text accompanying plate 2).
13. The Lansdowne head, whether or not originally part of Cardinal Albani's collection, almost certainly came from Rome. The circumstances under which Townley's head was acquired raise some doubt: he bought it from Michel Ferdinand, 8th Duc de Chaulnes, and Townley's accounts for 27 April 1795 record a payment 'To Charle Paris his draft for an Isis in basalte'. While this suggests acquisition in Paris, as apparently does Townley's handwritten list of the

best pieces in the collection (TY14/4/5, Townley Archive, The British Museum), it does not clarify the ultimate origin of the piece. Richard Payne Knight, who purchased a statuette of a ram-headed god from the Duke's collection, attributed it to Egypt (see M. Clarke and N. Penny (eds), *The Arrogant Connoisseur: Richard Payne Knight 1751–1824* (Manchester, 1982), 134 no. 38). Townley's head, however, possibly had been inherited by the Duke from a relative who had been ambassador to Rome in the seventeenth century.

14. O. Lollio Barberi, G. Parola and M. Toti, *Le antichità egiziane di Roma imperiale* (Rome, 1995) looks at the various collections formed during the sixteenth to eighteenth centuries.
15. J. Wortham, *The Genesis of British Egyptology 1549–1906* (Norman, 1971), 24–47; J. Black, *The British Abroad. The Grand Tour in the Eighteenth Century* (New York, 1992), 72.
16. So John Montagu, Earl of Sandwich, and William Ponsonby, Earl of Bessborough. Both men had visited Egypt in the late 1730s; B. Redford, 'The measure of ruins: Dilettanti in the Levant 1750–1770', *Harvard Library Bulletin* n.s. 13 (2002), 5–36.
17. These figured prominently in the collections of Dr Richard Mead, Sir Hans Sloane and Colonel William Lethieullier, which were donated to the British Museum on its foundation in 1753. See S. Moser, *Wondrous Curiosities. Ancient Egypt at the British Museum* (Chicago/London, 2006), 33–41; some pieces were included in K. Sloan (ed.), *Enlightenment. Discovering the World in the Eighteenth Century* (London, 2003). As Moser pointed out (p. 73), it was not until Britain's imperial presence in Egypt during the post-Napoleonic age that there were naval resources to ferry colossal monuments back to England.
18. A 1749 capriccio depicts an Egyptian obelisk framed by a Roman triumphal arch (Paris, Musée Nationale du Louvre MNR312; F. Arisi, *Gian Paolo Panini e i fasti della Roma del '700* (Rome, 1986), 426 no. 391).
19. In the final version of the painting, now in Frankfurt, the hieroglyphs are nearly invisible, but the painter's intent is known from a contemporaneous copy made *c.* 1787 as well as its original title 'Wanderer auf dem Obelisk' (Weimar, Goethe-Nationalmuseum, Grafische Sammlung); J. Endrödi, 'Die Ewigkeit der Ägyptomanie', in W. Seipel (ed.), *Ägyptomanie* (Vienna, 2000), 161 fig. 2. For a similar mix of Roman and Egyptian antiques see the 1797 portrait of Allen Smith by François-Xavier Fabre, set implausibly in Tuscany (Cambridge, The Fitzwilliam Museum; S. Allard, R. Rosenblum, M. Stevens and G. Scherf, *Citizens and Kings: Portraiture in the Age of David and Goya, 1770–1830* (London, 2007), 320–1 no. 113, fig. on p. 255).
20. Augsburg, Städtische Kunstsammlungen inv. no. 12634. See S. Roettgen, *Anton Raphael Mengs, 1728–1779* I. *Das Malerische und Zeichnerische Werk* (Munich, 1999), 154–6 no. 104, col. pl. 6.
21. Formerly Ince Blundell Hall, now Liverpool Museums, Ince 11; B. Ashmole, *A Catalogue of the Ancient Marbles at Ince Blundell Hall* (Oxford, 1929), 29 no. 54 pl. 18. Restorations include the head with the *nemes* head-cloth and uraeus.
22. This type of figure is documented amply in Rome, from a monumental granite column that once decorated the Sanctuary of Isis in the Campus Martius (now in the Museo Capitolino; A. Roullet, *The Egyptian and Egyptianizing Monuments of Imperial Rome* (Leiden, 1972), 58 nos. 17–19, pl. 30) to an *opus sectile* wall from the Basilica of Junius Bassus in Rome (now in the Museo Nazionale Romano 375830; illustration on p. 256 and catalogue entry by E. Calandra in A. La Regina (ed.), *Palazzo Massimo alle Terme* (Milan, 1998)).
23. R. Venuti, *Vetera Monumenta quae in Hortis Caelimontis et in Aedibus Matthaeiorum Adservantur, nunc Primum in Unum Collecta et Adnotationibus Illustrata* III (Rome, 1779), 5.49, pl. 26.2. The relief is now in the Musei Vaticani, Cortile del Belvedere 55; W. Amelung, *Die Sculpturen des Vatikanischen Museums* II (Berlin, 1903), 142–5 no. 55, pl. 7.
24. J.J. Winckelmann, *Geschichte der Kunst des Altertums* (Dresden, 1764), I.3 102 and 107 (J.J. Winckelmann, *Schriften und Nachlass* (ed. A. Borbein *et al.*) (Mainz, 2006), 4.1, 162 and 170).
25. Winckelmann, *History of Ancient Art* (above, n. 12). But that he considered the two together marked a major intellectual development, which I shall discuss below. Winckelmann's writings on Egyptian art were highly influential, not only for his criticisms but also specific points of chronology — he was the first to recognize that some works that looked Egyptian were actually Roman. Echoes of this thinking, if not direct quotations, can be found in Dallaway, *Anecdotes* (above, n. 12) and Blundell, *An Account* (above, n. 6).
26. On his attitudes towards the male and female bodies, see A. Potts, *Flesh and the Ideal. Winckelmann and the Origins of Art History* (New Haven/London, 1994).
27. Blundell, *An Account* (above, n. 6), 284–5 app. 4.
28. So Ince 11, 28, 80 and 150 (entries in Blundell, *An Account* (above, n. 6), although 28 is an archaistic female and 150 is an Apollo). Ironically, Ince 58 and 59 are called male but instead do represent the female goddess or one of her priestesses.
29. British Museum GR 1805.7-3.79; A. Smith, *The British Museum. A Catalogue of Sculpture in the Department of Greek and Roman Antiquities* III (London, 1904), no. 1874.
30. Burnley, Townley Hall Art Gallery and Museums; Cook, *Townley Marbles* (above, n. 7), fig. 30; B. Cook, 'The Townley marbles in Westminster and Bloomsbury', *Collectors and Collections. British Museum Yearbook* 2 (1977), 34–78; M. Webster, *Johan Zoffany 1733–1810* (London, 1966).
31. Although it bears similarities to the lotus, the bifurcated, longish leaf with a slightly curved tip is not in fact found on actual specimens of the water plant. For a sample of Egyptian plant forms, see E. Wilson, *Ancient Egyptian Designs* (London, 1986), figs 40–4. B. de Montfaucon, *Antiquité expliqué* II (Paris, 1719; English translation by D. Humphreys (London, 1721)), pl. 38 no. 19, had identified the subject of a gem as Isis seated on a flower; perhaps this influenced Townley.

32. Over the years the statue's identification has coursed through history and myth, changing from Agrippina (the identification probably closest to the truth) to Libera to Clytie, the deserted lover of Helios who was changed into a flower.
33. Townley Notebook C, quoted by G. Vaughan, *The Collecting of Classical Antiquities in England in the 18th Century. A Study of Charles Townley (1737–1805) and His Circle* (D.Phil. thesis, University of Oxford, 1988), 221 n. 162. My discussion owes much to Vaughan's observations.
34. For example, the 'Isis in basaltes' discussed above (p. 171). See as well in Catalogue of Ancient Marbles Collected in Mr. Townley's House (above, n. 8), a statuette of Isis or Libera (Staircase no. 4, Dining Room no. 47); a statuette of Isis 'in her character of Fortune' (Dining Room no. 16).
35. See Giovanni Battista Piranesi's engraving, *Veduta del tempio di Iside* (E. Arslan, *Iside. Il mito. Il mistero. La magia* (Milan 1997), 339).
36. Contemporary listeners described him as a 'vivacious raconteur' (F. Haskell, 'The Baron d'Hancarville: an adventurer and art historian in eighteenth-century Europe', in F. Haskell, *Past and Present in Art and Taste. Selected Essays* (New Haven/London, 1987), 30).
37. *Recherches sur l'origine* (above, n. 12). See P. Funnell, 'The symbolical language of antiquity', in Clarke and Penny (eds), *The Arrogant Connoisseur* (above, n. 13), 50–64. S. de Caro (ed.), *Il gabinetto segreto del Museo Archeologico Nazionale di Napoli* (Naples, 2000), 10, discussed d'Hancarville's interest in erotica.
38. These descriptions are found in various seventeenth-century sources cited in H. Whitehouse, 'Egyptology and forgery in the seventeenth century: the case of the Bodleian Shabti', *Journal of the History of Collections* 1 (2) (1989), 187–95. The attitude of William Guthrie and John Gray is typical: '... idolatry seems at length to have over-run all Egypt, to a degree almost incredible. Notwithstanding their boasted wisdom, the Egyptians paid divine honours to several beasts, and even to vegetables, as leeks and onions' (*A General History of the World* (London, 1764), 70).
39. See also Moser, *Wondrous Curiosities* (above, n. 17), 57.
40. Both of these are Egyptianizing rather than Egyptian. Male: Ince 548 (Blundell, *An Account* (above, n. 6), no. 548; baboon: Ince 78 (Ashmole, *Catalogue of the Ancient Marbles at Ince Blundell Hall* (above, n. 21), 30 no. 57).
41. De Montfaucon, *Antiquité expliqué* II (above, n. 31), 171–2.
42. C. Dupuis, *Abrégé de l'or. Origine de tous les cultes* (Paris, 1822).
43. J. Assmann, 'Jehova-Isis. Egypt and the quest for natural religion in the age of Enlightenment', in Seipel (ed.), *Ägyptomanie* (above, n. 19), 289–96.
44. For a general survey, see D. Haycock, 'Ancient Egypt in 17th and 18th century England', in P. Ucko and T. Champion (eds), *The Wisdom of Ancient Egypt: Changing Visions through the Ages* (London, 2003), 133–60. On Egypt, India and China, see J. Bryant, *A New System: or an Analysis of Ancient Mythology* (London, 1774). Major proponents of connections between the Druids and the Egyptians included William Stukeley and Alexander Gordon; see R. Sweet, *Antiquaries. The Discovery of the Past in Eighteenth-century Britain* (London/New York, 2004), 130–1.
45. E. Iversen, *The Myth of Egypt and its Hieroglyphs in European Tradition* (Copenhagen, 1961); S. Marchand, 'The end of Egyptomania: German scholarship and the banalization of Egypt, 1830–1914', in Seipel, *Ägyptomanie* (above, n. 19), 125–33.
46. B. Curran, *The Egyptian Renaissance: the Afterlife of Ancient Egypt in Early Modern Italy* (Chicago, 2007); J. Curl, *The Egyptian Revival. Ancient Egypt as the Inspiration for Design Motifs in the West*, third edition (London/New York, 2005), especially chapters 2 and 3.
47. Comte de Caylus, *Recueil d'antiquités égyptiennes, étrusques, grecques et romaines*, 7 vols (Paris, 1761). See also n. 12.
48. The *Geschichte* was not translated into English until 1849–73; rather, it was Winckelmann's earlier *Gedanken über die Nachahmung der Griechischen Werke in der Malerei und Bildhauerkunst* (Friedrichstadt, 1755) that was translated into English by Henry Fuseli in 1767.
49. Winckelmann, *History of Ancient Art* (above, n. 12), II, 167. The adjectives 'primitive' and 'imitative' appear frequently.
50. The first was sold to Friedrich August II of Saxony in 1728 (now Dresden, Staatliche Kunstsammlungen) and the second to Clement XII in 1733 (for what is now the Capitoline Museum).
51. P. Bol (ed.), *Forschungen zur Villa Albani: Katalog der Antiken Bildwerke* I (Berlin, 1988), 135; S. Curto, *Le sculture egizie e egittizzanti nelle ville Torlonia in Roma* (*Études préliminaires aux religions orientales dans l'empire romain* 105) (Leiden, 1985).
52. For a view of the Gabinetto see the drawing of Charles Percier from the early 1770s. What Percier called the 'Appartement des Bains' no longer exists and is possibly a fiction. Both are reproduced in J. Humbert (ed.), *Egyptomania. L'Égypte dans l'art occidental 1730–1930* (Paris, 1994), 20.
53. Hope's so-called 'Egyptian room' (above, n. 10) adheres to this new trend, but this has been described more as a 'decorative concept than an overriding historical theme' (W. Ernst, 'Frames at work: museological imagination and historical discourse in neoclassical Britain', *The Art Bulletin* 75 (1993), 484).

From Homer to Faustina the Younger: representations of antiquity in Batoni's British Grand Tour portraits

Edgar Peters Bowron

Pompeo Batoni (1708–87) first attracted the attention of the British in Rome with the drawn copies of classical statuary that he began to produce shortly after his arrival in the city in May 1727.[1] For a brief period the artist joined the ranks of the professional copyists who worked for antiquarians, amateurs and engravers, and his drawings after the antique provided both a source of income and the basis of his earliest local reputation. Francesco Benaglio (1708–59) made clear in his early account of Batoni's life that it was his copies of the classical sculptures in the Belvedere Courtyard of the Vatican that first attracted his English patrons.[2] Batoni appears to have gained this entrée through the painter Francesco Fernandi, called Imperiali (1679–1740), who served as an antiquary and specialist in guiding British visitors on their excursions around the sights of Rome, and played the role of agent and entrepreneur for those amateurs who wished to obtain drawings of the classical sculptures they had admired during their visit to the city.

The most important of Imperiali's clients to come to light is Richard Topham (1671–1730) of Windsor, whose drawings of classical antiquities in Rome by various Italian artists, some from the sixteenth and seventeenth centuries but the majority from the eighteenth, constitute a survey of the classical sculptures contained in Roman collections of the period 1725–30.[3] Among Batoni's 53 drawings in the Topham Collection at Eton College are records of the most celebrated antiquities in the collections of Cardinal Alessandro Albani (1692–1779) (Plate 13.1), drawn before Albani was forced to sell a group of antiquities in 1733–4 to Pope Clement XII (1652–1740), who made it the nucleus of a new museum on the Capitol. He drew as well the ancient marbles in the Villa Ludovisi, Palazzo Ruspoli, Palazzo Farnese and Palazzo Barberini, among other collections in Rome. One of the most famous antiquities recorded by Batoni at the time is the so-called *Cupid and Psyche* belonging to Count Giuseppe Fede (*c.* 1700–77), a collector-excavator who made important finds at Hadrian's Villa near Tivoli.[4]

The importance of Batoni's activity as a professional copyist for his development as a painter should not be underestimated, because in the course of making hundreds of drawings after ancient statues, busts and sarcophagi, he acquired an extraordinary grasp of the problems of conveying three-dimensional form onto a two-dimensional surface, and he quickly learned the means of imparting a vigorous sculptural quality to the forms in his drawings and paintings. Even after the Topham commission of about 1730, Batoni continued his activity as a professional copyist. The evidence for this exists in the engraving after his drawing of one of the two centaurs that were uncovered during the excavations of Monsignor Giuseppe Alessandro Furietti (1685–1764) at Hadrian's Villa in December 1736. Batoni's bold depiction of the young centaur, the basis of the reproductive engraving by Giovanni Girolamo Frezza (1659–after 1741) (Plate 13.2), is extraordinarily faithful to the original[5] and remarkable for the handling of contour, silhouette and tonality.

Although this youthful practice of drawing antiquities in Roman collections provided Batoni with an understanding of ancient art rivalled by few painters in the city — Gavin Hamilton (1723–98) and Anton Raphael Mengs (1728–79) come to mind — he did not employ his knowledge of classical antiquity to significant advantage in Grand Tour portraits until two decades later. Although we associate Batoni's portraits of young Irish, English and Scots visitors to Italy with his emblematic use of antiquities and views of Rome to establish both the presence of the young men in Rome and their status as learned, cultivated, yet leisured, aristocrats, antiquities are in fact notably absent in his earliest portraits. Joseph Leeson (1701–83), 1st Earl of Milltown, who sat to Batoni in 1744, and his son, the 2nd Earl, in 1751,[6] are both shown before a simplified background of draped curtain and architectural frame of columns and pilasters that provide no indication of the sitters' presence in Rome. The series of fanciful half-length portraits at Uppark commissioned in 1751 by Sir Matthew Fetherstonhaugh (*c.* 1715–74), 1st Baronet, of himself and his relations[7] depict the sitters in various rustic or hunting guises that provide no hint of where they were painted. And well into the 1750s Batoni continued to present the majority of his sitters in formats that underplayed their identities as visitors to Italy, such as the portraits of *John, Lord Brudenell, Later Marquess of Monthermer*, of 1758,[8] depicted with a musical instrument and the score of a Corelli violin sonata, and *Frederick, Lord North, Later 2nd Earl of Guildford*,[9] *c.* 1753–6, shown writing at a table.

By the middle of the eighteenth century, when Batoni took up portraiture in earnest, nearly all the features associated with the Grand Tour portrait — ancient architectural monuments, curtained backgrounds, finely carved furniture, classical busts, still lifes of globes, writing implements and books — had been anticipated by earlier Roman painters, beginning with *Robert Spencer, 2nd Earl of Sunderland* (*c.* 1661) by Carlo Maratti (1625–1713),[10] in which the sitter is depicted out-of-doors in Roman dress with his arm resting on a pedestal carved with a bas-relief and an antique fragment at his feet. Other precedents for the Grand Tour portrait include *William Johnstone, 1st Marquis of Annandale* (1713) by Andrea Procaccini (1671–1734),[11] in which the sitter is seated at a table with coins and a cameo, with a marble fragment at his feet, while presenting a statuette to the beholder; *Thomas Coke, 1st Earl of Leicester* (1717) (Fig. 7.10),[12] by Francesco Trevisani (1656–1746), whose subject is seated grandly with his dog in an ornate Baroque setting before a curtain parted to reveal a gallery of classical sculptures; and the same artist's portrait of *Sir Edward Gascoigne* (1725) (Plate 7.3),[13] showing Gascoigne seated at a table with a copy of Horace, pointing to a window that commands a view of the Colosseum.

Exactly why Batoni took so long to incorporate antique motifs into his portrait repertory, much less fully develop the format of a casually posed sitter in an open-air setting, surrounded by classical statuary and antique fragments or set against the backdrop of a classical building, is something of a mystery. Only after he had painted some 30 portraits of British sitters did Batoni employ a reference to classical antiquity as a portrait accessory, with *Robert Clements, Later 1st Earl of Leitrim* (Fig. 13.1), who presumably sat for his portrait in the late spring or early summer of 1753. Although Batoni painted more than 200 individual British visitors to Rome, there is no extant record of a sitter instructing the painter how he was to be portrayed. Presumably Batoni, or an intermediary like Thomas Jenkins (1722–98) or, later, James Byres (1734–1817), would have discussed in detail with each client the proposed presentation and resolved in advance such matters as pose, costume and accessories. That certain demands and concessions were made by both parties in the selection of the latter is inevitable, but the question remains open as to whether the archaeological insertions in Batoni's Grand Tour portraits held a personal meaning for either the sitter or commissioner of the portrait, or for both.

The bust of *Homer* in Clements's portrait, one of the most celebrated ancient portraits, corresponds in all essentials to a marble then in the Palazzo Farnese in Rome (Fig. 13.2).[14] Clements himself noted 'the famous bust of Homer, Antich & extremely fine' during his visit to the Farnese Collection in spring 1753, and thus the inclusion of the sculpture in his portrait may reflect a personal response to the aesthetic qualities of the work, as well as an appreciation of Homer as an eminent signifier of the classical tradition. For a number of contemporary observers, including Peter Beckford (1740–1811) — who noted in a letter to a friend following his visit to the Capitoline Collections, 'You will see many excellent busts of Homer, which will bring the Iliad to your remembrance' —, the ancient Greek author embodied the classical virtues that visitors to Italy sought to revive and imitate, and thus it is hardly surprising that the bust of Homer appears in at least two other Batoni portraits.[15] The contemporary appreciation for images of the poet in both Rome and England may be supported by many examples, such as its presence on a marble chimney-piece in the Saloon at Uppark carved by Thomas Carter (d. 1756) for Sir Matthew Fetherstonhaugh in about 1750.[16]

James Caulfield (1728–99), 4th Viscount Charlemont, later 1st Earl of Charlemont, who sat to Batoni in the second half of 1753,[17] also admired the Farnese *Homer*, and in March 1754 was permitted to export a number of marbles from Rome, including a copy of the bust.[18] His half-length portrait also stands at the very beginning of Batoni's evolution of a specifically

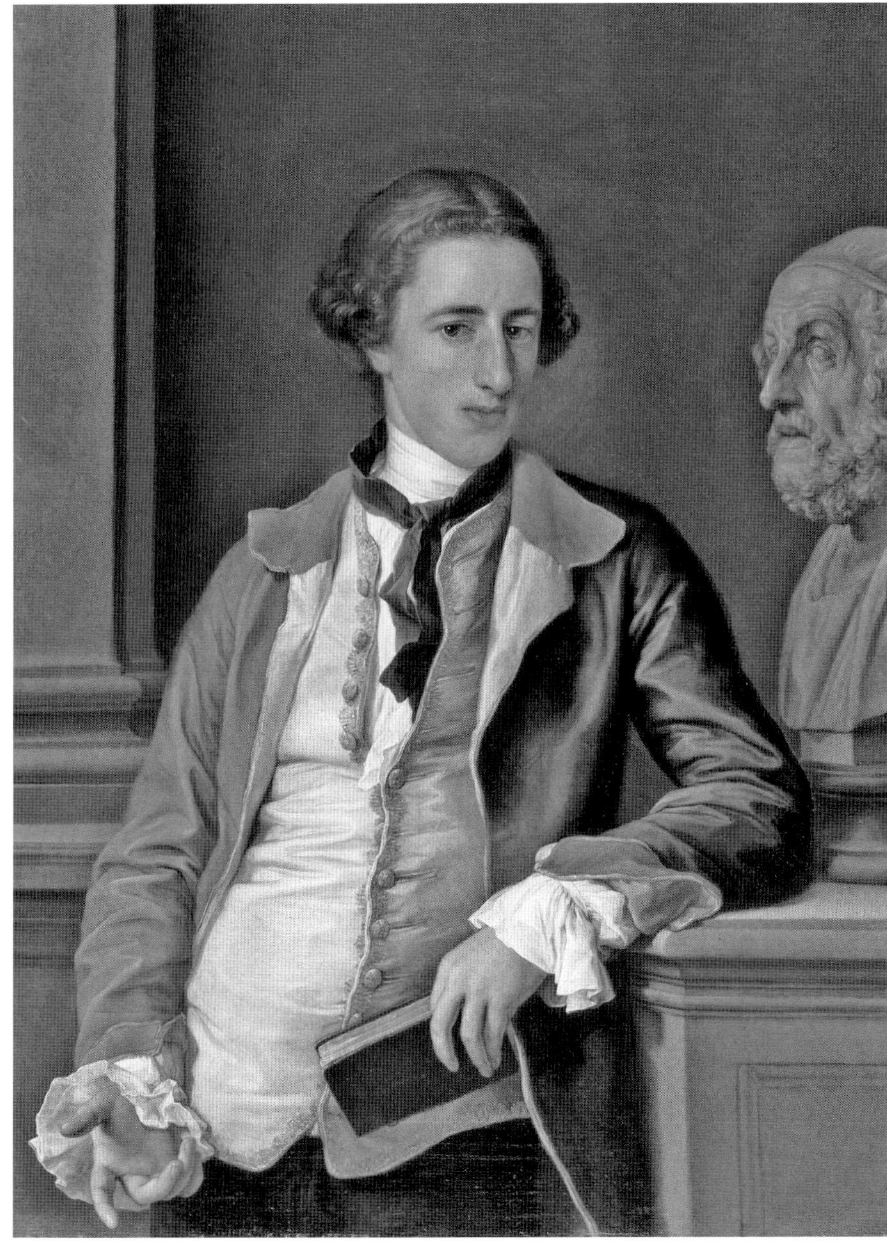

FIG. 13.1. Pompeo Batoni (1708–87), *Robert Clements, Later 1st Earl of Leitrim (1732–1804)*, c. 1753–4. Oil on canvas, 101 × 73 cm. Hood Museum of Art, Dartmouth College, Hanover, New Hampshire. Purchased through a gift from Barbara Dau Southwell, Class of 1978, in honour of Robert Dance, Class of 1977, a gift of William R. Acquavella, and the Florence and Lansing Porter Moore 1937 Fund. *(Reproduced courtesy of the Hood Museum of Art.)*

'Grand Tour' formula, but he is shown with a view of the Colosseum glimpsed in the background through the open window, rendered as if it were a small painting, in contrast to Batoni's later, more accomplished integration of the motif within a spatial continuum that convincingly includes the sitter.

In the late 1750s, Batoni established his *métier* as a Grand Tour portraitist with two full-length portraits of *Charles Compton, 7th Earl of Northhampton*, and *Sir Wyndham Knatchbull-Wyndham, 6th Bt.*, each of about 1758.[19] The latter in particular epitomizes Batoni's ability to transmute the seventeenth-century Baroque portraits of Sir Anthony van Dyck (1599–1641) into a sophisticated and subtle hybrid that persuasively assimilates the heritage of English painting to the sitter's presence in Rome. The debonair stance of Sir Wyndham (1737–63) was intended to evoke one of the most famous antiquities of the time, the *Apollo Belvedere*, which may account for the response of the German antiquarian Johann Joachim Winckelmann (1717–68), who considered it 'one of the best portraits in the world'.[20]

The bust at the left of each composition is derived from a full-length marble statue of *Minerva*, a Roman adaptation of a bronze original of the fourth century BC.[21] Batoni employed the *Minerva* as a table-top

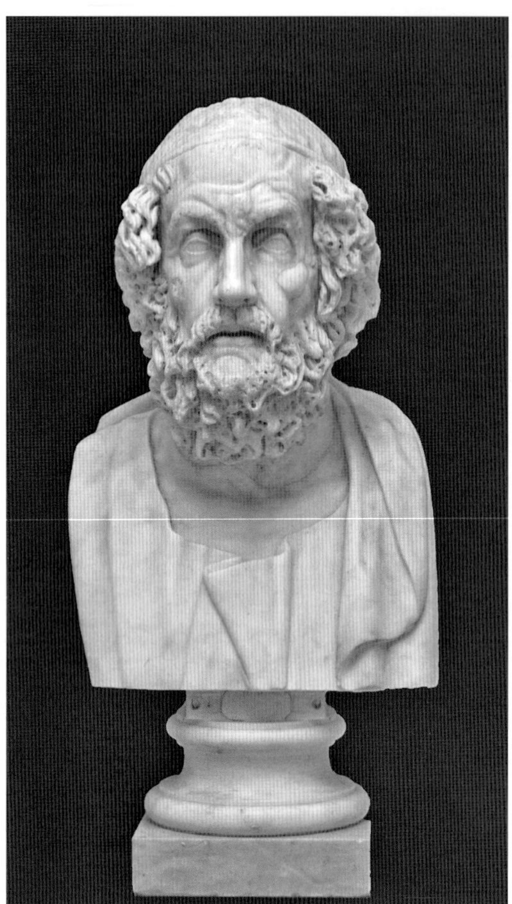
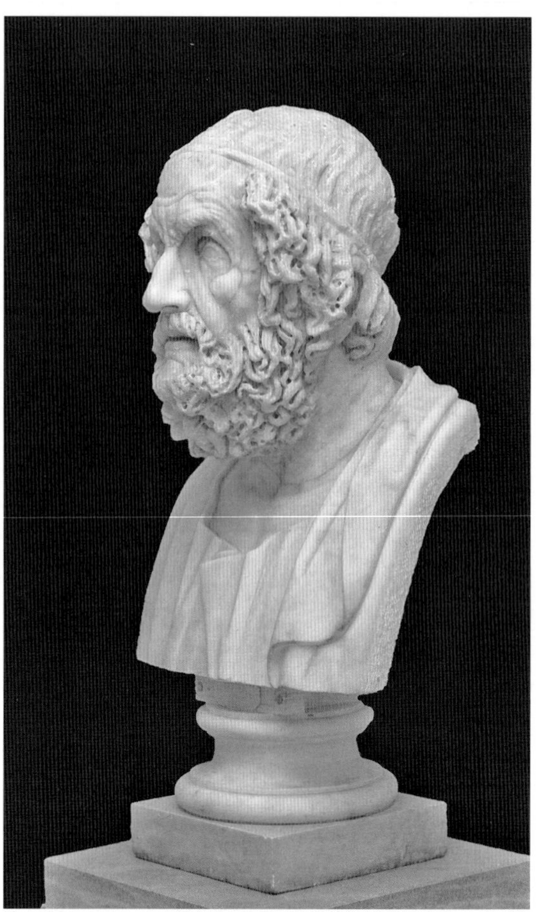

FIG. 13.2. Unknown sculptor, *Bust of Homer*, mid-second century BC. Marble. Naples, Museo Archeologico Naples. *(Photo: Giulio Archinà, Cosenza.)*

bust in at least twelve other portraits of British visitors to Rome during the next three decades, perhaps because the English in particular worshipped the statue; Johann Wolfgang von Goethe was told by the custodian of the Giustiniani Collection that they kissed one of its hands so frequently that it was whiter than the rest of the marble.[22]

The so-called Temple of the Sibyl at Tivoli in the background, another of Batoni's favorite antique references, was first employed in the full-length portrait of Sir Wyndham. The depiction of the temple is quite accurate, both by comparison with other eighteenth-century representations and with the ruin as it still exists. Tivoli was to contemporary Britons a powerful image, both because of its classical associations and because it was familiar to them as the sketching ground of the seventeenth-century landscape painters they most admired, Claude Lorrain (*c.* 1602–82) and Gaspard Dughet (1615–75). Batoni incorporated the ruin into nearly a dozen portrait compositions of Grand Tourists in the 1760s and 1770s.

For the most part, the antiquities Batoni depicted as portrait accessories were well established in the guidebooks his clients brought with them, along with maps, phrase books, lists of recommended inns and money conversion tables. Early in the century guidebooks like the Richardsons' *Account of Some of the Statues, Bas-reliefs, Drawings, and Pictures in Italy* were already directing tourists to the antique sculptures and monuments in Rome that were to appear later in Batoni's portraits.[23] The continued repetition of a relatively small number of ancient works in the guidebooks and travel diaries in the first half of the eighteenth century meant that after 1750 the majority of Batoni's sitters responded more or less conventionally to the sights of Rome and were favourably inclined towards a canonical group of antiquities in whose company they would be shown. The familiarity of a handful of motifs in Batoni's portraits alluding to the architecture and sculpture of ancient Rome — the Colosseum (incorporated into nearly a dozen portraits), for example, and the *Ludovisi Mars*, which appeared in five full-length portraits between 1768 and 1782, exactly when the popularity of the statue was at its height following Winckelmann's praise of the figure's repose[24] — has led to the belief that Batoni employed antique references willy-nilly, as mere 'studio props'. The ease with which he could orchestrate his sitters' poses, accessories and settings into agreeable and pleasing compositions — reversing a sculpture or the direction of a staircase so that it could be displayed at the left or right of a composition — contributes further to this view.

That Batoni was much more thoughtful and deliberate with regard to his use of archaeological allusions is confirmed by the number of antiquities employed in only a single portrait each; for example, the bust of the young *Marcus Aurelius* in the Capitoline displayed on a table beside a Grand Tourist identified as *Richard Milles* (*c.* 1758).[25] Other examples of antiquities making a single appearance in Batoni's British portraits include:

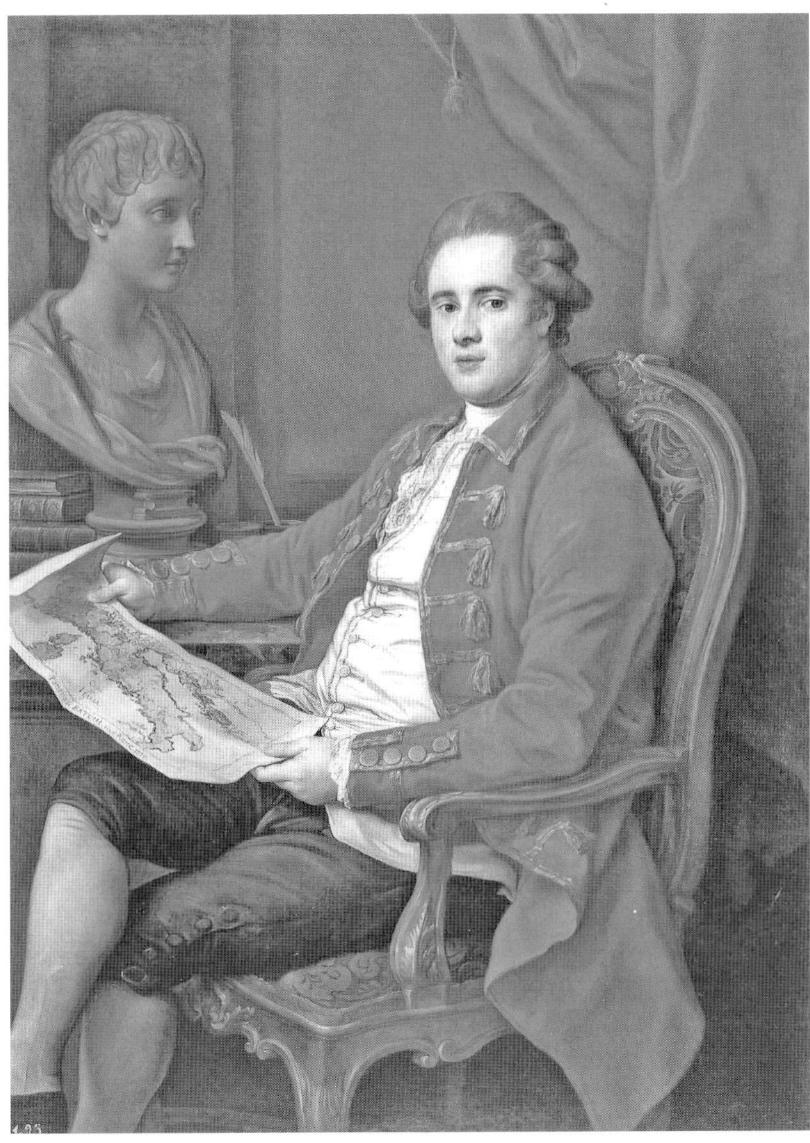

FIG. 13.3. Pompeo Batoni (1708–87), *George Legge, Viscount Lewisham (1755–1810)*, 1778. Oil on canvas, 127 × 100 cm. Museo Nacional del Prado. *(Photo: © Museo del Prado.)*

- a bust of the *Apollo Belvedere* embellishing *Edward Dering, Later 6th Bt.* (*c.* 1758–9),[26] although in fact the bust was quite common in Roman sculpture collections such as that in the Palazzo Giustiniani;
- a terracotta statuette of the *Farnese Hercules* shown on a table along with a reduction of the *Vatican Ariadne* in the portrait of *c.* 1761–2 of *Charles John Crowle* (1738–1811);[27]
- a marble krater beside *John Wodehouse, Later 1st Baron Wodehouse* (1764),[28] recorded in the encyclopedia of classical antiquities by Bernard de Montfaucon (1655–1741), *Antiquity Explained and Represented in Sculptures*,[29] but otherwise unknown;
- a marble urn, adorned with the relief figures of Mercury and the infant Bacchus, the so-called vase of Gaeta, which in the eighteenth century, after having been mutilated for 'decency', was employed as a baptismal font in the local cathedral and noted by numerous travellers in the south of Italy, incorporated into the portrait of *William Cavendish, 5th Duke of Devonshire* (1768);[30]
- a seated *Agrippina* in the Capitoline Collections well-known in the eighteenth century and admired by English visitors to Rome like Dr Charles Burney (1726–1814), who noted that it possessed 'such drapery and expression as I never saw in sculpture',[31] against which stands *John, Lord Montstuart, Later 4th Earl and 1st Marquess of Bute* (1767);[32]
- an unidentified sitter in the dress of a cavalry officer leaning on a pedestal beside a head of Menelaos from the so-called *Pasquino* group (1774);[33]
- and a bas-relief of the *Papirius* group in the Ludovisi Collection, whose popularity in the seventeenth, eighteenth and nineteenth centuries was reflected

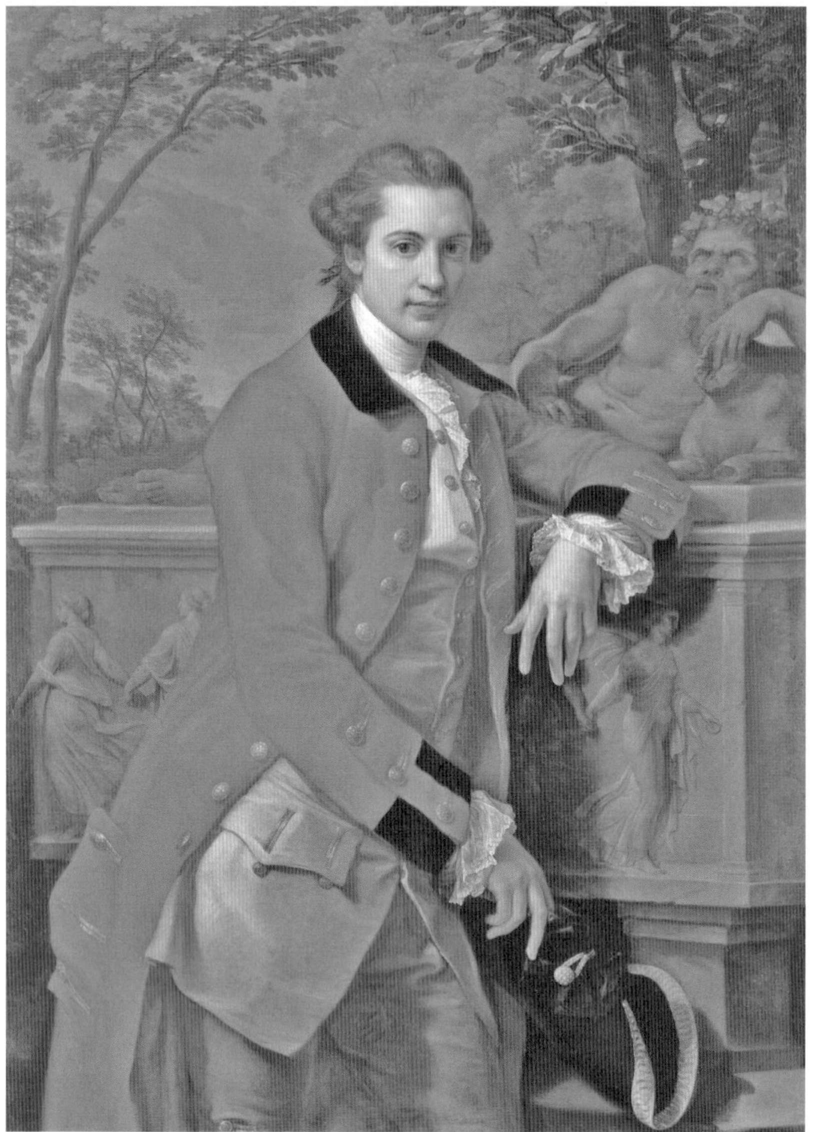

FIG. 13.4. Pompeo Batoni (1708–1787), *Edmund Rolfe (1738–1817)*, c. 1761–2. Oil on canvas, 137 × 98.5 cm. Private Collection. *(Photo: Edgar Peters Bowron. Reproduced courtesy of the owner.)*

> in illustrated anthologies, in copies and in the comments of travellers,[34] which adorns the portrait of *Francis Bassett, Later Baron de Dunstanville* (1778).[35]

The single use of the bust of *Faustina the Younger*, discovered in Hadrian's Villa at Tivoli and donated in 1748 by Benedict XIV (1675–1758) to the Capitoline Museum, where it was restored a year later by Bartolomeo Cavaceppi (1716–99) and widely copied by him and others for the trade, in the portrait of *George Legge, Viscount Lewisham* (Fig. 13.3),[36] underscores further the artist's measured invocation of Rome's classical heritage.

Batoni was even discreet in his use of the *Apollo Belvedere*, *Laocoön*, *Belvedere Antinous* and *Vatican Ariadne*, the canonical statues on display at the Vatican that made a visit to Italy such an important part of the education of the cultured British gentleman. He employed them as a group only twice, once in the fictitious arrangement before which *Thomas Dundas, Later 1st Baron Dundas* (1763–4) (Fig. 2.2)[37] stands in a pose that carries the cross-legged stance of English portraiture to extremes, and two years later in an even grander full-length portrait of *Count Kirill Grigoriewitch Razumovsky* (1766).[38] Their rarity in Batoni's work may be explained by the fact that each of these sitters was among the very wealthiest of Batoni's clients, and it is certain, if unproven, that he would have charged them accordingly for the extra work entailed in the inclusion of the most famous marbles of antiquity. Even the famous *Antinous* bas-relief belonging to Cardinal Albani, excavated in 1735 at Hadrian's Villa and first recorded in an engraving after a drawing by Batoni published the following year, appears in his entire portrait *oeuvre* but once (Plate 13.3).

That only about 50 of Batoni's portraits of British sitters, roughly one-quarter of the total, actually contain antique references further underscores his calculated use of ancient sculptures, monuments, ruins and maps to situate unmistakably his subjects in Rome. Unfortunately, as indicated at the outset, little evidence exists to establish whether such motifs really imply some specific interest in ancient art on the sitters' part, if there were any actual give and take between painter and patron, or if their presence should be more or less attributed exclusively to Batoni's creative artistic licence. The model for inquiry into an individual work of portraiture is a recent close and informed reading of the pictorial complexity of one of Batoni's most remarkable Grand Tour images, *Colonel the Hon. William Gordon* (1765–6) (Plate 20.2).[39] Taking into account such issues as the highly politicized nature of Colonel Gordon's belted tartan costume, the proprietary swagger and martial

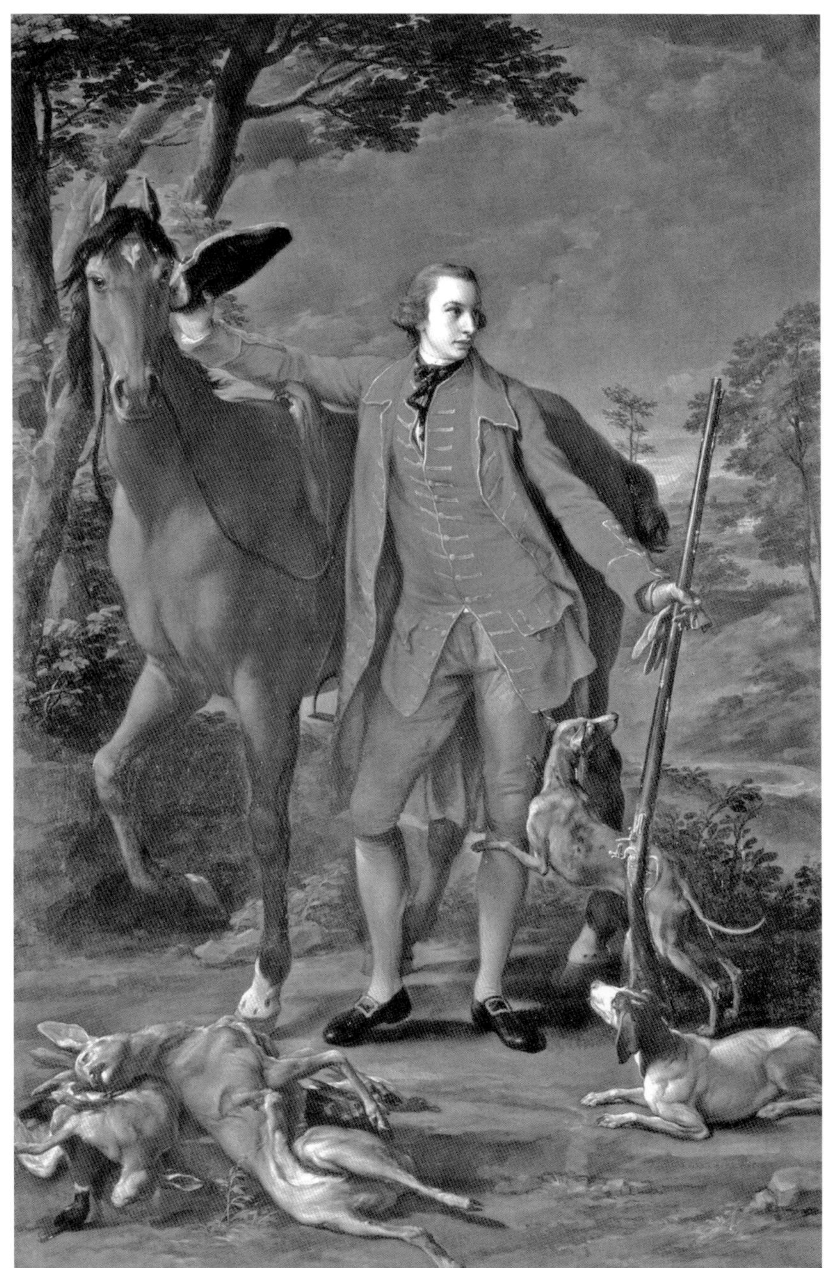

FIG. 13.5. Pompeo Batoni (1708–87), *Alexander Gordon, 4th Duke of Gordon (1743–1827)*, 1763–4. Oil on canvas, 292 × 192 cm. National Gallery of Scotland, Edinburgh. *(Photo: National Galleries of Scotland.)*

saw the artist painting during a visit to his studio during Holy Week in 1765.[40]

The contemporary gossip surrounding the commissioning of the full-length portrait of *Thomas William Coke, Later 1st Earl of Leicester* (1774)[41] by the Young Pretender's wife, Princess Louise of Stolberg-Gedern, Countess of Albany (1752–1824), with whom Batoni is said to have had an affair, and the inference that the *Vatican Ariadne* held a specific reference to the Countess, whose features were said to have been recognized in the sculpture, probably contains enough truth to suggest that here, too, there was an unusual degree of complicity between painter and patron in the choice not only of the salmon-pink and silvery white Vandyke costume — possibly the very outfit that Lord Coke wore to a fancy-dress ball given by the Countess the previous year — but also of the sculpture itself, thought at the time to represent Cleopatra, or Venus.[42]

But these are only two instances in which it is possible to speculate with some degree of confidence on what the images really meant to those who went to considerable effort and expense to have them painted. There are many more Batoni portraits begging for a closer and detailed look at the archaeological insertions and their relevance to the sitter's life, station and character. One is the portrait of a Norfolk traveller, *Edmund Rolfe (1738–1817)* (Fig. 13.4),[43] who leans against a sarcophagus adorned with a relief frieze adapted from the *Borghese Dancers*, frequently admired in the highest terms in the eighteenth century, surmounted with a reclining Silenus probably derived from the central figure in the group of the *Nile*, installed as a fountain in the middle of the Belvedere statue court.[44] Another is the portrait of *George Gordon, Lord Haddo (Died 1791)* (Plate 13.4), which includes a statue of a priestess carrying a vessel in the Capitoline collections, used only once previously by Batoni. The presence of the sarcophagus of a child depicting the myth of Prometheus, which Batoni has shown in reverse,

self-possession of his pose, the iconography of the accessories of the Colosseum and the fictive statue of Roma, and contemporary debates about Scotland and Scots cultural and national identity, Christopher Johns has suggested convincingly that there must have been a genuine interchange between painter and patron over the choice and disposition of the antique references, and that Gordon actively engaged Batoni's interest in his choice of costume, which James Boswell

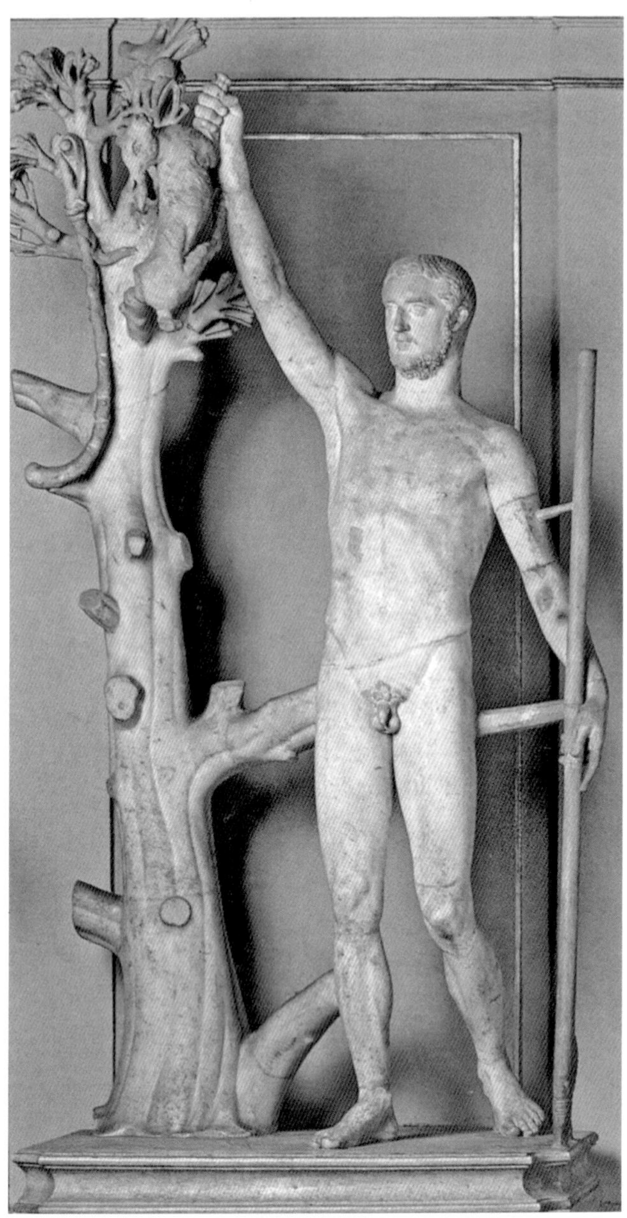

FIG. 13.6. Unknown sculptor, *Hunter with a Hare*, pastiche from the mid-third century BC. Marble, 198 cm high. Museo Capitolino, Rome. *(Photo: Musei Capitolini, Rome.)*

entered the Capitoline Museum in 1733 from the collections of Cardinal Albani, where it had been published by de Montfaucon,[45] would suggest a serious interest in antiquity on the part of Lord Haddo, but his inclinations in such matters, or why he is surrounded by these particular statues, are not known.

One of Batoni's sitters who demonstrably possessed no interest in the beauties of antiquity, much less in the learned paraphernalia of Grand Tour portraits, was Alexander, 4th Duke of Gordon (1743–1827) (Fig. 13.5), who sat expressionless in his carriage while no less a *cicerone* than Winckelmann himself attempted to arouse his interest in ancient Rome.[46] But back home, admiring the striking and unusual portrait in which he is shown beside his handsome bay horse, surrounded by a profusion of dead game such as might be found in the Scottish highlands, His Grace might well have been surprised to learn that even in this rustic setting he could not escape the reach of Rome's classical past: his dogs evoke such classical precedents as the companions of the mythological hunter Meleager; his horse, by means of the placement of the duke's hat, appears as if winged and thus becomes Pegasus, its hoof raised to strike the blow that brought forth the sacred spring, the Hippocrene, on Mount Helicon; and his pose is strongly reminiscent of a life-size third-century statue of a hunter with his prey, a hare, found near Porta Latina in 1747 (Fig. 13.6).[47]

Notes

1. For Batoni and his works cited herein, see A.M. Clark, *Pompeo Batoni. A Complete Catalogue of His Works*, edited and prepared for publication by E.P. Bowron (New York, 1985); see also E.P. Bowron and P.B. Kerber, *Pompeo Batoni: Prince of Painters in Eighteenth Century Rome* (New Haven/London, 2007), esp. pp. 78–87.
2. F. Benaglio, 'Abbozzo della vita di Pompeo Batoni pittore', in A. Marchesan (ed.), *Vita e prose scelte di Francesco Benaglio* (Treviso, 1894), 41–2.
3. H. Macandrew, 'A group of Batoni drawings at Eton College, and some eighteenth-century Italian copyists of classical sculpture', *Master Drawings* 16 (1978), 131–50.
4. Macandrew, 'A group of Batoni drawings' (above, n. 3), 150, no. 47, pl. 23.
5. The original is in the Museo Capitolino, Rome.
6. Both portraits are in the National Gallery of Ireland, Dublin.
7. Fetherstonhaugh Collection, Uppark, The National Trust.
8. The Duke of Buccleuch & Queensbury KT, Boughton House, Northamptonshire.
9. National Portrait Gallery, London.
10. Althorp, Northumberland.
11. Hopetoun House, Edinburgh.
12. Holkham Hall, Norfolk.
13. Lotherton Hall, Leeds.
14. Bowron and Kerber, *Pompeo Batoni* (above, n. 1), 185, n. 9.
15. P. Beckford, *Familiar Letters from Italy to a Friend in England* (Salisbury, 1805), II, 122; Clark and Bowron, *Pompeo Batoni* (above, n. 1), nos. 277, 346.
16. C. Rowell, *Uppark: West Sussex. The National Trust*, revised edition (London, 2004), 19, illustrated.
17. Now in the Yale Center for British Art, Paul Mellon Collection, New Haven, Connecticut.
18. B. Ford and J. Ingamells, *A Dictionary of British and Irish Travellers in Italy, 1701–1800. Compiled from the Brinsley Ford Archive* (New Haven/London, 1997), 198.
19. The former is in the Fitzwilliam Museum, Cambridge, the latter in the Los Angeles County Museum of Art.
20. J.J. Winckelmann, *Briefe*, edited by W. Rehm and H. Diepolder (Berlin, 1952–7), II, 53.
21. Today in the Vatican Museums, then in the Giustiniani Collection.
22. F. Haskell and N. Penny, *Taste and the Antique: the Lure of Classical Sculpture 1500–1900* (New Haven/London, 1981), 270.
23. J. Richardson and J. Richardson, *Account of Some of the Statues, Bas-reliefs, Drawings, and Pictures in Italy* (London, 1722).
24. Haskell and Penny, *Taste and the Antique* (above, n. 22), 260.
25. The National Gallery, London.
26. Private Collection, on loan to the Art Institute of Chicago.
27. Musée du Louvre, Paris.
28. Allen Memorial Art Museum, Oberlin College, Ohio.
29. B. de Montfaucon, *Antiquity Explained and Represented in Sculptures by the Learned Father Montfaucon*, 5 vols, trans. D. Humphreys (London, 1722).
30. Chatsworth House, Derbyshire.
31. Quoted by Haskell and Penny, *Taste and the Antique* (above, n. 22), 133.
32. Private Collection.
33. Private Collection.
34. Haskell and Penny, *Taste and the Antique* (above, n. 22), 288.
35. Museo Nacional del Prado, Madrid.
36. For the identification of the sitter, see A.M. Suárez Huerta, 'A portrait of George Legge by Batoni', *The Burlington Magazine* 148 (April 2006), 252–6.
37. The Marquess of Zetland, Aske Hall, North Yorkshire.
38. Private Collection.
39. The National Trust for Scotland, Fyvie Castle, Aberdeenshire. C.M.S. Johns, 'Portraiture and the making of cultural identity: Pompeo Batoni's *The Honourable Colonel William Gordon* (1765–66) in Italy and north Britain', *Art History* 27 (3) (2004), 382–411.
40. Johns, 'Portraiture and the making of cultural identity' (above, n. 39), 384–5.
41. Holkham Hall, Norfolk.
42. Haskell and Penny, *Taste and the Antique* (above, n. 22), 184–7.
43. Musée du Louvre, Paris.
44. Haskell and Penny, *Taste and the Antique* (above, n. 22), figs 101, 142.
45. De Montfaucon, *Antiquity Explained* (above, n. 29), III, 152, pl. 74, no. 4.
46. Winckelmann, *Briefe* (above, n. 20), II, 297–8.
47. W. Helbig, *Führer durch die Öffentlichen Sammlungen Klassischer Altertümer in Rom*, fourth edition (ed. H. Speier) (Tübingen, 1966), 194–5, no. 1388.

Romanizing frescoes: from the Villa Negroni to Ickworth

Andrew Wallace-Hadrill

> Tis difficult to say wh. pleases me the most: the magnificence of ancient or the elegance of modern Rome, for my own part I have been singularly fortunate — several ancient rooms have been unearthed since my arrival — the ptgs were in fresco & almost as perfect as at first — the secret was soon found of detaching the ptd stucco from the walls, & I have bought three complete rooms with which I propose to adorne the Downhill & *le rendre un morceau unique*.

So, on 9 November 1777, Frederick Hervey, 4th Earl of Bristol and Bishop of Derry, wrote to his daughter.[1] The paintings he purchased were among the finest examples of fresco wall-decoration ever found in Rome. Today they are seemingly lost, and consequently largely ignored in discussions of Roman mural decoration.[2] What I have to say is not new. But the story just happens to offer a vivid case-study of the deep involvement of British milordi, dealers, artists and architects in the late eighteenth-century rediscovery of antique Rome, and of the impact of that rediscovery on British taste. It also just happens to offer an excuse to draw attention to one of the jewels in the extraordinary collection of books and prints built up by Thomas Ashby of which the British School is the custodian, the series of twelve plates produced by Camillo Buti of the frescoes from the Villa Negroni, some of which the Earl-Bishop purchased.

Let me start from the back-end of my story. In 1997, I received from one knowing my interest in things Pompeian a postcard depicting a room in Ickworth House in Suffolk (Plate 14.1). It is called the 'Pompeian room', and decorated with scenes that at first glance seem reasonably faithful reproductions of Pompeian frescoes. It struck me that I knew these scenes, and that they were not at all from Pompeii. Only the previous year, the Museo Nazionale delle Terme had put on an important exhibition called *Antiche stanze*, and had borrowed the School's set of Villa Negroni prints. The purpose of the exhibition was to reconstruct an entire quarter of ancient Rome excavated in the late 1940s during the construction of the new metro line. The structures were immediately demolished, the frescoes and mosaics put into storage in the Terme museum, and no publication of any sort shared this knowledge with the public. Yet, half a century on, it was possible from notebooks and photographs made at the time, and the fragments that have survived, to reconstruct in detail what had been lost. Mariarosaria Barbera, Rita Paris and their collaborators took the inspired decision to gather what was known about other lost material from earlier excavations in the Termini area, and revived the story of the Villa Negroni, turning to the British School at Rome to borrow the best surviving set of illustrations.[3]

The 'Pompeian room' from Ickworth House evidently was based on the Villa Negroni prints (Plate 14.2; Fig. 14.1); and the fact that its Roman origin had been suppressed only further underlined a vital theme of the exhibition, of the traditional indifference to antique Roman housing in Rome. Rome is seen as the city of monuments, not of domestic spaces. If you want to understand Roman houses, you go to Pompeii. And so, when excellent specimens of housing actually are excavated in Rome, they are demolished, or buried in oblivion, or both. The Villa Negroni house was not merely demolished and sold off to foreigners, but its memory faded so far that a room drawing closely upon it could be called 'Pompeian'. The choice of this Roman model for later imitation in Ickworth House, as we shall see, was no coincidence; and as a case-study it well illustrates not only the two-way theme of *Roma Britannica*, but the complexity of the relationship between Roman and Pompeian.[4]

Let us go back to 1777. At that time, the Marchesi Negroni, owners of the Villa Montalto, had secured a papal licence to excavate within their grounds.[5] They struck a deal with the procurator

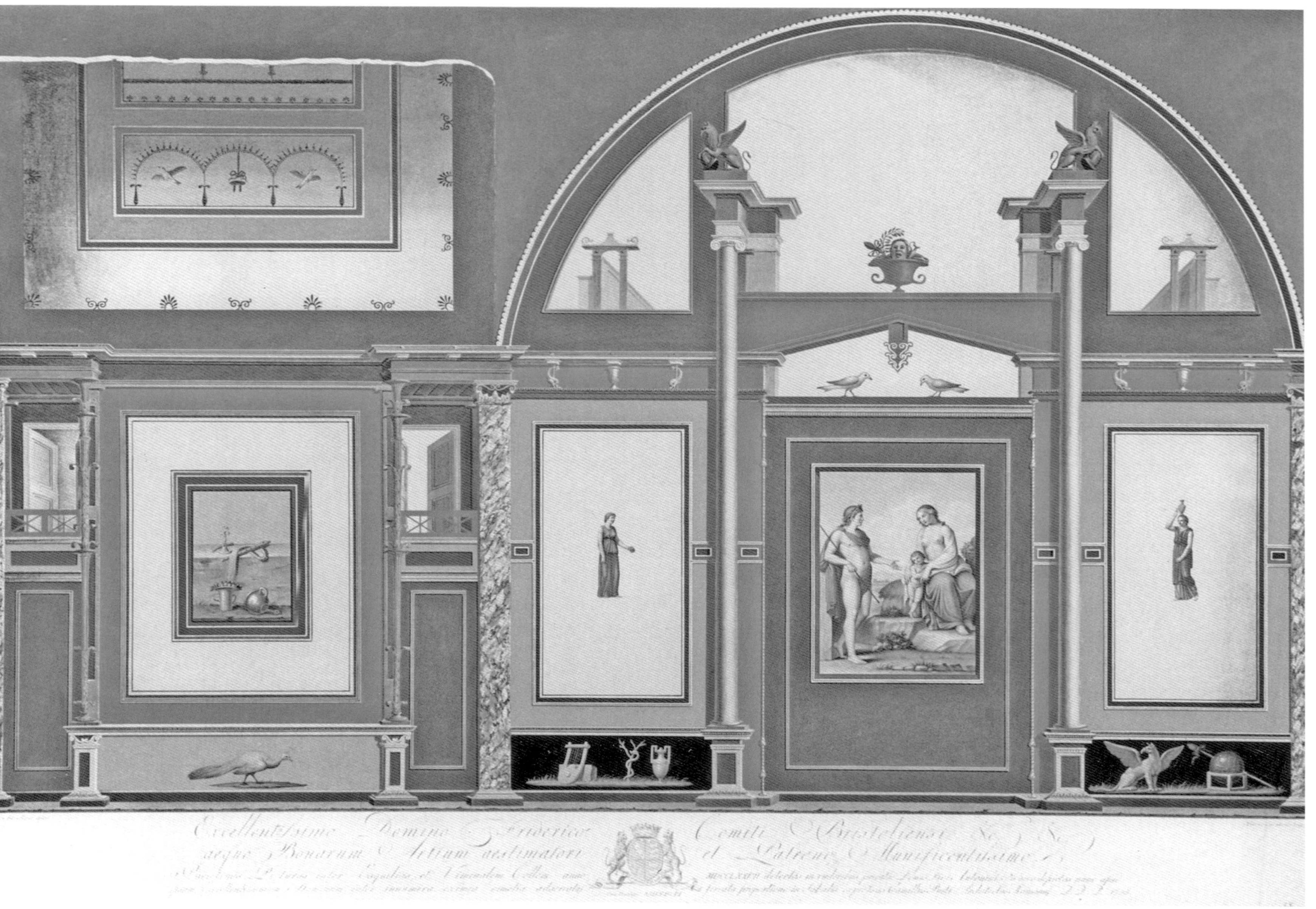

FIG. 14.1. Camillo Buti (1747–1808), *Wall design from the Villa Negroni* (Buti, plate IX). British School at Rome. *(Photo: British School at Rome Library and Archive.)*

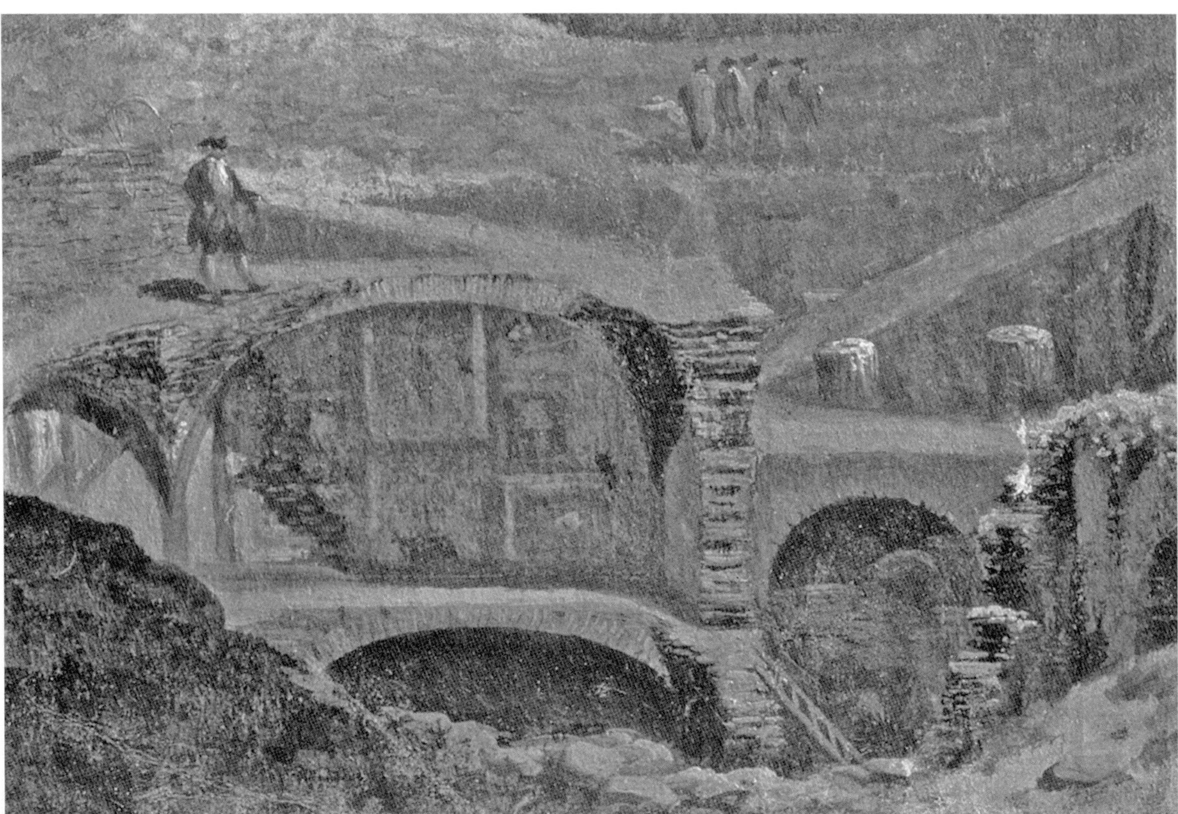

FIG. 14.2. Detail of PLATE 14.3, showing the wall paintings.

of Charles III of Spain, Cavalier José Nicolàs de Azara, who was their guest in the villa, that he should excavate and keep one-third of the antiquities found. This was, of course, precisely the period during which the Bourbons were coming towards the end of 40 years of excavation in Herculaneum, and were beginning their new excavations in Pompeii. Charles III, who had initiated the excavation of Herculaneum in his early years as King of the Two Sicilies, and to whom were dedicated the volumes of the *Antichità di Ercolano* that were still being published at this time, certainly appreciated the value of digging, and for once the universal British diggers, Gavin Hamilton, Thomas Jenkins and Robert Fagan, were not called to the share of the spoils.[6] The discovery of a Roman house with frescoes in near-perfect condition caused a sensation, and attracted many visitors.

Among these, to our good fortune, was the Welsh artist, Thomas Jones, in Rome since 1776 on his own Grand Tour, which was to fetch up so successfully in Naples in the following year. The quality of his work has been made the more visible by the 2003 exhibition by the Welsh National Galleries.[7] The loving precision of Jones's Neapolitan views encourage us to take seriously the accuracy of his sketch of the new excavations at the Villa Negroni (Plate 14.3). He went there on 5 July 1777 at the invitation of Henry Tresham, the dealer who at once purchased the frescoes for 50 crowns, and was to sell them on to the Earl-Bishop. In his memoirs, Jones described the frescoes as 'painted Ornaments much in the Chinese taste'. It is a pity he did not attempt to reproduce them in detail (Fig. 14.2).[8]

Jones's subsequent painting records a number of important details.[9] First, it ought to provide the clue to the location of the excavation. Paris, in the *Antiche stanze* catalogue, located it at a point just south of the Servian *agger*, on the junction of via Carlo Alberto (formerly via di Sant'Eusebio) and the suppressed via di Porta San Lorenzo (in modern terms, on the edge of the rectilinear mesh of streets between Santa Maria Maggiore and the Termini stations) (Fig. 14.3).[10] But this is contradicted not only by Rodolfo Lanciani, who showed quite different structures at this point, but also by Thomas Jones's painting, which shows clearly in the background to the left a church, which has been identified with the convent of Sant'Eusebio all'Esquilino.[11] The sun, which is high in the sky and so presumably to the south, is behind the viewer and

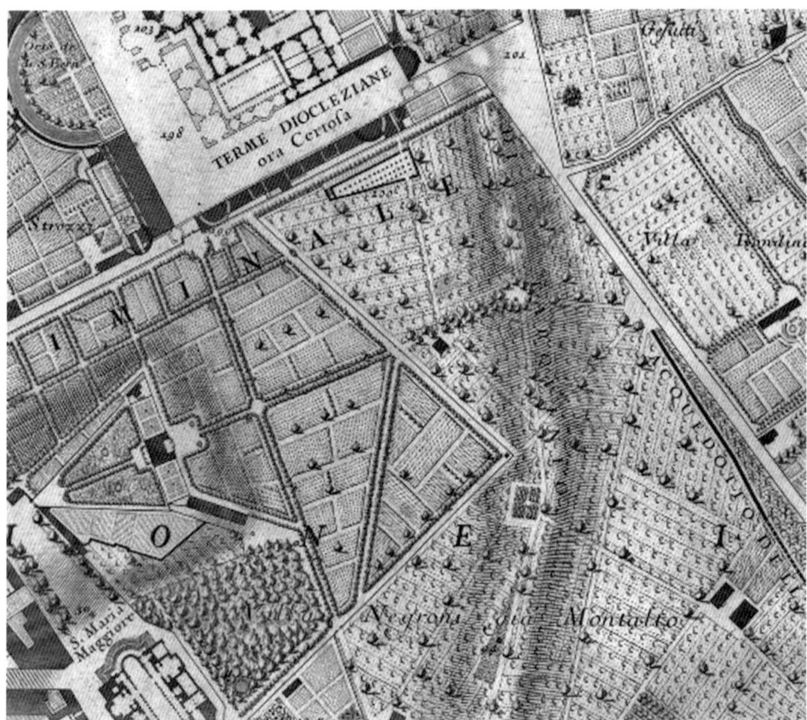

FIG. 14.3. Detail of the plan of Rome by Giovanni Battista Nolli (1701–56), 1748, area southeast of the Baths of Diocletian, with the proposed location of the Villa Negroni excavations.

to the right, suggesting a view to the northeast, in which case the excavation was to the southwest of the church, which is hard to reconcile with the position suggested, northwest of the church. The heap of earth to the right, which might initially be taken for the Servian *agger*, is rather, as the figures with wheelbarrows make clear, the growing spoil heap of the excavation itself. But this is, as we have seen, incompatible with the orientation of the convent. There is a puzzle here still to work out.

The second point of some interest (one not noted in previous discussion) is that Jones distinctly shows a structure on two floors. This apparently contradicts Buti's statement that nothing remained of the upper storey at the time of excavation. On the contrary, we see clearly two frescoed walls of a room with a cross vault; beneath it in the shadows is a second vault, and to the right a ladder leads downwards (Fig. 14.2). To the right of the ladder are further vaulted rooms, but set at a level intermediate between the two vaulted storeys to the left. It is by no means easy to reconcile this with Buti's plan of the house, which shows two sets of vaulted rooms joined by a narrow peristyle (Fig. 14.4). I take it that Jones's ladder goes down into this peristyle area. In any case, Jones's view suggests that the Buti plan is at the very least oversimplified.

Jones, Tresham and the Earl-Bishop were not the only British visitors drawn to the Roman remains. The English architect Thomas Hardwick, who had arrived in Rome that year, executed two drawings of the frescoes. Hardwick was the old classmate and travelling companion of John Soane, who arrived in Rome exactly in the spring of 1778, and made the acquaintance of the Earl-Bishop, who gave him various commissions.[12] Though this is not explicitly attested, Soane must have visited the Villa Negroni excavations, for he drew on its images for his first London home, Pitzhanger Manor in Ealing, and had a framed set of the first eight of Buti's plates on the walls of the Breakfast Room of the house that became his museum.[13]

Before I turn in more detail to the decorations themselves, I would like to complete the trail to Ickworth. The Earl-Bishop evidently took an intense interest in these frescoes.[14] Not only did he purchase some — at least three rooms as he claimed to his daughter — of the stuccoes themselves, but he took a close interest in the series of drawings that Buti was commissioning for the Spanish. The fact that Hardwick, who was surely working on commission for the Bishop, produced only two drawings might be due not to lack of interest but to difficulties with the Spanish. The official artist commissioned to record the walls was the Spanish court painter, Anton Raphael Mengs. Despite intense public interest in acquiring reproductions, Mengs succeeded in 1778 in producing only three plates. He complained that the damp conditions were damaging his health (those working in the Bourbon excavations in Herculaneum complained with equal vigour and equal reason), and indeed died the next year. The task was taken over by his brother-in-law, Anton von Maron, who between 1779 and 1786 produced five more, dedicating the first to the memory of Mengs, and the rest to the excavator, Azara. These first eight plates must have been issued separately as a set, since many collections, including the Sir John Soane, the Victoria & Albert Museum and two sets in the British Museum, have only these eight. There is then an interval of seven years, and only in 1793, 1800, 1801 and 1802 were the final four produced, to complete the set. The fact that the

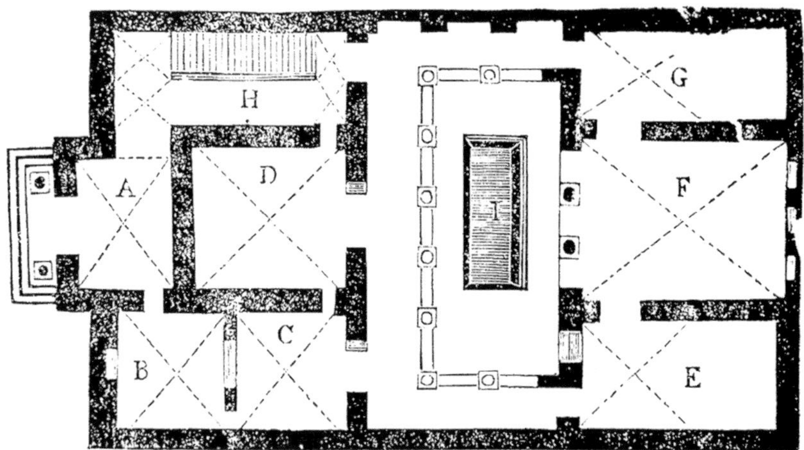

FIG. 14.4. Plan of the ancient house in the Villa Negroni, made for Buti.

last four were dedicated to the Earl of Bristol shows that his interest persisted.

What happened to the frescoes themselves, which were destined to adorn the Earl-Bishop's Irish seat of Downhill Castle? Hetty Joyce, whose meticulous article of twenty years ago is the most detailed source on these questions, enquired at Downhill, and could find no trace of the frescoes in the records, let alone the physical remains, and could offer no explanation.[15] But we know that in 1798 the French army of occupation in Rome confiscated much of his collection, still stored in Rome, and dispersed it despite a petition from 345 artists. The Earl-Bishop himself spent nine months in confinement in Milan. I suggest that the frescoes were still in Rome in 1798, at a time when he was pressurizing Maron to complete his drawings and complete the transaction. Had they fallen into French hands, we might have expected them, given their outstanding quality, to be in the Louvre. So perhaps they were lost at sea in transit, or were otherwise destroyed, unwitting victims of the French Revolution.

In any case, it sounds as if in 1798 the Earl-Bishop still had not succeeded in getting his precious frescoes to Britain, yet was still thinking about them. And by now he had a new context for them. As a third son, he had never expected to succeed to the family title, and hence his move, through unashamed nepotism thanks to his father's court connections, to secure a bishopric. But by 1779, his brother Augustus John, the 3rd Earl, died and he succeeded, able at last to take over the family seat at Ickworth House in Suffolk. He did not abandon Derry, and indeed in 1780 invited Soane to propose plans for the rebuilding of Downhill Castle, though he rejected them. The central feature of the building actually commissioned was an oval rotunda, intended as a museum to house his art collection. But by 1796 his efforts were focused on the rebuilding of Ickworth House, the central feature of which was also an oval rotunda. He died in 1803, before the building was completed, but the project was taken on by his son, the 5th Earl and 1st Marquis of Bristol, who had accompanied his father on the voyage to Italy of 1777. However, he abandoned his father's plans to create a museum, and developed his own Regency style.[16]

The destruction of the Hervey papers (as noted in the *Dictionary of National Biography*) means that the vital information is missing, but it seems hard to resist the inference that when, in 1879, the 3rd Marquis commissioned the artist John Dibdee Crace, great-grandson of the John Crace who had worked at Soane's Pitzhanger Manor, to decorate a room in the Roman style, the family had not forgotten the Earl-Bishop's passion for the frescoes he had tried so hard to acquire. In any case, the family possessed a set of the Buti prints that he could conveniently use as his model. What had changed was that the memory of Rome as a location of the frescoes was dead, and Pompeii had assumed its total dominance in the popular imagination. It was hard to think of this style of decoration as anything other than Pompeian. Faithful though its adherence to the Buti prints was, it had to be the Pompeian room.

But just how Roman were the Buti prints in truth? The problem is not simply one of location (Rome versus the bay of Naples), but of period. The Villa Negroni house was clearly dated by brick stamps of AD 134 to the reign of Hadrian, a good half-century after the eruption of Vesuvius. A curiosity of the history of Roman wall-painting is that the confident scheme of four successive 'styles', one that is a persistent feature of discussions of Pompeian decoration, collapses in the second century AD. This is due partly to the state of the evidence. The Vesuvian cities produce so many hundreds of examples that August Mau was able to categorize them confidently. For the next century, we have a scattered handful, and categorization collapses. Joyce's excellent study is driven to the conclusion that the style was eclectic, drawing on Pompeian second, third and fourth styles.[17]

The architecture of the house points strongly to a second-century date, and to a contrast with Pompeian standards: the use of brick and concrete cross-vaulting, unknown in Pompeii, is paralleled in tombs in the

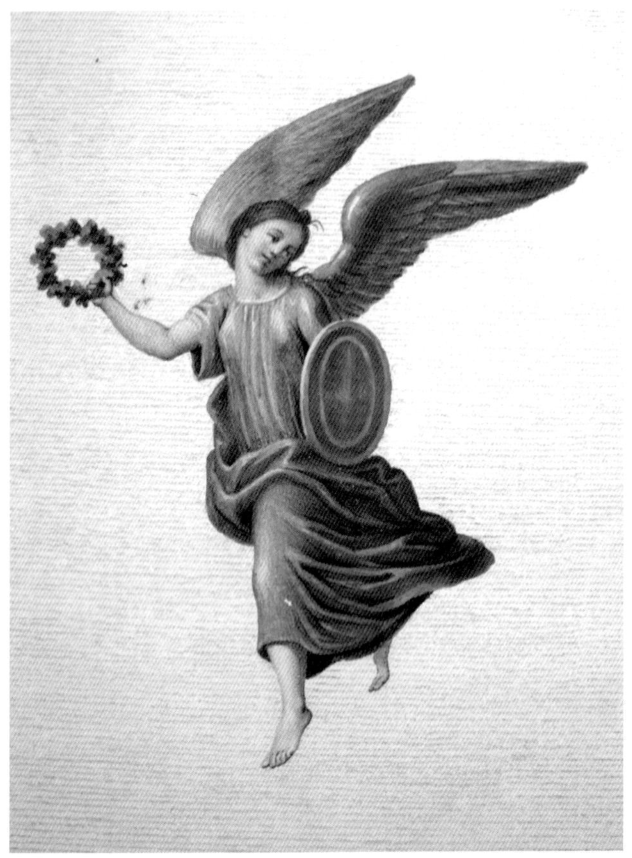

FIG. 14.5. Camillo Buti (1747–1808), *Winged Victory*, detail of Buti, plate XI. Coloured engraving. British School at Rome. *(Photo: British School at Rome Library and Archive.)*

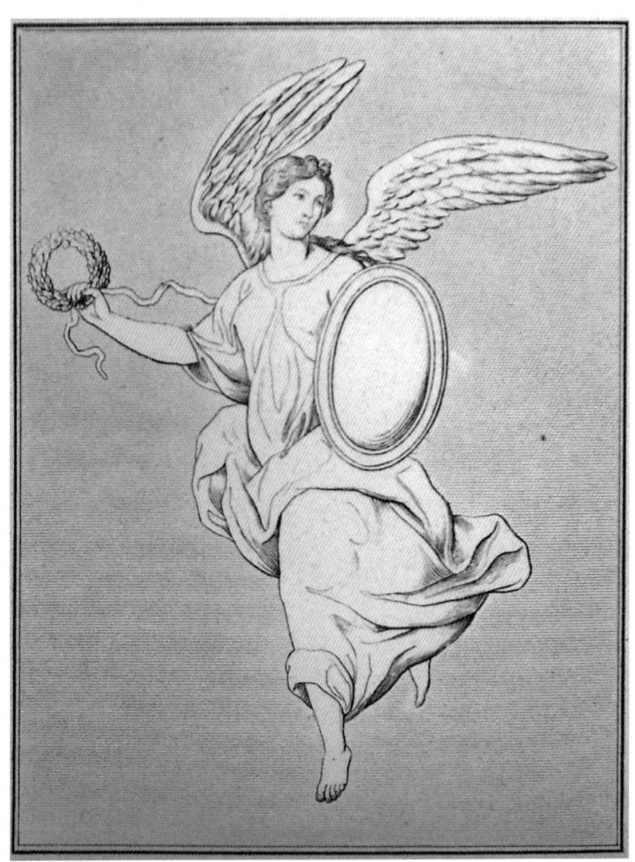

FIG. 14.6. Detail of a winged victory, from *Antichità di Ercolano* vol. 2, plate XL.

Vatican. The layout of the house also shows how far the Pompeian atrium house model has been left behind. An entrance framed by two columns and an aedicule leads into a vestibule in which, rather than offering an axial view through the house, the view is brought up short by three niches containing statues. It is necessary to circumnavigate to the private peristyle area to reach the main reception rooms. Exactly the same pattern is seen at Ostia in the Casa del Protiro: the porch that gives the house its name, the niched vestibule that blocks the axial view, the courtyard around which the principal rooms open.

If architectural style had changed, so surely had decorative style. Yet the Villa Negroni frescoes, seen through the spectacles of Mengs and Maron, are most unusual even within the second-century corpus. Mythological schemes, rare elsewhere, are the dominant feature here. And many features of the decorative detail and colour schemes seem more reminiscent of Pompeii than contemporary parallels. One need only contrast the frescoes rescued from the Termini metro from the *Antiche stanze* exhibition, dated a few decades later, to see another, much simpler, decorative world. The suspicion then arises that Buti's artists, in reconstructing these paintings, were influenced by their knowledge of the Vesuvian cities, and indeed were anxious to produce a Roman answer to the great discoveries of the bay of Naples.[18]

In defence of the authenticity of the paintings are two strong arguments. The first is that contemporary eyewitnesses commented on the excellent state of their preservation: as the Earl-Bishop put it, 'almost as perfect as at first'. On the other hand, common experience of excavations suggests that a few fragments of vividly painted plaster are enough to provoke the 'perfectly preserved' reaction, and that, in practice, it is incredibly rare, even in the circumstances of the Vesuvian cities, to find a completely preserved wall. The strongly symmetric schemes of decoration always allow the artist to reconstruct confidently much of what he cannot in fact see. The second argument is that when Hardwick painted the same scene as Mengs, he offered the same details. The problem here is that we do not know what access the artists had to each other's work, and one may be derivative from the other, or a common source.

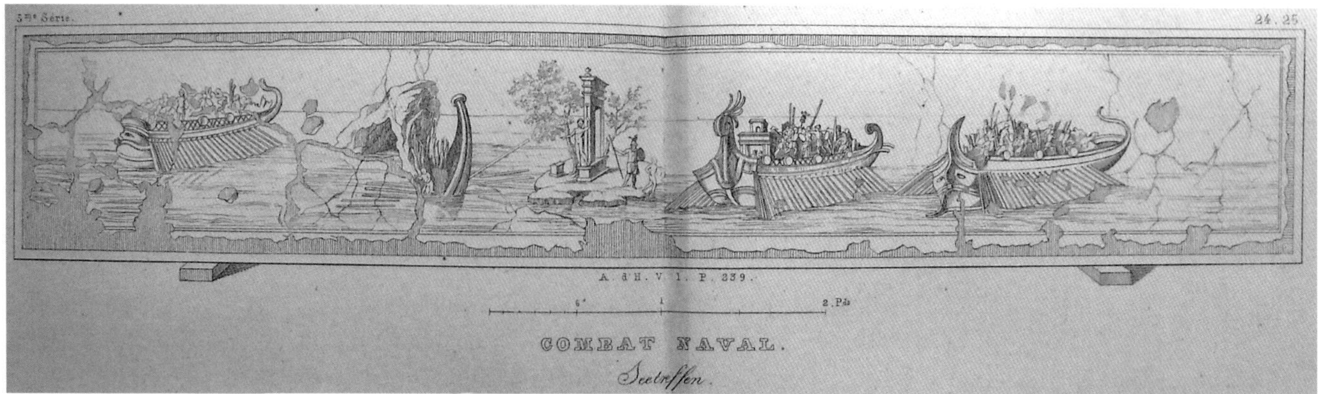

FIG. 14.7. Detail of a scene with warships, from *Antichità di Ercolano* vol. I, plate XLV.

It is almost certain that Buti's artists used sources other than the remains themselves. Joyce was able to show that a number of decorative details have extremely close parallels in the *Antichità di Ercolano*, which in the 1770s was the principal repertory of Vesuvian art. Joyce pointed to some candidates for copying: a lamp with winged torso (pls II and IV), the sphinxes serving as acroteria, and the leaping deer (pl. IV) all have close parallels from Herculaneum, while the winged victory in the centre of a side panel on plate XI is too close to plate XL of volume 2 of the *Antichità* (published in 1760) to be anything other than a copy (**Figs 14.5** and **14.6**). Indeed, one may worry about how an accurate knowledge of remains that seem to have been demolished rapidly after their discovery (the Negroni were after reusable bricks) could be preserved for the entire 25-year period over which the production of Buti's set of illustrations was dragged out. Only if Mengs and Maron produced very accurate drawings in 1777–9 can the whole set be reliable. It is not unreasonable to suggest that they are a complex product of accurate observation and reconstruction based on educated guesswork, the guesswork informed by a knowledge of Vesuvian paintings that pre-dated Mau's identification of the four styles by a century, and therefore allowed eclectic use of elements from paintings of very different styles.

On the other hand, it would be impossible to argue that the Villa Negroni drawings were derived entirely

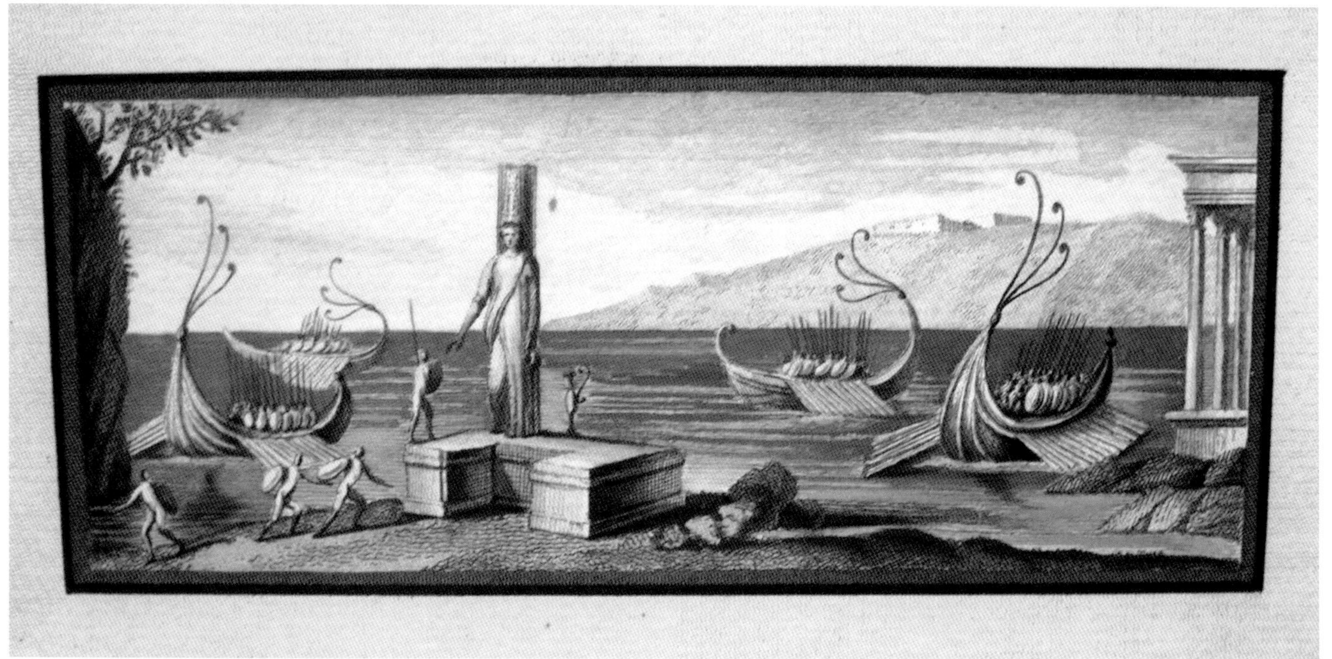

FIG. 14.8. Camillo Buti (1747–1808), *Scene with Warships*, detail of Buti, plate VI. Coloured engraving. British School at Rome. *(Photo: British School at Rome Library and Archive.)*

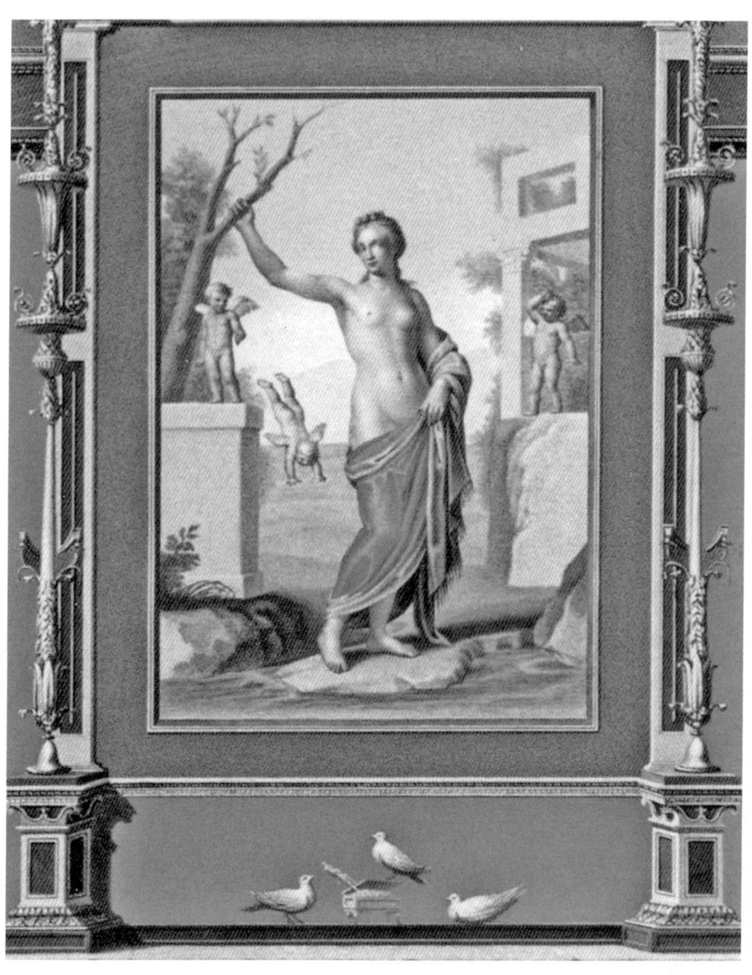

FIG. 14.9. Camillo Buti (1747–1808), *Venus with Cupids*, detail of Buti, plate I. Coloured engraving. British School at Rome. *(Photo: British School at Rome Library and Archive.)*

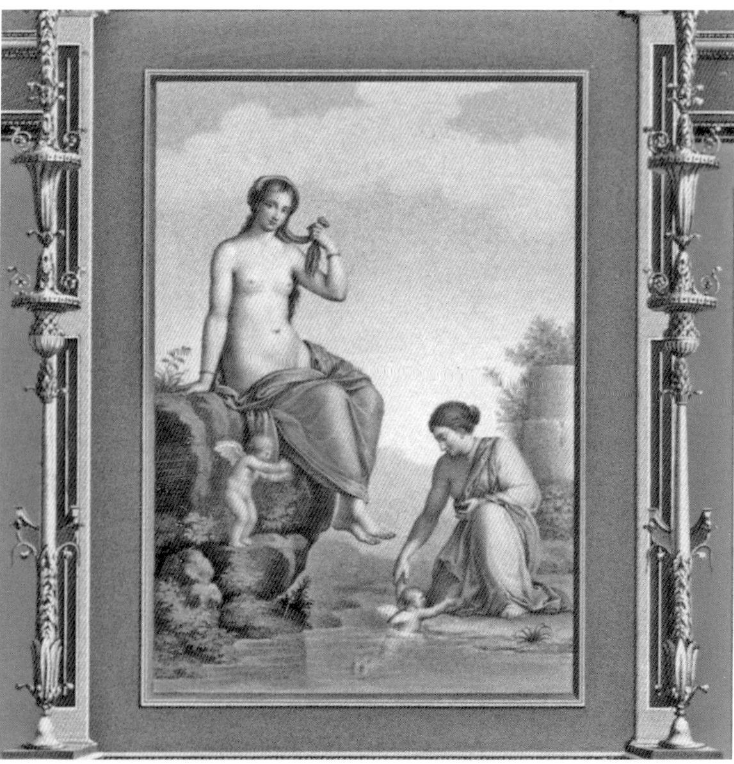

FIG. 14.10. Camillo Buti (1747–1808), *Venus and Companion with Cupids*, detail of Buti, vol. 2, plate III. Coloured engraving. British School at Rome. *(Photo: British School at Rome Library and Archive.)*

from models in Herculaneum and Pompeii. The parallel with scenes from Pompeii and Herculaneum is an argument that can cut both ways. When a figure like the winged victory (above) is reproduced almost exactly, one can assume copying at work, and in this case, as Joyce suggested, we may be looking at a special case of pastiche in plate X, produced on the Earl-Bishop's insistence two decades after the original discovery. On the other hand, when Joyce pointed to a *generic* similarity of the sea-battle scene on plate VI to no less than three scenes from the *Antichità di Ercolano*, it might be taken as reassurance that, far from being a copy (to lift details from just one scene would be easier), it is evidence that the Villa Negroni scene was yet another sample of a genuine Roman repertory (Figs 14.7 and 14.8). Many other such scenes have been discovered subsequently, none quite the same as the Villa Negroni example. The same argument applies even more forcefully to the mythological scenes that are the most remarkable feature of this series. While it is certain that the Villa Negroni paintings have extraordinarily close affinities with Pompeian painting, it is also clear that they are wholly independent of them. Now that Jürgen Hodske has assembled all known variants of mythological scenes from Pompeii, it is far easier to make the comparison, to acknowledge the similarities, and to recognize the differences.[19]

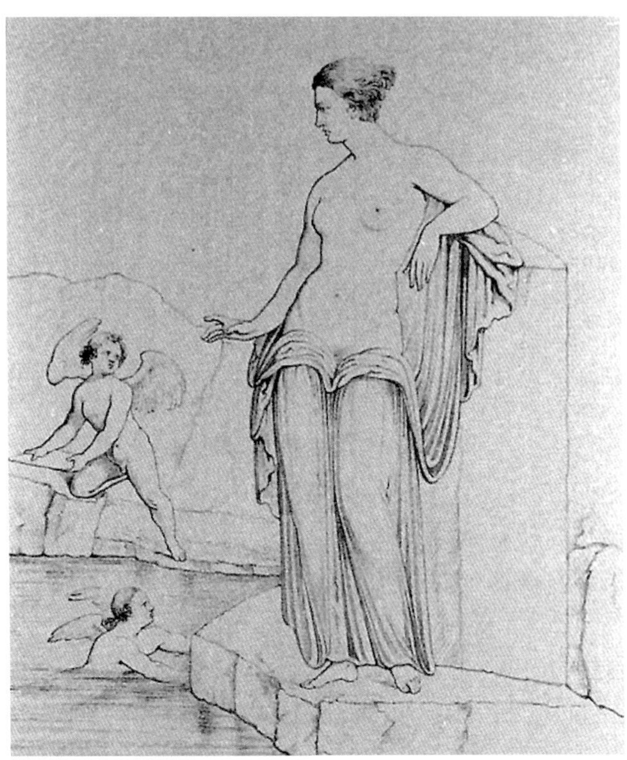

Fig. 14.11. Venus with two cupids, scene from the House of M. Lucretius, Pompeii (IX 3,5), excavated 1846, now destroyed. From W. Helbig, *Wandgemälde der vom Vesuv Verschütteten Stadte Campaniens* (Leipzig, 1868), no. 820b.

It is enough to consider two of the series of mythological scenes, showing Venus/Aphrodite with cupids or putti. In the first (Fig. 14.9), Venus stands on a rock at the edge of water, her right hand stretched above her head towards the branch of a tree; around her, three winged Cupids play to left and right, one diving into the water. The dress of Venus is draped to reveal the upper half of her body, and hint at her groin; she looks towards the viewer with the coquetry fit for the goddess of love; her hair is gathered above her head in a style familiar from statues of the second century AD.[20] In the second scene (Fig. 14.10), Venus is seated to the left on a rock above water, her body similarly revealed, but her long hair held up to dry, again a gesture familiar from first-century statues. Here, too, cupids play in the water, while a female companion, more fully

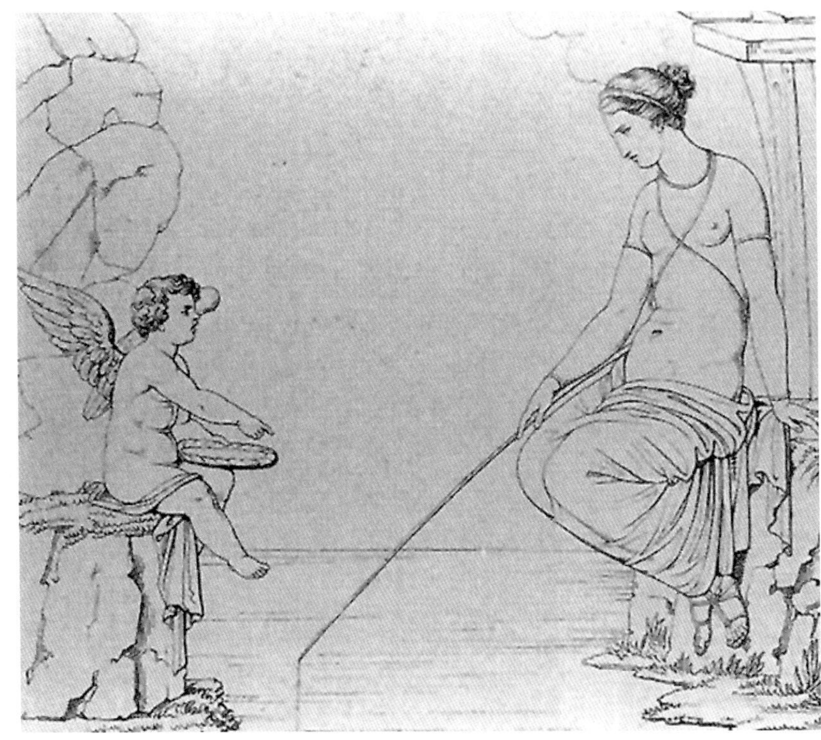

Fig. 14.12. Venus fishing with a cupid, scene from the House of Ganymede, Pompeii (VII 13,4), excavated 1824, now destroyed. From W. Helbig, *Wandgemälde der vom Vesuv Verschütteten Stadte Campaniens* (Leipzig, 1868), no. 352.

attired, kneels to the right. These scenes are strongly reminiscent of a number of paintings from Pompeii showing Venus and cupids on rocks by water. In one version, Venus stands to the right, leaning on a rock, again half-draped, this time not fishing but watching two cupids bathe (Fig. 14.11). In another, known in at least a dozen versions, Venus sits on a rock, to the right (or occasionally left), semi-draped just as in the Villa Negroni scenes, and fishes in the water below, assisted by a cupid, and in some variants accompanied by a female companion, fully draped (Fig. 14.12). These form part of a larger series of scenes of Venus with cupids: from the House of the Punished Cupids comes a scene of the female companion bringing back a contrite cupid for punishment.[21] We are evidently in the world of Hellenistic epigrams, such as those met in the Palatine Anthology, peopled by playful and naughty erotes. But what is striking is that, though the Villa Negroni scenes reflect the same set of iconographic traditions, they do not in either case show scenes that could be said to copy the Pompeian ones, which in any case were excavated in the course of the nineteenth century, long after Mengs had produced his copies. Similarly, if we compare the Villa Negroni scene of Venus and Adonis with the variants from Pompeii, we can see both similarities in the seated, semi-naked, Adonis with hunting spear, and fundamental differences in composition that guarantee its independence.[22] That is to say, we may be reassured that the drawings reproduce authentic Roman paintings, and are not an ingenious eighteenth-century forgery.

What we are looking at are high-quality metropolitan versions of the same sort of language of images that are more familiar from Pompeii. The error that led to their description at Ickworth House as 'Pompeian' is a significant one. The sort of art that came to be thought of as Pompeian could indeed be found at Rome, the workshops of which were more likely to have generated the sort of variations on standard Hellenistic themes that we encounter in Campania. Were it not for the Hadrianic brick stamps, we would surely attribute them to the late first century BC, and place them in series with the decoration of the house of Augustus on the Palatine. One of the pities of the loss of the excavated structures is that we cannot test whether in fact the house had more than one phase, with the Hadrianic phase later than the paintings. For the same reason we must regret the more that the eccentric and colourful Earl-Bishop failed to get his shipment of frescoes to a place of safety, one that would allow us today to check the reliability of Buti's remarkable series of plates. In any case, they illustrate vividly both the world of British collectors and artists in eighteenth-century Rome, the impact of that experience on the British country house, and the value of the documentation they generated for recovering knowledge of lost Roman monuments.

Notes

1. Cited by H. Joyce, 'The ancient frescoes from the Villa Negroni and their influence in the eighteenth and nineteenth centuries', *The Art Bulletin* 65 (1983), 423–40, at p. 426.
2. Thus passed over by F. Wirth, *Römische Malerei vom Untergang Pompejis bis ans Ende des Dritten Jahrhunderts* (Berlin, 1934). Attention was drawn to the frescoes by the excellent study of Hetty Joyce, 'The ancient frescoes' (above, n. 1); see also H. Joyce, *The Decoration of Walls, Ceilings, and Floors in Italy in the Second and Third Centuries A.D.* (Rome, 1981). They are also mentioned briefly in R. Ling, *Roman Painting* (Cambridge, 1991), 176; R. Paris, 'Le testimonianze pittoriche a Roma', in A. Donati (ed.), *Romana pittura: la pittura romana dalle origini all'età bizantina* (Rome, 1998), 82.
3. M. Barbera and R. Paris (eds), *Antiche stanze. Un quartiere di Roma imperiale nella zona di Termini (Museo Nazionale Romano Terme Diocleziano, Roma dicembre 1996–giugno 1997)* (Milan, 1996).
4. On Ickworth and 'Pompeian rooms' in general, see J. Wilton-Ely, 'Pompeian and Etruscan tastes in the neo-classical country house interior', in G. Jackson-Stops (ed.), *The Fashioning and Functioning of the British Country House* (Washington DC, 1989), 51–73; and now V. Coltman, *Fabricating the Antique: Neoclassicism in Britain, 1760–1800* (Chicago/London, 2006), esp. pp. 111–21, underlining the frequency with which 'Pompeian' rooms drew on non-Pompeian sources. I thank both authors for friendly advice.
5. See Barbera and Paris (eds), *Antiche stanze* (above, n. 3), 29–35.
6. On the British excavators, see the study of I. Bignamini and C. Hornsby, *Digging and Dealing in Eighteenth-century Rome* (New Haven/London, 2010); also I. Bignamini, 'The Grand Tour: open issues', in A. Wilton and I. Bignamini (eds), *Grand Tour: the Lure of Italy in the Eighteenth Century* (London, 1996), 31–6; I. Bignamini (ed.), *Archives & Excavations. Essays on the History of Archaeological Excavations in Rome and Southern Italy from the Renaissance to the Nineteenth Century* (*Archaeological Monographs of the British School at Rome* 14) (London, 2004). My debt to Ilaria Bignamini for all that affects the Grand Tour is unforgotten.
7. A. Sumner and G. Smith (eds), *Thomas Jones (1742–1803): an Artist Rediscovered* (New Haven/London, 2003), especially the essay by C. Riopelle, 'Thomas Jones in Italy', 47–67 for his visit to Rome and links with Jenkins, Anton Raphael Mengs and the Earl of Derby.
8. Cited in Sumner and Smith (eds), *Thomas Jones* (above, n. 7), 175.
9. Reproduced in Sumner and Smith (eds), *Thomas Jones* (above, n. 7), pl. 65; Wilton and Bignamini, *Grand Tour* (above, n. 6), nos. 174, 225.
10. Barbera and Paris (eds), *Antiche stanze* (above, n. 3), 15.
11. Barbera and Paris (eds), *Antiche stanze* (above, n. 3), 25, n. 20.
12. For the links of Soane, Hardwick and the Earl-Bishop, see D. Watkin, 'Sir John Soane's Grand Tour', in C. Hornsby (ed.), *The Impact of Italy: the Grand Tour and Beyond* (London, 2000), 101–19.
13. D. Cruickshank, 'Soane and the meaning of colour', *Architectural Review* 185 (1989), 46–52.
14. On Frederick Augustus Hervey, 4th Earl of Bristol, see *Dictionary of National Biography* IX (London, 1908), 730–3; J. Turner (ed.), *The Dictionary of Art* XIV (London, 1996), 485–6; B. Fothergill, *The Mitred Earl: an Eighteenth-century Eccentric* (London, 1974).
15. Joyce, 'The ancient frescoes' (above, n. 1), 426.
16. A. Laing, *In Trust for the Nation: Paintings from National Trust Houses* (London, 1995), 230; G. Jackson-Stops (ed.), *Ickworth* (London, 1979).
17. A. Mau, *Geschichte der Decorativen Wandmalerei in Pompeji* (Berlin, 1882); Joyce, 'The ancient frescoes' (above, n. 1). H. Krieger, 'Dekorative Wandgemälde aus dem II. Jahrhundert nach Christus', *Römische Mitteilungen* 34 (1919), 24–52, argued for a reversion to schemes based on the second style under Hadrian, comparing the Villa Negroni frescoes to the tomb of the Nasonii and other Hadrianic buildings. Joyce drew attention to elements from the third and fourth styles, especially in the mythological paintings; however, we may note that none of the decorative 'tapestry' borders that are the best sign of the fourth style occur in the Villa Negroni paintings.
18. Discussed in detail by Joyce, 'The ancient frescoes' (above, n. 1), 433–6.
19. J. Hodske, *Mythologischen Bildthemen in den Häusern Pompejis: die Bedeutung der Zentralen Mythenbilder für die Bewohner Pompejis* (Ruhpolding, 2007).
20. Compare the Campo Iemini Venus from the British Museum, excavated in 1794 (that is, later than the engraving of the plate), Wilton and Bignamini, *Grand Tour* (above, n. 6), 269–70.
21. See Hodske, *Mythologischen Bildthemen* (above, n. 19), Taf. 18.
22. See Hodske, *Mythologischen Bildthemen* (above, n. 19), Tafn 7–10.

CONSTRUCTING THE FUTURE ON THE RUINS OF THE PAST: THE BRITISH AND THE ROMAN PRACTICE OF ARCHITECTURE

Roma Communis Patria: Filippo Juvarra and the British

Tommaso Manfredi

The biography of the architect-priest from Messina, Filippo Juvarra (1678–1736), written posthumously by his brother Francesco, chronicles a journey Juvarra made to Portugal, when, for a period of about six months, from the end of 1719 until the middle of 1720, he was a guest at the court of King João V, with the permission of his principal patron, King Vittorio Amedeo II of Savoy.[1] According to the biography, during this period the architect received a commission from the king to design the patriarchal church and royal palace of Lisbon, and immediately afterwards went to Britain and France, staying for about a month in each country. While Francesco's account of the period Juvarra spent in Portugal was interwoven with numerous references concerning the honours João V awarded the architect, his account of Juvarra's visit to England, which was apparently based on a personal desire of the architect to see that country, instead focused on a dramatic mishap. While travelling on horseback outside London with the Portuguese ambassador, en route to an as yet unidentified lady's residence, the coach in which Juvarra was travelling was attacked and robbed by four armed bandits.[2]

The absence of other documentation regarding Juvarra's English sojourn has stimulated the imagination of scholars, who have speculated about possible contacts the architect may have had with British patrons and architects. For example, it has been proposed that Juvarra may have met Lord Burlington, and that he was introduced into Burlington's artistic and cultural circle.[3] In this context, the similarity first noted by Rudolf Wittkower between the pyramidal bell-tower of Saint George's, Bloomsbury, designed by Nicholas Hawksmoor in the first years of the second decade of the eighteenth-century (**Fig. 15.1**), and the crowning element of a monumental bridge that features in an unpublished presentation drawing by Juvarra of 1719 in Turin (**Plate 15.1**), appears highly significant.[4]

However, Hawksmoor and Juvarra probably arrived at these unusual, yet similar, architectural solutions independently, and far earlier than 1719: Hawksmoor, in the graphic transposition of a textual reconstruction of the Mausoleum of Halicarnassus written by his teacher, Christopher Wren, and already used by Hawksmoor for a model of a church (**Fig. 15.2**),[5] and Juvarra, in a design for theatrical scenery dating from at least ten years previously (**Plate 15.2**).[6] The primary source of inspiration for both architects was most likely the 'temple with a pyramid and obelisk' illustrated in Francesco Colonna's *Hyperotomachia Poliphili* (Venice, 1499). This was also the basis for the 1721 design by Johann Bernhard Fischer von Erlach for a reconstruction of the Mausoleum of Halicarnassus. Fischer von Erlach, moreover, would have had the opportunity to meet both Wren and Hawksmoor during his 1704 visit to England.[7]

None the less, the fact that Juvarra's drawing of a covered tower in the form of a pyramid coincides chronologically with Hawksmoor's extraordinary idea of actually saddling a religious building with such a structure must be re-examined in the light of the possibility that the projects of both Juvarra and Hawksmoor were planned in London and were the fruit of reciprocal influence between the two architects. Contrary to what Wittkower believed, Juvarra's Portuguese visit took place not in the first months of 1720, as Francesco Juvarra had mistakenly reported, but almost a year earlier, from January to July 1719.[8] Consequently, the dates of the architect's trips to England and to France must now also be backdated, to August and September 1719 respectively.

Juvarra's Turin drawing shows a pyramidal tower crowning the prow of a fantastic vessel on the central arch of a majestic bridge. To a trained eye, this bridge can be recognized easily as a double version of Andrea Palladio's famous design for the Rialto bridge in Venice, which was published originally in the Vicentine architect's *Quattro libri di architettura*. As an edition of Palladio's text

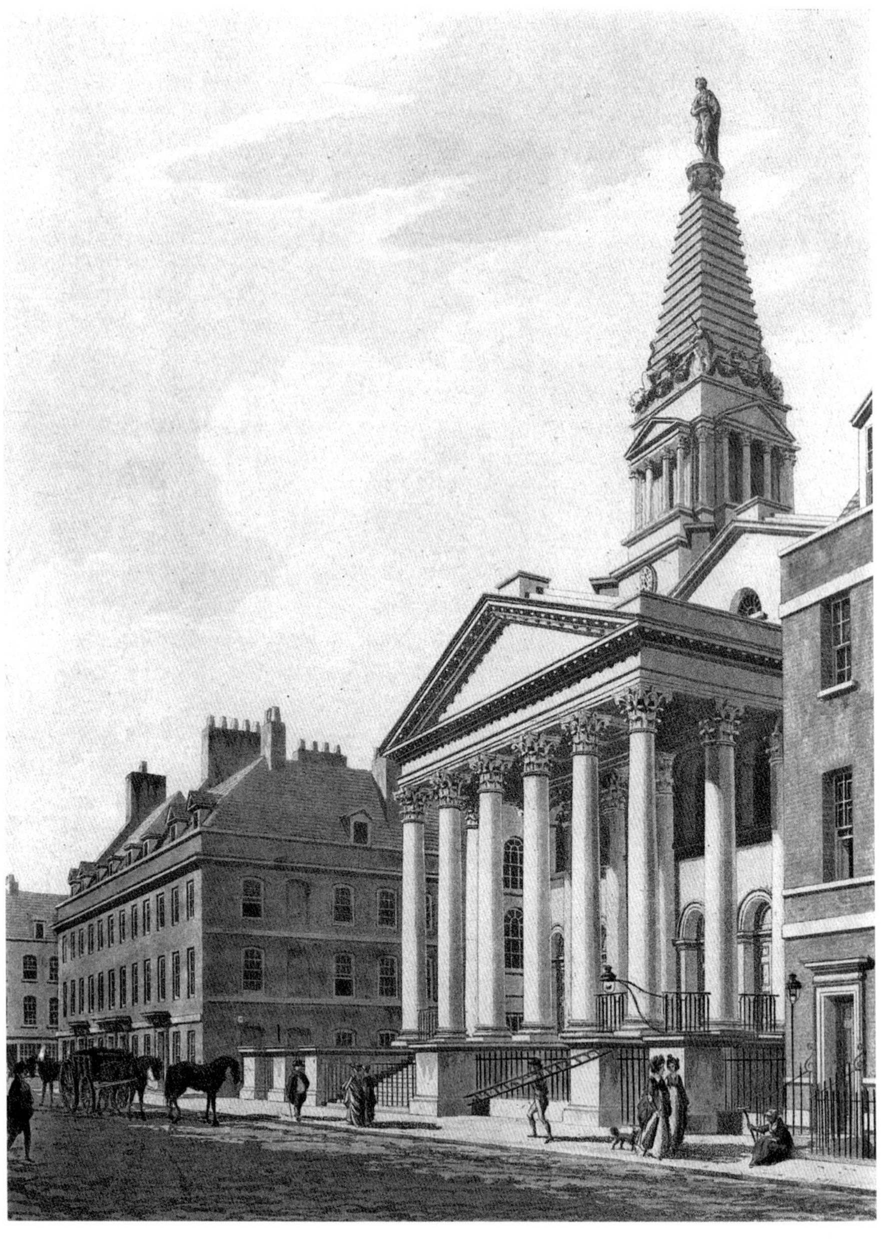

FIG. 15.1. Nicholas Hawksmoor (1661–1736), Saint George's, Bloomsbury, London. Acquatint after Thomas Malton (from *Picturesque Tour through the Cities of London and Westminster*, 1792).

had been published in London only four years earlier, in 1715, this reference undoubtedly would have been of interest to the city's cultural élite. Juvarra certainly incorporated the bridge motif intentionally, while combining it with figurative themes and expressive modes that were dear to him and that he used regularly. The motif of a ship tied to a bridge probably derives from Pirro Ligorio's *Anteiquae Urbis Imago* (1561) or a capriccio by Giovanni Antonio Dosio. However, the bridge, both 'magnificent' and 'triumphal', is a recurring element in Juvarra's imaginary architectural drawings, which unite experimental forms inspired by Rome's past, from antiquity to the seventeenth century.[9] The architect had become famous for such sketches during his Roman residence of 1704–14, and subsequently at the court in Turin, and he often presented them as gifts to illustrious personalities. Indeed, Juvarra's sketches were so popular that, according to an account by his literary friend, Scipione Maffei, nobles contested the drawings that Juvarra hastily sketched in the cafés of Turin, wishing to exhibit them in their studies or libraries.[10] It is possible, therefore, that Juvarra's Turin presentation drawing of a monumental bridge with a pyramidal tower may have been intended for an illustrious English collector, perhaps even Lord Burlington.

Two other unpublished drawings from the Turin album, both of which are *tondi* (roundels), may have

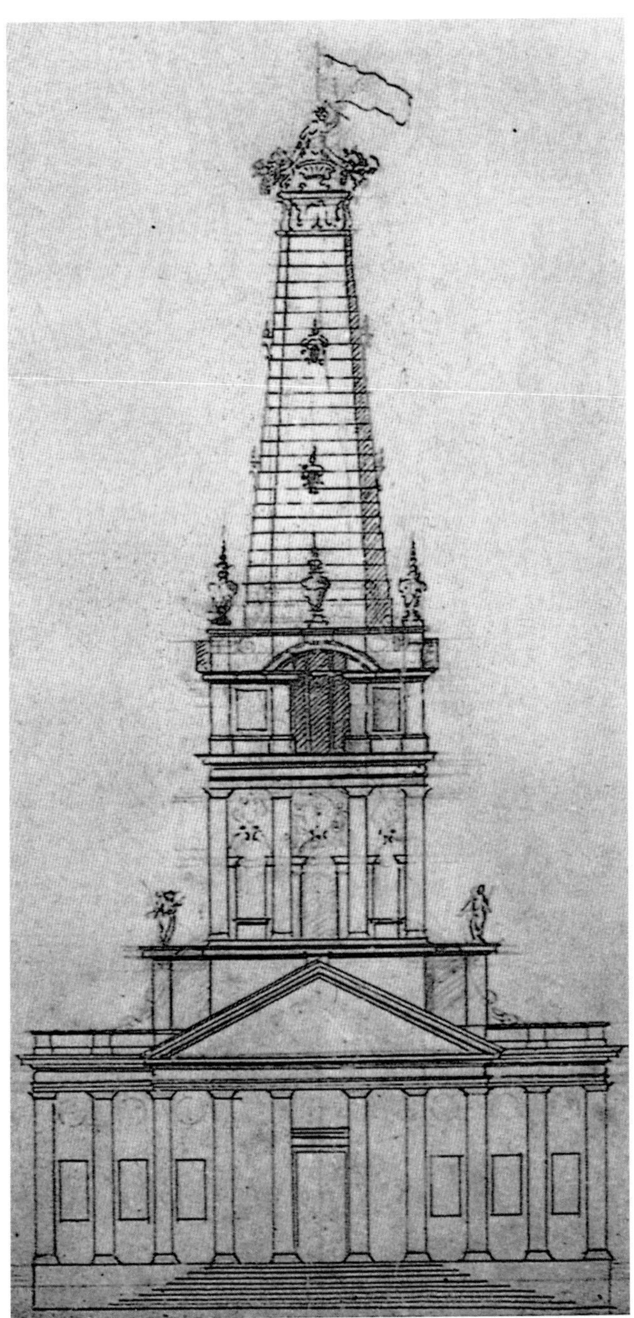

FIG. 15.2. Nicholas Hawksmoor (1661–1736), Project for a church. (After K. Downes, *Hawksmoor* (London, 1996), fig. 133.)

been destined for Burlington also. The first shows a celebratory tower that is designed like a circular interpretation of Colonna's *Hyperotomachia Poliphili* 'temple with pyramid and obelisk' (Fig. 15.3).[11] The second features the same pyramidal theme, but in this case the pyramid has been transposed to a church tower, with obelisks at each of the four corners, lending the design antique connotations (Plate 15.3).[12] These two *tondi* can be dated to 1719 for stylistic reasons and because they are contiguous in the album with a drawing that can be linked unequivocably to the complex for the palace, basilica and convent of Mafra in Portugal, which was under construction at that time (Plate 15.4). Curiously, this last drawing hitherto has not been connected to Juvarra's Portuguese *oeuvre*, although it is a rare drawing that can be ascribed with certainty to the architect's sojourn in Portugal.[13]

Another unpublished sketch that probably dates to 1719 in the same album shows the plan and elevation of a large open area surrounded by a portico, based on antique models (Fig. 15.4).[14] This drawing can be singled out as the architectural invention of Juvarra that best exemplifies his poetic interpretation of antiquity, which at this time was inspired by the monumentality and minimal ornamentation of the giant order employed by architects in the great tradition of Roman architecture from Michelangelo to Borromini. This and the other Turin album drawings can be placed at the beginning of a series of projects from the second period of Juvarra's artistic activity, and are characterized by a severe, almost minimalist, character, which is particularly evident in the elevations. Seen in the context of the evolution of Juvarra's poetic sensibility, this change can be exemplified by comparing the first project for the façade of the church of San Filippo Neri in Turin of 1715–16 (Fig. 15.5), in which the decorative ornament is integrated with the structure in a balanced way, with the definitive project of 1730 (Fig. 15.6), in which the decoration is understated with respect to the dominant linearity of the architectural composition. In fact, a nineteenth-century project for the completion of the church façade further accentuates the severity of Juvarra's last design, by eliminating the decorative bas-reliefs altogether.[15] The delicate equilibrium that Juvarra had struck between the structure and the decoration in his final design was the fruit of an aesthetic sensibility that was as controversial as it was contradictory. This artistic paradox is reflected perfectly in a famous excerpt from a dedication Juvarra wrote in an album of drawings for Count Roero di Guarene:

> In these [drawings] emerges as fully as possible the solidity of art, according to the teaching of Vitruvius and Palladio, and of all the most celebrated Authors: I have always been a lover of this solidity, and of that simplicity, in which every art, I believe, achieves perfection; Not that however, I have neglected ornament, but I have applied it with sobriety and I have tried with all my powers of imitation to follow the style of the Cavalier Borromini in this respect, who, more than any other, enriched his designs with ornament and thus introduced this taste to the people ...[16]

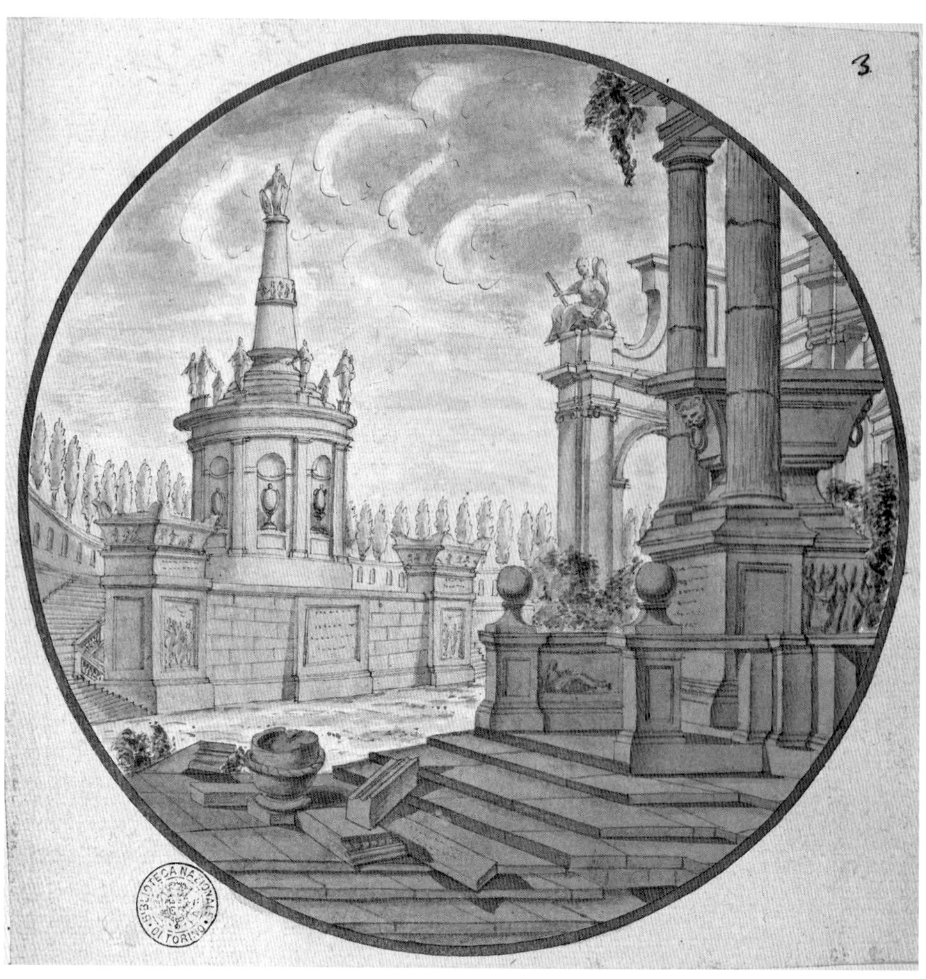

FIG. 15.3. Filippo Juvarra (1678–1736), *Architectural Fantasy*. Pen and watercolour in various shades of sepia, blue and light green, 22.3 cm diameter. BNT, album Ris. 59,6, fol. 3r. *(Reproduced courtesy of the Ministero per i Beni e le Attività Culturali, Biblioteca Nazionale Universitaria di Torino. Reproduction prohibited.)*

Juvarra's declared adherence to a 'solidity' inspired by the architectural theories of Vitruvius and of Palladio, and the 'simplicity, in which every art ... achieves perfection', implicitly relegates the decorative vocabulary of Borromini's style to second place as far as architectural models are concerned. This is in direct contradiction to the vast majority of Juvarra's projects, for these are palpably indebted to the works of Borromini even in their spatial concepts. However, some Juvarra projects that can be dated to the period immediately after the architect's visit to Britain do exhibit a notable tendency towards 'solidity', 'simplicity' and extreme decorative sobriety. Among these are the second project for the palace of the Savoy Senate (1720), which also remained unfinished until the nineteenth century, and which was designed by the architect with uncharacteristically severe Doric façades (Fig. 15.7). Another is the design for Juvarra's own house in Turin, which manifests an almost revisionist confluence of classical intensity with northern abstraction (Fig. 15.8).[17]

Even when viewed within the framework of Juvarra's vast and varied architectural activity, the stylistic progression from the architect's first design for the façade of the church of San Filippo, which is still fully consistent with traditional Roman models, to his final project, which is strikingly similar in many of its aspects to the trends in contemporary English architectural circles, raises the question of whether Juvarra may have been influenced by English cultural developments, and what he may have taken from them to add to his already huge architectural repertory. In order to seek answers to this novel and stimulating line of enquiry, it is first necessary to take a step backwards in time, and to examine the origins of Juvarra's contacts with the British. This leads us back to Rome in the first years of the eighteenth century.

*****

At the beginning of the eighteenth century in Rome even young foreign artists had the opportunity to be

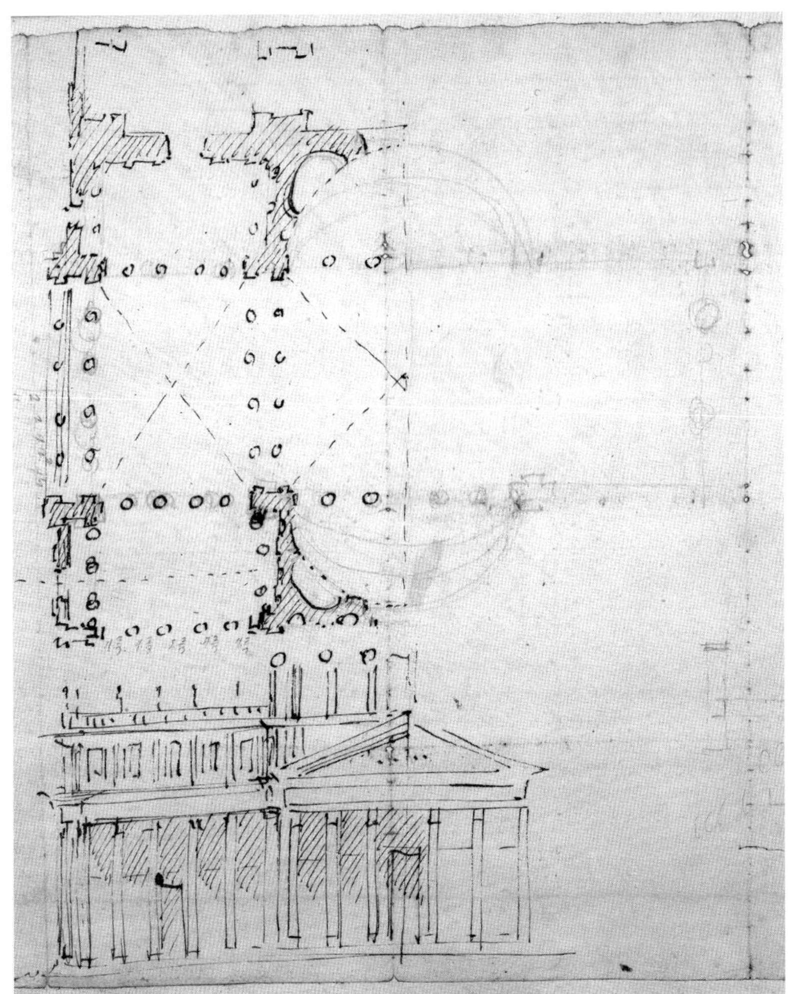

FIG. 15.4. **Filippo Juvarra (1678–1736), *Plan and Elevation of a Monumental Portico.* Pen and chalk, 23.1 × 28.2 cm. BNT, album Ris. 59,6, fol. 33r.** *(Reproduced courtesy of the Ministero per i Beni e le Attività Culturali, Biblioteca Nazionale Universitaria di Torino. Reproduction prohibited.)*

apprenticed to, or work alongside, professional artists and architects, either in their workshops or in their architectural studios.[18] In the most important architectural studio in the papal city, that of Carlo Fontana, Juvarra would have had the chance to come into contact with the Scottish architect James Gibbs. Gibbs had arrived in Rome at the end of 1703, a few months before Juvarra arrived in Rome from Sicily.[19] While a relationship between the two can be documented securely by the existence of a group of drawings given by Juvarra to Gibbs around 1706, the two men also shared personal and artistic affinities. Both Juvarra and Gibbs had had architectural training, both had trained as painters, both had taken religious vows (even though Gibbs revoked his, on account of his maltreatment by the Scottish College in Rome), and finally, although both men were firmly grounded in Roman architectural practice, they took an eclectic approach to architectural design, adapting their style to suit each commission according to its geographical context.[20]

As a participant in the *Concorsi Clementini* organized by the Accademia di San Luca in 1704–5, and after 1707 as an instructor at the Accademia, Juvarra would have had the opportunity to make the acquaintance of young British artists and architects. These included the Irish painter Henry Trench, who was in Rome in 1704 and who, like Juvarra, won some of the *Concorsi Clementini* between 1705 and 1711,[21] and also, and more significantly, the English painter William Kent, whom Juvarra probably had known since his arrival on the scene in 1710. It is a little known fact that Kent participated unsuccessfully in the second class of the *Concorso Clementino* in 1711, before winning second prize in that of 1713.[22] The young British artists and architects who came to the Eternal City regularly found themselves bitterly competing for the patronage of their noble countrymen, proposing themselves to these rich visitors as artistic advisers, *ciceroni*, copyists, or would-be professors of painting and architecture. Gibbs described the unhappy situation frankly when he lamented that he only remained in Rome from the necessity to perfect himself 'in this most miserable business of architecture', as 'things go so ill here, and there is such a pack of us, and Jealous of one another, that the one would see the other hanged'.[23]

Until his departure from the papal capital in 1708, Gibbs was most likely the conduit for Juvarra's interaction with the British Grand Tour scene in Rome. But after Juvarra joined the court of Cardinal Pietro Ottoboni in the summer of 1709, practising principally as a set designer and teacher of architecture, he came to the attention of both the Roman nobility and foreign visitors. Even after his transfer to Turin in 1714,[24] Juvarra continued in his role as set designer and adviser during trips back to Rome. Profoundly influenced by Juvarra's ability and inventiveness as a set designer to the Ottoboni court, Kent sought to present himself as the ideal go-between for Juvarra and the British patrons he kept in touch with.[25] It is not unreasonable to

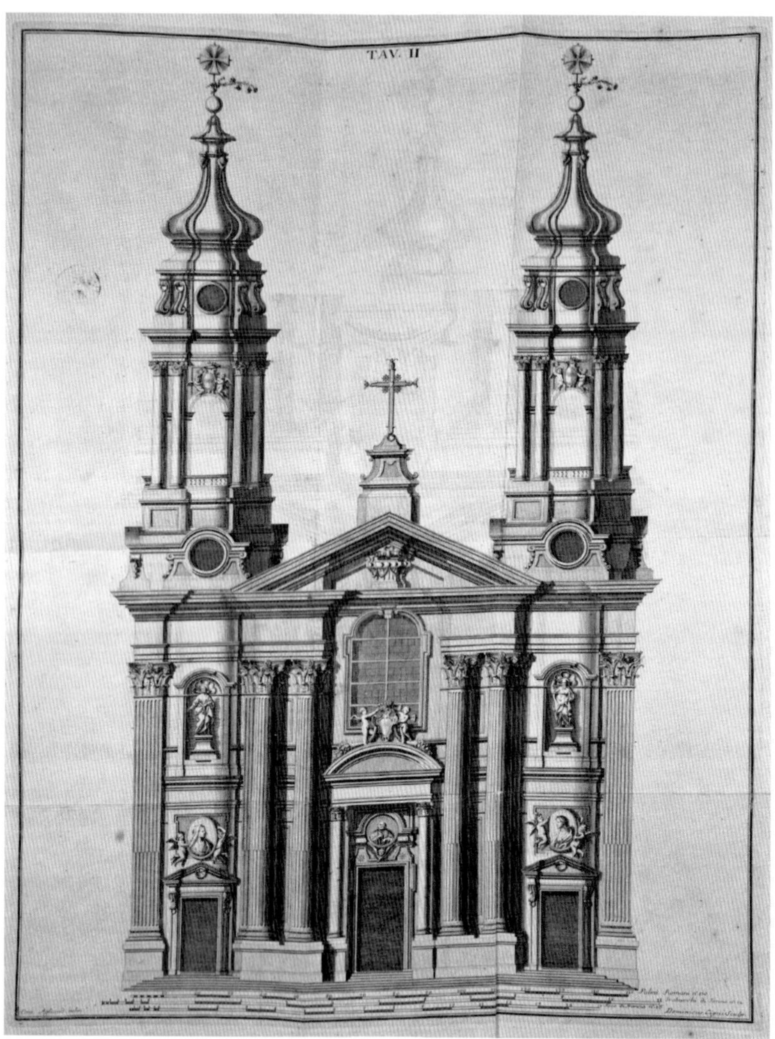

FIG. 15.5. Domenico Cigni (active c. 1760) after a drawing by Gian Pietro Baroni di Tavigliano (Ignazio Agliaudi) (1705–69), *First Project by Filippo Juvarra for the Façade of the Church of San Filippo Neri in Turin*. Copper etching with engraved retouching. After G.P. Baroni di Tavigliano, *Modello della chiesa di San Filippo Neri* (Turin, 1758), tav. II.

assume, therefore, that it was Kent who engineered an introduction for Juvarra with the youthful Thomas Coke, the future Baron Lovell and Earl of Leicester, who visited Italy from 1713 to 1717.[26]

A first meeting between Juvarra and Coke may have taken place in Rome at the Ottoboni court by mid-April 1714;[27] if not there, it would certainly have taken place in Turin, where the young aristocrat attended the military academy for a period of four months, from the middle of December 1714 until the middle of April 1715, when Juvarra was also resident in the city.[28] Moreover, Coke visited Parma together with the ubiquitous Kent[29] from 18 November until 23 December 1716, at the same time that Juvarra was slowly making his way from Turin to Rome, travelling via Parma, as can be attested by a surviving autograph drawing of 6 December 1716 of Giovanni Battista Aleotti's Ducal Theatre in Parma.[30] Juvarra's first meeting with Richard Boyle, 3rd Earl of Burlington and a friend of Coke, also may have taken place at the Ottoboni court in Rome during the same brief window of time from the middle of January 1715 until 5 February of the same year, when Burlington departed from Rome.[31] At that juncture it would surely have been Burlington's great passion for opera, for which the Ottoboni court was renowned, rather than his later, and much-celebrated, interest in architectural theory that drew him to this ambient.[32]

Whatever specific artistic rapport existed between the two British nobles and the Messinese architect, it certainly formed part and parcel of the larger cultural involvement of Juvarra with the personalities of the Grand Tour, and especially with the Jacobite circle that patronized Kent.[33] This circle, which was secretly frequented by Coke and, above all, by Burlington, came under the protection of Cardinal Ottoboni in his role as the Cardinal Protector of France, since it was France that had given political asylum to James II and his heir, James III, and to the Imperial ambassador, Johan Wenzel, Count Gallas, who had previously served as ambassador to London and who had remained a staunch supporter of the Jacobite cause in his new role as Imperial envoy to Rome.[34]

If the political implications of Juvarra's involvement with British visitors to Rome remains hypothetical, his artistic ties to these tourists can be documented securely. After the architect's death on 31 January 1736, his pupil, Giovanni Battista Sacchetti, in an inventory of Juvarra's drawings that had remained in the possession of the Savoy family, labelled a group of projects from 1716 as 'Drawings of different ideas made for a variety of English Milordi'.[35] While it is not known whether any of these projects were intended for Coke or Burlington, it can be established that some were certainly commissioned by another young English aristocrat on the Grand Tour, Anthony Grey, Earl of Harrold. Grey, son of the Duke of Kent, had left Britain in January 1715, together with his instructor and tutor, Mr J. Gerrard, with the precise intention of improving his talent as an architect, and in particular to specialize in

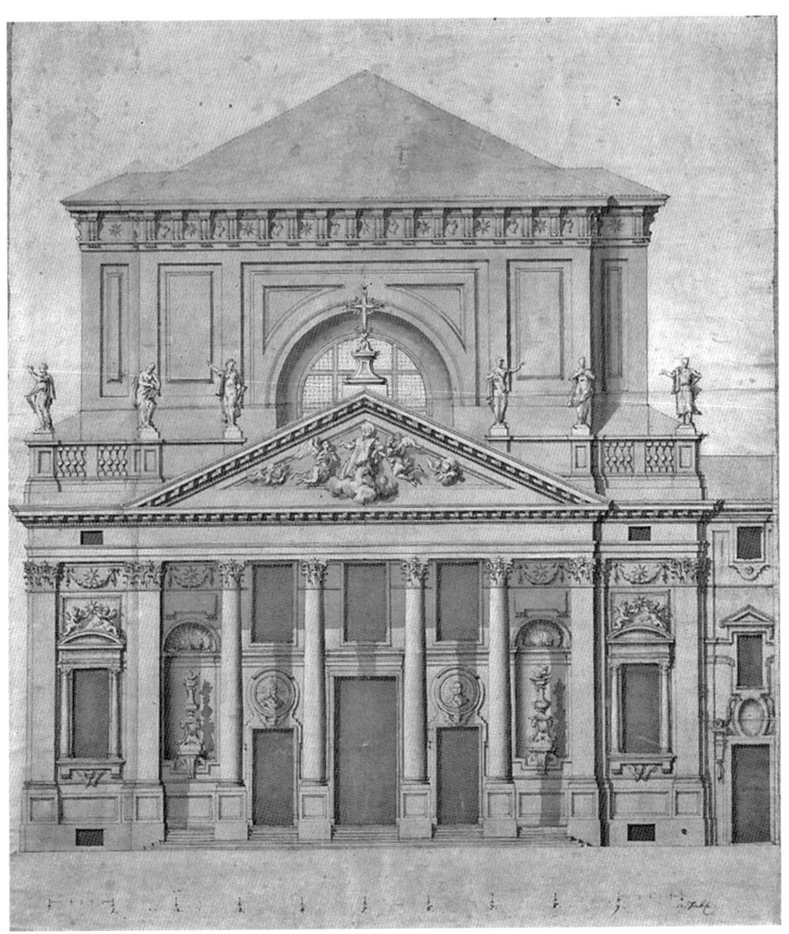

FIG. 15.6. Filippo Juvarra (1678–1736), *Definitive Project for the Façade of the Church of S. Filippo Neri in Turin*, 1730. Watercolour with traces of chalk on canvas, 45.9 × 54 cm. Museo Civico di Torino, armadio 4, palchetto 13, cartella B, 'Juvarra', Deposito dell'Archivio dei RR. PP. di San Filippo Neri. After Gritella, *Juvarra* (n. 3), I, 306 fig. 377.

domestic architecture.[36] Grey's mission was at the instigation of his father, who wished to update the family residence, Wrest Park in Bedfordshire. To this end, the Duke of Kent simultaneously had demanded a project for the house from his courtier, the Venetian architect Giacomo Leoni; however, only a drawing for the ground-plan for the first of two projects by Leoni survives (Fig. 15.9).[37]

Harrold and Gerrard received Leoni's project by mail in Genoa, at the end of August 1715, with instructions that they present it for critiquing to the best Italian architects.[38] Juvarra, in Genoa on his way back to Turin from Rome, and renowned as Italy's most important architect, was the first to be asked to give his opinion.[39] Subsequently, when he arrived in Turin, Vittorio Amedeo commissioned Juvarra to produce an alternative project for Wrest Park, *ex novo*.[40] Unfortunately, Juvarra's drawings for this project, which he began planning during his trip back to Turin and which only reached Harrold in Venice after a long interval in August 1716, have all been lost, except for some that feature two variants for a garden pavilion (Figs 15.10 and 15.11).[41] However, the stunned reactions of Harrold and Gerrard, who described Juvarra's project as magnificent but frightening, survive in letters written to the Duke, giving a clear idea of what Juvarra had planned. The nobleman and his tutor were particularly astonished by a double-height central oval *salone*, which could be seen rising up out of the body of the palace over the main façade, an idea perhaps more suited to the Vatican sacristy than to an English country house. But they were quick to assure the Duke that the huge number of pilasters and columns that were distributed along the exterior walls could be reduced drastically to make the grandiose project more feasible. Not surprisingly, Juvarra's project never saw the light of day, and neither did that of Leoni.

Notwithstanding the fact that Juvarra had attempted to comply with the Duke's preference for 'plainness' in the planning of the buildings,[42] as we know from correspondence concerning the project, ultimately the architect was unable to satisfy his client's brief. Indeed, Juvarra had designed a Roman villa suitable for a competition at the Accademia di San Luca, a design that would have been totally incongruous with the aesthetic of the Duke, who was an exponent of the current trend of British cultural patronage that was centred on the rediscovery of Palladio. The Duke promoted the publication of the first edition of Colen Campbell's *Vitruvius Britannicus*, and was also behind the first English edition of Palladio's *Quattro libri*, edited by Leoni, both of which had appeared in the previous summer, in 1715.

At the time that Juvarra travelled to Portugal, Britain and France, with his first Turin projects well in hand, he was still under the sway of his earliest Roman training and had not been able to respond to the design challenges presented by foreign contemporary architectural developments. Despite having freed himself from the kind of project he had designed for the Accademia di San Luca competition, his work had not satisfied the expectations of the Duke of Kent, nor of his son and

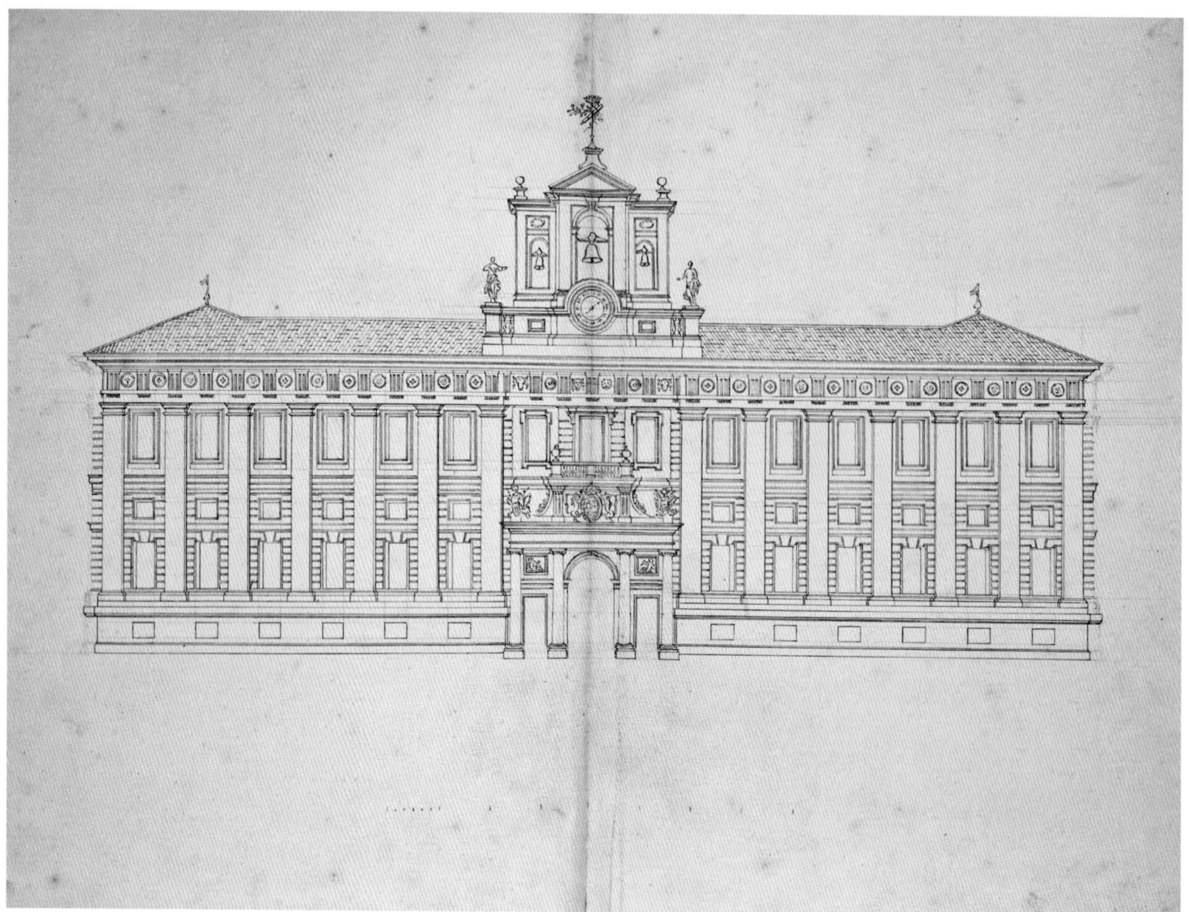

FIG. 15.7. Studio of Filippo Juvarra, *Second Project for the Main Façade of the Palazzo del Senato Sabaudo, Turin*. Pen and ink and chalk, 58.2 × 45.9 cm. BNT, album Ris. 59,3, fol. 37. *(Reproduced courtesy of the Ministero per i Beni e le Attività Culturali, Biblioteca Nazionale Universitaria di Torino. Reproduction prohibited.)*

his tutor. He had not been able to make headway with contemporary developments in France, which traditionally served as a model for the Turin court; nor had he responded to the English architectural scene, which at the time was the most effervescent in Europe for its capacity for self-renewal.

It was Juvarra's intention to engage with new architectural developments that must have been one of the

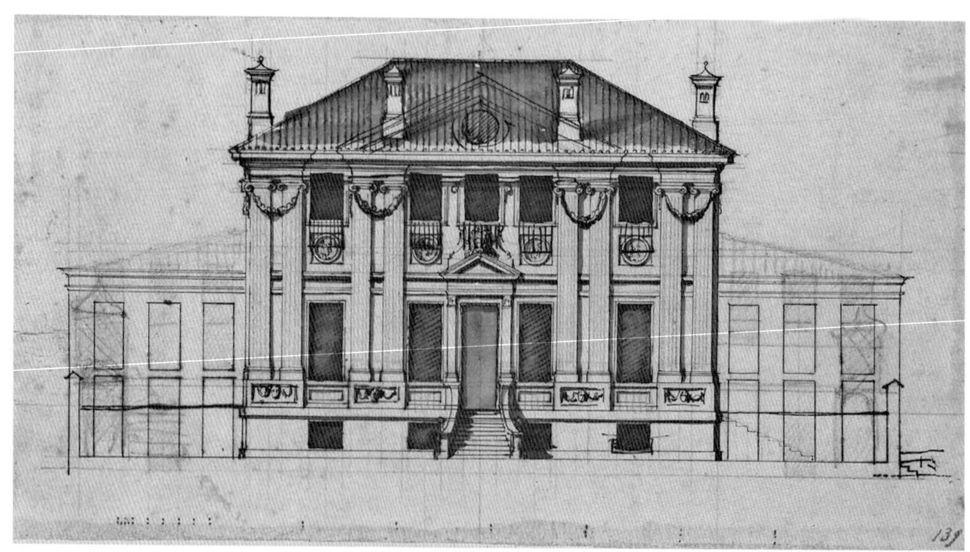

FIG. 15.8. Filippo Juvarra (1678–1736), *Project for Juvarra's House in Turin*, c. 1724. Ink, watercolour and chalk on paper, 33.6 × 17.8 cm. Museo Civico di Torino, Disegni di Filippo Juvarra, vol. I, fol. 89, n. 139. After Gritella, *Juvarra* (n. 3), II, 475 fig. 563.

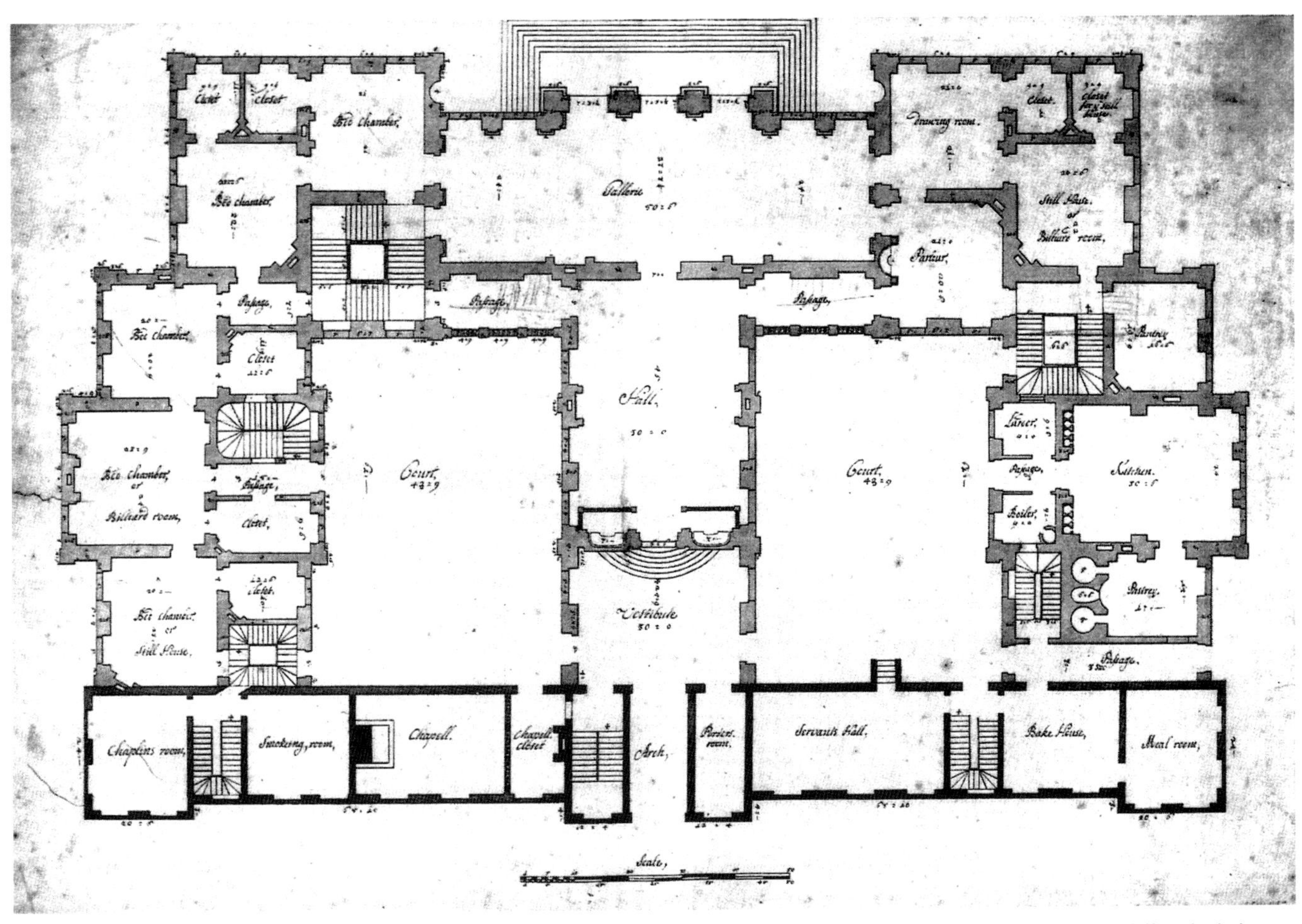

FIG. 15.9. Giacomo Leoni (c. 1686–1746), *Plan of a Project for Reconstructing Wrest Park*, 1715. Bedfordshire County Record Office, Lady Lucas Collection, L33/46. After Friedmann, 'Lord Harrold in Italy 1715–1716' (n. 36), 837, fig. 29.

factors behind his mysterious trip to London. He arrived in the English capital on 10 August 1719, 21 days after his departure from Lisbon on a fast packet-boat.[43] Dressed in civilian attire to hide his identity as a priest in the anti-Catholic climate of Britain, Juvarra surely employed the recommendations and credentials given to him by João V to establish contacts with the highest levels of English aristocracy. Juvarra also may have been involved in covert diplomacy, as his principal patrons, in the House of Savoy, were at that time indirectly involved in a war that saw France, Holland, Britain and Austria opposing Spain over the question of the latter's attack in 1718 on Savoy-held Sicily. Juvarra's trip to Lisbon surely formed part of the diplomatic process of reconciliation that led to the re-establishing of official relations between the Savoy state and Portugal. Moreover, in addition to such overtly political factors, the ever present and inflammatory issue of the Jacobites must have played a part, as it was a cause that secretly involved more or less all of Juvarra's possible London contacts. In the circle of his former Roman acquaintances then in London, such as the engraver Nicholas Dorigny and the violoncellist Filippo Amadei (in the service of Lord Burlington), the primary role must have been played by Juvarra's friend Gibbs, who was both Catholic and Jacobite. It is tempting to picture Gibbs as Juvarra's guide to the capital's religious architecture, and above all to his own recently-completed church of Saint Mary-le-Strand (1714–17), an iconic example of the mix of Roman traditions and local practices. But Gibbs may have shown Juvarra around civil structures as well, including the austere and monumental public buildings of London, where, independently of their specific styles, the Italian architect could finally come to terms with that 'plainness' that had been required of him four years previously by the Duke of Kent's son. Juvarra may well have met Lord Harrold in London, and also probably encountered Thomas Coke and Lord Burlington, both of whom were in the English capital during the architect's visit.

In the absence of further documentary evidence, the clues regarding a probable London meeting between Burlington and Juvarra, paradoxically, induce one to hypothesize that the two also may have left the capital together to travel to France.[44] This hypothetical voyage, moreover, lends itself to another intriguing line of speculation, namely that Burlington's trip was in reality a secret mission connected to the cause to restore James III to the British throne, since it was just at this time, the summer of 1719, that the exiled Stuart King was attempting a return to power.[45] That Juvarra may have associated himself with Burlington's entourage is supported by the coincidence of dates of their French sojourns.[46] According to Francesco Juvarra's biography of his brother, once in France Juvarra was accompanied to the royal sites by Louis XIV's architects, probably including the first architect to the King, Robert de Cotte, whom Burlington surely knew. Like Bernini before him, Juvarra opined about contemporary architectural developments, and did not fail to criticize the inadequate monumentality of buildings in relation to the splendour of their patron, rebuking architects who 'were unable to take an idea of antique, imperial grandeur, to allude to grandiosity'.[47] For both Juvarra and Burlington, this 'idea' constituted the foundation of architecture suited to the status of a nobleman.

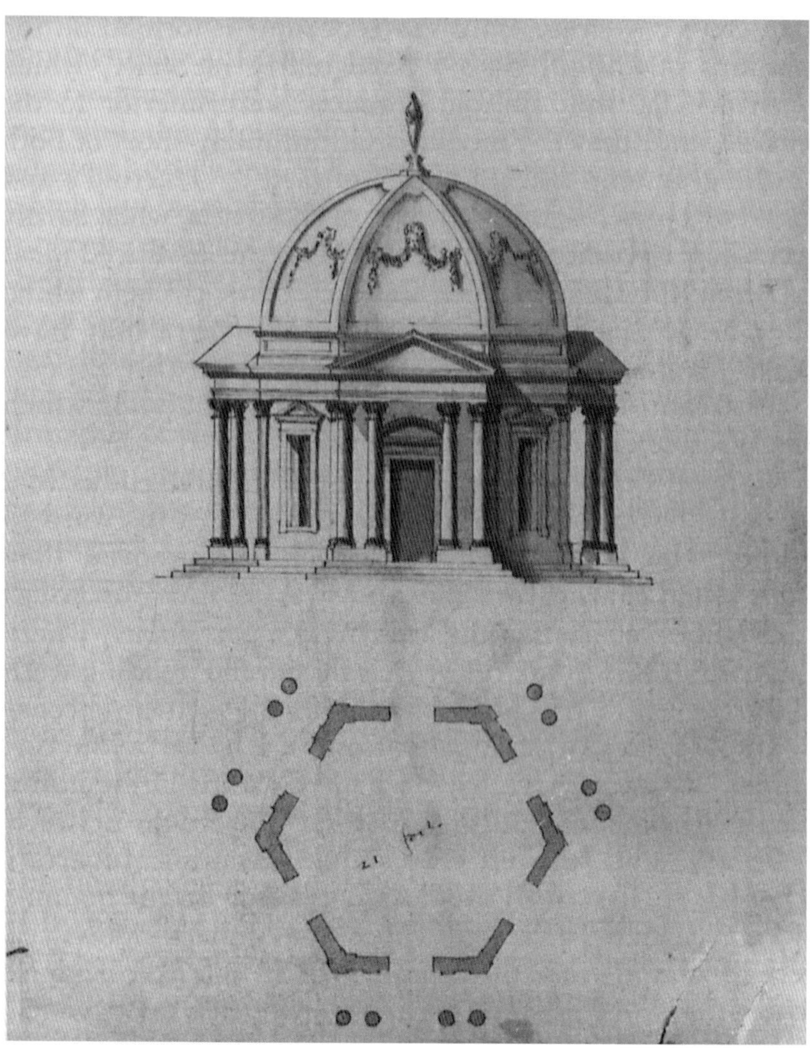

Fig. 15.10. Filippo Juvarra (1678–1736), *Garden Pavilion for Wrest Park*, plan and elevation, 1715–16. Bedfordshire County Record Office, Lady Lucas Collection, L33/101. After Friedmann, 'Lord Harrold in Italy 1715–1716' (n. 36), 839, fig. 30.

The date of Burlington's arrival in Genoa, at the beginning of October, as well as the date of Juvarra's return to Turin, a few days before 11 October, also fit with the hypothesis of a continuation of their trip into Italy. Such a journey, apart from its eventual political implications, would for Burlington at least have had only one goal: to arrive in the Veneto and organize a systematic campaign to record all of Palladio's buildings. This information comes to us at first hand from a letter written by Kent, who, with his usual alacrity, was in Genoa when Burlington arrived on his way back to England. He wrote that Burlington 'was going towards Vicenza & Venice to get Archetects to draw all ye fine buildings of Palladio, and return back here (Paris)'.[48] With characteristic opportunism, after Burlington had praised his architectural drawings, Kent was then invited by Burlington to precede him to Paris and await his arrival there, so that they might return to Britain together. Once home, Burlington determined that they would finally be able to change the 'Dam'd Gusto' that in his opinion dominated the British architectural scene.[49]

Even if we consider these events to be a series of accidents and not part of a complex plan organized by Burlington and Juvarra before they left Britain, it is nevertheless highly probable that Burlington's intention to achieve a deeper understanding of Palladio through studying his designs on site was in some way related to Juvarra's manner of reasoning and of interpreting architecture. Indeed, after his stay in the

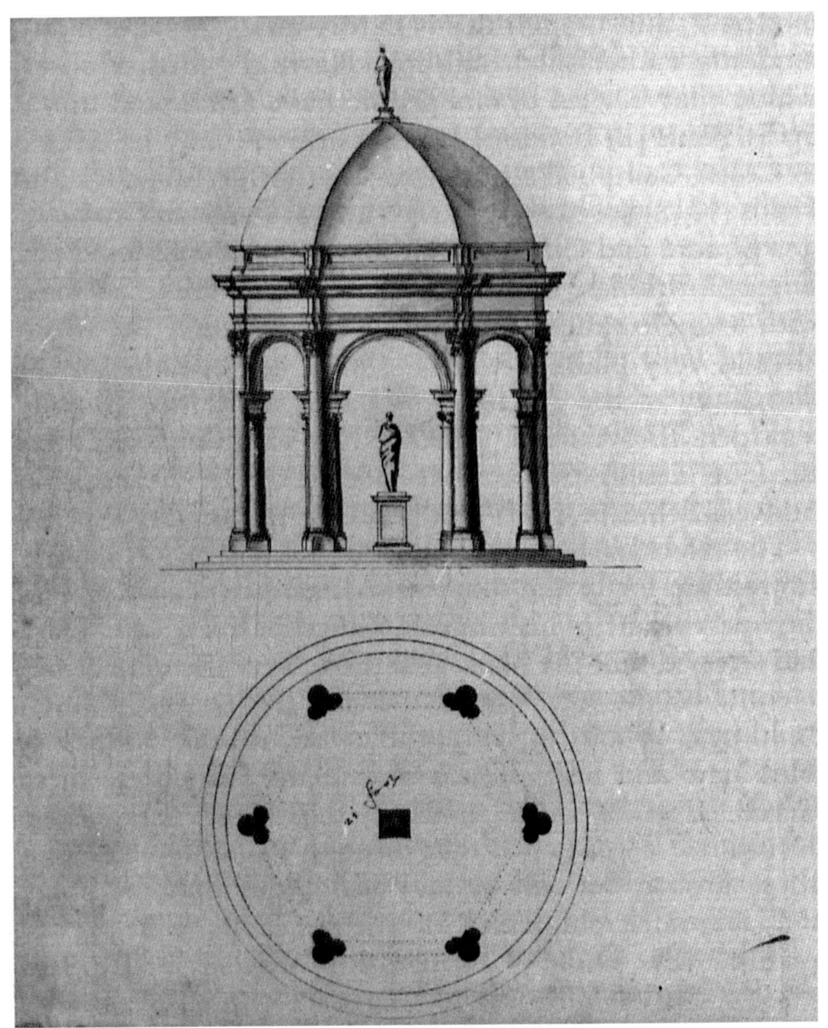

FIG. 15.11. Filippo Juvarra (1678–1736), *Garden Pavilion for Wrest Park*, plan and elevation, 1715–16. Bedfordshire County Record Office, Lady Lucas Collection, L33/101. After Friedmann, 'Lord Harrold in Italy 1715–1716' (n. 36), 839, fig. 31.

Veneto, carrying with him not the drawings of Palladio's buildings that he had set out to commission — which on account of extreme weather conditions he had been unable to order — but a bundle of original Palladio drawings after Roman baths, Burlington caught up with Juvarra in Turin, where he can be documented on 6 November 1719. It was at the court of Vittorio Amedeo II Savoy, where the culture was dominated by Juvarra, that Burlington made his last stop on this second, fleeting and final voyage to Italy, before returning to Britain with a new-found determination. This saw him transformed from the enthusiastic connoisseur and dilettante architect that he had been at the time of Juvarra's arrival in London, into an international icon of neo-Palladianism, Roman style, which had been developed by his favoured courtier Kent under the influence of Juvarra.[50]

In this context, it is notable that one of the first connections between the works of Juvarra and those of Kent is designs for grotesque decorations for royal apartments, both inspired by the same Roman antiquarian models. During a brief period Juvarra experimented with this type of ornamentation in the ceiling decoration of five rooms at Vittorio Amedeo II's Castello di Rivoli (1720–5), at the same time that Kent was designing three rooms in the same idiom at Kensington Palace for George I (the King's Bedroom, 1723; the Council Room and the Presence Room, 1724).[51] Even if these projects evolved independently, they display a common interest in mixing antique prototypes with Roman and French sixteenth-century designs (the last of which both architects had been able to study during their separate visits to Paris). Moreover, the inventiveness of Kent's designs was certainly indebted to Juvarra. As we have seen, the same mix of architectural models characterize Juvarra's 'pseudo-Palladian' period in Turin, following his European trip.

This period partly overlaps with the presence in Turin of John Molesworth as British Consul. Molesworth was a great connoisseur of architecture and a patron of Alessandro Galilei, and was perhaps the only person to understand the influence that English architectural culture had on the stylistic development of Juvarra.

Finally, it cannot be coincidental that immediately following the publication of Palladio's drawings after Roman baths by Burlington in 1730, Juvarra dedicated a volume of architectural and antiquarian capriccios to Burlington that are today at Chatsworth. Some of these drawings reflect themes and subjects related to Juvarra's European trip of ten years earlier: the pyramidal crowning element recurs, as do monumental bridges, while two drawings were inspired by memories of the royal architecture Juvarra saw in France, the Collège des Quatre-Nations by Le Vau in Paris, and the Pont du Gard at Nîmes. Inserted within an eclectic mix of references appears a small, circular temple set upon a podium articulated with staircases, which, as Wittkower has demonstrated, influenced Burlington's decision to add a similar base to Hawksmoor's mausoleum at Castle Howard, profiting from the latter's death in 1736, even though Hawksmoor had been staunchly opposed to any type of modification.[52] With this decision Burlington not only established a striking connection between Hawksmoor and Juvarra, both of whom shared a sensibility towards antiquarian themes, but also celebrated symbolically, on English soil, an epilogue to the intense and fruitful rapport that the Sicilian architect had cultivated with his British colleagues and patrons.

Notes

1. F. Juvarra, 'Vita del cavaliere don Filippo Juvara. Abbate di Selve e Primo architetto di S.M. di Sardegna [*c.* 1736]', ed. A. Marabottini, in L. Pascoli, *Vite de' pittori, scultori ed architetti viventi, dai manoscritti 1383 e 1743 della Biblioteca Comunale 'Augusta' di Perugia* (Treviso, 1981), 276–88. Francesco Juvarra fixed the date of his brother's departure for Lisbon, presumably from Turin, as 'in the month of November 1719' ('nel mese di novembre del 1719').
2. Juvarra, 'Vita' (above, n. 1), 284–6: 'Spirava intanto il tempo della licenza datagli dal suo Re, et andatose a' Piedi di S. Maestà [João V] gli ricordò l'obbligo che avea di ritornarsene in Torino, che con dispiacere gl'accordò il ritorno accompagnandolo con doni di galanterie della Cina d'infinito valore . . . e perché D. Filippo aveva detto a detta S. Maestà che voleva fare il giro per l'Inghilterra, e la Francia gli comandò espressamente che arrivato in Londra, e Pariggi si portasse da suoi Ministri, e colà si trattenesse tutto il tempo che dovea dimorare in quel luogo, et oltre ciò gli donò per il viaggio delle Casse di Cioccolata, di Cera, di Zuccaro, molti castrati, pollami, et infinita altra robba dimostrazioni degne veramente della generosità, e magnanimità dell'animo della Maestà di quel Gran Re.

   Vestitosi da secolare s'imbarcò nel vascello che si spedisce per le lettere alla volta di Londra che in poco tempo vi pervenne andando secondo gli ordini del Re di Portogallo in casa del di lui Ministro che fu accolto con indicibbile allegrezza dal medesimo e trattato con tutta distinzione, e mentre una mattina lo conduceva seco a diporto assiemi con altro cavaliere per far visita ad una dama fuori di Londra alcune miglia s'incontrarono per strada con quattro a cavallo con pistole alla mano che fattigli smontare da loro cavalli gli levarono ciò che avevano indosso, et a D. Filippo gli fu levato l'orologio, tabbacchiera d'argento, et una borza di doppie, e ciò fu motivo di ritornarsene immediatamente in Londra e la mattina il Sig. Ambasciadore fece trovare sul tavolino a D. Filippo altro orologio, altra tabbacchiera, et una borza di doppie, et anche di più di quelle gli erano state tolte tanto era la stima, e l'onore che gli portava, e non trattenutosi che un mese di Londra si partì alla volta di Parigi ove giunto fu trattato con grande onore, e dall'ambasciatore di Portogallo secondo gli ordini di quel Re e dal primo Architetto di Luiggi XIV, che lo portò seco vedendo tutte le cose magnifiche di quella città, e di Versaglia, et interrogato dagl'architetti del suo paese su le lor fabbriche le lodò molto, ma per esser secche, e senza grandiosità gli diede una bella risposta, che essendogli state ordinate le fabbriche da quel gran Re non avevano saputo prendere un idea dell'Imperatori antichi, per alludere alla grandiosità, e trattenutosi colà un mese o poco più tornò speditamente in Torino al servizio del suo Re'. On the attack whilst in the company of the Portuguese ambassador, see also the contribution of Katrina Grant in this volume.
3. R. Wittkower, 'Un libro di schizzi di Filippo Juvarra a Chatsworth', *Bollettino della Società Piemontese d'Archeologia e di*

Belle Arti n.s. 3 (1–4) (1949), 94–118, esp. p. 75 (English edition 'A sketchbook of Filippo Juvarra at Chatsworth', in R. Wittkower, *Studies in the Italian Baroque* (London, 1975), 187–210); V. Viale, 'Regesto della vita e delle opere di Filippo Juvarra', in V. Viale (ed.), *Filippo Juvarra, architetto e scenografo* (Messina, 1966), 69; S. Boscarino, *Filippo Juvarra architetto* (Rome, 1973), 303; G. Gritella, *Juvarra. L'architettura*, 2 vols (Modena, 1992), I, 58; G. Dardanello, 'Juvarra e l'ornato da Roma a Torino: repertori di motive per assemblaggi creativi', in G. Dardanello (ed.), *Disegnare l'ornato. Interni piemontesi di Sei e Settecento* (Turin, 2007), 170–2.

4. Wittkower, 'Un libro di schizzi' (above, n. 3), 114. Wittkower noted the presence of the stepped pyramidal motif on fol. 49 of album Ris. 59,6 in the Biblioteca Nazionale di Torino [henceforth BNT], showing the triumphal bridge, as well as on fol. 4. of the same album and on fols 2 and 10 in the album at Chatsworth given by Juvarra to Lord Burlington in 1730.
5. For a possible dating of the written description of the Mausoleum of Halicarnassus in Wren's *Parentalia* to a date after 1680, and for the subsequent translation by Hawksmoor of this written description into a design for a bell-tower for the Church of All Souls and for its realization as the bell-tower for Saint George's at Bloomsbury, see G. Worsley, *Classical Architecture in Britain. The Heroic Age* (New Haven/London, 1995), 50–6.
6. BNT, album Ris. 59,4 fol. 40r.4. This drawing was described by M. Viale Ferrero (*Filippo Juvarra, scenografo e architetto teatrale* (Turin/New York/London, 1970), 342) as representing the 'exterior of a temple' and as forming part of a group of drawings for Cardinal Ottoboni for an unidentified opera.
7. This is the reconstruction that Fischer von Erlach proposed in his *Entwurf einer Historischen Architektur*, published in 1721, but begun after 1705 following his London trip of 1704, where he probably met Wren. See Worsley, *Classical Architecture* (above, n. 5), 51.
8. Regarding the circumstances of the trip and the presence of Juvarra in Portugal, see A. Scotti, 'L'attività di Filippo Juvarra a Lisbona alla luce delle più recenti interpretazioni critiche della sua architettura con una appendice sui rapporti Roma–Lisbona', *Colóquio Artes* s. II, 18 (1976), 28; A. Scotti, 'L'accademia degli Arcadi e i suoi rapporti con la cultura portoghese nel primo ventennio del 1700', in *Actas do congresso a arte em Portugal no séc. XVIII, Bracara Augusta*, t. XXVII, 63, I (1973), 122; Gritella, *Juvarra* (above, n. 3), 462–9; A. Delaforce, *Art and Patronage in Eighteenth-century Portugal* (Cambridge, 2002), 181–7; W. Rossa, 'Lisbon's waterfront image as an allegory of Baroque urban aesthetics', in H.A. Millon (ed.), *Circa 1700: Architecture in Europe and the Americas* (Washington, 2005), 167–75.
9. The folio drawing in the album Ris 59,6 represents the first combination of the model for the 'magnificent' and 'triumphal' bridge in the specifications put forward by D.R. Marshall, 'Piranesi, Juvarra, and the triumphal bridge tradition', *The Art Bulletin* 85 (2003), 321–52, to which the reader is referred for the other Juvarra drawings of this subject. Among these, two capriccios based on the 'Tiber Island of antiquity' can be singled out as the most relevant for the present discussion. One is from the first years of Juvarra's Roman sojourn of 1704–17 (Turin, Fondazione Antonio Maria e Mariella Marocco (previously Tournon Collection), vol. II, fol. 104) and the other comes from the album *Disegni di prospettiva ideale*, bearing a dedication to King Augustus of Poland, 12 April 1732 (Dresden, Kupferstich-Kabinett, Ca 66, n. 17449).
10. S. Maffei, 'Elogio di Filippo Juvarra', in *Osservazioni letterarie che possino servire di continuazione al Giornale de' Letterati d'Italia* III (Verona, 1738), 193–204.
11. BNT, album Ris. 59,6, fol. 3r.
12. BNT, album Ris. 59,6, fol. 4r.
13. BNT, album Ris. 59,6, fol. 31bis–v. The drawing depicts the Mafra complex, still under construction, as shown by the incomplete terminating elements of the bell-towers and the buttresses; these last were planned by Juvarra to be completed with crowning elements different to those that were eventually realized. The connection of this drawing with the Mafra project has been proposed only tentatively so far, by the cataloguer of the drawing at the Biblioteca Nazionale di Torino.
14. BNT, album Ris. 59,6, fol. 33r.
15. On the various projects for the church of San Filippo Neri and on the *prospetto* undertaken in the nineteenth century, with some variations with respect to the definitive project, see Gritella, *Juvarra* (above, n. 3), 287–317, with a vast previous bibliography, and especially V. Comoli Mandracci, *Le invenzioni di Filippo Juvarra per la chiesa di San Filippo Neri in Torino. Con notizia dei vari disegni e della realizzazione dell'opera* (Turin, 1967).
16. The dedication of the volume, entitled *Studio d'architettura civile sopra gli ornamenti di porte e finestre disegniate dal Cav. Yvarra 1725*, is dated 24 December 1725 (Turin, Fondazione Antonio Maria e Mariella Marocco (previously Tournon Collection, vol. II)) (cited in L. Rovere, V. Viale and A.E. Brickmann, *Filippo Juvarra* (Milan, 1937), 81–2); G. Dardanello, 'Filippo Juvarra: 'chi poco vede niente pensa'', in G. Dardanello (ed.), *Sperimentare l'architettura: Guarini, Juvarra, Alfieri, Borra, Vittone* (Turin, 2001), 158, n. 119.
17. On Juvarra's house in Turin, in the via di San Domenico, see Gritella, *Juvarra* (above, n. 3), II, 55–6, 474–5; Dardanello, 'Filippo Juvarra' (above, n. 16), 176, pl. 64. Although construction of Juvarra's house was begun in 1724, the residence was almost certainly planned already in 1720, the date when Vittorio Amedeo II made the architect a gift of the site.
18. For Juvarra's early formation in Messina and his residency in Rome until 1714, see T. Manfredi, *Filippo Juvarra. Gli anni giovanili* (Rome, 2010); H.A. Millon, *Filippo Juvarra. Drawings from the Roman Period. 1704–1714* (Rome, 1984); T. Manfredi, *Filippo Juvarra a Roma (1704–1714).*

La costruzione di una carriera (Ph.D. thesis, Politecnico di Torino, 1997); T. Manfredi, 'Filippo Juvarra', in *Dizionario biografico degli Italiani* LXII (Rome, 2004), 710–19. On the architect's subsequent connection with Rome, see T. Manfredi, 'Juvarra e Roma (1714–1732): la diplomazia dell'architettura', in Dardanello (ed.), *Sperimentare l'architettura* (above, n. 16), 177–96; T. Manfredi, 'Filippo Juvarra e il giovane Vanvitelli', in A. Gambardella (ed.), *Luigi Vanvitelli, 1700–2000. Atti del convegno internazionale, Caserta, 14–16 dicembre 2000* (Caserta, 2005), 233–42; T. Manfredi, 'Filippo Juvarra a Roma: i progetti per la chiesa dei Santi Cosma e Damiano dei Barbieri', *Palladio* 20 (2007), 55–68. For the dates that Juvarra was present in Rome (between 1715 and 1732), see T. Manfredi, 'La biblioteca di architettura e i rami incisi dell'eredità Juvarra', in V. Comoli Mandracci and A. Griseri (eds), *Filippo Juvarra. Architetto delle capitali. Da Torino a Madrid 1714–1736* (Milan, 1995), 287–90, nn. 4–14; T. Manfredi, 'La professione del Virtuoso', in G. Bonaccorso and T. Manfredi, *I Virtuosi al Pantheon. 1700–1758* (Rome, 1998), 40.

19. T. Friedman, *James Gibbs* (New Haven/London, 1984); B. Ford and J. Ingamells, *A Dictionary of British and Irish Travellers in Italy, 1701–1800. Compiled from the Brinsley Ford Archive* (New Haven/London, 1997), 398–9. Gibbs arrived in Rome in October of 1703, after having been to Holland, Germany and France, and made contact with Juvarra in Fontana's studio, where he was accepted as an architectural student (until the end of 1704). Later, Gibbs would say that, other than Fontana, his master had been Abraham Paris. The group of six 'targhe' (plaques for coats-of-arms) entitled 'invenzione del Juvarra', given by the Messinese architect to Gibbs before his departure from Rome in 1708, can be dated to around 1706 (Friedman, *James Gibbs* (above), 87; V. Assandria, C. Gauna and G. Tetti, 'L'architettura descritta: viaggiatori e guide a Torino tra Sei e Settecento', in Dardanello (ed.), *Sperimentare l'architettura* (above, n. 16), 335.

20. For a young, aspiring and ambitious architect to frequent the studio of the father–son team of Carlo and Francesco Fontana was comparable to attending the Accademia di San Luca itself, as the Fontanas were effectively in control of that institution's architectural mission. None the less, even though Gibbs did not participate in the *Concorsi Clementini*, he surely attended the academic courses, because in later life he declared that Pier Francesco Garoli, a professor of perspective, had been his teacher at the Accademia before 1708. Bearing this in mind, it is probable that Gibbs was present at Juvarra's victory in the first-class competition of 1705, winning with a magnificent project for a 'villa for three princes'.

21. Ford and Ingamells, *Dictionary of British and Irish Travellers* (above, n. 19), 950–2; T. Mowl, *William Kent. Architect, Designer, Opportunist* (London, 2007), 30–1, 38–41, 47, 49. Trench won the first prize 'ex aequo' of the third class of 1705, the first prize of the second class of 1706 and the second prize of the first class of 1711 (A. Cipriani and E. Valeriani (eds), *I disegni di figura nell'archivio storico dell'Accademia di San Luca* II (Rome, 1989), 55, 67, 71, 82, 141, 145).

22. While Kent's participation in the second class of the *Concorso Clementino* for painting in 1711 was unsuccessful (Cipriani and Valeriani (eds), *I disegni di figura* (above, n. 21), 143), this indicates that he evidently frequented the Accademia di San Luca from the moment he arrived in Rome in April 1710. At exactly this time Juvarra was teaching perspective to future painters and architects, and so came into contact with the architect earlier than has been assumed previously (cf. Viale Ferrero, *Filippo Juvarra* (above, n. 6), 56; M. Wilson, *William Kent. Architect, Designer, Painter, Gardener, 1685–1748* (London, 1984), 233). For Kent's painterly training in Rome, which he began under Giuseppe Chiari, see Wilson, *William Kent* (above); C.M. Sicca, 'On William Kent's Roman sources', *Architectural History* 29 (1986), 134–57; Ford and Ingamells, *Dictionary of British and Irish Travellers* (above, n. 19), 569–71; Mowl, *William Kent* (above, n. 21). For the broader context of Juvarra's academic activity, see my forthcoming monograph on the architect. Trench and Kent's regular attendance at the Accademia, and the fact that both artists came from the Marattesque studio of Chiari, along with the numerous surviving letters from Kent, testify to their close contacts, even if this did not extend to friendship. These contacts may have included also a third young British painter, the unknown John Taylor, identified as 'Gioani Telor scocese', who, together with an unknown Irishman ('ibernese') David Roger, participated unsuccessfully in the third class of the *Concorso Clementino* in painting in 1707 (Cipriani and Valeriani (eds), *I disegni di figura* (above, n. 21), 90). As we know, moreover, from a letter of Kent, Roger was still in Rome in 1714 (Ford and Ingamells, *Dictionary of British and Irish Travellers* (above, n. 19), 932).

23. From a letter from Gibbs to Sir John Perceval of 3 December 1707: Friedman, *James Gibbs* (above, n. 19); Ford and Ingamells, *Dictionary of British and Irish Travellers* (above, n. 19), 398. In these difficult circumstances, Gibbs often turned to tour guiding and to architectural instruction for hire, while Kent and Trench busied themselves giving lessons on art to illustrious visitors, and also procuring architectural teachers for them.

24. See the bibliography in n. 18.

25. For the notable influence that Juvarra and the theatrical ambience of the Ottoboni court exercised on the artistic formation and production of Kent, see the article by Grant in this volume, pp. 225–39. In any case, it is clear that, both before and after his transfer to Turin, the rapport between Juvarra and Kent was consolidated in court circles and that it had huge consequences for the artistic formation of the young British artist. Kent's ripening openness to the extraordinary artistic possibilities offered by viewing the stage designs exhibited between 1710 and 1714 in Ottoboni's private theatre at the Cancelleria, in the public theatre of the Palazzo Capranica, and in that of the Queen of Poland (which, contrary to general belief, was not situated in the Palazzo Zuccari, but in

the nearby Villa Torres), must be considered, together with the prevailing influence of Juvarra's presence.

26. Ford and Ingamells, *Dictionary of British and Irish Travellers* (above, n. 19), 225–6.
27. The young Thomas Coke, animated by a grand passion for the arts, arrived in Rome on 7 February 1714 and remained until 6 June (except for a trip he made to Naples from 10 to 22 March). As Wittkower suggested (R. Wittkower, 'Documenti sui modelli per la sacrestia di San Pietro a Roma', *Bollettino della Società Piemontese d'Archeologia e di Belle arti*, n.s. 3 (1949), 105), while in Rome Coke could have met up with Juvarra before the middle of April 1714, at which date the architect left for Lucca (where he can be documented between 20 April and 21 May 1714).
28. Coke made contact with both Trench and Kent, and on 6 June 1714 he undertook a long study trip to the south of Italy with the latter. We know that Kent left Coke in Padua in early August to study in Parma (although there are payments for 9 and 24 August from Coke to Trench). Thereafter, Coke continued travelling, visiting Vicenza, Verona, Mantua, Modena and Parma, until he reached Turin. He arrived in the Savoy capital on 3 December 1714 and departed 12 April 1715, after having attended a local military academy, a favoured choice of the English nobility. In Turin, Coke could have met Juvarra at any time from the middle of December 1714, when Juvarra returned from Rome (the architect was sworn in as royal architect on 18 December), until the middle of January 1715. At that date Juvarra left for a six-month trip to Rome, as he was participating in the competition for the design for a new Vatican sacristy. Thereafter, Coke travelled extensively through France, Switzerland and Germany, until December 1715, when he travelled by boat to Sicily, where he remained between January and February 1716, also visiting Malta. Finally, from the port of Amalfi he made his way back up the Italian peninsula. Coke's unusual decision to include Sicily and Malta in his Grand Tour may well have been the result of Juvarra's influence, as it would not be surprising that the Messinese architect would have told the young Englishman about his native Sicily. Similarly, the decision to stay for such a long period in Turin to attend the military academy, in the same city in which Juvarra was royal architect, lends credence to the possibility that there was a pre-existing rapport between the two that had begun with Coke's tour to Rome, and may have been tied to his architecture lessons. Juvarra did not meet Coke in the winter of 1715–16 in Rome, as the architect had left Rome before Coke's arrival from the south, on 2 June 1716 (see below, n. 29).
29. Coke, together with Kent who had met up with him in Naples in May, and who was probably on his umpteenth tour, after a stopover in Rome, continued on to northern Italy, in search of the paintings and architecture that were increasingly interesting the young Lord.
30. The drawing of Aleotti's Parma theatre is one of a group of eleven drawings, made on site, of churches by architects of the sixteenth and seventeenth centuries. These included: San Sebastiano in Milan (Pellegrino Tibaldi); the Annunziata dei Minimi (Giovanni Battista Fornovo) and Santa Maria della Steccata (Giovanni Battista Zaccagni) in Parma; the Madonna dei Servi di Maria o della Ghiara (Alessandro Balbi and Francesco Pacchioni) in Reggio Emilia; San Giorgio (Gaspare Vigarani) in Modena; and Santi Salvatore e Paolo (Magenta) in Bologna. These on-site drawings map the route that Juvarra was travelling to Rome (A. Griseri, 'Itinerari juvarriani', *Paragone (Arte)* 93 (1957), 51–4, figs 38a–40b; Boscarino, *Filippo Juvarra* (above, n. 3), figs 35–6). Coke and Kent can be documented in Parma at the end of 1716 (18 November–23 December), Reggio Emilia (23 December), Modena (24 December), Bologna (26 December 1716–1 January 1717). Therefore, the possibility exists that Juvarra accompanied them on their return trip to the papal capital, which can be documented on 8 January 1717, and Coke probably kept in touch with the architect for the remainder of the winter season, until 5 April 1717, when the Englishman left. Coke reserved enough time, however, to have Trevisani, who was a friend of Juvarra, paint his portrait (Fig. 7.10), and also to commission drawings from Trench, and to take architecture lessons from Giacomo Mariani, an ex-student from the Accademia di San Luca (and who was remunerated by Coke for a drawing of the ground-plan of the villa).
31. For Burlington's sojourns in Italy, see Ford and Ingamells, *Dictionary of British and Irish Travellers* (above, n. 19), 159–61; J. Carré, *Lord Burlington: (1694–1753); le connaisseur, le mécène, l'architecte* (Clermont-Ferrand, 1994). He arrived in Rome on 18 September 1714 and he departed on 5 February 1715, but he spent the first three months of his visit confined to his bed, gravely ill. In fact, on 24 November 1714, Kent, who had recently returned to Rome from the northern leg of Coke's trip, reported that no one had so far seen Burlington in Rome, and, according to Kent's correspondence, Burlington only made his entrance into society on 27 December 1714, when Kent probably met him for the first time. A meeting between Burlington and Juvarra could have taken place only during the last few days of January 1715, when the architect returned to Rome from Turin, until 5 February 1715, when, as we have seen, Burlington left the city.
32. Through Ottoboni, with whom he had a common passion for music and opera, and also frequenting the Cardinal's court, where he probably met Juvarra, Burlington came into contact with the famous violoncellist, Filippo Amadei, called Pippo. After Ottoboni released Amadei from his service, Burlington engaged him and brought him to London. Thereafter, in 1720, from London, Burlington hired Giovanni Bononcini (who had arrived in Rome between 1714 and 1715), whom he had heard perform in Rome at the Capranica theatre in 1715.
33. Both of the families that sponsored the Roman stays of Kent, John Chester and Burrell Massingberd were Jacobites. See J. Clark, 'Lord Burlington is here', in T. Barnard and J. Clark

(eds), *Lord Burlington. Architecture, Art and Life* (London, 1995), 270.

34. On the relationship between Burlington and the Jacobites, see Clark, 'Lord Burlington is here' (above, n. 33). Relations between Juvarra and Count Gallas can be documented by a Juvarra drawing for a silver vase, dated 1715, destined for the Count (kindly pointed out to me by Giuseppe Dardanello).
35. 'Disegni di più idee fatti per diversi Milordi inglesi': Rovere, Viale and Brickmann, *Filippo Juvarra* (above, n. 16), 30. On the rapport between Juvarra and the British artists and tourists, see also Griseri, 'Itinerari juvarriani' (above, n. 30), 50–1.
36. T. Friedman, 'Lord Harrold in Italy 1715–16: four frustrated commissions to Leoni, Juvarra, Chiari and Soldani', *The Burlington Magazine* 130 (1988), 838–41; Ford and Ingamells, *Dictionary of British and Irish Travellers* (above, n. 19), 469–70. Harrold and Gerrard's Grand Tour began in January 1715 in France, including time in Paris, and then progressing through Italy during all of 1716.
37. Lady Lucas Collection, L33/46, on deposit in the Bedfordshire County Record Office. Friedman, 'Lord Harrold in Italy' (above, n. 36), 837, fig. 29.
38. At the end of July, Harrold and Gerrard were staying for an extended period at Genoa, as part of their Grand Tour. Leoni's project had been prepared after the departure of the two from England in January 1715 and had been sent to them attached to a letter dated 28 July. They received it by the end of August.
39. The last documentation of Juvarra's presence in Rome is on 3 July 1715 (Wittkower, 'Documenti sui modelli' (above, n. 27)), 158–61). This makes sense as, if Juvarra arrived in Genoa at the end of August, he probably would have had to have set out from Rome more than a month before. In Genoa, Juvarra provided Harrold with an initial oral opinion, of which nothing is known, except that it seems to have impressed the young Lord: an 'Architect ... att present in this Town [who has] made some plans for the King of Sicily And seems to have a good Judgment in Building'. Letters from Gerrard to Kent from Genoa of 9 September 1715, cited in Friedman, 'Lord Harrold in Italy' (above, n. 36), 838.
40. Friedman, 'Lord Harrold in Italy' (above, n. 36), 838. According to a letter of 20 October 1715, written by Gerrard, who was in Turin, to Kent, Vittorio Amedeo II had engaged Juvarra to 'wait upon [Harrold] to give his opinion upon the Plans he had brought or make a New design'. The last letter that Gerrard wrote to Kent, from Genoa, dates from 22 September. The first letter sent to Kent from the two architects, in Turin, was that sent by Harrold on 10 October 1715.
41. Lady Lucas Collection, L33/101, on deposit in the Bedfordshire County Record Office (Friedman, 'Lord Harrold in Italy' (above, n. 36), 837, figs 30–1). Based on these premises, and on the flood of news arriving from Rome about the grandiosity of Juvarra's project for the new Vatican sacristy, the expectations for the Wrest residence plans grew apace with the prolonged wait because of the architect's many obligations, even though Harrold and Gerrard continued during their Tour to ask other architects for their opinions. At the beginning of November they were again in Genoa; they reached Venice at the start of December; and finally Rome, where they lodged from February to July 1716. In a letter written to his father from Rome, dated 22 February, Harrold informed him that the drawings had been consigned to the architect and that they were still waiting on 'something both handsome and noble'. In all probability, Harrold met Juvarra in Rome between February and Easter 1716. In a letter of 14 April he described the architect as 'the most able [architect] in Italy', still hoping that Juvarra would 'doe something [for Wrest] that shall be handsome and noble', once he had overcome his illness. In May, after Juvarra had returned to Turin, only the hope remained that 'the beauty of the design will make amends for the Long delays'. In a letter to the Duke of Kent, dated 9 May 1716, Gerrard declared himself to be hopeful of receiving the project even though Juvarra had 'so much business for his Majesty who is building a Church and his Pallace of the Venerie that he had not time to make the draughts'. In a letter to his father of 13 June 1716, Harrold reported some news that he had heard from the Savoy ambassador, according to whom, despite his workload and illness, Juvarra was ready to send the project, which he wanted to exhibit to experts in the field, anxious to have their admiration more than to receive their opinion. The diplomatic correspondence of the Savoy court (not taken into account by Friedmann, 'Lord Harrold in Italy' (above, n. 36), but cited by Gritella (*Juvarra* (above, n. 3), I, 378), who in turn did not consider Friedmann's research), completes the information about this affair. A letter from Vittorio Amedeo II to his ambassador in Rome, Provana, dated 3 June 1716, informed him that he had given Juvarra the commission to design the villa for the Duke of Kent, and that he had sent the designs: 'supponiamo che a voi sia noto l'arrivo costà del figlio del Duca di Kent inglese qual havendo lasciato nel suo passaggio per Torino a questo D. Filippo Juvarra nostro architetto di fargli un dissegno per la sua casa che il detto Duca suo padre ci ha fatto pregare di fargli tenere ve lo inviaremo'. On 19 June the project finally left Turin (or Venaria Reale) attached to a second letter from Vittorio Amedeo II to his ambassador: 'Qui giunto vi trasmettiamo il consaputo disegno fatto dal Nostro Architetto D. Filippo Juvarra di cui vi habbiamo scritto nella penultima nostra per il Duca di Kent, a cui va pure unito quello rimesso al detto D. Filippo dal figlio d'esso Duca nel di lui passaggio per costà a Torino'. But Harrold had departed for Venice already, taking with him a project by an unknown architect, perhaps the one who had given him architecture lessons (18 April 1716). Finally, at the end of August, he received Juvarra's new project, as well as his opinion on Leoni's plan.
42. In Gerrard's letter to the Duke of Kent, sent from Turin on 20 October 1715, a letter to Harrold is cited in which he declared he was 'against making Many breaks, and is for a plainness in the building'.
43. Archivio di Stato di Torino, Corte, Lettere Ministri, mazzo 25, letter of 17 August 1719. According to the papal nuncio, Monsignor Vincenzo Bichi, Juvarra left Lisbon to get to

Turin 'by way of England, Holland and France, travelling by English 'Paquebot'' (see above, n. 8, for bibliography).

44. Burlington was still in London on 6 August 1719, four days before the arrival of Juvarra. On 31 August he was in Paris: Carré, *Lord Burlington* (above, n. 31), 297; J. Harris, *The Palladian Revival: Lord Burlington, His Villa and Garden at Chiswick*, new edition (New Haven/London, 1995), 61.
45. Clark, 'Lord Burlington is here' (above, n. 33), 266–73.
46. Lord Stair, from Paris on 9 September 1719, reported that Burlington was to leave for Italy in a few days time, and on 22 November he noted Burlington's return of about two days previous (Clark, 'Lord Burlington is here' (above, n. 33), 270). The Count of Vernone, Savoy ambassador to Paris, wrote on 26 September to Del Borgo, Minister of Foreign Affairs in Turin, that Juvarra had left a few days earlier, headed toward the Savoy capital (Viale, 'Regesto della vita' (above, n. 3), 67).
47. Juvarra, 'Vita' (above, n. 1), 285–6.
48. The letter written by Kent to Massingberd in Paris on 15 November 1719 constitutes a valuable source for understanding the movements of Burlington in Italy. Burlington took Kent along to see 'two fine palaces of Vitruvio [these are the two villas by Galeazzo Alessi, who was known as 'Vitruvio'] ... that My Ld carry'd me to see, wich he has order'd to be drawn', to teach him a 'better gusto than the Dam'd Gusto that's been for this sixty years past' (Carré, *Lord Burlington* (above, n. 31), n. 22). Kent, therefore, at an undetermined date (probably at the beginning of October 1719) met Burlington in Genoa. Burlington seemed to want to rush to the Veneto to find architects to draw the works of Palladio. Burlington's itinerary in the Veneto is not clear, but he was certainly in Venice in the last two weeks of October (he is documented there on 21 October). There is the possibility that Juvarra and Burlington may have travelled together toward Genoa, and that together they may have met Kent in that city. Thereafter Juvarra would have left Burlington and Kent to go on to Turin, where his recent return was noted in a letter of del Borgo, dated 11 October 1719, to Vernone (Viale, *Filippo Juvarra, architetto e scenografo* (above, n. 3), 67).
49. See the preceding note.
50. On 3 November 1719 a British diplomat in Venice noted his departure from that city on 1 November to return to England. He arrived in London before 30 November; presumably after having caught up with Kent in Paris. An important piece of information is in a letter written by Burlington to Andre Fontaine from Carignano (or from Turin) on 6 November 1719, in which Burlington wrote that he was 'in constant hurry' and that he was forced 'to make my stay in Vicenza much shorter than I intended for the waters were so out that there was no possibility of seeing any of the villas at any distance from the town ... here has been such violent rains that the road from Venice to [Turin] looks like a sea, I left a great many passengers on the road and I was the only one that ventured to come on'. In the same missive he revealed that he had acquired 'some tables at Genoa and some drawings by Palladio at Venice'. In Vicenza he bought a copy of the *Quattro libri* by Palladio and 'some papers relating to Palladio's life and some of his designs from the owner of the Villa Maser'. On 3 November 1719, James Hay, doctor, fencing master, and instructor of languages and architecture to the young Charles Compton, wrote regarding Burlington: 'I Wish we could afford to travel after his maner, but without his train'. Burlington was in London with Kent on 24 November 1719.
51. For a comparison between the two works, see Dardanello, 'Juvarra e l'ornato' (above, n. 3), 170–2, who suggested that the derivation of the English model stems from possible discussions between Juvarra and Kent. It should in any case be noted that the last possible direct contact between the two architects could not have occurred in 1720 in London, as Dardanello suggested, but in October 1719 in Genoa (see above, nn. 48 and 50), another important centre for the development of picturesque and grotesque decoration.
52. See the bibliography in n. 4.

Planting 'Italian gusto' in a 'Gothick country': the influence of Filippo Juvarra on William Kent

Katrina Grant

After a lacklustre attempt to become a painter, William Kent (1685–1748) developed a career as a garden designer, working mainly for Lord Burlington and other patrons in his circle.[1] His gardens represent some of the earliest gardens of a style that became known as the 'English Landscape Garden', exemplified by Stourhead in Wiltshire, Rousham in Oxfordshire and Stowe in Buckinghamshire; so named in part because, in the past, scholars have pointed to landscape painting as the primary influence on the creation of this new style.

The idea that the landscape garden is a representation of the 'natural' landscape belongs to a later period, that of Horace Walpole at the end of the eighteenth century. However, Walpole applied it retrospectively to designers like Kent in an effort to prove that the garden designers of the early eighteenth century had been aiming for an ideal that ultimately would be achieved by the 'high' phase of landscape gardening, the Picturesque School.[2] In addition, Walpole, as well as Joseph Addison and Alexander Pope, argued that the landscape park was a purely English invention, quite at odds with the European style of gardening, which was stereotyped as the symmetrical parterres and neatly clipped box-hedges of gardens, such as was to be found at Versailles.[3] Walpole's viewpoint was subsequently accepted as fact in much garden history written during the twentieth century.

In recent years this point of view has fallen from favour. Laurie Olin, for example, has criticized the way landscape painting has been considered to be not simply a possible influence on some gardens of the period, but the sole influence on all gardens.[4] Yet despite this criticism, the idea that these gardens were three-dimensional representations of landscape paintings has remained popular. For example, an article published in 2002 dealing with a project at Stourhead that involved the reconstruction of various lost eighteenth-century structures referred to the garden as 'a living Claudian landscape',[5] in spite of the fact that the project involved the recreation of various later eighteenth-century features, including a Turkish Tent and a Steel Bridge, which never appeared in the landscapes of Claude. Clearly there were other influences at work within these eighteenth-century English gardens. Olin convincingly demonstrated the influence of the park-like *vigne* of sixteenth- and seventeenth-century Italy, such as the Villa Madama in Rome, but the theatre has been proposed also. Susan Lang suggested that, in addition to Italian gardens, Kent was influenced by the theatre he had known in Rome during his time spent in Italy,[6] and John Dixon Hunt has also pointed to Kent's close involvement with theatre as a possible influence on his garden designs.[7] Yet despite the general acceptance of Kent's involvement with theatre both as a spectator and designer, we still lack a clear idea of exactly how this may have impacted upon his garden designs.

In this paper, therefore, I shall present a way of approaching Kent's garden designs that focuses on his experiences in Rome and his subsequent position within the musical and theatrical milieu of Lord Burlington. I shall explore the influence of Italian set design upon the garden style that Kent introduced to England in the 1720s, and go from there to the wider question of the 'theatricality' of the English Baroque garden.

*****

In 1720 Kent, newly returned to England from Italy, wrote to his patron, Burrell Massingberd, that 'I keep my little room only twice a week [then] I go to the operas where I am highly entertained and then think my self out of this Gothick country'.[8] Kent was clearly dissatisfied with England after his long stay in Italy, which took place from 1709 to 1719. During his time in Italy, Kent often wrote of his intention to introduce 'ye Italian gusto' to the arts of England, and it seems that, back in 'Gothick' England, Kent was pining for Italian culture by recalling his theatrical experiences in Rome. In England, Kent was at this time much engaged with garden design. If his mind was so focused on his memories of Italian opera, as this passage suggests, it is likely that the garden style he introduced into England in the 1720s was shaped in some way by his experience of Italian opera, where garden sets were not uncommon.

The leading set designer in Rome during the first half of Kent's stay there was Filippo Juvarra (1678–1736).[9] Between 1708 and 1714 Juvarra was architect to Cardinal Pietro Ottoboni, and during this period his work consisted almost exclusively of designing sets for operas. These sets were for operas staged in Ottoboni's private theatre in his residence, the Palazzo della Cancelleria, and for operas sponsored by the cardinal at the public Teatro Capranica.[10] Juvarra also worked for other patrons as a set designer, including Queen Casimira of Poland.[11] Kent was deeply involved with the artistic community in Rome at this time.[12] He studied at the Accademia di San Luca, where Juvarra was teaching architecture between 1707 and 1709, and then again in 1711 and 1712, and he won the second prize in the second class in painting at the *Concorso Clementino* of 1713.[13] During this time Kent also attracted the attention of Cardinal Ottoboni. In 1716, Kent wrote to Massingberd that:

> I cannot do less then to inform you of my success with Cardinal Ottoboni though, [I] am assham'd for fear it should be thought vanity, you know at Rome its the custom to expose pictures at feasts, I having done mine which happened to be a great subject, reps't: Cyrus king of Persia a given liberty to the Jews to return to Jerusalem to build the temple, I was desir'd to expose it at the feast of the St Rock [San Rocco] which I did and by good fortune was lik'd both by the Italians and English that was here, the Cardinal made me a handsome present and took it (it) now hangs up in his house ... the Cardinal ... told me when I return [from a tour of Lombardy] I shall do another ...[14]

In another letter of 1717 Kent wrote that 'I have been with the cardinal since I came [back to Rome]', suggesting that the artist was now resident with him.[15] Nevertheless, Kent was not listed in Ottoboni's household at the Palazzo della Cancelleria for 1715, 1716 or 1717, so he may have meant only that he had entered the cardinal's milieu.[16] Although this contact with the cardinal comes after 1714, when Juvarra had moved to Turin, Juvarra returned regularly to Rome, notably to produce a design for the new sacristy at the Vatican in January 1715, when he stayed in Rome for seven months.[17]

An acquaintance with Juvarra may have come about also through Kent's friendship with Sir Thomas Coke, who was mentioned regularly in the former's letters to Massingberd.[18] The two appear to have been close friends. While in Rome Coke engaged an architectural tutor, possibly Giacomo Mariari, and took a keen interest in architecture.[19] For his part, Juvarra was known to English patrons. The catalogue of his works by Giovanni Battista Sacchetti, published with an anonymous life of the artist in 1847, but written around 1736, refers to 'Disegni di più idee fatti per diversi milordi inglesi' made in 1716.[20] One of these 'milordi inglesi' was Anthony Grey, Earl of Harrold, who, on his Grand Tour, sought critical comments from architects on the designs for the remodelling of the family mansion at Wrest Park in Bedfordshire, and to this end he sought out Juvarra in Turin in 1715.[21] Juvarra apparently produced a new design for the house, as well as offering comments upon a design already executed by Giacomo Leoni (Fig. 15.9). Juvarra also produced two drawings for a small garden pavilion (Figs 15.10 and 15.11).[22]

Juvarra was acquainted also with Lord Burlington, although whether they met during his Grand Tour in 1714–15 or when he revisited Italy in 1719 is unknown.[23] Burlington, however, must have been acquainted with Cardinal Ottoboni, since on his return to England in 1715 he took several of the Cardinal's court musicians with him.[24]

To sum up, Kent, Juvarra and Burlington belonged to overlapping circles of acquaintanceship centred on the court of Cardinal Ottoboni. All three were in Rome in the winter of 1714–15.[25] All three met in London in 1719. In July 1719 Juvarra had left Portugal, where he was working, to visit London. He was the guest of the Portuguese ambassador for a month, and during this time was a frequent visitor to Lord Burlington.[26] A letter of 1719 written by Paolo Antonio Rolli, an Italian librettist living in England and a member of the Burlington circle, to Giuseppe Riva recorded this visit by Juvarra to London.[27]

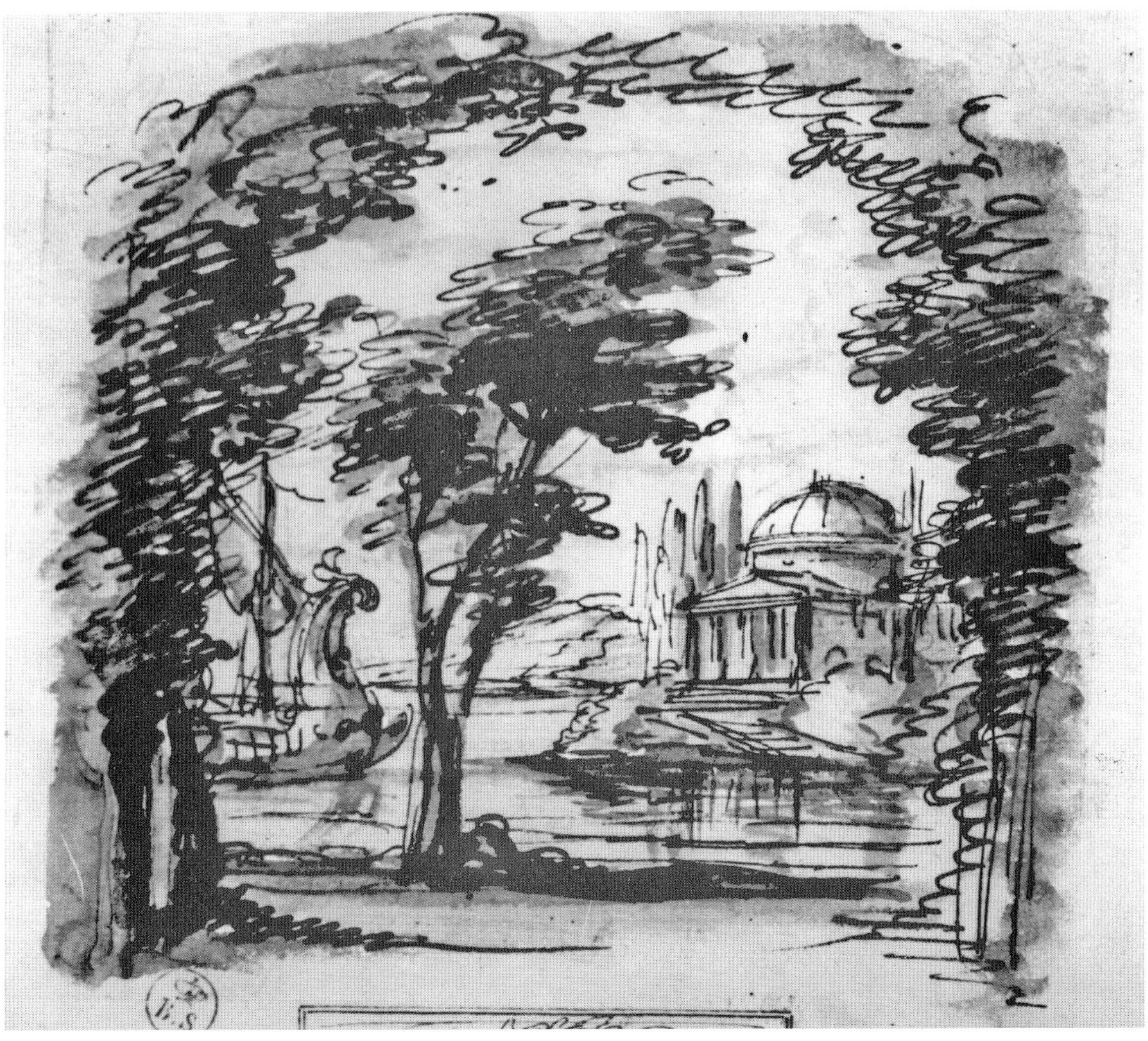

FIG. 16.1. Filippo Juvarra (1678–1736), Set design for *Iphigenia in Tauris* performed in Rome in the theatre of the Queen of Poland, in the Palazzo Zuccari, 1713. Pen and ink. Turin, Biblioteca Nazionale, Ris. 59/4, fol. 85 (1). *(Reproduced courtesy of the Ministero per i Beni e le Attività Culturali, Biblioteca Nazionale Universitaria di Torino. Reproduction prohibited.)*

The conclusive evidence of a relationship, albeit at a later date, is a volume of drawings of architectural fantasies by Juvarra at Chatsworth, from the collection of Lord Burlington, which bears a dedication from Juvarra to Burlington in 1730.[28] Aside from these fantasies for Burlington, the designs by Juvarra for the opera *Teodosio il Giovane* (Palazzo della Cancelleria, 1711) were copied by the English set designer John Devoto, who worked as a set designer for Handel operas. This proves that at least some of Juvarra's sets were known in eighteenth-century London.[29]

As Kent's letter indicates, he had attended operas in Italy. In a letter to Massingberd, written during his Italian stay on 26 January 1714, Kent wrote that, 'Operas are begun at Queens & Capranica'.[30] This is a reference to the public opera at the Teatro Capranica, and to the private operas put on by the widowed Queen Casimira of Poland, resident in Rome from 1699 until her death in 1716. The Queen sponsored productions in a small theatre in her palace, the Palazzo Zuccari. In 1713 the operas performed in Queen Casimira's theatre, which was under the direction of Domenico Scarlatti, were *Iphigenia in Tauris* and *Iphigenia in Aulis*, with music by Domenico Scarlatti and sets by Filippo Juvarra.[31] As it seems that Kent must have seen one or both of these operas, this is a good place to begin to explore Kent's experience of Roman theatre.

Around seven of Juvarra's sketches have been identified securely as connected with these two operas.[32] A sketch for Scene I of *Iphigenia in Tauris* shows a body of water surrounded by trees with a ship approaching from the left, a classical temple with a columned portico and a dome reminiscent of the Pantheon rising behind (Fig. 16.1). This drawing resembles a view at the garden of Stourhead in Wiltshire, with its 'Pantheon' by the lake (Plate 16.1). This comparison is not the usual one made between works of art and this view at Stourhead.[33] More commonly Claude Lorrain's *Coast View of Delos with Aeneas* in the National Gallery, London, is invoked, and it is assumed that Henry Hoare was inspired by this image to create the view of the Pantheon in his garden.[34] (In fact, Hoare owned copies of two paintings by Claude in the Galleria Doria Pamphilj in Rome, and although one of them, the *View of Delphi with a Procession*, is related in composition to the *Coast View of Delos with Aeneas*, it does not make reference to the Pantheon.)[35]

Further, the only contemporary reference that links the painting with the landscape at Stourhead refers to Gaspard Dughet, not to Claude. Hoare wrote in a letter that a view of Stourhead, once completed, '[w]ill be a charming Gaspard [Dughet] picture at the end of the water'.[36] Hence, in spite of the visual similarity between Claude's paintings and views at Stourhead, there is no concrete evidence that Hoare intended to recreate scenes from particular paintings by Claude. Neither do we have any record of Kent taking a particular interest in landscape painting. In his letters he stated that he had acquired 'landskips' for his patron, but he did not express a direct engagement with landscape imagery in the way that he engaged with the theatre, or with the works of Correggio in Parma, or the pages written upon the work of Giulio Romano at the Palazzo del Te.[37]

On a formal level, the similarity between the Juvarra set and the Stourhead 'view' is very close. Is it reasonable to connect the two images, or is the connection merely fortuitous? The Stourhead temple was erected in 1754, six years after Kent's death, but it may well have been designed earlier. There is no direct evidence as to who designed the Pantheon, but it appears to have been a collaborative effort, involving Hoare, his architect, Henry Flitcroft, and Kent.[38]

If Juvarra's theatre set, filtered through Kent, did play a role in the conception of the site, then we might like to reconsider the emphasis on the iconographical programme of the garden that flows from connecting the structure with either Claude's *Coast View of Delos with Aeneas*, or the *View of Delphi with a Procession*, which has dominated art historical accounts of Stourhead.

Kenneth Woodbridge, after reviewing the possible designers of the Stourhead Pantheon, supported his preferred option — that Flitcroft and Hoare collaborated[39] — by reference to an account of the iconographical programme of the garden, which, he argued, was based on Virgil's *Aeneid*.[40] Woodbridge observed that the view 'bears more than a casual relation' to Claude's painting, which illustrates an episode from the third book of the *Aeneid*.[41] He pointed out that the inscription 'procul, o procul este profani' on the Temple of Flora further round the lake comes from the sixth book of the *Aeneid*; hence, he concluded, the path around the lake symbolizes Aeneas's journey. This has set the direction of research for most subsequent scholars.[42] However, if the idea of a Pantheon beside the lake derives, however indirectly, from Kent's experience of Juvarra's set, it provides little encouragement for such an iconographical account, since the set design represents the Temple of Diana on the island of Taurus where Iphigenia, rescued from being sacrificed herself, is now a priestess preparing unfortunate travellers for sacrifice to Diana.[43]

A set for the pendant opera, *Iphigenia in Aulis*, provides a more direct link to William Kent's garden design. This set design shows an army encampment (Fig. 16.2), with in the centre a large tent shown with its curtains drawn aside so that a view of a distant city can be glimpsed beyond. The tent acts like a second proscenium, repeating the stage curtains. We find in Kent's designs for landscape gardens a number of similar motifs. One drawing, not connected with an extant garden structure, shows a grand tent (Fig. 16.3), while another shows a tent to be erected over a river (Fig. 16.4). Both designs have echoes of Juvarra's set design. Such campaign tents later became a feature of landscape gardens, where they are usually identified as Turkish tents. One was recently reconstructed at Stourhead during 2002, based upon the structure described by F.M. Piper on his visit to the garden in 1779: he stated that it was positioned so as to provide a view across the lake to the Pantheon.[44] A similar tent was constructed at Painshill Park in Surrey in 1760.[45] Kent's drawings would appear to constitute some of the first proposals to incorporate tents into garden design, and may derive directly from his experience of these Roman operas.

If we move now beyond these two operas to Juvarra's designs for opera sets and Kent's garden design more generally, there are many other intriguing connections. For example, designs for groves with small circular temples and obelisks appear both in Juvarra's designs for the stage and those by Kent for gardens. Although we only have direct evidence of Kent attending the operas of 1714, we must assume that he

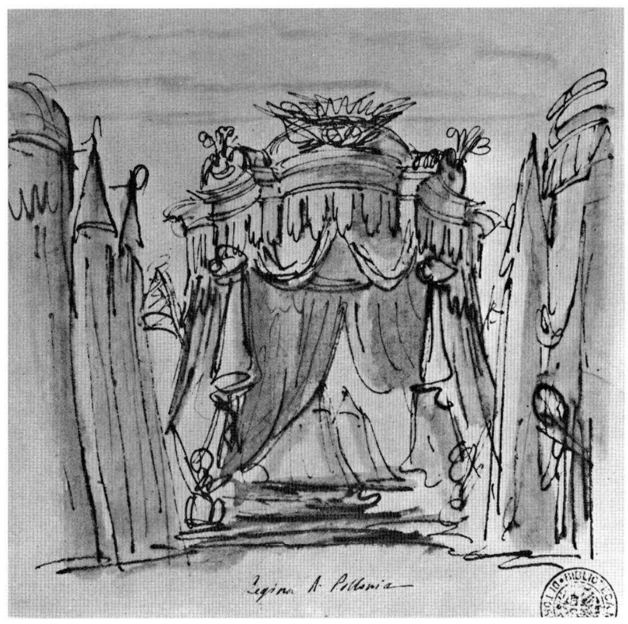

FIG. 16.2. Filippo Juvarra (1678–1736), *Encampment*, set design for *Iphigenia in Aulis*, performed in Rome, in the theatre of the Queen of Poland, 1713. Pen and ink. Turin, Biblioteca Nazionale, Ris. 59/4, fol. 69 (1). *(Reproduced courtesy of the Ministero per i Beni e le Attività Culturali, Biblioteca Nazionale Universitaria di Torino. Reproduction prohibited.)*

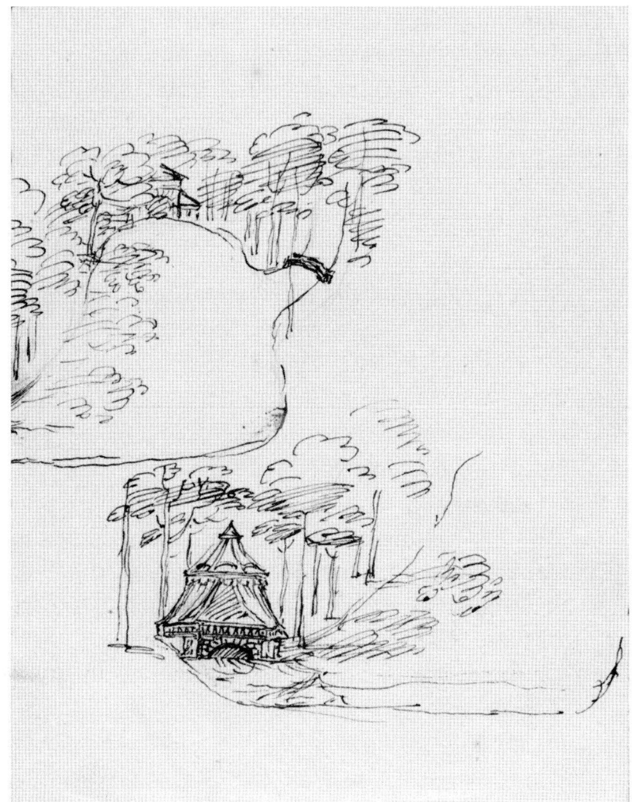

FIG. 16.4. William Kent (1685–1748), *Two Designs for Buildings and Water*. Pen over pencil. London, Victoria and Albert Museum, E.393-1986. *(Photo: © V&A Images/Victoria and Albert Museum, London.)*

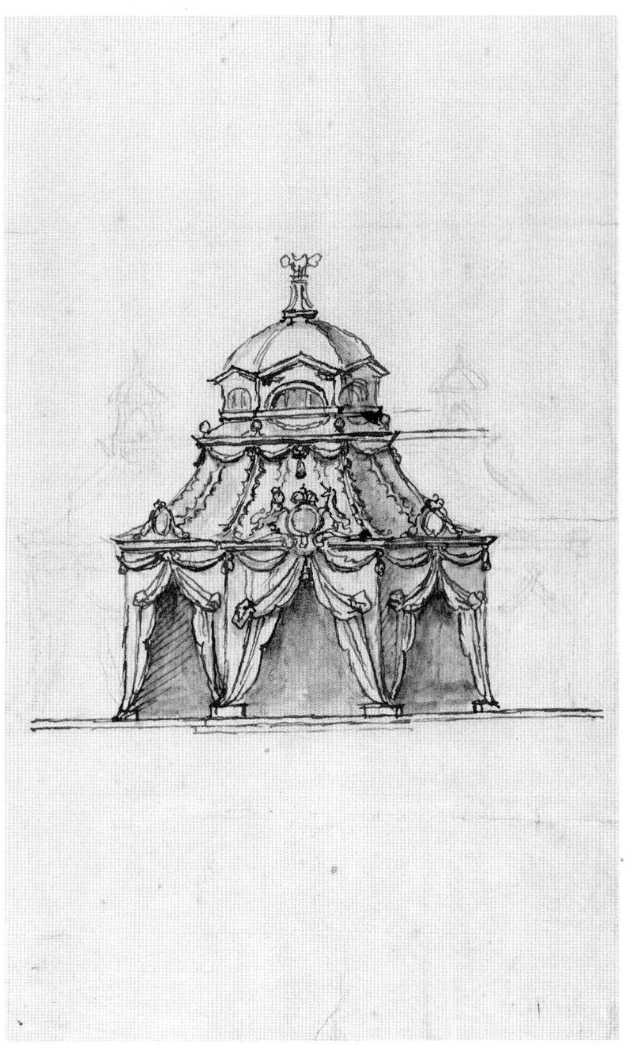

FIG. 16.3. William Kent (1685–1748), *Design for a Royal(?) Tent*. Pen and wash over pencil. London, Victoria and Albert Museum, E.387-1986. *(Photo: © V&A Images/Victoria and Albert Museum, London.)*

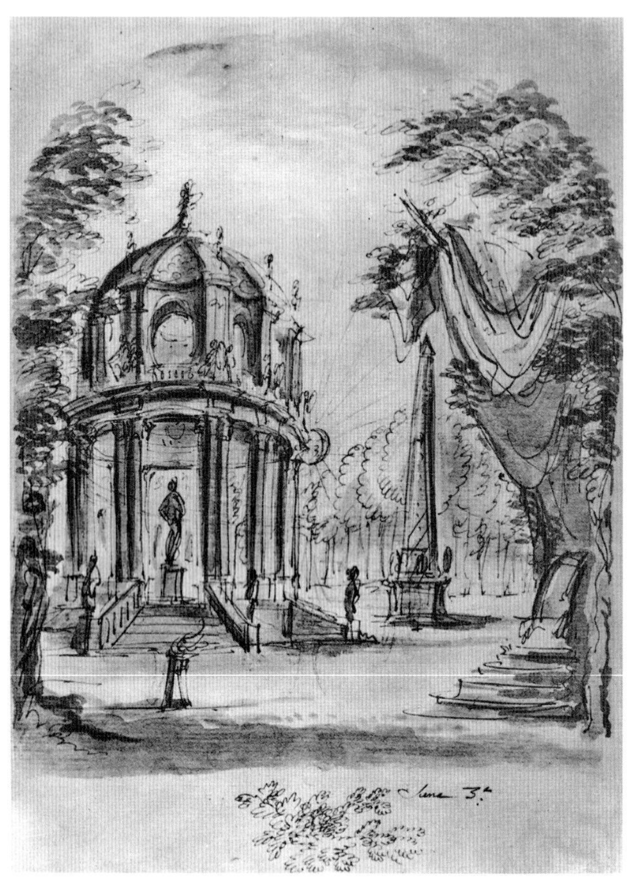

FIG. 16.5. **Filippo Juvarra, *Tempietto and Altar Prepared for Sacrifice*, set design for *Il Ciro*, performed in Rome, Teatro Ottoboni, 1712. Pen and ink. London, Victoria and Albert Museum, print room reg. 8426: 118.** *(Photo: © V&A Images/Victoria and Albert Museum, London.)*

regularly attended the Roman opera seasons during his time in Italy, and so it is plausible to search for further inspirations for Kent's gardens in Juvarra's other set designs.

The opera *Il Ciro*, with sets by Juvarra, was performed in 1711, when Kent was resident in Rome.[46] The design for Scene III exists in two versions. The first shows 'A Temple prepared for Sacrifice' (**Plate 16.2**). In the foreground is a small altar, behind which stands a circular temple with six pairs of Solomonic columns and a small domed roof. This tempietto is set within a sort of amphitheatre, the scene is surrounded by trees and a cloth ceiling hangs above the tempietto. The second drawing also has a small altar in the foreground with a circular tempietto behind (**Fig. 16.5**). This example evokes Kent's Temple of Ancient Virtue at Stowe, where a small circular temple with single evenly-spaced Ionic columns and a small domed roof nestles amongst bushes and trees (**Fig. 16.6**).[47]

A version of this temple also appears in much the same form in a number of other designs by Kent, including several showing his proposal for a cascade upon the hillside at Chatsworth, in Derbyshire (**Fig. 16.7**), and the Chiswick cascade (**Fig. 16.8**), and also a design for 'Buildings on lawn' for the gardens at Badminton House. Although such temples have other obvious sources, such as the Temple of Vesta at Tivoli, there is an undeniable affinity between the set

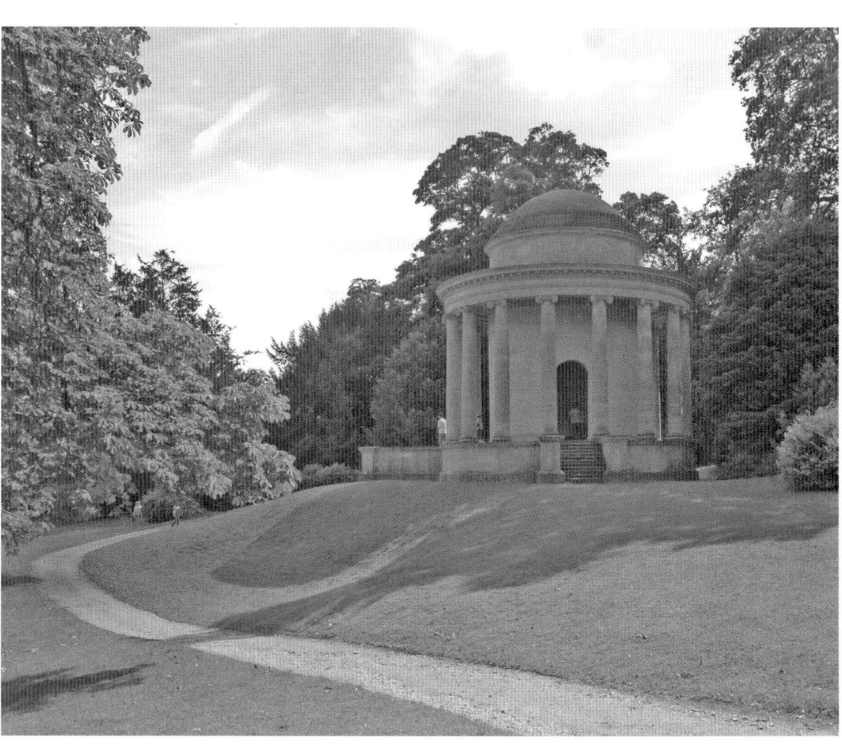

FIG. 16.6. **William Kent (1685–1748), *Temple of Ancient Virtue, Stowe, Buckinghamshire*.** *(Photo: © David R. Marshall, 2009.)*

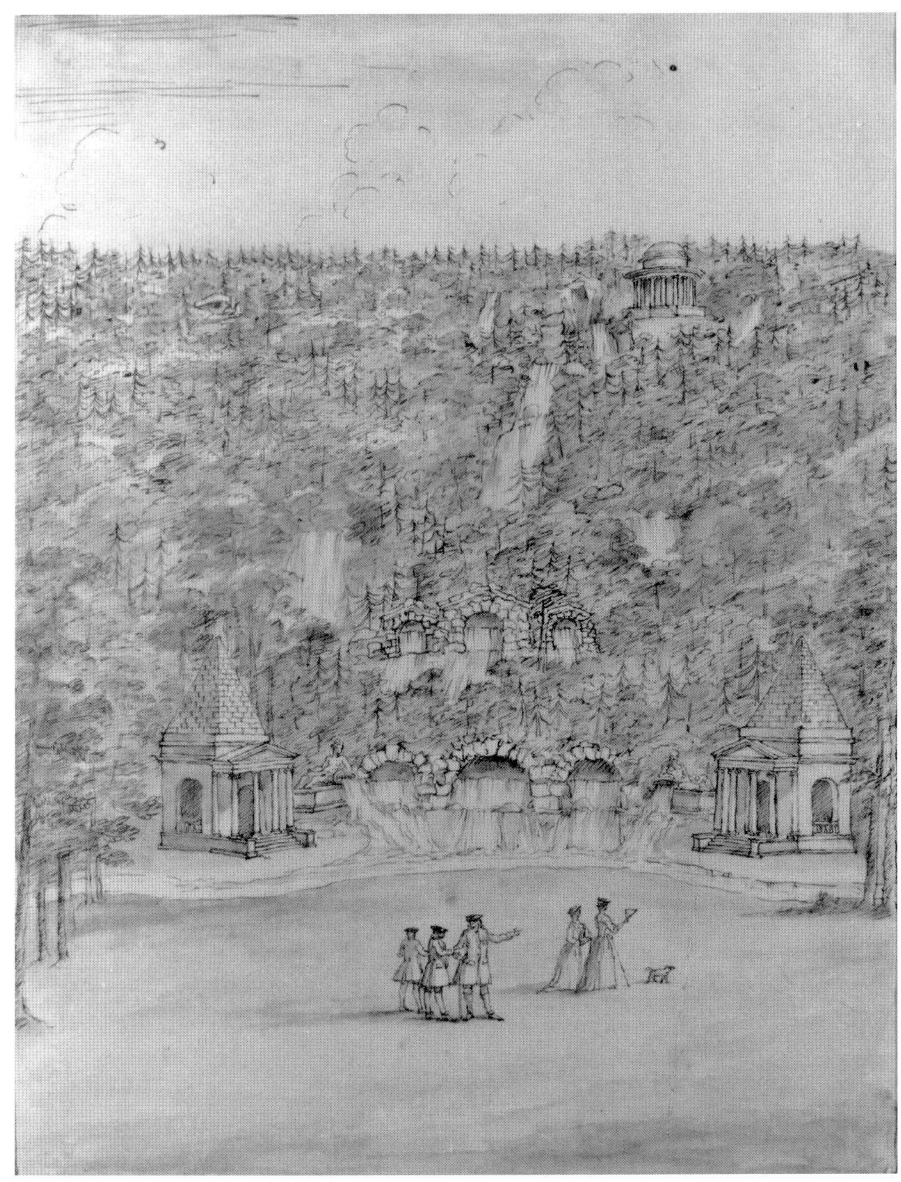

FIG. 16.7. William Kent (1685–1748), *Design for a Cascade at Chatsworth*. Sepia ink and wash over pencil. Chatsworth, Derbyshire, Devonshire Collection, inv. no. 26a/4. *(Photo: Photographic Survey, Courtauld Institute of Art. © Devonshire Collection, Chatsworth. Reproduced by permission of Chatsworth Settlement Trustees.)*

designs by Juvarra and Kent's ideas for temples within wooded groves. Furthermore, there are a number of circular temples in the sketches by Juvarra dedicated to Lord Burlington in 1730, which show that such imagery was part of Juvarra's repertory, and may have flowed from there to Kent.

GARDEN DESIGN AND THEATRE

Kent was clearly inspired by the theatre designs he encountered during his Italian sojourn. Furthermore, Kent's involvement with two of the greatest musical patrons of the early eighteenth century, Ottoboni and Burlington, would have ensured that his perception of the classical and mythical past was more likely to have been shaped by attendance at the opera than by landscape paintings. For us, today, landscape paintings by Claude present a more powerful image than do the preparatory sketches and engravings by which we know eighteenth-century opera sets. But if we try and imagine the sets as they first appeared, as magnificent backdrops to operas, we can begin to understand how influential they must have been. One of the best images in this regard is Giovanni Paolo Panini's view of the interior of the Teatro Argentina painted in 1747 and showing a performance of a secular cantata (Plate 1.2).[48]

In order to try to recreate the nature of the early eighteenth-century theatrical experience, and the effect this may have had on garden design, we need some basic concepts. The obvious terms are 'theatrical'

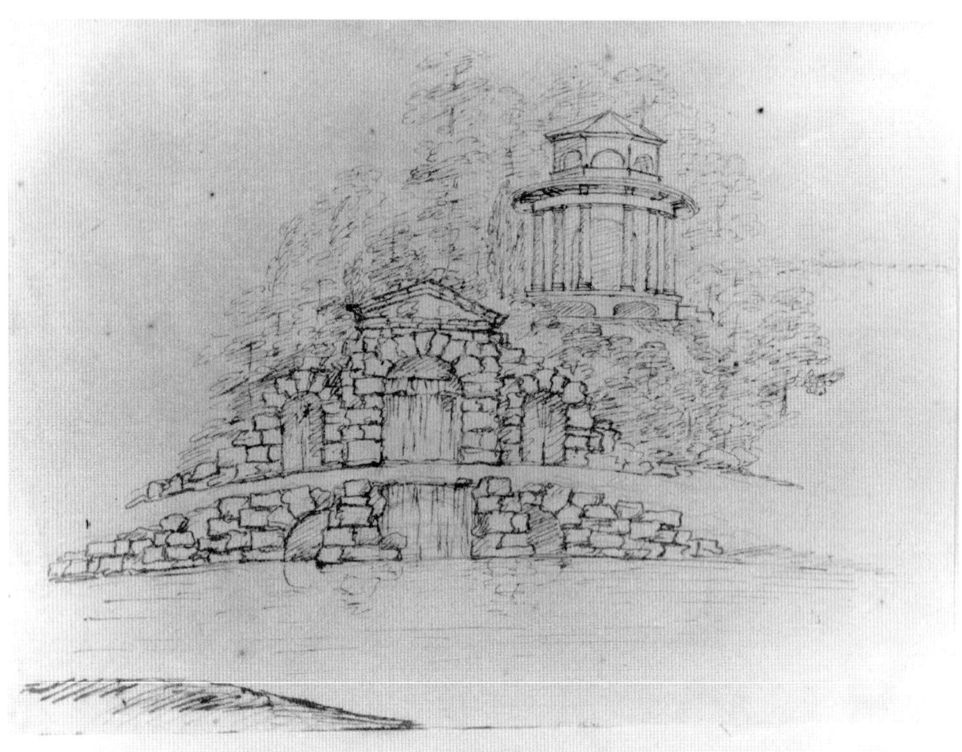

FIG. 16.8. William Kent (1685–1748), *Design for a Rustic Cascade with Temple Behind.* Pen over pencil. Chatsworth, Derbyshire, Devonshire Collection, inv. no. 26a/39. *(Photo: Photographic Survey, Courtauld Institute of Art. © Devonshire Collection, Chatsworth. Reproduced by permission of Chatsworth Settlement Trustees.)*

and 'theatricality', but the usages of these terms are problematic. Is a theatrical art one that has the style of a dramatic performance, one that is showy and spectacular, one that is assumed, or artificial, or one that invokes spectatorship? It can be all or any of these things, and its very imprecision makes it difficult to work with. Besides, the term 'theatrical' has so many negative connotations that it distorts our understanding from the start.

Instead, what I propose is to discuss Kent's garden designs in terms of the 'Theateresque'. This term obviously takes its cue from the concept of the 'Picturesque'. At its simplest level, the Picturesque garden contains qualities 'after the manner of painters'. A handful of statements concerning the 'Picturesque' qualities of the Early English landscape garden have been brought to bear on them. These include Pope's statement that 'All gardening is landscape painting. Just like a landscape hung up';[49] or Hoare's aforementioned statement that one view of Stourhead, when completed, 'will be a charming Gaspard [Dughet]'.[50]

Consequently 'Theateresque' must be defined as art that takes 'after the manner of theatre'. But what elements constitute the 'Theateresque'? These elements may include such formal derivations as I have proposed, but they may also extend into ways of experiencing the garden. One consequence of the Picturesque approach is that it leads to considering the landscape garden as one to be taken in as a single view, or as a series of single views, each of which corresponds to a notional painting. Yet such a static experience is at odds with the actual experience of gardens, which invariably involves moving through them. Theatre, however, although using static sets based on one-point and multi-point perspectives, is an art form involving living people who move through space, a space that is partly real and partly fictive, a description that applies equally well to the Baroque garden. The concept of the 'Theateresque' can accommodate the experience of movement in a way that the Picturesque cannot.

If we assume, then, that Kent's intention was more 'Theateresque' than Picturesque, other designs by Kent must be analysed in terms of this and other aspects of the concept of the 'Theateresque', both in order to understand better Kent's influences and also to refine the concept.

In some sketches by William Kent for a sea-horse pavilion we see an overt similarity to theatre sets in the designs themselves. In the first of two sketches on the same sheet the pavilion appears either to sit upon the water or to be situated directly at the water's edge (Fig. 16.9). In the second there seems to be an idea for it to be positioned at the end of a grassed avenue. Forward of the portico there is the suggestion of a ship's hull, from which rises a figurehead in the form of a horse, not dissimilar to the figurehead in Juvarra's

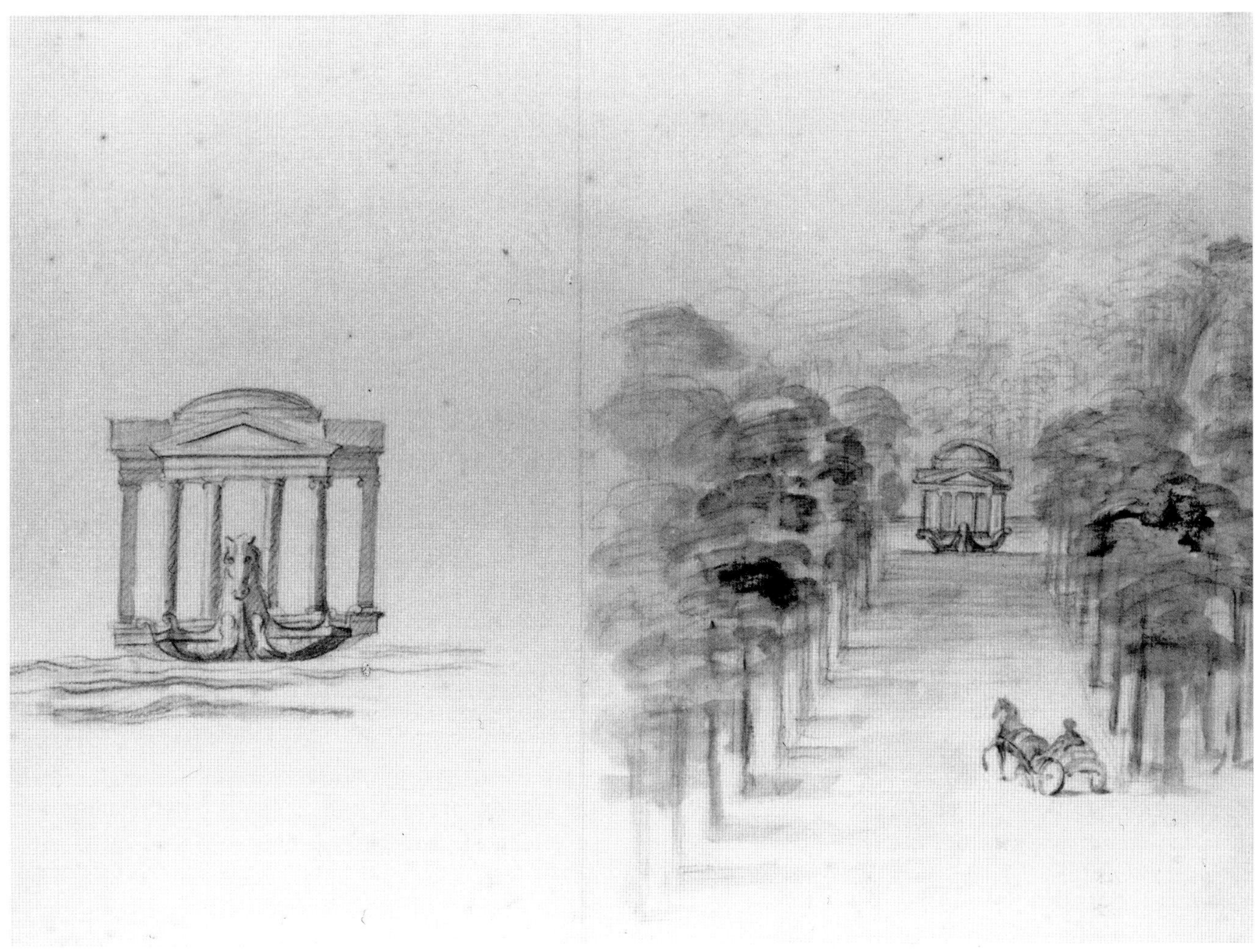

FIG. 16.9. William Kent (1685–1748), *Sea Horse Pavilion: Elevation and Siting*. Chalk and washes. Chatsworth, Derbyshire, Devonshire Collection, inv. no. 26/121. *(Photo: Photographic Survey, Courtauld Institute of Art. © Devonshire Collection, Chatsworth. Reproduced by permission of Chatsworth Settlement Trustees.)*

design for Scene I of *Iphigenia in Tauris*. The temple is similar in both, and in both is situated upon the water's edge. This drawing therefore may be a conflation of two ideas from Juvarra's set design.

This type of fantastical structure is certainly similar to the types of invention found on stage in other Juvarra sets, such as the designs for Scene I of *Theodosius the Younger* (1711) (Fig. 16.10).[51] The sets of this opera must have been known in London as the English set designer Devoto made copies of them, possibly after a printed edition of the libretto.[52] Here a small circular temple sits upon the waters in a port surrounded by classical buildings. Staircases from this temple lead upwards to a floating garden in the clouds. This spirit of extravagant fantasy is associated much more readily with theatre than with the Picturesque.

Another aspect of the 'Theateresque' in Kent's work is the way that he would design garden areas that clearly are intended to resemble, and even to be representations of, set designs. In these the design emphasizes the central perspective views, rather than the asymmetry that we associate with Claude and the Picturesque. An example is his design for a cascade on the hillside at Chatsworth (Fig. 16.7). Designed symmetrically, it has a strong central axis running up the hill and two inventive classical buildings flanking the cascade. A similar set design with a central perspective of a garden was made by Juvarra for the opera *Junius Brutus*. Other designs include forms typical of outdoor theatre forms, such as a sketch of a design for the exedra at Chiswick, which is very similar to exedrae found in Italian garden theatres, such as at the Villa Aldobrandini, which we know Kent visited.[53]

Another example is Kent's amphitheatre of orange trees, which was laid out in the gardens of Chiswick, and is depicted in a painting by Pieter Andreas

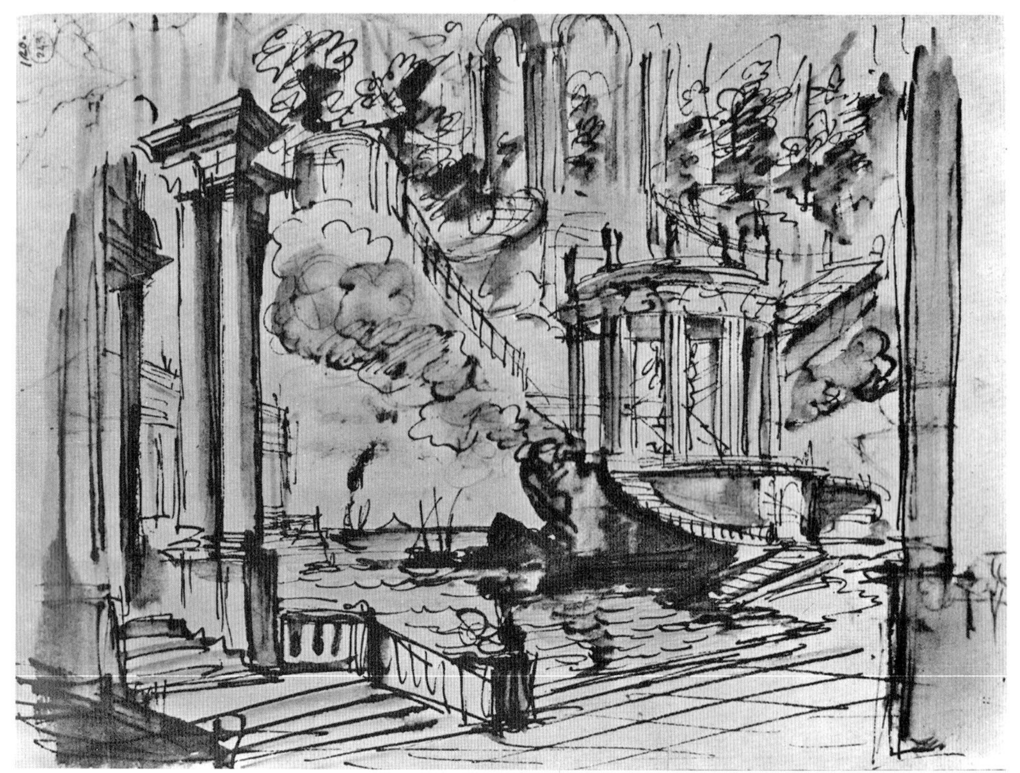

Fig. 16.10. Filippo Juvarra (1678–1736), *Seaport with Macchina*, set design for *Theodosius the Younger*, performed in Rome, Teatro Ottoboni, 1711. Pen and ink. London, Victoria and Albert Museum, print room reg. 8426: 14. *(Photo: © V&A Images/ Victoria and Albert Museum, London.)*

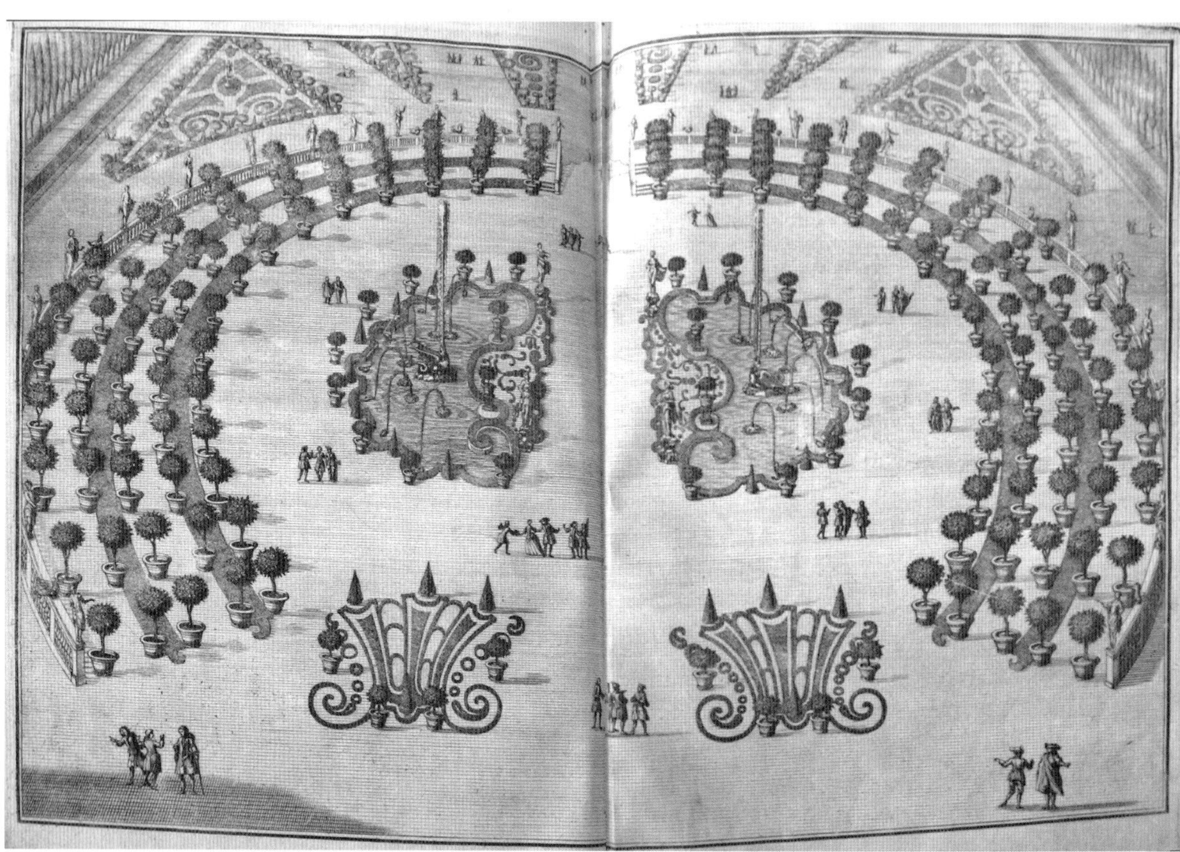

Fig. 16.11. Antonio Fritz and assistants, *Anfiteatro d'agrumi* from *Delizia Farnesiane*, c. 1723. Engraving. *(Photo: Katrina Grant.)*

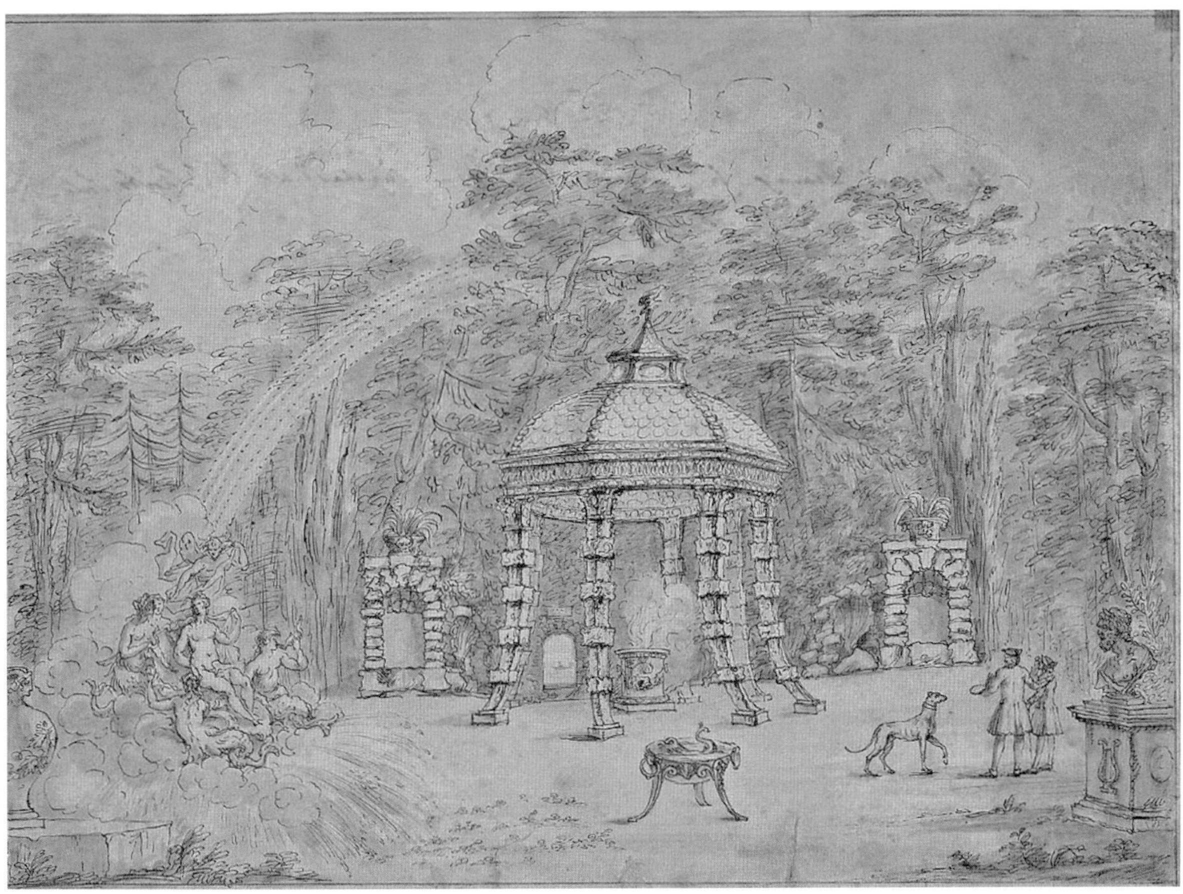

FIG. 16.12. William Kent (1685–1748), *View in Pope's Garden with His Shell Temple*. Pen and ink with wash. London, British Museum, Department of Prints and Drawings (1872-11-9-878). *(Photo: © The Trustees of the British Museum.)*

Rysbrack.[54] This closely resembles the *Anfiteatro d'agrumi* (Fig. 16.11) in the gardens of the Farnese villa at Colorno near Parma, which Kent had visited in 1714.[55] This amphitheatre was constructed between 1708 and 1712, during the first phase of this garden's design, and was designed by Ferdinando Galli Bibiena, one of the eighteenth century's greatest set designers.[56]

Finally, we turn to the 'Theateresque' and the experience of the garden. In Kent's illustration of his friend Pope's garden at Twickenham (Fig. 16.12), we see two typically Kentian figures standing to the right, and the shell temple before them. But to the left the image diverges from the real, and deities descend upon clouds. A similar mix of the real and the fantastic exists in a capriccio by Kent of Hampton Court and Esher Palace (Fig. 16.13), where a man and woman stand observing the scene while a triton drives his sea horses down the river before them. Kent's gardens sought to create an alternative reality, or a type of idealized Arcadia: an experience that would have been heightened by the visitor's experience of the garden as a three-dimensional space. Such drawings demonstrate a fascination with the idea of the garden space as an enchanted one, in which an alternative reality could be entered into and experienced.

In conclusion, it is evident that we should read the influence of theatre set designs on Kent's garden designs as the consequence of a desire to create, in three dimensions, the semi-pictorial world of the stage. More than this, it then represents a desire to realize the world enacted within those sets. Kent was in pursuit of a fictive world that was intended to be experienced not simply as a landscape cleverly imitating a painting, but as something that could be experienced not only by the eye, but by the other senses and by the spectator's body itself. The visitor could move through the garden and discover a succession of scenes; but, more importantly, these scenes became spaces that could be entered, and within them the kind of dramas shown on the stage could be re-enacted.[57] In this way, the ideal world alluded to in the garden could become as alive, or even more alive, as the world of opera, with its illusionism, special effects and singers.

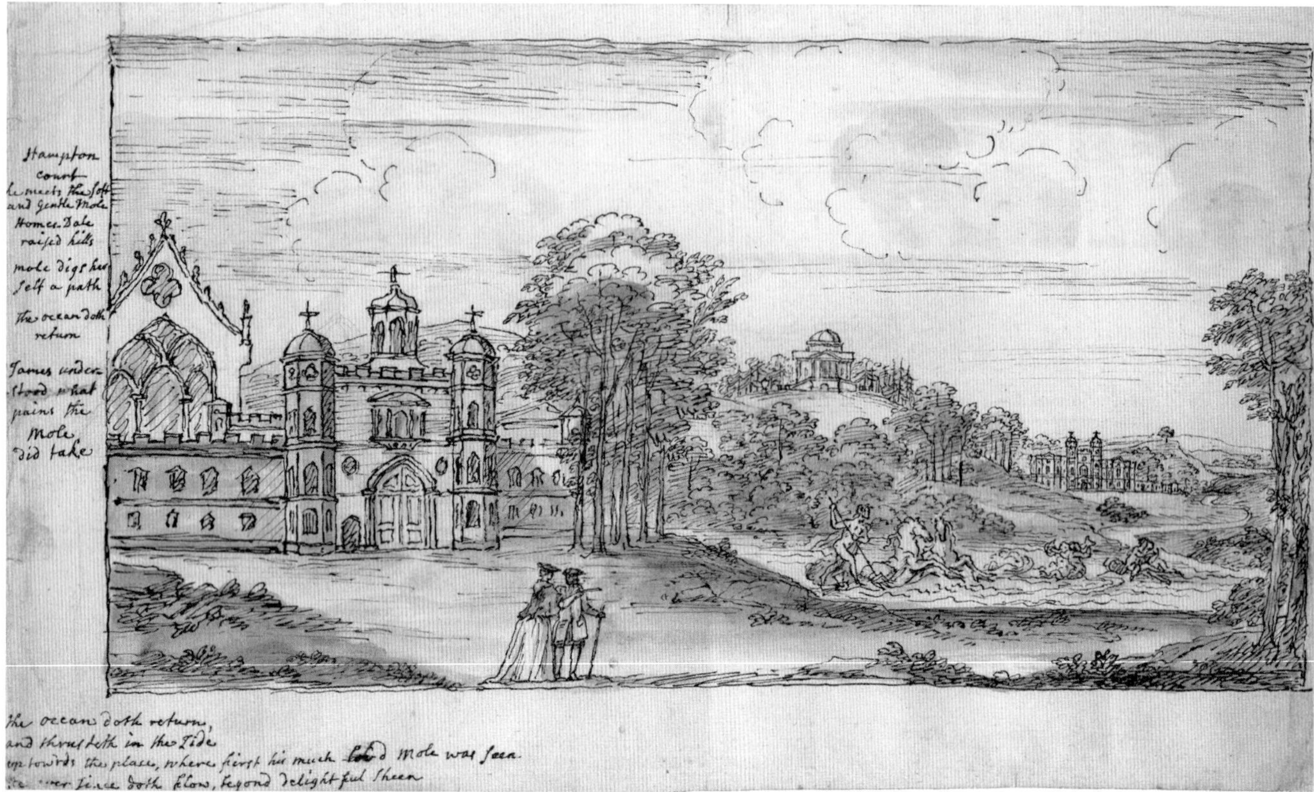

FIG. 16.13. William Kent (1685–1748), *Landscape Capriccio with Hampton Court, Esher and River*. Pen and wash over pencil. London, British Museum, Department of Prints and Drawings (1927-7-21-5). *(Photo: © The Trustees of the British Museum.)*

NOTES

1. William Kent's life and works are the subject of three monographs: M. Jourdain, *The Work of William Kent: Artist, Painter, Designer and Landscape Gardener* (London, 1948); M. Wilson, *William Kent. Architect, Designer, Painter, Gardener, 1685–1748* (London, 1984); and, most recently, T. Mowl, *William Kent. Architect, Designer, Opportunist* (London, 2006). On Kent's time in Italy, see C.M. Sicca, 'On William Kent's Roman sources', *Architectural History* 29 (1986), 134–47.
2. H. Walpole, *The History of the Modern Taste in Gardening* (New York, 1995). Walpole declared that Kent was 'the inventor of an art that realizes painting and improves Nature'. The issue of the retrospective application of the ideals of the landscape and picturesque style on to Kent's work has been discussed in J.D. Hunt, *The Picturesque Garden in Europe* (London, 2002), 26–8, 35–7. Hunt has suggested that, as well as Walpole, other writers in the decades following Kent's death, such as the poets William Shenstone and William Mason and the essayist Henry Home (Lord Kames), also made similar declarations that promoted Kent's place in the development of the picturesque. On the issue, see also S. Lang, 'The genesis of the English landscape garden', in N. Pevsner (ed.), *The Picturesque Garden and its Influence outside the British Isles* (Washington, 1974), 6. Lang suggested that 'nobody before Walpole, it appears, mentions Claude in connection with gardening', though she also acknowledged that the link with painting was not 'entirely a *post factum* invention'.
3. Hunt, *The Picturesque Garden in Europe* (above, n. 2), stated that Walpole's *The History of Modern Taste in Gardening* 'sets up a new, modern, natural and above all English garden against the horrid artificialities of French and Dutch design'. Hunt emphasized the fact that this firm distinction was driven as much by patriotic concerns as by actual differences in style. He gave the example of Joseph Spence, who claimed that Kent was among the first to use 'perspective, prospect, distancing and attracting', which is directly contradicted by the use of perspective in the garden of André le Nôtre in seventeenth-century France. Addison made frequent remarks upon the genesis and individual quality of the English garden in his various letters published in *The Tatler* and *The Spectator*: see, in particular, his letter published in *The Spectator* no. 414 (25 June 1712). For comments by Pope, see his *An Epistle to Lord Burlington* (1731), reproduced in J.D. Hunt and P. Willis, *The Genius of the Place: the English Landscape Garden 1620–1820* (London, 1975), 211–14.
4. L. Olin, 'William Kent, the Vigna Madama, and landscape parks', in A. von Hoffman (ed.), *Form, Modernism, and History: Essays in Honor of Eduard F. Seckler* (Cambridge (MA)/London, 1996), 125–50.

5. A. Mead, 'Stourhead revisited', *Architectural Journal* 216 (2002), 46–7, referred to the garden as 'The Classical dream in the paintings of Claude, Poussin and Gaspar Dughet ... apparently made real in eighteenth-century Wiltshire'.
6. Lang, 'Genesis of the English landscape garden' (above, n. 2), 28, n. 90, acknowledged that the Juvarra scholar, Mercedes Viale Ferrero, had also noted a similarity between Kent's garden designs and Juvarra's theatre designs.
7. J.D. Hunt, *William Kent, Landscape Garden Designer: an Assessment and Catalogue of His Designs* (London, 1987), 30–3.
8. Lincolnshire Archives Office [henceforth LAO], 2MM/19A, letter from William Kent to Massingberd, dated London 30 January 1720.
9. On Juvarra, see G. Gritella, *Juvarra. L'architettura*, 2 vols (Modena, 1992) for the architectural works; and M. Viale Ferrero, *Filippo Juvarra, scenografo e architetto teatrale* (Turin/New York/London, 1970) for the theatre designs.
10. See J.H. McDowell, 'The Ottoboni theatre: a research adventure', *The Ohio State University Theatre Collection Bulletin* 11 (1964), 34–6; F.E. Warner, 'The Ottoboni theatre', *The Ohio State University Theatre Collection Bulletin* 11 (1964), 37–45; Viale Ferrero, *Filippo Juvarra* (above, n. 9). For theatrical patronage in early eighteenth-century Rome more generally, see M. Boyd, 'Rome: the power of patronage', in G.J. Buelow (ed.), *The Late Baroque Era: from the 1680s to 1740* (Englewood Cliffs, 1993), 39–65; R. Strohm, Dramma per musica*: Italian Opera Seria of the Eighteenth Century* (New Haven/London, 1997).
11. W. Rozkowska, 'Filippo Juvarra al servizio dei Sobieski', in M. Bristiger, J. Kowalczyk and J. Lipiński (eds), *Vita teatrale in Italia e Polonia* (Warsaw, 1984), 245–63.
12. Details of Kent's acquaintances in Italy can be found in the many letters he exchanged with Massingberd now in the Lincolnshire archives. The letters were published recently in C. Blackett-Ord, 'Letters from William Kent to Burrell Massingberd from the Continent, 1712–1719', *Walpole Society* 63 (2001), 75–109. Further details on these travellers, including detailed itineraries, can be found in B. Ford and J. Ingamells, *A Dictionary of British and Irish Travellers in Italy, 1701–1800. Compiled from the Brinsley Ford Archive* (New Haven/London, 1997).
13. H.A. Millon, *Filippo Juvarra. Drawings from the Roman Period 1704–1714* (Rome, 1984), xxii.
14. LAO, Kent to Massingberd, letter dated Rome 8 October 1716. Blackett-Ord, 'Letters from William Kent' (above, n. 12) recorded the painting as untraced.
15. LAO, Kent to Massingberd, letter dated Rome 15 February 1717. That Kent may have lived with the cardinal has been proposed also by J. Harris, *The Palladian Revival: Lord Burlington, His Villa and Garden at Chiswick* (New Haven/London, 1994), 39.
16. Archivio Vicariato di Roma [henceforth AVR], San Lorenzo in Damaso: 1715, n. 409, Palazzo della Cancelleria; 1716, n. 414, Palazzo della Cancelleria; and 1717, n. 410.
17. See Gritella, *Juvarra. L'architettura* (above, n. 9), 58, for Juvarra's travels. See also Tommaso Manfredi's contribution to this volume, above, Chapter 15.
18. This possibility is suggested also in the essay by Manfredi in this volume. For mentions of Coke in the letters, see, for example, LAO, Kent to Massingberd, letter dated Rome 16 May 1714; and Kent to Massingberd, letter dated Rome 24 November 1714.
19. Wilson, *William Kent* (above, n. 1), 25.
20. Sacchetti's catalogue was published, with an anonymous life of Juvarra, in 1874 by Adamo Rossi. Dated to *c.* 1730–6, it is reproduced in V. Viale (ed.), *Filippo Juvarra, architetto e scenografo* (Messina, 1966), 31–103.
21. T. Friedman, 'Lord Harrold in Italy 1715–16: four frustrated commissions to Leoni, Juvarra, Chiari and Soldani', *The Burlington Magazine* 130 (1988), 836–45.
22. The drawings are now in the Bedfordshire County Record Office, Lady Lucas Collection, L33/101.
23. This point is also discussed in the essay by Manfredi in this volume (pp. 207–24). He strongly suggests that a meeting could have taken place in 1714–15.
24. See R. Strohm, *Essays on Handel and Italian Opera* (Cambridge, 1985); S. Boorman, 'Lord Burlington and music', in J. Wilton-Ely (ed.), *Apollo of the Arts: Lord Burlington and His Circle* (Nottingham, 1973), 16–18.
25. This relationship was first discussed by R. Wittkower, 'A sketch-book of Filippo Juvarra at Chatsworth', in R. Wittkower, *Studies in the Italian Baroque* (London, 1975), 187–210, where he maintained that it was unlikely that Burlington and Juvarra met in Italy, as their paths only came close to crossing in early 1715. However, more recent studies, in particular those by Manfredi, have suggested that a meeting between them was indeed possible. See T. Manfredi, 'Juvarra e Roma (1714–1732): la diplomazia dell'architettura', in G. Dardanello (ed.), *Sperimentare l'architettura: Guarini, Juvarra, Alfieri, Borra, Vittone* (Turin, 2001), 177–96, esp. p. 178; also the contribution by Manfredi in this volume.
26. Cf. the contribution by Manfredi in this volume.
27. Rolli wrote: 'E stato in Londra D. Filippo Juvara, quel bravo Architetto siculo che facea le belle scene d'Ottoboni in Cancelleria a Roma. Egli è al servizio del Re dell'Alpi a venia da Portugallo, dove fudal suo Re mandato a quell'altro Re [John V] per la direzzione d'un Palazzo e d'una Catedrale. Fu rubato di molta somma, mentre andava a spasso presso all'alto Bosco nel Coppé con l'Inviato portughese [Jacinta Borges Pereira de Castro], ma che importa? È stato pensionato da quel re di 1 000 scudi annui a fatto Cavaliero del su'ordine, oltre la paga del suo Padrone'. From L. Lindgren, 'The staging of Handel's operas in London', in S. Sadie and A. Hicks (eds), *Handel Tercentenary Collection* (London, 1987), 93–119, esp. p. 118 n. 40.
28. See Wittkower, 'Sketchbook of Filippo Juvarra' (above, n. 25).
29. E. Croft-Murray, *John Devoto: a Baroque Scene Painter* (London, 1953).

30. LAO, letter of Kent to Massingberd, dated Rome 26 January 1713/14.
31. Rozkowska, 'Filippo Juvarra al servizio dei Sobieski' (above, n. 11), 261.
32. Viale Ferrero, *Filippo Juvarra* (above, n. 9), 353 cat. 85 (1) and tav. 146.
33. It is the sets of this opera that most often have been singled out as a possible influence on Kent, but the fact that Kent was certainly in attendance has not been noted hitherto. A possible link between Kent and Juvarra was first noted by Viale Ferrero, *Filippo Juvarra* (above, n. 9), 56, which was expanded upon in Lang, 'Genesis of the English landscape garden' (above, n. 2), 29.
34. K. Woodbridge, 'Henry Hoare's paradise', *The Art Bulletin* 47 (1965), 83–116, esp. pp. 94–5. Woodbridge stated that Hoare did not own a copy of the *Coast View of Delos with Aeneas*, but he suggested that Hoare might have viewed the original as it was 'in a sale in 1737, about the time when Henry was travelling abroad forming the nucleus of his picture collection'. See also K. Woodbridge, *The Stourhead Landscape. Wiltshire* (London, 2002) (the National Trust guidebook, first published in 1981), who reproduced the National Gallery painting and asked (p. 20) 'Had Henry Hoare at some time seen the *Coast View of Delos with Aeneas*?'. Woodbridge noted that Walpole saw a painting by Claude in the Hoare collection in 1762 (K. Woodbridge, *Landscape and Antiquity: Aspects of English Culture at Stourhead 1718 to 1838* (Oxford, 1970), 23 n. 36). The painting in question was described by Röthlisberger as a simple pastoral landscape without architectural features, which he did not attribute to Claude (M. Röthlisberger, *Claude Lorrain: the Paintings* (New Haven, 1961), I, 499–500; II, fig. 343).
35. Woodbridge, 'Henry Hoare's paradise' (above, n. 34), 94–5; also Woodbridge, *Landscape and Antiquity* (above, n. 34), 31. Neither publication discussed the history of the paintings, but they are assumed to have been acquired by Henry Hoare (see the National Trust guidebook, *Stourhead. Wiltshire*, revised edition (London, 2005), 26). Since the rehang of the Picture Gallery in 1994–5 they have hung on the South (entrance) wall of the Picture Gallery. For the original of the *View of Delphi with a Procession* in the Galleria Doria Pamphilj, Rome, see Röthlisberger, *Claude Lorrain* (above, n. 34), I, 293–7; II, fig. 207. Röthlisberger did not cite the copies owned by Hoare, but they were discussed in St John Gore, 'Prince of Georgian collectors: the Hoares of Stourhead — I', *Country Life* 135 (1964), 210–12, who stated that they were recorded in the 1785 inventory of the collection (Wiltshire County Record Office, Trowbridge, 383.919) as by Andrea Locatelli.
36. Hoare to Lady Bruce, 23 October 1762, quoted in Woodbridge, 'Henry Hoare's paradise' (above, n. 34), 109. The original letter is in the Tottenham House Archive.
37. See, for instance, LAO, letter from Kent to Massingberd dated Rome 5 February 1717, and his diary of travels to northern Italy, Bodleian MSS Rawl. D.1162.
38. Woodbridge, 'Henry Hoare's paradise' (above, n. 34), 95.
39. Woodbridge, 'Henry Hoare's paradise' (above, n. 34), 95, put forward four options: '1. It was Henry Hoare's conception and he employed Flitcroft for the technical details of the buildings; 2. Although Flitcroft was employed by Henry Hoare, the concept was his; 3. Both contributed to the idea; 4. Flitcroft consulted Kent, who was still alive in 1744'.
40. Woodbridge, 'Henry Hoare's paradise' (above, n. 34), 95.
41. This interpretation was put forward by Woodbridge most strongly in *Landscape and Antiquity* (above, n. 34), in particular pp. 30–7.
42. The idea appears to have originated with Walpole, who frequently mentioned Claude in relation to his descriptions of garden designs, both in Walpole, *History of the Modern Taste in Gardening* (above, n. 2) and H. Walpole, *Journal of Visits to Country Seats* (New York, 1982). It was picked up and further reinforced by Woodbridge in 'Henry Hoare's paradise' (above, n. 34) and *Landscape and Antiquity* (above, n. 34), and followed by R. Paulson, *Emblem and Expression: Meaning in English Art of the 18th Century* (London, 1975), 29, and W.J.T. Mitchell, C.W. Moore and W. Turnbull, Jr (eds), *The Poetics of Gardens* (Cambridge (MA), 1988), 141. M. Kelsall ('The iconography of Stourhead', *Journal of the Warburg and Courtauld Institutes* 46 (1983), 133–43) argued against the idea that the garden at Stourhead can be interpreted as having an overall programme: 'Let us accept the supposition that an eighteenth-century visitor would have recalled Claude's *Coast View of Delos with Aeneas* on entering the garden. If he possessed such remarkably precise powers of recall then the Pantheon/Temple of Hercules across the lake would be incorrectly associated with Apollo, or Latona . . . Nothing is in the right order. Even allowing for the eclectic powers of associationism this is a very odd programme. Moreover, what is Father Tiber doing in hell and why should either image recall Aeneas landing on the coast of Africa?' (p. 136).
43. The major studies of the construction and iconography of the garden at Stourhead are by Kenneth Woodbridge ('Henry Hoare's paradise' (above, n. 34); *Landscape and Antiquity* (above, n. 34)). He later revised a number of his conclusions in *Stourhead Landscape* (above, n. 34). Other interpretations of the construction and iconographical programme include J. Turner, 'The structure of Henry Hoare's Stourhead', *The Art Bulletin* 61 (1979), 68–77; M. Charlesworth, 'On meeting Hercules in Stourhead garden', *Journal of Garden History* 9 (1989), 71–5. See also S. Ross, *What Gardens Mean* (Chicago/London, 1998) for a summary of a number of the iconographical interpretations.
44. A published record of this reconstruction is in Mead, 'Stourhead revisited' (above, n. 5), 46–7. Piper's drawings are published in K. Woodbridge, 'The planting of ornamental shrubs at Stourhead: a history, 1746 to 1946', *Garden History* 4 (1976), 88–109.
45. On the tent at Painshill, see M. Collier and D. Wrightson, 'The re-creation of the Turkish Tent at Painshill', *Garden History* 21 (1993), 46–59.

46. Pietro Ottoboni and Alessandro Scarlatti, *Ciro dramma per musica* (Rome, 1712). A copy of the printed libretto is in the Biblioteca Casanatense, Rome, comm. 445/2.
47. Lang, 'Genesis of the English landscape garden' (above, n. 2), 28, also indicated a stage design by Inigo Jones that may have influenced Kent's design for this temple.
48. Giovanni Paolo Panini, *Musical Performance Given by the Cardinal de la Rochefoucauld in the Teatro Argentina in Rome on 15 July 1747 for the Marriage of the Dauphin of France*, 1747. Paris, Louvre, inv. 414-140.
49. Quoted in Hunt, *The Picturesque Garden in Europe* (above, n. 2), 15.
50. See p. 228, n. 36.
51. Pietro Ottoboni and Filippo Amadei, *Teodosio il giovane* (Rome, 1711). A copy of the printed libretto is in the Biblioteca Apostolica Vaticana, St.Ferr.V.8047 (int. 5).
52. Croft-Murray, *John Devoto* (above, n. 29); Lindgren, 'The staging of Handel's operas' (above, n. 27), *passim*.
53. LAO, letter dated Rome 16 April 1715 (2MM/19A).
54. Pieter Andreas Rysbrack, *The Ionic Temple and the Orange Tree Garden*, *c.* 1729. Derbyshire, Chatsworth, oil on canvas.
55. Sicca, 'On William Kent's Roman sources' (above, n. 1), 138.
56. C. Mambriani, 'La versaglia dei duchi di Parma: prototipi e metamorfosi dei giardini di Colorno', in M. Macera (ed.), *I giardini del 'Principe': IV convegno internazionale, parche e giardini storici, parchi letterari* (Savigliano, 1994), 149–58, esp. pp. 152–3. For the prints, see D. Lenzi, J. Bentini, S. Battistini and A. Cantelli (eds), *I Bibiena: una famiglia europea* (Venice, 2000), 351–2 — recently they have been identified by Mambriani as being by the engraver Antonio Fritz and his collaborators.
57. Movement as it relates to the understanding of gardens was the subject of a set of papers published by Dumbarton Oaks — M. Conan (ed.), *Landscape Design and the Experience of Motion* (Washington, 2003) —, and was also discussed by J.D. Hunt, *The Afterlife of Gardens* (London, 2004), 145.

'My Holy See of pleasurable antiquity': Robert Adam and his contemporaries in Rome

John Wilton-Ely

The late eighteenth century was exceptional in its recognition of the need to create a vital, contemporary language of design. In responding to this situation, the Adam brothers were fully aware that they were launching a major revolution within the visual arts. They set out consciously to fashion an attractive and flexible style applied across the full spectrum of the fine and decorative arts, from architecture, landscape and urban design to decorative painting, furniture, plasterwork, metal-work, ceramics and textiles — this wide range of the applied arts being skilfully orchestrated within the integrated interior. Fundamental to the creation of this style were the Grand Tours in Italy by Robert and James Adam, made 1755–7 and 1760–3 respectively, during which their stays in Rome — unusually well documented by correspondence and a wide range of drawings — were to prove of major consequence. Not only did Robert absorb a prodigious amount of material, extending from classical antiquity to the contemporary world, but both brothers were to benefit from a series of critical contacts with their Italian, British and French contemporaries in terms of professional practice and patronage. This paper explores the complexity of Robert Adam's artistic development, particularly under the influence of Charles-Louis Clérisseau and, above all, Giovanni Battista Piranesi and his circle. While, ultimately, Robert was to prove the creative force behind the emerging partnership, various roles fulfilled by James in Italy were to become essential factors in his more energetic brother's professional strategy.

Robert Adam (1728–92) (**Plate 17.1**) and two of his three brothers, John (1721–92) and James (1732–94), were trained under their father William (1689–1748), the leading architect of his time in Scotland. Their younger brother William (d. 1822) was eventually to follow Robert and James to London, where he undertook business contracting in their considerable property speculations in the 1770s.[1] On William Adam senior's death the brothers inherited a considerable practice, along with access to timber-yards, iron-works and quarries, as well as a landed estate north of Edinburgh, at Blair Adam. This substantial business and financial background was to prove an essential factor in their rapid success, and particularly influenced the scope and scale of the visits to Italy by Robert and James. Coming to maturity in the age of the Enlightenment, they mixed in the intellectual circles of Edinburgh with figures such as David Hume and Adam Smith, William Robertson and Adam Ferguson. Although Robert matriculated at the University, he left his studies prematurely in 1746 to join his father's office at a time of critical development for the firm. When their father died in 1748, Robert and John entered into partnership in order to continue the practice, and James subsequently followed. Along with six sisters, they were a tightly-knit family presided over by their mother, Mary, the sister of the Reverend William Robertson, minister of Greyfriars in Edinburgh and a strongly Protestant force in their upbringing. Another conditioning factor was the family's allegiance to the Hanoverian government, which was associated with a highly lucrative business constructing military communications and fortifications in the Highlands, such as Fort George, in the wake of the 1745 Jacobite uprising. An upwardly mobile family, the Adams were characteristic of the new professional class emerging in the latter half of the eighteenth century, aspiring to be on closer terms with the intellectual and aristocratic world they served. In particular, they enjoyed an especially good relationship with their clients, the Hopes of Hopetoun House. The brothers took over the construction of this substantial seat from their father and completed it in a neo-Palladian style in 1754.[2]

By the 1750s the Adams were becoming increasingly aware of the major cultural significance of Rome, not only as the focus of the Grand Tour but as a key centre in the revaluation of antiquity closely associated with significant contemporary developments in architectural design. The neo-Palladian revolution, which had affected the work of their father, was seen as increasingly out of date in the light of major archaeological finds, epitomized by the discoveries in Herculaneum and publications such as Robert Wood's folios on Palmyra and Baalbec, together with a developing interest in the significance of ancient Greece. In a conscious decision, the family decided to finance Robert, and, in turn, James, on what amounted to be a Grand Tour. More than one generation of the Hopes had made the tour, and it was the 2nd Earl's suggestion that Robert should accompany his younger brother, the Hon. Charles Hope, to Italy in 1754. At this point in the story, we have an almost unique insight into the career developments of Robert and James through a series of letters written to each other and to members of the family up until James's return from Italy in 1763, first revealed by John Fleming in his seminal book some two centuries later.[3]

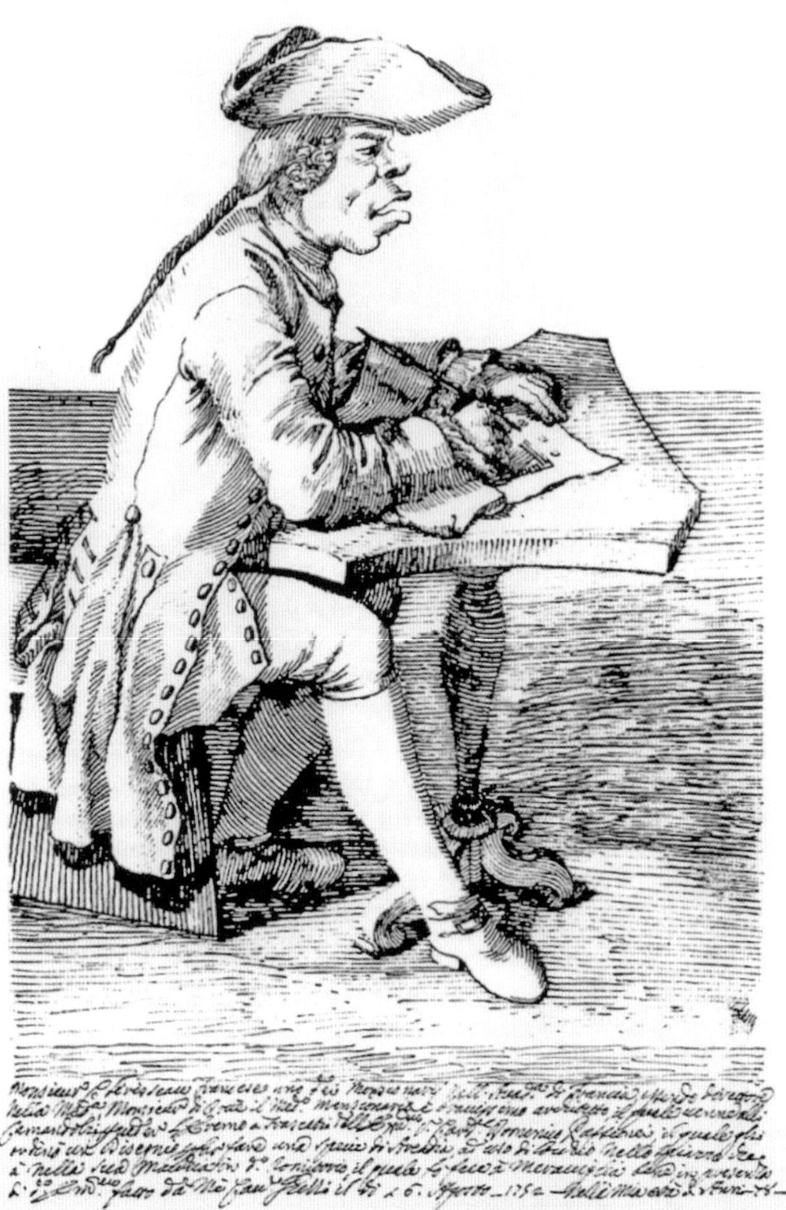

FIG. 17.1. Pier Leone Ghezzi (1674–1755), *Charles-Louis Clérisseau*, 1752. London, British Museum. *(Photo: © The Trustees of the British Museum.)*

Unlike other British artists and designers visiting Italy, Robert adopted, early on, a strategy of distancing himself from fellow professionals by assuming aristocratic attitudes and undertaking social activities that would bring him closer to the circles where he could develop future client relationships. With a capital of some £5,000, he was able to dress accordingly and attend the appropriate functions to a degree that the term masquerade was to have a double significance in his early months in Italy. As his contemporary the painter Nathaniel Dance wrote: 'I assure you the acquaintances one makes with English noblemen in Rome are of very great consequence when one meets them in England. Their having known you abroad, makes them interest themselves for you more than they would otherwise think of'.[4] Robert, thus assuming the role of a well-bred connoisseur, arrived at Genoa in January 1755 and was soon attending the opera as well as exploring the social world of Livorno and Pisa. However, by the time he reached Florence for the last fortnight of the Carnival, he was also making professional contacts through such key personalities as the collector and scholar Baron Stosch, the painter and dealer Ignazio Hugford, as well as the sculptor Joseph Wilton. Most significant of all was his cultivation of the former *pensionnaire* of the Académie de France in Rome, Charles-Louis Clérisseau (Fig. 17.1), who had fallen foul of the Académie after a series of protracted quarrels and was then seeking a career without the normal benefits of state promotion open to former students.[5] With five years' training in the foremost school of design in Europe, the Frenchman was taken on as a paid tutor to the Scot in order to impart a formidable range of skills in draughtsmanship and a systematic method of training characteristic of the Académie. As Robert justified this expensive decision in a letter to James of February 1755, he considered that Clérisseau possessed:

> the utmost knowledge of Architecture, of perspective, and of designing and colouring I ever saw, or had any conception of; he raised my ideas, he created emulation and fire in my breast. I wish'd above all to learn his manner, to have him with me at Rome, to study close with him and to purchase of his works. What I wished for, I obtained. He took a liking to me.[6]

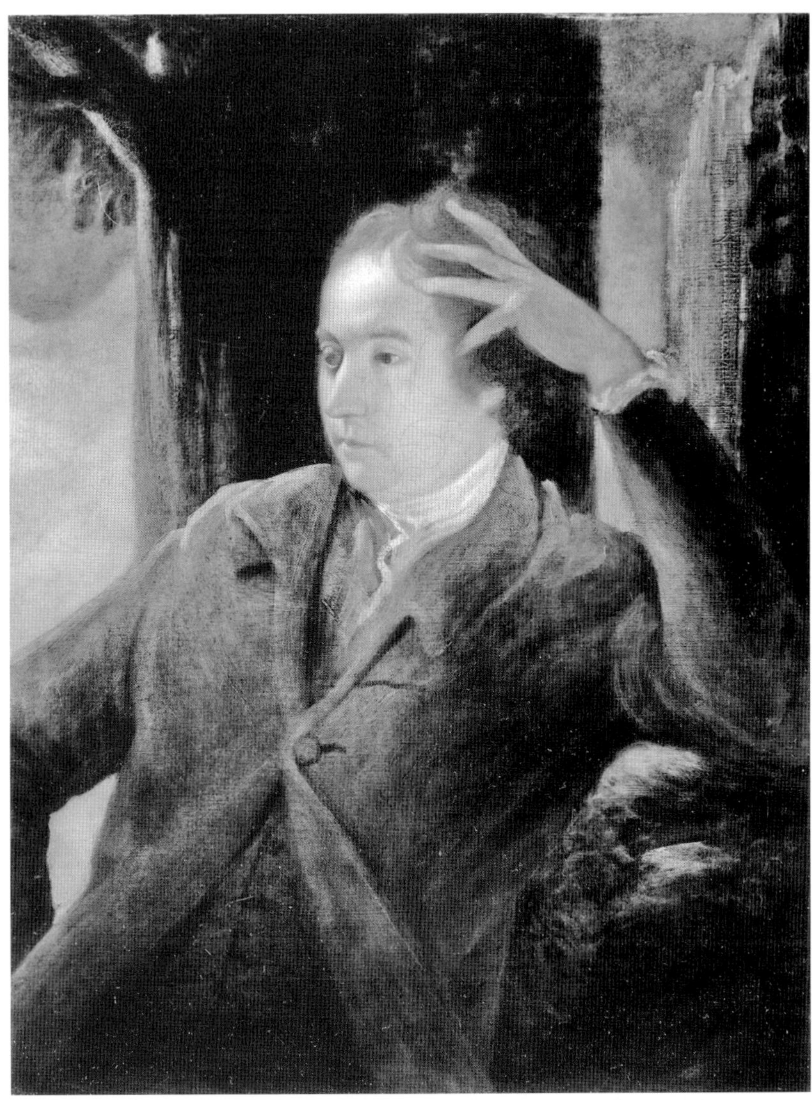

FIG. 17.2. Sir Joshua Reynolds (1723–92), *Sir William Chambers*, *c.* 1756–60. London, National Portrait Gallery, no. 27. *(Photo: © National Portrait Gallery, London.)*

Robert arrived in Rome with Clérisseau in late February 1755 and they established their base at the Casa Guarnieri, just off the Via Sistina at the top of the Spanish Steps. The social advantages were considerable, with the close proximity of tenants such as the young Duke of Bridgewater and his 'bear leader', the scholar Robert Wood.[7] However, during the early months in Rome, Robert, aged 27, with several years of practical experience working in his father's office in Scotland behind him, was keenly aware of the advantages possessed by potential rivals such as William Chambers (Fig. 17.2), then nearing the end of his stay.[8] The latter, five years older than Robert, had some six years' start on him in Continental training and experience. Before arriving in Rome, he had trained in Jacques-François Blondel's School of Architecture in Paris, as well as benefiting earlier from travels to India and China. However, Robert was not to be discouraged. As he wrote to his sister Peggy:

> To be the man I may be, much is to be done and I don't exaggerate when I assure you I as yet, with all I have seen, studied and done hitherto, think myself a mere beginner ... Chambers who has been here six years, is as superior to me at present as I am to Deacon Mack for greatness of thought and nobility of invention, drawing and ornamenting. But damn my blood but I will have fair trial for it and expect to do in six months as he has done in as many years. But then it will require study and attention, with application.[9]

After a visit in July 1755 with Clérisseau to Naples and Herculaneum, where the keeper of the museum, Camillo Paderni, conducted them through the buried amphitheatre and other sites, he wrote his first letter from Italy to James, who was proposing that they set up an office in London. Again, the threat from Chambers was still uppermost in his mind. As he wrote with a cool assessment:

> Chambers is a mortal check to these views in several ways. All the English who have travelled for these five years are much prepossessed in his favour and imagine him a prodigy for genius, for sense and good taste. My own opinion is that he in great measure deserves their encomiums, though his taste is more architectonic than picturesque ... His taste for bas-reliefs, ornaments and decorations of buildings, he both knows well and draws exquisitely ... Was I conscious to myself of having superior genius for drawing as well as being as well provided in good hints for designing and as many grand designs finished, finely drawn and coloured, as he had to show away with, it would be a different thing. But that can only come with time — and time alone can determine whether I am meet to cope with such a rival.[10]

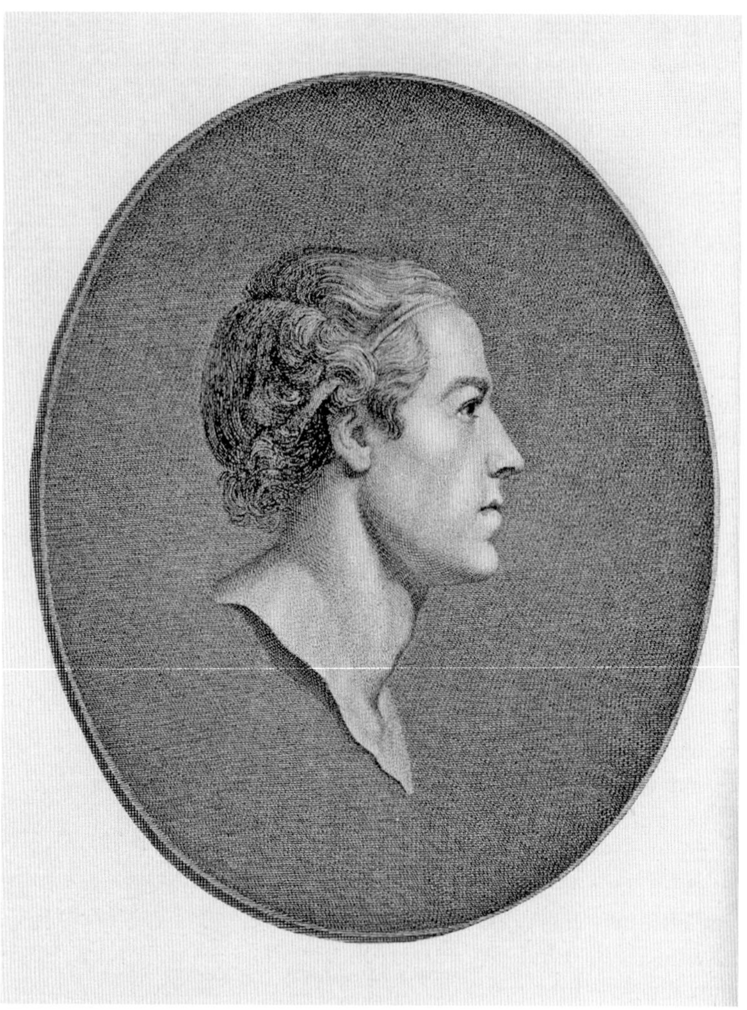

FIG. 17.3. Vangeliste after Richard Brompton (1734–83), *Robert Mylne, c.* 1757–8. Author's Collection. *(Photo: J. Wilton-Ely.)*

Therefore, Robert redoubled his efforts to mastering the basic rudiments of perspective and ornamental vocabulary from Clérisseau, as well as being instructed in figure drawing by Laurent Pecheux and in landscape composition by Jean-Baptiste Lallemand.[11] He not only learnt from Clérisseau to record the ancient monuments more accurately but appears to have made careful copies of the Frenchman's own topographical sketches with their precise effects of texture and light.[12] In fact, so impressed was Robert of the value of this rapid instruction course that he was soon urging James to follow him swiftly to Rome for this purpose before Clérisseau returned to France. According to Robert's correspondence, at this early stage his tutor actively discouraged him from premature experiments in devising imaginative compositions. As Robert confided to James in July 1755, 'Clérisseau preaches to me everyday to forbear inventing or composing either plans or elevations till I have a greater fund'. However, he went on to confess that: 'in spite of these admonitions I must still be scrawling a plan of a temple, or a bit of a front now and then makes its appearance ...'.[13]

Another potential architectural rival was his fellow Scot, Robert Mylne (**Fig. 17.3**), five years younger, who, with his brother William, had accomplished most of their journey to Rome on foot and were not inclined to be impressed by the lordly behaviour of Robert. As Robert Mylne wrote to his father, 'He makes a great figure here by keeping a coach and a couple of footmen but I assure you, as an architect he makes no more figure than we do ourselves for I see that a little study will make more than one family of architects in Scotland'.[14] Robert Adam, on the other hand, felt more insecure as he swiftly recognized the calibre of the competition, writing to James that:

> There are two sons of Deacon Mylne's in Rome at present, studying architecture. One of them had studied in France and has that abominable taste to perfection: the other [Robert], who came straight from Scotland, has made great progress and begins to draw extremely well, so if he goes on he may become much better than any of those beggardly fellows who torment our native city. For which reason, to keep all superiority in our hands, it will be

> absolutely necessary that the family of Adam all see foreign parts, without which that Mylne may turn to our disadvantage — as I assure you he promises well and having it to say he was so long abroad may have sway with many of our Scotch dons for whom, as he is poor, he will work much cheaper than we can do.[15]

Robert's fears were to be partially justified when Mylne became the first Briton to win the *Concorso Clementino* in 1758 and, on return to Britain, was successful in the Blackfriars Bridge competition in 1760.[16] This was even more to be the case with Chambers, who swiftly rose to royal preferment under George III, first as royal tutor in architecture and later as the leading government architect. He went on to design the monumental scheme for Somerset House in the 1770s and helped found the Royal Academy of which, as Treasurer, he persistently blocked the Adams' membership.[17]

With such incentives, therefore, Robert settled down to his methodical process of re-education. When, however, Clérisseau introduced him to Piranesi in June 1755 this pedestrian training was clearly disrupted by the sheer catalytic force of the Venetian's personality and visionary designs (**Fig. 17.4**).[18] The latter's initial reaction to Robert was swiftly communicated home, even if Robert was likely to have been wary of such fulsome praise on his hitherto modest achievements.

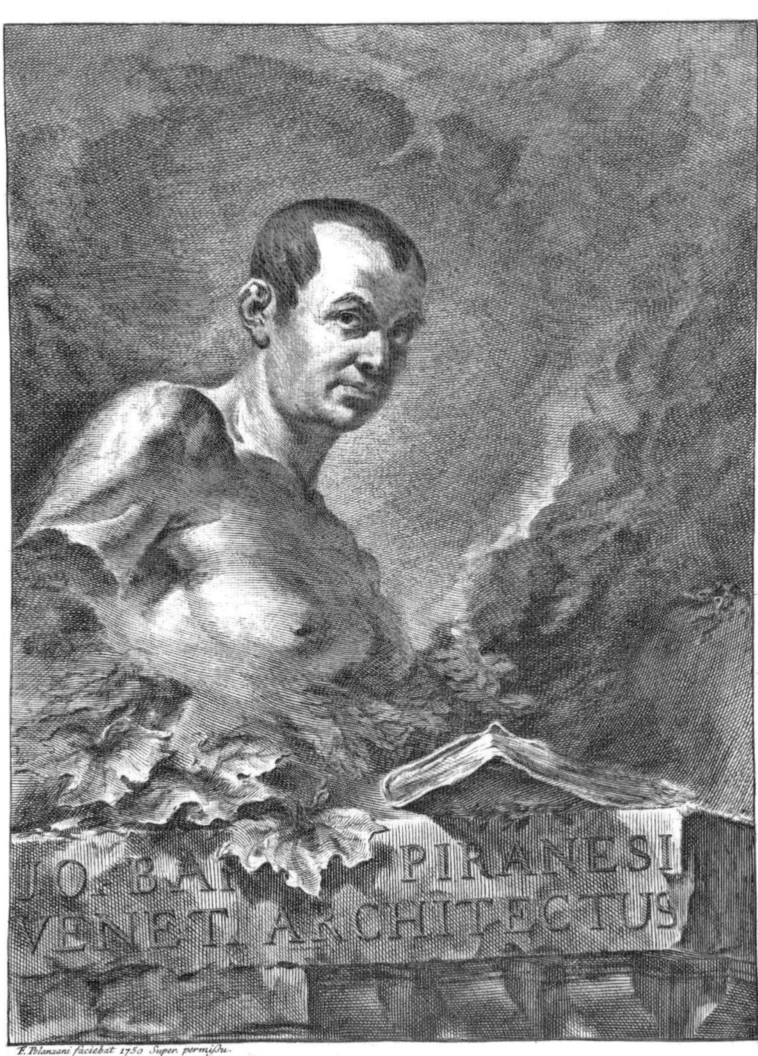

FIG. 17.4. **Felice Polanzani (1700–83),** ***Piranesi as an Antique Sculpture,*** **1750. Author's Collection.** *(Photo: J. Wilton-Ely.)*

> Piranesi, who is I think the most extraordinary fellow I ever saw, is become immensely intimate with me and as he imagined at first that I was like the other English who had love of antiques without knowledge upon seeing some of my sketches and drawings was so highly delighted that he almost ran quite distracted and said that I had more genius for the true noble architecture than any Englishman ever was in Italy.[19]

Robert nevertheless retained his faculty for a cool assessment and his initial reactions to Piranesi referred to him having 'such disposition as bars all instruction, his ideas in locution so ill arranged, his expression so furious and fantastic, that a Venetian hint is all that can be got from him, never anything fixed or well-digested so that a quarter of an hour makes you sick of his company'.[20] On the other hand, the Scot was already swift to recognize in Piranesi the stimulation he missed in Clérisseau's methodical instruction. As he went on to recognize: 'so amazing and ingenious fancies [as] he has produced in the different plans of the temples, baths and palaces I never saw ... are the greatest fund for inspiring and instilling invention in any lover of architecture that can be imagined'. Then, in somewhat gloating terms, Robert reported that:

> Chambers, who courted Piranesi's friendship with all the assiduity of a lover, never could bring him even to do a sketch of any one thing, and told me I would never be able to get anything from him. So much is

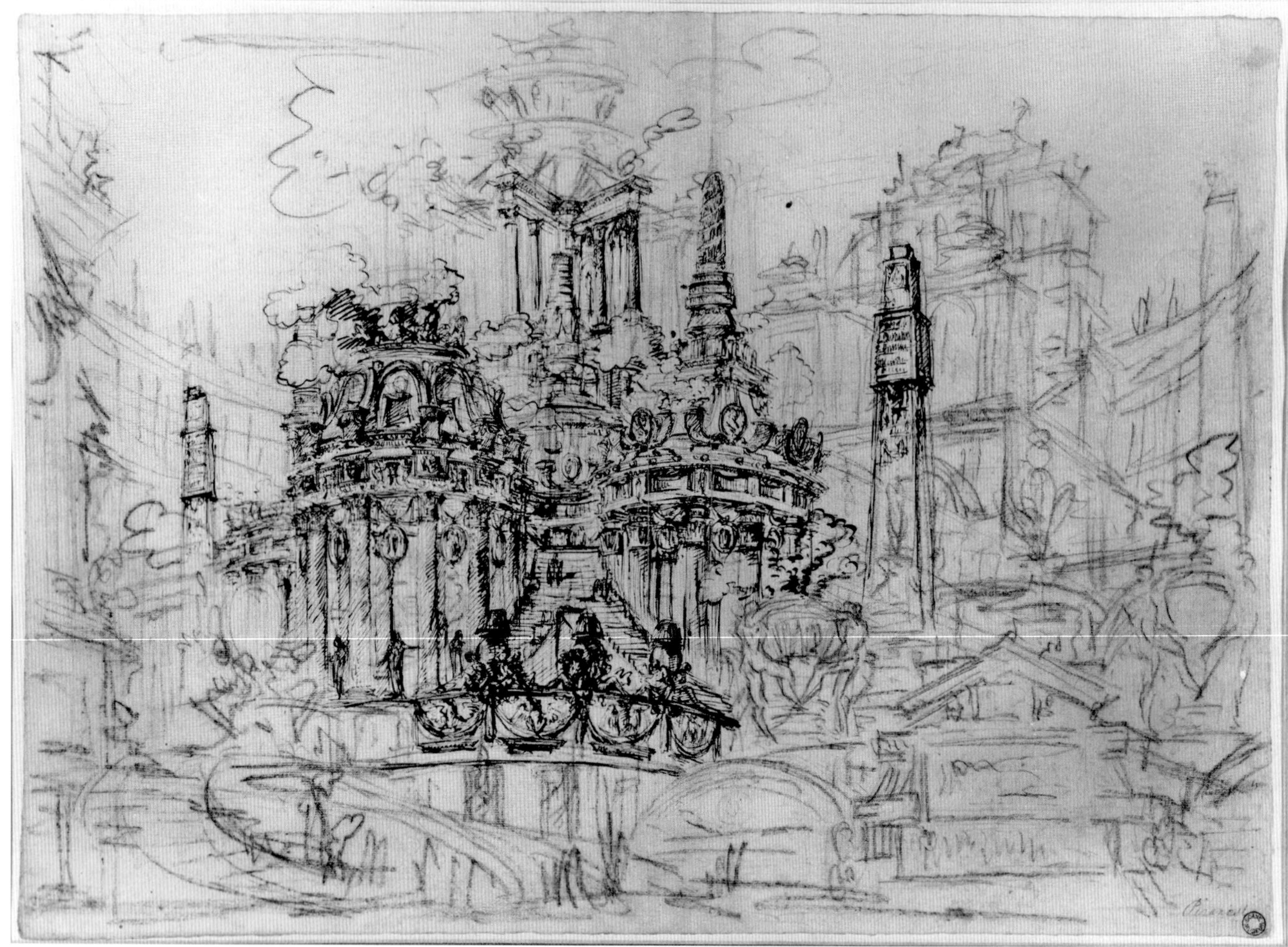

FIG. 17.5. Giovanni Battista Piranesi (1720–78), *Imaginary Architectural Composition*, c. 1755. London, Sir John Soane's Museum. *(Reproduced courtesy of the Trustees of Sir John Soane's Museum.)*

> he [Chambers] out of his calculation that he [Piranesi] has told me that whatsoever I want of him he will do for me with pleasure, and is now doing two drawings for me which will be both singular and clever.[21]

Indeed, one of the two Piranesi sketches in the Adam collection at Sir John Soane's Museum is likely to be one of these (Fig. 17.5).[22]

Piranesi's development of the drawn and engraved architectural fantasy as a 'test bed' for developing and communicating experimental ideas already had had its impact during the early 1740s in the imaginative development of several generations of *pensionnaires* at the Académie de France, from Charles Michel-Ange Challe, Jean-Laurent Legeay, Louis-Joseph Le Lorrain and Enemmond-Alexandre Petitot, to Charles De Wailly and Marie-Joseph Peyre.[23] Clérisseau was to fall within this same influence, even if he owed even more to the leading *vedutista* Gian Paolo Panini in terms of pictorial composition. Robert, coming from a more pragmatic tradition as well as an eclectic training under his father, who had been able to mix Baroque and neo-Palladian chacteristics in his style, was clearly receptive, unlike Chambers with his rigorous French training, to Piranesi's highly speculative approach to design, and a strong creative friendship soon developed between them.

On the surface, Robert's relationship with Clérisseau continued to appear harmonious. Robert referred to sketching expeditions in search of new antiquities, especially at Hadrian's Villa, Tivoli, with whom he termed his 'three friends Cronys & Instructors', Piranesi, Clérisseau and Pecheux.[24] A number of surviving views of the same subject drawn from similar angles by members of the group survive to indicate their respective approaches and capabilities. However, within a year of Robert's arrival in Rome, we can discern growing tensions in his relationship with

Clérisseau, both in human as well as in aesthetic terms. The Frenchman's initial dominance as tutor and sole channel of contact with the Roman artistic scene was to be increasingly undermined by Piranesi's influence. The former was no longer sole mentor of Robert, but found himself increasingly treated as a mere employee and a 'ghost' draughtsman. He began to experience the ruthless careerism of Robert, who was quite prepared to take over other people's ideas as his own. Robert not only assumed greater confidence in design but aspired to higher social circles, continuing to project himself as a dilettante and patron, and actively avoiding his fellow artists, even if he maintained a closer, if slightly patronizing, relationship with his fellow Scots, the painter and scholar Allan Ramsay and his wife.[25]

Robert's assimilation of Piranesi's formal ideas, meanwhile, is increasingly evident, although socially their relationship was to prove more complex. On the one hand, Robert saw himself sharing with Piranesi the same creative vision of Rome. This is testified by the Venetian's inclusion of an inscribed funerary monument to him (along with another one to Ramsay) in the Via Appia fantasy frontispiece to volume II of *Le antichità romane* of 1756, which was triumphantly reported by Robert in a letter to James.[26] Such a 'puff' was soon reinforced by the dedication of not only the large visionary map of the *Campo Marzio* to Robert (dated 1757) (Plate 17.2), but also the entire volume incorporating it, which was eventually published in 1762. Here Robert was treated as a patron by a fellow architect — itself an exceptional gesture almost without parallel in the eighteenth century. Even so, Piranesi, in the long dedicatory text, discussed their collaboration as equals in investigating the archaeological material on site when preparing the volume.[27]

In terms of his professional profile, Robert seems to have avoided entering the various *concorsi*, although he did submit a scheme for rebuilding Lisbon after the devastating earthquake in 1756.[28] He certainly made sure, however, of being elected to the Accademia di San Luca, as well as the academies of Florence and of Bologna. As for closer relationships with the artistic organizations in Rome, however, he was to a certain extent distanced from them through his close friendships with Clérisseau and Piranesi. From their side, they found considerable advantages through their relationship with Robert, since both were effectively 'outsiders', being excluded from the conventional architectural and patronage establishment of Rome by the time the Scottish architect had arrived on the scene. They were equally notable for their highly temperamental and over-sensitive natures, particularly where institutional life or rivals were concerned. As already mentioned, Clérisseau was *persona non grata* with the Académie de France in Rome after a series of protracted quarrels. Meanwhile, Piranesi had shown little respect for the contemporary architectural profession in Rome since his arrival from Venice in the 1740s, as he made clear in his disparaging comments in the texts both of his *Prima parte di architetture e prospettive* of 1743 and *Le antichità romane* of 1756. By the 1750s he had distanced himself even from his useful contacts within the Académie de France, as this institution became involved increasingly with the Hellenic side of the Graeco-Roman controversy, through the French support of Greek protagonists such as Marc-Antoine Laugier and Julien-David Le Roy. Like Clérisseau, Piranesi was seeking different fields of activity and influence, finding a new and more receptive audience for his eccentric ideas among visiting British designers such as Chambers, Mylne and Adam. Piranesi's acrimonious dispute with the Irish patron Lord Charlemont and his circle over the funding of *Le antichità romane* in the mid-1750s and with the Accademia di San Luca over the proposal for the Balestra monument in Santi Martina e Luca in the early 1760s were to continue this pattern of conflict.[29] Both Clérisseau and Piranesi, therefore, continued their close rapport with Robert. For the Frenchman it provided a source of employment, both by the Scottish architect and his brother as well as other British patrons, well into the 1770s. After Robert's return to Britain in Janary 1758, via the expedition to document Diocletian's Palace at Spalato with Clérisseau, his productive relationship with Piranesi was to develop into a lifelong friendship. While the Venetian found a kindred spirit in the Scot, given an opportunistic streak in the characters of both men, this association continued to produce a series of mutually-beneficial results.

While Adam maintained a relentless process of assimilation and recording from classical antiquity to contemporary design, he was energetically pursuing a social life to make the most advantageous contacts, both in the social world of Rome and the continually changing scene of the Grand Tour. A key agent in gaining him access to the ecclesiastical world was the Jesuit Abbé Peter Grant (Fig. 17.6), who represented the Scottish Mission for 46 years and had an unrivalled knowledge of and access to every level of the Roman

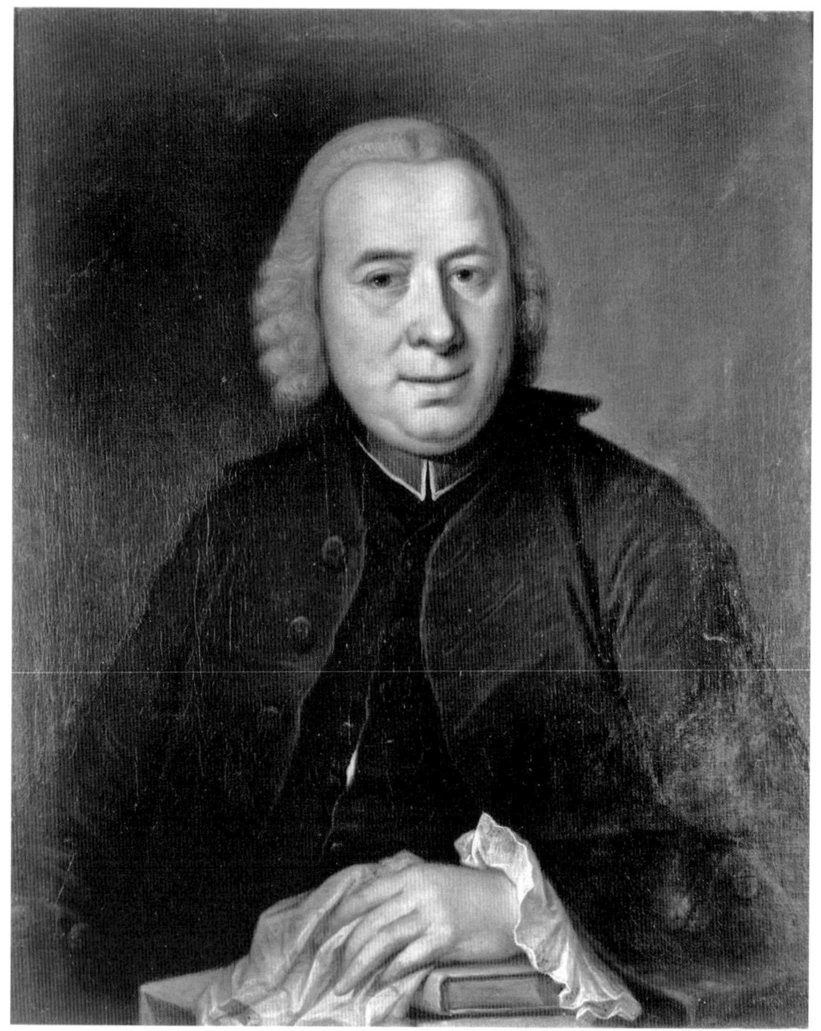

FIG. 17.6. Angelica Kauffman (1741–1807), *Abbé Peter Grant*. Private Collection, Scotland. *(Reproduced courtesy of the owner.)*

scene.[30] He had initially made the Scottish priest's acquaintance through Hope and referred:

> to my good friend the Abbé Grant who, if I mistake not, is as good a Jacobite and as good a Catholic, as true a friend and as worthy a man, as e'er a Christian in Europe. We are two brothers. He is constantly with me, for four or five hours at a time.[31]

While Robert was firmly made aware of compromising his family's lucrative Protestant allegiances, to his staunchly Presbyterian mother's concern he continued to mingle with the clerical establishment in a variety of assemblies and *conversazioni*, frequenting, in particular, the literary salon of Contessa Cheroffini at the Palazzo Frascara. His clear objective in this case was to make the acquaintance of one of the greatest patrons and collectors in Rome, Cardinal Alessandro Albani, whose intimate relations with the Countess were widely known. This contact appears to have developed fast, and by May 1755 he wrote:

> Cardinal Albani and I are turned very thick as he has discovered my hidden talents for the hidden treasures of antiquity. He has given me allowance to mould several things from his originals, shakes me by the hand like an honest goddam and claps my shoulder. In short *son éminence* and me are as grit as dogs' heads.[32]

Albani was then in the process of building his celebrated villa on the Via Salaria, in which to display his major collection of antiquities, presided over by Johann Joachim Winckelmann, Piranesi's chief opponent in the developing Graeco-Roman controversy, and recently appointed the Cardinal's librarian.[33]

Inevitably the question arises of Robert's possible social contacts with members of the Stuart court in exile, and it is clear that his close friendship both with Grant and the Stuart's physician, James Irvine, with whom he dined, was a source of increasing concern back home. However, apart from the mention of once catching sight of Cardinal York in his coach returning from Saint Peter's, he allayed his mother's anxiety by reassuring her that in the case of Irvine — 'a very sensible clever old man' — 'the best Whigs go to see him so that it is no stain and he is so sensible as not to say or do anything to offend them'.[34]

By 1757, although Robert was in no frame of mind to leave 'my holy see of pleasurable antiquity', as he put it, the family was getting impatient for his return, especially when he mentioned the possibility of a trip to Greece and the eastern Mediterranean.[35] Reluctantly leaving Rome in May, he was accompanied by Clérisseau, his servant Donald, and two young draughtsmen, the Belgian Laurent-Benoît Dewez and the Italian Agostino Brunias.[36] After a swift survey of Diocletian's palace at Spalato (to be published in 1764 in a handsome folio, dedicated to George III) he was back in

England by January 1758.[37] There he swiftly joined James at their new London office in Lower Grosvenor Street, from which a rapid career of major architectural commissions developed.

Robert had barely entered this revolutionary phase in his professional life when James now left London for Italy in spring 1760, accompanied by George Richardson, one of the senior draughtsmen in the Adam office. While James shared the same educational objectives that had taken his brother abroad six years earlier, he had, of course, considerable advantages due to Robert's preparatory briefing and well-established contacts with Clérisseau and Piranesi. Even so, James appears to have made little use of either of these two exceptional designers in comparison with his energetic brother. As he himself admitted later: 'I believe that biographers will choose to pass over this part of my life in profound silence'.[38]

James first met Clérisseau in Venice in June 1760, where the latter was supervising the work of the engravers Bartolozzi, Zucchi and Santini on the Spalato volume. After touring the Veneto together, they journeyed south, reaching Rome the following February, and then made another expedition further south, to the Naples area, before returning to Rome in December. By then their relationship had begun to deteriorate, since Clérisseau considered that James lacked his brother's application to study in favour of fashionable diversions, and found himself treated increasingly as a superior kind of servant, styled as *segretario al Cavaliere*.[39] For all his lack of application, however, James proved of considerable use in reinforcing Robert's social contacts and in acquiring paintings and sculpture for the family business, particularly to augment the display developed at their London office in order to impress future clients.[40] Assisted by the Abbé Grant's contacts, he had accumulated some 500 pictures 'besides drawings, antiquities, modellos, gessos &ca valued at £1,500 more'.[41] His greatest coup, however, was undoubtedly arranging the purchase of Cardinal Albani's unparalleled collection of Old Master drawings for George III, despite the considerable reluctance of the owner.[42] However, the pressing need for money to furnish a dowry for the daughter of the Cardinal's liaison with Contessa Cheroffini settled the matter, and James saw the collection dispatched from Livorno in July 1762.

Despite his failure to benefit from Piranesi's artistic influence, another useful task fulfilled was to hasten the publication of the latter's folio, *Il Campo Marzio dell'antica Roma*. This lavish work, with its flattering dedication to Robert, was recognized as a valuable form of publicity, and a considerable number of copies were ordered to give to clients in Britain.[43] Piranesi, however, appears to have been impressed by James's design for a British Order, as part of a hastily prepared scheme for a Houses of Parliament, the finished designs of which being greatly enhanced by Clérisseau.[44] Later published in *The Works in Architecture of Robert and James Adam* in 1779, this conceit was based on the capital from the Temple of Mars Ultor, and ingeniously incorporated the lion and unicorn as supporters of the British royal coat of arms.[45] Later on, Piranesi, in his polemical dialogue between two fictitious architects, the *Parere su l'architettura* of 1765, was to refer to this work (significantly attributing it to Robert, rather than James) as a striking example of the imaginative application of antiquity to a contemporary need.[46] Predictably, when James sat for his portrait around 1763, his left arm is shown resting elegantly on a wax model of this capital (Fig. 17.7).[47]

The last months of James's time in Rome are documented sparsely, apart from his activities in securing material for his brother's work at Syon House for the Duke of Northumberland, such as the marble columns for the Ante-room, copies of major statues and the commissioning of a marble relief by Luc-François Breton.[48] He also may have had a hand in commissioning the four etched plates by Piranesi of the Entrance Hall and Ante-room from drawings by Robert, dated 1761, later published in the brothers' *The Works in Architecture*.[49] Leaving Clérisseau behind in Rome as the brothers' chargé d'affaires — a device to avoid his influence on Robert becoming common currency in London gossip —, James finally left for England in April 1763. By the time he had joined his brother in London the main principles of the Adam style had been established without his contribution, and any serious threat that they might have expected from Clérisseau as a rival was of little significance by the time that the Frenchman eventually reached England in 1771. On the other hand, Piranesi's influence was reinforced with the publication of his final testament of design, the *Diverse maniere d'adornare i cammini* of 1769, making important contributions to a new phase of experiment by Robert and providing a basic theoretical defence for the Adams' innovations, which they rephrased (without acknowledgement) in their theoretical text in *The Works in Architecture*, as largely drafted by James.[50]

If there is an aspect of the mature Adam style that directly shows the collective impact of these Roman

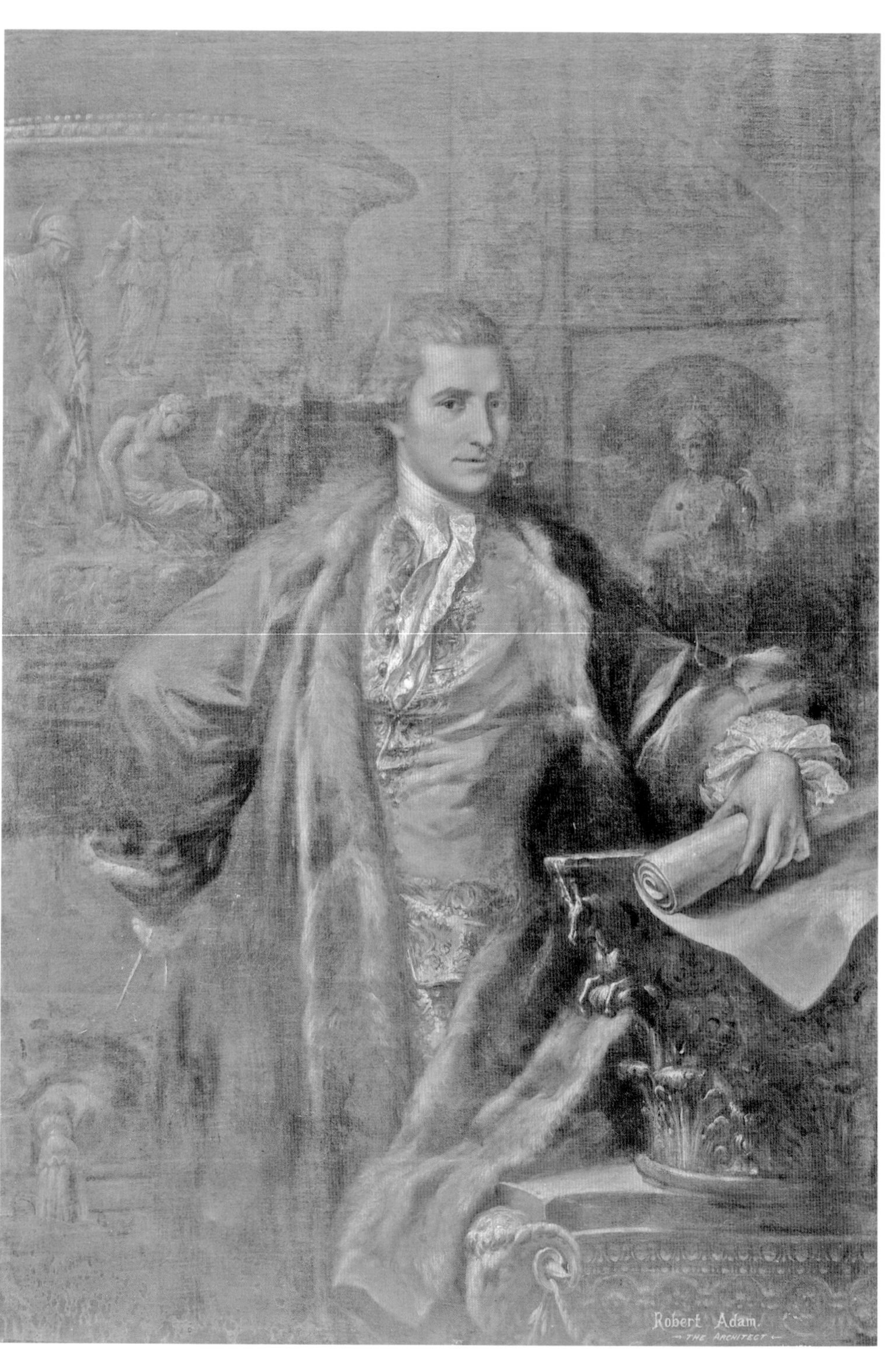

Fig. 17.7. Attributed to George Willison (1741–97), *James Adam*, 1763. Private Collection. *(Reproduced courtesy of Christie's.)*

influences, particularly through Clérisseau and Piranesi, it is the exceptional series of Etruscan rooms devised by Robert during the 1770s.[51] The most complete surviving one at Osterley Park (**Fig. 17.8**), painted by Pietro Borgnis with a contribution by Antonio Zucchi, shows considerable debts to Piranesi's advocacy in the *Diverse maniere* of an eclectic system of design applying antiquity to contemporary needs. In the Osterley interior Robert combined the pergola or trellis-like themes of Second Style Roman wall paintings (as also found in the Cinquecento grotesque decorations by the School of Raphael) with the colours and motifs of the so-called 'Etruscan' vases, published by Sir William Hamilton between 1767 and 1776. He also drew considerable

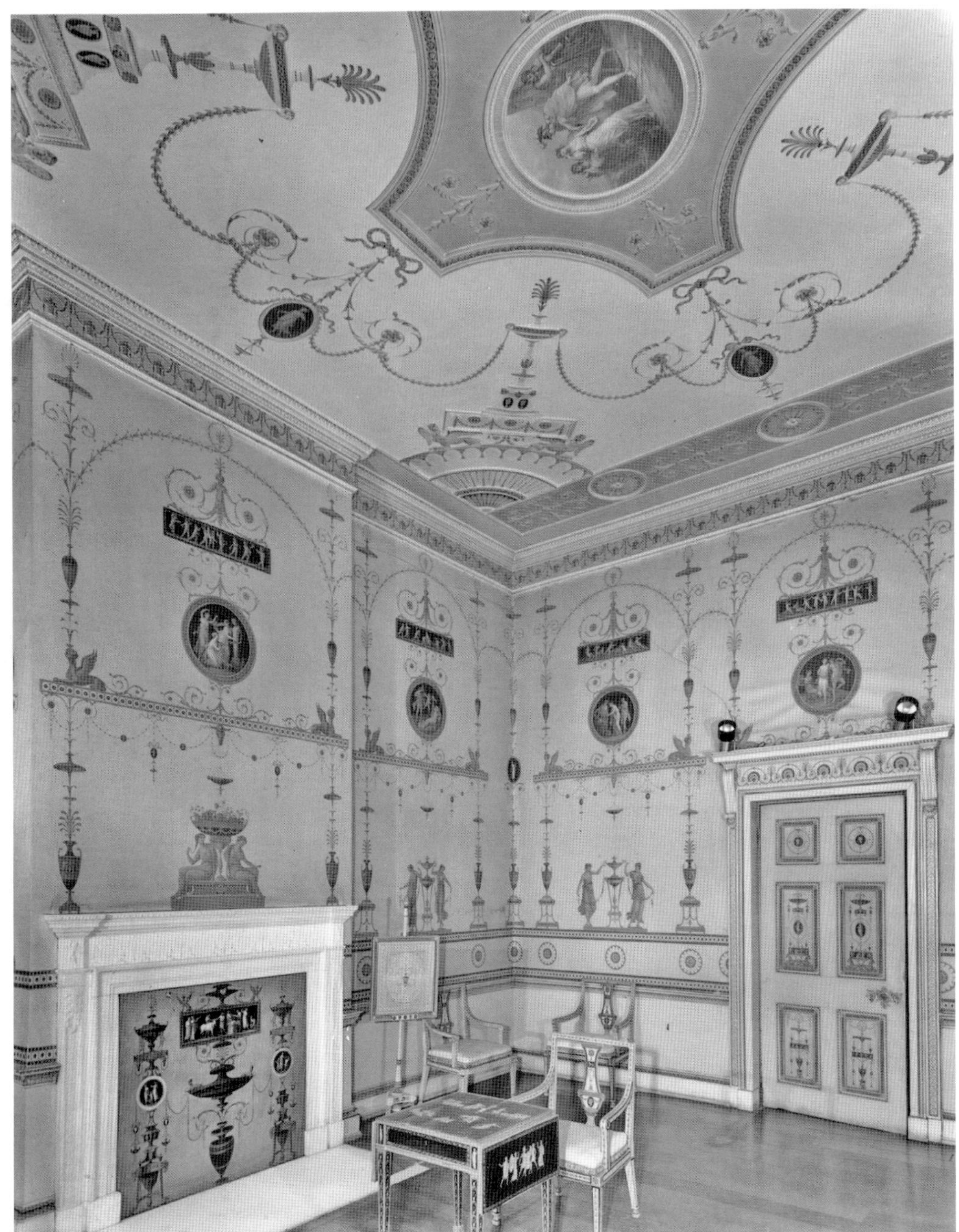

FIG. 17.8. Robert Adam (1728–92), *The Etruscan Dressing Room, Osterley Park*, 1775. *(Photo: A.F. Kersting.)*

inspiration from Piranesi's idiosyncratic interior schemes in certain plates of the *Diverse maniere*. However, the sheer elegance and finesse with which this ornamental composition is handled originates from the careful teaching of Clérisseau, as can be discerned when Robert's Osterley composition is compared with the French designer's documented scheme for the second of his two interiors at the Hôtel Grimod de la Reynière, Paris, of 1779–81.[52] On the other hand, where Clérisseau's scheme is more accomplished and fits well within the Louis XVI style, Robert's more exploratory manner, with its highly ingenious application of motifs to the integrated furniture and hangings of the room shows a far higher calibre of speculative mind at work. While paraphrasing Piranesi's words in the *Diverse maniere*, the Adam brothers' claim in the 1773 preface to their *The Works in Architecture* was not entirely unjustified when they asserted that: 'we flatter ourselves, we have been able to seize, with some degree of success, the beautiful spirit of antiquity, and to transfuse it, with novelty and variety, through all our numerous works'.[53]

Notes

1. For the early training and subsequent careers of the Adam brothers, see G. Beard, *The Work of Robert Adam* (Edinburgh/London, 1978); D. King, *The Complete Works of Robert and James Adam* (Oxford, 1991); E. Harris, *The Genius of Robert Adam. His Interiors* (New Haven/London, 2001). For William Adam junior, see A. Rowan, 'William Adam and Company', in 'After the Adelphi: forgotten years in the Adam brothers' practice', *Journal of the Royal Society of Arts* 122 (1973–4), 659–76. For their father's career, see J. Gifford, *William Adam 1689–1748. A Life and Times of Scotland's Universal Architect* (Edinburgh, 1989). For the Scottish architectural context in general, see also J. Macaulay, *The Classical Country House in Scotland: 1660–1800* (London, 1987). For the portrait of Robert Adam (London, National Portrait Gallery, no. 2953), attributed to George Willison (although David Martin has also been suggested), see J. Ingamells, *National Portrait Gallery. Mid-Georgian Portraits: 1760–1790* (London, 2004), 6–8.
2. For the Adam family's work on Hopetoun House, see Gifford, *William Adam* (above, n. 1), 87–90; J. Fleming, *Robert Adam and His Circle in Edinburgh and Rome* (London, 1962), 44–8; A. Rowan, ' The building of Hopetoun', *Architectural History* 27 (1984), 183–209.
3. Fleming, *Robert Adam and His Circle* (above, n. 2). Robert Adam's approach to achitecture during his years in Rome through surviving drawings is examined in A. Rowan, *'Bob the Roman'. Heroic Antiquity and the Architecture of Robert Adam* (London, 2003).
4. Dance writing from Rome, 3 February 1762, quoted in Fleming, *Robert Adam and His Circle* (above, n. 2), 245.
5. For Clérisseau's background and Robert's initial encounter with him, see Fleming, *Robert Adam and His Circle* (above, n. 2), 135–41. See also A. Braham, *The Architecture of the French Enlightenment* (London, 1980); T.J. McCormick, *Charles-Louis Clérisseau and the Genesis of Neo-classicism* (Cambridge (MA), 1990). For another caricature portrait of him by Pier Leone Ghezzi, see M.N. Benisovich, 'Ghezzi and the French artists in Rome', *Apollo* 85 (May 1967), 346, fig. 13.
6. Fleming, *Robert Adam and His Circle* (above, n. 2), 135.
7. Robert's skilful acquisition of his apartment at the Casa Guarnieri and its facilities, occupied from February 1755 until May 1757, are described in Fleming, *Robert Adam and His Circle* (above, n. 2), 150–1. His new outlook is recorded in a brief ink drawing entitled 'Sketch from my window in palazzo Guarnieri': see A.A. Tait, *Robert Adam. The Creative Mind: from the Sketch to the Finished Drawing* (London, 1996), 12, no. 4. The Duke of Bridgewater's tutor, who had published the key archaeological folio *Ruins of Palmyra* (1753) and who was to produce the *Ruins of Balbec* in 1757, gave Robert considerable advice on the social hazards of Roman society; see Fleming, *Robert Adam and His Circle* (above, n. 2), 148–9.
8. Chambers's early career and training in France as well as in Italy are examined in J. Harris, *Sir William Chambers. Knight of the Polar Star* (London, 1970), 18–31; J. Barrier, 'Chambers in France and Italy', in J. Harris and M. Snodin (eds), *Sir William Chambers. Architect to George III* (New Haven/London, 1997), 19–33. Chambers is recorded as staying in the palace of Count Tomati, 73 Strada Felice (now Via Sistina) between 1750 and 1752, during his initial years in Rome. Subsequently, Piranesi was to establish his lodgings and print establishment there in 1761. See J. Scott, *Piranesi* (London/New York, 1975), 311, n. 1. Chambers, while highly critical of Piranesi's more experimental ideas, considered him a valuable contact for one of his students, Edward Stevens. Writing to the latter in 1774, he added: '... forget not Piranesi, who you may see in my name; he is full of matter, extravagant 'tis true, often absurd, but from his overflowings you may gather much information'. See Harris, *Sir William Chambers* (above), 21–2. For Sir Joshua Reynolds's portrait of Chambers in the National Portrait Gallery (no. 27), see Ingamells, *National Portrait Gallery. Mid-Georgian Portraits* (above, n. 1), 97–9.
9. Fleming, *Robert Adam and His Circle* (above, n. 2), 152.
10. Fleming, *Robert Adam and His Circle* (above, n. 2), 160.
11. Robert's various instructors, such as Pecheux and Lallemand, and the process of his re-education under Clérisseau in Rome, are discussed in A.A. Tait, *Robert Adam: Drawings and Imagination* (Cambridge, 1993). See also Tait, *Robert Adam. The Creative Mind* (above, n. 7).
12. For an example of Robert's study of a monument with an almost identical one by Clérisseau, inside the Pantheon, see Rowan, *'Bob the Roman'* (above, n. 3), 17, nos. 2–3. For other examples, see McCormick, *Charles-Louis Clérisseau* (above, n. 5), *passim.*
13. McCormick, *Charles-Louis Clérisseau* (above, n. 5), 25.
14. Quoted in Fleming, *Robert Adam and His Circle* (above, n. 2), 188.
15. Quoted in Fleming, *Robert Adam and His Circle* (above, n. 2), 188.
16. For Mylne's time in Rome, see C. Gotch, 'The missing years of Robert Mylne', *Architectural Review* 110 (September 1951), 179–82. Piranesi was to etch a view of the prize-winning design of Blackfriars Bridge under construction ('A view of part of the intended bridge at Blackfriars, London, in August MDCCLXIIII by Robert Mylne, Architect, engraved by Piranesi at Rome'), discussed and reproduced in J. Wilton-Ely, *Piranesi. The Complete Etchings* (San Francisco, 1994), II, 1106–7, no. 1014. For the portrait of Mylne in Rome, drawn by Richard Brompton between 1757 and 1758, and engraved in Paris by Vangeliste in 1783, see B. Ford and J. Ingamells, *A Dictionary of British and Irish Travellers in Italy, 1701–1800. Compiled from the Brinsley Ford Archive* (New Haven/London, 1997), 133, 694. For Mylne's British career, see A. Richardson, *Robert Mylne. Architect and Engineer, 1733 to 1811* (London, 1955). See also Fleming, *Robert Adam and His Circle* (above, n. 2),

356–7. A significant study of Mylne, both as architect and engineer, is provided in R. Woodley, *Robert Mylne (1733–1811): the Bridge between Architecture and Engineering* (Ph.D. thesis, University of London (Courtauld Institute), 1999).

17. For Chambers's design of Somerset House, London, see Harris, *Sir William Chambers* (above, n. 8), 96–106; J. Newman, 'Somerset House and other public buildings', in Harris and Snodin (eds), *Sir William Chambers* (above, n. 8), 112–23. Piranesi's influence is shown particularly in the monumental treatment of the substructure fronting the Thames, which owes much to his technical analysis of the similar arcuated structure supporting the Temple of the Divine Hadrian in *Le antichità romane* (Rome, 1756), IV, pl. LIII; see Wilton-Ely, *Piranesi. The Complete Etchings* (above, n. 16), I, 578, no. 524. The remarkable Navy Staircase at Somerset House also shows affinities with Piranesi's compositional use of bridges and galleries in the *Carceri d'invenzione* (Rome, 1761).

18. For Piranesi's relationship with Robert, see D. Stillman, 'Robert Adam and Piranesi', in D. Fraser, H. Hibberd and M.J. Lewine (eds), *Essays in the History of Architecture Presented to Rudolf Wittkower* (London, 1967), 197–206; J. Wilton-Ely, *The Mind and Art of Giovanni Battista Piranesi* (London, 1978), 60–2; Tait, *Robert Adam: Drawings and the Imagination* (above, n. 11), 28–32.

19. Fleming, *Robert Adam and His Circle* (above, n. 2), 165.

20. Fleming, *Robert Adam and His Circle* (above, n. 2), 166.

21. Fleming, *Robert Adam and His Circle* (above, n. 2), 167.

22. For a discussion of the character and dating of the two Piranesi fantasy drawings from the Adam collection in Sir John Soane's Museum (**Figure 17.5** being the most likely one referred to in this quotation), see J. Wilton-Ely, *Piranesi, Paestum and Soane* (London, 2002), 8.

23. Piranesi's use of the architectural fantasy as medium for formal experiment is examined in J. Wilton-Ely, *Piranesi* (London, 1998), 24–6; see also Wilton-Ely, *The Mind and Art of Piranesi* (above, n. 18), 11–23. For Piranesi's critical impact on the *pensionnaires* of the Académie de France in Rome, see J. Harris, 'Le Geay, Piranesi and international neo-classicism in Rome, 1740–50', in Fraser, Hibberd and Lewine (eds), *Essays in the History of Architecture* (above, n. 18), 189–96; A. Chastel and G. Brunel (eds), *Piranèse et les Français, 1740–90* (Rome, 1976); R. Middleton and D. Watkin, *Neo-classical and 19th-century Architecture* (London, 1980), 69–75; J. Rykwert, *The First Moderns. The Architects of the Eighteenth Century* (Cambridge (MA), 1980), 357–63.

24. Fleming, *Robert Adam and His Circle* (above, n. 2), 165. On 5 July 1755 Adam wrote: 'I am going out tomorrow Morning, being Sunday on a party of antiquity hunting with Piranesi, Clérisseau & Pecheux, my three friends Cronys & Instructors'. See also Scott, *Piranesi* (above, n. 8), 109.

25. For Robert's relationship with the Ramsays, see Fleming, *Robert Adam and His Circle* (above, n. 2), 147–8. Apart from his activities as a portraitist, Ramsay was in the process of preparing a book on the remains of what he considered was Horace's Sabine villa, northeast of Tivoli, as published and discussed in B.D. Frischer and I.G. Brown (eds), *Allan Ramsay and the Search for Horace's Villa* (Aldershot, 2001).

26. The inscription of Robert's monument, in the left foreground, reads as follows: *Dis Manib – Roberti Adams Scot – Architecti – Praestantiss – I.B.P. – Fac Coeravit.* According to Robert, writing to James in April 1765: 'In one of the frontispieces representing the Appian Way in all its ancient splendour, with all the mausoleums of the Consuls, Emperors &ca., he has taken the occasion to put in Ramsay's name and mine, with all our Elogiums, as if buried in these tombs'; Fleming, *Robert Adam and His Circle* (above, n. 2), 207.

27. Robert's first surviving reference to the future *Ichnographia*, or visionary map of the *Campo Marzio*, appears to be in a letter to James on 18 June 1755, where, according to Robert, Piranesi 'threatens dedicating his next plan of ancient Rome to me, but of this I have no certainty ...' (Fleming, *Robert Adam and His Circle* (above, n. 2), 354). Subsequently, on 5 July 1755, he wrote: 'You will soon see my name in print as Piranesi has absolutely rejected the Cardinal he intended to dedicate his plan of ancient Rome to and has dedicated it to me under the name of Architect, Friend and Most Knowing in and Lover of the Antique' (Fleming, *Robert Adam and His Circle* (above, n. 2), 354). On his farewell visit to Piranesi's studio in April 1757, Robert was delighted to find the artist at work on the flattering dedication to the map (actually dated to that year). See Fleming, *Robert Adam and His Circle* (above, n. 2), 230–1. The place of *Campo Marzio* (Rome, 1762) within the Graeco-Roman debate, in which Robert became involved temporarily, is discussed in J. Wilton-Ely, 'Vision and design: Piranesi's 'fantasia' and the Graeco-Roman controversy', in G. Brunel (ed.), *Piranèse et les Français: actes du colloque tenu à la Villa Médicis, 1976* (Rome, 1978), 529–52. Robert's role within its production is examined in J. Wilton-Ely, 'Utopia or megalopolis? The *Ichnographia* of Piranesi's *Campus Martius* reconsidered', in A. Bettagno (ed.), *Piranesi: tra Venezia e l'Europa* (Florence, 1983), 293–304.

28. Adam's designs for rebuilding Lisbon are discussed in Fleming, *Robert Adam and His Circle* (above, n. 2), 204–7.

29. For Piranesi's quarrel with Charlemont, in which Robert became marginally involved, see Scott, *Piranesi* (above, n. 8), 108–16. For the Balestra affair, see C. Bertelli, 'Un progetto per Poets' Corner e una picca all'Accademia', *GRAFICA grafica* 2 (2) (Rome, 1976), 117–20.

30. For Grant's significant role in both Robert and James's 'neworking' activities, see Fleming, *Robert Adam and His Circle* (above, n. 2), *passim.*

31. Fleming, *Robert Adam and His Circle* (above, n. 2), 146.

32. Fleming, *Robert Adam and His Circle* (above, n. 2), 165.

33. For the Villa Albani, see Rykwert, *The First Moderns* (above, n. 23), 342–51; O. Collier, 'The Villa of Cardinal Alessandro Albani, Hon. FSA', *The Antiquaries Journal* 67 (1987), II, 338–47; also the two volumes in *Studi sul Settecento romano* (ed. E. Debenedetti): *Committenze della famiglia*

Albani. Note sulla Villa Albani Torlonia 1/2 (1985); *Alessandro Albani patrono delle arti, architettura, pittura e collezionismo nella Roma del '700* 9 (1993). For the British dimension of the Albani circle, see L. Lewis, *Connoisseurs and Secret Agents in 18th-century Rome* (London, 1961).

34. Fleming, *Robert Adam and His Circle* (above, n. 2), 246.
35. Fleming, *Robert Adam and His Circle* (above, n. 2), 232.
36. For the Belgian Dewez, who had joined Robert in Rome by 1756 as 'the plan man and line drawer', and who later worked at Spalato as well as in the London office, see Tait, *Robert Adam. Drawings and Imagination* (above, n. 11), 24–7. For the Italian draughtsman Brunias (acquired at about the same time), who later worked on the designs for Kedleston and whom Adam described as doing 'all my ornaments and all my figures vastly well', see Fleming, *Robert Adam and His Circle* (above, n. 2), 216–17.
37. For Robert's Spalato expedition and the resulting *Ruins of the Palace of the Emperor Diocletian at Spalatro* [sic], 1764, see I.A. Brown, *Monumental Reputation. Robert Adam and the Emperor's Palace* (Edinburgh, 1992). See also J. Fleming, 'The journey to Spalatro', *Architectural Review* 123 (1958), 103–7; E. Harris (with N. Savage), *British Architectural Books and Writers, 1556–1785* (Cambridge, 1990), 71–81. While Robert's survey team included Clérisseau, he was unable to persuade Piranesi to join them. See McCormick, *Charles-Louis Clérisseau* (above, n. 5), 75–98.
38. Fleming, *Robert Adam and His Circle* (above, n. 2), 303.
39. Fleming, *Robert Adam and His Circle* (above, n. 2), 303.
40. For the display arrangements at the Adams' establishment at Lower Grosvenor Street, see Tait, *Robert Adam: Drawings and Imagination* (above, n. 11), 77–85, figs 65, 67–8; R. Guilding, *Marble Mania. Sculpture Galleries in England: 1640–1840* (London, 2001), 38, no. 59.
41. Fleming, *Robert Adam and His Circle* (above, n. 2), 296. See also J. Fleming, 'Messrs Robert and James Adam: art dealers', *The Connoisseur* 144 (1959), 168–71.
42. For the sale of Albani's collection, see Fleming, *Robert Adam and His Circle* (above, n. 2), 297–8.
43. For James's protracted dealings with Piranesi over the completion of the *Campo Marzio* volume, see Fleming, *Robert Adam and His Circle* (above, n. 2), 374.
44. James's designs for a British Parliament are discussed in Tait, *Robert Adam: Drawings and Imagination* (above, n. 11), 55–68. See also Fleming, *Robert Adam and His Circle* (above, n. 2), 303–6.
45. The *Design of the Entablature and Britannic Order*, as reused for the projected gateway to the royal residence at Carlton House, London, was published in *The Works in Architecture of Robert and James Adam* I, part V (London, 1779), pl. II. There is a drawing for this work in the Avery Architectural Library, Columbia University, New York, and a smaller preliminary design in the Metropolitan Museum, New York (Harris Brisbane Dick Fund, 1934).
46. For Piranesi's reference to the Adam parliament project in the *Parere su l'architettura*, see the reprint of this publication in G.B. Piranesi, *The Polemical Works* (ed. J. Wilton-Ely) (Farnborough, 1972). On p. 13 of Piranesi's text, the architect Didascolo, taking up a reference to the Adam project in the *Gazette Litéraire de France*, praises the invention shown by a design for a British Order as following the artistic precepts of Roman antiquity (as, in fact, derived from an illustration in the *Libro d'Antonio Labacco*). See also G.B. Piranesi, *Observations on the Letter of M. Mariette; with Opinions on Architecture, and a Preface to a New Treatise on the Introduction and Progress of the Fine Arts in Europe in Ancient Times*, introduction by J. Wilton-Ely (Los Angeles, 2002), 41, 42, 109.
47. See Fleming, *Robert Adam and His Circle* (above, n. 2), 281. The portrait of James with the model of the capital of his British Order, illustrated by Fleming (fig. 88) and attributed to Pompeo Batoni on the basis of a later inscription, is no longer accepted as being by this artist. Among the artists working in Rome around 1763, Angelica Kauffman has been considered, but the far more likely candidate is George Willison, to whom the portrait of Robert Adam in Plate 17.1 already is attributed. (The author would like to thank Edgar Peters Bowron, Francis Russell and Wendy Wassyng Roworth for invaluable advice.) It was acquired by the Anstruther-Thomson family of Charleton House, Fife, through the marriage of John Anstruther-Thomson with Clementina Adam, only daughter of William Adam of Blair Adam (one of John Adam's sons) and later entered the collection of Baron Knut Bonde. (The author is indebted to Stephen Astley for this information.) The painting was sold at Christie's in 1964 to an anonymous buyer and can no longer be traced. According to James in a letter to Robert: 'This capital is modelled in wax and bronzed and has altogether the air antique, and has surprised everybody that has seen it who, indeed, are very few besides Natoire [Director of the Académie de France], my two English friends Crispin and Richardson. This same celebrated capital is for the great portico of my project, as I suppose you may guess'. Fleming, *Robert Adam and His Circle* (above, n. 2), 306.
48. For James's role in his brother's transformation of Syon House, see D. Stillman, *The Decorative Work of Robert Adam* (London, 1966), 64; Harris, *The Genius of Robert Adam* (above, n. 1), 66, 69, 74 and 341 n. 44.
49. Piranesi's four plates of Syon, based on drawings by Robert, were published in *The Works in Architecture by Robert and James Adam* (London, 1779), II, part 4, plates I, III, IV and V (although each plate is signed by Piranesi and dated 'Roma, 1761'). See Wilton-Ely, *Piranesi. The Complete Etchings* (above, n. 16), II, 1101–5, nos. 1010–13.
50. The theoretical significance of the *Diverse maniere*, especially its prefatory text, is discussed in Piranesi, *Observations on the Letter of M. Mariette* (above, n. 46), 51–5. The original text and illustrations are reprinted in Piranesi, *The Polemical Works* (above, n. 46). Piranesi's critical impact on the later Adam style is discussed in Stillman, 'Robert Adam and Piranesi' (above, n. 18). For the genesis and complex publication

history of *The Works in Architecture*, see Harris and Savage, *British Architectural Books and Writers* (above, n. 37), 83–94; R. Middleton, '*The Works in Architecture* of Robert and James Adam', in *The Mark J. Millard Architectural Collection* II. *British Books: Seventeenth through Nineteenth Centuries* (Washington, 1998), 12–18; Tait, *Robert Adam: Drawings and Imagination* (above, n. 11), 103–34.

51. Besides Etruscan interiors at Derby House, London, and the Dressing Room at Osterley Park, Middlesex, Robert designed examples at Apsley House, Cumberland House, Home House, 'Mr. Adamson's Parlour' (The Adelphi), all in London; a small room under the stairs of the garden façade at Osterley Park; and Harewood House and Byram Hall, both in Yorkshire. New assessments of this achievement are provided in Harris, *The Genius of Robert Adam* (above, n. 1), 177–9, and in J. Wilton-Ely, 'Le 'stanze etrusche' di Robert Adam: una rivoluzione stilistica', in E. Debenedetti and A. Griseri (eds), *Il Settecento e le arti: dall'Arcadia all'illuminismo: nuove proposte tra le corti, l'aristocrazia e la borghesia* (*Accademia Nazionale dei Lincei. Convegno internazionale 2005*) (*Atti dei convegni lincei* 246) (Rome, 2009), 325–39. Robert's Etruscan style is examined within the remarkable development of such painted interiors 'all'antica' in J. Wilton-Ely, 'Pompeian and Etruscan tastes in the neo-classical country house interior', in G. Jackson-Stops (ed.), *The Fashioning and Functioning of the British Country House* (Washington, 1989), 51–73. For Piranesi's contribution to this style, in particular see Stillman, 'Robert Adam and Piranesi' (above, n. 18).
52. For the interiors at the Hôtel Grimod de la Reynière, see McCormick, *Charles-Louis Clérisseau* (above, n. 5), 164–78.
53. *The Works in Architecture of Robert and James Adam* I (London, 1773), preface.

Vincenzo Brenna and his drawings from the antique for Charles Townley

Letizia Tedeschi

This paper will explore the biography of the architect Vincenzo Brenna (1741–) and his work in Rome, with a special focus on his meeting with the Grand Tourist Charles Townley (1737–1805). This meeting, which took place shortly before 1768, was most likely brought about by the English agent Thomas Jenkins, and its result was to give Brenna new prominence in the international circle of the devotees of the antique who were in Rome at this time. The meeting with Townley favoured Brenna's subsequent hiring by Stanislaw Kostka Potocki, who, after involving Brenna in his project for rebuilding the Villa Laurentina based on Pliny's description of the villa,[1] invited him in January 1781 to Poland. In this way he launched the architect, at the age of 40, on his international career, which eventually took him to the court of Saint Petersburg.[2]

This brief summary of the facts brings out the importance of the Roman milieu and of Vincenzo Brenna's training and early work in Rome, where he was born. Bearing this in mind, it is worth emphasizing the close ties between the English colony in Rome and Giovanni Battista Piranesi, with whom Brenna seems to have worked at least until 1772,[3] as well as Brenna's debut as an engraver of ancient architecture in his contributions to the volume *Del tempio tiburtino detto volgarmente della Sibilla*, published in 1767. The notebook of the purchases made by Townley on his first visit to Italy significantly contains records of payments for two copies of the volume.[4]

In my earlier studies I have reconstructed Brenna's Roman period in detail, including correcting the existing biographies. I shall confine myself here to a brief summary.

Francesco Gioacchino Aloisio Vincenzo Brenna (Brenna's full baptismal name as it appears in the records) was born in the Palazzo Colonna in Piazza Santi Apostoli on 20 August 1741. His parents were Paola Specchi and Francesco Antonio Brenna, a gentleman of the household of the Constable Prince Fabrizio Colonna.[5] On his mother's side he was the nephew of the architect Alessandro Specchi, who in 1714 had been commissioned by the Camera Capitolina to compile 'the state or plans of all the antiquities of Rome belonging to the Roman People'.[6] The boy therefore grew up under the aegis of the Colonna, and moved in their orbit. He was assisted in this by his elder brother, the Canon Nicola Brenna, who was secretary to Cardinal Pietro Colonna Pamphilj.[7]

Brenna completed his training in Rome in about 1762, in his twentieth year, in the workshop of the painter Stefano Pozzi (1699–1768). Pozzi had been active in the Palazzo Colonna in 1750 and 1758–61, where he had been summoned by Paolo Posi (1708–76), another of Brenna's teachers, to decorate a number of rooms. An authoritative reference to Brenna being in Pozzi's company occurs in a note written by Giacomo Quarenghi, sent from Saint Petersburg on 1 March 1785 to Luigi Marchesi of Bergamo.[8]

In 1766, the 25-year-old Brenna — who had evidently made some progress in his career and had won a corresponding reputation — was recorded as an Arcadian with the name of *Lindaro*, together with his brother Nicola, who took the name *Neleo Messenio*.[9] In 1767 he began his study and reproduction of Roman remains. In the same year Townley arrived in Rome on the Grand Tour, where he began one of the most important Grand Tour collections of antique statuary. He was to return to Italy again in 1772–3 and 1776–7.[10]

Townley must have met Brenna at some point during his first stay in Rome, since the correspondence between them begins shortly afterwards.[11] The contact between the two was doubtless favoured by the personal interests of Townley, who may have hired Brenna as a draughtsman through Jenkins. He also employed Brenna, together with the *abate* Matteo Fregiotti, as his agent for small purchases of antiquities.[12]

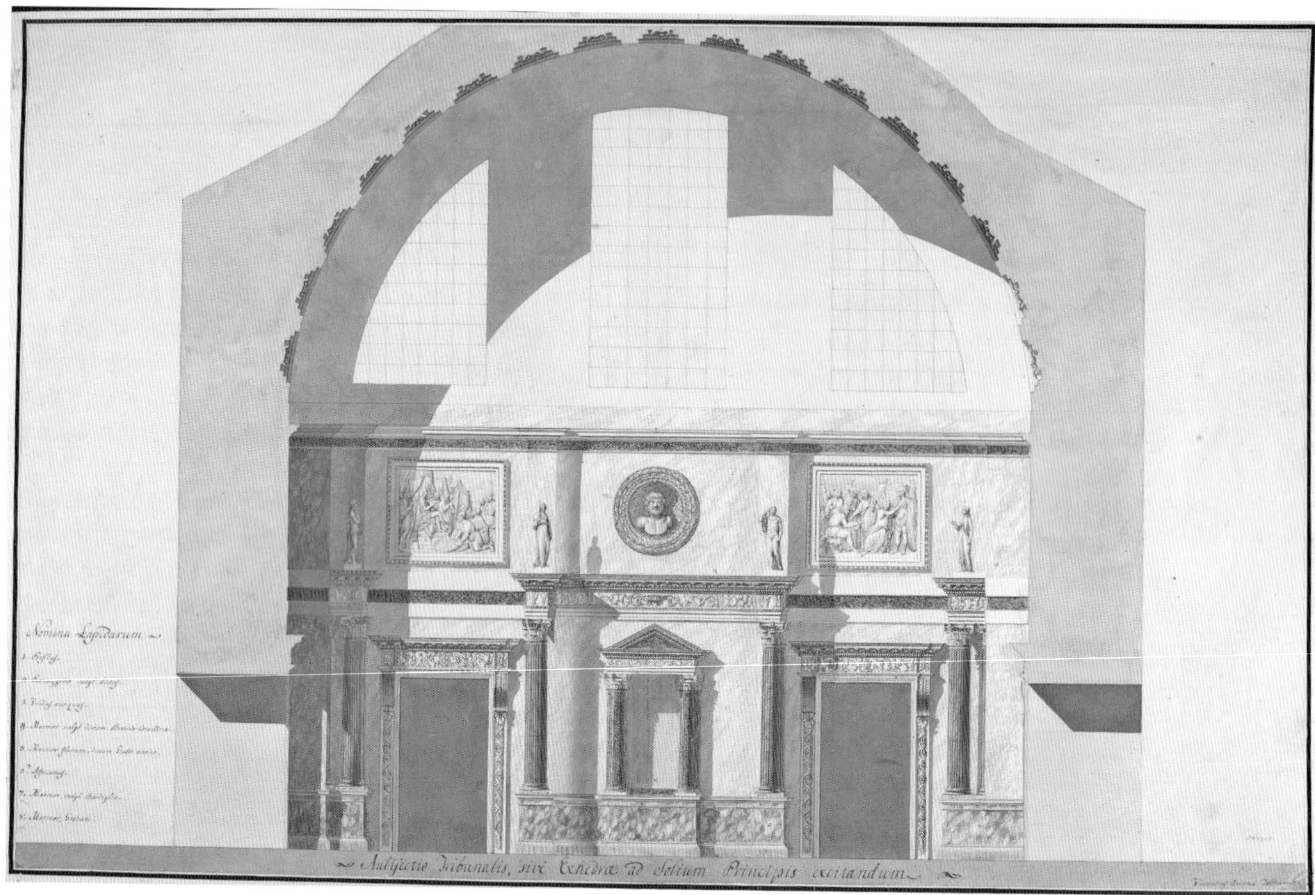

FIG. 18.1. Vincenzo Brenna (1741–), *Transverse Section of the Audience Chamber (Aula Regia) of the Palace of Domitian on the Palatine*, 1770. Indian ink, watercolour and tempera. London, Victoria and Albert Museum. *(Photo: © V&A Images/Victoria and Albert Museum, London.)*

A further point in Brenna's favour must have been his emergence as an engraver of ancient architecture in *Del tempio tiburtino detto volgarmente della Sibilla*, printed in 1767. In the two introductory folios we learn that the proportions of the Temple of the Sibyl at Tivoli 'have been drawn on the site itself with all possible fidelity and diligence'.[13] The words sound like a declaration by Brenna, for whom accuracy in rendering ancient architecture was paramount. Townley certainly knew the volume: his notebook records payments made for two copies.[14]

The existence of the letters between Brenna and Townley in the British Museum was noted by Jenkins and Vaughan in 1996,[15] and they were fully transcribed and published with a commentary by the present author in 2008.[16] They provide an implied chronology for Townley's Italian sojourns and, taken with his correspondence with Jenkins, his own account books, and recent archival discoveries regarding Brenna, they enable us to date and reconstruct the context of drawings executed by Brenna for Townley now in the Department of Prints, Drawings and Paintings of the Victoria & Albert Museum, datable to between 1768 and 1777.[17] Brenna's correspondence offers us a lively commentary on his career and the Roman antiquarian scene. Numbering some hundred sheets, they contain illustrations of the Round Temple at Tivoli, the Pantheon, the Audience Chamber of Domitian (Aula Regia) on the Palatine (Figs 18.1 and 18.2), the Colosseum, the Baths of Diocletian, the Baths of Titus, the Temple of Isis at Pompeii, the Temple of Serapis at Pozzuoli, the Temples at Paestum, and many other structures. His work for Townley was followed by a collaboration during the 1770s with the painter Franciszek Smuglewicz. Together they produced an inventory of the decorations in the rooms of the Domus Aurea discovered in excavations by Ludovico Mirri, who also promoted their publication in *Le vestigia delle Terme di Tito e loro interne pitture* (1776).[18]

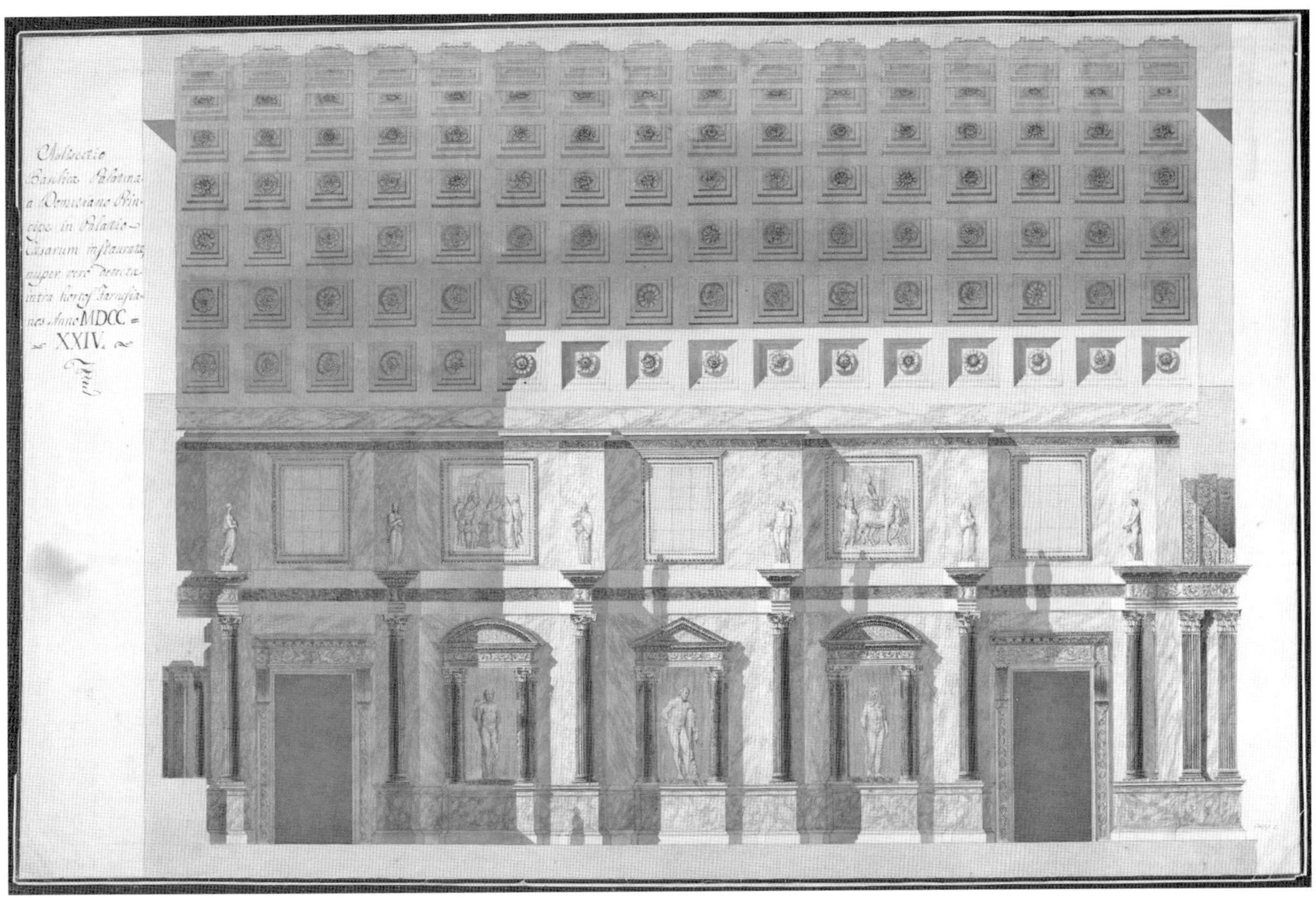

FIG. 18.2. Vincenzo Brenna (1741–), *Longitudinal Section of the Audience Chamber (Aula Regia) of the Palace of Domitian on the Palatine*, 1770. Indian ink, watercolour and tempera. London, Victoria and Albert Museum. *(Photo: © V&A Images/Victoria and Albert Museum, London.)*

THE RECONSTRUCTION 'WITH ALL POSSIBLE FIDELITY' OF THE ROUND TEMPLE AT TIVOLI

The first letter dates from November 1768, after Townley had left Rome in July. It begins by describing the excellent memories he had left behind with 'all those who had the fortune to deal with him and know him'.[19] His departure — a 'very sorrowful' one for Brenna — makes clear the influence exerted by his English patron while he was in Italy, and especially in Rome. From the same letter we learn that Brenna 'delivered to Signor Ginchÿs the drawings of the large sections of the Temple at Tivoli, namely the capital, cornice and base, and the plan of the Pantheon'.[20]

Among the sheets preserved in the Victoria & Albert Museum, four are dedicated to the details of the entablature, architrave, frieze and base of the columns of the Round Temple at Tivoli (Fig. 18.3).[21] In addition to the method already declared by Brenna in *Del tempio tiburtino volgarmente detto della Sibilla*, of 1767 ('it will be sufficient for us to describe the proportions currently visible in the ruins of the Temple ... drawn on the site itself'),[22] we should also bear in mind related fields of study. They comprise numismatics, stone carving, statuary (the object of specialized comparative studies), cartography and topography (in its own way a compendium of different forms of knowledge, involving geometry and mathematics, astronomy and natural sciences, as was clear to the followers of Cardinal Albani).[23] All these are relevant to a correct understanding of Brenna's cork model of the Temple, a work of unusually large dimensions made for Townley between June and October 1769.

We need to understand the significance of the detailed architectural renderings found in the drawings of columns, capitals, cornices, entablatures and ornaments in the plates, which accurately represent the form, and analytically measure the structure, of the

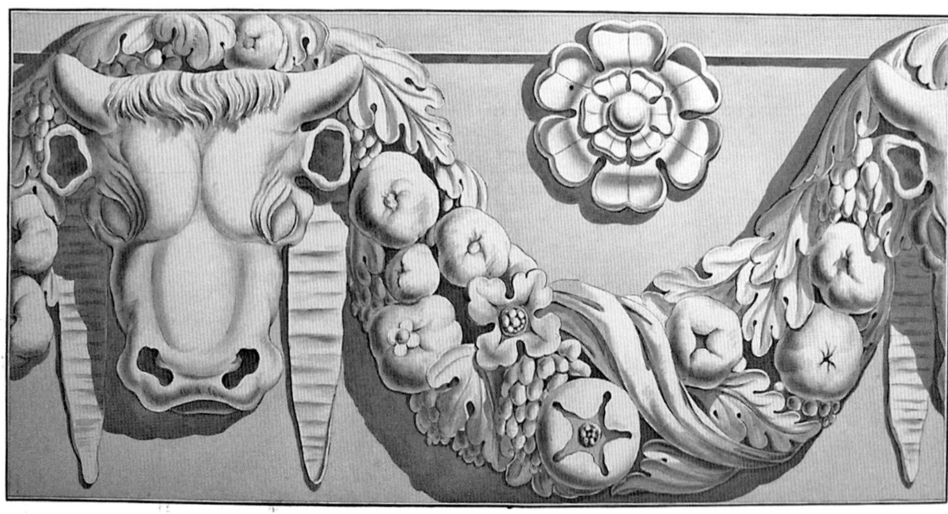

FIG. 18.3. Vincenzo Brenna (1741–), *Detail of the Frieze of the Round Temple at Tivoli*, 1768. Indian ink and watercolour. London, Victoria and Albert Museum. *(Photo: © V&A Images/Victoria and Albert Museum, London.)*

temple. It is as if they were the warp and weft in which every architectural element gains its substance; and we need to understand the instruments and methods used, so making his objective clear. Here Brenna seems to go beyond both generic and dispassionate typologies and emotional and impressionistic representations. In attempting to reconstruct the temple, he refuses to indulge in invention, his aim being to keep as close as possible to the original. He verified the measurements on the site, seeking within the temple correspondences (that is, equivalences and complementarities) that responded to proportional elements, in this way discovering a unity in the structural and formal features of the building and in the full set of its measurements (the height, width and volume of each masonry structure).[24] This approach, which we can call analytic, was based on a careful revision of earlier measurements made by artists from Andrea Palladio to Antoine Babuty Desgodetz, and it reveals their errors.[25]

THE EXPLORATION AND STUDY OF THE TEMPLES AT PAESTUM

Between 23 and 27 March 1768, Brenna, together with the painter Pierre-Jacques Antoine Volaire[26] and Fregiotti, accompanied Townley on a visit to Paestum, one of the archaeological attractions of the age.[27] Brenna took measurements that he used, on his return to Rome, to make drawings and engravings of the celebrated temples (Plate 18.1; Fig. 18.4),[28] as well as models, which he fashioned in cork and other materials. These added further fuel to the debate sparked off by the rediscovery of Paestum, which shed new light on Magna Graecia. Greece and the Aegean had by now become the subjects of systematic research, and careful study was devoted to the Doric order, especially by professional architects and English dilettanti. This study focused on the simplicity of form and lucidity of structure in relation to the order's generally harmonious proportions. Furthermore, Paestum was now being used as an example in the well-known polemic that pitted Greek and Roman *exempla* against each other in an attempt to assert the primacy of either Athens or Rome, depending on whichever historical prejudice was prevalent. Various writings by Julien-David Le Roy, James Stuart and Nicolas Revett contributed to the debate. On one side of this polemic appeared Winckelmann's *Osservazioni sull'architettura degli antichi* (1762), which was the first analysis free from the constraints of Vitruvius regarding Greek architecture, which it presented as a model of absolute beauty. Piranesi championed the primacy of Rome in his *Magnificenza e architettura dei romani* (1761), published in polemical opposition to statements by Ramsay (1755)[29] and Pierre-Jean Mariette (1764)[30] in an attempt to contest the primacy of Greek architecture.

Townley's tour of 1768, which also took in Naples, the Museum of the Royal Palace at Portici, Pompeii and Herculaneum, Pozzuoli, Caserta and Salerno, has been studied by Vaughan,[31] so I shall only highlight some details here.[32] There were many reasons why Townley should have decided to visit Paestum. As noted above, Paestum had become an *exemplum* of the Greek style in the Graeco-Roman polemic. A precedent for such a visit had been established by the French architect Jacques-Germain Soufflot, who had visited the temples in 1750 accompanied by Claude-Nicolas Cochin and the Marquis de Marigny, and whose drawings were

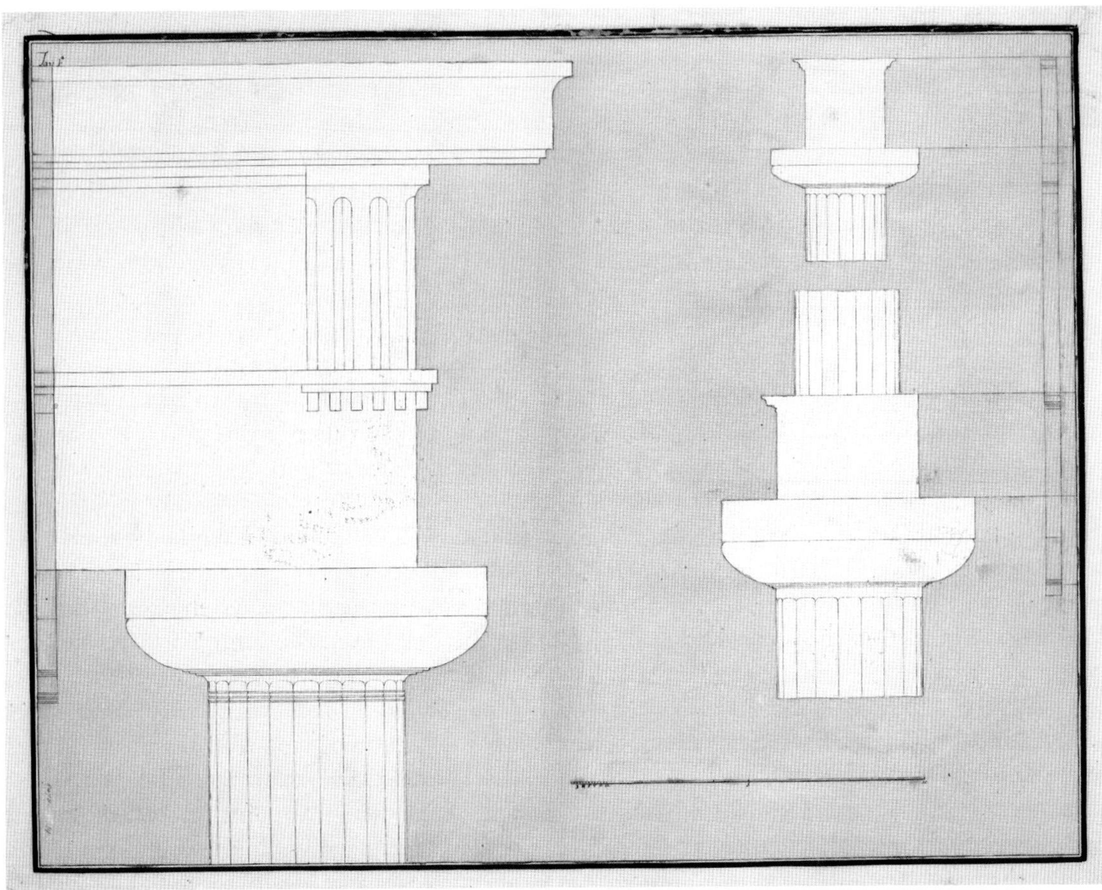

FIG. 18.4. Vincenzo Brenna (1741–), *Details of the Temple of Poseidon and Temple of Hera at Paestum*, 1768. Pen and watercolour. London, Victoria and Albert Museum. *(Photo: © V&A Images/Victoria and Albert Museum, London.)*

published by Gabriel-Pierre-Martin Dumont in 1764 and again in 1769. Furthermore, Thomas Major's *The Ruins of Paestum* (1768) (probably conceived by Robert Wood), illustrated with engravings after drawings now in Sir John Soane's Museum in London, had just been published.[33] This had been preceded by a series of projects going back (as far as English-language publications are concerned) to the 1750s.[34] A comparison between the plates by Major and Soufflot establishes that the designs in the English publication were indirectly dependent on the drawings by the French architect. Major's plates were based partly on drawings by Gaetano Magri and Robert Mylne, who had combined elements of Soufflot's drawings procured through Stephen Riou with those by Magri supplied by 'Horne'. Major also used drawings he had made himself when he visited Paestum in 1756.[35]

In any case, there must have been another factor behind the journey beyond the desire to verify and learn from the archaeological evidence and the urgent need to participate in the Graeco-Roman polemic. The entire party, not just Townley himself, must have had a new awareness of the various parameters, approaches to measurement and investigative methods that could be applied to ancient ruins and archaeological finds. From the summary testimony of Townley's diary, we know much was achieved in a little less than two days spent on the site taking measurements directly from the temples.[36] This time spent on the site seems to have allowed Brenna to make a qualitative breakthrough, partly because he shared the experience with Townley. Townley clearly wanted to verify *in situ* what had been stated by Major, to whom Brenna seems to have been indebted in his own drawings, in accordance with the 'archaeological science' maturing in Britain at this time. Furthermore, it may not be fortuitous that Townley's purchases in Naples included several editions of Vitruvius, ranging from the old translation by Daniele Barbaro (1566 and 1567),[37] by way of *Les dix livres* translated by a 'modern', Claude Perrault (1673),[38] to *L'architettura di Marco Vitruvio Pollione* by Berardo

Galiani (1758),[39] a text intended to supersede Perrault's.[40]

'REGARDING THE MODELS'

In addition to the five sheets with Brenna's drawings of the temples at Paestum, we have his own words in the letter of November 1768 mentioned above. 'Regarding the models of Paestum', he wrote:

> I already have the first at home, a very fine one, as well as the second, of the Basilica. But a difficulty has arisen, namely that you said I should make the cork models of the same size as the drawings I made for you in Rome — and so the first one of which I made a large drawing, Temple A, has come out fine on that scale. But the other two, B and C, being half the size of A, came out very small, since their columns are the size of drawing D. The result is that instead of producing a good effect they look like cages.[41]

Evidently, therefore, the architect intended to recreate the temples to scale and accurate in detail; to create models capable of representing architecture rather than its caricature. 'Therefore', he continued, 'I have seen fit to have them all made as big as A'.[42] This is confirmed by another letter, written on 4 March 1769, in which he declared that the models comprised 'two made out of cork and one of pumice, combined with other materials, which makes a better imitation of nature'.[43]

A few months after their exploration of Paestum, Brenna wrote to Townley about the models, and specifically about a model of the Round Temple at Tivoli:

> I have made for my own pleasure the model of the Temple of Tivoli out of pumice and cork. Namely everything that is [*illegible*] in pumice, and all that is coarser in cork. The said model stands about three English feet high ... you may rest assured that it has come out very well, since I have made it with my own hands.[44]

The construction of the model began in June 1769 and ended on 20 October of the same year: it was sent to England in February 1770. It is original both in dimensions and technique (the use of both cork and pumice). It may be considered an immediate rival of the first documented cork model, which, according to Valentin Kockel, dates from 1767. This was the model made by Giovanni Altieri for Jenkins, who exhibited it in December 1767 at Carlton House in London, in the chambers of the Society of Antiquaries.[45] This, too, was a scale model of the Round Temple at Tivoli.

The dimensions of Brenna's model can be established by reading his correspondence, in which he makes repeated reference to the question of measurements. The first letter gives a height of about 3 English feet, then 3½, and finally 3¾ feet, while the width is stated to be 4¼ feet.[46] Brenna emphasized that he made it with his own hands, paying close attention to the quality and successful use of the materials (pumice and cork). He then added that it was 'not in the least like others made of cork, since it has been studied in every part, and especially the ornaments, which have been modelled very exactly, and not like those made of cork and worked with a knife'. Relief was not something secondary, which suggests how important Brenna believed mouldings and decorations to be, not complementary to the architecture but integral and constitutive parts of it. Moreover, he used pumice: it is worth recalling that Agostino Rosa used terracotta elements during the 1770s, and that he and others used small decorative elements made of fine gesso casts that could be worked in an extremely detailed manner.[47] Evidently Brenna used pumice for a similar purpose.

THE PANTHEON, A GRAND ARCHITECTURAL AND ANTIQUARIAN BUILDING

The Pantheon, which Brenna tackled at the same time as the drawings and models of the temples at Paestum and Tivoli, offers further evidence (Figs 18.5 and 18.6; Plate 18.2). Not only was it a monument of ancient Rome that, despite many alterations and a problem concerning whether or not the existing building was the one described in the ancient sources,[48] had survived as a consequence of its consecration as a church; it was also notable for the technical expertise of its grand cupola, as well as for its proportions and spatial unity, which closely resembled the most audacious fantasies of the neoclassical period.

Palladio had already paid special attention to the building. During the seventeenth and eighteenth centuries measurements were taken *in situ* and there were numerous new studies, including those by Famiano Nardini (the first of the moderns, or post-Galileans) in 1666.[49] Antoine Desgodetz (1682),[50] Rodolfo Venuti (1767)[51] and Francesco Piranesi (1790)[52] made their own interesting contributions. They also tackled the

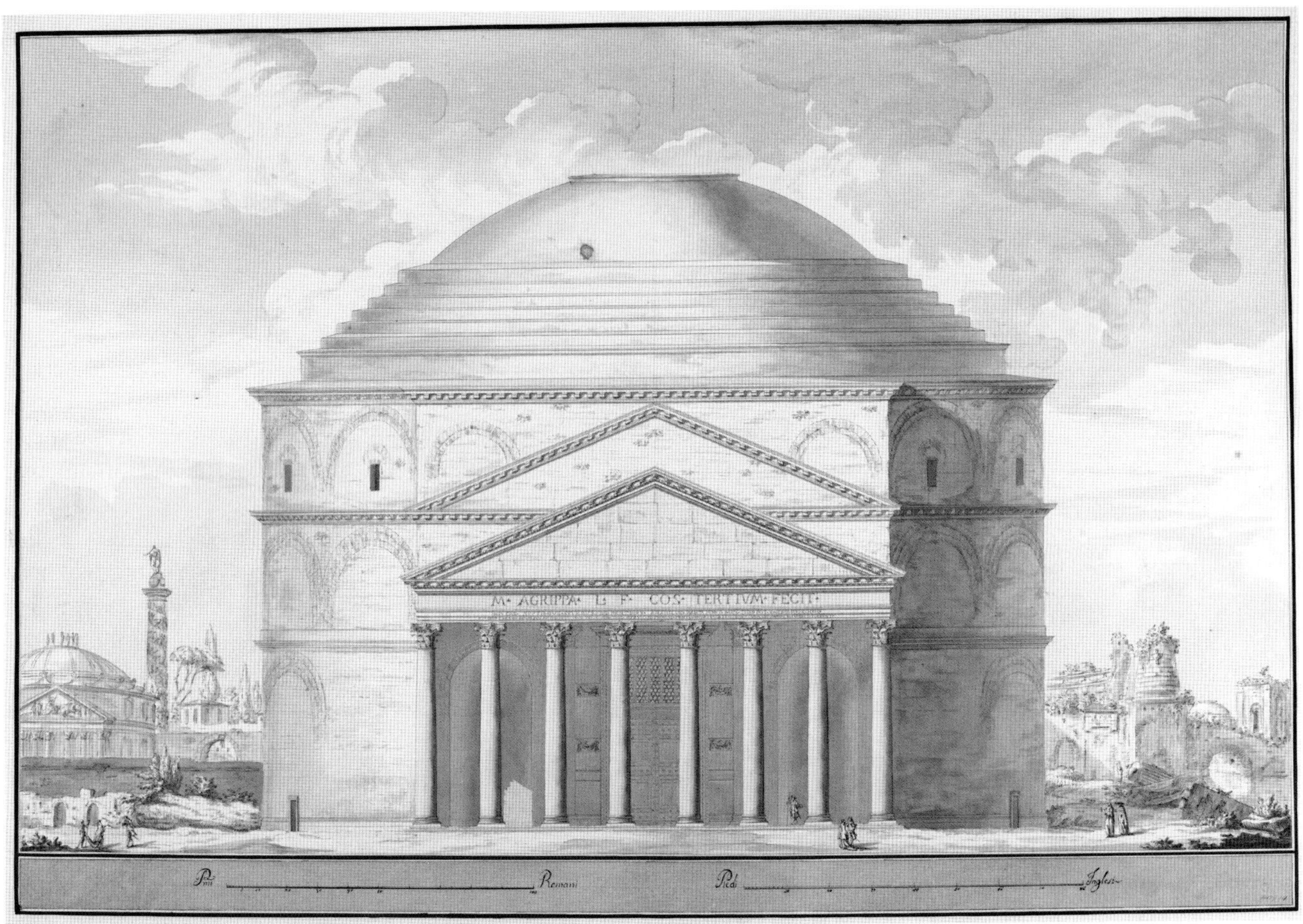

FIG. 18.5. Vincenzo Brenna (1741–), *Exterior Elevation of the Pantheon*, 1769. Indian ink, watercolour and tempera. London, Victoria and Albert Museum. *(Photo: © V&A Images/Victoria and Albert Museum, London.)*

interpretative problem of its ideal reconstruction, which had for some time evolved in different directions, and on which Brenna was to leave his mark.

In 1996 Susanna Pasquali carefully reconstructed the polemic about the complex question of 'architecture and antiquarianism' that centred on the Pantheon during the eighteenth century, as the subtitle of her book indicates.[53] She discussed the role of the architect who was responsible for the 'restoration', Alessandro Specchi, who in 1711 worked on the chapels, exedrae, aediculae and the reconstruction of the main altar. She also dealt with the polemic regarding the rearrangement of the attic storey by Posi, who aimed to unify and enhance the building's internal space.

We could also make a lengthy and careful examination of the whole subject, guided by the studies undertaken hitherto. We might, for instance, consider Fontana versus Desgodetz (and Palladio), and Specchi versus Posi, but we also might involve the painters as well, beginning with Giovanni Paolo Panini in his paintings of the Pantheon dating from about 1734, in order to demonstrate how and to what extent his canvases failed to match reality (they are to some extent ideal and imaginative interpretations) (**Fig. 9.2**). This would all fit into a series of interpretations, differing in their outcome, as proposed by one or other of the architects and artists involved; even Piranesi's contribution gives rise to a whole range of interpretative problems. All but a few authors muddle their sources and thus lose all sense of chronology, in homage to the lively debate over the recovery of the antique that, in the absence of documentary descriptions, had to be extracted from the very fabric of the building.

What remains is the fact that the Pantheon is a special monument, in which the remote past encounters and is related to the present without any break or disruption, through the combined effects of perfect volumes and spaces, uncommon constructional audacity, and elegance of form. All this reveals its complex

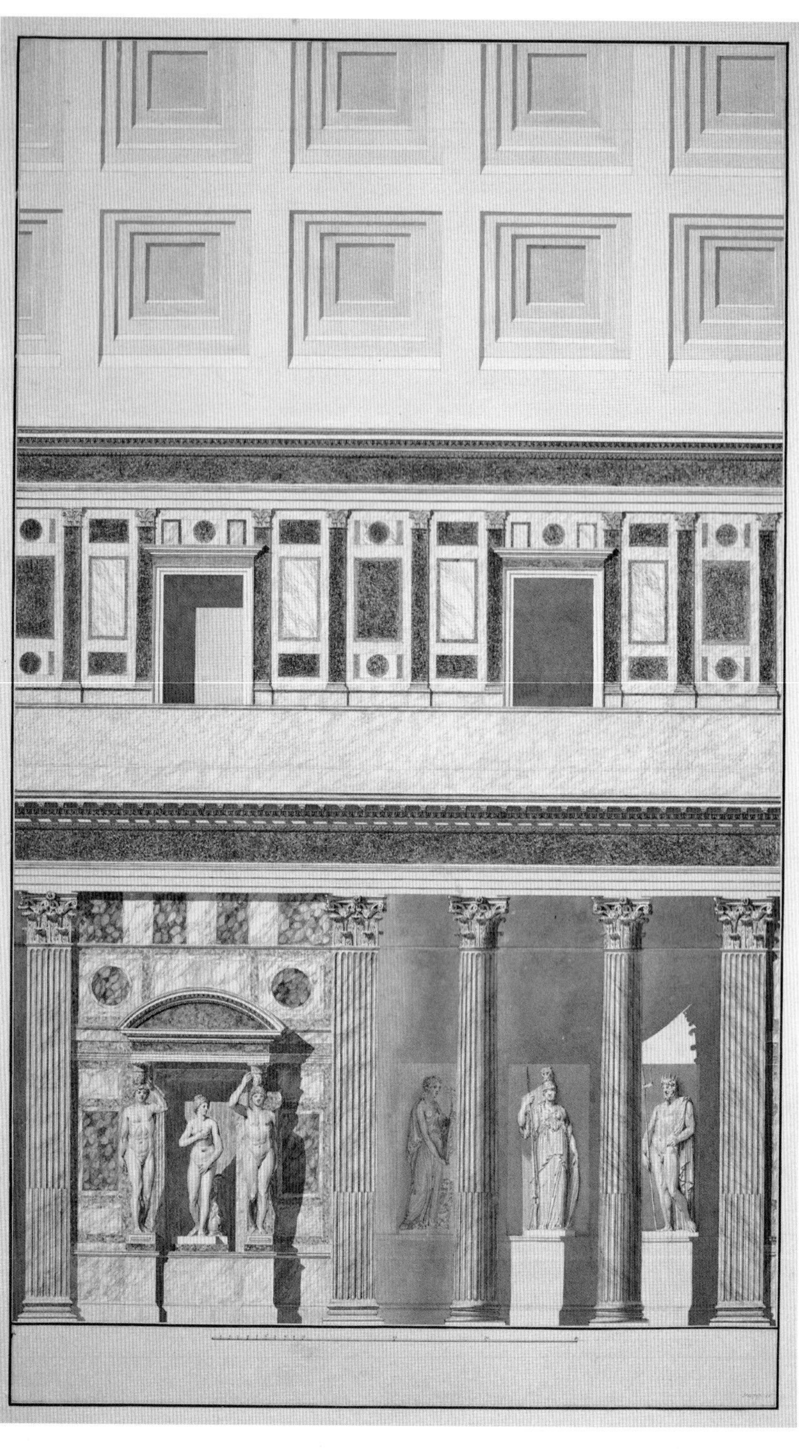

FIG. 18.6. Vincenzo Brenna (1741–), *Detail of the Interior of the Pantheon*, 1769. Indian ink, watercolour and tempera. London, Victoria and Albert Museum. *(Photo: © V&A Images/Victoria and Albert Museum, London.)*

Nietzschean timelessness, and Brenna's awareness of this enabled him, it seems, to relate himself closely to Desgodetz, drawing on his surveys, elevations and plans, yet without negating a personal interpretation of the grand structure itself. In his use and appropriation (paradoxically) of Pliny's reference to the caryatids within the building, he placed them in the aediculae ranged around the perimeter of the floor level (Fig. 18.6);[54] and he sets the statues of ancient deities between the columns, deducing their appearance from original antique models, namely the sculptures in the Capitoline Museum. Ideally, then, like Townley, Brenna once again kept pace with the vanished steps of the ancients.

Notes

1. In 1778 Brenna agreed to make an ideal reconstruction of the Villa Laurentina for Potocki, based on the text of Pliny the Younger's letter to Gallus (II.17). The count's manuscript, written in French, is now part of the Archiwum Główne Akt Dawnych, Warsaw [henceforth AGAD] under *Archiwum Główne Potockich*, MS no. 244, *Notes et idées sur la ville de Pline*. The sheets exist in two folders in the Warsaw National Library's Department of Iconographic Collections as 'La Ville de Pline ditte Laurentina restaurée par Cte Stanislas Potockij pendant son séjour à Rome en 1778' and 'Intérieurs de la Villa de Pline le jeune par Brenna', 1778, WAF 67 and 68 (I. Rys. 4999–5026 and 5027–5034). The sheets have been published in their entirety by K. Gutowska-Dudek, *Rysunki z Wilanowskiej Kolekcji Potockich w Zbiorach Biblioteki Narodowej* [*Drawings in the Potocki Collection of Wilanów in the Collections of the National Library*], 4 vols (Warsaw, 1997), I, nos. 210–43. They were studied for the first time by S. Lorentz, 'Domus Aurea Nerona i Villa Laurentina', *Meander* 1 (1946), 6, 314–24, and subsequently have been analysed by P. de la Ruffinière du Prey, *The Villas of Pliny from Antiquity to Posterity* (Chicago, 1994), in particular chapter IV, and by J. Miziolek, *Villa Laurentina. Arcydzielo-Eepoki Stanislawowskiej* (Warsaw, 2007). An extensive literature exists on Potocki's travels to Italy, the Polish élite's presence there, and the rediscovery of the antique in Poland; here reference will be made only to T. Mikocki, *A la recherche de l'art antique. Les voyageurs polonais en Italie dans les années 1750–1830* (Wroclaw/Warsaw/Kraków/Gdańsk/Łód, 1988), esp. pp. 70–4. See also *Grand Tour. The Birth of a Collection of Stanisław Kostka Potocki* (Warsaw, 2006).
2. For all further references, see L. Tedeschi, 'La cultura architettonica e il culto dell'antico nella Roma del Settecento. Vincenzo Brenna, i suoi anni romani: 1741–1781', in P. Angelini, N. Navone and L. Tedeschi (eds), *La cultura architettonica italiana in Russia da Caterina II a Alessandro I* (Mendrisio, 2008), 401–50, with full archival and bibliographical sources regarding Brenna; this establishes his first biography and early activity.
3. Brenna worked with Piranesi between 1768 and *c.* 1772. His first letter to Townley, datable to November 1768, makes clear reference to his familiarity with the *cavaliere*: 'Great quantities of things accumulate every day in Piranesi's house, generally Antiquities, but nothing special, just as nothing special is coming in to compare with what you acquired'. Brenna also worked on the volume *Vasi candelabri cippi sarcofagi tripodi lucerne ed ornamenti antichi disegni ed inc dal cav Gio Batta Piranesi pubblicati l'anno MDCCLXXIIX*, in which the plate entitled 'Tripode antico di Bronzo che si conserva a Portici nel Museo Reale di Sua Maestà Il Re delle due Sicilie' is signed 'Vincenzo Brenna disegnò'.
4. British Museum Archives, London [henceforth ABM], Townley Archive, *Lists of papers relating to purchases of antiquities. Book of lists of antiquities, drawings & books bought in Italy & expenses in transporting them to England 1768–73*, TY10/2, fol. 23, reprinted in *Catalogue of priced lists of articles bought in Italy 1767–8*, TY10/1, fol. 23v 'Due Copie del Tempio della Sibilla del Sig.r Vincenzo Brenna'.
5. Archivio del Vicariato di Roma [henceforth AVR], Santi XII Apostoli, Lib. bapt., 1733–51, vol. XIII, fol. 83. In the *Stati d'anime* the family of Francesco Brenna, 'Gentil.o del S.r Contest.e', the father of Vincenzo, is recorded as residing in the Palazzo Colonna in Piazza Santi Apostoli (AVR, Santi XII Apostoli, LSA (Libro degli Stati delle anime), 1740, fol. 4).
6. Active in the early decades of the century in the employ of Filippo and Fabrizio Colonna, Specchi designed the machinery and ephemeral structures for the festivals of the Chinea in Santi Apostoli. Francesco Antonio Brenna, the father of Vincenzo, and his uncle, the canon of San Celso, Filippo Brenna, were the executors of his will, which is published in B. Principato, 'Documenti inediti per la vita e l'opera di Alessandro Specchi', *Palladio* 2 (1990), 97–118, on pp. 117–18.
7. During this period in Rome there were significant numbers of French and English architects, foreign artists from every part of Europe, agents, mediators and Grand Tourists, as well as figures like Paolo Posi and Carlo Marchionni, not to mention Johann Joachim Winckelmann and Anton Raphael Mengs.
8. See V. Zanella (ed.), *Giacomo Quarenghi architetto a Pietroburgo. Lettere e altri scritti* (Venice, 1988), 83. Quarenghi appears to have been Pozzi's pupil from 1762 to 1764.
9. See A.M. Giorgetti Vichi, *Gli Arcadi dal 1690 al 1800* (Rome, 1977), 165.
10. Townley was preparing to make a fourth journey in 1779, but cancelled it when war broke out with France. He employed Brenna during his first and second stays in Rome. Travelling via France, he boarded ship at Toulon for Livorno, but because of a storm had to disembark at Lerici and reach Pisa by land. His stopping-points on this journey can be reconstructed through diaries, account books and letters from his personal archives, now in the British Museum. After a brief visit to Massa, he arrived in Lucca on 20 November 1767 and Pisa two days later, reaching Florence on 27 November. On 16 December he proceeded to Siena, where he remained for six days, then to Viterbo on 24 December. He finally reached Rome on Christmas Day and remained there until July 1768. His Roman sojourn was interrupted only once, by a six-week trip to Naples between late February and March.
11. Brenna's letters to Townley are in ABM, Townley Archive, *Incoming letters and correspondence, Brenna, Vincenzo*, March 1768–March 1803, 14 letters, TY7/1030–43; and in the Bodleian Library at Oxford University, MS Add. D. 70. See S.J. Hill, *Catalogue of the Townley Archive at The British Museum* (*Occasional Paper* 138) (London, 2002). Such letters allow us to date the drawings by Brenna commissioned and acquired by Townley during his Italian sojourns, now

housed in the Victoria & Albert Museum, London (Department of Prints, Drawings and Paintings, 8478.1–66 and 8479.1–32), consisting of 98 sheets, *c.* 1768–77. On Townley and Brenna, see G. Vaughan, *The Collecting of Classical Antiquities in England in the 18th Century. A Study of Charles Townley (1737–1805) and His Circle* (D.Phil. thesis, University of Oxford, 1988), esp. chapters I and II; G. Vaughan, "Vincenzo Brenna Romanus, architectus et pictor': drawings from the antique in late eighteenth-century Rome', *Apollo* 144 (October 1996), no. 416, 37–41; I. Jenkins, 'Drawings by Vincenzo Brenna', in A. Wilton and I. Bignamini (eds), *Grand Tour: the Lure of Italy in the Eighteenth Century* (London, 1996), 236–8, nos. 185–9; Tedeschi, 'La cultura architettonica' (above, n. 2).

12. See Vaughan, "Vincenzo Brenna Romanus, architectus et pictor" (above, n. 11).
13. 'si sono estratte sul luogo istesso con tutta la possibile fedeltà, e diligenza.' See *Del tempio tiburtino detto volgarmente della Sibilla. In Roma MDCCLXVII, per Michelangelo Barbiellini nel Palazzo Massimi, 1767*, with two folios of text and three of engraved plates. Brenna worked on the volume together with Francesco Ferrari, who was among the *Virtuosi del Pantheon* in 1781 and the architect for the *Tribunale delle Strade*.
14. See n. 4.
15. See n. 11.
16. See L. Tedeschi (ed.), "Il mio singolar piacere' in 18 missive di Vincenzo Brenna a Charles Townley e a Stanisław K. Potocki', in *La cultura architettonica italiana in Russia* (above, n. 2), 451–94.
17. See n. 4.
18. In 1776–7 Brenna made the following sheets for Townley relating to the 'Terme di Tito': detail of the vault of room no. 33 (Room of Bacchus) (8479.24); decoration of the 'Black Vault' (8479.22); wall of the room of the 'Black Vault' (8479.21); decoration of the wall and vault 'of the Eagles' (corridor no. 50), signed at lower left, 'Vincenzo Brenna Arch.o disegnò' (8479.20); detail of the 'Gilded Vault', signed at lower right, 'Vincenzo Brenna Architetto disegnò 1777' (8479.25); decoration of a Room (8479.23). Earlier, in 1768, he had drawn the plan of the Baths of Titus, a sheet signed at lower right 'Vincenzo Brenna Arch. Disegnò', and inscribed at lower centre, 'Terme di Tito in Roma', in 'Piedi romani' and 'Piedi inglesi' (8478.4). Regarding the publication of *Le vestigia delle Terme di Tito e loro interne pitture*, published by Mirri in 1776, and on Brenna's participation in the project, see: Tedeschi, 'La cultura architettonica' (above, n. 2); L. Tedeschi, 'Incontri romani di Vincenzo Brenna. Un contributo alla storia della pubblicazione delle *Vestigia delle Terme di Tito e loro interne pitture* del Mirri', in C. Frank (ed.), *Rome and the Constitution of a European Cultural Heritage in the Early Modern Period: the Impact of Agents and Correspondents on Art and Architecture* (Rome, forthcoming); and L. Tedeschi, 'Vincenzo Brenna i ruiny Term Tytusa. Próba rekonstrukcji rzymskiego okresu działalności artysty [Vincenzo Brenna and the remains of the Baths of Titus]', in J. Guze (ed.), *Złoty Dom Nerona. Wystawa w 200.lecie mierci Franciszka Smuglewicza (1745–1807)* [*The Domus Aurea of Nero. Exhibition Held for the Bicentenary of the Death of Franciszek Smuglewicz (1745–1807)*] (Warsaw, 2008).
19. 'Qui non si fa altro, che rammentar la sua Persona domandandomene tutti le nuove con rammemorare le sue Ottime qualità, il suo bel'genio e buon gusto, ed affabilissima maniera, con cui qui in Roma nella sua permanenza, hà dimostrato, con tutti quelli che anno avuto la sorte di trattarlo e conoscerlo'. ABM, Townley Archive, *Incoming letters and correspondence, Brenna, Vincenzo*, TY7/1031. See Tedeschi, "Il mio singolar piacere" (above, n. 16), doc. 1.
20. 'hò consegnato al Signor Ginchÿs li Disegni delle parti in grande del' Tempio di Tivoli, cioè il Capitello cornice e Base, e la pianta dell'Pantheon'. ABM, Townley Archive, *Incoming letters and correspondence, Brenna, Vincenzo*, TY7/1031. The letter is not dated but must be from early November 1768 as it refers to a letter from Jenkins to Townley, sent on 9 November 1768 (ABM, Townley Archive, *Incoming letters and correspondence, Jenkins, Thomas*, September 1768–April 1798, TY7/295–550). Passages regarding the Round Temple at Tivoli also occur in letters of 24 June 1769, 26 August 1769, 20 October 1769, 8 September 1769, 11 September 1769 and 20 February 1770. See Tedeschi, "Il mio singolar piacere" (above, n. 16), docs 1, 5–9.
21. The four drawings are entitled: *Base of column. Detail*, with an autograph note on the verso at upper right, 'Base de Tempio di Tivoli nella proporzione / che ivi si ritrova / Lad [*sic*] è la metà' (8478.21); *Cornice. Detail*, inscribed 'Fregio' at lower left, with an autograph note on the verso, 'Cornice dell'Ordine del Tempio di Tivoli nella / proporzione come ivi si ritrova / La quale nell contrassegno * unisce con il Fregio' (8478.18); *Cornice. Particolare*, inscribed 'Fregio' at upper left, and 'Architrave' at lower centre, with an autograph note on the verso at upper right, 'Architrave del Tempio di Tivoli nella sua proporzione / come ivi si ritrova' (8478.19); and *Decoration of the frieze. Detail*, with an autograph note on the verso, 'Fregio del Tempio di Tivoli nella sua proporzione come si ritrova. Il / medesimo hà il festone da una Testa di Bove all'altro alternativamente' (8478.20). See also ABM, Townley Archive, *List of papers relating to purchase of antiquities* (above, n. 4), TY10/2, fol. 32v, which also includes a drawing of the Temple at Tivoli.
22. 'ci basterà di descrivere le proporzioni, che si veggono attualmente nei residui del Tempio . . . le quali si sono estratte sul luogo istesso.' See *Del tempio tiburtino* (above, n. 13).
23. See M. Bevilacqua, *Roma nel secolo dei lumi. Architettura erudizione scienza nella pianta di G.B. Nolli 'celebre geometra'* (Naples, 1998).
24. Beyond the conventional Vitruvian approach, Brenna appeals to empirical evidence, taking it for granted that what is verified analytically on site, with recourse to modules (a correlation of proportional relationships), should satisfy criteria and

methodologies quite different from the recent — and not just ancient — past. Indeed, this is borne out by a reading of *Del tempio tiburtino*, where the first plate with the plan of the temple is discussed: 'The module of the said [plan] is divided into 18 parts. The width of the column is the same as that of the wall of the cella. The internal width is equal to the height of the column including the base and capital, as Vitruvius (book IV, chapter 7) says should be the case in such temples. The inter-columniation is of four modules. The ambulatory is four modules, and seven parts. All other measurements are described on the third plate, in the respective large-scale images' (Il modulo di detta, è diviso in parti 18. La grossezza della Colonna è uguale alla grossezza del muro della Cella. La larghezza interiore della Cella è eguale all'altezza della Colonna con base, e Capitello, come dice Vitruvio dover essere in questa specie di Tempj al lib. IV Cap. 7. L'inter-colonio è di quattro moduli. L'ambulatorio d'intorno è di moduli quattro, e parti sette. Tutte le altre misure poi sono descritte nella Tavola terza nei loro rispettivi pezzi in grande). This is even explained in detail on the second plate, where we read that 'the module is divided into 36 parts. The height of the pedestal including the base and top is six modules and four parts. The height of the column including the base and capital is nineteen modules and eight parts. The architrave, frieze and cornice, three modules and eight parts, which constitutes the fifth part of the column including the base and capital, so that all together from the ground level to the top of the cornice this makes 28 modules and 21 parts' (Il modulo è diviso in parti trentasei. L'altezza del zoccolo con base, e cimasa, è alto moduli sei e parti quattro. L'altezza della Colonna con base, e capitello moduli diecinnove e parti otto. L'architrave, fregio, e cornice moduli tre e parti nove, che viene ad essere la quinta parte e fa circa dell'altezza della Colonna con base, e capitello, sicché tutto assieme dal piano del basamento a tutta l'altezza della cornice, e moduli vent'otto e parti ventuno).

25. A.B. Desgodetz, *Les édifices antiques de Rome dessinés et mesurés tres exactement*, first published in Paris in 1682, which reproduces nearly all such monuments known at the time, in both plan and elevation. In *Del tempio tiburtino* it is stated that 'Both Serlio and Palladio represent the said Temple', but — it is emphasized — 'there is little or nothing that conforms between one and the other, and this applies not only to how each relates to the other, but in how far they stray from the measurements of the Temple itself, resulting in something alien from its principal character' (Tutti e due poco o nulla si conformano, non solamente tra loro, ma anche si allontanano affatto dalle misure del suddetto ed in tutto aliene dal suo carattere principale). We read subsequently that 'in his work, the celebrated Desgodetz shows the variations these authors made, but he too varies the dimensions, forms and ornaments — particularly in the frieze and the capital, to which he assigns neither the beauty nor grandeur found in the original; and he has made the stalks below the flower smaller than the usual style of the Corinthian order, even though they have an entirely novel appearance in the antique, one not so common in other capitals. He places the architrave directly above the abacus of the capital ... so creating darkness above it. He errs in the form of the column base, where the flutes end, by graduating them above the bottom of the shaft, and cuts them off like those straight above, because at the meeting point they project above the said column base and form a slanting plane; and then these flutes are twenty in number, not twenty-four, as he affirms' (Il celebre Degodetz mostra nella sua opera le variazioni che i medemi anno fatto, ma contuttociò esso ancora ha variato nelle misure nelle forme, ed ornati; particolarmente nel fregio, e Capitello, al quale non assegna quel bel carattere grandioso, che in opera si ritrova ed ha fatto sotto il fiore i caulicoli minori del consueto stile dell'ordine Corintio, quantunque nell'Antico siano di una maniera del tutto nuova, non troppo comune in altri capitelli. Fà egli posare l'architrave immediatamente sopra la tavola del Capitello ... che forma dello scuro sopra a detto. Sbaglia nella base della Colonna in quanto alla forma, nella quale finiscono le scannel-lature, facendole terminare sfumando sopra l'imo scapo, e le fa tagliare come le superiori dritte, che all'incontro queste vengono risaltate sopra detto imo scapo, che gli forma piano in pendenza, e dette scannellature sono venti di numero, e non ventiquattro, come egli asserisce).

26. Volaire worked in France with Vernet until 1763, when he moved to Italy. He became a member of the Accademia di San Luca in 1764. He settled in Naples some time after 1769. He specialized in nocturnal views of Vesuvius in eruption.

27. A brief diary contains an account of the visit (ABM, Townley Archive, *Diaries and memoranda books, travel diaries, Naples to Paestum & back with Monsieur Volaire*, 23–27 March [1768], TY1/3, fols 1–12), now transcribed and published in E. Beck-Saiello, *Le chevalier Volaire. Un peintre français à Naples au XVIIIe siècle* (Naples, 2004), 194–7. On this occasion Townley made numerous purchases, as shown by the record of payments (ABM, Townley Archive, *Lists of papers relating to purchases of antiquities. Catalogue of priced lists* (above, n. 4), TY10/1, fols 1–10v), containing lists of 'Robbe prese à Napoli in Marzo 1768. Nota di diverse Specie della Collezzione del Vesuvio fatto da Tommaso Valen-ziani Custode delle Pitture in Portici', fol. 1; 'Nota di Marmi comprate nel Regno di Napoli nel Mese di Marzo 1768', fol. 4; 'Libri e Stampe Comprate in Napoli nel Mese di Marzo 1768', fol. 7. On Townley's journey to Naples and Paestum, see also Volaire's letters to him of 17 April 1768, 3 May 1768, 19 May 1769 and a fourth undated letter (ABM, Townley Archive, *Incoming letters and correspondence, Volaire, Le Chevalier*, April–May 1768, TY7/1572–1576), and in particular the letter from Volaire to Brenna, dated from Naples on 17 May 1768 (TY7/1576), which refers to the drawings of the temples of Paestum and the aqueduct of Vietri, which Townley commis-sioned from the painter together with two paintings on canvas representing, respectively, a fire and a waterfall.

28. The following pen and wash drawings can be identified: *Elevation and Section of the Temple of Poseidon and Side Elevation of the First Temple of Hera (Basilica)* (8478.12), published by Jenkins in 'Drawings by Vincenzo Brenna' (above, n. 11), 236, no. 185; *First Temple of Hera (Basilica) and Temple of Athena*, (8478.15: the upper part of the sheet shows the side elevation of the first Temple of Hera, and the lower part shows the façade of the Temple of Athena, with details of capitals and entablature); *Corner of the Entablature of the Temple of Poseidon and of the First Temple of Hera (Basilica)* (8478.14); *Plan of the Temple of Athena* (8478.17); *Plan of the Temple of Poseidon* (8478.13); *Plan of the Temple of Hera, Formerly Described as a Basilica* (8478.16). One may suppose that it was during this journey that Brenna also executed the plans of the Temple of Isis in Pompeii (8478.38, 8478.40); the drawing of a floor preserved in the second room of the Museum in Portici, from Herculaneum (8478.51); the plan of an ancient house (8478.41); the plan and section of a public bath-latrine (8478.35); and the capital of the 'Tempio di Anxur' at Terracina (8478.45). He also made a drawing of the mausoleum near San Vito at Pozzuoli (8478.43, 8478.44), and there are two sheets of the Temple of Jupiter Serapis (8478.37, 8478.39). Some of these can be found in ABM, Townley Archive, *List of papers relating to purchases of antiquities* (above, n. 4), TY10/2: 'Un Antico Mosaico della Città di Ercolano che serviva di Pavimento', fol. 31v; 'Due Disegni di un antico Scaldarone di Acqua ritrovato à Pompeja', fol. 32; 'Pianta del Tempio di Giove Serapide in Pozzuoli', fol. 32v; 'Veduta del Tempio di Giove Serapide a Pozzuoli, e suoi Studj', fol. 33.
29. Anon. [A. Ramsay], 'A dialogue on taste', *The Investigator* 332 (*c.* 1755, reissued 1762).
30. P.-J. Mariettte, 'Lettre de M. Mariette aux auteurs de la Gazette littéraire de l'Europe', *Gazette Littéraire de l'Europe*, Supplément (4 November 1764), 232–47.
31. Vaughan, "Vincenzo Brenna Romanus" (above, n. 11).
32. Having reached Salerno, where they visited the Cathedral and its ancient Roman columns, they went to Paestum on 24 March, arriving at two o'clock in the afternoon. They immediately headed for the ruins, but were discouraged by strong winds and returned to their lodgings as guests of a canon of the cathedral. The following day saw them rise at six and return to the temples. Volaire made a perspective drawing of all three temples in a general view, while Townley and Brenna applied themselves to measuring the largest one. The group returned to Salerno on 26 March and reached Naples the next day.
33. See M. McCarthy, 'Una nuova interpretazione del 'Paestum' di Thomas Major e di altri disegni inglesi di epoca successive', in J. Raspi Serra and G. Simoncini (eds), *La fortuna di Paestum e la memoria moderna del dorico 1750–1830* (Florence, 1986), I, 41–56.
34. The first detailed account of the temples at Paestum in England was written by Lord North in 1753, and was thus almost contemporaneous with that of Soufflot.
35. McCarthy, 'Una nuova interpretazione del 'Paestum' di Thomas Major' (above, n. 33).
36. McCarthy, 'Una nuova interpretazione del 'Paestum' di Thomas Major' (above, n. 33).
37. D. Barbaro, *Dieci libri dell'architettura di M. Vitruvio tradutti et commentati da Monsignor Barbaro* (Venice, 1556); D. Barbaro, *M. Vitruvii Pollionis de architectura libri decem* (Venice, 1567).
38. C. Perrault, *Les dix livres d'architecture: corrigez et traduits nouvellement en françois, avec des notes & des figures de Vitruve* (Paris, 1673).
39. *L'architettura di M. Vitruvio Pollione. Colla trauzione. italiana e comento del Marchese Berardo Galiani* (Naples, 1758).
40. Townley also acquired an edition of Serlio; the first five volumes of *Le antichità di Ercolano esposte*; A.C. Pigonati, *Stato presente degli antichi monumenti siciliani* (Naples, 1767), a modest work by a military engineer; *La Reggia di Caserta: dichiarazione dei disegni del Real Palazzo di Caserta* (1756); and *Le antichità etrusche greche e romane 1766–1776* by Pierre Hugues d'Hancarville. See ABM, Townley Archive, *List of papers relating to purchases of antiquities* (above, n. 4), TY10/2, fol. 7.
41. 'Circa alli Modelli di Pesto hò già in Casa il primo molto bello ed il secondo che è la Basilica, ma vi è nata una difficoltà, cioè che lei mi disse, che li facessi fare in Sugero della grandezza delli disegni che a lei io in Roma avevo fatti, il primo che ho disegnato grande che era il Tempio più grande A è venuto bene di tal grandezza ma li altri Due B C che erano la metà di A venivano molto piccoli, essendo le Colonne della loro grandezza, tali eguali al'disegno D si ché in cambio di far bene parevano due Gabbie.' See Tedeschi (ed.), "Il mio singolar piacere" (above, n. 16), doc. 1.
42. 'Dunque hò stimato bene di far farli fare tutti della grandezza di A'; ABM, Townley Archive, *Incoming letters and correspondence, Brenna, Vincenzo*, TY 7/1031, undated letter, but written in November 1768. This contains a sketch of the temple plans, marked A (Temple of Poseidon), B (Temple of Hera, formerly called the Basilica), C (Temple of Athena), and of a Doric column, indicated with the letter D. See Tedeschi (ed.), "Il mio singolar piacere" (above, n. 16), doc. 1.
43. 'fatti due in Sugaro, ed uno in Pomice misturata con altre materie, che molto meglio inmitano il naturale'; ABM, Townley Archive, *Incoming letters and correspondence, Brenna, Vincenzo*, TY7/1030, letter of 4 March 1768 [1769]. See Tedeschi (ed.), "Il mio singolar piacere" (above, n. 16), doc. 2.
44. 'Hò fatto per mio piacere il Modello del Tempio di Tivoli, in Pomice e Buchon, cioè tutto ciò che è p ... in Pomici e ciò che è materiale in Buchon; il dett[o] Modello, è dell'altezza di tre piedi in circa inglesi ... si assicuri che è venuto molto bene, avendo fatto tutto con le mie proprie mani'; ABM, Townley Archive, *Incoming letters and correspondence, Brenna, Vincenzo*, TY7/1034, letter of 24 June 1769. See Tedeschi (ed.), "Il mio singolar piacere" (above, n. 16), doc. 5.

45. The model made in 1767 — the oldest one of which we have any mention — is now lost, and we know nothing of its appearance or dimensions; it must have been the prototype for many other models. See V. Kockel, *Phelloplastica. Modelli in sughero dell'architettura antica nel XVIII secolo nella collezione di Gustavo III di Svezia* (Stockholm, 1998).
46. Thus *c.* 127.5 cm wide and 105 cm high. Compared to Brenna's, the model by Altieri now in Sir John Soane's Museum, for example, measures 39.5 × 52.3 × 51.5 cm. The passages regarding the Temple at Tivoli are as follows, each as described in Brenna's letters. 26 August 1769: 'The model of the Temple of Tivoli is 4¼ English feet wide and 3½ feet high, so it may be understood that this is a model of great size ... and if it arrives intact you may see it with your own eyes, and by comparing it with the sheets you have by both Piranesi and myself you will be able to see the precision of the measurements, and the taste for fragments; and I have made it this size so that it may be intelligible, and of good form' (Il'Modello del'Tempio di Tivoli, è della larghezza di piedi 4 e un ¼ Inglesi e dell'altezza di piedi 3 e ½, siché puol capire, che è un Modello di una proporzione grande..., il lavoro, se gli arriverà felice, lo considererà sotto l'Ochio, è vedrà con il confronto delle Stampe, che hà si di Piranesi, come le mie l'esatezza delle misure, ed il gusto delli framenti, ed io l'hò fatto di detta grandezza, acciò sia intelligibile, e di buona forma); 20 October 1769: 'The model ... is completely finished, and has come out very well, and its height is about 3¾ feet; and you will thus be able to tell from its size that all its parts are of very intelligible proportions. This completely follows the original in Tivoli, with the same breaks and joints in the stone masonry, not only in its ornaments; but in the joints and in every part it is carved as it is in Tivoli; so that seeing the model is like seeing the original, and everyone who has seen it so far has been very happy with it. It not in the least like others made of cork, since it has been studied in every part, and especially the ornaments, which are modelled very exactly, and not like those made of cork and worked with a knife' (Il'Modello ... è tutto terminato, ed è riuscito molto bene, e l'altezza del detto è di piedi 3 e ¾ in circa; siché potrà conoscere dalla detta misura che tutte le sue parti sono di una proporzione molto intelligibile; Il medemo è in tutto e per tutto secondo l'Originale in Tivoli con le medeme rotture, e comissure di pietre non solamente nell'Ornato, come nelle commisure, ed ogni suo pezzo è tagliato secondo è quello in Tivoli; siché vedendo questo è come vedesse l'Originale, ogniuno che fin ad ora l'hà veduto ne è rimasto molto contento; non avendo che fare niente con quelli altri fatti in Buchon essendo questo studiato in ogni sua parte e particolarmente li Ornati che sono modellati con l'istesso Carattere non come quelli di Buchon lavorati con il Cortello); 11 September [but November] 1769: 'I have completely finished the Temple of Tivoli, which has turned out exactly as it should in all its parts ...; all those who see it say nothing truer to the original is possible, since it is not only similar in the joints and the workmanship, but precise in its measurements and ornaments. But it is not right for me to praise it. I hope you will see it with your own eyes' (Hò terminato affatto il Tempio di Tivoli, il quale è riuscito esattamente bene in tutte le sue parti ...; tutti quelli che lo vedono, dicono che più verisimile al'Originale di questo non si puol'dare, essendo non solamente consimile alle piene commisure e lavori, ma esattissimo nelle sue misure ed Ornati; e poi che io lo esalti non và bene spero che con li suoi Ochi lo vedrà). See Tedeschi (ed.), "Il mio singolar piacere" (above, n. 16), docs 6–8.
47. Rosa preferred this technique, which was not used by Altieri. Rosa was in touch with Piranesi, whom he accompanied to Paestum in 1777. There he executed a prototype for a cork model of the celebrated temple, and subsequently made several copies of it.
48. The fact that Latin sources (Vitruvius and Pliny) spoke of an earlier structure and only the *Historia Augusta* cited the Pantheon among the projects of the Emperor Hadrian meant that from the fifteenth century onwards the sources spoke of an older Pantheon, while none mentioned the existing structure.
49. *Roma antica di Famiano Nardini* (Rome, 1666).
50. *Les edifices antiques de Rome dessinés et mesurés tres exactement par Antoine Desgodetz* (Paris, 1682).
51. *Accurata, e succinta descrizione topografica, e istorica di Roma moderna opera postuma [di] Ridolfino Venuti. Ridotta in miglior forma, accresciuta e ornata di molte figure in rame* (Rome, 1767).
52. F. Piranesi, *Tempi antichi* II (Rome, 1790).
53. S. Pasquali, *Il Pantheon. Architettura e antiquaria nel Settecento a Roma* (Modena, 1996).
54. There are five drawings of the Pantheon, all dimensioned in 'Palmi Romani' and 'Piedi inglesi': *Plan* (8479.16); *Plan* (8479.17); *Elevation* (8479.14); *Section* (8479.15); *Detail of the Interior with an Aedicule and Chapel* (8479.18). Also listed in ABM, Townley Archive, *List of papers relating to purcahses of antiquities* (above, n. 4), TY10/2, fol. 32v, 'Disegno del Panteon'.

UNIVERSAL NEOCLASSICISM:
OLD ROME AND NEW BRITAIN

Commemoration 'in a more durable and grave manner': portrait busts for the British in early eighteenth-century Rome

Malcolm Baker

As a glance at a Pompeo Batoni portrait of a nobleman on the Grand Tour makes clear, sculpture figured prominently in the cultural experience of many British visitors to Rome during the eighteenth century. It is hardly an exaggeration to say that Rome meant sculpture. It is not surprising, then, that discussions of the Grand Tour have made constant reference to those works of antique sculpture that made such an impression on such visitors, or that the perceptions of eighteenth-century visitors to Rome constitute much of the evidence assembled by Francis Haskell and Nicholas Penny in their remarkable study of the reception of antique sculpture.[1] The importance of the sculptural was already evident of course in the accounts of Roman collections, such as those to be seen in the Palazzo Farnese or the Villa Mattei, in *Account of Some of the Statues ... in Italy*, by Jonathan Richardson Senior and Jonathan Richardson Junior.[2] As if in response to such texts, and the advice of their *ciceroni*, wealthier British visitors purchased copies and casts of the more celebrated works, and — whenever possible — acquired original examples of antique statuary that were to form an integral and prominent part of the interiors of their London palaces and country houses. But along with examples of antique sculpture, a number of these visitors also showed an active interest in the work of contemporary sculptors, such as Camillo Rusconi, Pierre-Étienne Monnot and Pierre Legros the Younger, whose recent sculpture — the Apostles lining the nave of Saint John Lateran, for example — was to be seen in the palazzi and churches of contemporary Rome.[3] Works by these artists — sometimes models for works that remained in Rome, sometimes modestly-sized marbles — were brought back to form part of British collections.[4] Whether antique or modern, these imported pieces provided a context for the sculpture commissioned from sculptors in Britain. Increasingly, histories of sculpture in Britain have made much of the way in which the importation of both ancient and modern sculpture played a part in conditioning the expectations of British patrons and, indeed, in the new importance of sculpture for the British during the eighteenth century.

One framework for understanding the significance of Rome for the history of British sculpture has, of course, been the Grand Tour, the study of which has been advanced greatly by the work of the late Ilaria Bignamimi, the Tate's 1996 exhibition, and, perhaps most importantly, the publication by John Ingamells of *The Dictionary of British and Irish Travellers in Italy*, using Sir Brinsley Ford's archive.[5] Another, closely related, set of debates has been concerned with the collecting of antique sculpture. This field has been a very active one during the past few years, with the pioneering work of Haskell and Penny being developed through studies by Jonathan Scott, Ruth Guilding and Viccy Coltman.[6] But the emphasis of work in both of these areas has been largely on the implications for our understanding of eighteenth-century Britain and its art world. The operation of the art market in Italy, and in Rome in particular, has been seen principally as a condition of British patronage and collecting, rather than being examined as a multifaceted international phenomenon. Although close attention has been paid in these studies to the social networks and mechanisms operating in Italy that made possible these processes of collecting and commissioning, most accounts are conceived in terms of the outcome for the British.[7]

Another factor has skewed our view of the British and sculpture in Rome in the early decades of the eighteenth century. Although the role of collectors of sculpture has been accorded more attention recently, histories of sculpture have, for the most part, been structured around the lives of individual sculptors, still following a pattern seen in Horace Walpole's *Anecdotes of Painting* and continued in

Allan Cunningham's *Lives of the Most Eminent British Painters, Sculptors and Architects*.[8] This biographical emphasis has meant that discussions of the British and sculpture in Rome have tended to focus on the activity of those British sculptors who spent time in Rome. This, for the most part, has meant sculptors working during the second half of the eighteenth century. The extended stays in Italy of figures such as Joseph Wilton, Joseph Nollekens and Thomas Banks, all of whom produced significant works there, not to mention the permanent residency of Francis Harwood and Christopher Hewetson, mean that any reasonably full account of sculpture by British sculptors of this period must involve discussion of the works created in Rome. The same does not apply, however, to sculptors working earlier in the century. Michael Rysbrack never went to Rome and Louis-François Roubiliac only travelled to Italy late in his career. Because Rome does not figure prominently in their biographies, the importance of the city for sculpture in Britain (and British patrons of sculpture) has tended to be underplayed.

Of course, sculptors such as Rysbrack and Roubiliac were hardly unaware of contemporary and earlier sculpture in Rome. The figure of Minerva on Roubiliac's Argyll monument — one of the turning-points in the history of the monument in Britain — appropriates the pose of a figure on Rusconi's monument to Pope Gregory XIII Boncompagni, though the sculptor had yet to see Rusconi's work.[9] Similarly, the motif of an heraldic dragon emerging from beneath the scarcophagus of this same papal monument was picked up by Rysbrack in his monument to the Duke of Marlborough.[10] Quite apart from these individual borrowings, it is clear that a knowledge of the format and compositional details of papal monuments by Rusconi, Monnot and Legros played a part in the development of those large-scale and aesthetically ambitious funerary monuments that form a major achievement of British art in the early eighteenth century. In part, these Roman qualities may be attributed to the role played by architects such as James Gibbs and Wiliam Kent in the design of many monuments. For most of the sculptors themselves, this awareness of contemporary sculpture in Rome was mediated through the print. Of the major sculptors working in Britain during the first half of the eighteenth century, only Francis Bird and Peter Scheemakers had had the opportunity to visit and spend an extended period in Rome.

The relationship between Rome and sculptors in Britain is, then, largely an indirect one. But if we shift the focus from sculptors to patrons, the British no longer appear distant observers. Indeed, sculpture in Rome during the early eighteenth century involved the British more than has been recognized generally, especially if we see these patrons as participants in a wider international aristocratic culture. Nowhere is this seen more clearly than in the case of the portrait bust. Busts and monuments formed the two categories of sculpture required by the British.[11] Although a few monuments — Monnot's tomb for the Earl of Exeter is the most striking example — were ordered from sculptors working in Italy, the commissioning of such large-scale works was unusual. But the commissioning of portrait busts was another matter. In this paper I shall argue that the sculptural portraits produced in Rome for British patrons by non-British sculptors do not form simply part of the history of sculpture in Britain, but belong to a more complex and broader history of the portrait bust in the eighteenth century. Although all the examples were sent to Britain and so have a role in that history, they also have distinctive features that set them apart from sculptural portraits produced in Britain. Conversely, while these images were produced within a Roman context and so share many characteristics within contemporary — or at least, slightly earlier — Roman sculptural portraits, they also have qualities that make them different from the busts commissioned by Italian or French patrons.

How, then, was the portrait bust perceived by these British visitors and patrons, and what expectations did they have? For one patron, at least, the portrait bust was seen as an Italian genre. In 1729 Sir Thomas Robinson wrote to the Earl of Carlisle at Castle Howard, suggesting that he should 'destroy the side board for plate (too mean an object for so noble a room) and in its place . . . have your Lordship's own statue'.[12] This statement in itself signals a shift towards the sculptural as far as the furnishing of interiors was concerned. But Robinson went further. He continued by saying that this would follow the practice of Italian noblemen of 'leaving themselves to posterity in a more durable and grave manner than by our method by pictures, that is by sculptures in either statues or busts'. By writing in this way, Robinson was thus explicitly connecting a move to the greater prominence of the sculpted portrait with the use of statues and portrait busts in Italy.

As far as we can tell from the surviving examples, portrait busts seem to be commissioned less frequently by Roman patrons in the eighteenth century than in the seventeenth, although the genre was alive and well in

Florence.[13] Robinson's view is more of a retrospective view — or a more broadly based account — than an observation of specific Roman practice at this date. None the less, his perception of the bust as a mode of representation favoured especially by the Italians presumably was based on his familiarity with the portrait busts to be seen in the Roman palazzi. Along with the antique portrait busts, these are described in the accounts of Rome written by Richard Lassels, John Breval, Edward Wright and, above all, the Richardsons.[14] It was these well-known publications that informed the viewing and commissioning practices of British visitors to Rome. Most of the references are brief and even cursory — something that might be said of most references to sculpture, other than celebrated antique figures —, but some comments are more expansive. Wright's account of the Palazzo Barberini, for instance, mentions 'a fine Chamber of Busts: *Julius Caesar*, *Scipio Africanus Marcus Aurelius*, *Lucius Verus*, and many others', and goes on to mention in 'another Chamber, a fine Bust, said to be of *Alexander*, with a Helmet: And, another of Pallas'. He then showed still greater enthusiasm for a bust by Gianlorenzo Bernini:

> In another Room is a most curious Portrait-Bust, carved by *Bernini*, a lady of the Family *Galeoti*, Wife to one of the *Barberini*. I have seen other Faces of his, full as well done as this: but there is somewhat in the Drapery almost surpassing Imagination. The Delicacy of the Lace about her Neck and Bosom, so wrought in Marble!—it is not to be express'd.[15]

Another Bernini is singled out for praise in the description of the Villa Borghese: 'A Ritratto Bust by *Bernini*: It is one of the Family, I think of Cardinal Scipio Borghese: It is most admirably perform'd. — This is the same in Sculpture, as the very best *Vandykes* are in Painting'.[16] Presumably it is works such as these, as well as at least a few more recent busts by contemporary sculptors, that Robinson had in mind.

However, when we turn to the portrait busts to be seen in Britain in the first half of the eighteenth century, Robinson's perception of the bust as an Italian genre seems to strike an odd note. Certainly, a few examples might seem to refer directly to Italian models. For instance, the monument to Sir Orlando Gee by Bird — one of the few British sculptors who had spent time in Rome — employs a compositional type, cut off at the waist and with gesturing arms, that is derived ultimately from the dramatic portraits by Alessandro Algardi and Bernini.[17] But, for the most part, the many portrait busts produced for British patrons during this period make use of formats and conventions associated more readily with French or Flemish sculpture. These consisted primarily of either busts showing male sitters in soft caps and informally open shirts or images that represented them in full wigs, with often more elaborate drapery. But even in the latter case, the scale was modest and the dress never as elaborately rich and flamboyant as that seen on, for example, busts by Giovanni Battista Foggini of the Medici family around 1700. Ironic though it might seem, it would appear that it was easier to adapt a motif from a papal monument for a tomb in Westminster Abbey than to appropriate the format of an Italian portrait bust for the image of a British nobleman. It is almost as if the use of the grandiloquent sculptural rhetoric characteristic of many portrait busts of late baroque Rome or Florence would have linked a British sitter too closely with a manner of self-presentation associated with the Catholic, absolutist world of the late Medici or the Pretender's court. By contrast, many of the marble busts of Rysbrack and Roubiliac have authority and power, but, in the main, this is achieved through more overtly modest means, appropriate to a polite culture and the visual language of an emergent public sphere.

Nevertheless, there was one mode of sculptural portraiture employed for British sitters that did bear a more direct and obvious link with the portrait busts described by Wright and the Richardsons, as well as with sculptural production in early eighteenth-century Rome. This was the classicizing bust showing the sitter with short hair, wearing antique armour, loose classical drapery, or bare-chested. This mode of portrait gained currency through the work of Rysbrack and Scheemakers, early examples being the former's bust of Daniel Finch, 2nd Earl of Nottingham (1723), and the latter's images of Lord Cobham and his political associates grouped together in the Temple of Friendship at Stowe (Fig. 19.1).[18] Scheemakers had, of course, spent several years in Italy and, even though his sketchbook from this period records details of monuments rather than any busts, he obviously took an interest in antique portraits, versions of which were among the models seen by George Vertue in 1730.[19] No such direct experience of works in Roman collections was possible for Rysbrack and others. Unlike antique figures, however, portrait busts were among the antiquities that could be acquired relatively easily, and so from early in the eighteenth

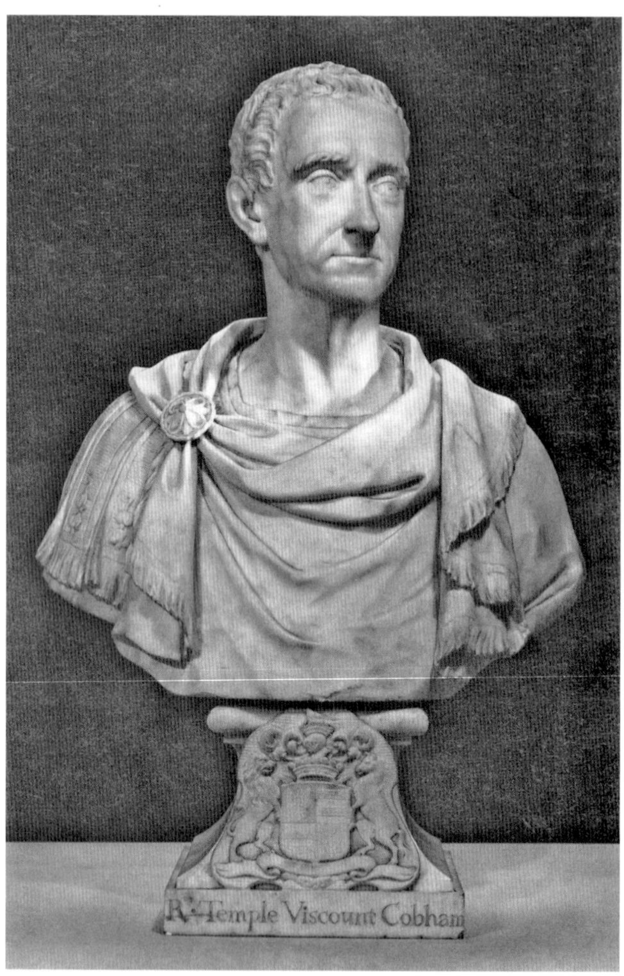

FIG. 19.1. Peter Scheemakers (1691–1781), *Richard Temple, Viscount Cobham*, c. 1740. Marble. Victoria and Albert Museum, London. *(Photo: © V&A Images/Victoria and Albert Museum, London.)*

century were to be seen in British collections. They figured prominently among the contents of the collection at Wilton House, assembled by Thomas, 8th Earl of Pembroke, and it was indeed said that 'Bustoes he was particularly fond of, as they expressed with more strength and exactness, the lineaments of the face'.[20] While a familiarity on the part of at least some sculptors and patrons with the antique busts in the Capitoline — from the 1730s displayed in large numbers in the Stanza dei Filosofi and the Stanza degli Imperatori — no doubt played a part in the formation of the classicizing bust as a distinctive and significant category of sculptural portraiture in eighteenth-century Britain, this development was not necessarily one that was linked directly with a knowledge of Roman collections.

There were, however, a number of other classicizing busts that are connected more directly with Rome and the experience of British patrons there. Commissioned not from British sculptors but from Italian and French sculptors active in Rome, these images should certainly form part of the history of the portrait bust in Britain, since they all found their way to Britain with their sitters or at least the patrons who paid for them. But, at the same time, they also constitute a distinctive aspect of sculptural portraiture in Rome during the first half of the eighteenth century. The two earliest of what might be more properly described as loosely-related examples of a type, rather than a group, was Monnot's marble bust of Lord Exeter (signed and dated 1701) (Fig. 19.2) and Francesco Maratti's portrait of Exeter's son, Lord William Cecil (Plate 19.1), to both of which Hugh Honour first drew attention in his important study of Italian sculptors and British patrons.[21] Both were apparently commissioned (along with Monnot's monument to Exeter at Stanford) when Exeter and his son were in Rome around 1700. According to Lione Pascoli in his biography of Monnot, the Earl met the sculptor in the church of Santa Maria del Popolo and admired his bust of Cardinal Savio Millini, which was then being placed in the family's chapel.[22] Both Exeter and Cecil are shown with short hair, though Monnot's bust of the

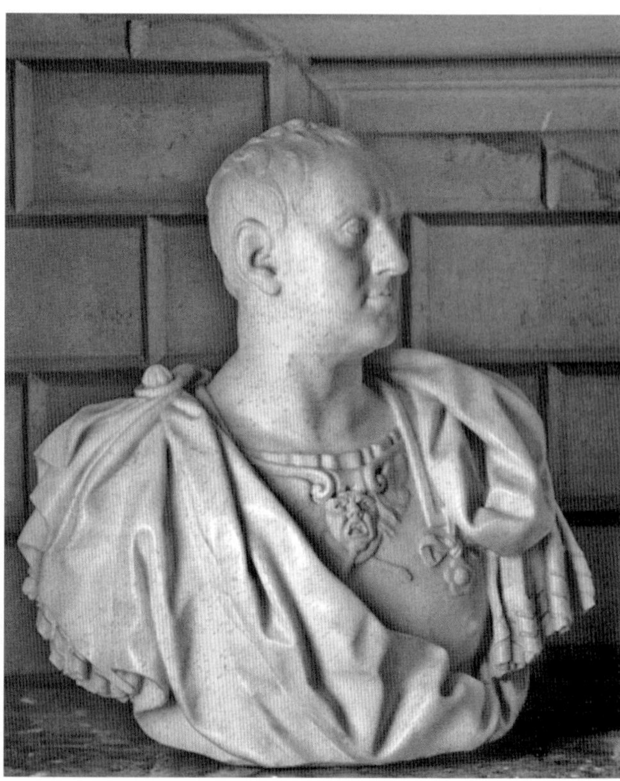

FIG. 19.2. Pierre-Étienne Monnot (1657–1733), *John, 5th Earl of Exeter*, 1701. Marble. The Burghley House Collection. *(Reproduced courtesy of the Burghley House Preservation Trust.)*

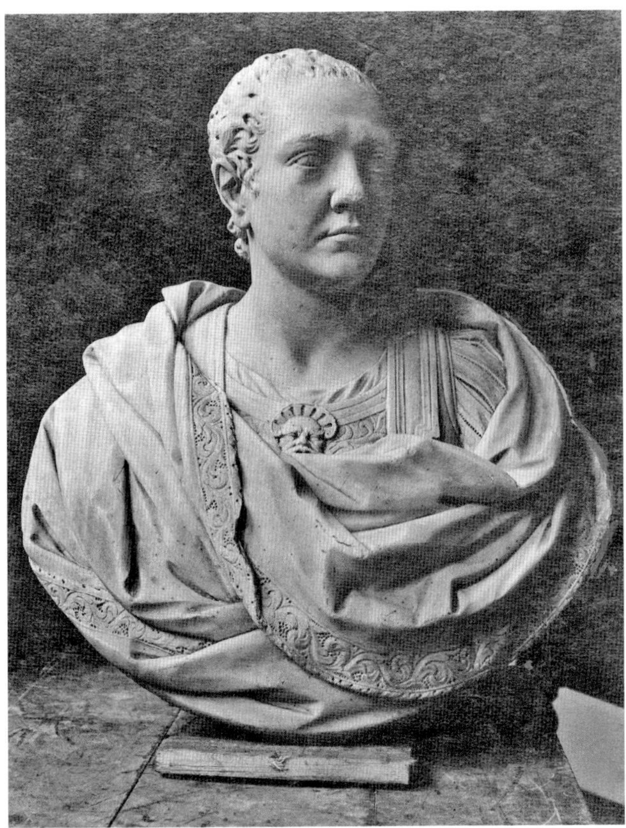

FIG. 19.3. Vincenzo Felici (fl. 1701–7), *Sir John Perceval (later 1st Earl of Egmont)*, 1707. Marble. London, National Portrait Gallery. *(Photo: © National Portrait Gallery, London.)*

former represents the sitter in armour with drapery above it, whereas Maratti's bust of the latter shows the son in classicizing drapery alone. Another, slightly later, portrait of a British sitter by an Italian sculptor employs a similar mode to that used for Exeter. This is the bust by Vincenzo Felici — the pupil and son-in-law of Domenico Guidi — of Sir John Perceval, later 1st Earl of Egmont, who spent part of 1707 in Rome (Fig. 19.3).[23] In this case, however, the drapery enfolding the bust proper is even more broad and expansive, especially when combined with the small head, with its tightly cropped curls. The overall impression is of a bust resembling those composite portraits made up of an antique Republican head and a Baroque bust.

As Honour pointed out in his discussion of the Exeter and Cecil busts, the style of bust used in all these cases — and, in particular, the short hair recalling Roman Republican models — is quite different from that seen in any of these others sculptors' portrait busts or, indeed, in any contemporary sculptural portraits being produced in Rome around 1700.[24] The choice of this manner, therefore, would seem to lie with the patrons rather than the sculptors. The formulation of this mode would seem to reflect that wish of the British to associate themselves with the civic humanist values of the Roman Republic, as reflected in the much-quoted passage from Jonathan Richardson's *An Essay on the Theory of Painting*:

> No Nation under Heaven so nearly resemble the ancient Greeks, and Romans as We. There is a Haughty Courage, an Elevation of Thought, a Greatness of Taste, a Love of Liberty, a Simplicity, and Honesty among us, which we inherit from our Ancestors, and which belong to us as Englishmen and 'tis in These this Resemblance consists.[25]

First seen in the busts commissioned in Rome in the first decade of the eighteenth century, this classicizing type of portrait was developed, through examples such as Rysbrack's Finch and Scheemakers' Stowe busts, into one of the principal types of sculptural portrait used in Britain, and by the end of the century was indeed the norm for the sculptural representation of male sitters. To put it in this simplistic way, however, is misleading, in that it suggests a direct linear connection between these Roman busts and the portraits by Nollekens via the images of Rysbrack.

The *all'antica* bust of course has a more complicated and varied history, and it was hardly a new invention of Roman sculptors for British patrons around 1700. Even in England the use of classical models for full-length statues of monarchs and nobility was almost standard by the late seventeenth century, as we see from Grinling Gibbon's images of James II and the Duke of Somerset.[26] But what is distinctive and striking about these Anglo-Roman portraits — these visual manifestations of *Roma Britannica* — is the way in which they combine the severity of Roman Republican portraits in the representation of faces and head with an expansive and showy swathe of drapery that allows the portrait to work on a confidently large scale. Here we can recognize a significant difference between the Exeter/Cecil/Egmont type and those classicizing images produced in Britain by Rysbrack and Scheemakers, such as the busts of Finch and Cobham (Fig. 19.1), mentioned earlier. Whereas the latter employ the classical mode to create images that are relatively modest and understated, in a way that is appropriate to a polite culture in which sculptural portraiture was no longer confined to the nobility, the busts of British sitters in Rome combine the severely classical with a grandiloquence

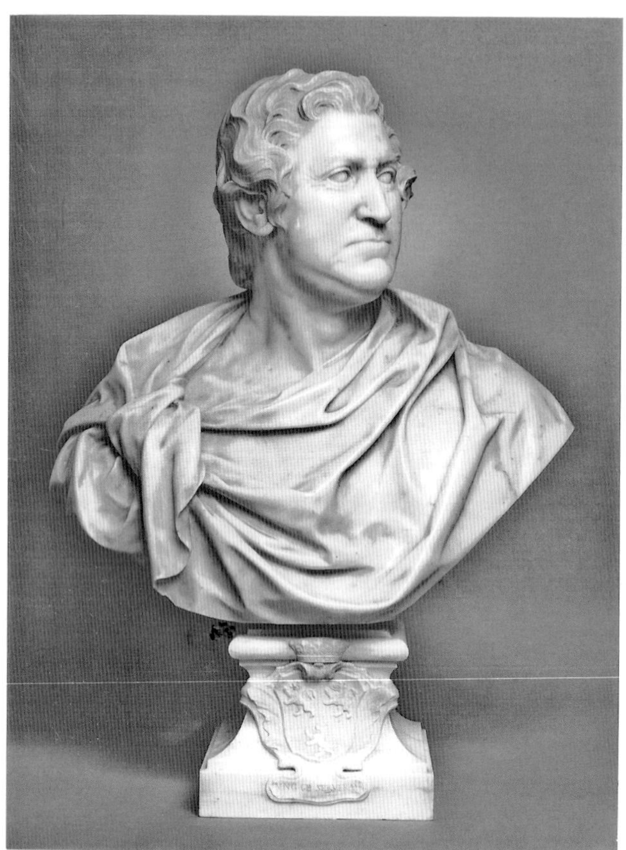

FIG. 19.4. Louis-François Roubiliac (1695–1762), *Henry, 9th Earl of Pembroke*, c. 1750. Marble. Private Collection. *(Reproduced courtesy of the owner.)*

associated not just with late baroque busts but with sculptural portraits of the aristocracy. Here we can glimpse that very connection that Robinson was making when he wrote about the bust as a genre preferred by Italian noblemen.

The assumption that the sculptural portrait of a nobleman required expansiveness, grandeur of scale and an abundance of drapery, in the Italian manner, may also account in part for the appearance of the later bust of Lord Binning, perhaps carved in Naples, where he died in 1732 (**Plate 19.2**).[27] Though later than the busts of Exeter and Egmont (and with its distinctive supporting scrolls, possibly a local Neapolitan feature), the bust of Binning, like them, combines a rich swathe of drapery with the severely cut hair and classicizing head.[28] (In this case, the severity of the image was intensified by the sitter's sickly mien; the bust may even be posthumous and based on a death mask.) A still later continuation of this association of nobility with grand scale is found in Roubiliac's various busts of Henry, 9th Earl of Pembroke (**Fig. 19.4**), which is in a markedly different mode from those portraits this sitter commissioned of his friends, Sir Andrew Fountaine and Martin Folkes.

Read in this context, Sir Thomas Robinson's suggestion to his friend the Earl of Carlisle seems very appropriate, but Carlisle does not seem to have taken this up.[29] Robinson himself, however, seems to have acted on his own recommendation by commissioning while in Rome busts of himself and his first wife, Lady Lechmere.[30] Robinson's bust (**Fig. 19.5**), executed around 1730 and described by him (in his will) as being by Filippo della Valle, employs, albeit in a more compact and modest way, the format of short hair and classicizing drapery seen earlier in the busts of Exeter, Egmont and Cecil.[31] But, if it might be seen as continuing this tradition, it also has connections with a rather different group of classicizing busts of male sitters produced around 1730 by Edmé Bouchardon, the sculptor responsible for the bust of his wife. Rather than linking it directly with the images of Exeter and others, we should instead see it as the latest in a series of busts produced in Rome by

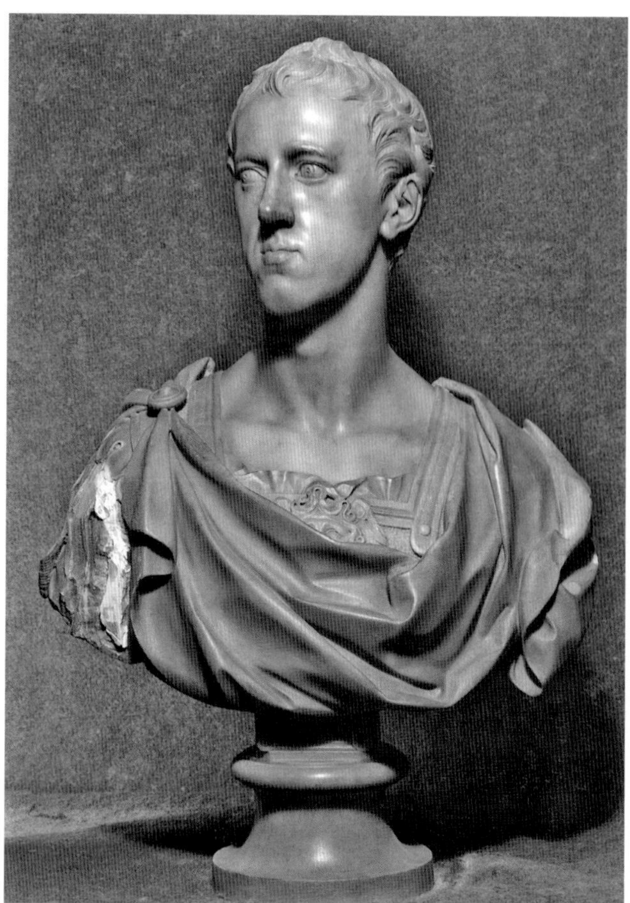

FIG. 19.5. Filippo della Valle (1698–1768) and (?) Edmé Bouchardon (1698–1762), *Sir Thomas Robinson*, c. 1730. Marble. Westminster Abbey. *(Reproduced courtesy of the Warburg Institute.)*

Bouchardon (and della Valle) for British sitters and constituting a distinct type of classicizing sculptural portrait.

A number of British visitors to Rome commissioned works from the young French sculptor and were among those foreign patrons about whom the Duc d'Antin complained when he reported that Bouchardon was neglecting his work as a *pensionnaire* at the Académie de France because of these commissions. It seems likely that these works for the British during the late 1720s played at least some role in establishing the sculptor's reputation and subsequent patronage of Cardinal Polignac, Cardinal Rohan and Clement XII. The earliest of these commissions was that for a bust of the young John Gordon, dated 1728 (Fig. 19.6). This was followed by a bust of Lord Hervey in 1729, the portrait of Lady Lechmere, executed around 1730, and, finally, an appropriately grand bust of the Duchess of Buckingham, completed in 1731. As well as producing these completed works, Bouchardon was also reported in 1730 to be occupied with a full-length statue of the Earl of Radnor, apparently never completed, though expected to be 'une chose très rare'.[32] Together, these British commissions constitute a substantial part of the French sculptor's *oeuvre* around 1730, but what is especially striking is the way in which all the male busts among these commissions employ a classicizing mode. Furthermore, for two of them — those of Gordon and Hervey — Bouchardon and his patrons rejected an antique model with drapery and opted instead for a more severe type involving bare chest and drapery only on one shoulder — a format that was clearly based on a bust of Trajan. In this case, however, the initiative for the adoption of a particular classicizing type lay not with a British patron but with an antiquarian, Philipp von Stosch, whose bust Bouchardon had carved in 1727.[33] Such a mode was especially appropriate for Stosch and we may assume that he was no doubt very much involved in the formulation of this type. But, with his close connections with the Pretender's court in Rome (about which he supplied intelligence to the British government) as well as through his contact with many British visitors to Rome, he must have been aware of the predilection that British patrons had shown already for a classicizing format for their sculptural portraits.

This mode, however, was not restricted to the portrait bust, and Stosch, as well as various British patrons — including those represented by Bouchardon —, were shown in a comparable classicizing manner, but on a smaller scale, in the form of ivory and wax reliefs, medals and engraved gems. Ten years before Bouchardon's portrait bust, Stosch had already been represented in a similar mode — following the Trajan model — in an ivory medallion by Giovanni Pozzo. The same ivory carver was later to produce a wax relief of John Gordon, bearing the same date as Bouchardon's bust and likewise showing him in a classicizing manner (Fig. 19.7). But before this Pozzo had also executed medals representing the antiquarians Conyers Middleton and Daniel Wray, each shown in a similar classicizing manner. This network between sitters and sculptors in different media may be extended further by linking Bouchardon's bust of Hervey with the *all'antica* profile of the same sitter carved as a gem by the gem-engraver Lorenz Natter, who was working in Rome at the same period. Given the antiquarian interests of many of these sitters and the concern they had not only with antique statuary but

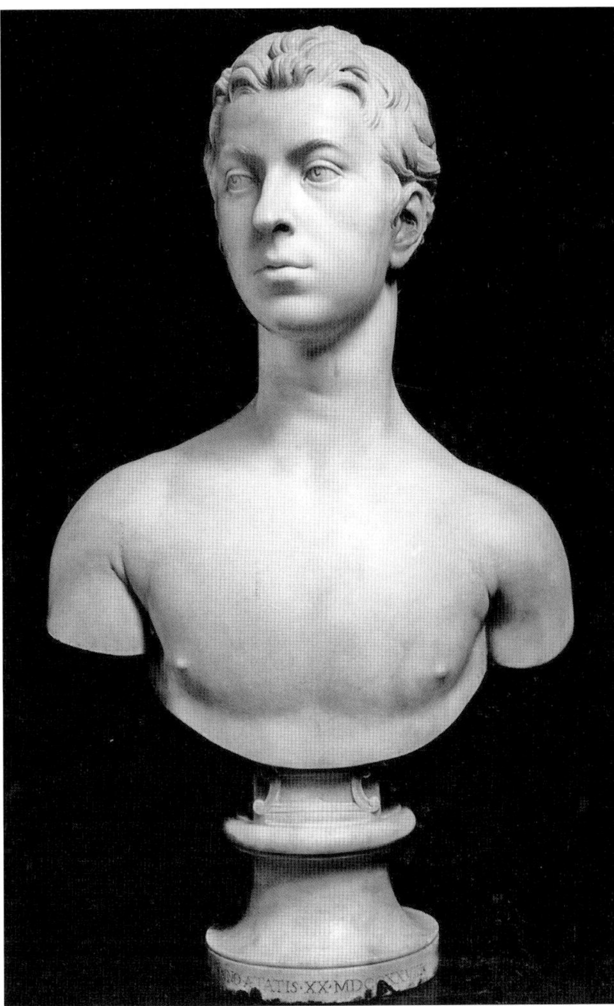

FIG. 19.6. Edmé Bouchardon (1698–1762), *John Gordon*, 1728. Marble. Highland Council. *(Reproduced courtesy of Inverness Museum and Art Gallery.)*

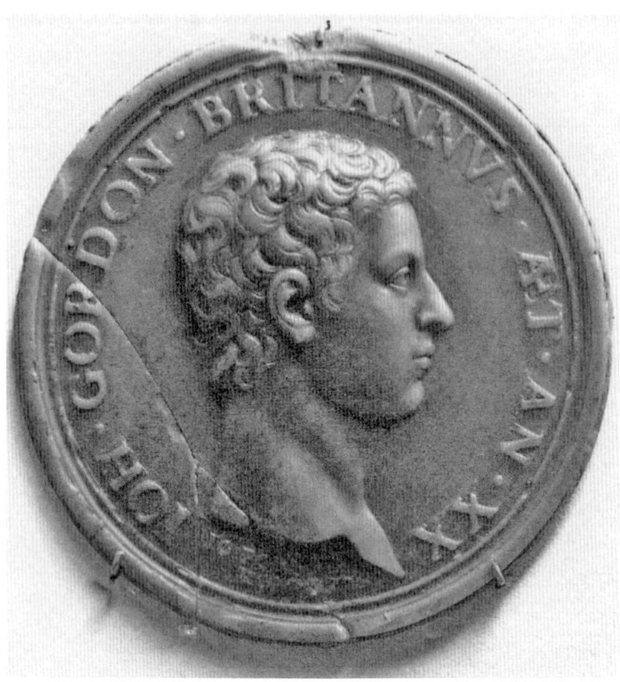

FIG. 19.7. Giovanni Pozzo, *John Gordon*, 1728. Wax. London, Victoria and Albert Museum. *(Photo: © V&A Images/Victoria and Albert Museum, London.)*

also with antique gems — Stosch described such gems as 'ma passion ... ma folie dominante'[34] —, these small-scale reliefs, which were evidently closely connected with the larger-scale portraits, need to be seen as more than merely marginal. Considering these various images as part of a broad continuum of sculptural portraiture, we should perhaps see the classicizing mode that they have in common as the outcome of the antiquarian preoccupations shared by most of these sitters. But it is striking how prominent a role British patrons played here.

From these various disparate examples, it would seem that classicizing sculptural portraits of various types, and across a range of scales, were being created by sculptors working in Rome during the first three decades of the eighteenth century. They seem to have been made predominantly for British patrons, and differ from the images produced by the same sculptors for patrons of other nationalities. But if the patrons were almost all British, the sculptors were certainly not, and it seems to have been the patrons who played an unusually significant directing role here. The agency for the formulation of this new type, then, lay with the patrons, rather than the sculptors. Though not by British sculptors (or indeed by foreign-born sculptors who then worked in Britain), these various busts need to be taken into account in any discussion of sculpture in Britain, and so form part of the history of British art. But, at the same time, they are equally very much part of the history of sculpture in early eighteenth-century Rome.

But at this point some distinctions should be made. While Monnot's bust of Lord Exeter and Bouchardon's bust of John, Lord Hervey may have within a few years of their making been viewed within the context of a British collection or domestic setting, it would be misleading to suggest a direct and continuous lineage that led to the classicizing busts being produced in significant numbers by Rysbrack and Scheemakers for British patrons of different social status by the middle of the century. By this point, the classicizing manner had become another mode of polite portraiture, considered to be as suitable for adoption by those of the middling sort as the more informal type of bust with soft cap and open shirt. The images discussed here, however, seem to have been more restricted in their usage, and more specific in their meanings and connotations. But just as a distinction should be made between the classicizing busts produced in Britain around 1750 and these earlier examples executed by foreign sculptors working in Rome for British patrons, so the differences between the earlier busts by Monnot and Felici and those by Bouchardon also need to be recognized.

For sitters such as Hervey, the classicizing manner as formulated by Bouchardon denoted an antiquarian engagement with antiquity that was a marked characteristic of these British patrons and visitors to Rome, as it was, of course, of Stosch. For sitters such as Exeter, the classical could be combined with a late Baroque grandeur in a way that signalled the way in which such sitters belonged to a pan-European aristocratic élite and yet, through the distinctive classicizing features, also showed them as being set apart as members of a nobility associated not with absolutism but with a constitutional monarchy. In Rome sculptural portraits were an aristocratic mode — part of a shared *ancien régime* culture —, and Robinson's remark to Carlisle assumes that the bust and the statue were types of representation appropriate to the nobility. What we see in the busts of sitters such as Exeter is an aristocratic mode of representation being inflected and nuanced through the distinctive use of the classical, for a member of the nobility who belonged to that élite but who was also different.

Both the early busts by Monnot, Maratti and Felici and those from the later 1720s by Bouchardon show, through their different appropriations of the antique, the ambiguous position of British visitors and patrons in Rome. In both cases, these busts of British patrons simultaneously registered that the sitters were part of a shared culture within early eighteenth-century Rome and made clear that they were in some way different, just as they were to appear different from those who sat to Rysbrack and Scheemakers in the 1750s.

Notes

1. F. Haskell and N. Penny, *Taste and the Antique: the Lure of Classical Sculpture 1500–1900* (New Haven/London, 1981).
2. J. Richardson and J. Richardson, *An Account of Some of the Statues, Bas-reliefs, Drawings and Pictures in Italy, etc, with Remarks* (London, 1722).
3. H. Honour, 'English patrons and Italian sculptors in the first half of the eighteenth century', *The Connoisseur* 20 (141) (1958), 220–6. Honour's study remains fundamental, and the present contribution is little more than a footnote to this. For assessments of eighteenth-century sculpture in Rome, see D. Walker, 'An introduction to sculpture in Rome in the eighteenth century', in E.P. Bowron and J.J Rishel (eds), *Art in Rome in the Eighteenth Century* (London/Philadelphia, 2000), 211–23, with catalogue entries on pp. 224–93; R. Enggass, *Early Eighteenth-century Sculpture in Rome* (University Park/London, 1976).
4. Examples include the model for Legros's relief of *Tobit Lending Money to Gabel* in the Monte di Pietà. For the marble, see Enggass, *Early Eighteenth-century Sculpture* (above, n. 3), 139–40; for the model and its British context, see M. Baker, 'That 'most rare Master Monsii Le Gros' and his Marsyas', *The Burlington Magazine* 127 (1985), 702–6. For British interest in Rusconi, see F. Martin, 'Camillo Rusconi in English collections', in C. Sicca and A. Yarrington (eds), *The Lustrous Trade. Material Culture and the History of Sculpture in England and Italy c. 1700–c. 1860* (Leicester, 2000), 49–66.
5. A. Wilton and I. Bignamini (eds), *Grand Tour: the Lure of Italy in the Eighteenth Century* (London, 1996); B. Ford and J. Ingamells, *A Dictionary of British and Irish Travellers in Italy, 1701–1800. Compiled from the Brinsley Ford Archive* (New Haven/London, 1997). See also C. Hornsby (ed.), *The Impact of Italy: the Grand Tour and Beyond* (London, 2000); and, for an overview of more recent literature, J. Wilton-Ely, ''Classic ground': Britain, Italy and the Grand Tour', *Eighteenth-century Life* 28 (2004), 136–65.
6. J. Scott, *The Pleasures of Antiquity. British Collectors of Greece and Rome* (New Haven/London, 2003); R. Guilding, *Marble Mania. Sculpture Galleries in England 1640–1840* (London, 2001); V. Coltman, *Fabricating the Antique: Neoclassicism in Britain, 1760–1800* (Chicago/London, 2006).
7. One notable and obvious exception to this sweeping generalization is, of course, F. Haskell, *Painters and Patrons* (second edition) (New Haven/London, 1980).
8. H. Walpole, *Anecdotes of Painting in England* (Strawberry Hill, 1765–80); A. Cunningham, *The Lives of the Most Eminent British Painters, Sculptors and Architects* (London, 1830–3).
9. For the Argyll monument, see M. Baker, 'Roubiliac's Argyll monument and the interpretation of eighteenth-century sculptors' designs', *The Burlington Magazine* 134 (1992), 785–97. From some of Rysbrack's unsuccessful designs for

this commission (for which see K. Eustace, *Michael Rysbrack Sculptor 1694–1770* (Bristol, 1982), 128–9) it would seem that he, too, was drawing on Rusconi's composition.

10. For the Marlborough monument, see M. Whinney, *Sculpture in Britain, 1530–1830* (second edition) (London, 1988), 173–6. One of the more striking among other appropriations of Roman monuments by British sculptors is the adaptation of the Gregory XIII pattern by Robert Taylor — the British-born sculptor most attuned to developments in French and Italian continental sculpture — in his design for the monument to Henry Petty, 1st Earl of Shelburne, for which see M. Baker, 'Lord Shelburne's 'Costly Fabrick': Scheemakers, Roubiliac and Taylor as rivals', *The Burlington Magazine* 132 (1990), 841–8.
11. The other major category of sculptural production — albeit one that has been marginalized in accounts of sculpture in Britain — is the chimney-piece. The importation of chimney-pieces from Italy, however, seems to have been greater in the second half of the century.
12. Letter from Sir Thomas Robinson to the Earl of Carlisle, 6 December 1730, Castle Howard Archives, and quoted by C. Saumarez Smith, *Charles Howard, Third Earl of Carlisle and the Architecture of Castle Howard* (Ph.D. thesis, Warburg Institute, 1986), 250. (I am grateful to Dr Saumarez Smith for drawing this to my attention.)
13. As Walker ('An introduction to sculpture' (above, n. 3), 215) remarked, 'Independent portrait busts were not nearly as prevalent as in the seventeenth century'. For the greater abundance of busts in Florence, see K. Lankheit, *Florentinische Barockplastik: die Kunst am Hofe der Letzten Medici, 1670–1743* (Munich, 1962).
14. R. Lassels, *The Voyage of Italy or a Compleat Journey through Italy. In Two Parts . . .* (London, 1670); J. Breval, *Remarks on Several Parts of Europe* (London, 1726); E. Wright, *Some Observations Made in Travelling through France, Italy, &c, in the Years 1720, 1721 and 1722* (London, 1730); Richardson and Richardson, *Account of Some of the Statues* (above, n. 2).
15. Wright, *Some Observations* (above, n. 14), 290. As Karin Wolfe has pointed out to me, the 'lady of the Family *Galeoti*' may be identified with the bust of Maria Barberini Duglioli, attributed to Giuliano Finelli, now in the Louvre; for which, see J. Montagu, 'Innovation and exchange. Portrait sculptors of the early Roman baroque', in A. Bacchi, C. Hess and J. Montagu (eds), *Bernini and the Birth of Baroque Portrait Sculpture* (Los Angeles, 2008), 47 and fig. 28. For the copy by Giuseppe Giorgetti placed on her tomb, see J. Montagu, 'Antonio and Gioseppe Giorgetti: sculptors to Cardinal Francesco Barberini', *The Art Bulletin* 52 (1970), 290–1.
16. Wright, *Some Observations* (above, n. 14), 342.
17. This was pointed out by Whinney, *Sculpture in Britain* (above, n. 10), 152.
18. For the Finch bust, see Whinney, *Sculpture in Britain* (above, n. 10), 166–7; M. Baker, 'Making the portrait bust modern', in J. Kohl and R. Müller (eds), *Kopf / Bild. Die Büste in Mittelalter und Früher Neuzeit* (Berlin, 2007), 347–66. For the Temple of Friendship busts, see I. Roscoe, 'Peter Scheemakers', *Walpole Society* 61 (1999), 268–9; M. Baker, *Figured in Marble. The Making and Viewing of Eighteenth-century Sculpture* (London/Los Angeles, 2000), 58–9.
19. G. Vertue, 'The notebooks of George Vertue, volume III', *Walpole Society* 22 (1934), 44, 139.
20. J. Kennedy, *Description of the Antiquities and Curiosities in Wilton House* (Salisbury, 1769), iv.
21. Honour, 'English patrons and Italian sculptors' (above, n. 3), 220–1.
22. L. Pascoli, *Vite de' pittori, scultori ed architetti moderni* II (Rome, 1730–6), 491.
23. For Perceval's Grand Tour, see Ford and Ingamells, *Dictionary of British and Irish Travellers* (above, n. 5). For his iconography, as well as this particular bust, see J. Kerslake, *Early Georgian Portraits* (London, 1977), 73. No mention was made of the bust or its commissioning in Perceval's extensive correspondence (British Library, Add. MS 47025) though reference was made here (fol. 80) to 'the Ivory Caesars heads wch. I bought at Rome', as well as to the 24 busts and three statues supplied by Massimiliano Soldani (fol. 81), all of which apparently were lost when a ship with a consignment of works of art and books was seized by French privateers. Interestingly, Perceval had contact in Italy with Gibbs (fols 81, 114–15), who would have come to work for him in Ireland, had he not accepted an offer from the Earl of Mar; for which, see T. Friedman, *James Gibbs* (New Haven/London, 1984), 7–9. For Felici, see C. Giometti, *Uno studio e i suoi scultori. Gli inventari di Domenico Guidi e Vincenzo Felici* (Pisa, 2007).
24. The same hairstyle was used for Exeter on the related monument.
25. J. Richardson, *An Essay on the Theory of Painting* (London, 1715), 209–10. For the wider context of Richardson's remark, see P. Ayres, *Classical Culture and the Idea of Rome* (Cambridge, 1997).
26. For James II, see Whinney, *Sculpture in Britain* (above, n. 10), 120; for Somerset, see M. Baker, 'The portrait sculpture', in D. McKitterick, *The Making of the Wren Library* (Cambridge, 1995), 112.
27. For Binning, see Ford and Ingamells, *Dictionary of British and Irish Travellers* (above, n. 5), 41–2 (under entry for Lady Grisel Baillie). For the bust, see M. Baker, 'Public fame or private remembrance? The portrait bust as a mode of commemoration in eighteenth-century England', in *Memory and Oblivion. Proceedings of the XXIXth International Conference of the History of Art held in Amsterdam, 1–7 September 1996* (Amsterdam/Dordrecht, 1999), 527–35.
28. Binning was also represented in a classicizing manner in the form of a medallion profile relief set in a *pietra dura* panel; for which, see Sotheby's sale, 28 September 1987 (*The Contents of Tyninghame, East Lothian, Scotland*), lot 58.
29. While the 3rd Earl of Carlisle does not seem to have been represented in this way, a classicizing bust, albeit truncated high on the shoulders and with only a modest amount of

drapery, was done of his grandfather, Charles, 1st Earl of Carlisle, and was set on a monument in York Minster, erected in the first few years of the eighteenth century by his daughter, Lady Mary Fenwick, to her executed husband, Sir John Fenwick, and her father. (On this monument see J.B. Morrell, *York Monuments* (London, 1944); G.E. Aylmer, 'Funeral monuments and other post-medieval sculpture', in G.E. Aylmer and R. Cant (eds), *A History of York Minster* (Oxford, 1977), 448. Aylmer attributed the monument to either John Hardy or Samuel Carpenter, and drew attention to its inscription as an extreme example of *supressio veri*, since it refers neither to Carlisle's Cromwellian career nor to Fenwick's attainder and execution for treason.) The bust, which might well have been carved before the monument was envisaged, is an early example of a classicizing image but may not be the first.

30. M. Baker, C. Harrison and A. Laing, 'Bouchardon's British sitters: sculptural portraiture in Rome and the classicising bust around 1730', *The Burlington Magazine* 142 (2000), 752–62. Detailed bibliographical references to works by Edmé Bouchardon, Giovanni Pozzo and Lorenz Natter may be found here.
31. The evidence about the bust's authorship is confusing. While various eighteenth-century writers listed it among della Valle's work, so corroborating Robinson's statement in his will, the bust has a socle that matches that on the bust of Lady Lechmere and, equally significantly, that used by Bouchardon on his other busts. While it is possible that della Valle may have carved the marble after Bouchardon's model, as suggested in Baker, Harrison and Laing, 'Bouchardon's British sitters' (above, n. 30), it seems odd that Robinson should name the carver rather than the sculptor to whom he sat. Perhaps some more complex form of collaboration was involved.
32. Letter from Philipp von Stosch to François Fagel, 19 June 1731, Collection Fagel, vol. 2048, letter 19, Algemeen Rijksarchief, The Hague (kindly brought to my attention by Philippe Senechal).
33. P. Senechal, 'Attaché entièrement à l'antique et à mon caprice': die Büste des Barons Philipp von Stosch von Edme Bouchardon', in U. Fleckner, M. Schieder and M.F. Zimmermann (eds), *Jenseits der Grenzen: Französische und Deutsche Kunst vom Ancien Régime bis zur Gegenwart: Thomas W. Gaehtgens zum 60. Geburtstag* (Cologne, 2000), 136–48.
34. Stosch to Fagel, 11 August 1713, quoted by J. Heringa, 'Die Genese von *Gemmae Antiquae Caelatae*', *Bulletin Antieke Bescheving* 51 (1976), 75.

'The Modern ... who recommends *himself*'; Italian painters and British taste in eighteenth-century Rome

Desmond Shawe-Taylor

In his *14th Discourse* of 1788, Sir Joshua Reynolds prophesied that:

> two of the last distinguished Painters of that country [Italy], I mean Pompeio Battoni, and Raffaelle Mengs, however great their names may at present sound in our ears, will very soon fall into the rank of Imperiale, Sebastian Concha, Placido Constanza, Massuccio, and the rest of their immediate predecessors; whose names, though equally renowned in their lifetime, are now fallen into what is little short of total oblivion.[1]

Pompeo Batoni is not mentioned in the *Discourses* before this, but several passages (quoted below) seem to have been written with him in mind. If so, the *Discourses* can be read as a sustained attack on 'Batonismo'.

Reynolds's feelings about Batoni hang upon his understanding of the concept of ideal beauty, which dominated artistic theory from the Renaissance until the death of Ingres. The definitive expression of this concept from the point of view of the eighteenth century was the introduction to Giovanni Pietro Bellori's lives of Italian artists (*Vite de' pittori, scultori e architetti moderni* (Rome, 1672)).[2] The idea was introduced into England through Charles Alphonse Du Fresnoy's *De arte graphica* (Paris 1668), translated into English in 1695, and Bainbridge Buckridge's 'An essay towards an English School' of 1706.[3] The purpose of the artist (according to these writers) is to depict an ideal, which might go by a variety of different names, some of which Reynolds listed in the *3rd Discourse* of 1770: 'The *gusto grande* of the Italians, the *beau ideal* of the French, and the *great style*, *genius*, and *taste* among the English, are but different appellations of the same thing'.[4] Two other names sum up the dual nature of this concept: *Idea*, an Italian word meaning 'imaginative image or conception', and *Nature*, used, in French and English, with a capital 'N' to mean a refined version of nature, also sometimes called 'La belle Nature' or 'Best Nature'. It is difficult in theory to reconcile these apparent opposites of imagination and nature, but in practice an artist can achieve the *gusto grande* in two easy stages: firstly, refine one's taste through the study of classical antiquity; then use that taste to select the beautiful parts when observing the works of nature. This range of beliefs was common to artists and academies throughout Europe, and it permeates Reynolds's thought.

Some scene setting is also needed when examining the history of the professional relationship between Reynolds and Batoni. A crucial figure in this respect is Allan Ramsay, the most Italianate and 'Batonian' of British eighteenth-century artists. Ramsay first met Batoni when he studied in Italy in 1736–8 with his master, Francesco Fernandi (Imperiale) (one of the artists mentioned in Reynolds's *14th Discourse* (see above)), and made copies of some Batoni drawings. During his second visit to Rome in 1754–7 he renewed the acquaintance and made sketches after two Batoni paintings.[5] During his fourth and final Roman visit in 1782–4, he asked Batoni to give drawing lessons to his son, John.[6] Batoni's studio in Rome seems to have been made available for British artists to study drawing. In 1750–2 two friends and fellow-pupils of Thomas Hudson (a portrait-painter and master of Reynolds and others) were in Rome; one, John Astley, studied with Batoni for some months; the other, Reynolds, did not.[7]

The professional rivalry between Reynolds and Ramsay was at its most intense in the years immediately after Ramsay's return from his second Roman trip in 1757. In most areas of patronage

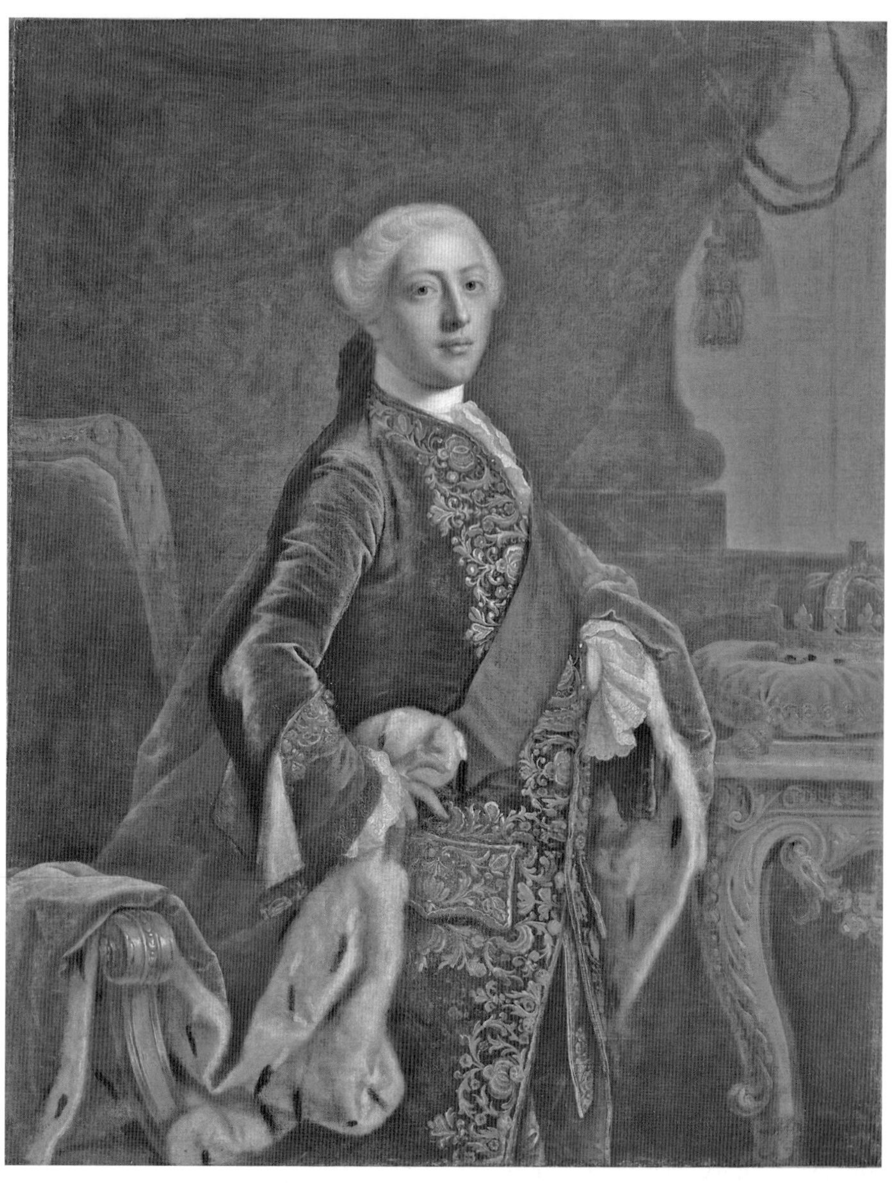

FIG. 20.1. **Sir Joshua Reynolds (1723–92), *George III as Prince of Wales*, 1759. Oil on canvas, 127 × 102. Royal Collection, OM 1011, 401034.** *(The Royal Collection © 2010 Her Majesty Queen Elizabeth II.)*

Reynolds gained the advantage over his older rival; however, in one — that of royal preferment — he was defeated outright. Ramsay's first portrait of George III, when Prince of Wales, was painted immediately after his return in 1757–8 for the 3rd Earl of Bute, and was followed up with the state portrait of the new king (**Plate 20.1**) painted soon after his accession in 1760.[8] As Alastair Smart has pointed out, these images are unusually Batonian, even by Ramsay's standards, and may be compared with Batoni's *Sackville Tufton, 8th Earl of Thanet* of 1752–4 or his *Karl Eugen, Duke of Württemberg*, 1753–4.[9] Reynolds countered with a portrait of the Prince of Wales of 1759 (**Fig. 20.1**) and an oil sketch for a large group portrait of George III's marriage to Queen Charlotte in 1761. Both these works are in the Royal Collection, but only because acquired during later reigns; they were undertaken with no royal encouragement (presumably as 'sales pitches') and remained on the artist's hands.[10] The portrait of George, Prince of Wales, is a conscious essay in the style of Ramsay, suggesting that Reynolds was prepared to go to some lengths to catch the royal eye.

In the same decade, the 1750s, Ramsay and Reynolds also became rivals in the field of artistic theory. Ramsay's *Dialogue on Taste* was published in 1755, and it did for the almost reverential respect for Old Master painting what his friend and philosophical mentor, David Hume, did for religious reverence.[11] Ramsay's dialogue is essentially a restatement of the familiar idea that there is no disputing taste. In the process he said three things calculated to offend advocates of the 'beau ideal': that the purpose of art is to copy nature and nothing more; that the layman can judge it as well, if not better, than the connoisseur; and that the measure of beauty is fashion, not some judgement of absolute value.[12] This last point applies to architecture as well as painting: 'Whatever pains those gentlemen [architects] may take to dignify the ornamental part of their art by scientific reasonings about propriety and fitness, it will be found at last to owe all its power of pleasing to custom only'.[13] For Ramsay fashion is, of course, arbitrary and contingent, but a philosophical artist or architect should acquiesce to it none the less. Ramsay even argued that antique art became stagnant precisely because it tried to hold in check the natural and healthy current of changing fashion. For Ramsay, the absolute notion of 'ideal beauty' was not only un-philosophical nonsense in theory but also dreary to behold in practice: 'a sort of common measure, but which falls mightily in its value when we consider that it is only of a negative kind, from which no excellence, no striking grace can be expected'.[14] The idea of selection — 'Best Nature' — is a 'common measure', a 'leaden' rather than a 'golden' mean: the Medici Venus is near enough to my notion of beauty not to disgust me and near enough to your (very different) notion of beauty not to disgust you; but it positively *delights* neither of us.

In the autumn of 1759 Reynolds wrote three articles for the *Idler*, a journal produced by his friend, Dr Samuel Johnson. Nowhere is Ramsay's recently published treatise mentioned, but the arguments seem to be aimed directly at it, even if the tone of enlightened scepticism is totally different from Giovanni Battista Piranesi's angry response to the same provocation.[15] Ramsay was also a friend of Johnson and a skilful prose writer; a bludgeoning refutation would have succeeded only in making Reynolds look foolish. In this spirit Reynolds cheerfully conceded that beauty grows out of familiarity in the eyes of many beholders, but he argued that this very familiarity creates an ideal. The distribution of variation within nature, Reynolds argued, is like a freely swinging pendulum; the form of beauty lies in the centre, and forms of ugliness or deformity lie all around. So while beauty is rare and ugliness common, all beauties are the same and all uglinesses are different. So beauty is more common than *any particular* ugliness, which means that the form of beauty is actually the most common form and its familiarity therefore breeds appreciation.[16] So convoluted an argument could have been undertaken only by someone familiar with Ramsay's ideas and keen to establish the idea of an absolute standard of beauty upon philosophical foundations. Elsewhere, however, he used the language of 'Best Nature' as if it could never have been a matter for dispute: 'The Italian', he pronounced, 'attends only to the invariable, the great and general ideas which are fixed and inherent in universal Nature, the Dutch, on the contrary, to literal truth and a minute exactness in the detail, as I may say, of Nature modified by accident'.[17] This contrast of low Dutch versus high Italian is familiar enough, but for Reynolds 'Nature modified by accident' can be recognized not by *ugliness* (as Bellori and previous theorists might have said) but by excessive attention to *detail*. In the Grand Style, he wrote, 'minute attention must be carefully avoided',[18] and elsewhere in this essay he talked about that 'servile attention to minute exactness or frivolous ornament, which is sometimes inconsistent with higher excellence and always lost in the blaze of expanded genius'.[19] This crucial shift in emphasis implies a tacit criticism of Ramsay's work as well as his thought, for his portraiture at this time certainly did pay more 'attention to minute exactness and ornament' than Reynolds's (whether or not one might want to call this attention 'servile' or 'frivolous').[20] The *Idler* articles put 'universal Nature' (as opposed to 'nature modified by accident') back on her throne; by the time of his *3rd Discourse* of 1770, Reynolds has also lost his tolerance of fashion. He expected artists to distinguish between what he called 'the genuine habits of nature' (another way of saying 'Best Nature') and 'those of fashion'; to recognize how nature is disguised by 'dancing-masters, hairdressers, and tailors, in their various schools of deformity'. 'However the mechanick and ornamental arts may sacrifice to fashion', he concluded, 'she must be entirely excluded from the Art of Painting'.[21]

The decade between Reynolds's *Idler* articles of 1759 and his *1st Discourse* of 1769 represents the high tide mark of Batoni's popularity with British patrons and of his influence on British painters. Benjamin West told Joseph Farington in 1814 that when he had first gone to Rome [in 1760] 'the Italian Artists of that day thought of nothing, looked at nothing, but the works of Pompeio Battoni'.[22] British artists were also influenced by this adulation: Nathaniel Dance worked so closely with Batoni that in 1762 they shared a business card, which read: 'Rome, Sigr. Pompeo Batoni & Mr Dance, for Portrait and History Painting'.[23] The fact that Dance enjoyed the patronage of George III, for whom he painted his *Timon of Athens* (Fig. 20.2) *c.* 1765–7, cannot have escaped Reynolds's

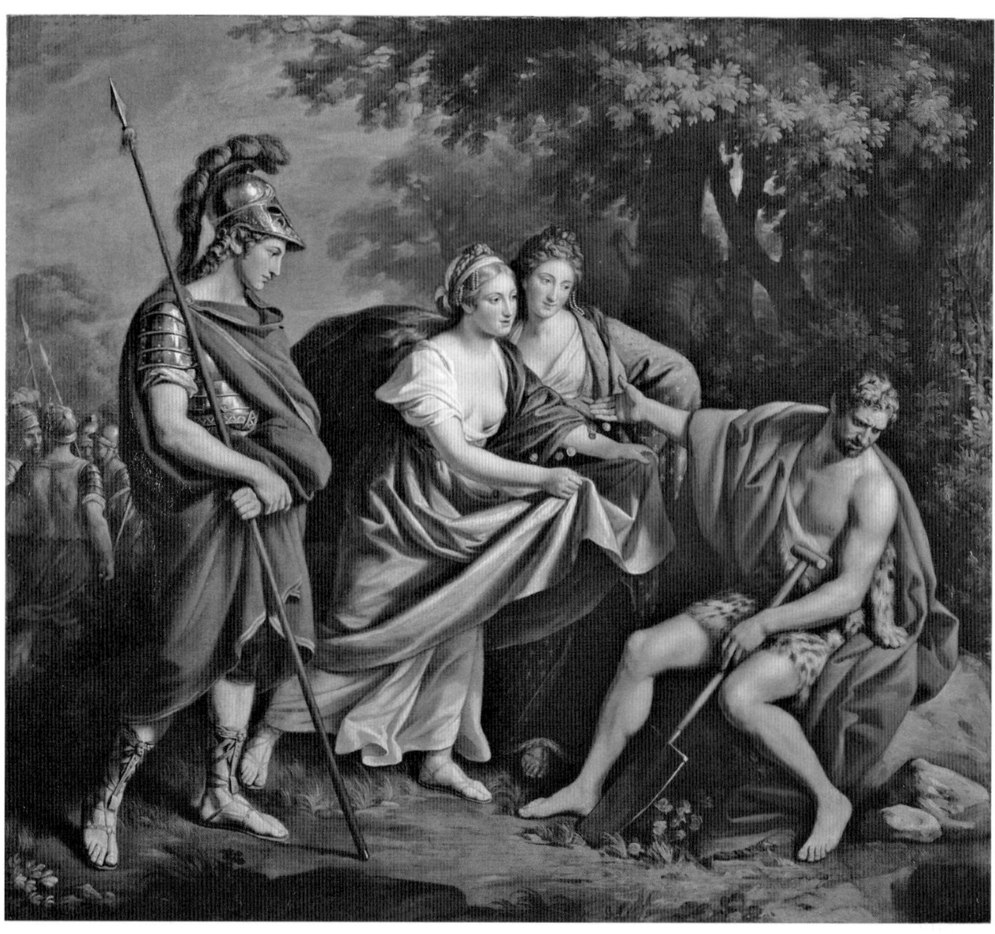

FIG. 20.2. Nathaniel Dance (1735–1811), *Timon of Athens*, c. 1765–7. Oil on canvas, 121.9 × 137.2 cm. Royal Collection, OM 725, 406725. *(The Royal Collection © 2010 Her Majesty Queen Elizabeth II.)*

notice.[24] Batoni was not only successful and influential, he was also competing within the arena of the 'grand style' of portraiture (Reynolds's special preserve), with timeless costume, expressive gestures and witty ideas. Christopher Johns has shown how brilliantly Batoni played with classicizing ideas in his heroic portrait of Colonel William Gordon of 1765–6 (**Plate 20.2**).[25] Gordon's head is seen in profile, with his powdered hair drawn back and out of the way, so as to resemble an antique coin. His plaid kilt and shawl is clearly intended to be read as a Roman soldier's skirt and toga, while his rolled-down hose impersonate Roman buskins, all costumes that a grand tourist could have seen on the equestrian statue and reliefs of Marcus Aurelius on the Capitoline.[26] As every schoolchild knew, the Colosseum (which appears directly behind the figure) was a place where swordsmen (*gladiatores* in Latin, from *gladius* for sword) did battle. These gladiators were recruited from the ranks of slaves captured in wars fought with countries, like Scotland, bordering the Empire. They also knew that the death of a gladiator was ordered by giving the 'thumbs down' sign. We are invited to recognize in Colonel Gordon a Caledonian gladiator predicting the death of anyone foolish enough to swing a net in his direction. Batoni's portrait seems to do everything that Reynolds requires of the grand style of portraiture.[27] This is *gusto grandissimo*. What is more, it is very good value for money: in the 1760s a Batoni full length cost 25 guineas, a Reynolds 150 guineas.[28]

Batoni was not universally admired: Johann Joachim Winckelmann, writing to Wilhelm Musel-Stosch on 3 January 1761, complained that his (now lost) *Hector's Farewell to Andromache* lacked 'the Homeric spirit', with exaggerated action, heads lacking in nobility and posture learned from a French dancing master.[29] Thomas Robinson wrote to his father on 9 August 1760 about the same picture in the same vein, explaining that Batoni's *Hector, Andromache and Astyanax* resembled 'il Signore Ettore, la Signora Andromache & il fanciullo Astyanax on the Theatre in Haymarket'.[30] The cult of Homer as the sublime rough-hewn genius was growing in these years: Winckelmann and Robinson might not have objected had Batoni illustrated Ovid in this 'Haymarket' manner. Robinson did, however, venture to criticize

Batoni's portraiture (in the same letter), which 'made one take Notice how well the Gold Lace was finished, how transparent the Linnen was', unlike Anton Raphael Mengs who 'dwelt on the Effect of his Whole Picture, on the Composition of it, its Force, & its Dignity, none of which things the Other with all his Accuracy had ever thought of'.[31]

These squibs set the agenda for Reynolds's sustained attack on Batoni and 'modern Italians' made throughout the *Discourses*. The first six *Discourses* (1769–73) were written to prepare Royal Academy students for their study trip to Rome; Reynolds had fought off two generations of British 'Batonians' — those of Ramsay and Dance — and seemed anxious to prevent the emergence of a third. In his *2nd Discourse* of 1769 he warned:

> To a young man just arrived in *Italy*, many of the present painters of that country are ready enough to obtrude their precepts, and to offer their own performances as examples of that perfection which they affect to recommend. The Modern, however, who recommends *himself* as a standard, may justly be suspected as ignorant of the true end, and unacquainted with the proper object, of the art which he professes. To follow such a guide, will not only retard the Student, but mislead him.[32]

The 'proper object' in question is surely the ideal that Ramsay tried to dismiss. At least Ramsay practised what he preached, with a realistic, fashionable and 'modern' style of portraiture. Batoni's *Colonel Gordon*, on the other hand, masquerades as something classical and timeless. In his *6th Discourse* of 1773, Reynolds again discussed the 'present Italian painters' with their 'common-place inventions', this time focusing on their neglect of the 'great artists with which they are surrounded'. He told the story of a conceited painter (who sounds like Batoni) who was commissioned to copy a Raphael, who claimed that 'he had not set his foot in the Vatican for fifteen years together'.[33] In Reynolds's view he should have gone 'at least once every month of his life'. He concluded by claiming that in this English Academy 'you contracted no narrow habits, no false ideas, nothing that could lead you to the imitation of any living master, who may be the fashionable darling of the day'.[34] Reynolds's successor as President of the Royal Academy, Benjamin West, warned in a similar vein against those '*schools* in art' that were 'destructive of it in every Country. Young Men became imitators of those works which were admired without looking beyond them, and from the Carach's at Bologna down to Carlo Maratt, & afterwards Pompeio Battoni'.[35]

Reynolds's *14th Discourse* of 1788 is devoted to a particular and (in his view) imperfect artist, Thomas Gainsborough, which gives him the opportunity to name names and to compare evils. After consigning Batoni and Mengs, along with Imperiale and others, to 'total oblivion' (the passage is quoted at the beginning of this paper), Reynolds went on:

> I do not say that those painters were not superior to [Gainsborough] in a certain routine of practice, which, to the eyes of common observers, has the air of a learned composition, and bears a sort of superficial resemblance to the manner of the great men who went before them. I know this perfectly well; but I know likewise, that a man, looking for real and lasting reputation, must unlearn much of the common-place method so observable in the works of the artists whom I have named. For my own part, I confess, I take more interest in, and am more captivated with, the powerful impression of nature, which Gainsborough exhibited in his portraits and in his landskips, and the interesting simplicity and elegance of his little ordinary beggar-children, than with any of the works of that School, since the time of Andrea Sacchi, or perhaps, we may say Carlo Maratti; two painters who may truly be said to be ULTIMI ROMANORUM.[36]

Reynolds here contrasted Carlo Maratti, the 'last of the Romans', with the next two generations: that of Imperiali, Sebastiano Conca, Agostino Masucci, Placido Costanzi; and that of Batoni and Mengs. Had he been comparing Gainsborough's 'powerful impressions of nature' with the work of Maratti, then it would have been a contrast (to the former's detriment) of low 'Dutch' versus high Italian. Instead, it is a contrast of something 'simple', but to be enjoyed on its own terms, with the 'air of a learned composition' executed with an excessive but pedestrian attention to surface and detail — with the shell of the grand style rather than its soul. Later remarks in this *Discourse* confirm this impression: Gainsborough is to be admired for working by candlelight, which gives 'a higher perception of what is great and beautiful in Nature. By candlelight, not only objects appear more beautiful, but from their being in a greater breadth of light and shadow, as well as having a greater breadth and uniformity of colour, nature appears in a higher style'.[37] Gainsborough formed 'all the parts of his pictures together; the whole going on at the same time, in the same manner as nature creates her works'. Batoni, by contrast, 'finished his historical pictures part after part; and in his portraits completely finished one feature before he proceeded to another. The consequence was, as might be expected; the countenance was never well expressed; and, as the painters say, the whole was not well put together'.[38] Later critics seem to have picked up on Reynolds's view: Cicognara referred to Batoni's 'laborious Dutch finish'.[39] In his *Celebrità italiane nell'architettura e pittura* of 1847, Melchior Missirini criticized his manner as 'perhaps too far gone down the road of simple nature'.[40]

Reynolds's opposition to Batoni led him to a new conception of the traditional concept of ideal beauty. Reynolds believed (like everyone) that grand style painting should be the result of thought, but he also believed that it should *look like* thought. For Reynolds, 'The great end of the art is to strike the imagination'.[41] In the same *Discourse* he explained:

> Whenever a story is related, every man forms a picture in his mind of the action and expression of the persons employed. The power of representing this mental picture on canvass is what we call Invention in a Painter. And as in the conception of this ideal picture, the mind does not enter into the minute peculiarities of the dress, furniture, or scene of action; so when the Painter comes to represent it, he contrives those little necessary concomitant circumstances in such a manner, that they shall strike the spectator no more than they did himself in his first conception of the story.[42]

Reynolds achieved this, at least according to Northcote: 'he enveloped objects in the same brilliant haze of a previous mental conception'.[43] Again this runs counter to Batoni's method of completing a painting with 'live models before his eyes'.[44]

This idea of 'thought-painting' became a popular one with the generation of British artists brought up on the *Discourses*. This 'brilliant haze of a previous mental conception' can be realized either by a certain cloudy indistinctness or a sketchy freedom of handling. According to Benjamin Robert Haydon, 'When a man polishes so highly as to get rid of all idea of touch, his work no longer awakens any association of thought, which is the result of an impression in the mind expressed rapidly by the hand'.[45] A story recounted in Farington's diary for 31 December 1812[46] sums up the change in taste that occurred during the years described in this paper and introduces a crucial concept for the Romantic period — feeling. Ramsay took Henry Fuseli to see a 'modern Italian' painter in Turin who 'could draw well and could reason upon the principles of art and compose pictures agreeably to rules commonly considered essential to be attended to, still His works produced little impression on an intelligent Spectator'. 'I see', said Ramsay to Fuseli on coming away, 'that common sense will not make a Painter. This man can shew you why He does this & that & attends to prescribed rules, but more is wanting to touch the feelings'.

Notes

1. Sir Joshua Reynolds, *Discourses on Art*, ed. R.R. Wark (New Haven/London, 1997), 248–9.
2. E. Panofsky, *Idea; a Concept in Art Theory*, trans. J.J.S. Peake (New York/Evanston/San Francisco/London, 1968).
3. C.A. Du Fresnoy, *De arte graphica. The Art of Painting ... Together with an Original Preface Containing a Parallel Betwixt Painting and Poetry. As also a Short Account of the Most Eminent Painters, Both Ancient and Modern, Continued down to the Present Times, According to the Order of Their Sucession* (London, 1695); B. Buckridge, 'An essay towards an English School', in R. De Piles, *The Art of Painting* (London, 1706).
4. Reynolds, *Discourses* (above, n. 1), 43.
5. A. Smart, *Allan Ramsay. Painter, Essayist and Man of the Enlightenment* (New Haven/London, 1992), 29–30, 119.
6. B. Ford and J. Ingamells, *A Dictionary of British and Irish Travellers in Italy, 1701–1800. Compiled from the Brinsley Ford Archive* (New Haven/London, 1997), 796–8.
7. Ford and Ingamells, *Dictionary of British and Irish Travellers* (above, n. 6), 32; A.M. Clark, *Pompeo Batoni. A Complete Catalogue of His Works*, edited and prepared for publication by E.P. Bowron (New York, 1985), 36–7.
8. The former is now in a Private Collection in Scotland. A. Smart and J. Ingamells (eds), *Allan Ramsay. A Complete Catalogue of His Paintings* (New Haven/London, 1999), nos. 191–2; O. Millar *The Later Georgian Pictures in the Collection of Her Majesty the Queen* (Oxford, 1969), no. 996.
9. In a Private Collection in England, and Württembergische Landesbibliothek, Stuttgart, respectively. Smart, *Allan Ramsay. Painter* (above, n. 5), 152; Clark and Bowron, *Pompeo Batoni* (above, n. 7), nos. 177–8.
10. Millar, *Later Georgian Pictures* (above, n. 8), nos. 1011–12.
11. Smart, *Allan Ramsay. Painter* (above, n. 5), 121, 139–48; D. Hume, *Dialogue Concerning Natural Religion* (London, 1779).
12. Smart, *Allan Ramsay. Painter* (above, n. 5), 142–6; A. Ramsay, *A Dialogue on Taste* (first published 1755) (second edition) (London, 1762), 71–2.
13. Smart, *Allan Ramsay. Painter* (above, n. 5), 146; Ramsay, *Dialogue on Taste* (above, n. 12), 28–9.
14. Ramsay, *Dialogue on Taste* (above, n. 12), 25–6.
15. Smart, *Allan Ramsay. Painter* (above, n. 5), 146–8.
16. Article III, *Idler* 82, 10 October 1759.
17. Article II, *Idler* 79, 20 October 1759.
18. Article II (above, n. 17).
19. Article I, *Idler* 76, 29 September 1759.
20. One of the few theorists who followed Ramsay rather than Reynolds on this and other issues is Jean-Etienne Liotard, whose *Traité des principes et des regles de la peinture* of 1781 suggests that art should simply copy nature; that the Dutch school should be imitated and that, as there are 'no brushstrokes in Nature', they should not be visible in art either.
21. Reynolds, *Discourses* (above, n. 1), 47–8.
22. Farington diary entry for 28 October 1814. J. Farrington, *The Diary of Joseph Farington*, various editors, 16 vols and index (New Haven/London, 1978–98), XIII, 4,600.
23. Ford and Ingamells, *Dictionary of British and Irish Travellers* (above, n. 6), 275.
24. Millar, *Later Georgian Pictures* (above, n. 8), no. 725.
25. C.M.S. Johns, 'Portraiture and the making of cultural identity: Pompeo Batoni's *The Honourable Colonel William Gordon* (1765–66) in Italy and north Britain', *Art History* 27 (3) (2004), 382–411; see also Clark and Bowron, *Pompeo Batoni* (above, n. 7), no. 298.
26. F. Haskell and N. Penny, *Taste and the Antique: the Lure of Classical Sculpture 1500–1900* (New Haven/London, 1981), nos. 55–6.
27. In his *7th Discourse* Reynolds advised a portraitist to dress his figures 'something with the general air of the antique for the sake of dignity', while preserving 'something of the modern for the sake of likeness': Reynolds, *Discourses* (above, n. 1), 140.
28. Clark and Bowron, *Pompeo Batoni* (above, n. 7), 41.
29. 'Die Zeichnung ist nicht fehlerhaft, aber es fehlet den Figuren den homerische Geist, ... die Handlung der Figuren ist übertrieben, Andromache ist ausgelassen wie eine Furie, Hector macht einen pas wie ein Schüler von Marcel, dem Lehrer der Mode-Gratie zu Paris, und die Ideen der Köpfe sind unedel' (The drawing is not faulty, but the figures lack the Homeric spirit, the action of the figures is exaggerated, Andromache is as unruly as a Fury, Hector steps out like one of the pupils of Marcel, the Parisian dancing master, and the expressions of the heads lack nobility): Clark and Bowron, *Pompeo Batoni* (above, n. 7), 277, no. 222.
30. Ford and Ingamells, *Dictionary of British and Irish Travellers* (above, n. 6), 817.
31. Ford and Ingamells, *Dictionary of British and Irish Travellers* (above, n. 6), 817.
32. Reynolds, *Discourses* (above, n. 1), 28.
33. Batoni certainly did copies of Raphael (Clark and Bowron, *Pompeo Batoni* (above, n. 7), 24) and had a reputation for conceit; Northcote said in 1778 that 'Pompeo thinks that all that ever has been, is now, or ever shall be, is like dirt in the street before him' (Clark and Bowron, *Pompeo Batoni* (above, n. 7), 18).
34. Reynolds, *Discourses* (above, n. 1), 111–12.
35. Farington diary entry for 28 October 1814, Farington, *Diary* (above, n. 22), XIII, 4,600.
36. Reynolds, *Discourses* (above, n. 1), 249.
37. Reynolds, *Discourses* (above, n. 1), 251.
38. Reynolds, *Discourses* (above, n. 1), 251.
39. L. Cicognara, *Storia della scultura*, 8 vols (Prato, 1823–4), VII, 51: 'laboriosa finitezza olandese'. See Clark and Bowron, *Pompeo Batoni* (above, n. 7), 23.
40. M. Missirini, *Celebrità italiane nell'architettura e pittura* (Florence, 1847), 111: 'forse troppo sulla via della semplice natura'. See Clark and Bowron, *Pompeo Batoni* (above, n. 7), 277.

41. *4th Discourse* of 1771; Reynolds, *Discourses* (above, n. 1), 59.
42. Reynolds, *Discourses* (above, n. 1), 58.
43. S. Gwynn (ed.), *Memorials of an Eighteenth Century Painter (James Northcote)* (London, 1898), 238.
44. Batoni, letter of 21 April 1742 to Lodovico Sardini. See Clark and Bowron, *Pompeo Batoni* (above, n. 7), 35, where another letter from Batoni to Sardini is quoted, dated 23 January 1745: 'a painting that illustrates a story for which all the necessary sketches must be made in advance, and afterwards must be perfected from reality, requires a few months of work'.
45. B.R. Haydon, *The Autobiography and Journals of Benjamin Robert Haydon*, ed. M. Elwin (London, 1950), 227.
46. Farington, *Diary* (above, n. 22), XII, 4274.

Between 'Old Tiber' and 'Envious Thames': the Angelica Kauffman connection

Wendy Wassyng Roworth

Angelica Kauffman, who was neither British nor Italian yet recognized as a member of the British School as well as a prominent artist in Italy, provided a unique link between artists and patrons in London and Rome. She was born in Switzerland, to a Swiss mother and Austrian father, and spent her early years in Como and Milan, growing up speaking fluent Italian as well as German. Her biographer, Giovanni Gherardo De Rossi, asserted that her parentage, as well as her professional status in England notwithstanding, he considered her an 'Italiana pittrice', for it was in Italy that her talent first took root and was cultivated.[1] As a rare successful female artist who did not belong to a particular nationality, especially at a time when the concept of 'nationalism' itself was evolving, Kauffman may be understood best as a truly international artist in that most international of cities, Rome.

She first made her mark in Rome in 1763 as a surprisingly ambitious young woman who aspired to produce history paintings of classical subjects, and by the following year, after returning to Rome from a sojourn in Naples, she painted her first history paintings, including *Penelope Mourning Ulysses*, *Bacchus and Ariadne*, and pendants representing *Chryseis Reunited with her Father Chryse* and *Coriolanus Entreated by His Mother and Wife*, for British patrons.[2] She met many British travellers in Naples, including James Boswell, who was captivated by this talented and clever young woman, and she made portraits of several visitors and residents, including the actor David Garrick, John Byng, the Anglo-Americans Dr John Morgan and Samuel Powel, the British Consul Isaac Jamineau, John Parker of Saltram, and Brownlow, 9th Earl of Exeter.[3] The last two gentlemen would become her most important patrons when she first arrived in England in 1766. She also met the artist-dealers James Byres and Thomas Jenkins, Abbé Peter Grant, and others in the English, Irish and Scots communities in Rome, in addition to tourists passing through the Eternal City. She studied English and by 1764 had become quite proficient.[4]

Her early paintings show the influence of Pompeo Batoni and Anton Raphael Mengs as well as her imitation of seventeenth-century Bolognese painters Guido Reni and Domenichino, whose works were greatly admired by artists of her generation. In addition, Kauffman's early history paintings suggest the direct influence of two British artists in Rome: Gavin Hamilton and Nathaniel Dance. Hamilton, whose sentimental-heroic classical subjects, such as *Brutus Avenging the Death of Lucretia* (1763) painted in Rome for Charles Hope, must have made a strong impression on her, remained a life-long friend and, though she was briefly engaged to marry Dance, the two parted ways either just before or soon after they moved to London in 1766.[5]

Kauffman and the Anglo-American painter Benjamin West also exchanged ideas in the heady atmosphere of the ancient city, and it was these two ambitious young artists who brought what they learned in Italy to London and pioneered the representation of British as well as classical history paintings in England. West, like Dance, never returned to Italy, but Kauffman's long career was divided between the two cities. She spent fifteen years in London as a fashionable society artist and later enjoyed a triumphant return to Rome in 1782, where she lived until her death 25 years later, in 1807.

In London Kauffman was one of several foreign artists invited to become Founding Members of the Royal Academy of Arts in 1768, a group that included Francesco Bartolozzi, Giovanni Battista Cipriani and Francesco Zucarelli.[6] Her future husband, the Venetian painter Antonio Zucchi, came to England at the invitation of Robert and James Adam, and he and his brother, Giuseppe Carlo Zucchi, were among Kauffman's closest friends in London. The Roman architect Joseph (Giuseppe) Bonomi, who also came to work with the Adam brothers, married Angelica's young cousin Rosa Florini in London in 1775, with Angelica, her father Johann Joachim Kauffman, Antonio and Giuseppe Carlo Zucchi as witnesses.[7] By the mid-1770s Kauffman enjoyed a thriving career in London among English and foreign friends, but she never felt at home the way she did in Rome.[8]

By the time she returned to Italy with her father and new husband in 1781 Kauffman had been contemplating a return for at least two or three years. Though she made a good living in London, especially through collaborations with printmakers and publishers such as Bartolozzi, Josiah Boydell, William Wynne Ryland and Thomas Burke, she longed for Rome with its great collections of antiquities and art-works, as well as the prospect of more commissions for large history paintings, including religious subjects for an international Catholic clientele. The hostile climate for Catholics in London, especially at the time of the Gordon riots in 1780, alarmed Kauffman and her elderly father.[9] Moreover, rivalry among portrait-painters in London, increasing xenophobia and competition for advantageous hanging space in the Royal Academy, and the occasionally critical London press, all may have contributed to her desire to leave that city.[10] In spite of her popularity and steady employment, she could not compete for the most profitable commissions with more influential male colleagues, especially Joshua Reynolds and West. Kauffman met West when they were both young foreigners in Florence, but as West gained accolades in London as an innovative painter of contemporary history, and rose to the positions of Royal Painter to King George III and President of the Royal Academy of Arts, Kauffman was not able to achieve fully her high aspiration to produce large-scale history paintings. Even when she was chosen as one of five artists for the aborted commission to paint the interior of the dome of Saint Paul's in 1775, she became the subject of an embarrassing pictorial joke in the form of Nathaniel Hone's satiric painting *The Conjuror*.[11] In contrast, her situation in Rome was very different. As Joseph Forsyth reported after his visit to Italy in 1802, 'This amiable woman is the idol of her invidious profession, the only artist beloved by all the rest'.[12]

After establishing themselves in Rome on the Via Sistina, Kauffman and Zucchi renewed their acquaintance with old friends, including the artist-dealers Jenkins and Hamilton, and cultivated new relationships with Italian and foreign artists. She continued to send art-works to England, and many of her pictures were engraved for the print market, so her reputation and the popularity of her decorative compositions continued to flourish in Britain.[13] Her most reliable patron was George Bowles of Wanstead Grove, who eventually owned about 50 paintings by Kauffman,[14] and she received numerous commissions from British visitors to Rome, including Bowles's nephew, John Rushout, 2nd Baron Northwick, who commissioned a painting of *Ulysses on the Island of Circe with Four of Her Maidens* in 1793.[15] Later the same year Thomas Noel-Hill, 2nd Lord Berwick, sat for his portrait and ordered two large pictures of classical subjects: *Ariadne Abandoned, Discovered by Bacchus* and *Euphrosyne Wounded by Cupid Complaining to Venus* (Plate 21.1).[16]

The author and artist De Rossi, who served as Director of the Portuguese Academy in Rome, composed an epigram inspired by Kauffman's painting of Euphrosyne, one of the Three Graces, that was later published in his *Scherzi poetici e pittorici*, accompanied by an illustration engraved by the Portuguese artist Jose Teixeira Barreto (Fig. 21.1).[17] This scene, as De Rossi's poem explains, depicts Euphrosyne, who has been wounded by Cupid's arrow, imploring the unsympathetic goddess Venus to punish her errant son. The poet addresses the 'Ingegnosa Pittrice' and enquires: 'What mystery is revealed by your pretty picture!'. The answer: 'one who is wounded by Love's arms and seeks Beauty's aid will find new abuses rather than pity'.[18]

As a popular artist in both London and Rome, Kauffman and her work were the subject of other poems that celebrated her virtues and talents, or commemorated important occasions in her life. This profusion of poems is not surprising, as so many of her friends and associates were writers, including the Germans Johann Wolfgang von Goethe and Johann Gottfried Herder, the Danish Frederike Brun, and Italians Vincenzo Monti and the illustrious Arcadian *improvvisatrici* Fortunata Sulgher Fantastici and Teresa Bandettini. A few poems about Kauffman have been discussed by scholars, such as George Keate's *An Epistle to Angelica Kauffman* (see below) and Fantastici's verses in praise of Kauffman that the artist depicted on a scroll in her portrait of her poet friend.[19] Other poems, however, have not been studied or even cited in the Kauffman literature. An examination of some poems on the subject of Kauffman's return to Rome in 1782 reveals, in addition to the individual poets' views of Kauffman as an artist and friend, how her identification with the cities of London and Rome sheds light on aspects of cultural exchange between Britain and Italy.[20]

In 1781 the poet, painter and travel-writer Keate, who was one of Kauffman's closest friends in England, as well as a great admirer of Rome, wrote *An Epistle to Angelica Kauffman* when Kauffman and Antonio Zucchi were about to depart for Italy.[21] In this lengthy appreciation of her talent, painting methods, variety of works from portraits to allegory to history, her career going back to her youthful seeking of 'Italy's soft scenes' under Minerva's guidance, Keate employed personifications of Rome and London's great rivers, the Tiber and Thames, to voice his views, a literary device he first employed in 1771, in *An Address from the Thames*, to celebrate the opening of his friends Robert and James Adam's 'new House in the Adelphi', between the Strand and the Thames embankment. In this poem the Thames, 'stretched on a sedgy couch ... a golden Trident at his side' articulates England's envy of Italy's many artistic splendours, though now, the river declares, with the Adams' new building on his shore, London poses a challenge to the rivers of Rome, Venice and Florence:[22]

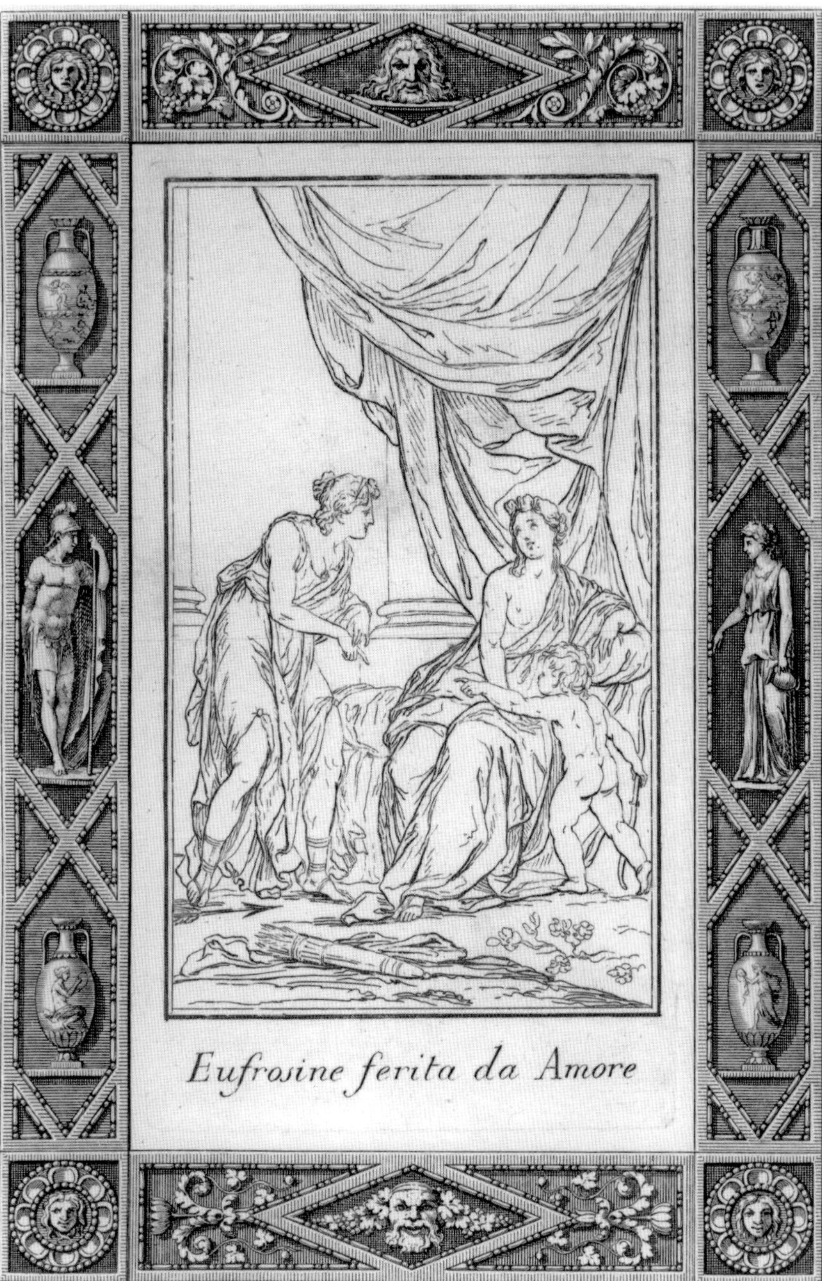

FIG. 21.1. Jose Teixeira Barreto (1763–1810) after Angelica Kauffman (1741–1807), *Euphrosyne Wounded by Cupid Complaining to Venus*. Engraving. From G.G. De Rossi, *Scherzi poetici e pittorici* (Parma, 1795), plate XL. *(Research Library, The Getty Research Institute, Los Angeles, California.)*

Jealous, have I heard too long
Tiber flow in ev'ry Song,
Arno's Torrent, Brenta's Stream
Live each lavish Muse's Theme:
They shall triumph now no more,
Equal Glories grace *my* Shore.

Ten years later Keate again invoked the voices of rivers to lament Kauffman's impending departure from London and to praise her contributions to the arts in England:[23]

All Italy with raptur'd Ears
The Wonders of your Pencil hears,
Rome's seven Hills your Praise resound,
Old Tiber rolls it wide around,
And distant Britain's Sea-girt Coast
Exults such Excellence to boast;
Exults, but sees its Joy o'ercast,
What Triumph ever long could last!
Griev'd, she th'approaching Day deplores,
Destin'd to bear you from her Shores;

To her, so well your Value known,
She sighs to reckon you her own;
Yet go where'er you will, she'll feel
For your fair Fame a Parent's Zeal.

The poet bemoans the impending loss of his friend to 'Old Tiber' and the hills of Rome, but his words also convey Britain's jealous desire to boast of Kauffman's 'excellence' and as a zealous parent to claim her as its own.

Another Kauffman friend, the minister and moralist Reverend James Fordyce, also wrote poems about Angelica. The first, composed in 1780, *On a Picture of Religion by Angelica Kauffman, an Ode*, praised her painting of *Religion* (shown at the Royal Academy in 1780), which she in turn had created from Fordyce's literary description of Religion in his allegorical essay *The Temple of Virtue.*[24] The painting as seen in Bartolozzi's engraving (**Fig. 21.2**) represented, in Fordyce's words, 'Religion ... as a Female Personage of great beauty, with her eyes full of mild devotion, and her right hand raised to Heaven ...'.[25] A few years later, in 1783, Fordyce composed *To Angelica Kauffman at Rome: an Elegy*, a work that has not been cited previously in Kauffman studies. This poem, like Keate's *Epistle*, mourns her move to Rome, though Fordyce's work, with its pious sentiments, focuses more on Kauffman's modesty and proper decorum than the artistic merits extolled by Keate. Nevertheless, Fordyce also expresses Britain's envy of Italy's advantages and contrasts 'fair Italia' with 'Britannia's' lamentable loss:[26]

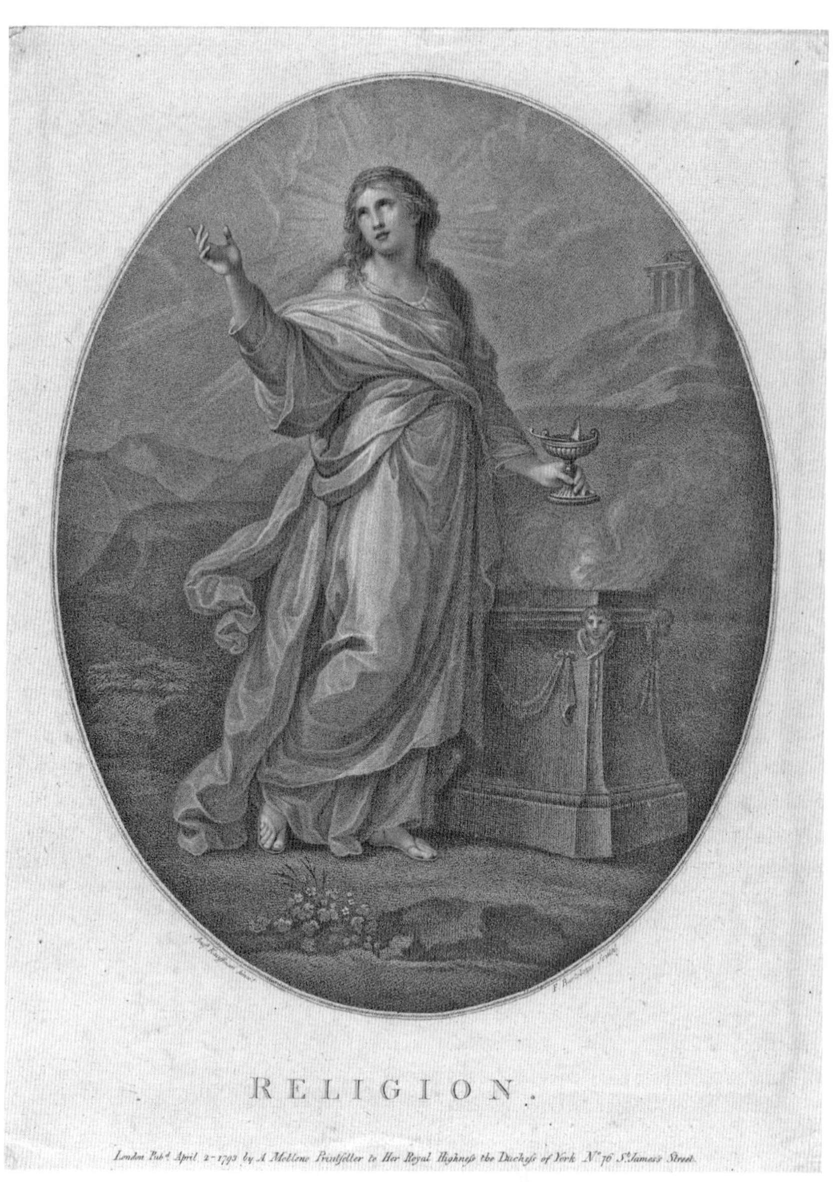

FIG. 21.2. **Francesco Bartolozzi (1727–1815) after Angelica Kauffman (1741–1807), *Religion*, 1793. Stipple engraving. Yale Center for British Art, Paul Mellon Collection B1977.14.19732.** *(Reproduced courtesy of the Yale Center for British Art.)*

Th' Original is vanish'd from our sight!
  I mourn thy absence, as I love thy worth.
I envy fair Italia's happier fate;
  Her sons I envy their more favour'ed taste.
Britannia's Isle thy merits knew too late;
  Blest in thy converse, in thy genius blest! ...
... Angelica, beyond the price of Kings,
  To us is lost, from us for ever gone!

In contrast to her British friends, the Italian poet Ippolito Pindemonte expressed the opposing view of Kauffman's move to Rome. In his 1784 epistle 'Alla Signora Angelica Kauffmann dipintrice celeberrima a Roma', published under the name of Polidete Melpomenio, he celebrated her return from Britain to Italy.[27] The poem describes how Minerva led Angelica to Italy in her early years and now brought her back to the Tiber, the embrace of the Campidoglio and the Vatican's welcome, her eyes filled with new fire at the sight of the statue of Apollo, Raphael's *School of Athens* and other fine sights. Pindemonte employed allegorical imagery very similar to Keate, which suggests he knew *An Epistle to Angelica Kauffman*. The Italian poet took up the metaphor of the Tiber versus the Thames, complaining that 'Tamigi invidioso', Envious Thames, the enemy wave, had stolen her from Rome. How could she have had the heart to change Italy's sky for Britain's fog?:[28]

> ... Donna felice
> I sette colli di lasciar, di gire
> Fin sul Tamigi, e con Britanna nebbia
> Il purpureo mutare Italo cielo?
> Tamigi invidioso, onda nemica,
> Dunque di tue rapine Italia sempre
> Dovrà lagnarsi? ...

The poet added that Italy wept for the loss of other artists and cited three of them in a footnote: 'Signor Locatelli, scultore distinto, Cipriani, pittore de' primi, ed il celebre incisore Signore Bartolozzi, tutti e tre stabiliti in Inghilterra'.[29] Italy's losses were England's gain, but now the poet rejoiced at Angelica's return, paying tribute to her 'Grecian soul within a German breast', and calling her the 'Sappho of Painting' never vanquished by a 'Pindar painter', alluding to Sappho's victory over the Greek poet in public competition, perhaps also an allusion to the female poet Corille Olimpica's triumph over her male rivals when she was crowned poet laureate in 1776 in Rome.[30]

Pindemonte took particular notice of an impressive painting he had recently seen in Kauffman's Roman studio in 1783 (Plate 21.2). This was the large portrait of King Ferdinand and Queen Maria Carolina of Naples with their children, which Kauffman had begun the previous year during a visit to Naples. We know from her letters that she made drawings of the royal family in Naples, but chose to complete the painting in Rome, the city she called 'the Residence of the Arts', rather than remain at the Neapolitan court. Pindemonte's verses exult in her return to Italy, the land dearest to her above all others, and especially to Rome, where with her inventive brush she recreated the Parthenopean divinities and their heavenly children:[31]

> Tornasti; e Roma, la difficil Roma,
> Spiando il dolce tuo sacro ricetto,
> Vede I Partonopèi Numi, e la Diva
> Prole, mercè tuo creator pennello,
> Nascere un' altra volta, e lieta applaude

As Pindemonte suggested, this impressive, complex portrait, which he referred to in a footnote as 'un quadro istoriato', was much admired in Rome. The *Giornale delle Belle Arti* devoted a couple of pages of the 20 March 1784 issue to a description and praise of Kauffman's painting. The *Giornale* article called attention to the picture's unusual setting, which was not inside a chamber or any part of the palace but a 'domestico giardino' left more to the liberty of nature than 'servitude of art', rendering the distant view to the horizon cheerful and bright. The writer described the life-size figures, hunting dogs, beautifully painted draperies, and especially the gentle delineations of the queen — 'conserva ancora scolpiti nell'alma la nostra Roma' — whose face revealed among her graces a simple, contented Mother worthy of the highest admiration.[32] This painting is Kauffman's largest portrait, and, at an impressive size of approximately ten by fourteen feet, has the informal air of an English conversation piece blown up to regal proportions.[33] This appreciation in Rome for what was essentially a British form of family portraiture, albeit on a grander scale than anything Kauffman painted in England, was reinforced a few years later when the same journal published an Italian translation of Sir Joshua Reynolds's Royal Academy *Discourses* over several issues at the end of 1788.[34]

The poems by Pindemonte, Fordyce and Keate demonstrate Kauffman's role as an artist who had connections with both London and Rome, yet did not quite belong to either place. Both cities could boast of her accomplishments and as rivals claim her as their own, though at times her work and success provoked resentment or ridicule, rather than praise. For example, when, after a gap of three years, she sent two paintings from Rome to the annual Royal Academy exhibition in 1785, they were rejected, ostensibly because they were submitted by an engraver and not by the artist herself.[35] Even the following year, when she exhibited three history paintings of ancient Roman subjects — *Cornelia, Mother of the Gracchi Pointing to Her Children as her Treasures*, *Virgil Writing His Own Epitaph at Brundisium*, and *Pliny the Younger with His Mother at Misenum* —, they were subjected to criticism. The exhibition review in the *Morning Chronicle* on 3 May 1786 declared: 'Angelica has lost perhaps something, and has got nothing by her trip to Italy — the Cornelia and the Younger Pliny are neither warm nor delicate ...'. This disparaging view of a painter who had abandoned London in favour of Rome underscores how British admiration for Italian art was tainted by envy, and highlights Angelica Kauffman's unique position as an artist who worked both sides of this cultural exchange.

Similarly, Kauffman could incite the jealousy of local artists in Rome. In 1788 she was one of five artists chosen to make paintings to be reproduced as mosaics for a renewed campaign of decoration under Pope Pius VI in the pilgrimage church of the Santa Casa di Maria, the Holy House of Mary in Loreto, a project completed in 1791. The other artists involved in this commission were Anton von Maron, Cristoforo Unterberger, Antonio Cavallucci and Gaspare Landi, who noted his good fortune as the youngest of the group to have achieved this honour without intrigue and to be among the first artists of Rome.[36] This commission, reminiscent of Kauffman's inclusion along with four male painters for the Saint Paul's commission in London fifteen years earlier, also resulted in an insult, though it was Kauffman herself and not her painting for Loreto of *Saint Joachim, Saint Anna, and the Young Virgin Mary* that was the subject of attack.

Kauffman's biographer, De Rossi, related the circumstances of the Loreto commission and followed his remarks with a curious digression. The Pope, he explained, used to visit artists' studios, and this time he decided to call on Kauffman. However, the cabal of common artists who surrounded the Pope dissuaded him, and, De Rossi added,[37]

> unfortunately, this Pontiff who conceived so many great projects to support the fine arts, almost always gave his confidence to men as weak in their accomplishments as they were clever in deceit, who twisted his ideas to promote their interests; thus fine projects were confounded or spoiled or given as booty to contemptible performers.

Her later English biographer, Frances Gerard, suggested, based on De Rossi's account, that her fellow artists were jealous because she was a foreigner, but since von Maron and Unterberger were also foreigners — assuming there is some truth in this story — it seems more likely that they resented the triumph of a woman who had returned to claim her place in Rome as a well-established artist and could now add the Pope to her long list of powerful patrons.[38]

In 1790, the same year as the Loreto commission, Kauffman produced a painting for her English friend Keate: a scene from his 1773 poem *The Monument in Arcadia, a Dramatic Poem in Two Acts* (Plate 21.3). This work was inspired by Nicolas Poussin's much admired painting *Et in Arcadia Ego*. Keate had never seen this picture of shepherds unexpectedly encountering a tomb in Arcadia, but he had read about it in Abbé du Bos's influential *Critical Reflections on Poetry and Painting*, which praised the painting's beautifully rendered expressions that captured the shepherds' changing emotions as they came upon the startling evidence of death in an ideal place.[39] Keate declared in the introduction to his poem:[40]

> Painting can but tell her Story. — The Pencil, even under the happiest guidance, must be confined to a single action, nor can express more than the present sentiment. — To unveil external appearances, and to paint that previous disposition of the mind which fixes them, and which can magnify familiar events into effects of moment, is an elder Sister's province, and the peculiar property of the Muse.

Kauffman rose to the challenge by rendering the poet's words back into pictorial form. Coincidentally, the first subject picture she sent from Rome to the Society of Artists exhibition in London in 1766 also represented *A Shepherd and Shepherdess in Arcadia, Moralising at the Side of a Sepulchre, whilst Others are Dancing at a Distance*.[41] Her later version represents a more complex composition based on Keate's poetic drama. In a woodland setting an elderly bearded man, the rich shepherd Dorastus, raises his face to heaven as he embraces his long-lost daughter, Euphemia, who gazes up at him with wonder and affection. This scene is witnessed by two men on the left, the Arcadian shepherd Musidorus and Euphemia's lover, the Spartan Lysander, who, like his fiancée, is crowned with flowers. Her friend Delia, standing just behind the father and daughter, expresses her delighted surprise at their reunion. In the background Musidorus's daughters, Daphne and Laura, observe the scene beside a large monument that had been built to commemorate Euphemia. This monument, topped by a statue of a reclining nymph and garlanded with flowers, bears the inscription: ET IN ARCADI(A) EGO.

Kauffman represented the climactic moment when Dorastus realizes the young woman before him is the daughter he believed had died in infancy. She had been abducted as an infant by Spartans and raised in their land, but she returned to Arcadia as a young woman to marry her Spartan lover in fulfilment of her mother's dying wish. After the tearful reunion the play ends with a joyous celebration of the marriage. Kauffman rendered the poet's words into a picture, closely following his language in her portrayal of the characters' appearance, poses and facial expressions to capture the subtle transitions of emotional changes. The challenge for painters, as Abbé du Bos and Keate stated, inspired Kauffman's attempt to portray grief becoming joy, surprise to growing awareness, and love's triumph over death in an idyllic Arcadian landscape.

This brings us full circle through Keate's poetry and Kauffman's painting to consider her role linking British and Italian artists and patrons between Old Tiber and Envious Thames. She owed her early success to contacts with British artists and clients in Rome who helped launch her career and encouraged her move to London. Later, as a mature and highly regarded member of both the Accademia di San Luca and the Royal Academy of Arts, she served as a model and perhaps a spur to artists of a younger generation in Rome, while she continued to receive commissions from English clients. Kauffman, like Keate's Euphemia torn between two nations — Arcadia and Sparta, Italy and Britain —, and like her romantic namesake in Ariosto's *Orlando Furioso*, was the perfect poetic heroine, an exotic foreigner who stirred both jealousy and desire. As Keate addressed the artist in his *Epistle*:[42]

> Yes, my Angelica, to you
> This I devote, a Tribute due;
> Who can misplac'd the Off'ring deem
> To Her who hath inspir'd the Theme?
> Justly to you it doth belong,
> Worthy of ev'ry Poet's Song!—

Notes

1. G.G. De Rossi, *Vita di Angelica Kauffmann* (Florence, 1810), 3. The artist's name is spelled differently depending on the language of authors and publications. She always signed her name 'Angelica Kauffman', the form used in this essay.
2. See W.W. Roworth (ed.), *Angelica Kauffman: a Continental Artist in Georgian England* (Brighton/London, 1992), 24–37; B. Baumgärtel (ed.), *Angelika Kauffmann, Retrospektive* (Düsseldorf, 1998), 134–9; O. Sandner (ed.), *Angelica Kauffmann e Roma* (Rome, 1998), 12–14.
3. W.W. Roworth, 'Angelika Kauffmann e gli artisti inglesi a Roma', in Sandner, *Angelica Kauffmann e Roma* (above, n. 2), 49–55; B. Allen, 'Die Grand Tour der Briten, Künstler und Reisende in Rom in der Mitte des 18. Jahrhunderts', in Baumgärtel, *Angelika Kauffmann, Retrospektive* (above, n. 2), 47–51.
4. Letter from Johann Joachim Winckelmann to Johann Francke, 11 August 1764, cited in E. Thurnher (ed.), *Angelika Kauffmann und die Deutsche Dichtung* (*Vorarlberger Schrifttum* 10) (Bregenz, n.d.), 78; Baumgärtel, *Angelika Kauffmann, Retrospektive* (above, n. 2), 120.
5. On Hamilton's painting (Yale Center for British Art, New Haven), see D. Macmillan, 'Woman as hero: Gavin Hamilton's radical alternative', in G. Perry and M. Rossington (eds), *Femininity and Masculinity in Eighteenth-century Art and Culture* (Manchester, 1994), 78–98. For Kauffman's relationship with Dance in Rome and London, see W.W. Roworth, 'Angelica in love: gossip, rumour, romance, and scandal', in T.G. Natter (ed.), *Angelica Kauffman, a Woman of Immense Talent* (Bregenz, 2007), 45–7.
6. S. West, 'Xenophobia and xenomania: Italians and the English Royal Academy', in S. West (ed.), *Italian Culture in Northern Europe in the Eighteenth Century* (Cambridge, 1999), 116–39.
7. Westminster Diocesan Archives, London, *Registrum Matrimoniale, Protocollum Matrimoniorum, Capella Imperialis, ab anno Domini 1765*, p. 5: 13 July 1775.
8. W.W. Roworth, ''The residence of the arts': Angelica Kauffman's place in Rome', in P. Findlen, W.W. Roworth and C. Sama (eds), *Italy's Eighteenth Century: Gender and Culture in the Age of the Grand Tour* (Stanford, 2009), 151–71.
9. M. Gandy, 'Catholics in Westminster. The return of papists of 1767', *Westminster History Review* 2 (1998), 19–22; S. Burney, 'Account of the Gordon riots in her letter-journal, 8 June 1780', London, British Library, Egerton MS 3691, fol. 132.
10. M. Hallett, ''The business of criticism': the press and the Royal Academy Exhibition in eighteenth-century London', in D. Solkin (ed.), *Art on the Line. The Royal Academy Exhibitions at Somerset House 1780–1836* (New Haven/London, 2001), 65–76; West, 'Xenophobia' (above, n. 6), 116–39.
11. M. Butlin, 'An eighteenth-century art scandal: Nathaniel Hone's 'The Conjuror'', *Connoisseur* 174 (1970), 82–99.

12. J. Forsyth, *Remarks on Antiquities, Arts, and Letters during an Excursion in Italy, in the Years 1802 and 1803*, ed. K. Crook (Newark/Delaware/London, 2001), 134.
13. D. Alexander, 'Kauffman and the print market in eighteenth-century England', in Roworth, *Angelica Kauffman: a Continental Artist* (above, n. 2), 141–78.
14. W.H. Bowles, *Records of the Bowles Family* (London, 1918).
15. C. Knight (ed.), *La 'Memoria delle piture' di Angelica Kauffman* (Rome, 1998), 64–5. Kauffman's *Memorandum of Paintings* is in the Royal Academy of Arts, London; O. Bradbury and N. Penny, 'The picture collecting of Lord Northwick: part I', *The Burlington Magazine* 144 (2002), 485–96.
16. Knight, *La 'Memoria delle piture'* (above, n. 15), 67; Roworth, *Angelica Kauffman: a Continental Artist* (above, n. 2), 76–7, 93–4. The story of the wounded Euphrosyne was taken from P. Metastasio, 'Le grazie vendicate' (1735), in B. Brunelli (ed.), *Tutte le opere di Pietro Metastasio* (Milan, 1954), II, *Opere varie*, 221.
17. G.G. De Rossi, *Scherzi poetici e pittorici* (Parma, 1795), XL, 67–9, illus. 68.
18. 'Ingegnosa Pittrice / La tua vezzosa tela / Quale arcano mi svela! / Chi dall' armi d'Amor reso è infelice, / Se folle chiede aita alla beltà, / Trova insulti novelli, e non pietà.'
19. On Fantastici's portrait (Florence, Uffizi), see A. Rosenthal, *Angelica Kauffman, Art and Sensibility* (New Haven, 2006), 174–6; Baumgärtel, *Angelika Kauffmann, Retrospektive* (above, n. 2), 259–60.
20. Other poems on Kauffman not discussed in this essay include a sheet of anonymous verses on her paintings of *Praxiteles Presenting His Statue of Cupid to Phryne* (Rhode Island School of Design Museum of Art, Providence) and *Phryne Seducing the Philosopher Xenocrates* (Private Collection), both painted 1794 (Poem in an anonymous manuscript, Getty Research Institute, Special Collections, 900170); L. Acquisti, *Per il pranzo dato dalla celebre signora Angelica Kaufman agli artisti amici* (1803); *Epigrammi all Egregia Signora Angelica Kauffman celebre pittrice* (Parma, 1803); and the Russian poet G. Romanovich Derzhavin's ode 'To Angelica Kauffman', 1795. I am grateful to Brian Allen for calling my attention to Derzhavin's poem.
21. G. Keate, *An Epistle to Angelica Kauffman* (London, 1781).
22. G. Keate, *An Address from the Thames* (London, 1771) (vv. 35–40). See C. Wainwright, 'The 'distressed poet' and his architect: George Keate and Robert Adam', *Apollo* 143 (1996), 39–44. Keate's poetic imagery may have inspired James Barry's allegorical painting *Commerce or the Triumph of the Thames* for the Society of Arts, 1777–84. On Barry, see W.L. Pressley, *The Life and Art of James Barry* (New Haven/London, 1981), 101–5, 233.
23. Keate, *Epistle* (above, n. 21), vv. 157–70.
24. J. Fordyce DD, *Poems* (London, 1786), 119–22; J. Fordyce, *The Temple of Virtue, a Dream*, second edition (London, 1775).
25. Fordyce, *Poems* (above, n. 24), 119; F. Bartolozzi after Angelica Kauffman, *Religion*, stipple engraving, published by A. Torre, 1 October 1783. This print was reissued by print-seller A. Molteno in 1793.
26. Fordyce, *Poems* (above, n. 24), 123–4.
27. P. Pindemonte, 'Alla Signora Angelica Kauffmann dipintrice celeberrima a Roma', in *Versi di Polidete Melpomenio* (Bassano, 1784), 99–105.
28. Pindemonte, *Versi* (above, n. 27), 103.
29. Pindemonte, *Versi* (above, n. 27), 104. These were the painter Giovanni Battista Cipriani, engraver Francesco Bartolozzi, and sculptor Giovanni Locatelli, all Italians who settled and worked in England.
30. Pindemonte, *Versi* (above, n. 27), 99: 'Così parlato avria talun, ma forse / Non saprebb' ei, come d'un suol beato, / E d'un beato ciel d'uopo non s'aggia / Talor; come talor chiudasi ancora / In Germanico petto un' alma Greca'; 100: 'Ma sa pur, che non mai sorse la Saffo / De la Pitura, e che per man di donna / Un Pindaro pittor non mai fu vinto'. On Olimpica, see P. Giuli, "Monsters of talent': fame and reputation of women improvisers in Arcadia', in Findlen, Roworth and Sama (eds), *Italy's Eighteenth Century* (above, n. 8), 303–30.
31. Pindemonte, *Versi* (above, n. 27), 103.
32. *Giornale delle Belle Arti*, no. 12 (20 March 1784), 89–90: 'traspira nel volto fra le sue grazie il Materno contento e con semplice, ma degna positura esige la prima considerazione degli ammiratori'.
33. Naples, Museo Nazionale di Capodimonte, 1782–4. Oil on canvas, 310 × 426 cm. This work was described in Kauffman's *Memoria delle piture* as life-size figures in 'un Giardino Boscareccio ... Tutta la Realle Famiglia in abito familiare e gracioso che rapresenta una specie di scena Rurale'. Sent to Naples on 24 March 1784; Knight, *La 'Memoria delle piture'* (above, n. 15), 23–4.
34. *Giornale delle Belle Arti*, no. 45 (8 November 1788) through to no. 50 (13 December 1788). Kauffman's only English works that come near in size are her portraits of British nobility: the King's sister *Augusta, the Duchess of Brunswick with Her Infant Son* painted for the Princess of Wales in 1767 (Royal Collection, 270 × 187 cm) and her portrait painted in Ireland in 1771 of *Henry Loftus, Earl of Ely*, with his wife the Countess and their two nieces (Dublin, National Gallery of Ireland, 258 × 287 cm).
35. W.T. Whitley, *Artists and Their Friends in England, 1700–1799* II (New York/London, 1928), 38; Alexander, 'Kauffman and the print market' (above, n. 13), 176.
36. Letter from Landi in Rome to Abate Gianpaolo Maggi in Piacenza, 4 June 1788 (Getty Research Institute, Santa Monica). Kauffman noted the completion of her painting in January 1791. Knight, *La 'Memoria delle piture'* (above, n. 15), 53–4.
37. De Rossi, *Vita* (above, n. 1), 73–4 (author's translation).
38. F. Gerard, *Angelica Kauffmann, a Biography* (London, 1893), 203–4.

39. G. Keate, *The Monument in Arcadia: a Dramatic Poem in Two Acts* (London, 1773); *Réflexions critiques sur la pöesie et sur la peinture, par M. l'Abbé Du Bos*, new edition (Dresden, 1760); R. Verdi, 'On the critical fortunes — and misfortunes — of Poussin's 'Arcadia'', *The Burlington Magazine* 121 (1979), 94–107.
40. *The Poetical Works of George Keate, Esq.* II (London, 1781), 197.
41. This painting is lost.
42. Keate, *Epistle* (above, n. 21), vv. 63–8.

Fuseli's phallus: art and erotic imagination in eighteenth-century Rome

Kevin Salatino

No century has been more explicit than the eighteenth in associating eroticism with travel.[1]

I do assure you the climate of Italy affects me much. It inflamed my hot desires . . .[2]

The degree to which Italy's classical past 'eroticized' the art of the eighteenth century has been, I think, explored insufficiently. Certainly, the existence of ancient erotica (much of it discovered in the excavations at Pompeii and Herculaneum), while no doubt shocking to many Grand Tourists, upsetting their received notions of antiquity, had a liberating effect on others — artists in particular. One has only to realize that the English sculptor, Joseph Nollekens, resident in Italy from 1761 to 1770, copied from memory (as he proudly noted on the base of his sculpture) the infamous *Pan and Goat* group (Figs 22.1 and 22.2), unearthed at Herculaneum in 1752, to understand the galvanizing effect such works had on adaptable, creative and, not infrequently, mercenary minds.[3]

But the remains of the ancient world were not the only source of inspiration to foreign artists, for whom Italy was an essential part of their education, both aesthetic and sentimental. Nollekens also owned, while living in Rome, a copy of the outlawed Renaissance book *I modi*, or *The Sixteen Pleasures*, published in 1523, with pornographic engravings by Marcantonio Raimondi (after drawings by Giulio Romano), accompanied by equally explicit verses by Pietro Aretino. Immensely rare even in the eighteenth century (Pope Clement VII allegedly ordered the prints and the copper-plates destroyed shortly after the book appeared), not one copy of *I modi* has survived into our century.[4]

The modern art historian cannot but despair over the sad story of Nollekens (having long since returned to England) and his priest confessor who, discovering the artist perusing the illicit volume, ordered its destruction, a rash act Nollekens immediately regretted. When asked by his friends how he could have done such a thing, he replied "the priest made me do it,' and he was now and then seen to shed tears for what he called his folly'.[5]

What is clear is that *I modi*, or individual prints from it, were passed from artist to artist in Grand Tour Rome, especially within the circle of the Swiss-English artist Henry Fuseli, who lived and worked there from 1770 to 1778. Already predisposed to rejecting societal conventions, the twin authorities of antiquity and the Renaissance gave Fuseli and his 'entourage' the weapons with which to launch this assault. That the visual erotica they produced led to a relatively clandestine existence does not diminish either the erotica's potency or its radicalism.[6]

The impact of *I modi* was immediate and overt. Fuseli's closest friend in Rome, the brilliant, eccentric Swede, Johann Tobias Sergel, freely adapted, for example, *I modi*'s Posture 18 in an ink sketch of creative copulation, the original (lost) source for which can be identified in one of the nineteenth-century copy drawings that constitute one of our only, though highly compromised, surviving records of the book.[7] The sinuous line of Sergel's masterful sketch — which replaces the source print's human male with a satyr, thus transferring the *mise en scène* more effectively to the realm of myth — participates somatically in the very act it depicts, the satyr's forward thrust enacted by the repetition of heavy pen strokes used to define his contours.

Another member of Fuseli's Roman circle, the Danish painter Nicolai Abildgaard, copied Posture 15, in which a young couple make love in a seated position. The shadow image incised into the paper on the right side of Abildgaard's sheet is a reverse copy (perhaps even a tracing) of yet another posture (no. 9), the so-called 'wheelbarrow' position.

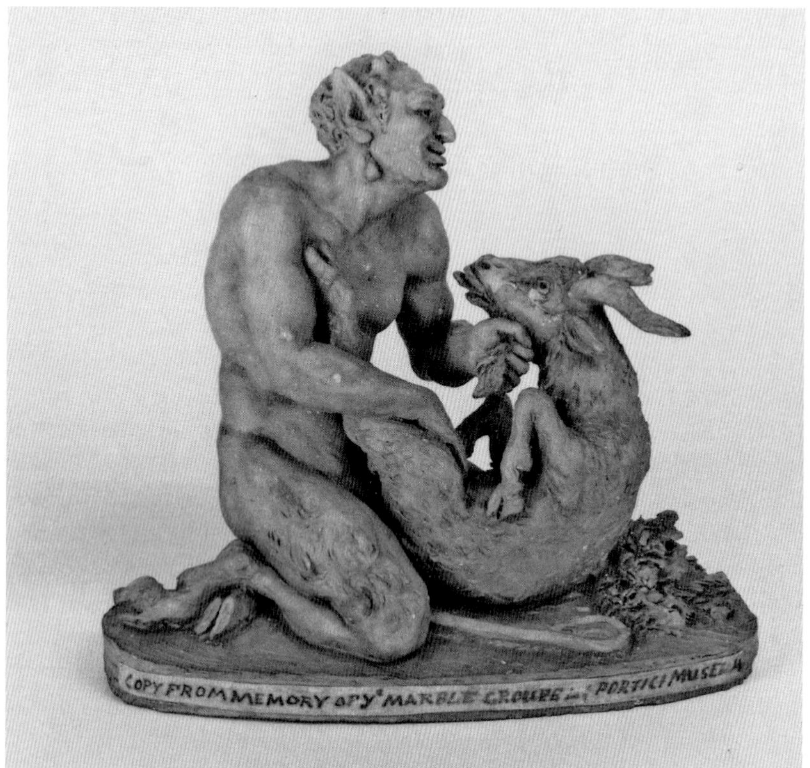

FIG. 22.1. Attributed to Joseph Nollekens (1737–1823), *Pan and Goat*. Terracotta. London, British Museum. *(Photo: © The Trustees of the British Museum.)*

Fuseli himself used *I modi*'s Posture 13 as the source for an exuberant ink and wash sketch of a pair of lovers coupling on a cloth-draped altar (Fig. 22.3), one of a remarkable group of erotic drawings the artist made during his eight years in Rome. Always creative in his borrowings, Fuseli has his male lover grasp — for support and perhaps inspiration — the enormous erect phallus of a leering herm. That the artist has transformed the original print's bed into an altar of Priapus underscores a trope common to his circle — the props of antiquity utilized as a pretext for libertinage.

In two other pen and ink drawings by Fuseli (one depicting exhausted post-orgiastic revellers, another, two 'courtesans' pleasuring a man; Fig. 22.4), and in several more discussed below, sexual excess becomes for the artist a form of liberation (from the conventions of polite society, for example), as well as an expression of his adherence to a philosophy of antinomianism, the radical view that a person is not bound by moral law.[8] At the same time, the drawings serve as sites of male/female conflict, of female domination and male submission. The worm's eye perspective that Fuseli employs in both sketches (that is, the foreshortening of the figures from ground level), is a typical Fuselian device, to which he ascribed tremendous importance as a recipe for 'Grandeur' and as a means of most effectively establishing the Sublime.[9] Indeed, these drawings are perhaps the earliest examples in art of what might be called the 'erotic sublime'.

In the sketch of a woman stimulating an ithyphallic man (Fig. 22.4), the latter's legs are forced into a spread-eagle position and his ankles bound, as are, presumably, his arms, which have been pulled tautly behind him. A second woman (as we shall see, the sexual threesome is a Fuselian commonplace) supports the supine male from behind, holding his barely visible head in her arms as she simultaneously tweaks his nipple and passionately kisses him. Aggressively objectifying the immobilized male-as-object, this ritual of sado-masochism positions him as passive sexual receptor.

The artist's lively rendering of the depleted participants of an orgy (Schiff no. 544[10] — as with Fig. 22.4, it appears to have been captured *in situ*) contains an implicit suggestion of male-on-male sex, particularly since the head of a sleeping male lies within inches of the still-erect phallus of the central reclining figure, whose legs are splayed open as if to emphasize the dominance of his tumescent member. Nor are the genders of the three other participants identified, a suggestive ambiguity that lends credence to a homophilac interpretation. The compositional similarities between these two scenes are noteworthy. In both, the central figure of a formal triad is a supine, aroused male observed in worm's eye perspective; even the disembodied doodle of a man's head appears in relatively the same position in each.

While the male is certainly pleasured in these orgiastic vignettes, as he is in two more of Fuseli's so-called 'symplegmas' (a Greek word that Fuseli himself used, meaning two or more entangled bodies) (Fig. 22.5),[11] there is, at the same time, an atmosphere of menace, an implicit and frequently explicit sado-masochism, the lurking fear of castration. In one of these (Fig. 22.5), the atmosphere of sado-masochism reaches a kind of fever pitch: a naked youth in obvious pain watches as a clothed woman, kneeling before him, inserts a key into a padlock attached to a ring in his foreskin, an act allegedly inspired by ancient Roman fibulation rites.[12] The scene is watched with insouciant

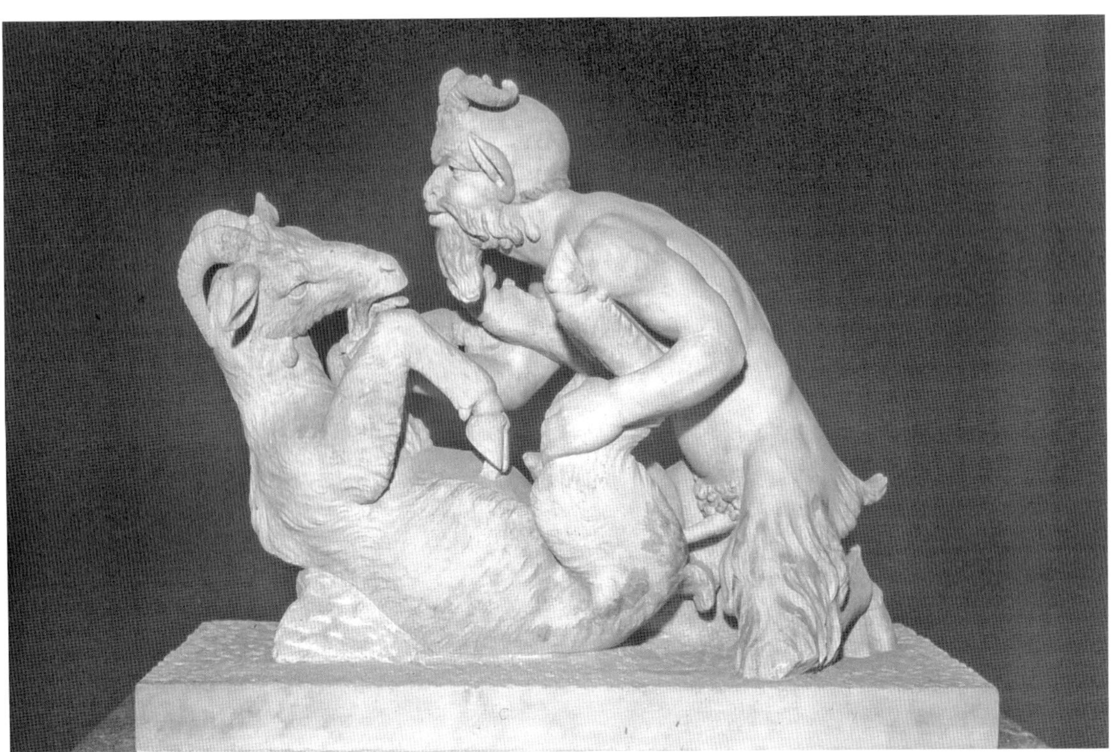

FIG. 22.2. Roman copy of a Greek original, *Pan and Goat*, second century BCE. Marble, height 47 × width 49 cm. Naples, Museo Archeologico Nazionale, Gabinetto Segreto. *(Reproduced courtesy of the Ministero per i Beni e le Attività Culturali, Soprintendenza Speciale per i Beni Archeologici di Napoli e Pompei.)*

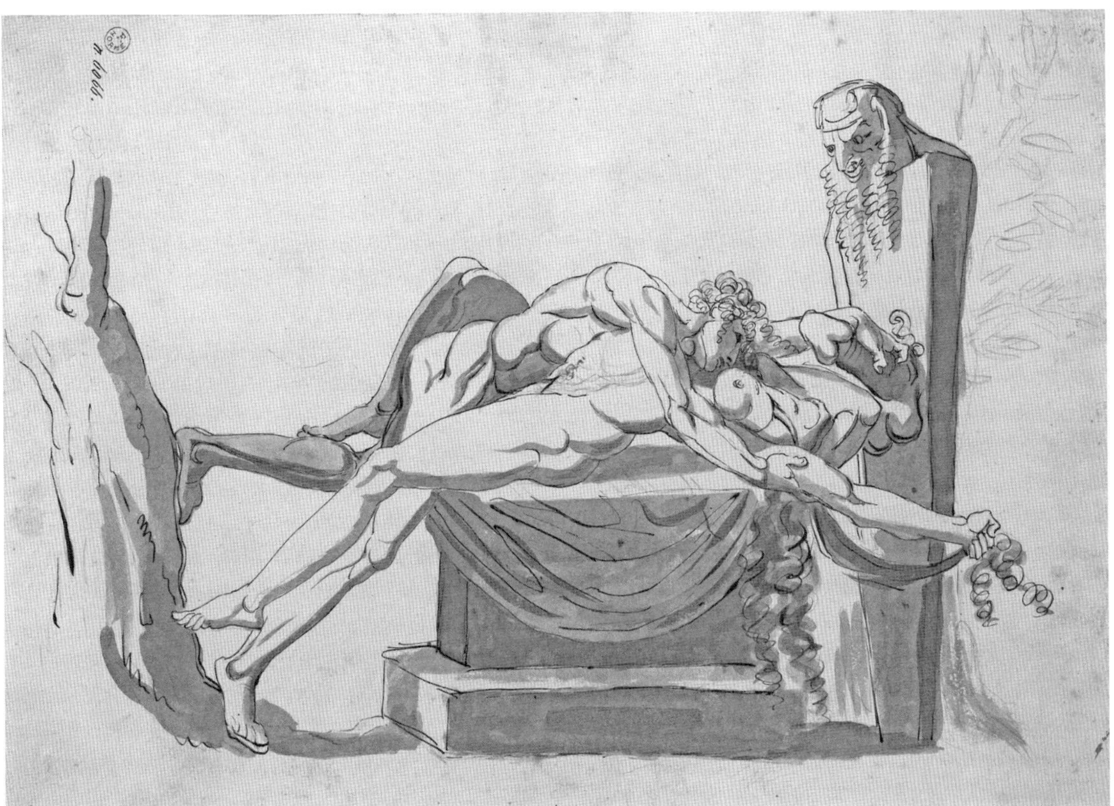

FIG. 22.3. Henry Fuseli (1741–1825), *Couple Copulating on an Altar of Priapus*, c. 1770–8. Pen and ink and wash over graphite, 26.1 × 37.6 cm. Florence, Museo Horne, inv. no. 6066. *(Photo: Fondazione Horne/Antonio Quattrone.)*

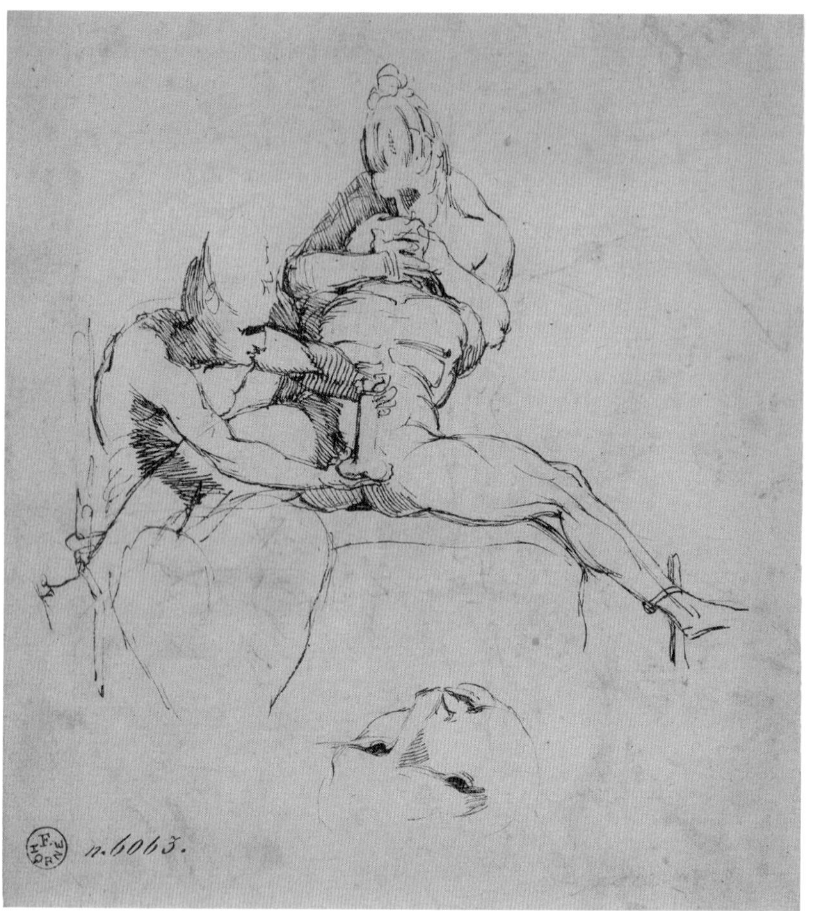

FIG. 22.4. Henry Fuseli (1741–1825), *Erotic Scene with Two Women and an Ithyphallic Man*, c. 1770–8. Pen and ink, 18.6 × 17 cm. Florence, Museo Horne, inv. no. 6063. *(Photo: Fondazione Horne/Antonio Quattrone.)*

sexual equanimity by a naked odalisque deployed languorously across a bed.

Greek inscriptions frequently appear on these drawings, added by Fuseli both as piquant commentary on their contents and to demonstrate his learning. They serve also to place these events in a pre-, post- or extra-Christian world beyond the strictures of a puritanical Church. The Greek word 'Perilambane' in the lower left of another of Fuseli's symplegmas (Schiff no. 541) means, roughly, 'grab it and stick it in'. (In this drawing, the sexual symbolism of the painting above the bed depicting Saint George slaying the dragon — the saint plunging his lance into the beast's gaping mouth — is too obvious to belabour, although, in its subversion of traditional Christian iconography, the scene's inclusion is decidedly anti-clerical.) The Greek word 'Klinopale' (here transliterated), which appears in the 'fibulation' symplegma (Fig. 22.5), may be translated as 'bed-wrestling', while in another of these impressive watercolours (Schiff no. 540), a symplegma in which the impending act of fellatio is paramount, a background pedestal supporting an outsize sculpture of an erect phallus bears the apposite phrase in Greek: 'grow large, male progenitor'.[13]

At this point, a clear distinction should be made between the fully-realized, finished ink and wash symplegmas and Fuseli's erotic sketches, or *pensées*. The latter (for example, Fig. 22.4) are quickly observed and incomplete, their pen strokes applied swiftly and calligraphically, doodles often meandering across the sheet. They are undeveloped studies, the stuff of sketch-books, ideas made manifest.[14] The finished drawings (for example, Fig. 22.5), on the other hand, are fully resolved, large in format, and as complete and compositionally complex as any of the 'public' drawings Fuseli executed in Rome, drawings upon which his reputation was made almost immediately. We must assume, then, that Fuseli saw the symplegmas as falling within the same class of production (if not marketing) as the less incendiary drawings that secured his fame.

Excepting their subject-matter, the symplegmas are topologically consistent with such iconic (and inoffensive) works as *The Witches Show Macbeth Banquo's Descendants*, or *Satan Starts from the Touch of Ithuriel's Lance*. In fact, both of these genera of drawings, non-erotic *and* erotic, share several analogous features: they are comparable in size and format; rendered in pen and ink and wash; focused upon a handful of central actors engaged in exaggerated theatrical gestures on a foreground stage; characterized by an overly dramatic contrast of light and dark; and virtually monochromatic (which has the effect of emphasizing action over setting). To Fuseli, the 'sublimity' of these drawings, whether erotic or chaste, is all of a piece — only the subject-matter (Shakespeare and Milton versus the erotic and ecstatic) differs. Indeed, a certain ecstasy of emotion, quintessentially Fuselian, may be their primary link.[15]

The *femmes fatales* who dominate Fuseli's erotic drawings, with their fetishized hair, their complete equanimity, their masterful control, are classic dominatrixes. Dominatrixes, in fact, form an essential component, indeed a leitmotiv, of Fuseli's aesthetic vocabulary from *The Henpecked Husband* (inscribed

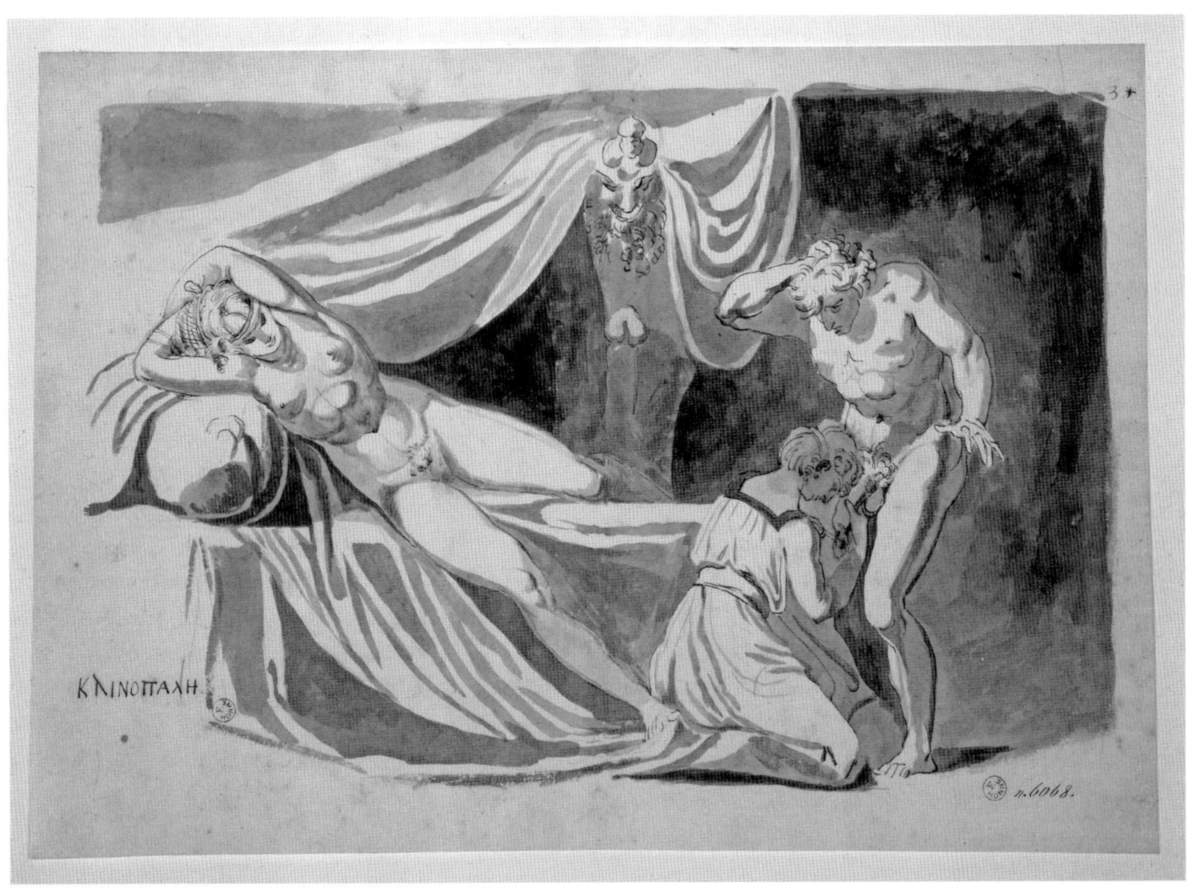

FIG. 22.5. Henry Fuseli (1741–1825), *Symplegma with a Man and Two Women*, c. 1770–2. Pen and ink and brown and grey wash, 29.3 × 42 cm. Florence, Museo Horne, inv. no. 6068. *(Photo: Fondazione Horne/Antonio Quattrone.)*

'you fool, your mare rides you', a precocious drawing he made at the age of sixteen, clearly referencing Aristotle and Phyllis), to the wedding-night scene from the Nibelungenlied, *Brunhild Watching Gunther Suspended from the Ceiling* (Schiff no. 1381), produced half a century later — these two works effectively framing, parentheses-like, a lifelong progression of fantasies of male submission to the emasculating power of viragos.

In one of the most extraordinary of Fuseli's dominatrix drawings from his Roman period (Schiff no. 547; an appropriate title for which might be 'The Great Dominatrix'), an aroused, submissive male kneels, naked — his hands apparently bound — at the feet of a fully-clothed woman who casually pulls back his head, one long-nailed finger placed threateningly against his throat, her only missing accoutrement a whip. The implicit violence of the drawing's content extends to the sheet itself. Torn into five pieces, it was, nevertheless, preserved and reconstructed. That Fuseli's erotic drawings have survived at all is nothing short of miraculous, especially when we consider that, in the words of the artist's early biographer, Allan Cunningham, '[f]ire... fell amongst most of these when he died — nor do I blame the hand of the widow who kindled it'.[16]

The most memorable drawing in the Rome group, however, the image that most explicitly defies conventional behaviour, dramatically realizing the sexual role reversal found only implicitly in the other drawings (with the exception, perhaps, of 'The Great Dominatrix'), may, in fact, be more remarkable than it seems (Fig. 22.6). Because a section of its right side has been torn off (like the previous drawing, it too was vandalized, though, oddly, not destroyed), we cannot know for certain if the passive partner being sodomized by a woman with a strap-on dildo is another woman or, in fact, a man.

This drawing demands close analysis. Several of Fuseli's interests, one might say obsessions, converge in it, not least among them the power struggle — the Fuselian dialectic between dominance and submission — that defines nearly all his work. That dialectic is characterized in much of Fuseli's *oeuvre* by *male*

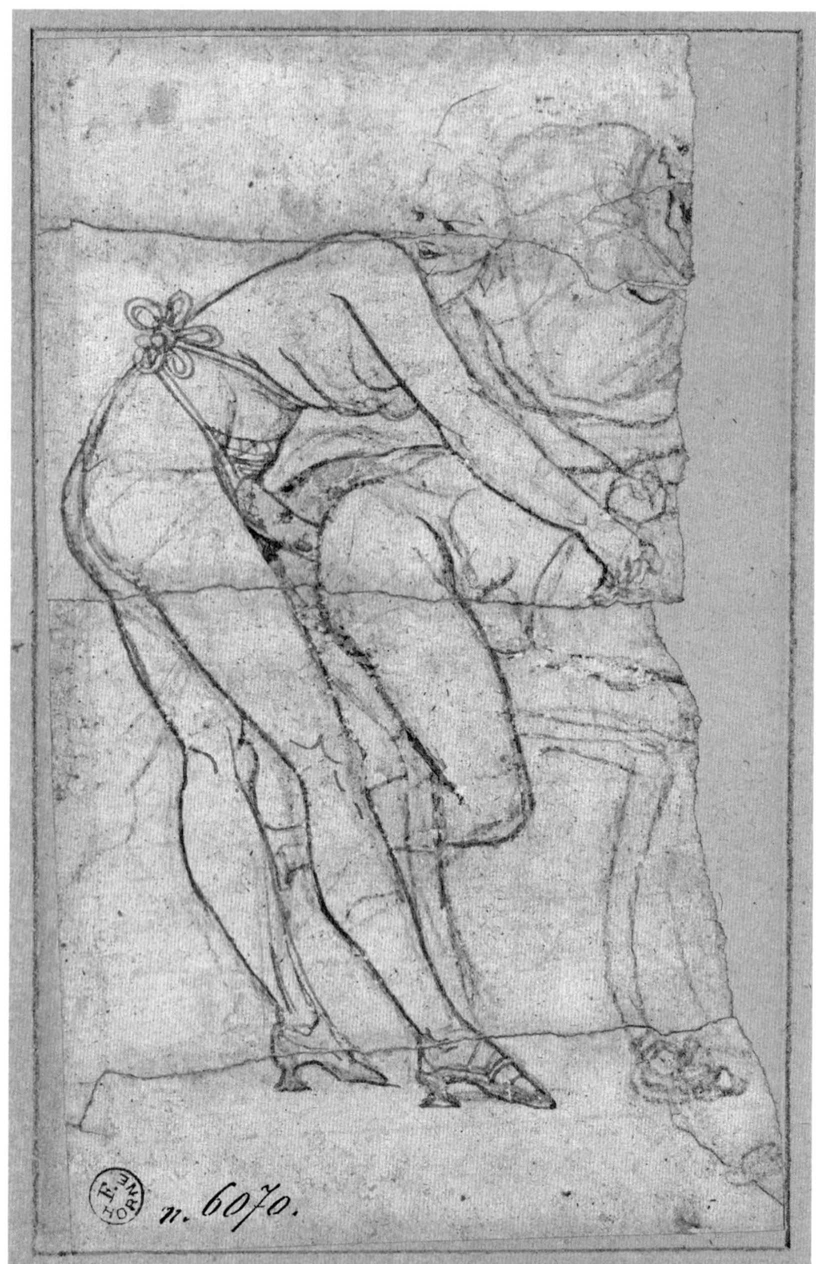

FIG. 22.6. Henry Fuseli (1741–1825), *Dominatrix with Strap-on Dildo*, c. 1770–8. Pen and ink over graphite, 18.7 × 11.5 cm. Florence, Museo Horne, inv. no. 6070. *(Photo: Fondazione Horne/Antonio Quattrone.)*

dominance and *female* submission, as, for example, in his late painting, *Jealousy* (1819–25; Schiff no. 1501), although even here the issue is problematized by the artist. For one thing, in *Jealousy* the male aggressor's active role is compromised, if not appropriated, by the spurned lover of whose presence he is unaware, occupied as he is. She, much more than her adulterous lover, dominates this scene of Grand Guignol. The murderous shears she wields, raised for the death blow, carry within them the implicit potential of the penetrating phallus, thus granting *her*, rather than her unfaithful lover, the active 'masculine' role, and him the passive 'feminine' one, even as he dominates his submissive prey. Their postures recall one of Fuseli's well-known aphorisms (no. 194): 'The forms of virtue are erect, the forms of pleasure undulate', suggesting that Fuseli's sympathies lie not with the undulating couple, but with the shears![17]

Nevertheless, what is covert in *Jealousy* is made overt in the dildoed dominatrix drawing. That Fuseli should devote such loving attention to the extravagantly tied bow that secures the device is itself worthy of mention, a transference of attention from her active role as penetrator to her more conventionally passive role as object of male, and female, gaze — as object, that is, of adornment. As David Weinglass has observed,[18] this establishes her from the outset (paraphrasing Roland Barthes) as an 'object in disguise', whose props of adornment (and these include her fetishized hair and heels — hair, especially, being a classic Fuselian signifier, as can be seen in a plethora of images of his much younger wife, Sophia Rawlins) function as a form of exorcism of female power. That she is, in fact, the object of spectatorial attention is made explicit by her own backward glance, notwithstanding its haughtiness, its barely concealed contempt for an unseen audience that includes, by extension, the viewer. In no other of Fuseli's erotic drawings do his subjects acknowledge, as here, a presence outside their notional world.

This sundering of fictional and actual space, this confusion of viewer and viewed, declares the drawing's particular significance. Its contested space — a site both active and passive — upsets a simple psychosexual interpretation of the subject, and brings to mind the following declaration by Fuseli: 'He who means to remain ignorant of the enormities of human debasement must remain ignorant of literature, history, and poetry… To point out these excrescences is to mark the rocks and whirlpools that endanger life...'[19] — a statement itself brimming with ambiguity.

It goes without saying that Fuseli's relationship with women was complex. And while it may be unsatisfactory to assert simply that Fuseli was a misogynist, he certainly was. In one of his better-known aphorisms (no. 226) he wrote, revealingly: '... in an age of luxury woman aspires to the functions of man, and man slides into the offices of woman. The epoch of eunuchs was ever the epoch of viragoes'.

In his post-Roman period watercolour, *The Debutante* (1807) (Plate 22.1), Fuseli simultaneously ridicules woman through the grotesque caricaturing of the accompanying duennas, and denounces woman's fate, enslaved as she is both by her own sex and by the conventions of a hypocritical society. Placed in a niche like a sculpture, leashed like a dog, she is good for little else but adornment, an act in which she herself engages via her embroidery — becoming thus an adorning adornment.

Benjamin Haydon — painter, diarist and former Fuseli student — wrote this memorable description of Fuseli's women (and men), a passage that may tell us as much, or more, about contemporary attitudes toward Fuseli, or about Haydon himself, than about the objects of his spleen:

> His women are all whores, and men all banditti. They are whores not from a love of pleasure but from a hatred, a malignant spite against virtue, and his men are villains not from a daring desire of risk, but a licentious turbulence of moral restraint; with the look of demons, they have the actions of galvanized frogs, the dress of mountebanks, and the hue of pestilential disease. Such a monstrous imagination was never propagated on lovely women.[20]

As if he could not restrain himself from launching an *ad hominem* attack, Haydon then vented his wrath upon the author of these 'galvanized frogs': 'Fuzeli' [sic], he asserted, 'was engendered by some hellish monster, on the dead body of a speckled hag, some hideous form, whose passions were excited & whose lechery was fired at commingling with fiery rapture in the pulpy squashiness of a decaying corpse'.[21]

*****

Why Fuseli made these drawings in Rome is not entirely clear. Certainly a climate of greater moral relativism (no doubt enhanced by the existence of a large community of foreign artists) had something to do with it, as well as a rather pronounced laxity and openness about sex and the easy availability of women, both high and low, for which Rome was notorious.[22] Fuseli's friendship with Sergel also provides part of the answer. It was, after all, Sergel (or so it is conjectured) who initiated Fuseli into a more debauched life than he had known previously, one that included participation in the infamous orgies the Swede is alleged to have orchestrated. In a particularly fine example of early modern art as therapy, Cunningham informed us that the artist's antidote to the licentious behaviour to which he succumbed in Rome was the self-enforced contemplation of Michelangelo's Sistine frescoes: '[he] lay on his back day after day, and week succeeding week, with upturned and wondering eyes, musing at the splendid ceiling of the Sistine Chapel...: [He claimed] that such a posture of repose was necessary for a body fatigued like his with the pleasant gratifications of a luxurious city'.[23]

The juxtaposition of debauchery and Michelangelo is not coincidental. The excesses of Michelangelo's exuberant style were suspect in an age that felt more comfortable with the easy classicism of Raphael while paying lip-service to the grandeur of Michelangelo (notwithstanding the last words of Joshua Reynolds's last discourse).[24] To a neoclassical aesthetic, as exemplified by Johann Joachim Winckelmann (whose *beau ideal* was famously expressed in the phrase 'noble simplicity and calm grandeur'), the art of Michelangelo was bloated, artificial, 'unnatural'. The opinion of Haydon (and I offer this cautiously — the issue is, of course, much thornier) may be taken as representative of one aspect of period English taste: 'Michael Angelo's forms', he wrote, 'have no refinement; they are heavy & not grand; they are forms of Porters and Mechanics'.[25] 'The more I see of Nature', Haydon earlier opined, 'and the more I see of Raphael, the more I abhor Fuzeli's mind, his subjects, and his manner; let me root his Pictures from my fancy forever, and banish them from my Soul'.[26] Note how Haydon thus set up the 'unnatural' alliance of Fuseli and Michelangelo in dialectical opposition to the 'natural' Raphael.

Against the grain, then (and he was famously contrarian), Fuseli adopted Michelangelo as his model.[27] As Cunningham related,

> In Rome [Fuseli] lived in a species of intoxication — affected the dress and mimicked the manners of Michael [Angelo]... He loved to dream along the road — to follow the phantasies of an unbridled imagination — to pen sarcastic remarks — sketch colossal groups,

> and would call out ever and anon, when some strange thought struck him, 'Michelangelo'.[28]

Fuseli's self-fashioning is bound up with his hero worship, and not just of Michelangelo, but of William Shakespeare, John Milton and Dante Alighieri, as well, all paradigmatic figures of the proto-Romantic sublime, of unbridled genius bordering upon frenzy.

Something of Fuseli's affect in the presence of Roman 'Grandeur' may be seen in two other of his drawings: *A Woman Astonished Before the Laocoön* (*c.* 1801–5; Schiff no. 1072), and the well-known *The Artist in Despair over the Magnitude of Antiquity* (1778–80). The stunned woman who stands before the Laocoön (the scene is invented, post-dating his Roman period by more than twenty years, and is almost certainly a portrait of Fuseli's wife), decorated with a large bow reminiscent of that of the dildo-sporting virago of our earlier drawing (and similarly fetishized), adopts an ambiguous, clench-fisted gesture of defiance and frustration, as if, confronted with such sublimity, she is incapable of absorbing its coiled energy. Indeed, she angrily, violently, resists it. That Fuseli should have made the agent of reception female calls to mind another of his aphorisms (no. 227): 'Woman . . . values, bears and wrangles with her equal; she adores what is above her'. The woman's highly emotional reaction to the sculpture stands in striking contrast to the disapproving observation of Fuseli's friend, John Moore, in *A View of Society and Manners in Italy* (1781) that 'Ladies who have remained some time at Rome and Florence, particularly those who affect a taste for *virtù*, acquire an intrepidity and a cool minuteness in examining and criticizing naked figures, which is unknown to those who have never passed the Alps'.[29]

The Artist in Despair over the Magnitude of Antiquity — in which a generic 'portrait of the artist' as Romantic exemplar confronts the fragments of the colossal sculpture of the Emperor Constantine with a mixture of anguish and empathy — more clearly reveals its sentiment.

But to return to Fuseli's friend, Sergel: while Sergel may, indeed, have been a catalyst for Fuseli's explorations into the darker realms of sexuality, his own forays into the erotic betray a radically different sensibility. His attitude to sex, and to male/female relationships in general, seems 'healthier' than Fuseli's, just another manifestation of his famously enormous appetites, his gluttony for life, his passion for extremes in all things.

Even in an eroto-pornographic context — as in his charming, uninhibited pen and wash sketch of a young couple making love beside their sleeping baby — the more domesticated, less tormented, Sergel invented a well-adjusted nuclear family. In the midst of lovemaking, Sergel's dutiful mother remembers her maternal duties, gently rocking her child's cradle with her foot. In contrast, Fuseli, in a drawing made late in life (*c.* 1810–20; Schiff no. 1619), imagined a pair of lesbian narcissists absorbed by their reflections in a mirror, as one absent-mindedly fondles the other. Fuseli's typically fetishized hair assumes a larger meaning in this drawing, as the fondled woman grasps the top-knot of her partner's phallic hairstyle in a gesture that mimics masturbation. The drawing's implied mutual stimulation thus suggests a blurring of male and female identities. But this is Fuseli's fantasy. That he should have had it sometime between the ages of 70 and 80, a period during which he revisited the erotic subjects of his Roman years, and by now a respected Professor of Painting and Keeper of the Royal Academy, is remarkable enough.

A more provocative drawing from the same late period imagines a fully dressed woman lost in concentration before the spectre of a naked, ithyphallic man (Schiff no. 1617).[30] His pallor and diminished detail suggest an otherworldly manifestation, conjured perhaps from the depths of the woman's unconscious, inchoate thoughts. This is Fuseli's *Nightmare* in reverse, the woman in charge — rather than victim — of her sexual fantasies. Or perhaps the ghostly erection — the fugitive phallus — is intended as a sign of creative energy born from idle thought. The whole of the man's right side (in actual fact, his front) is rendered in negative, defined by the white of the paper, devoid of outline or modelling. Through this device, Fuseli effectively erases him by erasing the site of his power, exorcizes his authority, castrates him. This is erection as fading memory, Fuseli's 'invisible man'. As such, the woman cannot see him. I would suggest that this is a self-portrait of the artist as old man — remembered potency now extinguished.

Several of Fuseli's late erotic drawings (those from 1809–10; for example Schiff no. 1620) return to the *mise en scène* of his Rome-period symplegmas. Adapted from the earlier, freer symplegmas, the late versions have a staid and finicky quality — recalled rather than felt. Unlike the Roman drawings, Fuseli now seems interested primarily in his women's fantastic hairstyles, which take on a life of their own, mini-sculptures fabricated with meticulous care. And while the earlier symplegmas were executed in monochromatic pen and black ink and grey wash, these, richly washed with colour, assume a decorative quality in tune with the props of adornment, from hair to jewellery, that seem to absorb Fuseli's attention.

At the same time, in the late drawings, to an even greater degree than before, the male is depersonalized, his head either lost in shadow or obliterated, his distorted body objectified for pleasure — the male as dildo. Their learned Greek inscriptions, longer and more ornate than those on his earlier symplegmas ('The inimitables about to die together', and 'Even so may love come, too, upon my enemies!'[31]), so overtly coupling sex with death, too literally announce this lifelong trope.

No one image so thoroughly encapsulates Fuseli's views on women in general and his wife in particular, nor was woman as object of male gaze ever rendered so flagrantly by the artist, than in the famous sketch of his wife as the Callipygian Venus (Schiff no. 1618).[32] Her back turned to us, her skirts raised, her buttocks exposed, Mrs Fuseli stands before an altar supported by two enormous erect phalluses — before, that is, the altar of Priapus. Staring at her reflection in the mirror that substitutes for, or functions as, an altarpiece, Sophia thus worships herself, a variation upon the theme of *amour propre* that characterizes the original *Venus Callipygia*, who herself admires that which she is admired for. In his drawing, Fuseli recalls both the Farnese *Callipygia*, as well as Sergel's sculpted copy after it, a work commissioned by Gustavus III of Sweden and completed in 1778, and to which Sergel gave the features of the royal mistress, Countess Ulla von Höpken, thus, like Fuseli, adapting the real to the mythic.

In Fuseli's drawing, auto-eroticism commingles with the implicit threat of sodomy, and both artist and viewer are implicated, are complicit, in this. The double meaning of the drawing's Greek inscription (which may be translated as 'I suffer pain' or 'I inflict pain') lends a typically Fuselian ambiguity to the image: 'I suffer pain' (signifying sexual violation?), 'I inflict pain' (meaning the cruelty of the *femme fatale*?). Or is it, in fact, the artist himself speaking? As we have seen, it is in Fuseli's nature to make the merely titillating perverse.

The initial and the essential impulse for Fuseli's erotic drawings — both those made in Rome and those made years later in England — their *fons et origo*, was Rome. The exposure to the ubiquitous remnants of the ancient world — an inexhaustible, dizzying mine of artistic riches — played a significant role in this. The grandeur of Rome, as idea and reality, more broadly fed the imagination of an artist as susceptible to such influences as Fuseli, deeply imbued with his age's philosophy of the terrible and the sublime, an artist whom Johann Kaspar Lavater described in 1774 as 'the most original genius I know... His spirits are storm-wind, his ministers flames of fire!... His laughter is the mockery of hell, and his love — a deadly lightning flash'.[33]

When Fuseli finally left Rome in 1778, after eight exhilarating years, he made an astonishing drawing (Schiff no. 568), which he included in a revealing letter sent from Lugano to his friend, the artist James Northcote, who was then studying in Rome. The sketch is an acute condensation of his emotions on departing Italy to return to England.

Depicting himself as one of his own tortured heroic male nudes — and simultaneously referencing the Sistine ceiling (specifically one of the *ignudi* adjacent to *The Drunkenness of Noah*), as well as the *Horse-tamers of Monte Cavallo* (that is, the Esquiline Dioscuri), the Laocoön, and the Belvedere torso, though in parodic form — he straddles a chamber-pot while defecating into a vessel inscribed 'Switzerland', the much-despised country of his birth (although this relationship, too, was complicated). A steaming mound of excrement floats gently past the shores of France, while England is beset by three mice, one labelled 'G[eorge] Romney', another 'Oz[ias] Humphrey' and the third, and largest, 'B[enjamin] West', three painters toward whom Fuseli clearly felt competitively dismissive ('Beware the mice', Fuseli warned Northcote in his accompanying letter). At the upper left, a winged phallus, emblem of energy, points, arrow-like, in the direction of Italy, 'seat of Passions, site of Grandeur, Sublimity, Terribilità!'.[34] Raising his right arm in a gesture that suggests wonder and dismay in equal measure, the giant Fuseli moves his left leg reticently but ineluctably in the direction of puny England, while his right leg holds back — one foot ever on Italian shores. The worm's eye perspective (Fuseli's recipe for 'Grandeur') lends weight to the image — functioning simultaneously as an exercise both serious and burlesque. This contradictory impulse is, as we have seen, typical of, indeed essential for, Fuseli. The heroic and the ludic converge in this extraordinary drawing, as they do, one suspects, in more of Fuseli's work than has been observed hitherto.

'At the sound of Rome, my heart swells, my eye kindles, and frenzy seizes me', the artist wrote in his letter to Northcote, and he referred to his 'lacerated heart and boiling brains'. And while there is evidence that he was recuperating from a love affair in Rome, this is insufficient to explain the wider meaning of the accompanying drawing. Indeed, in Fuseli's perpetually boiling brains the personal and the universal are ever one, united in his titanic soul.

Fuseli's experience of Rome fuelled his hot temperament: 'the Engines in Fuzeli's Mind [are] Blasphemy, Lechery and blood', to quote Haydon's memorable phrase.[35] Add to this the fracturing of art and morality that coloured his earliest views, strongly influenced by Jean-Jacques Rousseau, and a potent mixture results. An intensification of the dramatic, an exploration of the extremes of emotional experience, and what one contemporary called Fuseli's 'unbridled license of imagination'[36] — these are the features that came to characterize his art, influenced *by* as much as influencing the cultural climate in which he lived. What ultimately distinguishes the erotic drawings of Fuseli from any other of the ubiquitous visual erotica (by Thomas Rowlandson, for example) produced in eighteenth-century Europe (most of which existed in a public, if clandestine, sphere), is their intensely personal nature. Fuseli's drawings were not meant for public consumption; they were, to use anachronistic language, exercises in psychological self-examination.

Fuseli breaks out of his century, and his tortured, complex erotic drawings are perhaps the most potent symbol of that caesura. Though he may never have engaged fully the darker meaning of these extraordinary images, they make him modern in a way that can be said about no other of his contemporaries. Ironically, it was his experience of Rome, that most ancient of cities, that helped make Fuseli modern. His eight years there were an excursion of the mind and the spirit, as well as of the body, and it is Fuseli, activated by 'Rome' (and all that that word conjures), who most purely embodies the clash between transgression and sentiment, reason and passion, that would come to define the very notion of what it means to be 'modern'.

That we have been unable until relatively recently either to reproduce or talk in any meaningful way about his erotic drawings gives the following remark by William Blake, concerning his friend Fuseli, the air of prophecy: 'This country', Blake was apparently fond of saying (speaking of England), 'must advance two centuries in civilisation before it can appreciate him'.[37]

Notes

1. D. Porter, *Haunted Journeys: Desire and Transgression in European Travel Writing* (Princeton, 1991), 43.
2. James Boswell, quoted in F. Brady and A. Pottle (eds), *Boswell on the Grand Tour: Italy, Corsica, and France 1765–1766* (Melbourne/London, 1955), 110.
3. Though hidden from public view, the *Pan and Goat* group, housed at the Royal Museum at Portici, became a titillating 'must see' for the unsqueamish Grand Tourist. Among the instructions the Earl of Pembroke gave his son in 1779 concerning the boy's Tour, for example, was his directive that, when visiting the museum at Portici, 'Mind to have an order to see the Satyr f—ing the Goat' (Lord Herbert (ed.), *The Pembroke Papers: 1734–1780* (London, 1942), 197). A variation on the *Pan and Goat* appears as an illustration in one of the more obscure volumes of 'antiquarianism' produced by the self-styled Baron d'Hancarville (né Pierre François Hugues): *Veneres, uti Observantur in Gemmis Antiquis* (Naples, 1771), a book of pornography masquerading as archaeology, almost all of it entirely invented. The same volume contains an image of a female satyr pleasuring herself on the erect phallus of a herm, which d'Hancarville adapted from a Roman sarcophagus with scenes of Bacchanalian revelry in the Palazzo Farnese, Rome. A less graphic, intentionally burlesque variation on the Farnese sarcophagus was produced by the Swedish sculptor, Johann Tobias Sergel, for his relief of a nymph with an ithyphallic herm, which he completed in Rome in 1778. Prints after the sarcophagus by, for example, Marcantonio Raimondi, had been in circulation since the late Renaissance and were clearly known to Henry Fuseli's circle. It should be noted that John Kenworthy-Brown, who has published the Nollekens *Pan and Goat* ('Terracotta models by Joseph Nollekens, RA', *The Sculpture Journal* 2 (1998), 72–84) did not believe it to be by Nollekens.
4. The Bibliothèque Nationale, Paris, owns an impression by Raimondi of Posture 1 from *I modi*, which appears to have been largely reworked in pen and ink. As Bette Talvacchia has explained, 'this is the only scene from the series that has survived in more than one single-sheet example, most likely due to the more decorous... arrangement of its figures' (B. Talvacchia, *Taking Positions: on the Erotic in Renaissance Culture* (Princeton, 1999), 23; see also n. 3, pp. 238–9). On the subject of *I modi* and its critical fortunes, see Talvacchia, *Taking Positions* (above); L. Lawler, *I Modi, The Sixteen Pleasures: an Erotic Album of the Italian Renaissance* (Evanston, 1988); and, the clearest elucidation of *I modi*'s complex history, D. Foxon, 'Libertine literature in England, 1660–1745. II', *The Book Collector* 12 (1963), 159–77.
5. 'Mr. Nollekens was in possession of a set of those extremely rare engravings, from the Aretin subjects, so often mentioned by print-collectors; but it so happened, as he was glancing at them one day, that his Confessor came in, who insisted upon their being put into the fire, before he would give him absolution. I once saw them; and he lent them to Cosway, to make

tracings from them . . . [Nollekens] was frequently questioned thus: 'Where did you get them, Sir? whose were they?' His answer was, 'I brought them all the way from Rome"; J.T. Smith, *Nollekens and His Times* I (London, 1828), 367–8.

6. *I modi* was not the only Renaissance erotica to inspire Fuseli's circle. Two examples of several that could be cited include Agostino Carracci's engraving, *Il pendolino*, upon which Sergel based a sculptural relief, and L[eon] D[avent]'s print after Primaticcio of a nymph castrating a satyr, which may have been the inspiration for Fuseli's 'fibulation' symplegma (Fig. 22.5).
7. *I modi* as a visual source for Fuseli and his circle was first noted by J. Anderson, *De År i Rom: Abildgaard, Sergel, Füssli* (Copenhagen, 1989), 160–7. Concerning the nineteenth-century copy drawings, Lawler, *I modi* (above, n. 4), 10, explained that 'Count Jean-Frédéric-Maximilien de Waldeck . . . produced twenty ink and wash reconstructions of *I modi* based on eleven tracings by a French sculptor, François-Antoine Gérard, and original prints he claimed to have seen in a convent in Mexico . . .'. These drawings, of which there are two sets, are in the Bibliothèque Nationale, Paris, and the British Museum. 'Twenty' drawings immediately poses a problem, as there were only sixteen postures and, presumably, only sixteen original Raimondi engravings. Talvacchia, *Taking Positions* (above, n. 4) conjectured that Waldeck made an additional four drawings in order to conform to Vasari's assertion (which Talvacchia thinks an error) that Romano had produced twenty drawings. But the correspondence between Sergel's drawing and Waldeck's position 18 lends credence to the possibility that there were additional engravings.
8. On Fuseli's thinking about moral, aesthetic and intellectual matters, in his own words, see E.C. Mason, *The Mind of Henry Fuseli* (London, 1951).
9. See Mason, *Mind of Henry Fuseli* (above, n. 8), 218–19. This is seen most typically in Fuseli's several renderings of *The Horsetamers of Monte Cavallo*, sculptures that seem significantly to have influenced his theory of the Sublime.
10. The Schiff numbers refer to the entries in the *catalogue raisonné* of Fuseli's work: G. Schiff, *Johann Heinrich Füssli, 1741–1825*, 2 vols (Zurich/Munich, 1973).
11. While Gert Schiff began the practice of calling these drawings 'symplegmas', he took his cue from Fuseli, who used the term from time to time, as in the following passage: 'If the picturesqueness of objects be increased in proportion to their . . . intricacy of motion, two spiders . . . caressing or attacking each other, must . . . have greatly the advantage over every athletic or amorous symplegma left by the ancients' (Fuseli, in *Analytical Review* (November 1794), 265, quoted in Mason, *Mind of Henry Fuseli* (above, n. 8), 335.
12. Such rites are also occasionally to be found illustrated on Greek vases, where Fuseli may have seen them.
13. This rather loose translation is provided in the catalogue of the recent Tate Britain exhibition, M. Myrone (ed.), with C. Frayling and M. Warner, *Gothic Nightmares: Fuseli, Blake and the Romantic Imagination* (London, 2006), 166.
14. Two of Fuseli's Roman sketch-books survive intact, one in the British Museum, another in the Kunsthaus, Zürich. Others were obviously broken up, and their contents dispersed.
15. A further distinction should be made between the erotic drawings Fuseli produced in Rome in the 1770s and those he made 30 years later in London, some of them based on the earlier drawings. The London drawings are discussed later in this essay.
16. A. Cunningham, *The Lives of the Most Eminent British Painters* II (London, 1879), 'Henry Fuseli', 100.
17. J. Knowles, *The Life and Writings of Henry Fuseli* (London, 1831), 135, aphorism 194.
18. D.H. Weinglass, "The Elysium of fancy', aspects of Henry Fuseli's erotic art', in P. Wagner (ed.), *Erotica and the Enlightenment* (Frankfurt am Main, 1991), 309; R. Barthes, *Mythologies*, selected and translated by A. Lavers (New York, 1972), 84.
19. *Analytical Review* (September 1789), 29, quoted in Mason, *Mind of Henry Fuseli* (above, n. 8), 178.
20. W.B. Pope (ed.), *The Diary of Benjamin Robert Haydon*, 5 vols (Cambridge (MA), 1960–3), I, 488 (diary entry, December 1815).
21. Pope (ed.), *Diary of Benjamin Robert Haydon* (above, n. 20), I, 488–9.
22. Boswell wrote in his Roman journal (1765): 'I remembered the rakish deeds of Horace and other amorous Roman poets, and I thought that one might well allow one's self a little indulgence in a city where there are prostitutes licensed by the Cardinal Vicar' (Brady and Pottle (eds), *Boswell on the Grand Tour* (above, n. 2), 7). On Italian women in general, Boswell wrote: 'My desire to know the world made me resolve to intrigue a little while in Italy, where the women are so debauched that they are hardly to be considered as moral agents, but as inferior beings' (Brady and Pottle (eds), *Boswell on the Grand Tour* (above, n. 2), 30). In Rome in 1790, Auguste Marmont, who would later become one of Napoleon's generals, observed that 'the freedom of the women passes all belief and their husbands permit it, speaking cheerfully and without embarrassment of their wives' lovers'; quoted in M. Andrieux, *Daily Life in Papal Rome in the Eighteenth Century* (London, 1962), 109. On sex and morals in Rome in the period of the Grand Tour, see J. Black, *Italy and the Grand Tour* (New Haven/London, 2003), 118–31. On the Grand Tour as a sexual and sentimental journey, see Porter, *Haunted Journeys* (above, n. 1), especially chapter 1, 'Uses of the Grand Tour: Boswell and his contemporaries'.
23. Cunningham, *Lives* II (above, n. 16), 48.
24. 'MICHAEL ANGELO'.
25. Pope (ed.), *Diary of Benjamin Robert Haydon* (above, n. 20), 336 (9 January 1814).
26. Pope (ed.), *Diary of Benjamin Robert Haydon* (above, n. 20), 232 (27 April 1812).
27. He initially accepted Winckelmann's assessment of Michelangelo, changing his opinion only after actually seeing the Sistine Chapel. As Frederick Antal observed, Fuseli 'was

perhaps the first painter since the 16th century to single out Michelangelo as his favourite artist. Michelangelo now represented for him the genius par excellence in art... At the same time in England admiration for Michelangelo developed rather slowly'. That Fuseli 'placed Michelangelo, an artist out of favour with both Mengs and Winckelmann, above this canonical trinity [Raphael, Titian, Correggio], implied a bold reversal of the entire previous scale of values': *Fuseli Studies* (London, 1956), 31–2.

28. Cunningham, *Lives* II (above, n. 16), 53–4.
29. Second edition (London, 1781), vol. II, 424–5. On the reception of the antique by Grand Tourists, see C. Chard, *Pleasure and Guilt on the Grand Tour: Travel Writing and Imaginative Geography, 1600–1830* (Manchester/New York, 1999), esp. chapter 10, 'The feminine and the antique', 126–56. See also B. Dolan, *Ladies of the Grand Tour* (London, 2001).
30. D. Weinglass (Christie's sale catalogue, *British Art on Paper*, London, 3 June 2004, lot 79, p. 84) recently redated this drawing to the 1790s, rejecting Schiff's date of 1810–20 (Schiff, *Johann Heinrich Füssli* (above, n. 10). Whether or not this is true, the drawing would still represent a moment two decades removed from Fuseli's Roman period.
31. The latter quote is from Aeschylus's *Prometheus Bound* (1864), and refers to the sons of Aigyptos, who were murdered by their brides, the Danaids, on their wedding night. It is preceded in the text of the play by the following: 'Each wife shall rob her husband of his life, dipping in blood her two-edged sword': *Prometheus Bound*, in Aeschylus II (Chicago, 1956), 170, translated by D. Grene. As Grene noted in his introduction: 'In the eighteenth century the critics knew what they thought about the Prometheus of Aeschylus and knew why they thought it. It was a bad play because the structure was episodic, the characters extravagant and improbable, the diction uncouth and wild'. How appropriate, then, that Fuseli should take so 'Fuselian' a play as his source.
32. He had married Sophia, who was twenty years his junior, in 1788.
33. In a letter to Johann Gottfried Herder of 1774, quoted and translated in Mason, *Mind of Henry Fuseli* (above, n. 8), 67.
34. Fuseli's source for his flying phallus surely derives, at least in part, from his familiarity with ancient tintinnabula, or phallic apotropaic wind chimes, examples of which were discovered in Herculaneum and elsewhere. At least one of these, unearthed in Herculaneum in 1740, was reproduced in O. Baiardi and P. Carcani's *Delle antichità di Ercolano*, whose eight volumes were published between 1757 and 1792. John Knowles informed us that '[i]n 1775, [Fuseli] visited Naples, studied the works of art in that city, and examined the excavations at Herculaneum and Pompeii': Knowles, *The Life and Writings of Henry Fuseli* (above, n. 17), I, 50.
35. Pope (ed.), *Diary of Benjamin Robert Haydon* (above, n. 19), I, 488.
36. A. Cunningham, *The Lives of the Most Eminent British Painters, Sculptors and Architects* (London, 1843), 148.
37. A. Gilchrist, *Life of William Blake*, 2 vols (London, 1880), I, 336. Only 60 years ago Ruthven Todd (*Tracks in the Snow* (London, 1946), 82) could still write, 'These obscene drawings are among the finest of Fuseli's works... My only regret is that I am unable, under our present dubious legal system, to reproduce several of them here in their entirety; all that I can do is to give some details from six of these drawings lately in my own possession'.

Biographical notes on the contributors

MALCOLM BAKER is Distinguished Professor of the History of Art, University of California, Riverside. He has published widely on eighteenth-century sculpture and his books include *Figured in Marble: the Making and Viewing of Eighteenth-century Sculpture* (London/Los Angeles, 2000) and *Roubiliac and the Eighteenth-century Monument. Sculpture as Theatre* (co-authored with David Bindman) (New Haven/London, 1995) which was the winner of the 1996 Mitchell Prize for the History of Art. He is currently writing a study of the portrait bust in the eighteenth century, provisionally titled, *The Marble Index: Sculptural Portraiture in Eighteenth-century Britain*.

ELIZABETH BARTMAN is an independent scholar who specializes in ancient Roman sculpture. Currently she is engaged in publishing the ideal sculpture (for example, gods, mythic figures, personifications) collected in the second half of the eighteenth century by Henry Blundell for his house at Ince near Liverpool. She is currently the President of the Archaeological Institute of America.

EDGAR PETERS BOWRON is a native of Birmingham, Alabama. He received his BA from Colgate University and his MA and Ph.D. from the Institute of Fine Arts, New York University. He began his professional career at the Metropolitan Museum of Art and subsequently has worked in a number of American art museums. He was appointed Director and Professor of Fine Arts at the Harvard University Art Museums in 1985 and served as Senior Curator of Paintings at the National Gallery of Art, Washington, DC from 1990 until 1996, when he joined the staff of the Museum of Fine Arts, Houston, as the Audrey Jones Beck Curator of European Art. Responsible for the installation of European art in the Audrey Jones Beck Building, which opened in March 2000, Dr Bowron continues to supervise the Audrey Jones Beck Collection of Impressionist Paintings, the Kress and Straus Collection of European Old Masters, and the museum's wide-ranging collection of European art from the Middle Ages to 1913. A widely-respected scholar and connoisseur of European Old Master paintings, he has particular interest in French, Dutch and Italian painting of the sixteenth, seventeenth and eighteenth centuries, with especial enthusiasm for painting in Rome in the eighteenth century and Italian view-painting of the period. His writings include numerous collection and exhibition catalogues, the most recent of which are *Art in Rome in the Eighteenth Century* (Philadelphia Museum of Art and MFAH, 2000); *Bernardo Bellotto and the Capitals of Europe* (Museo Correr, Venice, and MFAH, 2001); *Best in Show: The Dog in Art from the Renaissance to Today* (Bruce Museum, Greenwich, and MFAH, 2006); *Pompeo Batoni: Prince of Painters in Eighteenth-Century Rome* (MFAH and National Gallery, London, 2007–8); and *Antiquity Revived: Neoclassical Art in the Eighteenth Century* (MFAH, 2011). During his museum career Dr Bowron has played a role in acquiring major works by such artists as Bellotto, Canova, Chardin, Courbet, Baron Gerard, Panini, Rembrandt, Guido Reni, Jacob van Ruisdael, J.M.W. Turner and Jan van Huysum.

EDWARD CHANEY is Professor of Fine and Decorative Arts and Chair of the History of Collecting Research Centre at Southampton Solent University. His books include *The Grand Tour and the Great Rebellion* (Geneva, 1985), *A Traveller's Companion to Florence* (Florence/London, 1986/2002); *The Evolution of the Grand Tour* (London/Portland (OR), 2000), *The Evolution of English Collecting: the Reception of Italian Art in the Tudor and Stuart Periods* (New Haven/London, 2003) and *Inigo Jones's 'Roman Sketchbook'*, 2 vols (London, 2006).

EDWARD CORP is Professor of British History at the University of Toulouse, and was the Paul Mellon Centre Rome Fellow at the British School at Rome in 2004–5. His books include *The King over the Water: Portraits of the Stuarts in Exile after 1689* (Edinburgh, 2001), *A Court in Exile: the Stuarts in France, 1689–1718* (Cambridge/New York, 2004) and *The Jacobites at Urbino: an Exiled Court in Transition* (Basingstoke/New York, 2009).

KATRINA GRANT recently has submitted her Ph.D. in Art History at the University of Melbourne on 'The Theatrical Garden in the Baroque, Filippo Juvarra, Gardens and Theatre in the Eighteenth Century', which is an exploration of how the Italian garden was related to theatre in the seventeenth and eighteenth centuries. In 2008 she was the Melbourne Rome Scholar at the British School at Rome.

JAMES HOLLOWAY has been the Director of the Scottish National Portrait Gallery since 1997. He studied History of Art at the Courtauld Institute before joining the Department of Prints and Drawings at the National Gallery of Scotland in 1972. He was an Assistant Keeper at the National Museum of Wales in the early 1980s. He returned to Edinburgh and to the National Galleries of Scotland in 1983.

CHRISTOPHER M.S. JOHNS received his Ph.D. in art history under the direction of Barbara Maria Stafford at the

University of Delaware in 1985. He has published monographic studies on the cultural patronage of Pope Clement XI (*Papal Art and Cultural Politics. Rome in the Age of Clement XI* (Cambridge/New York, 1993)) and Antonio Canova (*Antonio Canova and the Politics of Patronage in Revolutionary and Napoleonic Europe* (Berkeley/London, 1998)), in addition to his introductory essay in the exhibition catalogue, *Art in Rome in the Eighteenth Century* (London/Philadelphia, 2000), edited by E.P. Bowron and J.J. Rishel. He is Norman and Roselea Goldberg Professor of History of Art, Vanderbilt University, USA. He is presently completing work on a book-length manuscript entitled *The Visual Culture of Catholic Enlightenment*. He is Past President of the Historians of Eighteenth-century Art and Architecture and is a Fellow of the American Academy in Rome.

PETER BJÖRN KERBER is at the J. Paul Getty Museum, Los Angeles. He is co-curator of *Paris: Life & Luxury* at the J. Paul Getty Museum, Los Angeles and the Museum of Fine Arts, Houston, in 2011. He was co-curator of the Pompeo Batoni exhibitions at the Museum of Fine Arts, Houston, the National Gallery, London, and the Palazzo Ducale, Lucca, in 2007–9. Together with Edgar Peters Bowron, he wrote *Pompeo Batoni: Prince of Painters in Eighteenth-century Rome* (Yale University Press, 2007).

ALASTAIR LAING has been Curator of Pictures & Sculpture for The National Trust, with the oversight of the collections of works of art in some 150 houses in England, Wales and Northern Ireland, since 1986. He is also a specialist on François Boucher, and is a co-author (with M. Meade, J.W. Niemeijer, C. White, M. Jacobs, M. Snodin and K. Wolfe) of the *Catalogue of Drawings for Architecture, Design, and Ornament in the James A. de Rothschild Collection at Waddesdon Manor* (Aylesbury, 2006).

TOMMASO MANFREDI is an architect and researcher at the University 'Mediterranea' at Reggio Calabria, where he teaches the History of Architecture and Urbanism. His particular interests are Juvarra and Borromini, the Roman formation of the European architects of the eighteenth and nineteenth centuries, the urban history of Rome and the architectural treatises of the seventeenth and eighteenth centuries. He is the author (with G. Bonaccorso) of *I Virtuosi al Pantheon. 1700–1758* (Rome, 1998), *La costruzione dell'architetto. Maderno, Borromini, i Fontana e la formazione degli architetti ticinesi a Roma* (Rome, 2008), *Filippo Juvarra. Gli anni giovanili* (Rome, 2010) and of numerous articles that have appeared in national and international journals.

DAVID R. MARSHALL FAHA is Principal Fellow in Art History, University of Melbourne, and Adjunct Professor in Art History, La Trobe University. He has published widely on seventeenth- and eighteenth-century painting and architecture, and is the author of *Viviano and Niccolò Codazzi and the Baroque Architectural Fantasy* (Milan, 1993) and has edited several collections, including *Art, Site and Spectacle: Studies in Early Modern Visual Culture* (Melbourne, 2007). He is currently writing books on the Villa Patrizi and on the paintings of Giovanni Paolo Panini.

CAROL M. RICHARDSON is a Senior Lecturer in the History of Art at the Open University in the UK. Her research interests include the College of Cardinals, particularly in the fifteenth century, and the art and architecture of the Venerable English College, Rome. She has published in *Renaissance Studies*, *Apollo* and the *Papers of the British School at Rome*. Her book on the patronage of the College of Cardinals, *Reclaiming Rome: Cardinals in the Fifteenth Century*, was published by Brill in 2009. In 2008 she was awarded a Philip Leverhulme Prize. She is now completing a book on the English College.

WENDY WASSYNG ROWORTH is Professor of Art History at the University of Rhode Island. Her publications include: *Angelica Kauffman: a Continental Artist in Georgian England* (Brighton/London, 1992); 'Rethinking art in eighteenth-century Rome', *The Art Bulletin* 83 (2001), 134–44; catalogue essays in O. Sandner (ed.), *Angelika Kauffmann e Roma* (Rome, 1998) and T.G. Natter (ed.), *Angelica Kauffman: a Woman of Immense Talent* (Bregenz, 2007); and is editor (with P. Findlen and C.M. Sama) of *Italy's Eighteenth Century: Gender and Culture in the Age of the Grand Tour* (Stanford (CA), 2009), which contains her essay "The residence of the arts': Angelica Kauffman's place in Rome'.

FRANCIS RUSSELL has been a Director of Christie's since 1977, and is now a Deputy Chairman, Christie's International UK Ltd. He is a member of the Arts Panel of the National Trust and the author of numerous articles in *The Burlington Magazine*, *Country Life*, *Apollo*, *Master Drawings*, and other scholarly publications and exhibition catalogues, and of *Portraits of Sir Walter Scott* (London, 1987), *John, 3rd Earl of Bute: Patron *and Collector* (London, 2004) and *52 Italian Places* (Turin, 2007).

SUSAN RUSSELL is Assistant Director at the British School at Rome, on secondment from La Trobe University, Bundoora, Australia. She wrote her Ph.D. at the University of Melbourne on the fresco friezes of the Palazzo Pamphilj in the Piazza Navona and has published on Pirro Ligorio, the Dutch Italianate landscape painter Herman van Swanevelt and Pamphilj art and patronage.

KEVIN SALATINO is Director of the Bowdoin College Museum of Art (Maine, USA). Prior to that he was Curator and Head of the Department of Prints and Drawings at the Los Angeles County Museum of Art, and before that Curator of Graphic Arts at the Getty Research Institute. His book, *Incendiary Art: the Representation of Fireworks in Early Modern Europe* (Los Angeles, 1997), is being prepared for a French edition. He has published on topics as diverse as Renaissance Rome, the Grand Tour, James Ensor and Richard Pousette-Dart. He is currently writing a book on Henry Fuseli's erotic drawings.

DESMOND SHAWE-TAYLOR is Surveyor of the Queen's Pictures. From 1996 to 2005 he was Director of the Dulwich Picture Gallery, and from 1976 to 1996 was Lecturer in the History of Art at Nottingham University. He has published articles on seventeenth- and eighteenth-century art and numerous exhibition catalogues, including in *Shakespeare nell'arte/ Shakespeare in Art* (Ferrara, 2003) for the exhibition at the Palazzo dei Diamanti, Ferrara, and, at the Dulwich Picture Gallery, *Dramatic Art: Theatrical Paintings from the Garrick Club* (London, 1997) and *Genial Company: the Theme of Genius in Eighteenth-century Portraiture* (London, 1987) as well as the book *The Georgians: Eighteenth-century Portraiture and Society* (London, 1990).

LETIZIA TEDESCHI has been Founder and Director of the Archivio del Moderno in Mendrisio since 1996, the year when the Accademia di Architettura of the Università della Svizzera Italiana was established. Her research ranges from the eighteenth to twentieth centuries, with particular emphasis on the relationship between art and architecture. She has recently published (with N. Navone) *Dal mito al progetto. La cultura architettonica dei maestri italiani e ticinesi nella Russia neoclassica* (Mendrisio, 2004) and a number of papers on the architect Vincenzo Brenna (1741–1820). She is general editor of the series of books published by the Archivio del Moderno, the Mendrisio Academy Press.

ANDREW WALLACE-HADRILL is Master of Sidney Sussex College, Cambridge, and a former Director of the British School at Rome. Author of *Rome's Cultural Revolution* (Cambridge, 2008) and *Houses and Society in Pompeii and Herculaneum* (Princeton, 1994), and of articles on housing at Rome, he is director of projects at both Pompeii and Herculaneum.

JOHN WILTON-ELY, Emeritus Professor at the University of Hull, after teaching at Nottingham and Hull Universities, was Director of Education, Sotheby's London until 1992. He is a Visiting Professor at the Cooper-Hewitt National Museum of Design, New York, where he was guest curator of the exhibition, *Piranesi as Designer* in 2007. When this paper was delivered, he was the Paul Mellon Centre Rome Fellow at the British School at Rome, where he was undertaking research for a book on the Adam Style.

KARIN WOLFE is a Research Fellow at the British School at Rome. She did her Ph.D. at the Courtauld Institute on Cardinal Antonio Barberini, and specializes in Roman seventeenth- and eighteenth-century patronage, painting and architecture. She has taught at John Cabot University and Temple University, and has published on Cardinal Antonio Barberini, Caravaggio, Andrea Sacchi, Francesco Borromini, and Francesco Trevisani. She is co-author (with M. Jacobs) of the entries on Italian drawings in the *Catalogue of Drawings for Architecture, Design, and Ornament in the James A. de Rothschild Collection at Waddesdon Manor* (Aylesbury, 2006). She is currently preparing a monograph on Trevisani.

Contributors' addresses

MALCOLM BAKER
Department of the History of Art, University of California, Arts Building, 900 University Avenue, Riverside, California 92521-0319, USA.
mcbaker@ucr.edu

ELIZABETH BARTMAN
elizabeth.bartman@gmail.com

EDGAR PETERS BOWRON
The Museum of Fine Arts, Houston, PO Box 6826, Houston, TX 77265-6826, USA.

EDWARD CHANEY
Faculty of Media, Arts and Society, Southampton Solent University, East Park Terrace, Southampton, SO14 0YN, Great Britain.
Edward.Chaney@solent.ac.uk

EDWARD CORP
15 rue des Arts, 31000 Toulouse, France.
corp.edward@yahoo.fr

KATRINA GRANT
kat.grant@gmail.com

JAMES HOLLOWAY
Scottish National Portrait Gallery, 1 Queen Street, Edinburgh, EH2 1JD, Great Britain.

CHRISTOPHER M. S. JOHNS
Department of History of Art, Vanderbilt University, 230 Appleton Place, Box 0274 GPC, Nashville, Tennessee 37203, USA.
christopher.johns@vanderbilt.edu

PETER BJÖRN KERBER
J. Paul Getty Museum, 1200 Getty Center Drive, Los Angeles, CA 90049-1687, USA.

ALASTAIR LAING
The National Trust, 32 Queen Anne's Gate, London, SW1H 9AB, Great Britain.
alastair.laing@nationaltrust.org.uk

TOMMASO MANFREDI
Università 'Mediterranea' di Reggio Calabria, Facoltà di Architettura, Via Melissari, snc, 89124 Reggio Calabria, Italy.
tommaso.manfredi@unirc.it

DAVID R. MARSHALL
Art History, School of Culture and Communication, University of Melbourne, Australia.
david.marshall@unimelb.edu.au

CAROL M. RICHARDSON
Art History Department, The Open University, Walton Hall, Milton Keynes, MK7 6AA, Great Britain.
C.M.Richardson@open.ac.uk

WENDY WASSYNG ROWORTH
Department of Art and Art History, University of Rhode Island, 105 Upper College Road, Kingston, RI 02881, USA.
wroworth@uri.edu

FRANCIS RUSSELL
Christie's, 8 King Street, St. James's, London, SW1Y 6QT, Great Britain.
FRussell@christies.com

SUSAN RUSSELL
The British School at Rome, Via Gramsci 61, 00197 Rome, Italy.
s.russell@bsrome.it

KEVIN SALATINO
Bowdoin College Museum of Art, 9400 College Station, Brunswick, Maine 04011, USA.
ksalatino@bowdoin.edu

DESMONDE SHAW-TAYLOR
St James's Palace, London, SW1A 1BQ, UK.
desmond.shawe-taylor@royalcollection.org.uk

LETIZIA TEDESCHI
Archivio del Moderno, Via Lavizzari 2, CH-6850 Mendrisio, Switzerland.
letizia.tedeschi@usi.ch

ANDREW WALLACE-HADRILL
Sidney Sussex College, Cambridge, CB2 3HU, Great Britain.
aw479@sid.cam.ac.uk

JOHN WILTON-ELY
wiltonely.john@gmail.com

KARIN WOLFE
c/o The British School at Rome, Via Gramsci 61, 00197 Rome, Italy.
karinewolfe@tiscali.it

Index

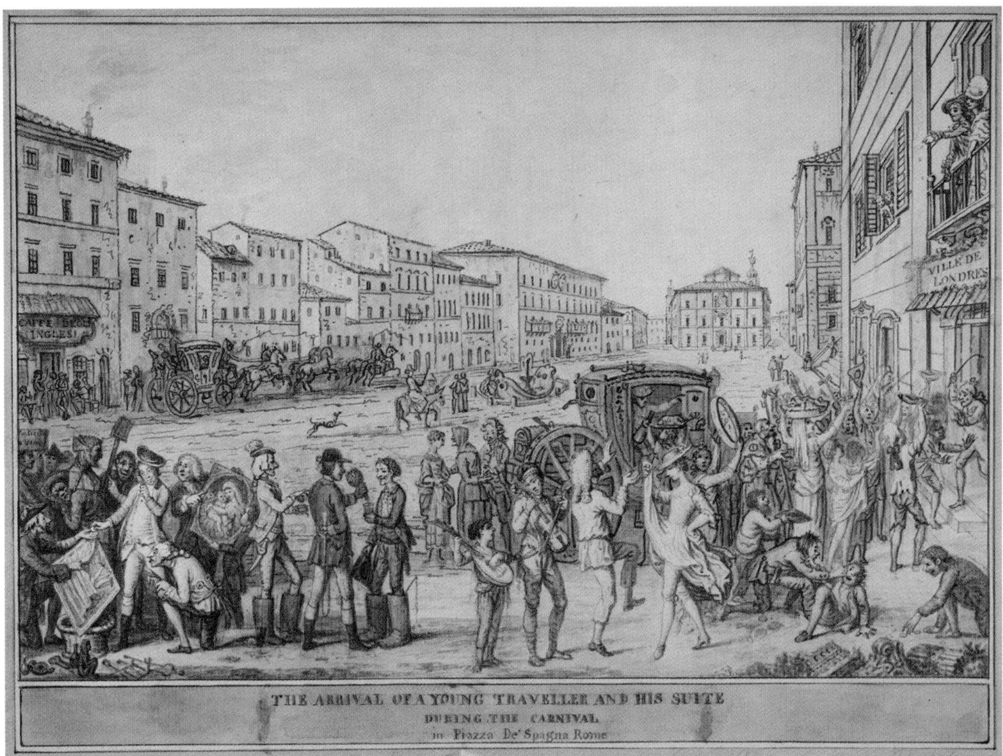

PLATE 1.1. David Allan (1744–96), *The Arrival of a Young Traveller and His Suite During the Carnival in Piazza di Spagna, Rome*, c. 1775. Pen and brown ink over pencil, partly redrawn in darker ink, 40 × 54 cm. *(The Royal Collection, © 2009 Her Majesty Queen Elizabeth II.)*

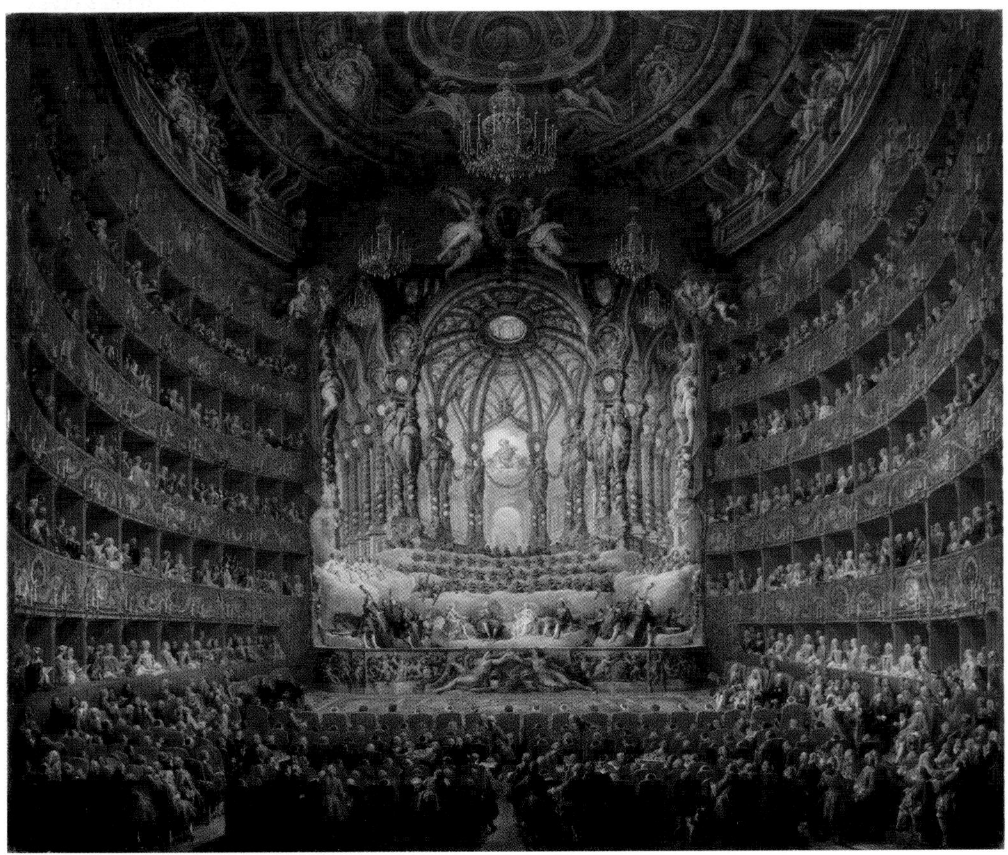

PLATE 1.2. Giovanni Paolo Panini (1691–1765), *Musical Performance Given by the Cardinal de la Rochefoucauld in the Teatro Argentina in Rome on 15 July 1747 for the Marriage of the Dauphin of France*, 1747. Paris, Musée du Louvre, inv. 414–140. *(Photo: © Réunion des Musées Nationaux/Gérard Blot.)*

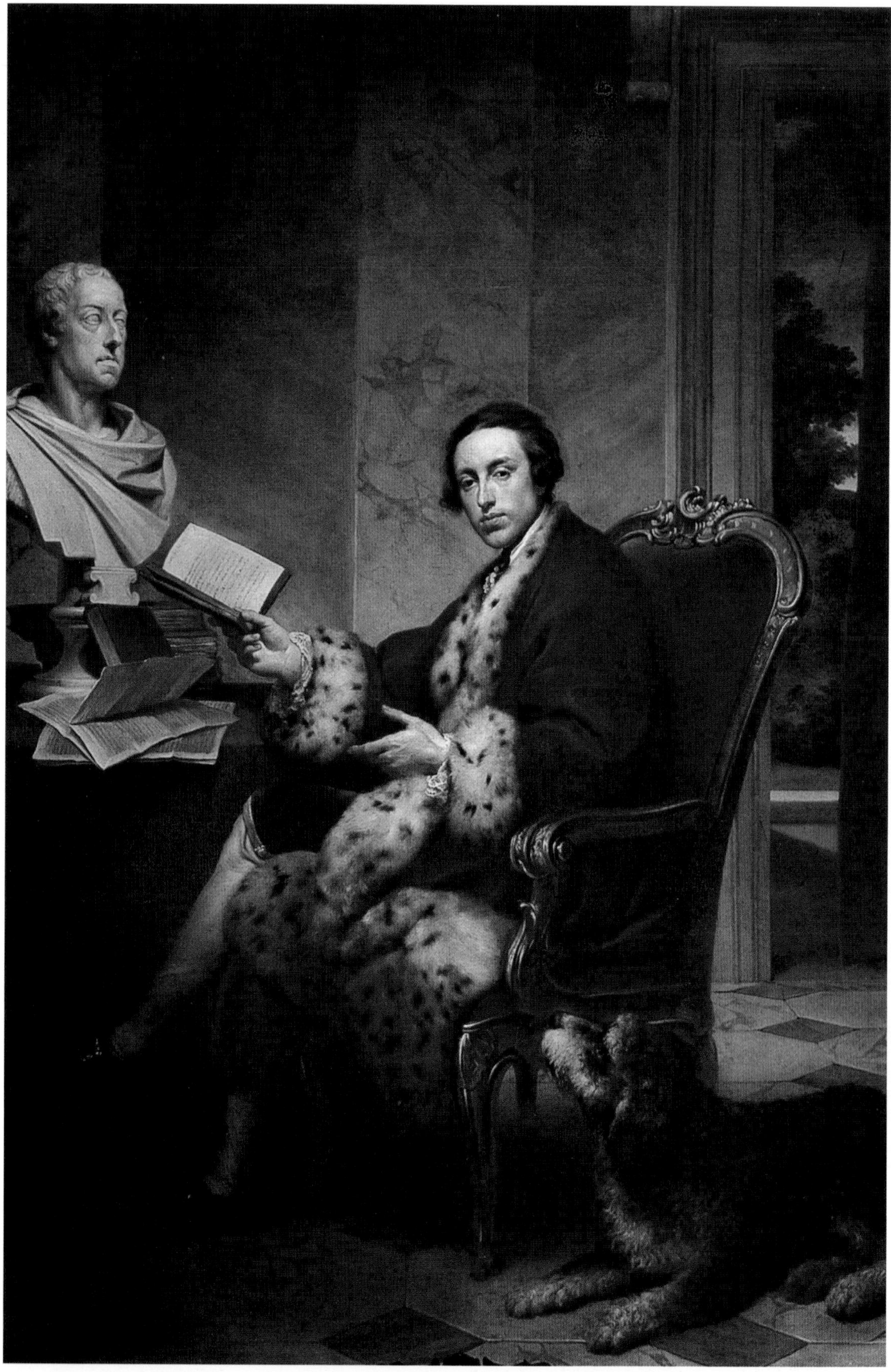

PLATE 2.1. Anton Raphael Mengs (1728–79), *John Brudenell-Montagu, Later Marquess of Monthermer*. Oil on canvas. Collection of the Duke of Buccleuch. *(Reproduced courtesy of the Trustees of the 9th Duke of Buccleuch's Chattels Fund.)*

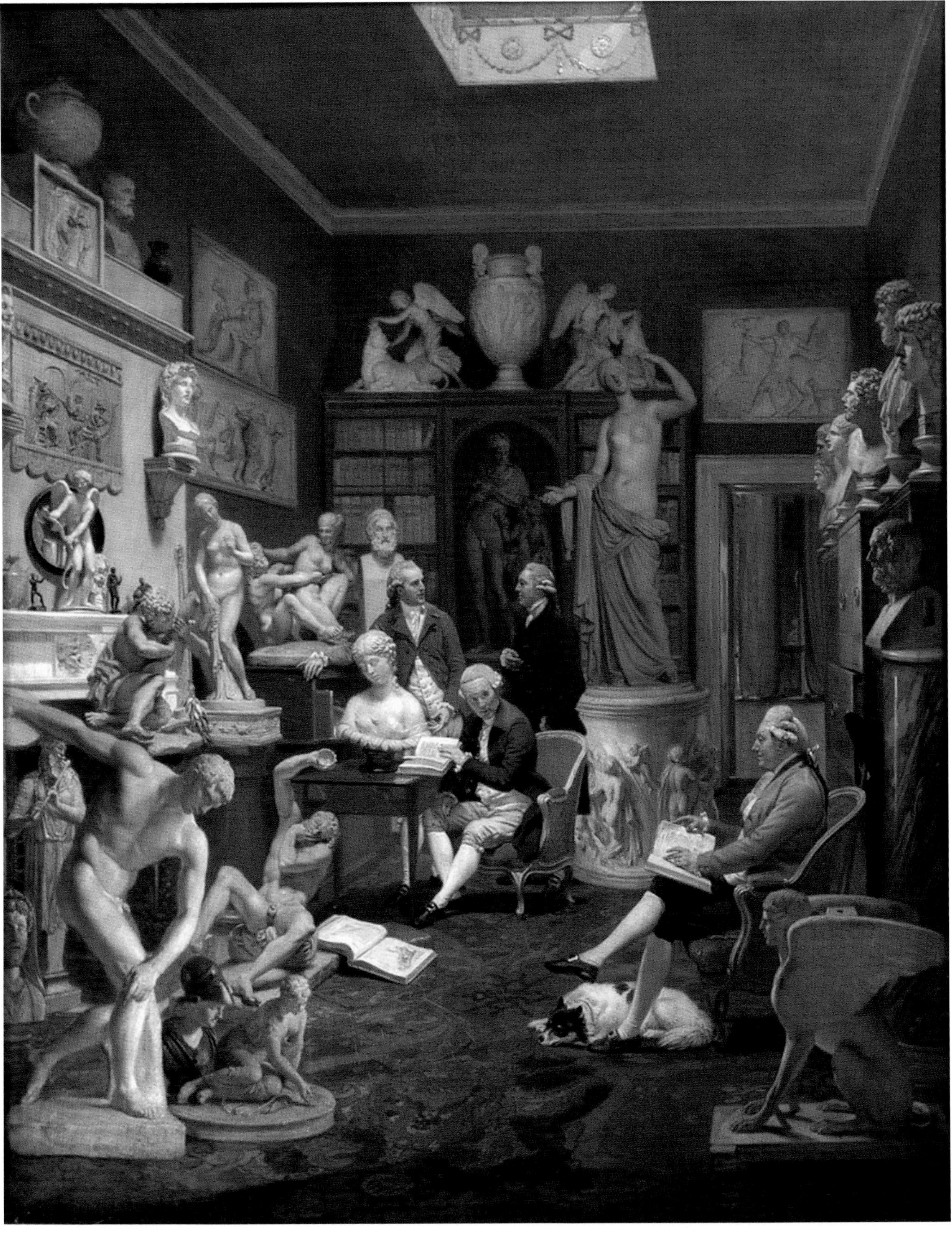

PLATE 2.2. John Zoffany (*c.* 1733–1810), *Charles Townley's Library at 7 Park Street, Westminster*, 1781–3. Oil on canvas. Burnley, Towneley Hall Art Gallery and Museum. *(Reproduced courtesy of the Towneley Hall Art Gallery and Museum, Burnley Borough Council.)*

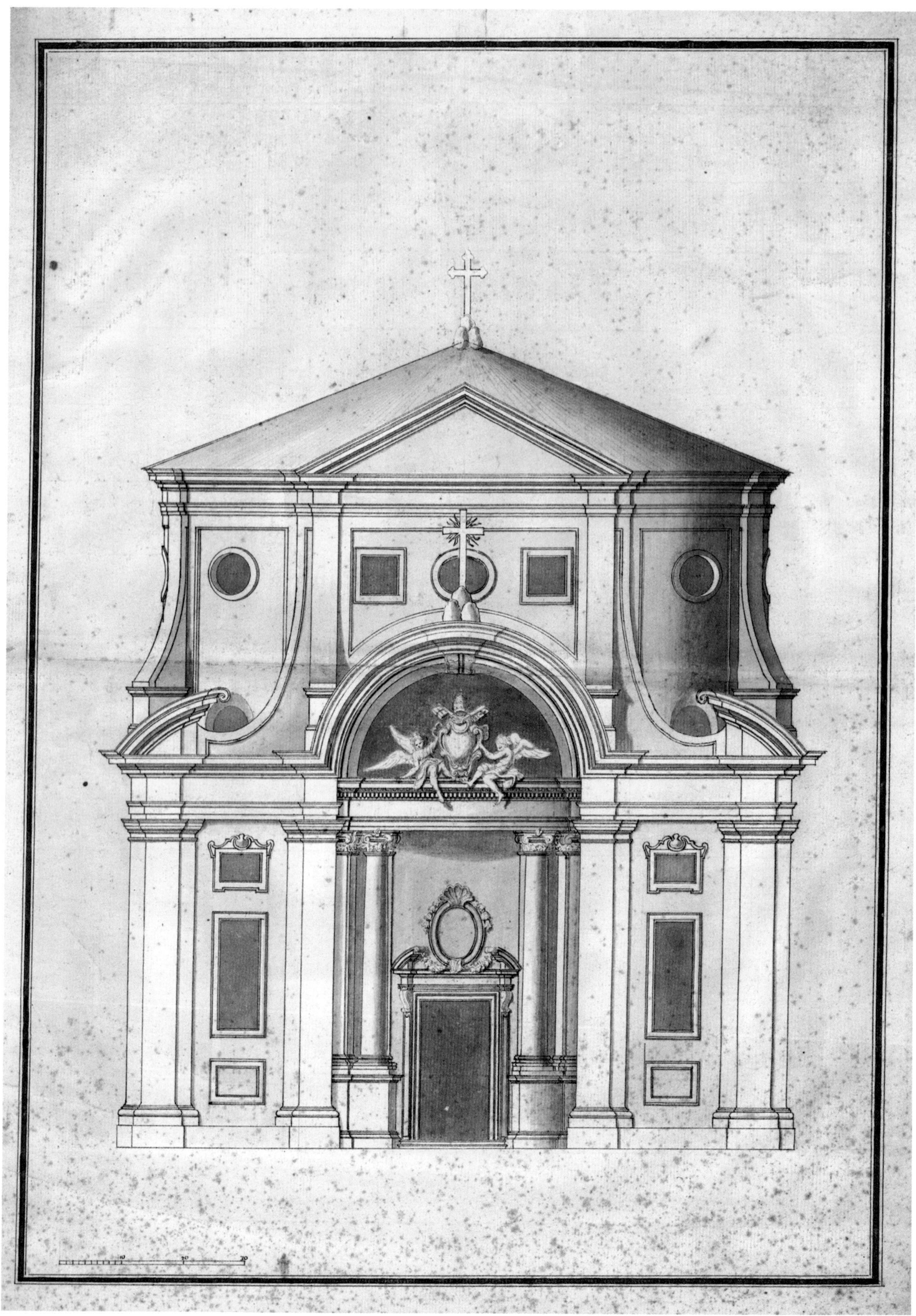

PLATE 3.1. Andrea Pozzo (1642–1709), *Design for the Façade of the New Church of the Venerable English College*, 1701–3. Pen and ink wash on paper. Venerable English College. *(Reproduced courtesy of the Venerable English College.)*

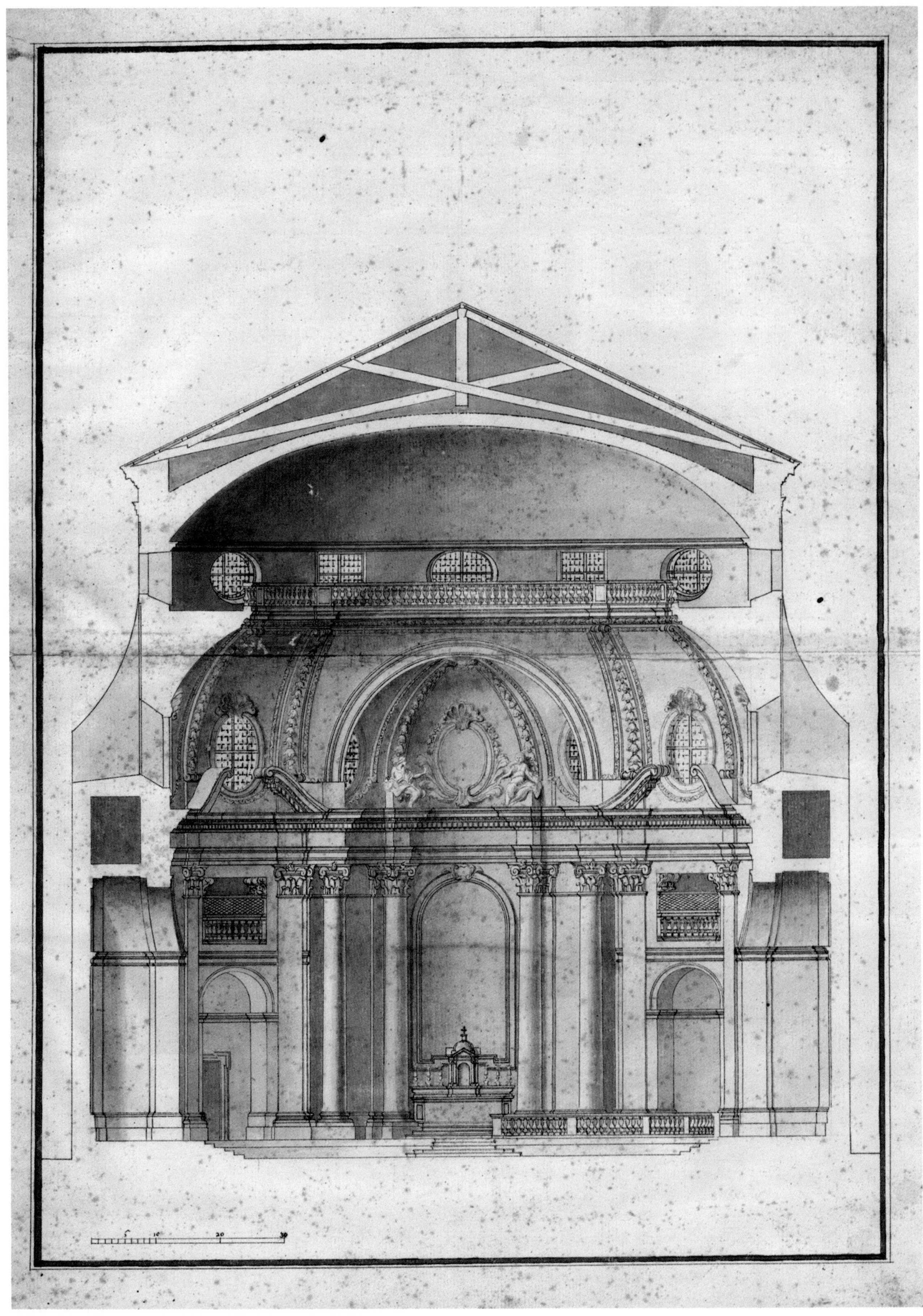

PLATE 3.2. Andrea Pozzo (1642–1709), *Design for the New Church of the Venerable English College, Transverse Section*, 1701–3. Pen and ink wash on paper. Venerable English College. *(Reproduced courtesy of the Venerable English College.)*

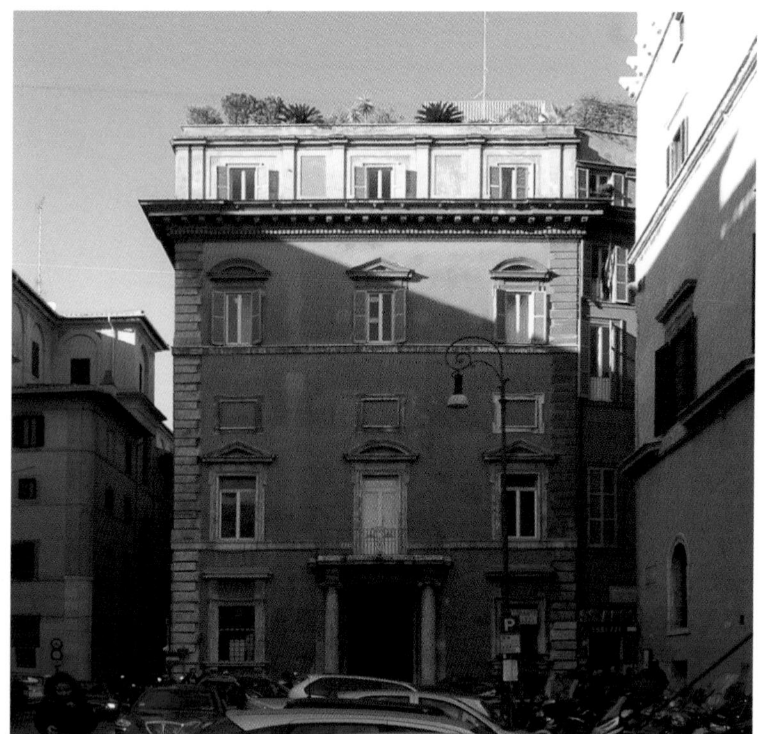

PLATE 4.1. Rome, 'Palazzo del Re', now Palazzo Balestra, from Piazza Santi Apostoli. *(Photo: © David R. Marshall, 2009.)*

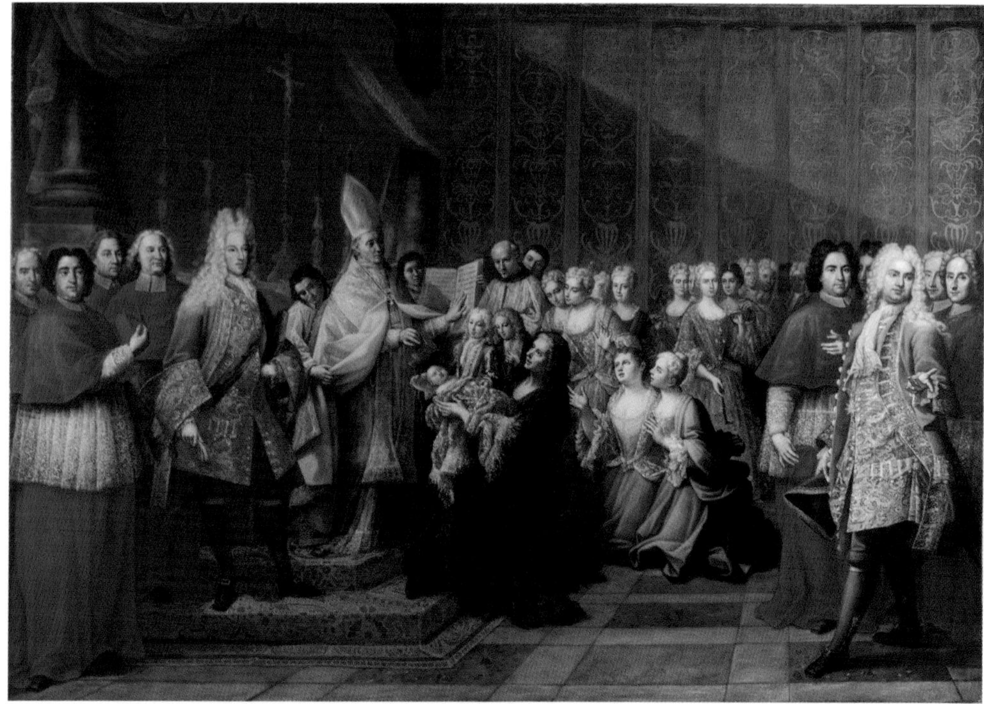

PLATE 4.2. Antonio David (1684–1737), *The Baptism of Charles, Prince of Wales on 31 December 1720*, 1725. Oil on canvas. Scottish National Portrait Gallery. From left to right: Cardinal Giuseppe Renato Imperiali, Cardinal Giuseppe Sacripanti and Cardinal Filippo Antonio Gualterio (the Cardinal Protectors of Ireland, Scotland and England), behind Cardinal Annibale Albani; James III; Lord Richard Howard (English), Lord William Drummond (Scottish), Antonio Ragazzi (parish priest of Santi Apostoli), and Father John Brown (Irish) with two boys, behind Sebastiano Bonaventura (Bishop of Corneto and Montefiascone); Contessa della Torre (better known as the Princesse des Ursins) kneeling and holding Charles, Prince of Wales; six Roman and Jacobite ladies (two of whom are kneeling); Ippolita Boncampagni (Principessa di Piombino) and her three daughters; four Roman and Jacobite gentlemen; Cardinal Francesco Aquaviva, Cardinal Francesco Barberini, Cardinal Fabrizio Paulucci and Cardinal Pietro Ottoboni, standing behind Don Carlo Albani. *(Photo: © Scottish National Portrait Gallery.)*

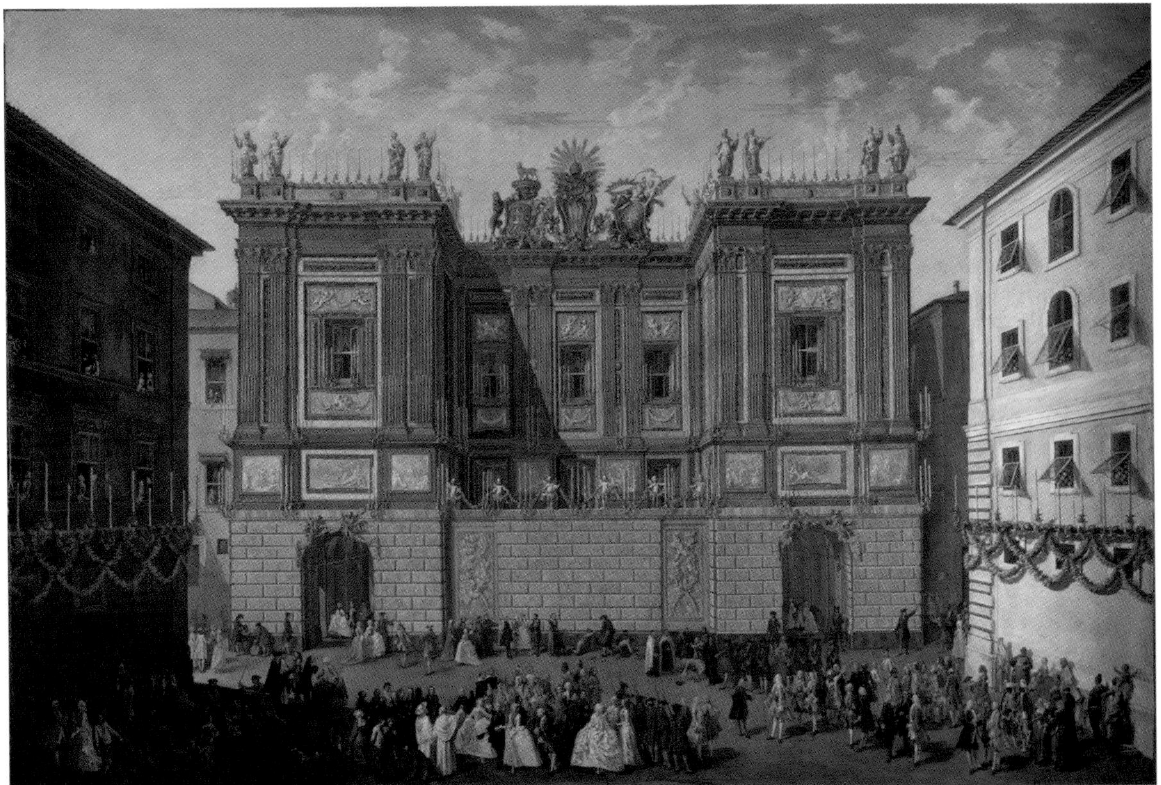

PLATE 5.1. Anonymous, *Prince James Receiving His Son, Prince Henry, in Front of the Palazzo del Re*, c. 1747. Oil on canvas, 195.58 × 297.18 cm. Edinburgh, Scottish National Portrait Gallery, accession no. PG 3269. Purchased with the support of the Heritage Lottery Fund and The Art Fund 2001. *(Photo: © National Galleries of Scotland.)*

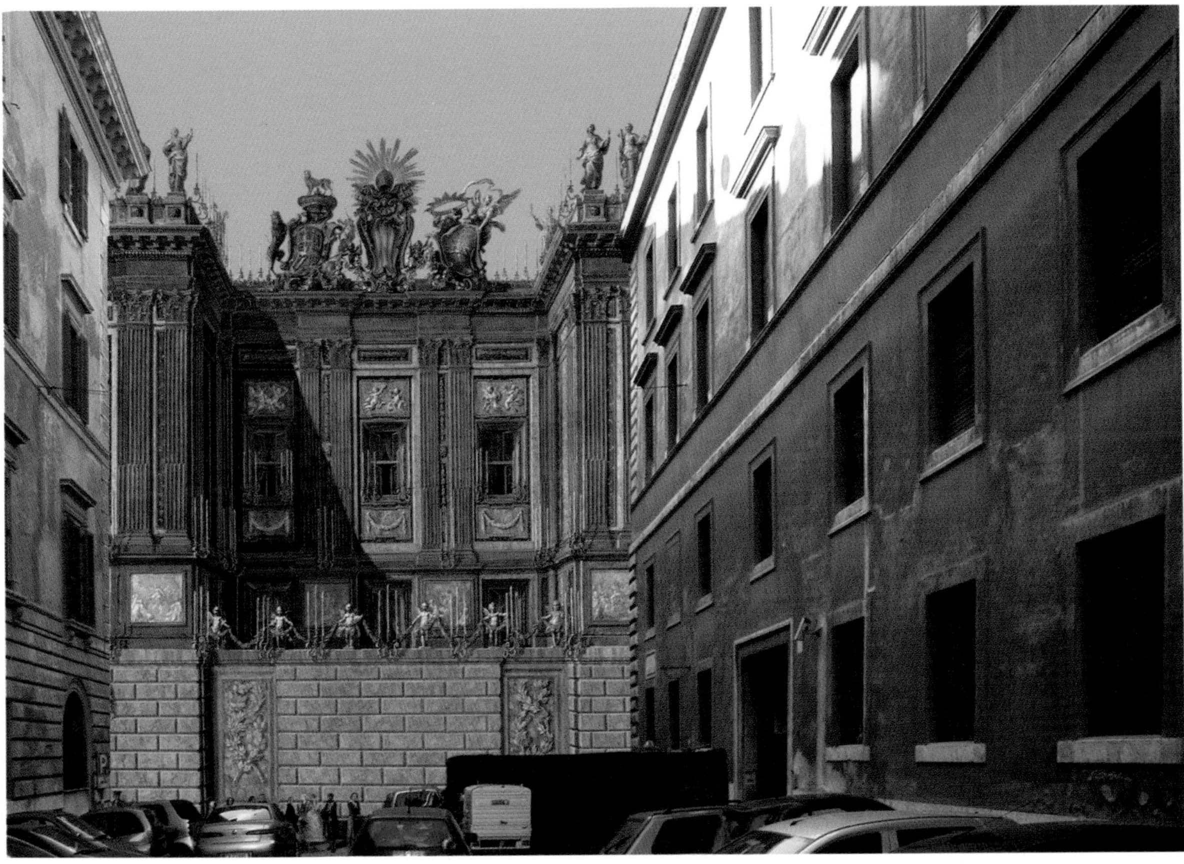

PLATE 5.2. Photomontage of *Prince James Receiving His Son, Prince Henry, in Front of the Palazzo del Re* (PLATE 5.1) with the rear façade of the Santi Apostoli palace. *(Photo: © David R. Marshall, 2009.)*

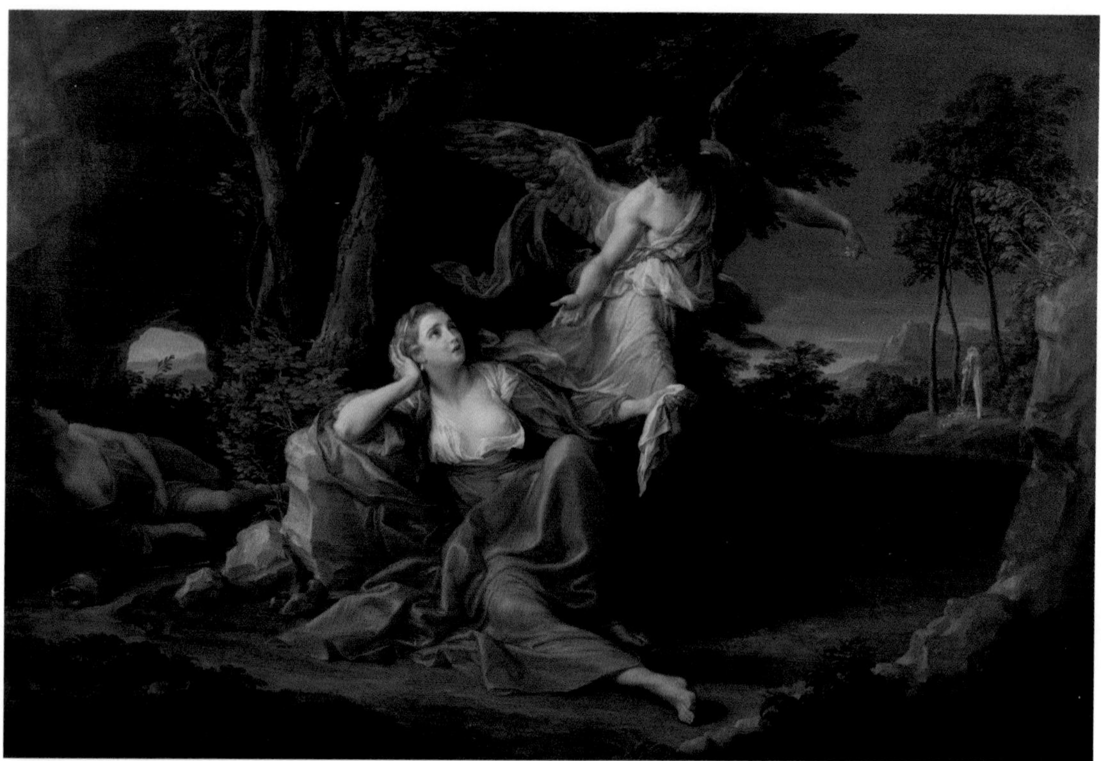

PLATE 6.1. Pompeo Batoni (1708–87), *The Appearance of the Angel to Hagar in the Desert*, 1774–6. Oil on canvas, 100 × 151 cm. Rome, Galleria Nazionale d'Arte Antica, Palazzo Barberini (2374). *(Reproduced courtesy of the Galleria Nazionale d'Arte Antica.)*

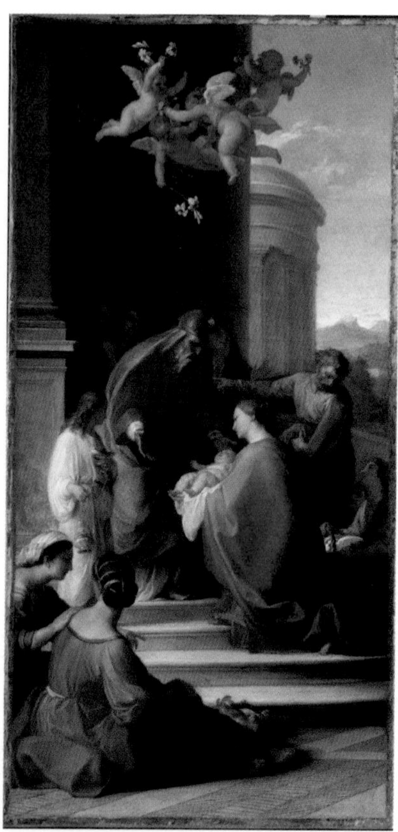

PLATE 6.2. Pompeo Batoni (1708–87), *The Presentation in the Temple*, 1735–6. Oil on canvas, 96.5 × 48 cm. Private collection. *(Reproduced courtesy of the owner.)*

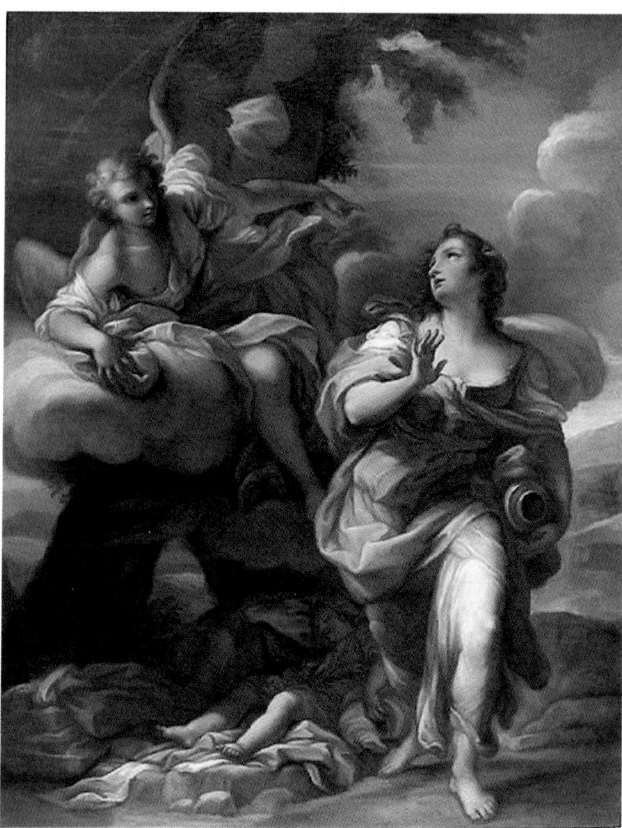

PLATE 6.3. Giuseppe Chiari (1654–1727), *The Appearance of the Angel to Hagar in the Desert*, c. 1705. Oil on canvas, 111 × 86 cm. Paris, Louvre, inv. no. R.F. 1997-35. *(Photo: © Réunion des Musées Nationaux.)*

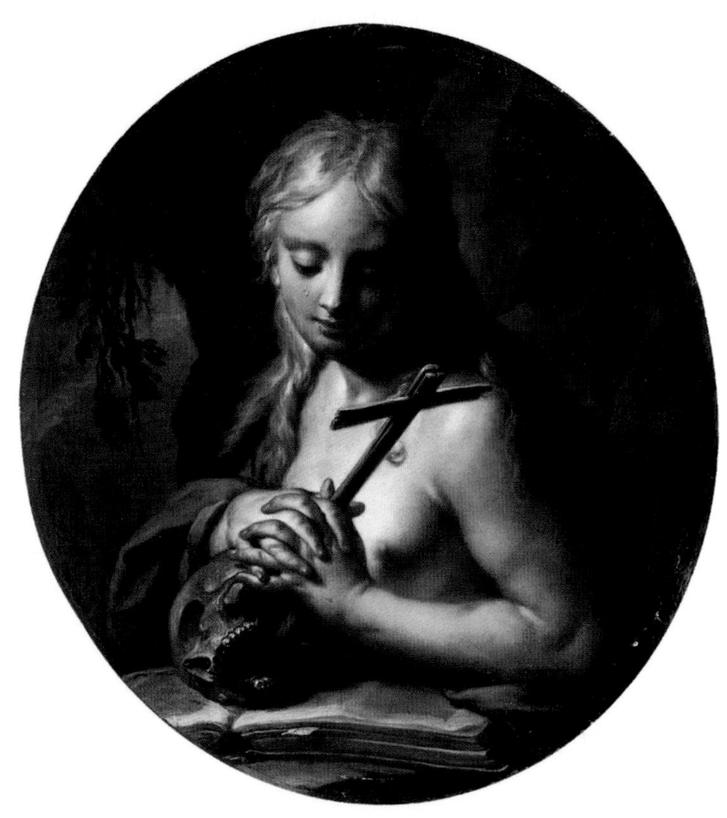

PLATE 7.1. Francesco Trevisani (1656–1746), *Penitent Magdalene*, signed 'F.T.' on the bookmark. Oil on canvas, oval, 70.8 × 65.7 cm. Christie's, New York, 28 January 2009, lot 239. *(Reproduced courtesy of the owner.)*

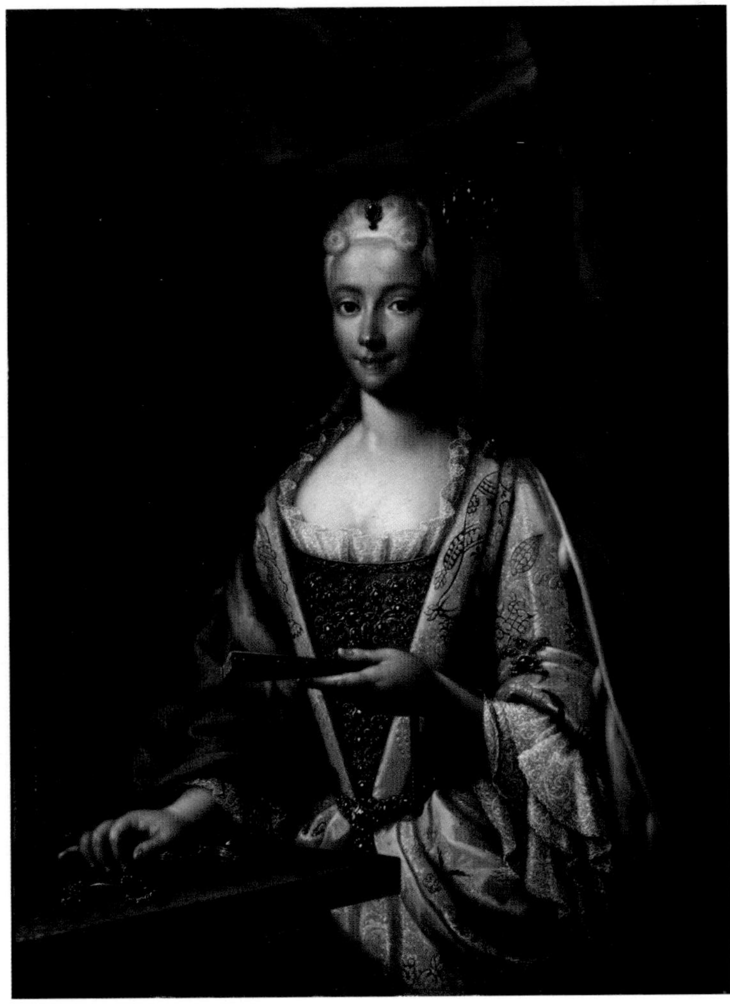

PLATE 7.2. Francesco Trevisani (1656–1746), *Portrait of Maria Clementina Sobieska*, 1719. Oil on canvas, 98 × 73 cm. Scottish National Portrait Gallery, Edinburgh, no. 886. *(Photo: National Galleries of Scotland.)*

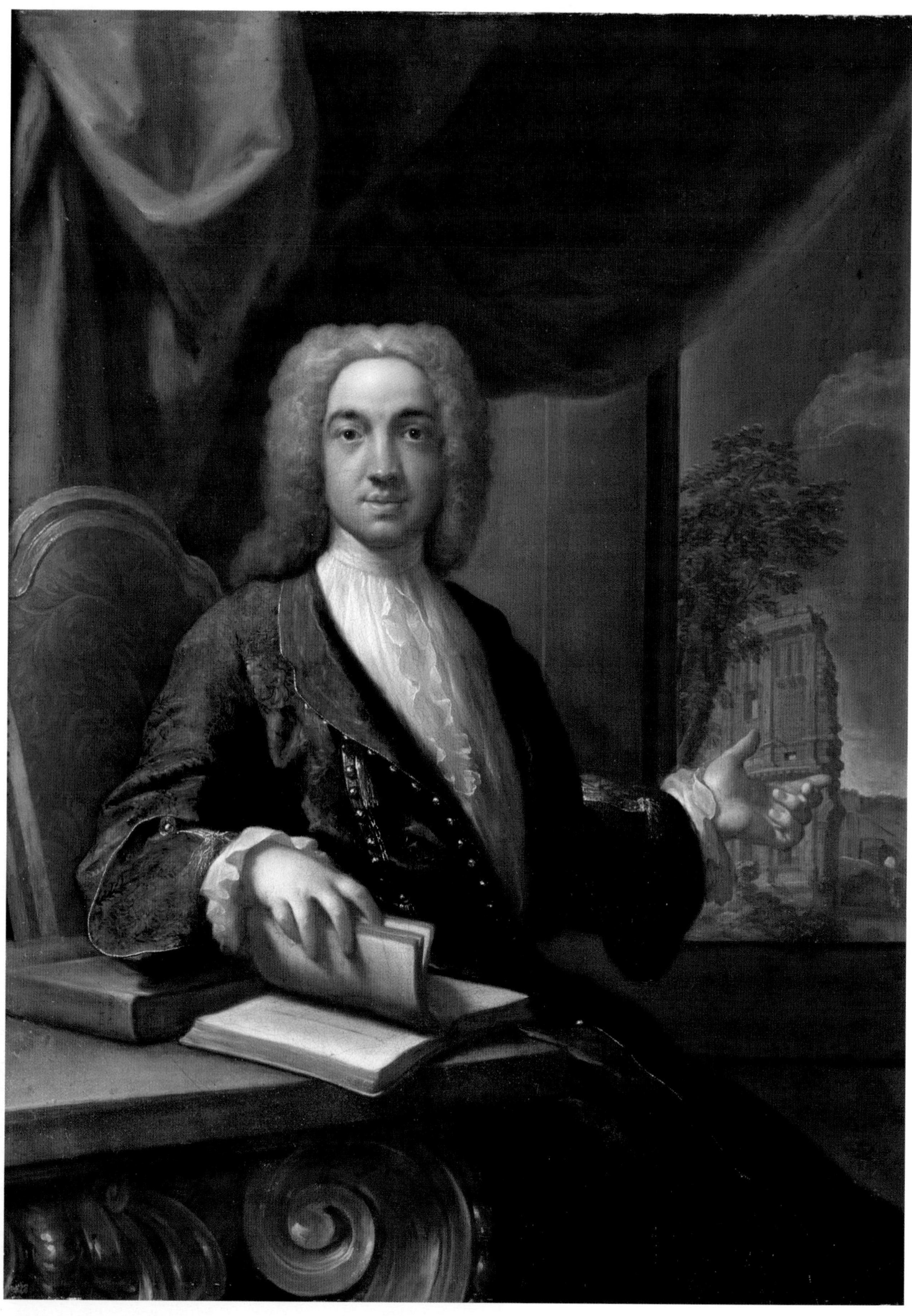

PLATE 7.3. Francesco Trevisani (1656–1746), *Portrait of Sir Edward Gascoigne, 5th Baronet*, 1725. Oil on canvas, 96.5 × 80 cm. Lotherton Hall, City Art Galleries, Leeds. *(Photo: © Leeds Museums and Galleries (Lotherton Hall) U.K.)*

PLATE 8.1. Antonio David (1684–1737), *Prince Charles Edward Stuart, 1720–1788. Eldest Son of Prince James Francis Edward Stuart*, 1732. Oil on canvas, 73.4 × 60.3 cm. Scottish National Portrait Gallery, acc. no. PG 887, purchased 1918. *(Photo: National Galleries of Scotland.)*

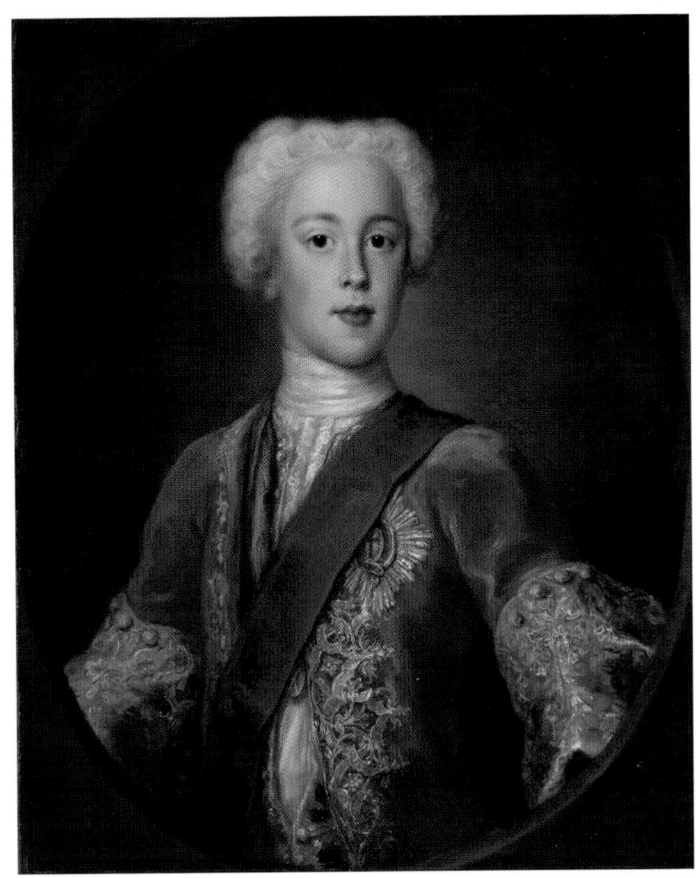

PLATE 8.2. Francesco Trevisani (1656–1746), *The Resurrection of Christ*. Oil on canvas, 202 × 149 cm. Private Collection. P. & D. Colnaghi and Co. *(Reproduced courtesy of the owner.)*

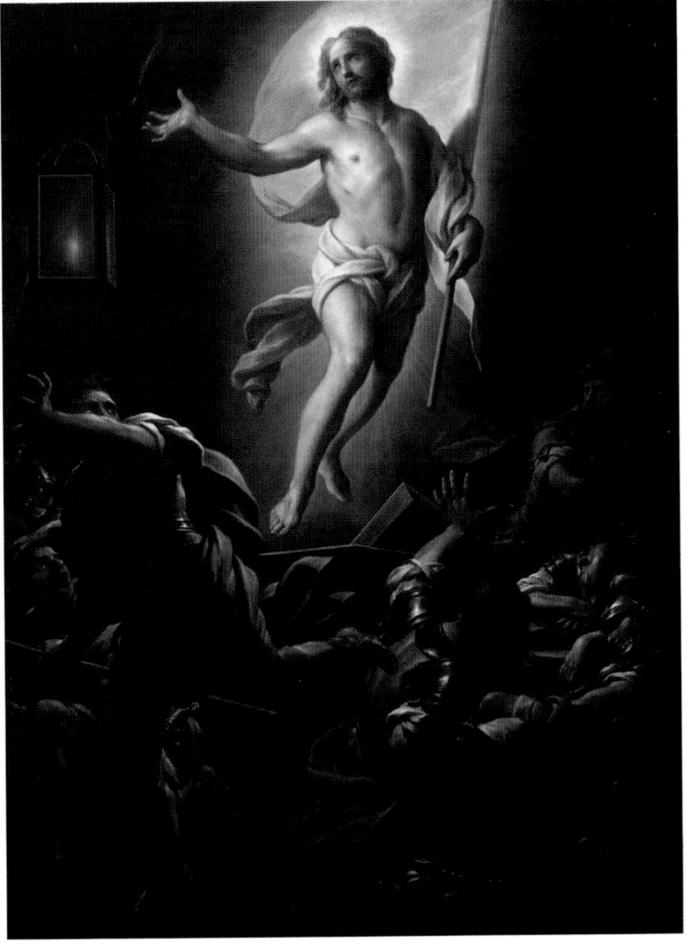

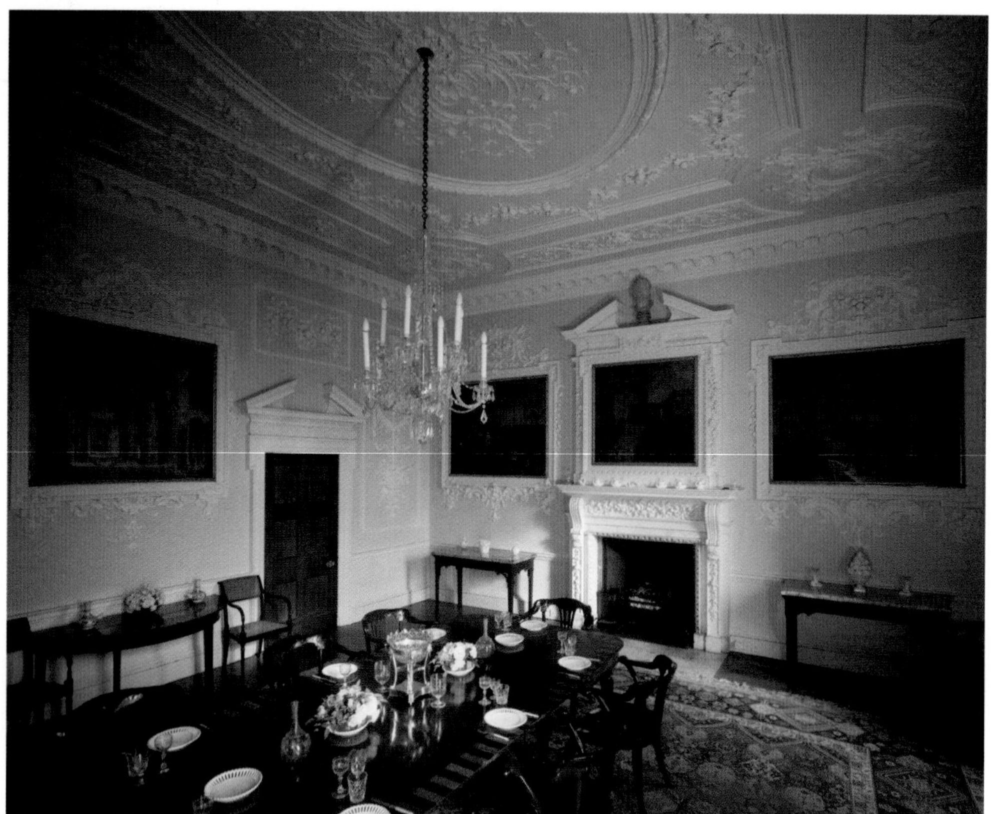

PLATE 9.1. View of the Dining Room at Farnborough Hall, Warwickshire, The National Trust. *(Photo: National Trust Picture Library.)*

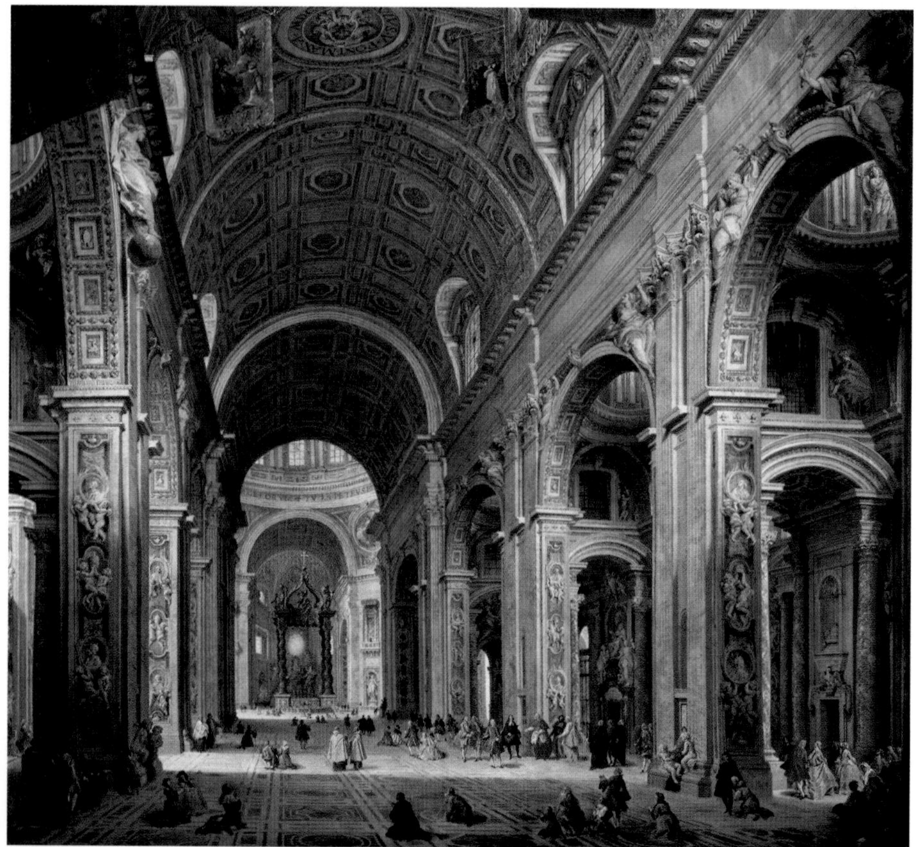

PLATE 9.2. Giovanni Paolo Panini (1691–1765), *Interior of Saint Peter's, Rome*, 1750. Oil on canvas, 132.7 × 145.6 cm. Detroit, The Detroit Institute of Arts, Gift of Mrs Edgar R. Thom, inv. 56.43. *(Reproduced courtesy of the Detroit Institute of Arts.)*

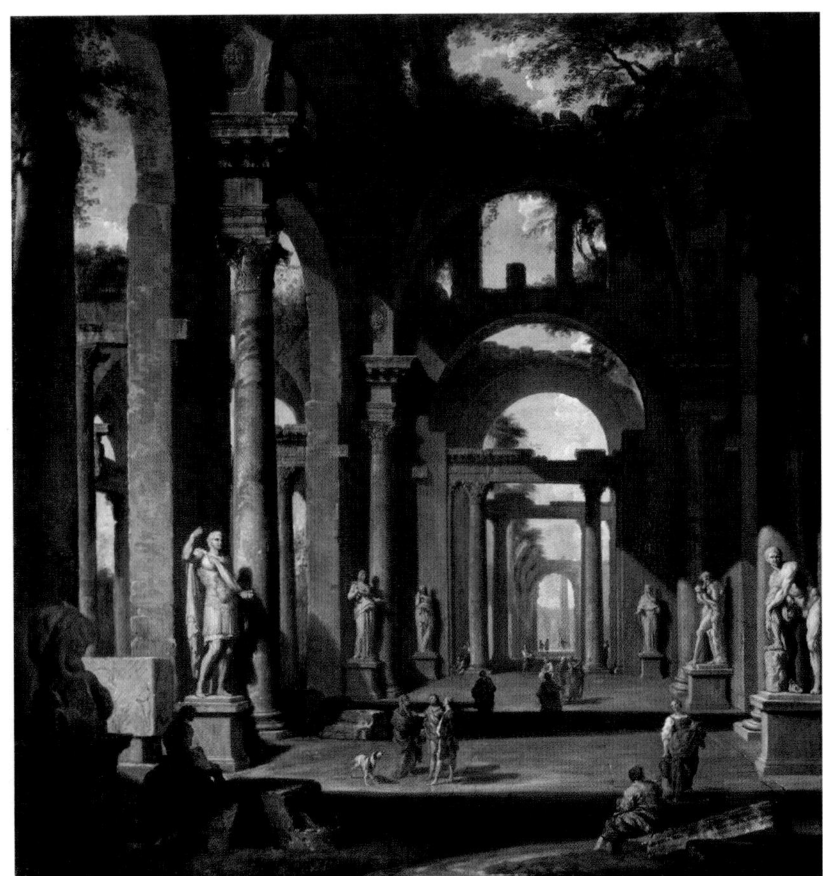

PLATE. 9.3. Giovanni Paolo Panini (1691–1765), *Statues in a Ruined Arcade*, 1738. Twickenham, Marble Hill House, English Heritage, inv. no. MH71. *(Photo: © English Heritage. Reproduced courtesy of English Heritage.)*

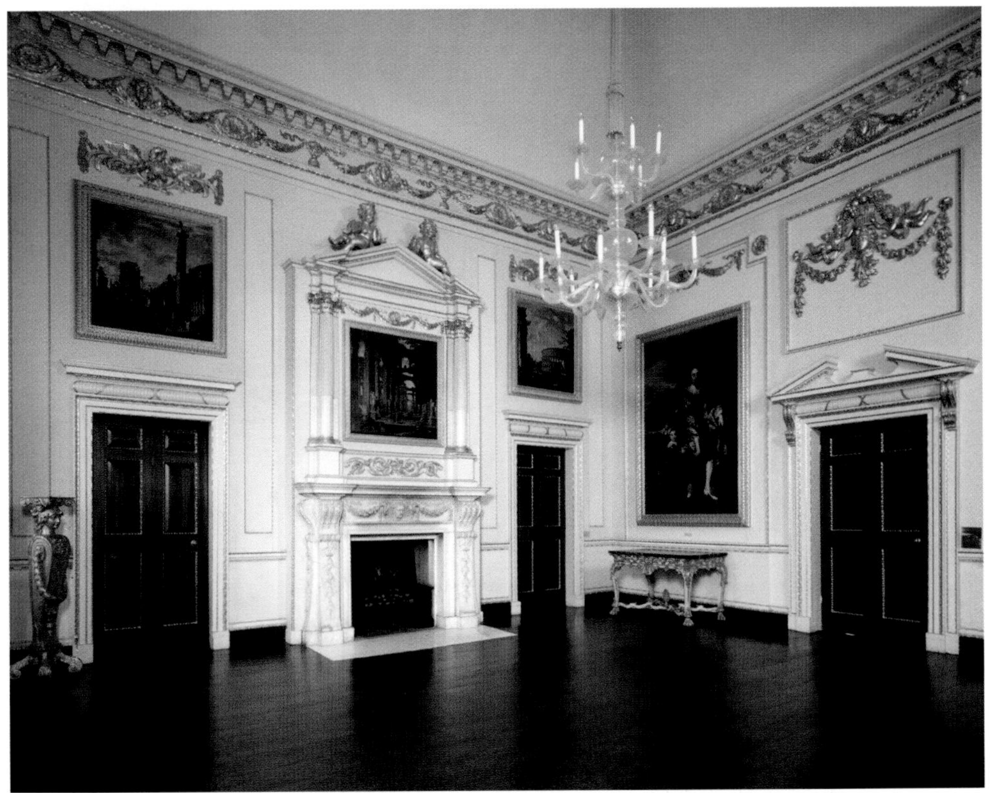

PLATE 9.4. View of the Great Room, Marble Hill House, Twickenham. English Heritage. *(Photo: © English Heritage. Reproduced courtesy of English Heritage.)*

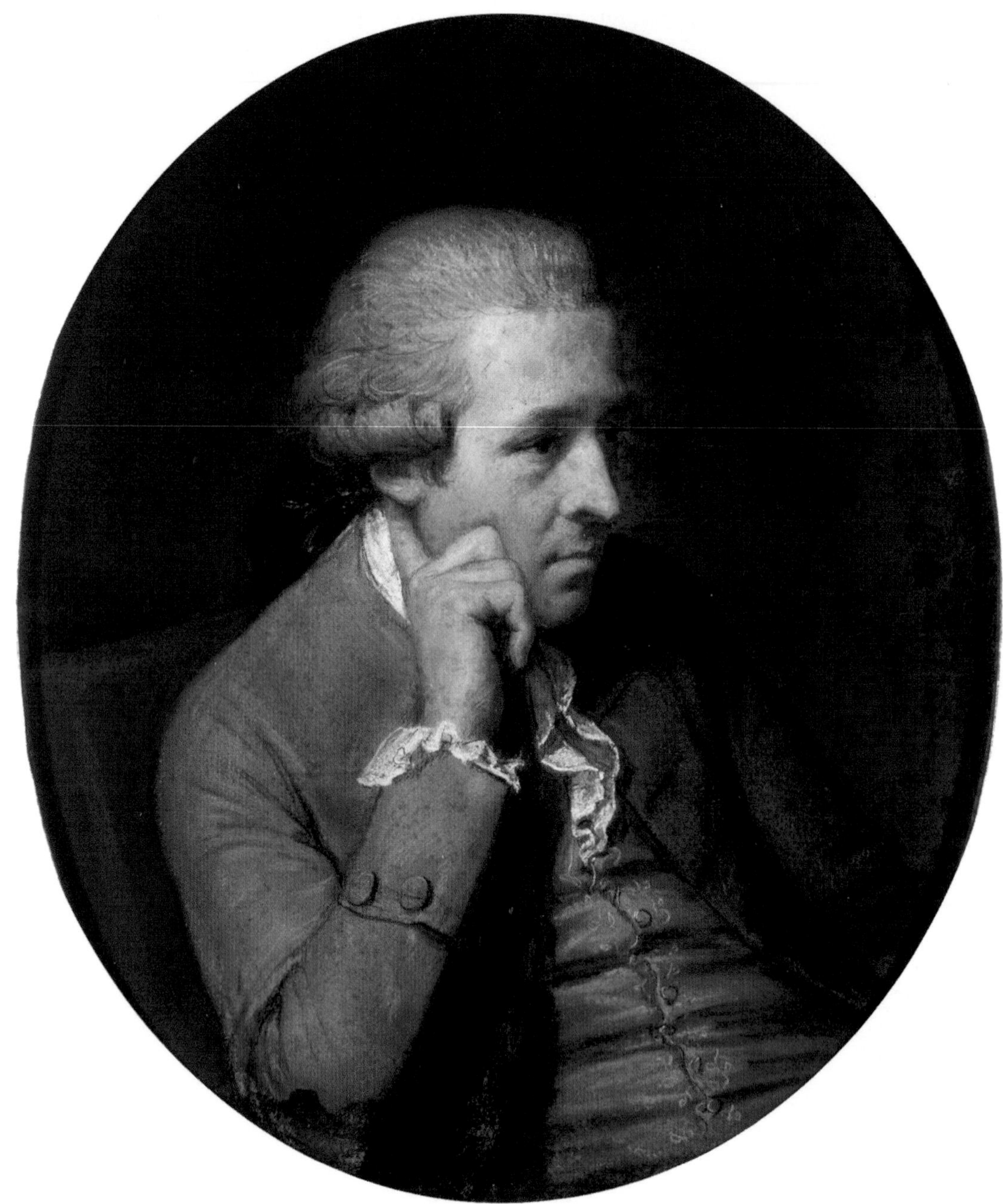

PLATE 10.1. Hugh Douglas Hamilton (*c.* 1739–1808), *James Byres*. Pastel on paper, 28 × 24. Aberdeen Art Gallery, acc. no. ABDAG000094, presented in 1978 by the National Art Collections Fund (Ramsay-Dyce Bequest). *(Reproduced courtesy of Aberdeen Art Gallery and Museums Collections.)*

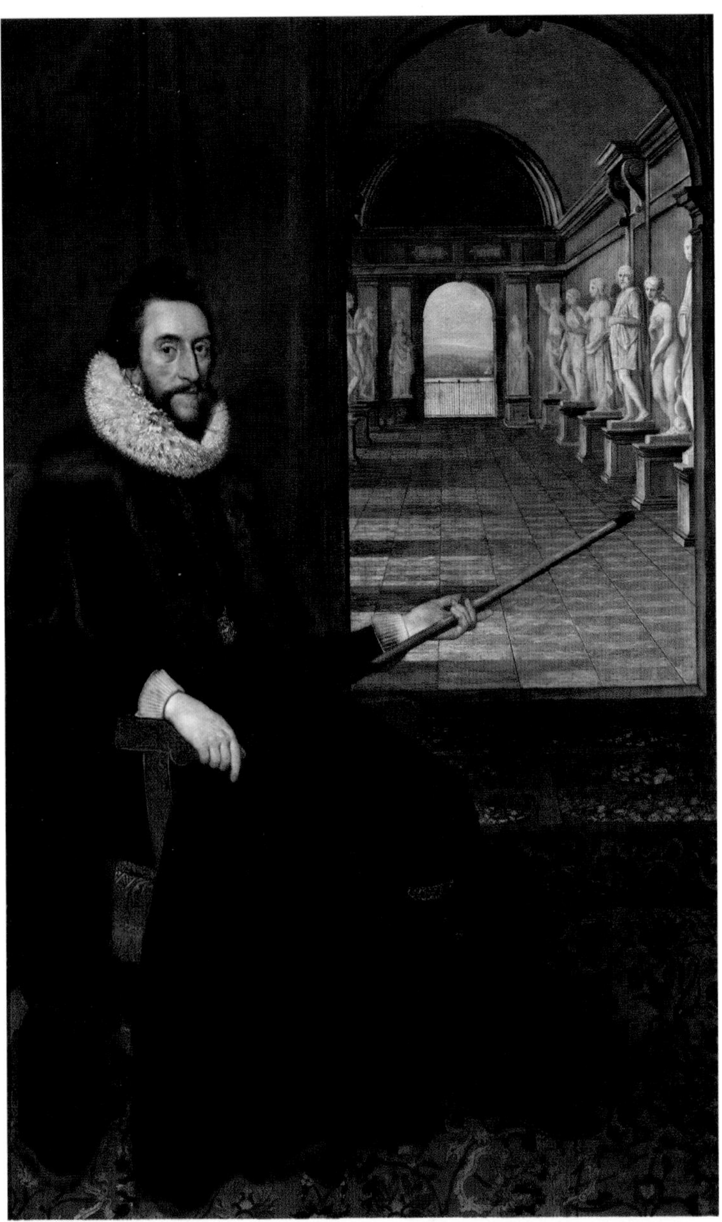

PLATE 11.1. Daniel Mytens (*c.* 1590–1647), *Thomas Howard, 14th Earl of Arundel and Surrey (1585–1646)*, c. 1618. Oil on canvas, 207 × 127 cm. London, National Portrait Gallery 5292. Accepted in lieu of tax by H.M. Government and allocated to the Gallery, 1980. *(Photo: © National Portrait Gallery, London.)*

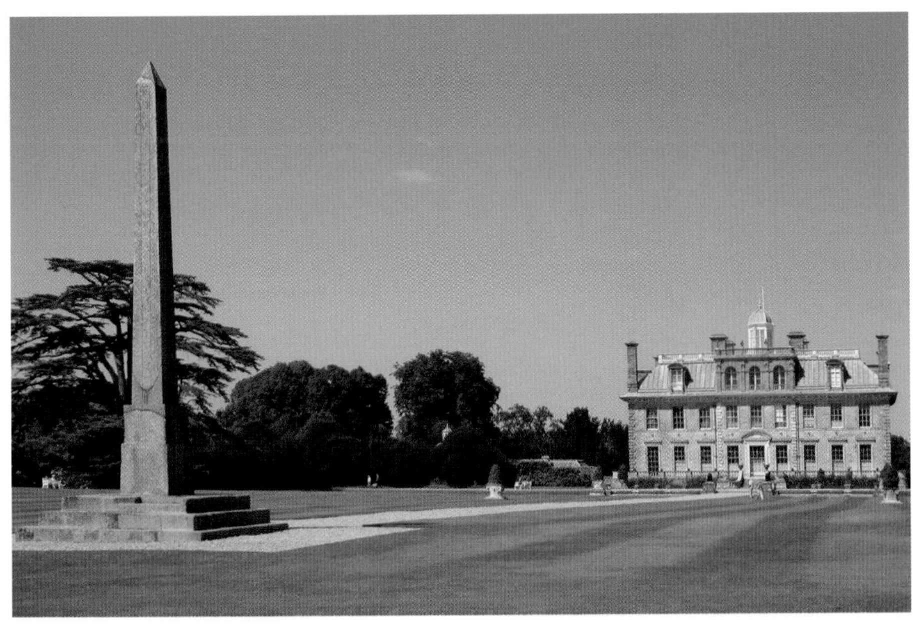

PLATE 11.2. ***The Philae Obelisk***, Kingston Lacy, Dorset. *(Photo: © David R. Marshall, 2009.)*

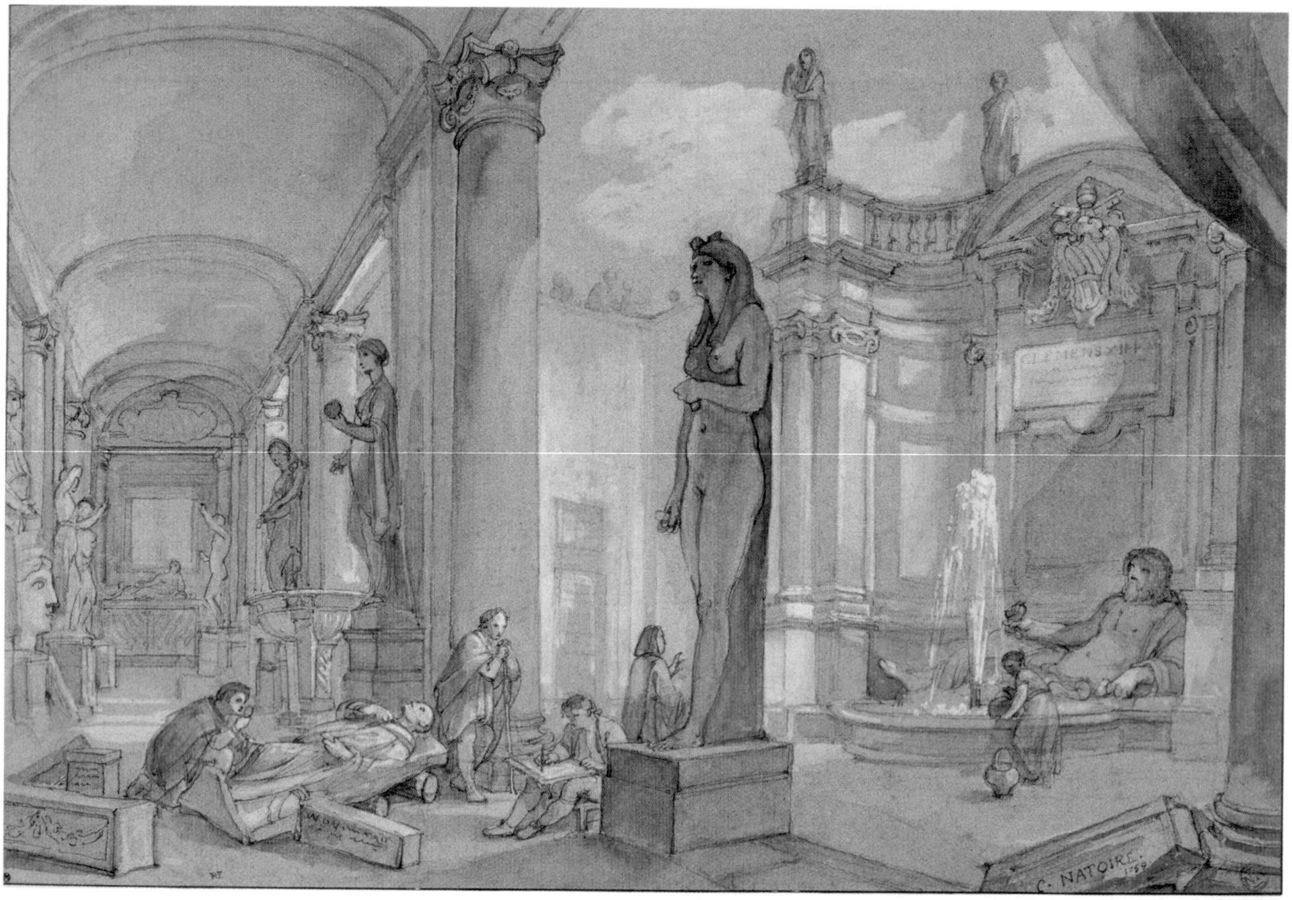

PLATE 12.1. *Above*: Charles-Joseph Natoire (1700–77), *Courtyard of the Capitoline Museum in Rome*, 1759. Pen and ink. Paris, Museé Nationale du Louvre, inv. 31381. *(Photo: Michèle Bellot, Réunion des Musées Nationaux/Art Resource, NY.)*

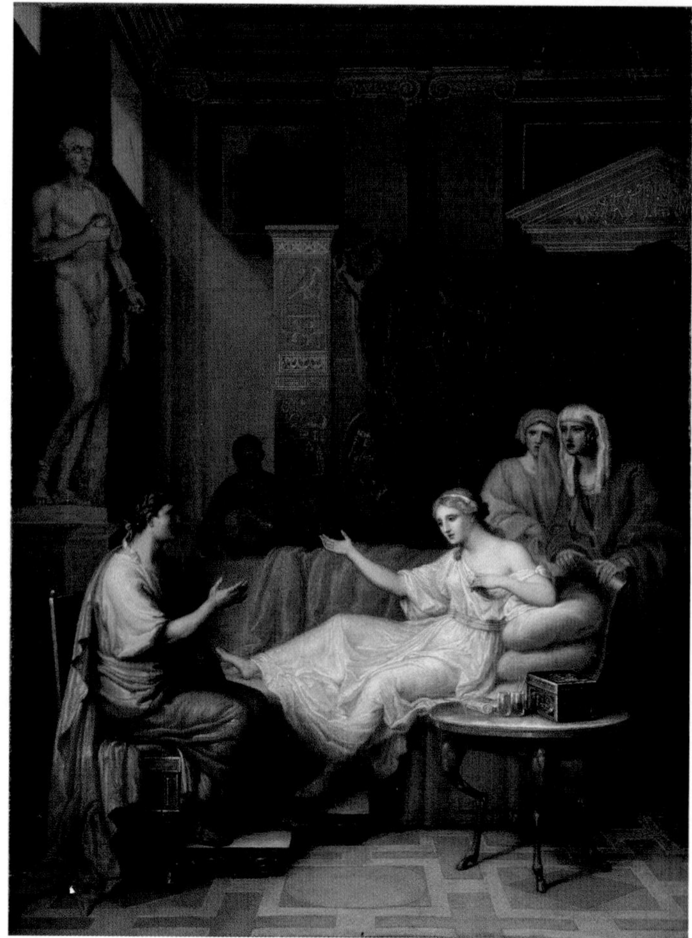

PLATE 12.2. *Right*: Anton Raphael Mengs (1728–79), *Augustus and Cleopatra*, 1759. Oil on canvas. Augsburg, Städtische Kunstsammlungen, inv. no. 12634. *(Reproduced courtesy of the Kunstsammlungen und Museen Augsburg.)*

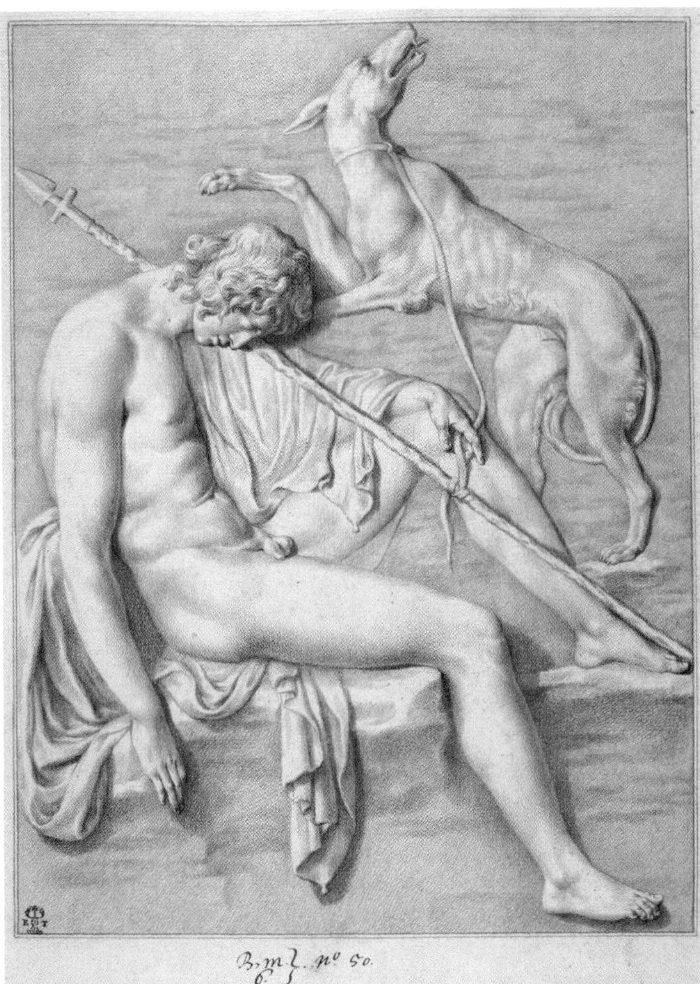

PLATE 13.1. Pompeo Batoni (1708–87), ***Endymion Relief***, *c.* 1730. Red chalk on white paper, 470 × 360 mm. Eton College, Windsor. *(Reproduced by permission of the Provost and Fellows of Eton College.)*

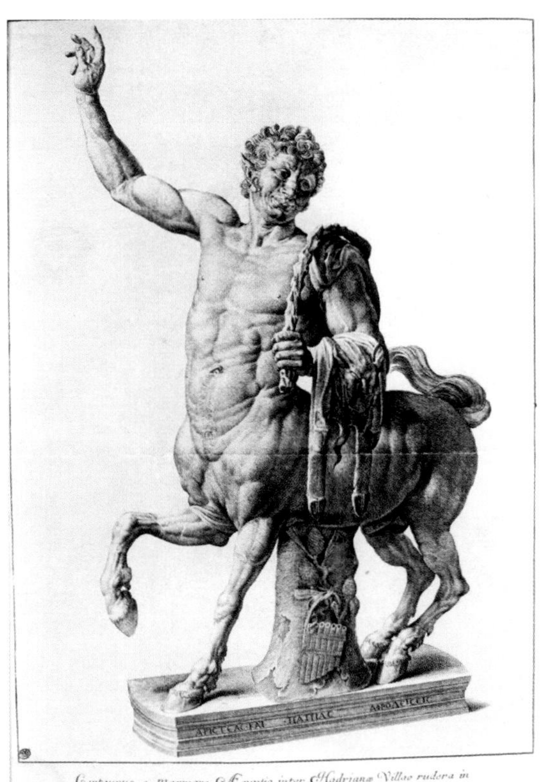

PLATE 13.2. Giovanni Girolamo Frezza (1659–after 1741), *The Younger Furietti Centaur* (after Batoni), 1739. Engraving, 493 × 334 mm. Private Collection. *(Photo: E.P. Bowron.)*

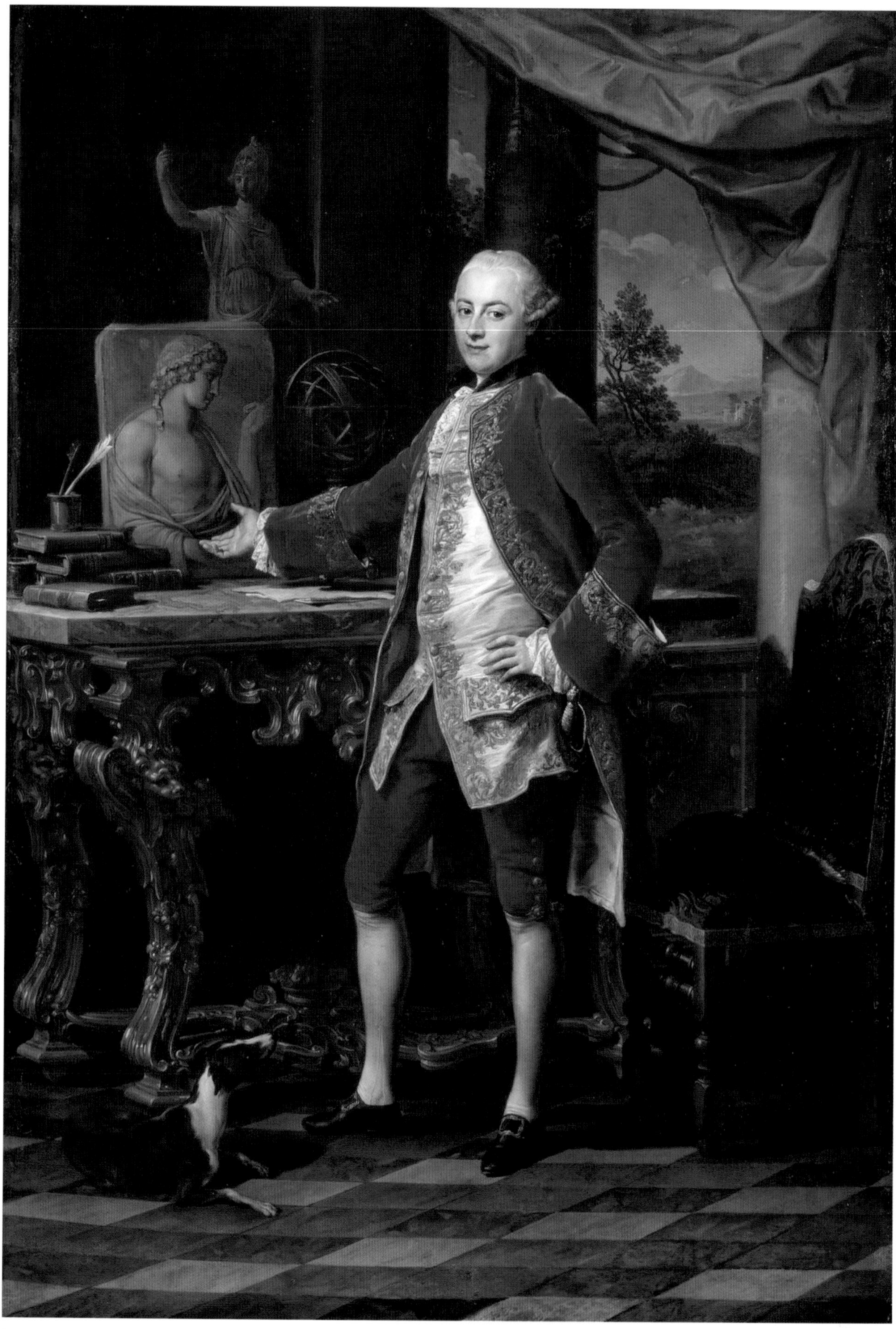

PLATE 13.3. Pompeo Batoni (1708–87), *Portrait of a Gentleman*, early 1760s. Oil on canvas, 246.8 × 176 cm. The Metropolitan Museum of Art, New York; Rogers Fund, 1903 (03.37.1). *(Image © The Metropolitan Museum of Art.)*

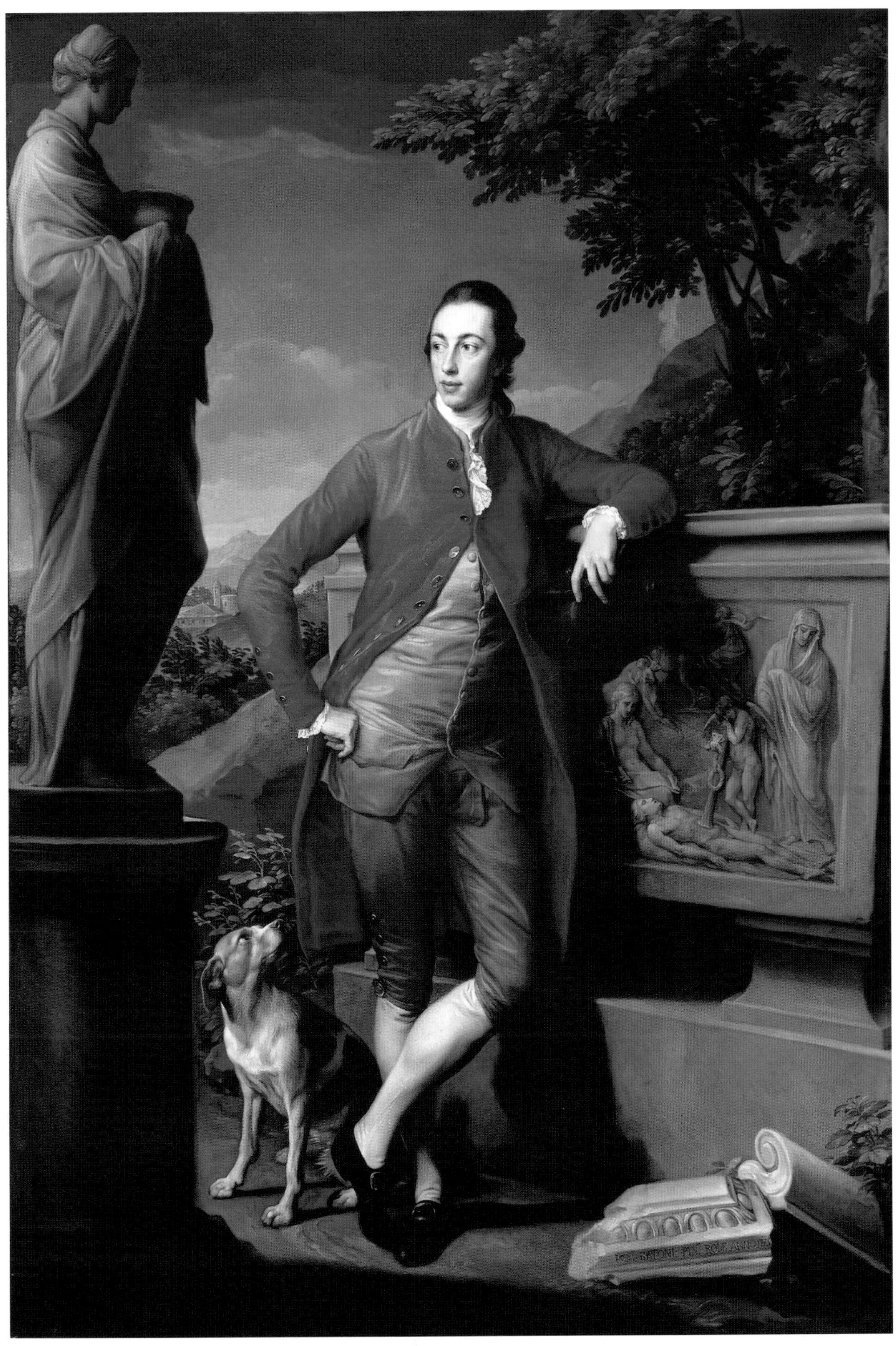

PLATE 13.4. Pompeo Batoni (1708–87), *George Gordon, Lord Haddo (Died 1791)*, 1775. Oil on canvas, 259.2 × 170.3 cm. The National Trust for Scotland, Haddo House, Aberdeenshire. *(Reproduced by kind permission of The National Trust for Scotland.)*

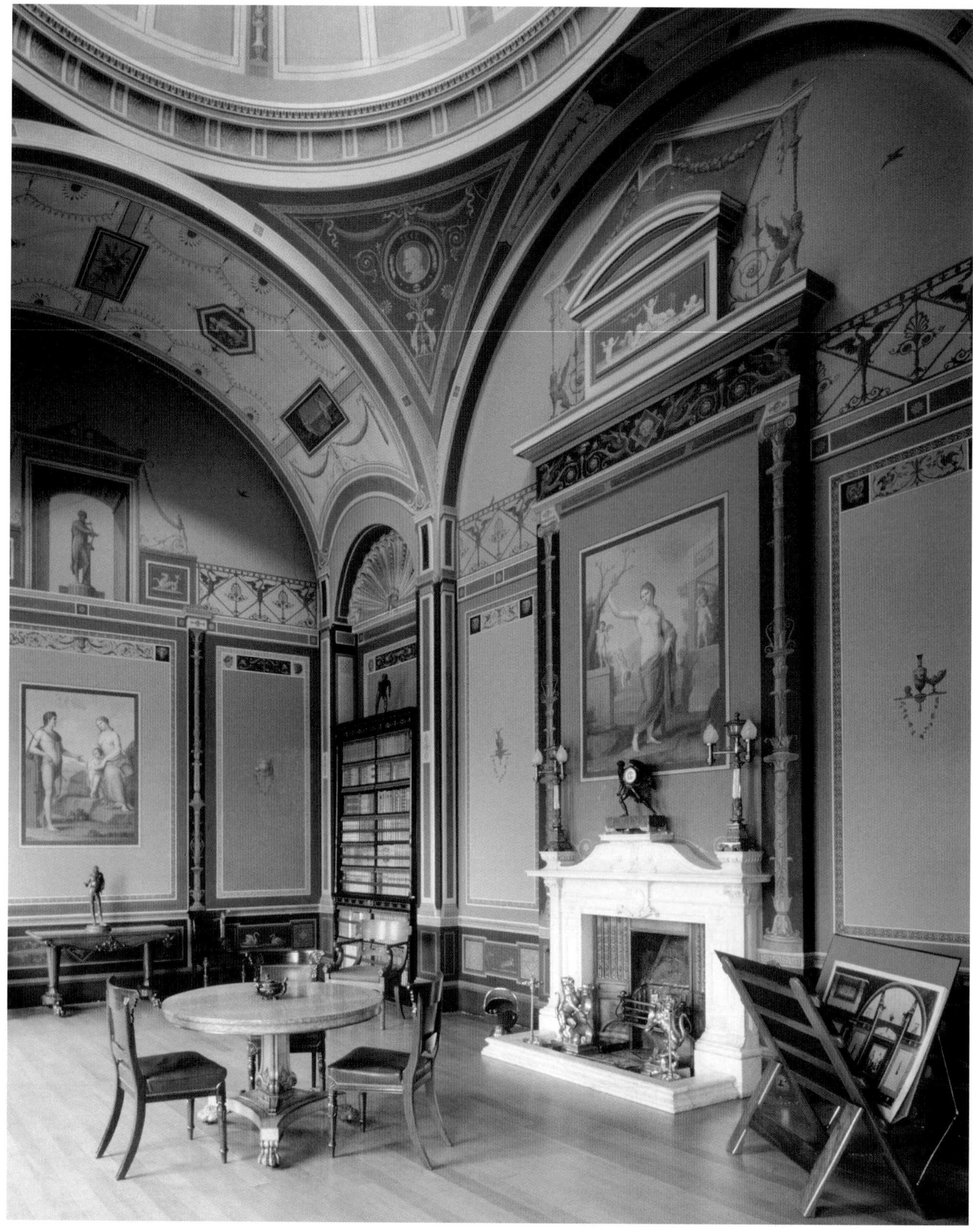

PLATE 14.1. **The 'Pompeian room', Ickworth House, Suffolk.** *(Photo: National Trust Photographic Library/Andreas von Einsiedel.)*

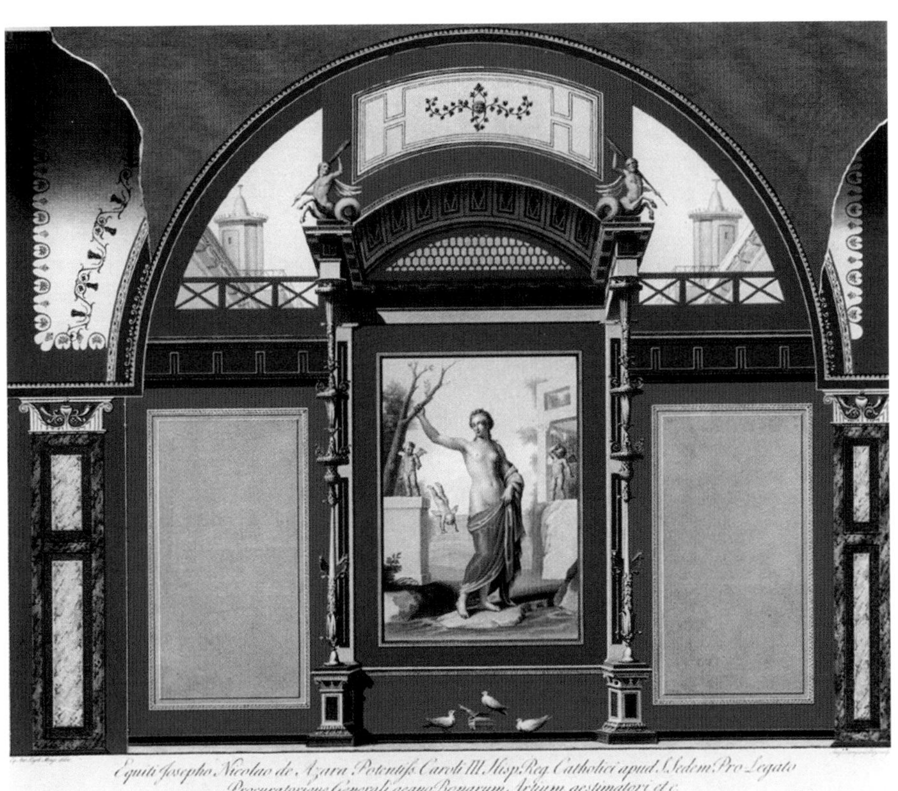

PLATE 14.2. *Left*: Camillo Buti (1747–1808), *Wall design from the Villa Negroni* (Buti, plate I). Coloured engraving. British School at Rome. *(Photo: British School at Rome Library and Archive.)*

PLATE 14.3. *Below*: Thomas Jones (1742–1803), *An Excavation of an Antique Building Discovered in a Cava in the Villa Negroni at Rome in the Yr. 1779*. Oil and chalk on paper, 406 × 552 mm. London, Tate Gallery, T03544, presented by Canon J.H. Adams, 1983. *(© Tate, London, 2010. Reproduced courtesy of the Tate Gallery.)*

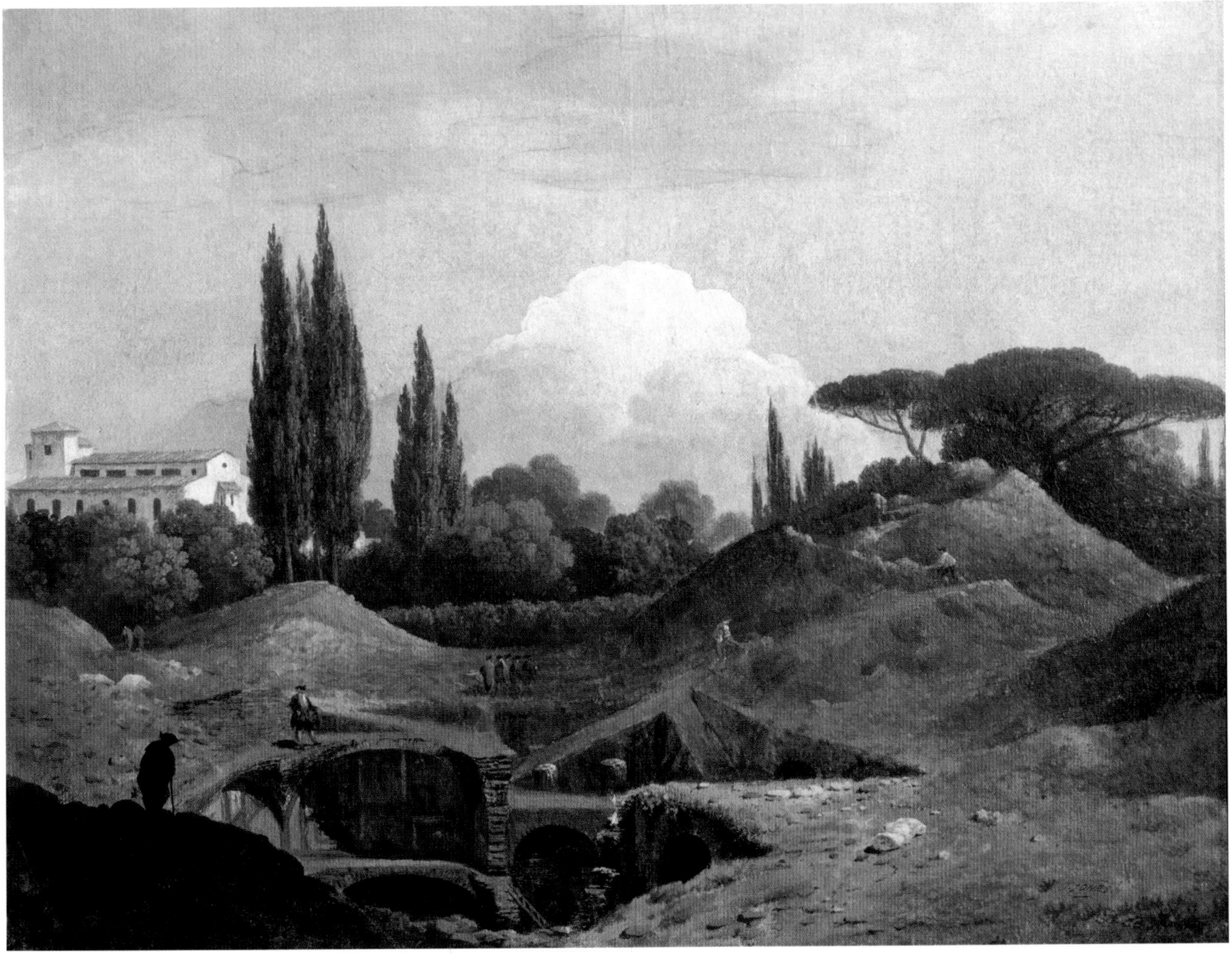

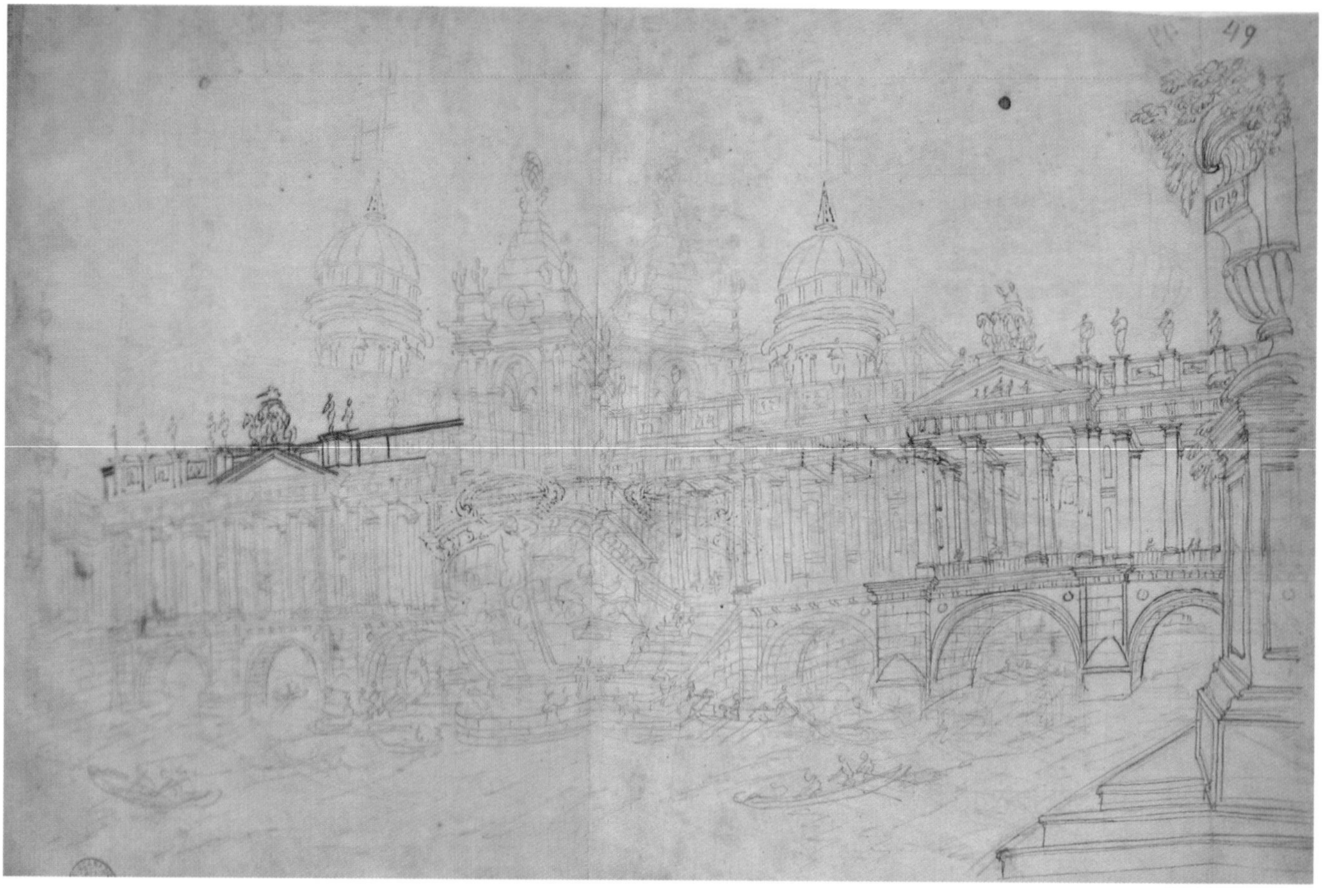

PLATE 15.1. *Above*: Filippo Juvarra (1678–1736), *Monumental Bridge*, 1719. Pen and red chalk, 18.5 × 50 cm. BNT, album Ris. 59,6, fol. 49. *(Reproduced courtesy of the Ministero per i Beni e le Attività Culturali, Biblioteca Nazionale Universitaria di Torino. Reproduction prohibited.)*

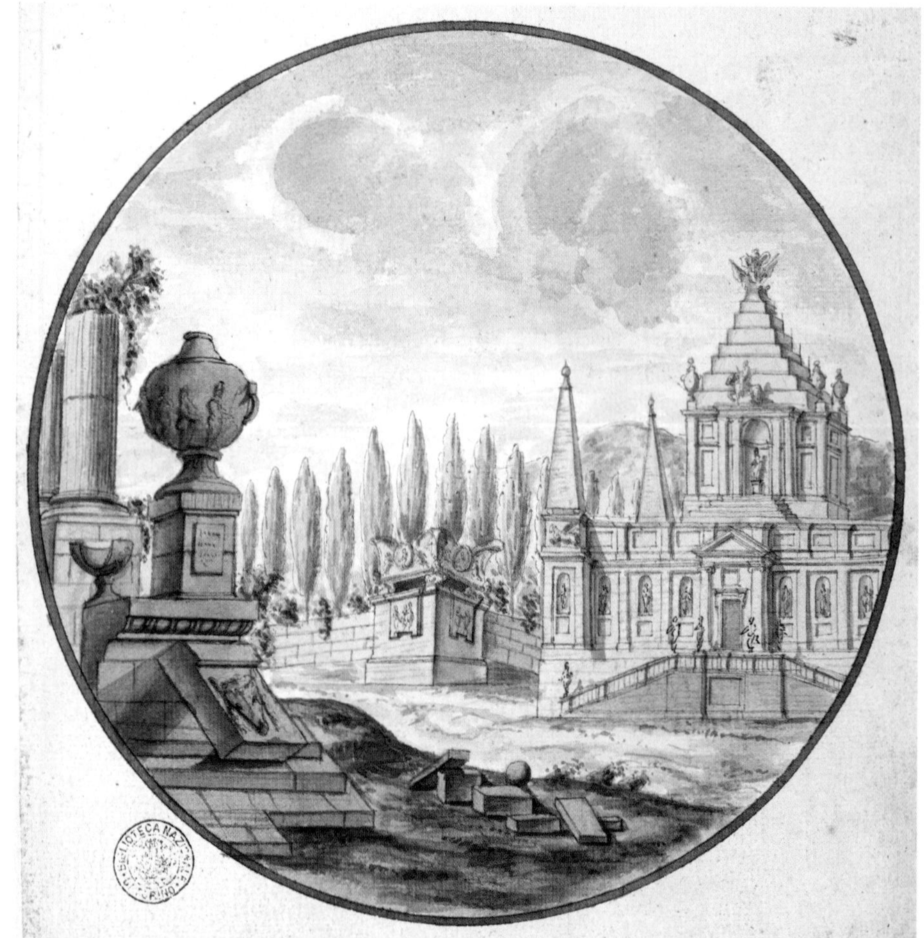

PLATE 15.3. *Right*: Filippo Juvarra (1678–1736), *Architectural Fantasy*. Pen and watercolour in various shades of sepia, blue and light green, 22.3 cm diameter. BNT, album Ris. 59,6, fol. 4r. *(Reproduced courtesy of the Ministero per i Beni e le Attività Culturali, Biblioteca Nazionale Universitaria di Torino. Reproduction prohibited.)*

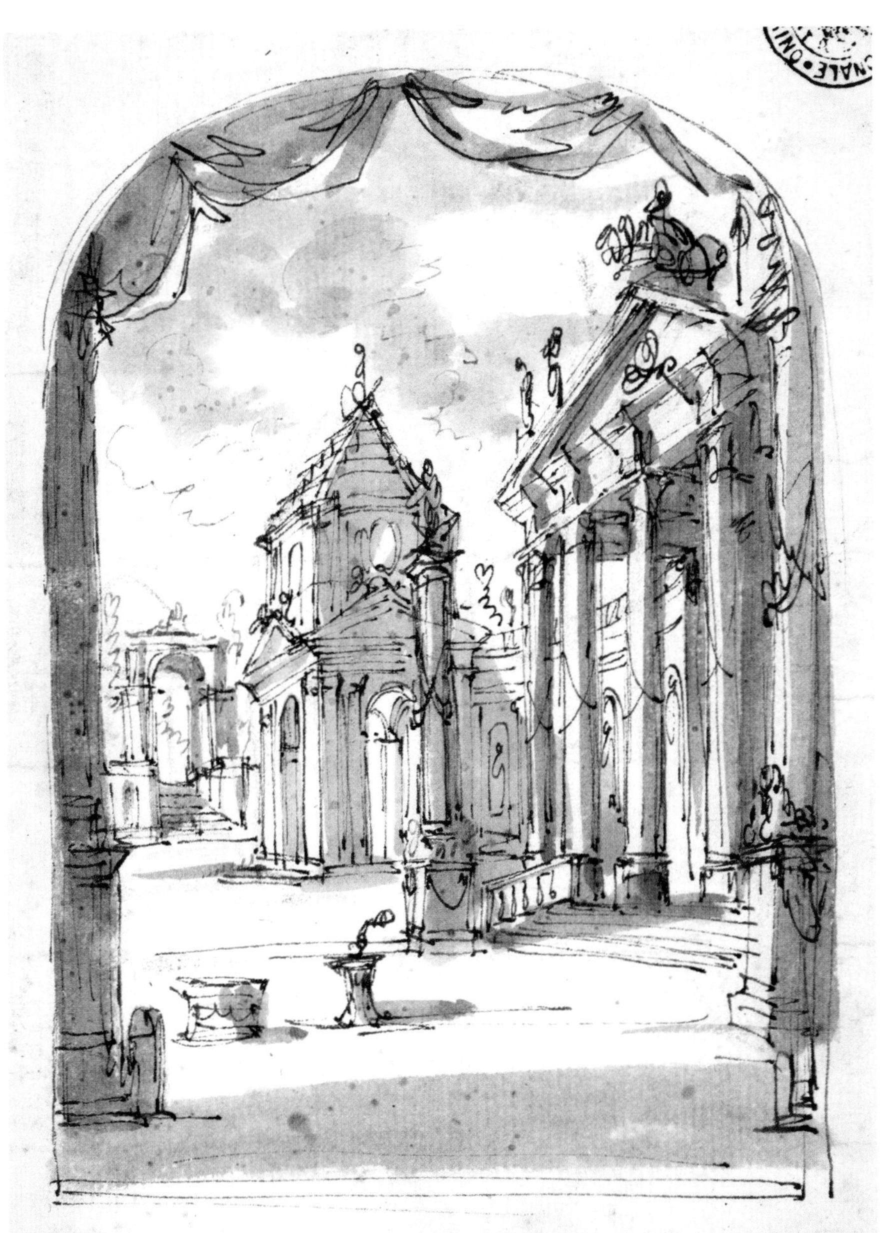

PLATE 15.2. *Right*: Filippo Juvarra (1678–1736), ***Set Design with Architectural Capriccio***. Pen and grey wash, 18.3 × 12.9 cm. BNT, album Ris. 59,4, fol. 40r.4. *(Reproduced courtesy of the Ministero per i Beni e le Attività Culturali, Biblioteca Nazionale Universitaria di Torino. Reproduction prohibited.)*

PLATE 15.4. *Below*: Filippo Juvarra (1678–1736), ***View of the Complex of the Palace, Convent, and Basilica of Nostra Signora e Sant'Antonio di Mafra***, 1719. Pen and traces of chalk, 24.5 × 35.3 cm. BNT, album Ris. 59,6, fol. 31bis–v. *(Reproduced courtesy of the Ministero per i Beni e le Attività Culturali, Biblioteca Nazionale Universitaria di Torino. Reproduction prohibited.)*

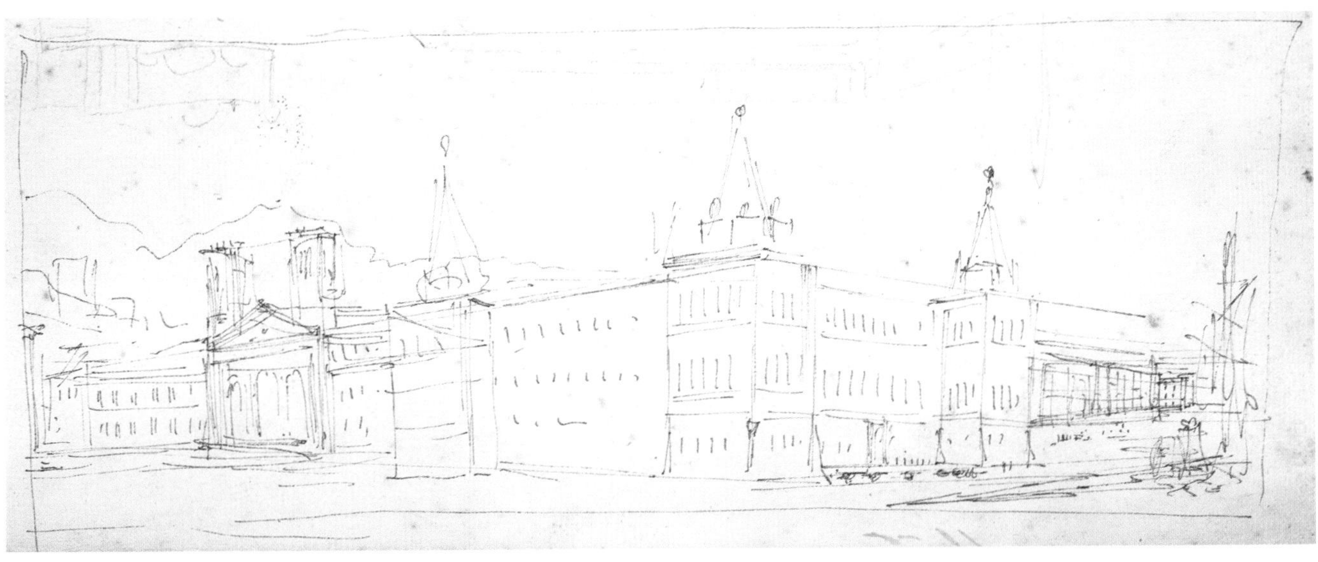

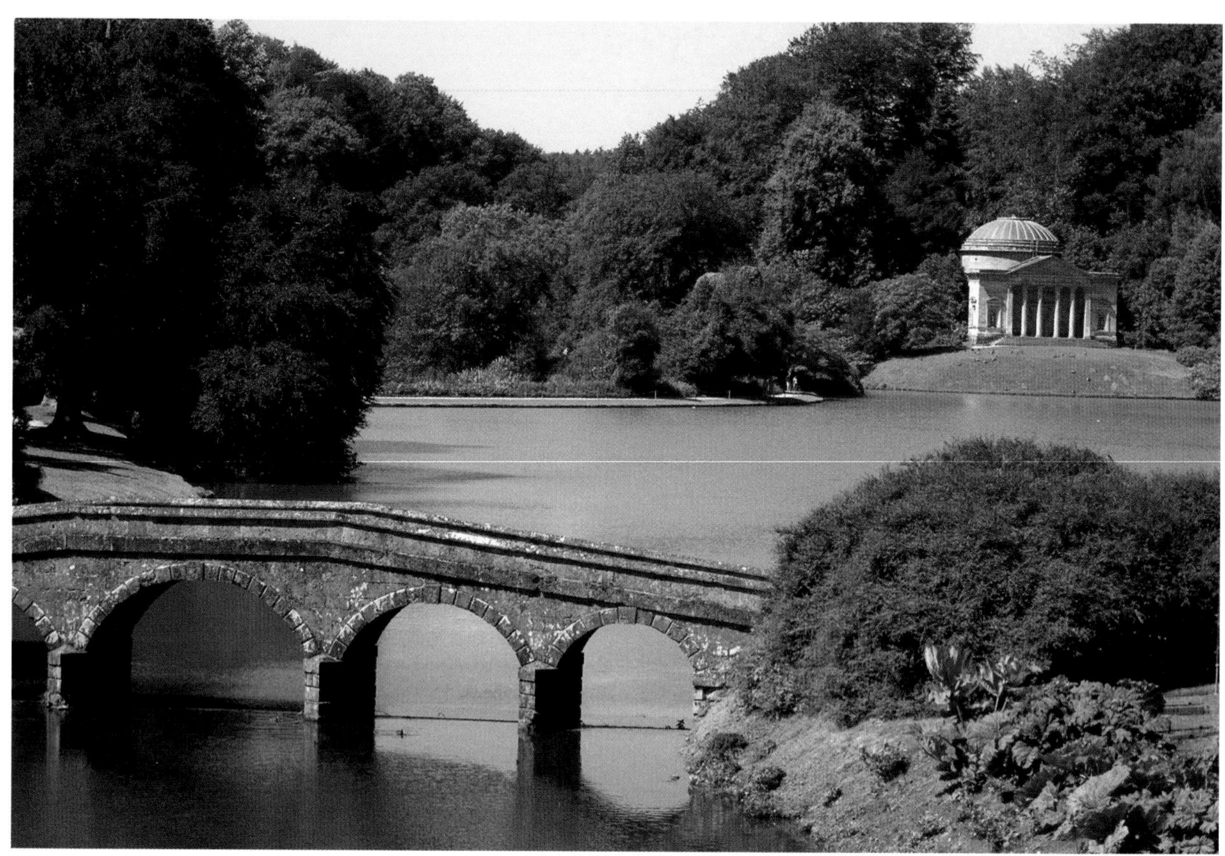

Plate 16.1. *Above*: **View of the Pantheon at Stourhead, Wiltshire.** *(Photo: © David R. Marshall, 2009.)*

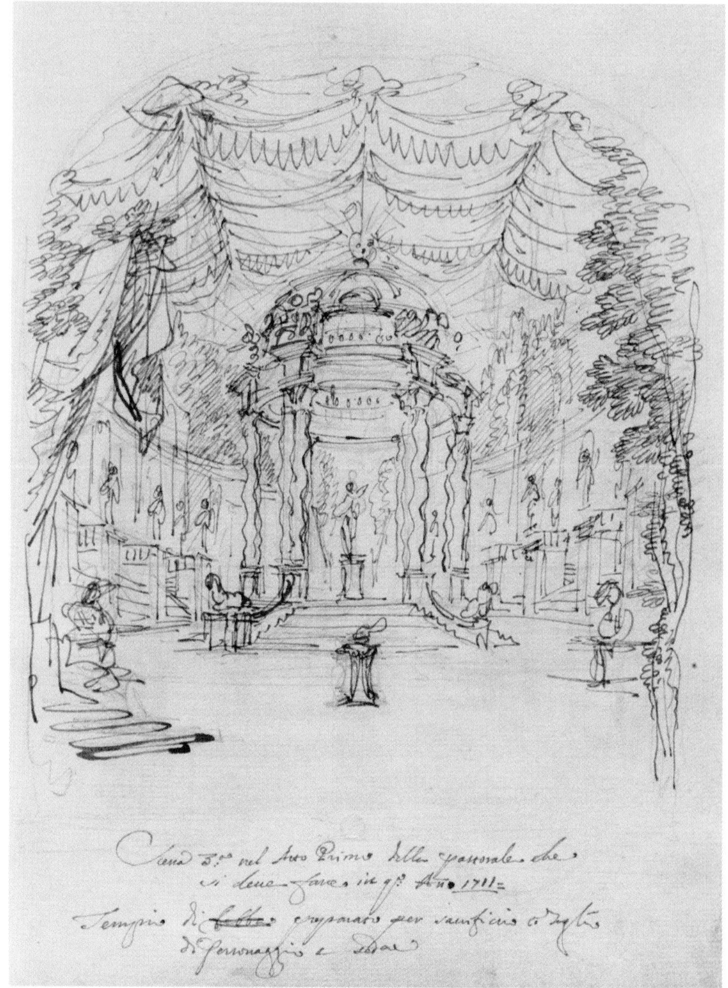

Plate 16.2. *Right*: **Filippo Juvarra (1678–1736), *A Temple Prepared for Sacrifice*, set design for *Il Ciro*, performed in Rome, Teatro Ottoboni, 1712. Pen and ink. London, Victoria and Albert Museum, print room reg. 8426: 17.** *(Photo: © V&A Images/Victoria and Albert Museum, London.)*

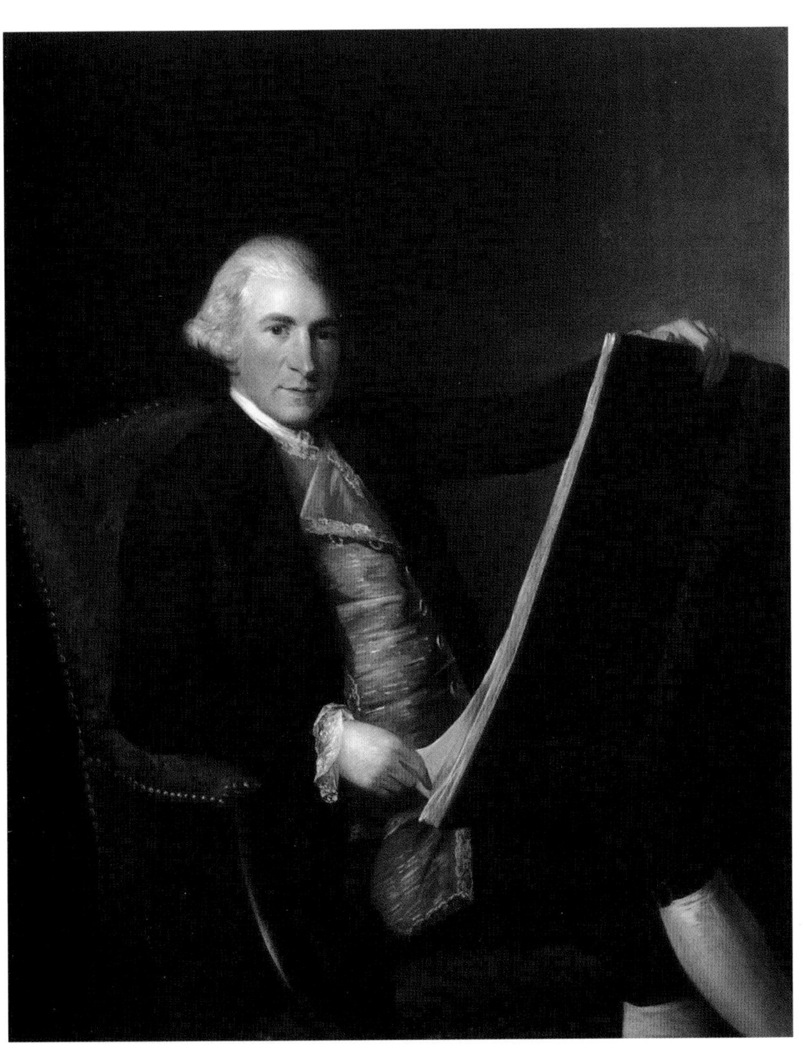

Plate 17.1. *Left*: Attributed to George Willison (1741–97), *Robert Adam*, *c.* 1763. Oil on canvas, 127.0 × 101.6 cm. London, National Portrait Gallery, no. 2953. *(Photo: © National Portrait Gallery, London.)*

Plate 17.2. *Below*: Giovanni Battista Piranesi (1720–78), *Ichnographia* (detail) from *Il Campo Marzio dell'antica Roma*, 1762. *(Photo: David R. Marshall/University of Melbourne, Baillieu Library.)*

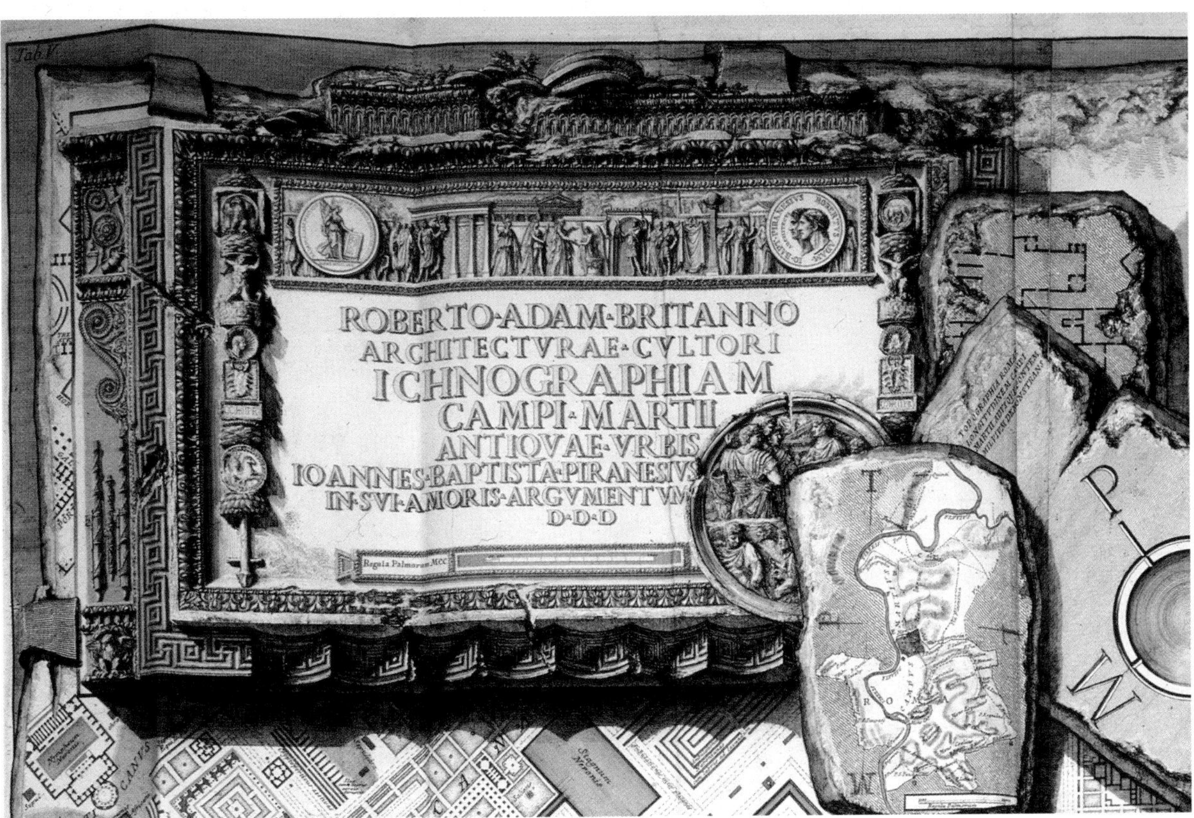

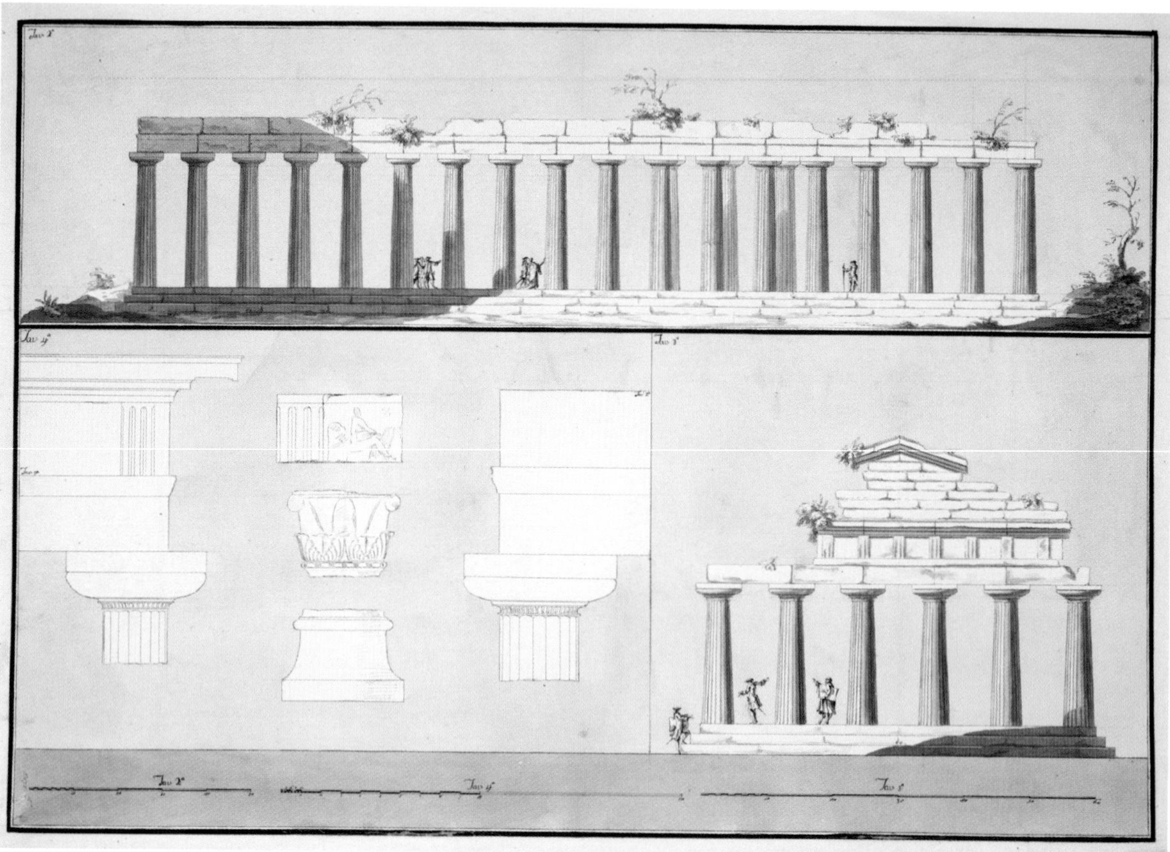

PLATE 18.1. Vincenzo Brenna (1741–), *First Temple of Hera and Temple of Athena at Paestum*, 1768. Indian ink and watercolour. London, Victoria and Albert Museum. *(Photo: © V&A Images/Victoria and Albert Museum, London.)*

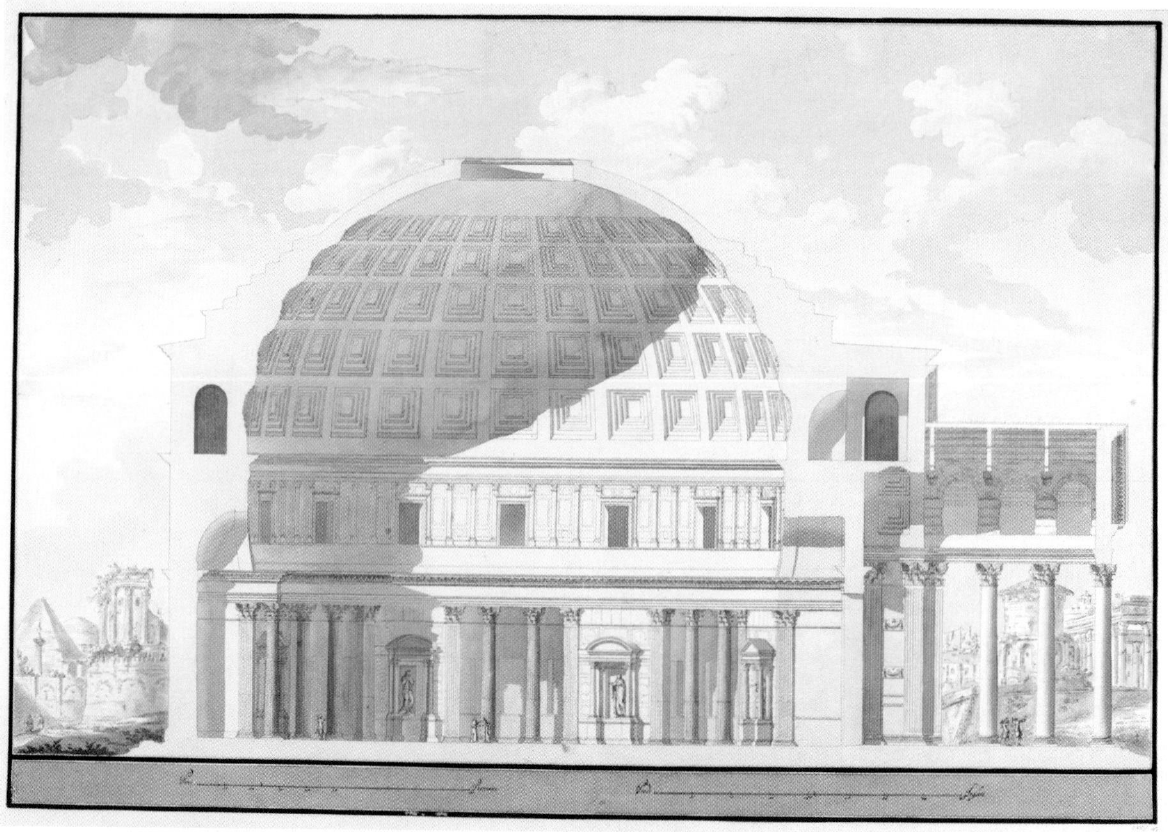

PLATE 18.2. Vincenzo Brenna (1741–), *Longitudinal Section of the Pantheon*, 1769. London, Victoria and Albert Museum. *(Photo: © V&A Images/Victoria and Albert Museum, London.)*

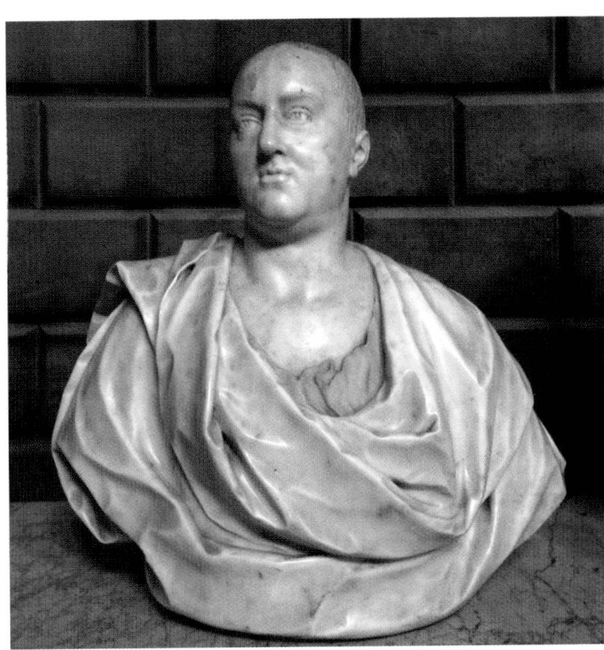

PLATE 19.1. Francesco Maratti (fl. 1686–1719), *Lord William Cecil*, *c.* 1701. Marble. The Burghley House Collection. *(Reproduced*

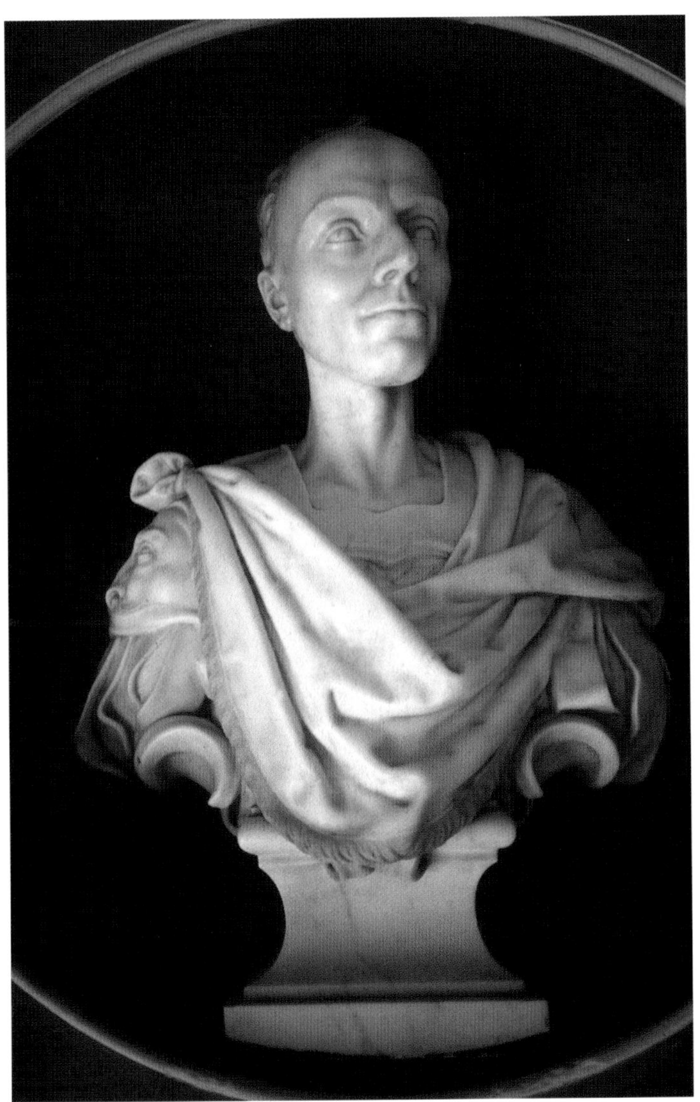

PLATE 19.2. Neapolitan(?), *Lord Binnning*, *c.* 1732. Marble. Earl of Haddington Collection, Mellertsain. *(Reproduced courtesy of the owner.)*

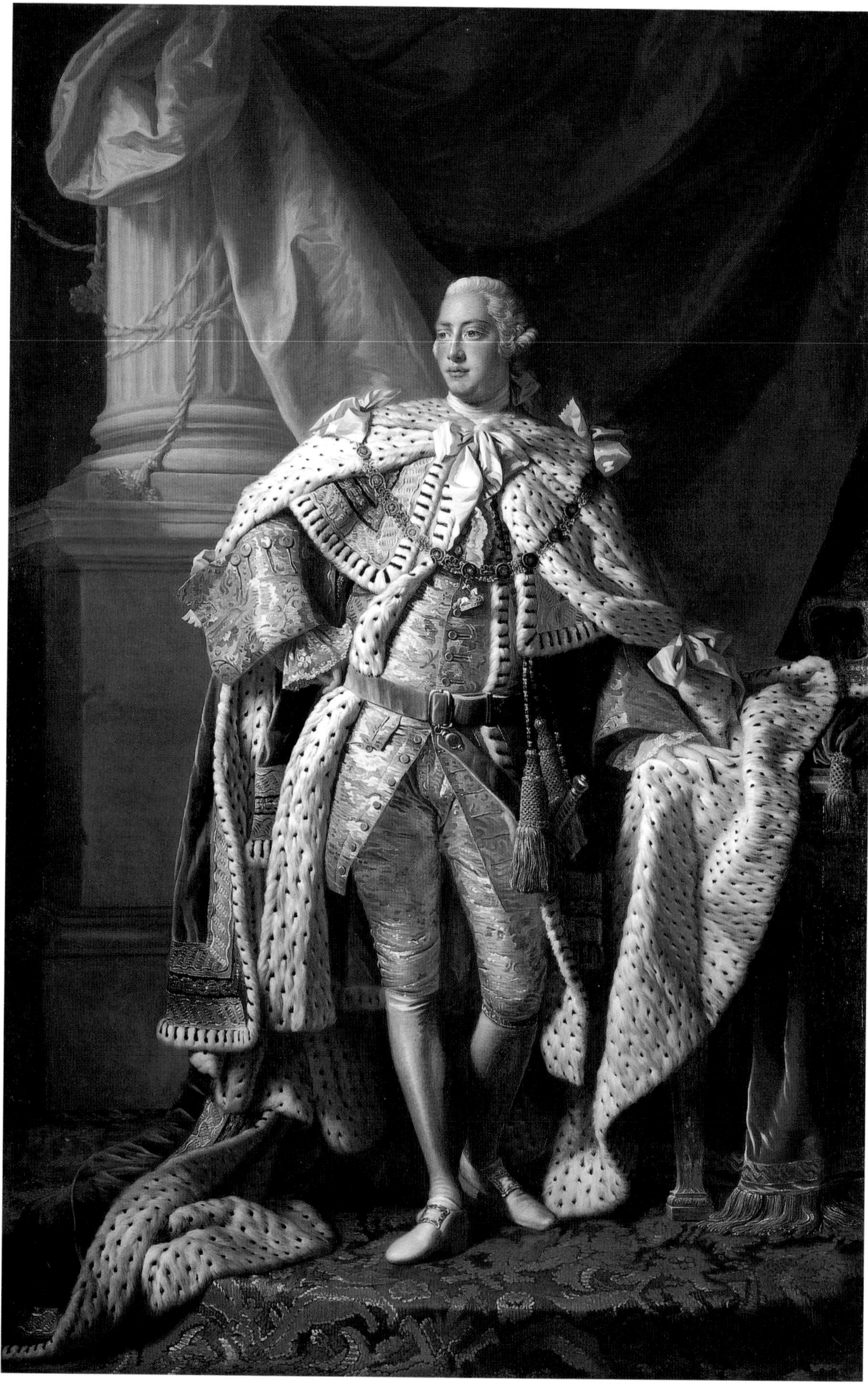

PLATE 20.1. Allan Ramsay (1713–84), *Portrait of George III*, 1761–2. Oil on canvas, 250 × 162 cm. Royal Collection, OM 996, 405307. *(Photo: The Royal Collection © 2010 Her Majesty Queen Elizabeth II.)*

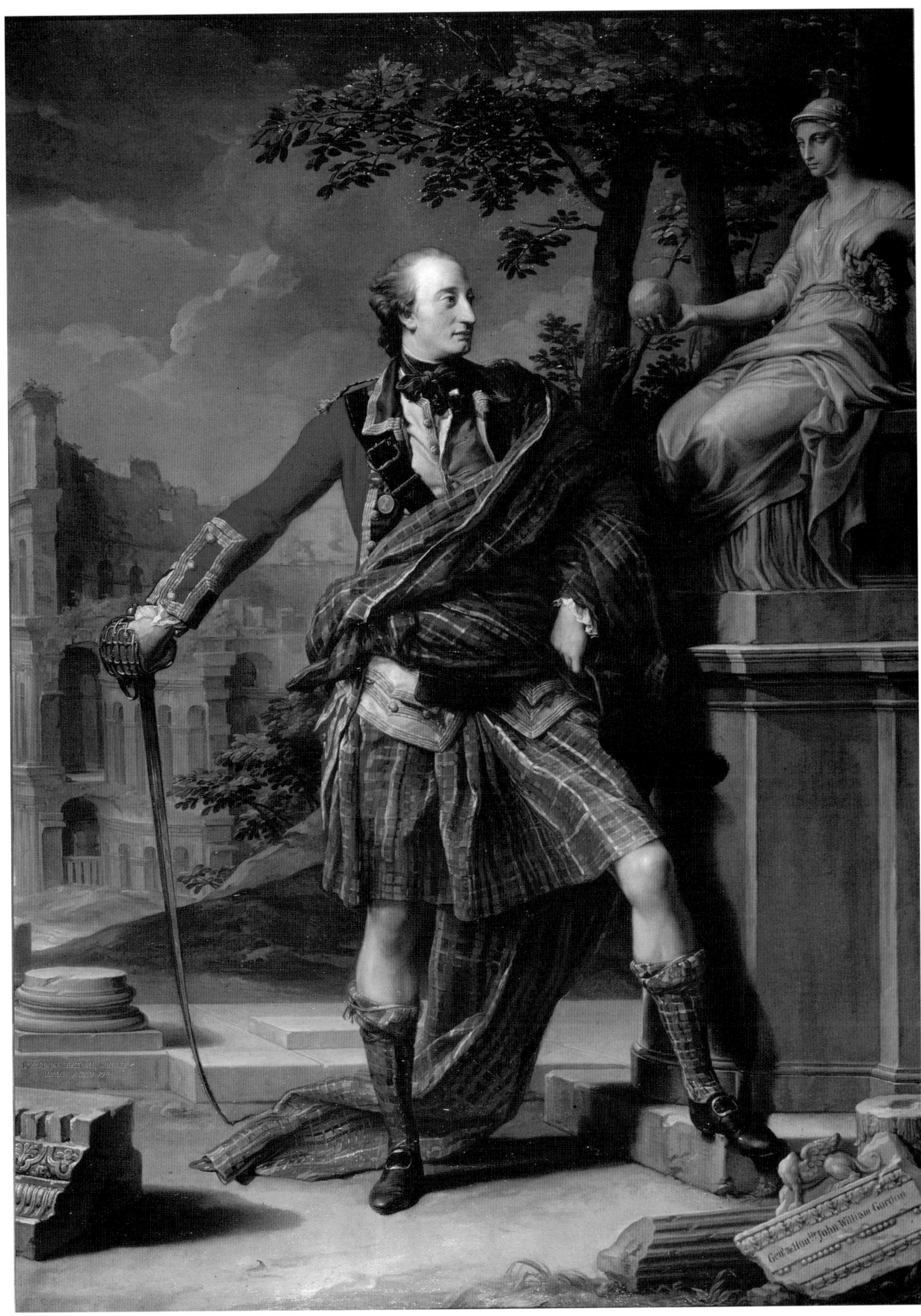

PLATE 20.2. Pompeo Batoni (1708–87), *Colonel William Gordon*, 1765–6. Oil on canvas. Fyvie Castle, National Trust for Scotland. *(Reproduced courtesy of the National Trust for Scotland.)*

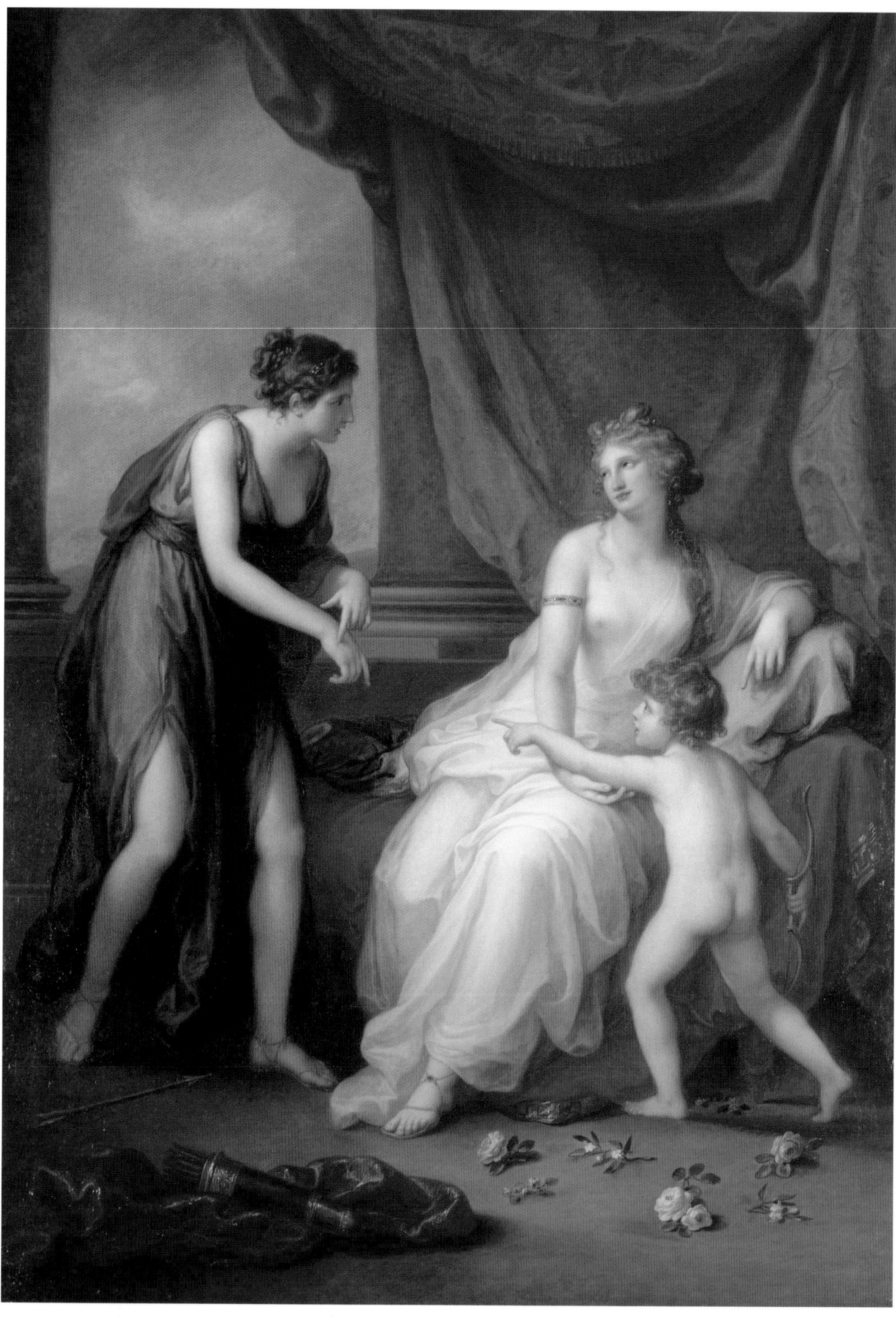

PLATE 21.1. Angelica Kauffman (1741–1807), *Euphrosyne Wounded by Cupid Complaining to Venus*, 1793. Oil on canvas. Attingham Park, The Berwick Collection (The National Trust). *(Photo: © National Trust Picture Library/Derrick E. Witty.)*

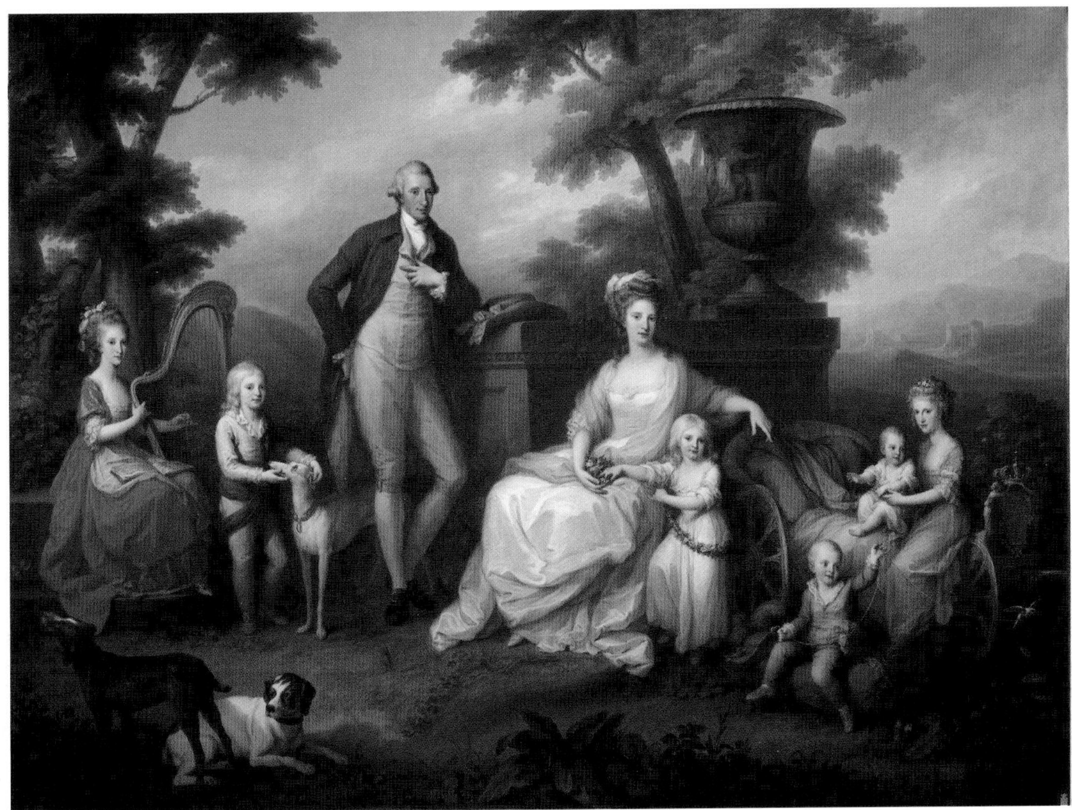

PLATE 21.2. Angelica Kauffman (1741–1807), *King Ferdinand IV and Queen Maria Carolina of Naples with Their Children,* 1782–4. Oil on canvas. Naples, Museo Nazionale di Capodimonte. *(Photo: Alinari/Art Resource, NY.)*

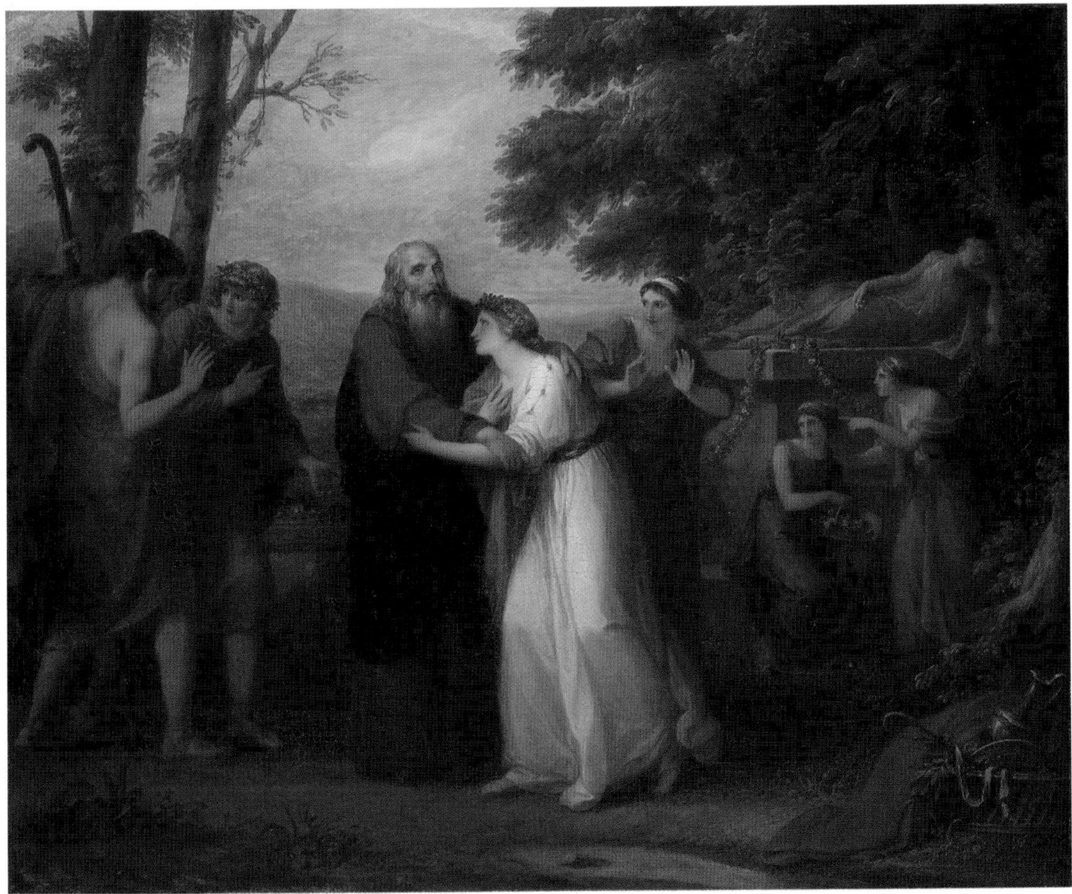

PLATE 21.3. Angelica Kauffman (1741–1807), *The Monument in Arcadia,* 1790. Oil on canvas. Private Collection. *(Reproduced courtesy of the owner.)*

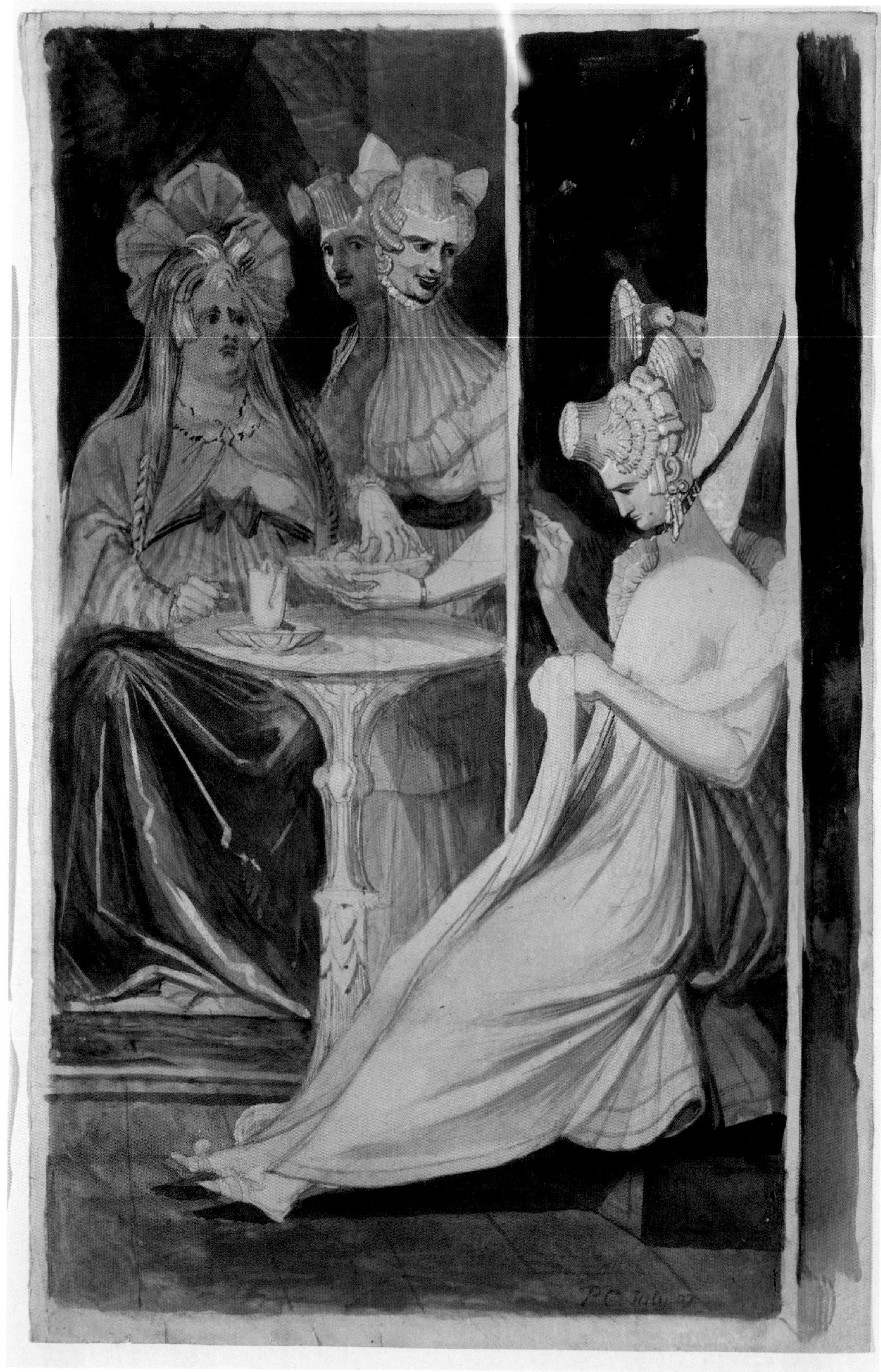

PLATE 22.1. Henry Fuseli (1741–1825), *The Debutante*, 1807. Watercolour over graphite with traces of gouache, 34 × 27 cm. London, Tate Gallery, N03396. *(© Tate, London, 2009. Reproduced courtesy of the Tate Gallery.)*